A CHILD'S GEOGRAPHY
OF THE WORLD

美国学生世界地理

（英汉对照）

〔美〕希利尔⊙著

欧阳瑾⊙译

台海出版社

图书在版编目（CIP）数据

美国学生世界地理：英汉对照 / (美) 希利尔著；
欧阳瑾译 . -- 北京：台海出版社，2018.3
ISBN 978-7-5168-1778-0

Ⅰ.①美… Ⅱ.①希… ②欧… Ⅲ.①英语—汉语—
对照读物②地理—世界—青少年读物 Ⅳ.① H319.4：K

中国版本图书馆CIP数据核字(2018)第037457号

美国学生世界地理：英汉对照

著　　者：〔美〕希利尔		译　　者：欧阳瑾	
责任编辑：高惠娟		装帧设计：同人阁文化传媒·书装设计	
版式设计：同人阁文化传媒·书装设计		责任印制：蔡　旭	

出版发行：台海出版社

地　　址：北京市东城区景山东街 20 号　　邮政编码：100009

电　　话：010 - 64041652（发行，邮购）

传　　真：010 - 84045799（总编室）

网　　址：www.taimeng.org.cn/thcbs/default.htm

E - m a i l：thcbs@126.com

经　　销：全国各地新华书店

印　　刷：香河利华文化发展有限公司

本书如有破损、缺页、装订错误，请与本社联系调换

开　　本：710mm × 1000mm　　　　1/16

字　　数：498 千字　　　　　　印　　张：22.75

版　　次：2018年5月第1版　　　印　　次：2018年5月第1次印刷

书　　号：ISBN 978-7-5168-1778-0

定　　价：45.00 元

Just suppose you could go way, way off in the sky, sit on a corner of nothing at all and look down at the World through a spy glass.

假设你能够走到天空中很远、很远的地方，坐在一个什么也没有的角落里，用望远镜来俯瞰整个世界。

TO

THE NINE-YEAR-OLD
WHO SAID,

"I wish there were a hundred more 'Lands' in the World for you to tell us about".

献给

那个年仅九岁、说"要是世界上还有一百块'陆地',可以让您来给我们介绍就好了"的孩子。

C目录
ontents

If you are under fifteen years, eight months and three days old

DON'T READ THIS INTRODUCTION

小朋友们，如果你们还不到十五岁八个月零三天，那就不要看这一部分。

This book is to give a traveler's view of the World—but not a commercial traveler's view.

本书旨在让孩子们能够用旅行家的眼光，而不是用旅行推销员的态度来看待世界。

It is to show the child what is beyond the horizon, from "Kalamazoo to Timbuktu."

本书旨在让孩子们明白，从"卡拉玛祖[1]到廷巴克图[2]"，地平线之外还有些什么。

It is to show him not only "the Seven Wonders of the World" but the seventy times Seven Wonders of the World.

本书不仅会让孩子们了解所谓的"世界七大奇迹"，而且会让他们了解到七十倍于"世界七大奇迹"的内容。

When I was a boy in New England we had for Thanksgiving six kinds of pie: apple, peach, cranberry, custard, mince, and pumpkin, but I was allowed to have only two kinds and I never could make a satisfactory choice. I have had the same difficulty in selecting geographical places and subjects to tell about. There are too many "most important" places in the World to be included in this first survey, and there will inevitably be those readers who will wonder why certain countries and certain places have been omitted, especially the place where the reader may live.

To me, as a child, geography was a bugbear of repellent names—Climate and Commerce, Manufactures and Industries, and *products*, products, PRODUCTS. It seemed

我小的时候，在新英格兰地区过感恩节时，记得有六种馅饼：苹果饼、桃饼、越橘饼、蛋奶饼、肉末饼和南瓜饼。可是，大人每次都只允许我吃两种，而我也从来没有做出过一种满意的选择。在选择可以介绍给小朋友们的地理位置和题材时，我也面临着同样的难题。世界上属于"极其重要"的地点实在太多，无法囊括讲本书这种初步性的概览之中，因此，有些读者必然会觉得奇怪，某些国家和某些地点，尤其是读者所在的国家和地方，为什么本书没有提及。

对小时候的我而言，地理就是一个大难题，充斥着令人反感的名称，比如气候与贸易、制造业与工业，以及物产、物产、物产。世界各地的主要物产，似乎不是玉米、小麦、大麦和黑麦，或者黑麦、大麦、小麦和玉米，就是大麦、玉米、黑麦和小麦。在我的地理概念中，现代希腊的内容只有短短的一段，因为我觉得，该国

---

[1] 卡拉玛祖（Kalamazoo），美国城市，属于密歇根州的五大城市之一。

[2] 廷巴克图（Timbuktu），非洲马里中部的一座城市，一译"通布图"。现亦用于指"遥远的地方"。

that the chief products of every place in the World were corn, wheat, barley, rye; or rye, barley, wheat, corn; or barley, corn, rye, wheat. In my geography modern Greece had but a paragraph—because, I suppose, it did not produce wheat, corn, barley, rye. Geography was a "stomach" geography; the "head" and "heart" were left out.

I loved the geography pictures and maps but hated the text. Except for an occasional descriptive or narrative paragraph the text was wholly unreadable—a confused jumble of headings and sub-headings and sub-sub-headings: Home Work, *NOTES*, Map Studies, *Suggestions to Teachers*, Helps, *Directions, Questions*, REVIEWS, Problems, *Exercises, Recitations*, LESSONS, Picture Studies, etc., etc., etc.

The World was an orange when I went to school, and there were only three things I can remember that I ever learned "for sure"—that the Dutch children wore wooden shoes, the Eskimos lived in snow houses, and the Chinese ate with chopsticks.

We had a question and answer catechism which we learned as we did the multiplication tables. The teacher read from her book:

Q. "What is the condition of the people of the United States?" and a thirteen-year-old boy in the next seat answered glibly: A. "They are poor and ignorant and live in miserable huts." At which astounding statement the teacher unemotionally remarked, "No, that's the answer to the next question, 'What is the condition of the Eskimos?'"

When my turn came to teach geography to beginners nine years of age, I found the available textbooks either too commercial and industrial, on the one hand, or too puerile

并不出产小麦、玉米、大麦或者黑麦。这种地理，属于只有"肚子"的地理，而其"头部"和"心脏"，则被我们抛弃了。

我很喜欢地理书上的图片和地图，却很讨厌书中的文字。除了偶尔有那么一段描述性的或者叙述性的文字之外，整个正文完全都是枯燥无味的，充斥着一堆混乱不堪的标题、小标题和小小标题，比如"家庭作业"、"注释"、"地图研究"、"给教师的建议"、"帮助"、"题目要求"、"题目"、"复习"、"问题"、"练习"、"背诵"、"功课"、"图片研究"，等等，等等，等等。

我上学之后，得知世界就是一个橙子。但如今还记得、当时我"很肯定"地了解到的，却只有三件事情：一是荷兰的孩子穿木屐；二是因纽特人住在冰雪建造的房子里；三是中国人用筷子吃饭。

我们在学习地理的时候，也像学习乘法口诀表那样，用的是问答式教学法。老师会照本宣科，看着课文朗读。

比如，老师会问道："美国人民的现状是怎样的呢？"坐在旁边座位上的一个十三岁的男孩，立即会不假思索地回答道："他们都很穷，没有文化，住在破烂的棚子里。"听到这种令人吃惊的说法，老师却丝毫不为所动，只是说："不对，那是下一题的答案。下一题就是：'因纽特人的生活状况是怎样的呢？'"

轮到我来向那些年仅九岁、刚刚入学的孩子讲授地理的时候，我却发现，手头可用的教科书一方面是要么太过注重商业，要么太过注重工业，另一方面则是要么太过幼稚，要么便是逻辑上没有连贯性。九岁的孩子根本无法理解统计数据和抽象

and inconsequential, on the other. Statistics and abstractions were entirely beyond the ken of the child of nine, and random stories of children in other countries had little value as geography.

As I had been a traveler for many years, had visited most of the countries of the Globe, and in actual mileage had been five times the distance around the World, I thought I would write a geography myself. Vain conceit! A class would listen with considerable attention to my extemporaneous travel talks, so I had a stenographer take down these talks verbatim. But when I read these notes of the same talk to another class, then it was that I discovered a book may be good—until it is written. So I've had to try, try again and again, for children's reactions can never be forecast. Neither can one tell without trial what children will or will not understand. Preconceived notions of what words they should or should not know are worthless: "Stupendous and appalling" presented no difficulties whatever but much simpler words were misunderstood.

I had been reading to a class from an excellent travel book for children. The author said, "We arrived, tired and hungry, and found quarters in the nearest hotel." The children understood "found quarters" to mean that the travelers had picked up 25-cent pieces in the hotel! Then again I had been describing the "Bridge of Sighs," in Venice, and picturing the condemned prisoners who crossed it. Casually I asked if any one could tell me why it was called the Bridge of Sighs. One boy said, "Because it is of big *size*." A little girl, scorning his ignorance, said, "Because it has *sides*." A boy from the country, with a farfetched

概念，而杂乱无章地选取出来的、关于其他国家一些孩子的故事，对于地理来说，其实也没有什么意义。

由于我多年来一直热衷于旅行，已经去过世界上绝大多数国家，而实际的旅行里程也已经相当于绕着地球转了五圈，因此我觉得，自己完全可以来编写一部地理书了。不过，这其实完全是虚荣和自负在作祟！一个班级的学生，会极为专心地听我即兴讲述自己的旅行见闻，于是，我请了一位速记员，一字不漏地将这些内容记录了下来。可待我把记录下来的相同内容读给另一个班的学生去听时，这才发现，虽然一本书的确可以很好，但要编写得好才是真的好。因此，我不得不试了一次又一次。因为孩子们的反应，是我们永远也预计不到的。而且，不经过尝试，我们也无法搞清楚哪些内容孩子们听得懂，哪些内容孩子们又听不懂。先入为主地假定他们应当了解哪些内容、不应该了解哪些内容，是没有意义的："举世瞩目和令人震惊"这样的词汇，无论用来修饰什么，孩子们都能够理解。而一些简单得多的话语，却经常让孩子们产生误解。

我曾经给一个班级朗读过一本专门针对儿童而编写的优秀游记。该书作者写道："我们到达后，又累又饿，便在最近的一家旅店里找了个住宿的地方。"孩子们却将"找了个住宿的地方"理解为，游客们在那家旅店里捡到了一些二十五美分的硬币呢[1]！而且，有一次我正在给孩子们介绍威尼斯的"叹息桥"，并且描述那

---

[1] 英语中，quarters一词既可指"住宿地"，又可指二十五美分的硬币，因此孩子们才会产生误解。

imagination, suggested it might be because they used "scythes"; and a fourth child said, "Because it belonged to a man named 'Cy.'"

The study of maps is interesting to almost all children. A map is like a puzzle picture—but new names are hard. And yet geography without either name or place is not geography at all. It is only fairyland. The study of maps and names is therefore absolutely essential and large wall maps most desirable.

Geography lends itself admirably to research on the part of the child. A large scrap-book arranged by countries may easily be filled with current pictorial news, clippings from magazines and Sunday newspapers, and from the circulars of travel bureaus. There is a wealth of such scrap-book material almost constantly being published—pictures of temples in India, wild animal hunts in Africa, parks in Paris—from which the child can compile his own Geographic Magazine. Furthermore, the collection of stamps offers a most attractive field, particularly for the boy just reaching the age when such collections are as absorbing as an adult hobby.

Of course, the best way to learn geography is by travel but not like that of the business man who landed in Rome with one hour to see the city. Jumping into a taxi and referring to a slip of paper, he said: "There are only two things I want to see here—St. Peter's and the Colosseum. Drive to them as fast as you can and back to the station." He was accordingly driven to St. Peter's. Sticking his head out of the window he said to the driver, "Well, which is this?"

些已经定罪、经过该桥的因犯。我随口问他们，看谁能跟我说一说，这座桥为什么会叫作"叹息桥"。一个男孩回答道："是因为它的尺寸非常巨大。"一个小姑娘嘲笑那个男孩很无知，说道："是因为这座桥有侧面。"还有一个乡下来的男孩子，他的想象力实在牵强得很，认为可能是因为那些因犯用的是"长柄大镰刀"。第四个孩子则说："因为那座桥是属于一个叫作'赛'的人。"[1]

学习地图的时候，差不多所有孩子都觉得很有意思。一幅地图，就像是一幅拼图。可地图上的新名称，记起来却很不容易。不过，要是没有名称或者地点，地理就根本不成其为地理，只是仙境了。因此，学习地图和地名绝对必要，而那种大型的挂图也是最合适的。

就孩子而言，地理其实极其适合于他们来进行研究。一本列有各国国名的大型剪贴簿，可以轻而易举地用当前的图片新闻、从杂志和周日报纸以及旅行社散发的传单上摘取下来的剪报填满。如今，人们几乎经常出版有许多这样的剪贴簿材料，比如印度寺庙的图片、在非洲狩猎野生动物的图片、巴黎各大公园的照片。孩子们可以用这些材料，汇编出一本属于自己的《地理杂志》来。此外，集邮也是一件极其吸引孩子们的事情，而对于那些刚刚达到一定年龄的男孩子来说，收集某种物品尤其有吸引力，他们甚至可能将这种业余爱好带到成人阶段。

当然，学习地理的最佳办法还是旅行，不过，这种旅行可不像是商人急急忙忙

---

[1]　"叹息桥"中的Sighs（叹息）一词，与后面孩子们所说的"尺寸"（sizes）、"侧面"（sides）、"长柄大镰刀"（scythes）及人名"赛"（Cy）都属于同音词。

In the little town where I was born, there lived an old, old man whose chief claim to distinction was the fact that he had never in his whole life been ten miles away from home. Nowadays travel is so easy that every child may look forward to traveling some day. This book is to give him some inkling of what there is to see, so that his travel may not be as meaningless as that of the simple sailor who goes round the world and returns with nothing but a parrot and a string of glass beads.

地到达罗马，只有一个小时看看那座城市那样。商人会跳上一辆出租车，看着一张纸条，说："我只想看看这里的两个地方：圣彼得大教堂和圆形竞技场。尽快开到这两个地方，然后赶回车站来。"于是，出租车便会带着他来到圣彼得大教堂。他把头伸出车窗，然后问司机："哦，这是哪儿呀？"

在我出生的那个小镇里，有一个年纪很大、很大的老人，他最主要的与众不同之处，便是一生中从未到过离家超出十英里[1]远的地方。如今，旅行已经变得非常容易，因此每个孩子可能都会渴望着自己将来哪天出去旅行。本书的目的，就是为了让孩子有个模糊的概念，知道到了那时他们可以看些什么，以便不让这种旅行变得毫无意义，不像那些愚笨的水手一样：他们虽说周游了整个世界，回来时却只带了一只鹦鹉、一串玻璃念珠，其余什么也没有。

---

[1]　英里（mile），英制长度单位。1英里约合1.609千米。

"ALL ABOARD!"

When I was a boy, my nurse used to take me to the railroad station to see the trains. A man in a blue cap and blue suit with brass buttons would call, "All aboard for Baltimore, Philadelphia, New York, and points north and east!" and wave his arm for the train to start. My nurse said he was a conductor.

So when I went home I used to put on a cap and play conductor shouting, "All aboard for Baltimore, Philadelphia, New York, and points north and east!" over and over, again and again, until I was told, "For pity sake, stop it!"

But some day I hoped, when I grew up, to be a real conductor in a blue cap and a blue suit with brass buttons. And now that I am grown up, I am still playing conductor, for in this book I am going to take you to Baltimore, Philadelphia, New York, and points north, east, south and west—round the World!

"全体上车！"

我小的时候，奶妈常常带我去火车站看火车。一个头戴蓝色帽子、身穿镶有黄铜扣子的蓝色制服的人会大声喊道："前往巴尔的摩、费城、纽约，以及往北往东各地去的乘客都上车了！"然后挥动手臂，示意列车启动。我的奶妈说，那人是个列车长。

于是，我回到家后，就会经常戴着一顶帽子，像列车员那样喊道："前往巴尔的摩、费城、纽约，以及往北往东各地去的乘客都上车了！"并且喊了一遍又一遍，直到大人对我说："天哪，别再喊了吧！"

不过，我还是希望，待我长大成人之后，有朝一日能够成为一名真正的列车长，真正头戴蓝色的帽子，穿上镶有黄铜扣子的蓝色制服。如今，虽说已经长大成人了，但我还是在扮演列车长的角色。因为在本书中，我将带领你们前往巴尔的摩、费城、纽约，以及往北、往东、往南、往西各地，到世界各地去！

1 The World Through a Spy-Glass

You have never seen your own face.

This may surprise you and you may say it isn't so—but it is so.

You may see the end of your nose.

You may even see your lips if you pout out—so.

If you stick out your tongue you may see the tip of it.

But you can't go over there, outside of yourself, and look at your own face.

Of course you know what your face looks like, because you have seen it in a mirror; but that's not yourself—it's only a picture of yourself.

And in the same way no one of us can see our own World—all of it—this World on which we live.

You can see a little bit of the World just around you—and if you go up into a high building you can see still more—and if you go up to the top of a high mountain you can see still, still more—and if you go up in an airplane you can see still, still, still more.

But to see the Whole World you would have to go much higher than that, higher than any one has ever been able to go or could go. You would have to go far, far above the clouds; way, way off in the sky where the stars are—and no one can do that, even in an airplane.

第1章　用望远镜俯瞰世界

大家从来都没有见到过自己的脸。

这话可能会让你们觉得惊讶，你们可能还会说不是这样的；可事实就是这样。

你们可以看到自己的鼻尖。

如果把嘴唇噘起来，你们甚至还看得见自己的嘴唇。

如果把舌头伸出来，那你们可以看见自己的舌尖。

但是，你们却没法走到自己的对面，走到自己的身外，去看一看自己的脸。

你们自然知道自己的脸是个什么样子，因为大家都在镜子里看到过，可镜中的样子，却并不是你们自己，只是你们自己的影像。

同样，我们当中也没有人能够看到自己所生活的这个世界，没有人能够看到整个地球。

大家只能看到自己周围的那一小部分世界。要是爬上一栋高楼，你们就能看到更大的范围；要是爬到一座高山的山顶，那就能看到更大、更大的范围；而要是坐在飞机里升到空中的话，你们就能看到更大、更大、更大的范围了。

不过，要想看到整个世界，大家必须爬得更高，比任何人曾经能够或者可以达到的高度更高才行。你们必须去得更远，到云层之上很远的地方，来到空中星星所在的遥远之地才行，就算是坐飞机，也没有人能够做到这一点哩。

Now you cannot see the World in a mirror as you can see your face. So how do we know what the World looks like?

A fish in the sea might tell her little fish, "The World is all water—just a *huge* tub; I've been everywhere and I know." Of course, she wouldn't know anything different.

A camel in the desert might tell her little camels, "The World is all sand—just a *huge* sand pile; I've been everywhere and I know."

A polar bear on an iceberg might tell her little polar bears, "The World is all snow and ice—just a *huge* refrigerator; I've been everywhere and I know."

A bear in the woods might tell her little bear cubs, "The World is all woods—just a *huge* forest; I've been everywhere and I know."

In the same way, once upon a time, people used to tell their little children, "The World is just a big island like a huge mud pie with some water, some sand, some ice, and some trees on it, and with a cover we call the sky over us all; we've been everywhere and we know."

When some inquisitive child asked, "What does the flat World like a mud pie rest on?" they really truly said, "It rests on the backs of four elephants."

But when the inquisitive child asked, "And what do the elephants stand on?" they really truly said, "On a big turtle."

Then when the inquisitive child asked, "What does the turtle stand on?" no one could say—for no one could even guess farther than that—so the turtle was left standing—on nothing.

注意，你们不能像在镜子里看到自己的脸那样，在镜子里看到整个世界。那么，我们又是怎么知道世界长得是个什么样子的呢？

大海里的一条鱼儿，可能会对自己的小鱼宝宝说："世界全都是水，就是一个巨大的盆子，我哪里都去过，所以我知道。"这条鱼儿，自然也不会知道别的什么东西。

沙漠里的一头骆驼，可能会告诉自己的骆驼宝宝说："世界全都是沙子，就是一个巨大的沙堆，我哪里都去过，因此我知道。"

冰山上的一头北极熊，可能会对自己的北极熊宝宝说："世界全都是冰雪，就是一个巨大的冰箱，我哪里都去过，所以我知道。"

森林里的一头熊，可能会对自己的熊宝宝说："世界全都是树林，就是一片巨大的森林，我哪里都去过，所以我知道。"

同样，在很久以前，人们也常常对自己的小宝宝说："世界是一个巨大的岛屿，就像一块巨大的泥饼，上面有点儿水、有点儿沙、有一些树木，并且所有人上面，都有一个我们称之为天空的罩子，我们哪里都去过，所以我们知道。"

如果有个喜欢刨根问底的孩子问道："这个像是一块泥饼、平平坦坦的世界，又是搁在什么东西上面呢？"那么，人们就会认认真真地回答说："是在四头大象的背上驮着呢。"

可是，如果这个喜欢刨根问底的孩子又问："那些大象又是站在什么东西上面呢？"那么，人们仍会认认真真地回答说："是站在一头巨龟上面呀。"

然后，要是这个喜欢刨根问底的孩子再问："那只巨龟，又是站在什么东西

That's the old story that parents long ago used to tell their children as to what the World was like. But just suppose you could go way, way off above the clouds; way, way off in the sky, sit on a corner of nothing at all, dangle your feet over the edge and look down at the World far, far below. What do you suppose it would really look like? I know—and yet I have never been there.

The World from way off in the sky and through a spy-glass would look just like a full moon—round and white; not round like a plate, but round like a huge snowball. Not exactly white, either, but bright—for the sun shines on this big ball, the World, and makes it light just as the headlight on an automobile shines on the road at night and makes the road light. Of course, the sun can shine on only one side of this big ball at a time; the other side of the World is dark,

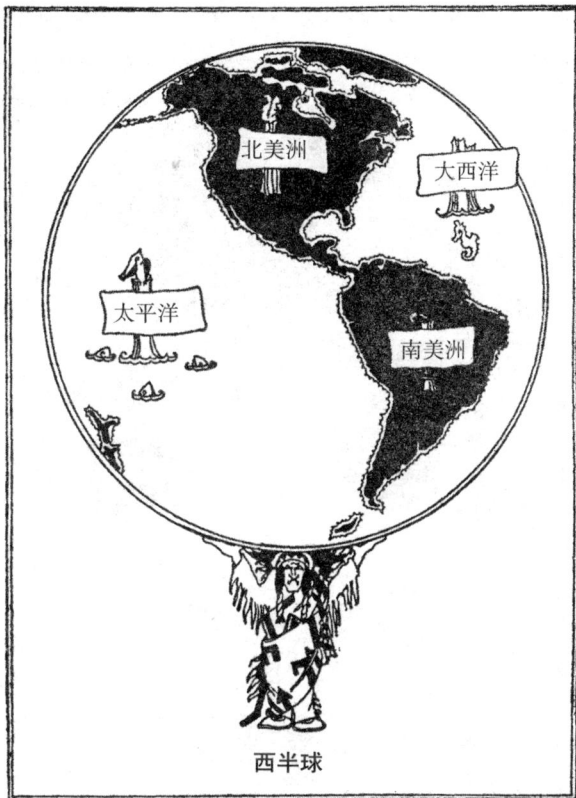

北美洲
大西洋
太平洋
南美洲

西半球

上面呢？"那就没人能够回答了，因为无人能够更加深入地去思考这个问题，于是，他们便任由这只巨龟脚下什么也没有地站在那里了。

这就是很久以前，在对自己的孩子介绍世界是个什么样子时，父母们经常讲述的那个古老故事。不过，假定你们可以来到云层之上很远、很远的地方，来到天空之上很远、很远的地方，坐在一个什么也没有的角上，双脚从边上垂下来晃呀晃，并且俯瞰着相距很远、很远的这个世界。那么，你们觉得，这个世界真正的模样会是怎样的呢？尽管从来都没有到过那个地方，可我知道。

从天空中很远以外的地方，用一架望远镜俯瞰起来的世界样子就是像是一轮满月，又圆又白，当然，它并不是像盘子那样既圆又平，而是像一个巨型雪球似的那么圆滚。它也并不是真正的白色，而是很明亮，因为太阳照耀着这个巨大的球体，使整个地球变得很亮，就像夜间马路上一辆汽车开着前灯，照亮了马路一样。当然，太阳每次都只能照亮这个巨型球体的一面，因而地球的另一面是暗的，不过，地球一直在阳光中不停地转动着。

要是用一副单筒望远镜来看一看地球，就像人们用望远镜去观察月亮一般，那你们就会看到，地球的一面上有两片形状非常古怪的阴影，而在地球另一面，

but the World keeps turning round and round in the sunlight.

If you looked at the World through a telescope—you know what a telescope is: one of those long spy-glasses that makc things seem closer and bigger—as men look at the moon, you would see on one side of the World two big patches that look like queerly shaped shadows and on the other side of the World twice as many big patches, four queerly shaped shadows. These patches which look like shadows are really land and are called by a long name: continents. These continents have names, and if their names were printed across them in letters a thousand miles high—which they are not—so that the man with a spy-glass could read them, he would read on one side of the World

NORTH AMERICA

SOUTH AMERICA

and if he waited until the World turned round, until the other side showed in the sunlight, as I've seen the World

东半球

这些斑纹的数量则有前者的两倍，即有四片形状古怪的阴影。大家都知道单筒望远镜是个什么东西吧，那就是一副使得物体看起来更近、更大的长望远镜中的一支。那些看起来就像是阴影的斑纹，其实都是陆地，叫作"大陆"。这些大陆各有名称，如果用高达一千英里的字体，将各自的名称打印出来贴在那些大陆之上（这一点当然是做不到的），从而让那个用单筒望远镜来观察的人能够看清的话，那他就会看到，地球的一面上有：

北美洲

南美洲

而等到地球转过去，它的另一面出现在阳光之下，就像我在《电影梦工厂》里看到的地球那样，我们又会看到欧洲、亚洲、非洲，以及面积最小、名称却最长的大洋洲[1]。这一面的最底下，就是南极洲了。

我们把一枚硬币的一面称为"头像面"（或者"正面"），因为这一面上通

---

[1] 大洋洲（Oceania），包括澳大利亚、新西兰等十四个国家。

do in "the movies," he would read on this continent EUROPE and on that continent ASIA and on the other continent AFRICA, and the smallest one would have the longest name, AUSTRALIA. At the very bottom would be ANTARCTICA.

We call one side of a piece of money "the head," because there is usually the head of some one on that side, and the other side we call "the tail," as that is opposite from the head. It would be easy to tell which side of the World was which if we could call one side heads and the other tails. But there are no heads or tails on the World—only these queer shadows—so we use two big words instead of "heads" and "tails" to tell which side of the World is which. We call one side the "Western Hemisphere" and the other side we call the "Eastern Hemisphere." Whew! Why don't they call it something easy?—well, let's call it "Half-a-Ball," for that is what Hemisphere means. The Western Half-Ball has two continents and the Eastern Half-Ball has four continents.

The tip top and the very bottom of the World are called the Poles, although there are no poles. Around the top and bottom Pole it would be all white—snow and ice—for the Poles are so cold there is snow and ice there all the time.

The part of the World that isn't patches of shadow or snow is water. The water all around the continents is the ocean, and though of course there are no walls nor fences dividing it into different parts, its different parts are called by different names.

Do you know your right hand from your left? Of course you do if you're over six years old. But do you know the west side from the east side? If you are over nine years old you

常都印有某个人物的头像；而另一面，我们则称之为"背面"，因为它与"正面"相对。要是把地球的一面也称为"正面"、而另一面也称为"背面"的话，那我们就能轻而易举地区分出地球的两面了。不过，地球上其实并没有什么"正面"或者"背面"，只有那些形状古怪的阴影，因此我们便用两个大词，取代了"正面"和"背面"，来区分地球的两面。我们把其中的一面称为"西半球"，而将另一面称为"东半球"。唷！为什么人们不用更简单的词来称呼呢？好吧，我们不妨称之为"半个圆球"，因为"半球"一词，指的就是这个意思。所以，西半球有两个大洲，东半球则有四个大洲。

地球的最顶端和最底部称为"两极"，但其实那里并没有什么柱子[1]。顶端的北极地区和底端的南极地区，全都是白茫茫的冰雪，因为极地非常寒冷，冰雪长年不化。

地球上不属于阴影斑片和冰雪的部分，全都是水。包围在各洲大陆周围的水体，就是大洋了，尽管自然界里并没有什么墙壁、篱笆将大洋分隔成不同的部分，可大洋中的各个部分，也有各自不同的名称。

大家分得清自己的左手和右手吗？只要过了六岁，你们自然分得清。不过，你们分不分得清东、西呢？要是超过了九岁，那你们也应该分得清了。东方就是太阳

[1] 英语中，"极"（包括物理学上的电极、磁极，以及数学上的轴极等）与"柱子"是同一个词，都是pole。作者为了不让孩子们混淆起来，才这么解释。

should. The east is where the sun rises, the west is where it sets. And if your right hand is east, your left hand is west, your face is north and your back is south.

The Atlantic Ocean is on the east side of North and South America. The Pacific Ocean is on the west. The ocean entirely in the Eastern Hemisphere is called "Indian." No, it is not named for our Indians. At the top of the World is the Arctic Ocean. At the bottom, all around Antarctica, is the Antarctic Ocean. The Arctic and Antarctic Oceans are mostly ice, for it is so cold there the water freezes and stays frozen. If we wanted to put names on the oceans so that a man off in the sky could read them, we would have to stick huge signs in the water, as we can't paint letters on the ocean.

There is no reason why I show you the World turned this way with North America on top. I might just as well show it upside down or sideways, for there is no upside nor downside on the World. I suppose the reason that the north side is always shown on top is because the people who made maps and geographies all lived in the north part of the World and they wanted their part of the World on top.

So this is our World. You may wonder, "Are there any other Worlds besides ours?" Some have guessed that there may be—that some of those sparks in the sky that look like stars at night may be other Worlds like ours with people living on them. But no one knows, for the strongest telescope is not strong enough for us to see what is on those far off sparks, so we can only guess about them.

升起的方向，而西方则是太阳落下的方向。要是让右手朝着东方，左手朝着西方的话，那么你们面对的就是北方，而背后就是南方了。

大西洋位于南、北美洲的东方，太平洋位于南、北美洲的西方。完全位于东半球的那个大洋，叫作"印度洋"。注意，这个大洋可不是用美国的印第安人来命名的[1]。地球的顶端，是北冰洋。而位于地球底部、环绕着南极洲的，则是南极海。北冰洋和南极海的绝大部分都被冰雪覆盖着，因为那里非常寒冷，海水都结成了冰，并且一直封冻着。假如大家想要给各个大洋标上名称，以便位于空中远处的人看得清的话，那就必须在水中插上巨型的标志才行，因为我们可没法在大洋的水面上描出字母来呢。

我为什么要给你们看这样一个将北美洲放在上方并转动着的地球，可没有什么理由好说。我也可以将地球颠倒过来，或者侧着给你们看，因为地球上本来并没有什么上下之分。我觉得，地球的北部之所以总是放在上方，是因为制作地图、进行地理研究的人全都住在地球的北部，并且希望将他们所住的这个地区放在上方吧。

这就是我们的地球。你们可能会想知道："除了我们的地球，还有别的地球吗？"有些人猜想，可能还存在着别的地球，认为那些在天空中闪烁着、夜晚看上去就像是星星的天体，可能会是其他与我们的相似的地球，也有人们居住。不过，这一点还没人知道，因为即便是最强大的望远镜，也不足以让我们看到如此遥远的那些星球上都有些什么，所以人们只能靠猜想了。

---

[1] 哥伦布发现美洲大陆时，以为自己到达的是印度，因而把当地的土著居民称为"印度人"（Indian）。后来，我们为了区分二者，便将美洲的土著译为"印第安人"。

2 The World Is Round, for I've Been Round It

Did you ever run away from home?

I did—once upon a time—when I was younger than you are.

I wanted to see the World.

My mother had told me the World was a huge ball and that if I kept on, straight ahead, following my nose, I would go round the ball and come back to where I started.

So early one morning, without telling anyone, I set out to go around the World.

But I didn't get very far before night came on, and a big kind policeman brought me back home.

When I was grown up and had no home, I started out once again to go around the World. This time I got on a train headed toward the setting sun. Night came on, but no big, kind policeman brought me back home; so I kept on and on, day after day, week after week, month after month—sometimes on trains, sometimes on boats, sometimes in automobiles, sometimes on the backs of animals—but always toward the side of the World where the sun sets, the side which the people call "the west."

I passed broad fields and thick forests, small towns and big cities—I went over bridges, round hills, and through holes in mountains—I reached a great ocean and sailed across it

第2章　地球是圆的，我曾环绕一周

大家有没有离家出走过呢？

很久以前，我比你们都要小的时候，就离家出走过一回。

当时，我希望去看一看世界。

我的妈妈告诉过我，说世界是一个巨大的圆球；因此，假如径直向前走，朝着自己鼻子所指的方向一直走下去的话，那我就会环绕地球一周，然后再回到出发的那个地方。

于是，有天清晨，在没有告诉任何人的情况下，我开始去环绕地球了。

不过，我还没走多远，天就黑了，一个好心的大个子警察，把我送回了家。

待到我长大成人、却还没有成家的时候，我又一次开始出发去周游世界了。这一次，我坐上火车，朝着太阳落下的方向而去。夜幕落下，可没有好心的大个子警察再把我送回家去了。因此，我一直不停地往前，日复一日、周复一周、月复一月地前进。虽说有时是坐火车，有时是坐小船，有时是坐汽车，有时是骑在牲口背上，但我始终都是朝着太阳落下的那一方而去，即始终朝着人们所称的"西方"而去。

我经过了许多辽阔的田野、茂密的森林，经过了许多小型的城镇、大型的城市，我跨过了许多桥梁，绕过了许多山岳，穿越了许多山间的隧道；我到达了一个

on a big ship to another continent—I came to strange lands where people dressed in strange clothes, lived in strange houses, and spoke strange languages ; I saw strange animals, trees, and flowers ; I crossed another great ocean and at last, after many, many months, always going in the same direction, I came back here to the exact spot from which I had started. So I knew the World was round, for I had been round it—but it was not round and smooth like a tennis ball, but humpety and bumpety, and so huge that it didn't seem like a ball at all.

It took me nearly half a year to go round the World—that seems like a long time, but then it was a long way—over twenty-five times a thousand miles. But others have been around the World in much faster time. The airship *Graf Zeppelin* flew around the World in three weeks. Two flyers took less than nine days to circle the globe in their airplane and return to their starting point, New York. An American Air Force plane flew around the World without stopping in less than four days.

If a man could start out when the sun rose in the morning and keep up with it all day long, go over the side of the World when the sun set, and keep up with it on the other side of the World, he would be back again where he started the next morning. He then would have gone round the World in one day. But to do that he would have to travel over 1,000 miles an

广袤的大洋，坐上一艘巨大的轮船，横跨这个大洋，到达了另一个大洲，我来到了许多陌生的国度，那里的人都穿着奇怪的服装，居住在奇怪的房子里，并且说着奇怪的语言，我看到了许多陌生的动物、树木和花草。我跨过另一个大洋，并且在始终朝着同一个方向旅行了许多许多个月之后，最终又回到了我出发的这个地方。因此，我知道地球是圆的，因为我已经环绕了它一周。不过，地球并不是像一个网球那样浑圆、滑溜的，而是坑坑洼洼，像个鸡蛋，并且极其巨大，因此看上去根本就不像是一个球呢。

我花了差不多半年的时间，才环绕了地球一周，这似乎是一段很久的时间，但在那时，这也是一段很长的距离，达到了两万五千多英里呢。不过，其他一些人环绕地球所花的时间，却要比我短得多。飞艇"格拉夫·齐柏林"号只用了三个星期，便绕着地球飞行了一圈。有两位飞行员，曾经驾驶着各自的飞机，不到九天便环绕了地球一周，然后回到了他们的出发地纽约。美国空军的一架战斗机要是连续飞行、中途不停的话，只需不到四天的时间，便可绕地球一周呢。

假如一个人能够在清晨太阳升起的时候出发，并且一整天都跟着太阳跑，到太阳落山的时候便走完了地球的一面，并且再跟着太阳走完地球另一面的话，那么他第二天早上便会回到自己的出发地。这样，他就是在一天之内环绕了地球一周。不过，要做到这一点，在一天一夜的二十四个小时内，他每个小时都必须走上一千多英里，才能赶上太阳的步伐。

hour to keep up with the sun for each of the twenty-four hours in a day and night.

All around the outside of the World—as you probably know—is an ocean of air that covers everything on the World as the ocean of water covers everything in the sea. What you probably don't know is that this ocean of air is wrapped only round the World—it does not fill the sky. Men and animals live in this ocean of air as fish live in the ocean of water, and if a huge giant picked you out of the air you would die just as quickly as a fish does when taken out of the sea. The air is thick near the ground but gets thin and thinner the higher up you go off the ground. That's why airplanes can go up but a few miles high—there is not enough air to hold up the plane, for the plane must have air to rest on and for its propeller to push against, just as a boat in the water must have water to rest on and water for its propeller to push against. Or if it's a jet plane, it must have air to feed its jet motors. An airplane could not rise beyond the ocean of air and sail off into the sky where there is no air any more than a steamship on the sea could rise out of the water and sail off up into the air.

There is only one thing that men can send up high enough to travel above the ocean of air. That is a rocket, which doesn't depend on air for its motor or to hold it up. Someday rocket ships will probably carry men on trips to the Moon or even to the planet Mars. How would you like to go exploring in a rocket ship beyond the World's atmosphere out through empty, airless space? How would you like to be the first Man in the Moon? You wouldn't find any living thing on the Moon, for the Moon is a dead, lifeless ball without any air on it at all. But if your rocket got to Mars you would almost certainly find some

你们很可能都知道，环绕在地球外部的，就是大气层。就像海水淹没了海中的一切那样，大气也淹没了地球上的一切。而你们很可能不知道的，就是这个大气层只是环绕在地球的外部，却没有填满整个天空。人类和动物都生活在这个大气层里，就像鱼儿生活在海水当中一样，要是一个巨人把你们拎起来扔出大气层，那你们很快就会死去，就像离开了海水的鱼儿一样。越是靠近地面的地方，空气密度越大，而离地面越高，空气就会变得越来越稀薄。飞机之所以只能飞到几英里高的地方，原因就在这里：高空中没有足够多的空气来支撑飞机，因为飞机必须有空气才能浮在空中，飞机的螺旋桨才能产生推力，这个道理，跟水中的船只必须有水才能浮在水上、船只的螺旋桨才能产生推力是一样的。就算是一架喷气式飞机，也必须有空气吸入其喷气式发动机才行。飞机没法上升到大气层以上的高度，无法进入太空，就像大海上的一艘汽轮没法浮到水面以上，没法在空中航行一样。

人类只能发射一种飞行高度能够达到大气层以上的设备。那就是火箭，因为它不依靠空气来驱动它的发动机，也不依靠空气来支撑其自身的重量。有朝一日，宇宙飞船很可能会把人类运送到月球、甚至是火星上去旅行呢。你们喜不喜欢乘坐宇宙飞船，到地球的大气层以外，去探索那空无一物、没有空气的宇宙空间呢？你们希不希望自己是第一个到达月球上的人类呢？你们在月亮上可不会找到任何生物，因为月亮是一个死气沉沉、没有生命的星球，上面根本就没有空气。不过，如果你们乘坐火箭来到了火星上，那就极有可能发现某些活体植物，甚至是某些活体动物。但这也是没准的事情，谁知道呢？

living plants—and perhaps, who knows?—even some living animals.

Some mountains are so high that their tops almost stick out of the ocean of air; at least, there is so little air covering their tops that people can't go all the way to the top unless they take along canned air to breathe.

You can't see air—you may think you can, but what you see is smoke or clouds, not air. When air is moving, we call it wind. Then you can feel it when it blows your hat off, you can hear it when it bangs the shutters and whistles round the house; but no one has ever seen air itself.

The World wasn't always as it is now. It was once a ball of fire—a huge burning ball. That was millions of years ago, and of course long before there were any people or animals or plants on the World. But the fiery ball got cooler and cooler until it was no longer burning but a hot ball of rock. There were then no oceans, no water on the World, for water won't stay on anything very hot—it won't stay on a hot stove—it turns to steam when there is fire under it; so there were only clouds of steam, an ocean of steam, around the World. But the World kept getting cooler and cooler until at last the steam turned to water and fell on the World—rain, rain, rain, until there perhaps was one big ocean covering the whole World.

But the World still kept on cooling and cooling, and as it cooled it shrank and shriveled and wrinkled and crinkled and puckered like the outside of a prune. You know a prune was once smooth and round when it was a plum. These little wrinkles and crinkles rose up out of the ocean and were the continents and mountains, so you see how big the wrinkles and

地球上有些高高耸立的山脉，山顶几乎伸到了大气层之上，起码来说，这些山脉顶上的空气非常稀薄，因此人类除非携带着呼吸用的罐装空气，否则便没法登上这些山顶呢。

大家是看不到空气的，虽说你们可能以为自己看得见，但其实你们见到的都是烟雾或者云朵，而不是空气。空气流动的时候，我们便称之为风。这样，当风吹落你们的帽子时，你们就可以感觉到空气，当风啪啪地敲击着百叶窗、在你们家房子周围呼啸而过的时候，你们也能听得到空气的声音，不过，迄今为止，还没有人见到过空气本身呢。

以前，地球并非始终都像如今这个样子。它曾经是一个大火球，一个巨大的、熊熊燃烧着的火球，那还是数百万年前的事情了。当然，也是在这很久以后，地球上才出现了人类、动物或者植物。不过，熊熊燃烧着的地球后来变得越来越冷，最终不再燃烧，成了一个由岩石组成的炽热球体。当时，地球上还没有海洋，没有水，因为任何炽热之物上都是存不住水的，下面有火加热时，水就会变成蒸汽，因此，当时地球上只有一团团的蒸汽，形成了环绕地球的一个蒸汽层。但是，地球继续变得越来越凉，最终这些蒸汽冷凝成水，落到了地球上，形成了雨，雨不停地、不停地、不停地下着，直到整个地球上可能都被一个巨大的海洋所淹没了。

但是，地球还在继续变得越来越凉爽，而在变冷的过程中，地球又开始变小、收缩、起皱、缩褶和皱起，就像梅干的外皮一样。你们都知道，梅干在新鲜的时候，原本都是又光滑又圆润的。这些小的褶子和皱纹升到了海洋之上，变成了大陆

crinkles really are. The earth is still wrinkling a bit even now, and when it does so it shivers and shakes and we say there has been an earthquake. But the earthquakes nowadays are as nothing to what may have been the tremendous shudder when the continents rose out of the first single ocean. The thunderous roar of that quake may have reached the stars with a stupendous and appalling boom of a bursting, cracking, rending, groaning World, as if the last day had come. Don't you know what stupendous and appalling boom means? Why, it means "stupendous and appalling boom." But that's all guess—for the continents may have risen out of the sea as softly, slowly, silently as a blade of grass grows out of the ground. No one knows. We only know the continents did rise out of the water—we can find seashells on the tops of high mountains, and we know they could only have been made under the water when the mountain was under the water.

地 球

地球曾经是一个大火球

海 洋

接下来，地球上下起了雨，
形成了海洋

陆 地

接下来，地球开始收缩起皱，
变成梅干的外皮那样

山 川

陆地、山脉从海洋当中耸立而出

和山脉，因此，你们完全可以想见，这些褶子和皱纹实际上有多巨大。即便是到了如今，地球也仍在轻微地收缩着。当地球收缩的时候，就会地动山摇，而我们则称这种现象是发生了地震。不过，如今的地震与当初陆地从一整片海洋中耸立而出的时候那种山崩地裂式的震动相比，根本就算不上什么了。这种震动所带来的巨大声音，伴随着爆炸、裂开、分裂、咆哮的地球发出巨大而可怕的轰鸣之声，可能响彻了宇宙，直抵各大恒星，仿佛是世界末日降临了一般呢。你们知道"巨大而可怕的轰鸣之声"是什么意思吗？嗨，它指的就是"巨大而可怕的轰鸣之声"。不过，这一切全都属于我们的猜测，因为各个大陆也有可能是轻柔、缓慢而无声地升出海面的，就像地上生长出的一片草叶那样。没人知道实际情况究竟如何。我们只知道各个大陆的确是从水中耸立出来的，因为在一些高山之巅，我们如今还能找到海贝，而我们也知道，这些海贝是在水下生成的，因此只可能是在山脉还位于海底的时候留下来的。

3 The Inside of the World

When I was a very little boy I was very inquisitive. At least, that's what my nurse called me. One day when I was walking with her along the city pavements, I asked:

"Jane, what's under the pavement?"

"Oh, just dirt," she replied.

"And what is under the dirt?"

"Oh, more dirt," she replied.

"Well, what's under that?" I asked. I wasn't satisfied.

"Oh, nothing—I don't know—why are you always so inquisitive?" she asked.

I knew there must be something underneath that, and I just wanted to know what it was—I was just inquisitive.

I had heard that the place had boys went when they died was down under the ground somewhere—a big cave, perhaps—and I wanted to know if that were so.

So I made up my mind I'd dig down through the World; down, down, down, till I came through on the other side, and then I'd know. I was a very little boy, you see. With a tin shovel I started a hole in the back yard behind the grapevines, where no one would know what I was doing. I wanted to keep it a secret until I had dug all the way through. Day

第3章　地球的内部

还在很小的时候，我就很喜欢打破砂锅问到底。至少来说，我的奶妈是这样认为的。

有一天，我正跟着她沿着市里的人行道散步，我问她说：

"简，人行道下面是什么？"

"哦，全都是土啊。"她回答道。

"土下面又是什么呢？"

"哦，还是土。"她回答道。

"好吧，那下面又是什么呢？"我问道。她的回答可没有让我觉得满意。

"噢，没有什么了吧，我可不知道。你为什么总是这样喜欢刨根问底呢？"她问道。

我知道，泥土下面肯定是有某种东西的，我就是想知道，那种东西究竟是什么，谁叫我喜欢刨根究底呢。

我曾经听说，坏孩子死后，会去地下的某个地方，或许是一个大洞穴吧，因此，我希望弄明白，究竟是不是那么回事。

于是，我便下定决心，要向下挖穿整个地球，并且一直向下、向下、向下挖掘，直到我抵达地球的那一边，那样一来，我就知道情况究竟是不是那样的了。你们都知道，当时我还是个很小很小的小男孩哩。我拿起一把锡制的铲子，开始在我家后院的葡萄架后挖出一个洞来。在那里进行挖掘，就没人知道我在干什么。我希

after day I worked, digging up first soft ground—that was easy—then I got down to solid ground; that was hard. I had a hole which I could stand in up to my waist.

Then one evening my father asked, "What's that hole in the back yard?"

My secret was out. He didn't laugh when I told him—at least, out loud—but he asked me if I knew how far I'd have to dig.

"Could you dig *down* as deep as the Washington Monument goes *up*?" he asked.

I thought perhaps I could, but I was a little doubtful, for the Washington Monument seemed terribly high.

"Men have dug wells many times as deep as the Washington Monument," my father told me, "but never all the way nor nearly all the way through the World. You would have to dig many thousands of times deeper than the Washington Monument to get down even to the center of the World. It's eight thousand miles straight through the earth and most all the way is rock—just rock, and more rock, that's all."

Then I gave it up.

"How do you know it's eight thousand miles if no one has ever been through the World?" asked the inquisitive

拿起一把锡制铲子，我便开始向下挖掘，准备挖穿整个地球

望在一路挖通之前，保守住这个秘密。我干了一天又一天，起初挖出的都是松软的泥土，很容易挖掘；可接下来，我就挖到结实的土层，很难挖下去了。我挖出了一个洞，站在里面，洞子只有我的腰部那么深。

然后，有天傍晚，我的父亲问道："后院里那个洞是干什么用的？"

我的秘密便公之于众了。我把这一切告诉父亲时，他并没有笑起来（起码也是没有哈哈大笑），而是问我，知不知道自己必须挖多远才能挖穿。

"你向下挖掘出的深度，能够达到华盛顿纪念碑[1]向上耸立的那种高度吗？"他问道。

虽然觉得自己可能做得到，但我还是有一点儿怀疑，因为华盛顿纪念碑看上去，可高得很呢。

"人类向下挖掘的深度，已经达到华盛顿纪念碑高度的好多、好多倍了，"父亲告诉我说，"可从来没有挖穿过，或者接近挖穿过地球呢。你必须挖到有华盛顿纪念碑高度的几千倍深，才能挖到地心。地球的直径有八千英里，而且其中绝大部分都是岩石，全都是岩石，好多好多的岩石，没有其他的东西。"

于是，我便不再挖下去了。

"如果说到现在为止，还没有人挖穿过整个地球，那您又怎么知道地球的直径是八千英里呢？"那个喜欢刨根问底的孩子问道。我不记得父亲当时是怎样回答我

---

[1] 华盛顿纪念碑（Washington Monument），美国为纪念首任总统乔治·华盛顿而建造的一座纪念碑，位于华盛顿市中心，是一座大理石方尖碑，底部宽22.4米，高169.045米。

child. I don't know what my father answered. I was too young to understand. I wonder if you are too young, if I tell you how we know it's eight thousand miles; for without ever having been through the World, we do know how far it is.

This is how we know. It's a funny thing, but every ball, whether it is a little ball or a medium-sized ball or a great big ball, is always just a little more than three times as big round as it is through. I have often wondered why this was so—why a ball shouldn't be exactly three times or four times or five times as big round as through, but it isn't. You can try it yourself if you don't believe it. Take an apple or an orange and measure it around and then cut it and measure it through.

Now we know the World is a ball, a huge ball, and yet as it is a ball it must, like all other balls, be a little more than three times as big around as it is through. It is twenty-five thousand miles round the World, because men have actually measured that. So we know that the distance through must be about eight thousand miles, as twenty-five is a little more than three times eight. That is not geography; it's arithmetic. If you want to use big words for "around" and "through," as they do in geographies, you must say "circumference" for "around" and "diameter" for "through"—which mean the same thing: the circumference of the World is twenty-five thousand and the diameter is eight thousand.

The outside of the World is a crust of rock like the skin of a baked potato over the hot inside. Some of the crust that you go through first is in layers, like layers in a jelly-cake, one layer after another, only these rock layers look as if they were made of sand and

的了。那个时候，我还太小，根本就理解不了。我不知道你们是不是也太小，要是我跟你们解释我们为何知道地球直径是八千英里的话，你们是不是能够理解，因为我们确实无须穿过整个地球，便知道地球的直径是多少。

下面就是我们得知地球直径的方法。有一个非常有意思的现象：任何一个球体，无论它是一个小球，还是一个中等尺寸的球体，抑或是一个非常巨大的球体，其最大一圈的长度始终都是球体对直距离的三倍多一点儿。我也一直都想知道，为什么会是这样：一个球体最大一圈的长度，为什么不是正好等于其对直距离的三倍、四倍或者五倍，可事实就是如此。要是不信的话，你们自己就可以试一试。你们不妨拿出一个苹果或者一个橙子，量一量它一圈的长度，然后再从中切开，量一量它们的对直距离。

既然我们知道地球是一个球体、一个巨大的球体，那么，作为一个球体，它最大一圈的长度，也必定是整个地球对直距离的三倍多一点儿。环绕地球一圈的长度是二万五千英里，因为人类已经实地测量过了。所以，我们便知道，地球的对直距离一定是八千英里左右，因为二万五千英里正好是八千英里的三倍多一点儿。这可不是个地理问题，而是一个算术问题了。要是你们想要像地理学上一样，用更难一点儿的词汇来代替"圈长"和"对直距离"的话，那么"圈长"对应的就是"周长"，"对直距离"对应的就是"直径"，它们所指的都是同一回事儿：地球的周长是二万五千英里，而直径就是八千英里。

地球的表面，是一层由岩石组成的地壳，它就像热乎乎的烤土豆外面包裹着的

shells, or coal or little stones, and that's what they *are* made of. If you could cut the World in half as if it were an apple, it might look something like the picture on the next page. We call it a "Cross Section."

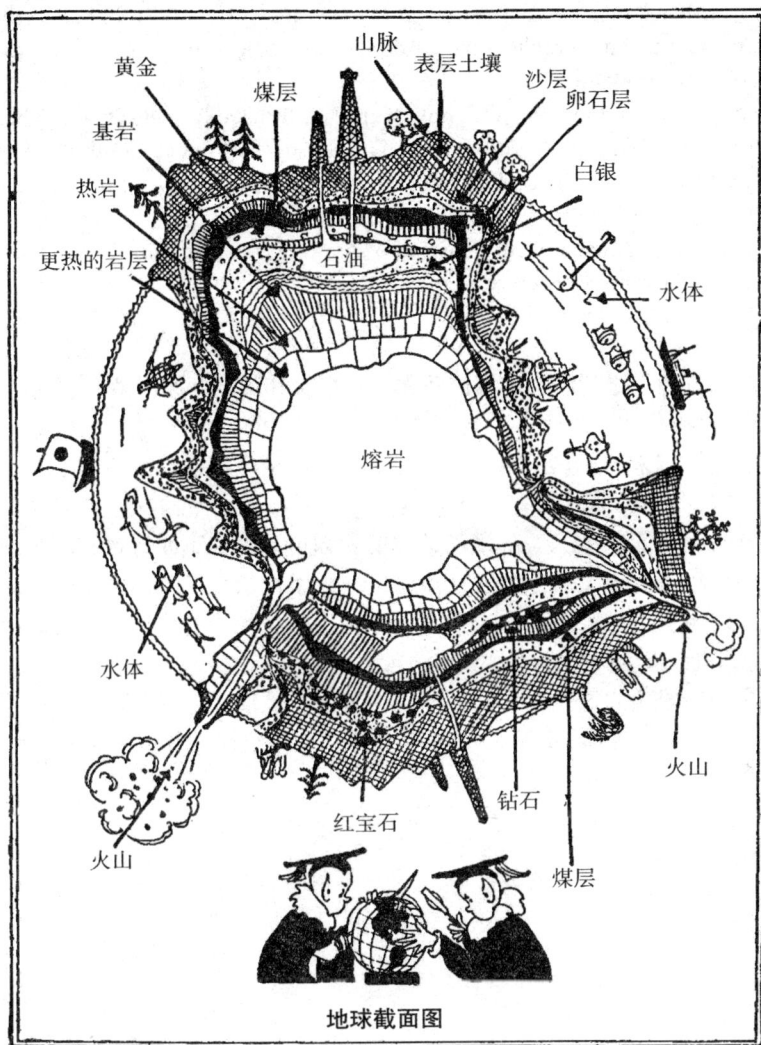

地球截面图

那层烤焦了的外皮一样。假如向下挖掘的话，那么最先挖到的那一部分地壳是分层排列的，就像果冻蛋糕那样，一层一层地堆叠着，只是地壳里的这些分层，似乎都是由沙子和贝壳或者煤炭和小石子构成的，而事实上，它们也的确是由这些东西组成的。如果你们能够像切苹果那样，把地球切成两半的话，就会呈现出上图所示的样子来。我们称之为"横截面"。

有些岩层之间还有煤炭，就像果冻蛋糕里的果冻似的，其他地方则有黄金、白银、钻石和红宝石，还有些岩层里则储存着石油。人们之所以会向下打井，钻穿这

Between some of the layers of rock there is coal like jelly in a jelly-cake and in other places there are gold and silver and diamonds and rubies, and in some of the rock there are pools of oil. That's why men dig wells down through these layers of rock to get oil, and that's why men dig mines to get coal and gold.

And still farther down the rock is not in layers—it is just solid rock; and still farther down it gets hotter and hotter where the world has not cooled off even yet, until the rock is no longer solid, but melted.

Whenever you see a chimney you know there is a furnace beneath it, and when smoke and fire come out of its top you know there is a fire in the furnace. Well, there are many places on the World where fire and smoke come out of the ground as if through a chimney from a fiery furnace. These places are called volcanoes.

Why was the World made of rock instead of brass or glass or china? Why is the World shaped like a ball and not like a box, a roller, or an old shoe?

些岩层来开采石油，之所以会挖掘矿井来开采煤炭和黄金，原因就在于此。

而岩石层之下更深的地方，就不再是分层排列的，而全都是基岩了。再往下去，岩石还变得越来越炽热，因为地球的这一部分至今都还没有冷却下来，使得岩石不再是固体，而成了熔岩。

无论什么时候，只要一看到烟囱，你们就知道，烟囱下面肯定有座炉子，如果烟囱顶上还冒出烟火来，那你们就会知道，炉子里肯定是生了火。好吧，地球上有好多的地方，地上也会冒出烟和火来，就像是从一座燃着的炉子上方的烟囱里冒出来似的。这些地方，就称为火山。

为什么地球是由岩石构成的，而不是由黄铜、玻璃或者瓷器构成的呢？为什么地球的样子会是一个球体，而不是像一个盒子、一个滚筒或者一只旧鞋子呢？

4 The Endless Parade

Did you ever see a parade—a very long one? I once saw a parade of soldiers that took all day to pass by. Tramp, tramp—tramp, tramp—tramp, tramp, hour after hour, all day long. I never had seen so many men in my whole life. There must have been a hundred thousand of them. It didn't seem possible that there were so many people in the World. But if all the people there are in the World should pass by in one long parade, it would take not one day but a lifetime for them to pass by, for there are over two billion people in the world.

A hundred new people—babies—are born every minute of the day and of the night; many are born while you are reading this, and with every tick of the clock some one has died. But more people are born than die each day, so that the World is getting fuller and fuller of people all the time.

The people on the World are all about the same size and shape. Only in fairy-tales are people as small as your thumb or as tall as a church-steeple. None have wings instead of arms or wheels instead of legs. They all have one head, one nose, one mouth; they all have two ears, two eyes, two arms, and two legs. And yet in all these two billion people there are no two alike, there is not a single person exactly like any other one. Even twins are not

第4章　没有尽头的游行队伍

你们有没有见过一支游行队伍，一支很长、很长的游行队伍呢？我曾经见过一支由士兵组成的行军队伍，他们整整走了一天，队伍才完全经过呢。嗵、嗵、嗵、嗵、嗵、嗵，过了一个小时又一个小时，一整天都在走。我的一生中，还从来没有见过那么多的人。那支队伍里，一定有十万人吧。地球上有这么多的人，这一点看起来似乎不可思议得很。不过，倘若全世界的人组成一支长长的游行队伍经过的话，那么需要的可不只是一天，而是需要一生的时间了，因为世界上如今总共有二十多亿人口呢[1]。

世界的一个昼夜当中，每一分钟都会新出生一百个人，即出现一百名新生婴儿。因此，就在你们看到这句话的时候，世界上又出生了许多的婴儿，并且，时钟每滴答一次，就有一个人死去。不过，由于每天出生的人数都比去世的人数要多，因此全球人口数量一直都在不停地增长。

世界上所有人的身材和模样都差不多。只有在童话故事里，才有小至大拇指、高至教堂尖顶的人物。人类没有翅膀，只有胳膊；没有轮子，唯有双腿。他们都只有一个脑袋、一个鼻子、一张嘴；他们都有两只耳朵、两只眼睛、两只胳膊和两条腿。而且，在所有这二十多亿人口当中，没有两个人的长相是相同的，也就是说，

---

[1] 作者编纂本书时是二十世纪四五十年代，当时全世界还只有二十多亿人口。到了2014年，全世界的人口总数则已经超过了七十二亿。

exactly alike.

The chief difference in people is their color. Most of the two billion are white, hut a great many are black and a larger number are halfway between white and black—they are sort of yellow-brown. These three colors of people we call "races." "It's a good day for the race," my father used to say. I thought he was talking of a horse-race or a boat-race, but when I asked, "What race?" he would smile and say, "It's a good day for the white race, the black race, all the races."

Each race used to live by itself in its own part of the World, but many have wandered away to other

全世界所有人组成了一支没有尽头的游行队伍
（玛丽·舍伍德·赖特·琼斯制图）

没有一个人长得与另一个人一模一样。即便是双胞胎，长相也不是完全一样的。

人与人之间的主要区别，就在于他们的肤色不同。这二十多亿人口当中，绝大多数都是白种人，但也有许多属于黑种人，还有更多介乎白人和黑人之间的人种，就是皮肤有点儿带黄棕色的人。我们把这三种肤色不同的人，分称为三个“种族”。“今天对种族来说可是个好日子呢。”我的父亲以前常常这样说。我以为他说的是赛马或者赛艇，可当我问道：“什么比赛呢？”他却会微笑着回答说：“对白种人、黑种人和所有种族的人来说，今天都是个好日子。”[1]

在过去，每个种族常常都独自居住在世界上属于他们自己的那个区域，可到了后来，许多人却漂泊到了其他的地方。在我们美国，绝大多数人都是白种人，但也有许多的黑种人，并且还有少量的黄种人。

---

[1] 在英语中，“种族”和“比赛”都用race表示，因此会引起小孩子误解。

parts. Most of the people in our part of the World are white, but there are also many black and a few yellow-brown.

Suppose you had been born black.

Suppose you'd been born yellow or red.

Suppose you had been born in

Africa or

Asia or

Australia.

Suppose you had been born with another father and mother.

Suppose you had been born in another world instead of this World.

Suppose you hadn't been born at all—where would you be now?

There are only six continents where people live, but on each of these there are several countries. *A* country doesn't mean *the* country. *A* country means cities, towns, villages *and* country under one ruler. There are eighty countries on the World. Some countries are small with only a few thousand people in the whole country, and some countries are large with many millions of people. Our country, the United States, has over one hundred and fifty million people, but there are several countries with more. China, which is on the other side of the World, has the most people. It has three times as many people as the United States; and India, another country on the other side of the World, has the next largest number of people. Both these countries are in Asia—the largest continent with the shortest name and

　　假设你出生的时候是个黑种人。

　　假设你出生的时候是个黄种人或者红种人。

　　假设你出生于非洲、亚洲或者大洋洲。

　　假设生你的是另一对父母。

　　假设你不是出生在地球上，而是出生在另一个世界里。

　　假设你根本就没有出生；那么，现在你又会在哪儿呢？

　　世界上只有六个大洲有人居住，但每个大洲上又分成了许多的国家。一个国家，指的可不是"乡村"[1]。一个国家，是由同一个统治者统治着的城市、市镇、村庄以及乡村所组成的。如今，世界上有八十个国家[2]。有些国家很小，全国只有数千人口；有些国家则很大，国内总人口达数百万。我们国家，即美利坚合众国，有一亿五千多万人口，不过，有几个国家的人口数量则更多。处于地球另一面的中国，是世界上人口最多的国家。该国的人口数量，达到了美国的三倍。还有同处于地球另一面的印度，人口数量则居世界第二。这两个国家都位于亚洲，虽说亚洲属于世界上面积最大的一个洲，但其名称最短，人口也最多。

　　每个国家都有一个统治者，就像每个家庭都有一位父亲、每支橄榄球队都有一位队长那样。有些国家的统治者是国王，有些国家则是总统，并且，在绝大多数国

---

　　[1]　英语中，"国家"和"乡村"都用country表示，只是前面所用的冠词不一样。

　　[2]　这是作者编纂本书时的数据。如今据统计，世界上共有二百二十多个国家和地区，其中主权国家就有一百九十多个。下文中列举的人口数量也是如此，请读者注意。

the most people.

Each country has a ruler, just as every family has a father or every football team has a captain. Some countries have a king for a ruler and some have a president, and most countries have other people to rule with the king and the president.

A king is a king because his father was a king, and his son will be king for the same reason. A president is president because he was chosen by the people in the country, just as the captain of a football team is chosen by his team. Choosing we call "voting." A king is king for his whole life, but a president is president for only a few years.

The country of a king is called a kingdom. If one man rules over several countries, he is called an emperor and the countries an empire. A country with a president is called a republic. Our country is a republic. The king or the president and the others who rule with him are called the government. The government makes the rules, but it also does two things that no one else is allowed to do. The government makes the money of the country and the postage-stamps. The money of one country is not good in another country and neither are the postage-stamps. And neither is the language of one country good in another—usually.

The people on the World speak many different languages. Even in the same country many different languages are spoken. There are over 3,000 different languages in all— 3,000, just think of that! You probably speak only one of these, and couldn't talk to any one nor understand any one who spoke any other language than your own. In the United States almost every one speaks English, which, strange to say, is the language of another

家里，还有许多其他的人，与国王或者总统一起治理着整个国家。

一位国王之所以成为国王，是因为他的父亲就是一位国王，而他的儿子，也会出于同样的原因而成为国王。一位总统之所以成为总统，是因为该国人民挑选他来当总统，就像橄榄球队队长是由队员们推选出来的那样。这种选择，我们称之为"选举"。国王是终身制的，但总统的任期却只有数年。

设有国王的国家被称为王国。假如一个君主统治着好几个国家，那么这个君主就被称为皇帝，而他统治下的那些国家则组成了一个帝国。设有总统的国家被称为共和国。美国就是一个共和国。国王或者总统，加上与之一起治理整个国家的人，就组成了政府。政府制定法律法规，但同时还拥有两种其他人不允许去做的特权。政府可以发行该国的货币和邮票。一国的货币到了另一国并不一定有效，邮票也是这样。而一国的语言到了另一国，通常也是行不通的。

地球上的人，说着许多种不同的语言。即便是在同一个国家里，人们也会说多种不同的语言。世界上总共有三千多种语言，想象一下吧，竟然达到了三千多种！你们很可能只会说其中的一种，并且，除了那些与你们说同种语言的人，你们很可能无法与说其他语言的人交谈，也无法听懂说其他语言的人的话。在美国，几乎人人都说英语，但说来奇怪，英语也是另一个国家即英国的语言。不过，在一个像欧洲这样的大陆上，如果出去走上一天，大家是很难不在街道上、商店内、旅馆里听到另一种不同的语言的。

country—England. But on a continent like Europe you could hardly go a day's journey without hearing a different language on the street, in the shops, at the hotel.

I happened to be born in the United States, and as I heard everybody around me speaking English I learned to speak English too. But I might have been born in Asia, a yellow boy, and learned to speak Chinese, or I might have been born in Africa, a black boy, and learned to speak a language I don't even know the name of. I know a man who speaks a dozen different languages, and I know *of* a man who speaks 100! You can understand how wonderful this is when it usually takes years to learn to speak *one* other language besides your own. Letters of most of these languages are like ours, like the letters on this page—they are called Roman, because a people called Romans first used them long ago. But letters of Chinese and Japanese and some other faraway languages are different—they look like this:

我碰巧出生在美国，由于周围的人全都说英语，因此我也学会了说英语。但是，我也有可能出生在亚洲，是一个黄种男孩，并且学会了说汉语，或者，我也有可能出生在非洲，是一个黑人小男孩，并且学会了说一种连名称我也说不上来的语言呢。我认识一个能说十几种不同语言的人，并且我还听说过，有个人竟然能说一百种语言！如果你们知道，除了自己的母语，学会另一种语言通常都要花上好几年的时间，那你们就能理解，这一点有多么神奇了。这些语言中，大部分所用的字母都像我们所说的英语一样，与我写作本书所用的文字一样，这种字母，叫作"罗马字母"，因为它们是很久以前一个叫作罗马人的民族率先使用的。但中国的汉字和日文字母，以及许多与我们相距遥远的语言，却不一样，它们的样子，就像是这样：

5　The 13 Club

A man may pay millions of dollars to have a hospital, a library, or a museum named after him, and another who has paid nothing, done nothing, deserved nothing, and asked nothing has two of the biggest things in the World—the two continents North and South America—named after him, and people will go on forever calling them America after him—an unimportant, almost unknown man named Amerigo.

Do you know the song that begins, "My Country, 'Tis of Thee"? What do you mean by "My Country"? It is a part, the smaller part, of North America.

Have you a buffalo nickel in your pocket—a 5-cent piece? If not, perhaps you can borrow one just to look at. On the head side is the picture of an Indian with feathers in his hair. Why do you suppose our country has the picture of an Indian instead of a white man on the nickel? On the tail side is the picture of a buffalo. Why do you suppose our country has a picture of a buffalo on the nickel instead of a horse or a cow?

Well, long before there were any white men here at all, or any horses or cows, there were a great many Indians and a great many buffaloes in this country. Now there are very few Indians and very few buffaloes in America, so these pictures on the nickel are to remind us that the Indian is the first American man and the buffalo is the first American animal.

第5章　"十三州"俱乐部

有人可能会花上数百万美元，来用自己的名字为一座医院、图书馆或者博物馆命名，但也有一个人，既没有花任何钱、没有做任何事，也没有要求什么，就让自己的名字变成了世界上两个最大地区的名称，即南、北美洲这两块大陆的名称；而且，人们还会继续下去，永远用他的名字来称呼这两块大陆呢。他就是一个并不重要、几乎名不见经传的人物，叫作亚美利哥。

你们知不知道有这样一首歌曲，开头是"我的祖国，也属于你"呢？你们知道"我的祖国"指的是什么吗？它就是北美洲的一部分，且属于北美洲的一小部分。

大家口袋里有没有一枚水牛镍币[1]，即一枚五分钱的硬币？要是没有的话，或许你们可以去借一枚来看一看。硬币的正面，是一幅头插羽毛的印第安人像。你们想一想，为什么美国的镍币上会用印第安人的头像，而不是用白人的头像呢？硬币的背面，是一头水牛的图案。你们想一想，为什么美国的硬币上会用一头水牛的图案，而不是用一匹马儿或者一头母牛的图案呢？

---

[1]　水牛镍币（buffalo nickel），美国政府于1913年发行并于1938年停止发行的一种硬币，其背面图案是一头水牛，目的提醒公众保护环境和水牛，正面图案则是一位土著印第安人，说明了美国社会的包容性前进了一步。亦称"野牛镍币"。它与自由女神像、美国哥特式、芭比娃娃及"山姆大叔"一起，称为美国文化的五大象征。

If you will look at the printing on the nickel you will see it says "United States of America." That's the full name of our country, but it is too long for us to say United States of America every time, so we usually say just United States or just America or use just the initials U. S. A.

Have you ever seen a picture of a tall man with a suit of clothes that looked as if it had been made out of a flag, with red and white striped breeches, a long-tailed coat, and a tall hat with stars on it? There never was such a man really, but he is supposed to be the picture of the United States. As the initials of the United States are U. S., some one said they stand for Uncle Sam, so the old fellow dressed in a flag we call Uncle Sam.

The map of the U. S. looks as if it were made like a patch-work quilt of patches of different sizes and shapes. These patches are the States that are United—that means, joined to one another. As a matter of fact, of course, there are no lines between the States. The lines on the map are marked on the ground by stone posts set so far apart that you may cross from one State to another without even knowing when you are in a different State. Each State has towns and cities and country. I live in a city and the city is in the State of Maryland. You may live in a city or a town or in the country in another State. But every one in the U. S. must live in some State unless—I'll

我们便把这个身披旗帜的
老伙计称为"山姆大叔"

好吧，在美国还没有出现任何白人、没有出现任何马匹或者母牛的很久以前，这个国家里就生活着大量的印第安人，生活着大量的水牛了。如今，美国的印第安人数量很少，而水牛数量也不多了，因此硬币上的这两幅图案，就是为了提醒我们，印第安人是美国最初的原住民，而水牛则是美国最早的动物。

假如看一看硬币上的文字，大家就会看到，上面写着"美利坚合众国"几个字。这是我们美国的全称，不过，由于这个全称太长，人们不可能每次都说"美利坚合众国"，因此我们通常都将其简称为"合众国"、"美国"，或者只用首字母U. S. A.来表示。

你们有没有见过这样一幅图画，上面是一个身材高高的男子，身穿一套似乎是用一面旗子制成的衣服，下身是红白条纹相间的马裤，上衣则是长长的燕尾服，头上还戴着一顶高高的、上面缀着星形的帽子呢？虽说现实当中根本就没有这样的一个人，可人们却认为，他就是美国的象征哩。由于"合众国"的首字母是U. S.，有人说它是"山姆大叔"（Uncle Sam）的缩写，因此，我们就把这个身披旗帜的老伙计称为"山姆大叔"，来指代美国人了。

美国的地图，样子就像是一条用布头拼成的被子，上面布满了大小和形状不同的各种补丁。这些"补丁"，就是"合众"起来，也即彼此联合起来的各个州。当然，各州之间事实上并没有真正的线条相隔。地图上的这些线条，在地面上是用石

北冰洋

格陵兰岛

阿拉斯加

加拿大

哈德逊湾

拉布拉多半岛

纽芬兰岛

大湖地区

哥伦比亚河

黄石公园

大盐湖

圣弗朗西斯科（旧金山）

洛杉矶

科罗拉多河

下加利福尼亚半岛

芝加哥

低特律

匹兹堡

华盛顿

丹佛

派克斯峰

安那波利斯

圣路易斯

密西西比河

波士顿

纽约

费城

巴尔的摩

美利坚合众国

大西洋

墨西哥

新奥尔良

墨西哥湾

太　平　洋

北美洲

tell you later the few places he may live without being in any State.

Some of the States have straight sides and some have one, two or more crooked sides. Some are big and some are little. The biggest State is Texas, at the bottom, near the center—only we don't say bottom, we say south. The smallest State is Rhode Island, which is not an island at all. It is near the upper right-hand corner—

桩标示的，但它们之间相距甚远，因此当你们越过一个州，进入另一个州时，甚至都不知道自己何时已经身处一个不同的州里了。每个州都有市镇、城市和乡村。我住在一座城市里，而这座城市则位于马里兰州。你们可能住在另一个州的一座城市、一个市镇或者乡

下。不过，美国境内的每个人，都必定居住在某个州，除非他可以住在几个不属于各州的地方，到了后面，我再跟你们来说一说那几个不属于各州的地方吧。

有一些州的边界都是笔直的，还有一些州则有两条或者更多条弯弯曲曲的边界。有些州的面积很大，有些州则很小。美国面积最大的州是得克萨斯州，它位于地图底下靠近地图中心的那个地方，只是，我们不说"底下"，而说"南部"。美国面积最小的州则是罗得岛州，但它其实根本就不是一个岛屿。该州位于地图的右

only we don't say upper right-hand corner, we say northeast. Texas would make more than 200 Rhode Islands. That is, you could put more than 200 Rhode Islands in Texas.

Not so long ago there was no United States. There were only thirteen little States along the shore of the Atlantic Ocean. These States were so small they thought they ought to form a club. There is an old story about a man who wanted to break a bundle of sticks. He tried and he tried but he couldn't break the bundle. Then some one told him to take the bundle apart and break each stick separately; so he did, and broke them easily. The States thought that they, in the same way, might be broken easily if separate, so they tied themselves together like a bundle of sticks in order that they might not be "broken" by an enemy. And so the 13 States formed a 13 club and called themselves the United States. They took as their motto "In Union is Strength," which means "In one bundle we are strong."

Now thirteen is generally considered an unlucky number, but these 13 States were not afraid of bad luck. In fact, as the new country had to have a flag, they made a flag with 13 stripes—seven red stripes and six white—and they put a white star for each State in a blue corner of the flag. Other parts of North America thought they'd like to join the club too, and more and more pieces kept on joining until there were forty-eight States, and these States that were united stretched from the Atlantic Ocean on one side to the Pacific Ocean on the other—that is, from where the sun rises from the ocean on one side to where it sets over the ocean on the other. Each time a piece joined the U. S. another star was put in the

上角，只是我们不说"右上角"，而是说"东北部"。得克萨斯州的面积，相当于两百多个罗得岛州的面积呢。也就是说，你们可以把两百多个罗得岛州，装入得克萨斯州里面。

就在不久之前，世界上还没有什么"合众国"。当时，只是大西洋沿岸有十三个小小的州。这几个州的面积都太小，因此它们都觉得，应该组成一个俱乐部才行。有个古老的故事，说的是一个人想要折断一把棍子。他试了又试，可怎么也没法折断那把棍子。后来，有人告诉他说，可以把那捆棍子分开，再一根一根地折断。他听从了这一建议，便轻而易举地把所有棍子都折断了。这十三个州觉得，要是各自为政的话，它们同样会被敌人轻而易举地各个击破，因此，它们便彼此团结起来，就像一捆棍子那样，从而不至于被任何敌人"折断"了。于是，这十三个州便组成了一个"十三州"俱乐部，并自称为"合众国"。它们把"团结就是力量"当成座右铭，这句话的意思就是："抱成一团，我们就很强大。"

如今，人们常常认为十三是个不吉利的数字，可在当时，这十三个州却并不担心它们会遭到噩运。事实上，由于新成立的这个合众国必须拥有一面国旗，因此它们便制作了一面镶有十三道条纹的旗子，其中有七道红色条纹、六道白色条纹，并且在旗帜上那个蓝色的角上，用白色的星形代表各个州。后来，北美洲的其他地区觉得，它们最好也加入这个俱乐部，因此，越来越多的地区不断加入进来，直到总数达到了四十八个州。而联合起来的这些州，从北美洲一侧的大西洋沿岸延伸到了另一侧的太平洋沿岸，也就是说，从太阳升起那一侧的海洋，一直延伸到了太阳落

corner of the flag, but the number of stripes was not changed, for there would have been too many; so now there are forty-eight stars—that means forty-eight States united into one country. That's why there are on our coins the words "*e pluribus unum*", which means "one from many."

Not all of America joined the club, however. The country north of the U. S. called Canada and the country south of the U. S. called Mexico did not join. And yet the people in Canada are Americans, and the people in Mexico are Americans too, but both Canada and Mexico have different rulers from what we have, for they are different countries.

Though there are very few Indians left in the U. S., we still use some of their names in naming our States. See if you can pick out some of the States on the map that have Indian names. Maryland and Virginia, of course, are *not*—for they are girls' names. States beginning with "New"—like New York, New Jersey, New Hampshire—of course are *not* Indian. They are named after old places in another country. But Minnesota, which means "sky blue water"; Ohio, which means "beautiful river" or "great"; and many others are Indian.

下的另一侧海洋。每当一个地方加入合众国，国旗角上便会增加一颗星星，但国旗上的条纹数却没有变化，因为要是每加入一个州就添加一道条纹的话，那么条纹数就会太多了。因此，如今美国的国旗上就有四十八颗星星，意味着四十八个州联合起来，组成了一个国家[1]。我国的硬币上印着一行拉丁文"e pluribus unum"，意思就是"合众为一"，原因就在这里呢。

然而，并不是北美洲的所有地区全都加入了这个俱乐部。美国北边的那个国家，叫作加拿大，而美国南边的那个国家，则叫墨西哥，它们都没有加入。虽说加拿大人和墨西哥人也都属于美洲人，但这两个国家的统治者都与美国不同，所以它们都是与美国不一样的国家。

尽管如今美国境内剩下的印第安人已经很少了，但我们还是用了印第安语里的一些名称，来给一些州命名。看一看，你们能不能在地图上找出一些拥有印第安名称的州来吧。马里兰州和弗吉尼亚州当然不是，因为它们都是女孩子的名字。凡是以"新"或音译"纽"开头的州，比如纽约州、新泽西州、新罕布什尔州等，用的自然也不是印第安名称。它们都是用另一个国家的老地名来命名的。不过，意思是"天空般湛蓝之水"的明尼苏达州、意指"漂亮河流"或者"巨大"的俄亥俄州，以及其他许多的州名，用的可都是印第安名称呢。

---

[1] 注意，如今美国已经有五十个州（增加了阿拉斯加州和夏威夷州），还有一个直辖特区（即华盛顿特区）。

6 A City Built in a Swamp

A cap which you wear on your head means "head."

A *cap*-tain also means "head"—he's the head of a company of soldiers.

A *cap*-ital means "head" too—it's the head city of a country or of a State.

When I was a boy I lived in the *capital* of the United States, but I did not live in the *Capitol* of the United States. That may sound funny, but it's true, for there are two kinds of capit$_a^o$ls. The capit-Al is a city, the Capit-Ol is a building, and of course I didn't live in the Capit-Ol building. Not even the President lives there.

When our country was started men tried to find a suitable place for the capital. Eight places were tried out and at last a swamp was chosen as the proper place to build the city, because it was then near the center of our country. So a city was built there and called Washington after George Washington, because he was the First President of the United States. Even when-I-was-a-boy there was a part of Washington which every one called "Swamp Puddle" or "Swam-poodle." I wonder if boys there still call it that. It is now one of the most beautiful cities in the World, with lovely parks and beautiful buildings. George Washington didn't live in Washington. He lived at a place in the State of Virginia about ten miles away called Mount Vernon. Washington is now on the edge of our country, over a thousand miles from the center. The capital hasn't moved, but the center of the country

第6章　建在沼泽里的城市

大家戴在脑袋上的帽子（cap），意思就是"头"。

一名上尉（captain），指的也是"头儿"，因为他是一个连队里的士兵的头儿。

而一座首府（capital），也有"头"的意思，因为它是一个国家或者一个州领头的城市。

我小的时候，就居住在美国的首都（capital），不过，那时我并没有在美国的国会大厦（Capitol）里住过。这听上去很好玩，但事实却正是如此，因为在英语里，这是两个同音词。capital指的是一座城市，Capitol指的则是一座大楼。我呢，自然没有在国会大厦这栋大楼里住过。连美国总统，也不住在那里呢。

美国刚刚建国的时候，人们想要找到一个适合的地方，来作为首都。他们考查过八个地方，最终选定了一处沼泽，认为那里最适合于建立首都，因为在当时，那里就在美国中部地区的附近。于是，人们在那里修建起了一座城市，并且根据乔治·华盛顿的名字，将那里命名为华盛顿市，因为乔治·华盛顿是合众国的第一任总统。甚至到了我小的时候，大家都还把华盛顿市里的一个地区称为"沼泽潭"或者"沼泽池"呢。我很想知道，目前住在那里的孩子们，是不是还会这样来称呼那个地区。如今，这里已经成为世界上最美丽的一座城市，里面有着许多秀美的公园和漂亮的建筑。乔治·华盛顿可没有在华盛顿市里居住过。他住在离该市大约十英

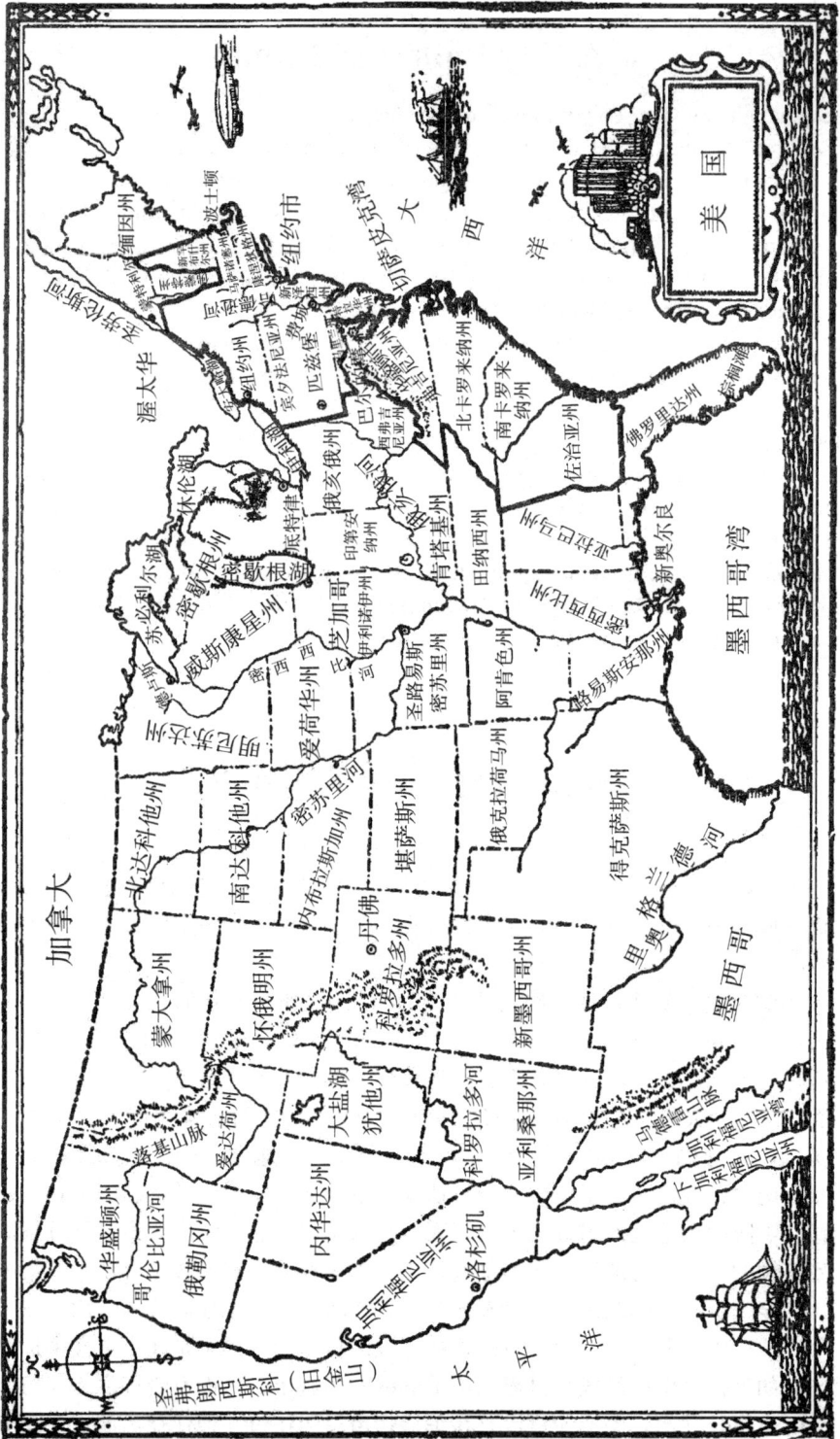

美国

加拿大

渥太华

大西洋

纽约市

切萨皮克湾

缅因州

新罕布什尔州

佛蒙特州

马萨诸塞州

罗德岛州

康涅狄格州

纽约州

宾夕法尼亚州

新泽西州

特拉华州

马里兰州

波士顿

黄夕法尼亚州

匹兹堡

巴尔的摩

西弗吉尼亚州

弗吉尼亚州

北卡罗来纳州

南卡罗来纳州

佐治亚州

佛罗里达州

墨西哥湾

新奥尔良

密西西比州

亚拉巴马州

田纳西州

肯塔基州

俄亥俄州

印第安纳州

伊利诺伊州

俄克拉荷马州

阿肯色州

路易斯安那州

圣路易斯

密苏里州

堪萨斯州

得克萨斯州

里奥格兰德河

墨西哥

新墨西哥州

亚利桑那州

科罗拉多河

下加利福尼亚州

马德雷山脉

苏必利尔湖

休伦湖

密执安湖

伊利湖

安大略湖

威斯康星州

明尼苏达州

密执根州

爱荷华州

内布拉斯加州

北达科他州

南达科他州

蒙大拿州

怀俄明州

科罗拉多州

丹佛

犹他州

大盐湖

内华达州

加利福尼亚州

洛杉矶

圣弗朗西斯科(旧金山)

华盛顿州

俄勒冈州

爱达荷州

哥伦比亚河

落基山脉

密苏里河

太平洋

has.

There are twenty-eight cities named "Washington" in the United States. Washington, the capital, looks on the map as if it were in the State of Maryland, but it isn't. It isn't in any State. The capital of all the States had to have a place all its own; so this piece of land is called the District of Columbia, or D. C. for short. The District of Columbia is named after Columbus, the man who discovered America. So if you write a letter to any one in Washington, the capital, you must be very careful to put "D. C." after Washington, for there are so many cities and towns named after Washington that your letter might not go to the right one.

When I was a boy I thought the Capitol was the most beautiful building in the World. Since then I have seen nearly all of the most beautiful buildings in the World, and I have changed my mind. I have even seen a building fit to be in Heaven. I used to make a copy of the Capitol as nearly as I could in my sand-pile. I would fill a shoe-box with wet sand, then turn it carefully upside down so as to empty it out without breaking, and I made the dome on top in the same way with a tea-cup.

I thought all capitols of other countries must have domes too. I didn't learn until later that not capitols but churches were the first buildings to have domes, and that many capitols have no domes. As a boy I used to climb to the top of the dome—for there was no elevator—to see the view of the city, and to look down on the inside at the floor far below where people walking seemed like ants crawling.

里以外、属于弗吉尼亚州一个叫作"弗农山"的地方。现在，华盛顿市处于美国的边上，距美国的中心地带有一千多英里远了呢。不是这座首都移动了，而是美国的中心地带转移了。

在美国，总共有二十八座城市，都叫"华盛顿"。首都华盛顿市在地图上看来，似乎位于马里兰州，可实际上并非如此。它没有位于任何一个州里。作为全国的首都，它必须有一块属于自己的地盘才是，于是，这处地盘便被称为"哥伦比亚特区"[1]，或者简称"特区"。哥伦比亚特区，是用发现美洲的哥伦布这个人物的名字来命名的。因此，假如你们要给首都华盛顿的哪个人写信的话，那就必须非常仔细，得在"华盛顿市"后面加上"特区"才行，因为美国有那么多以华盛顿的名字来命名的市镇和城市，如果不加上"特区"二字的话，你们的信件可能就到不了正确的城市呢。

小的时候，我曾经以为国会大厦是世界上最漂亮的一座建筑。自那以后，由于已经见过了世界上差不多所有最漂亮的建筑，因此我不再那样认为了。我甚至还见过一座堪称天上才有的建筑呢。以前在玩堆沙的时候，几乎只要做得到，我都会用沙子堆出国会大厦的模样来。我会用一个鞋盒子装满湿沙，然后小心翼翼地将盒子倒过来，倒出里面的沙子，不让沙子散开，接着再用同样的方法，用一只茶杯在上

---

[1] 哥伦比亚特区（District of Columbia），美国联邦直辖区，相当于我国的直辖市。其范围与首都华盛顿市相同，如今多称"华盛顿特区"。

On one side of the Capitol is a large room called the Senate, and on the other side is a still larger room called the House of Representatives. In both the Senate and the House of Representatives men sit at desks like boys in school. These men are the ones who make our laws, which are rules that everybody in the United States must obey. The men in the Senate are called Senators. The men in the House are called Representatives. When I say "men," I mean women too, for some of the Senators and Representatives are women.

Each State chooses two Senators to go to the Capitol in Washington. No matter whether the State is big like Texas or whether it is little like Rhode Island, it sends only two Senators. And each State also sends to the Capitol in Washington other men or women called Representatives, but the number of Representatives each State sends depends on the number of people in the State; New York has the most people, so it sends the most Representatives. Several States have so few people that they send only one Representative.

美国国会大厦

我曾经以为它是世界上最
漂亮的建筑

The Senate and the House of Representatives together are called "Congress," and when Congress is holding a meeting a flag is flying over the Capitol.

Look in the front of this book or any other book and you will see printed there "Copyright." Just across a park from the Capitol is a large building with a golden dome on top. This building is the Library of Congress. Every one in the United States

面做出一个穹顶来。

我曾经以为，其他国家的国会大厦，一定也都建有穹顶。直到后来我才知道，最先修建穹顶的可不是国会大厦，而是教堂，并且许多的国会大厦也没有修建穹顶。小的时候，我经常爬到那座穹顶上面（因为那时还没有电梯），去观看这座城市，去俯瞰国会大厦的内部，人们远远地在下面的地上走动，似乎就是一只只爬动着的蚂蚁呢。

国会大厦一侧，有一个巨大的房间，叫作参议院，而另一侧还有一个更大的房间，叫作众议院。在参议院和众议院里，人们都是像学校里的学生一样，坐在桌子旁边。这些人，就是为美国制定法律，即制定合众国里任何人都必须遵守的规定的人。参议院里的人，叫作参议员。众议院里的人，则叫众议员。我说的"人们"当中，也有女性，因为有些参议员和众议员就是女性议员。

每个州都会推选出两名参议员，入驻位于华盛顿市的国会大厦。不管一个州是像得克萨斯那样的大州，还是像罗德岛这样的小州，都只能派出两名参议员。每个州还会向位于华盛顿市的国会大厦派驻众议员，男女都有，可各州所派众议员的数量，却取决于各州的人口数量。纽约州的人口最多，因此该州派驻的众议员人数也最多。有好几个州，都由于人口太少，因此只能派出一名众议员呢。参议院与众议院合称为"国会"，每当国会举行会议的时候，国会大楼上方都会飘扬着一面美国国旗。

who prints a book sends two copies of it to this library, and the library sends him a "copy right," which means that no one else has the "right" to copy it or print it without his permission. In the Library of Congress there are more books than in any other building in the country.

Look on your camera or phonograph, or any other machine in your home, and see if you can find the word "Patented." Any one in the country who invents anything new and useful—whether it is a fountain-pen, an airplane, or a mouse-trap—sends one—a model, it is called—to another building in Washington called the Patent Office and asks for a patent. If the thing is really new and no one has ever made anything of the kind before, the Patent Office gives him the sole right to make and sell it, and no one else is allowed to make or sell it. That is called a patent. Some of the models are very curious. One model that some one had invented was a steam-engine that walked with iron legs. When-I-was-a-boy I invented a "snapback" handkerchief. I would blow my nose, then let go the handkerchief, and a rubber pulled it back into my pocket. But I didn't get a patent.

Parades! Soldiers! Bands of music! Flying flags! Some of the greatest parades have passed down a very wide street in Washington called Pennsylvania Avenue, or usually just "*The* Avenue." It might be called "Parade Avenue." It stretches from the Capitol to another building about a mile away that looks like a big bank. This other building is called the Treasury. There is a picture of it on the $10 bill. In the Treasury is kept money of the United States. We write United States with two letters, U. S., and we write the sign for

看一看本书的前部，或者看一看其他任何一本书的前部，大家就会发现，这些书上都印有"版权"两个字。与国会大厦隔着一个公园相对而立的，是一栋楼顶建有一座金色穹顶的大楼。这座大楼，就是国会图书馆。美国国内每个出版图书的人，都会送上两册到这座图书馆来，而这座图书馆则会把一种所谓的"复制权"授予给那个人，这就意味着，未经此人许可，其他任何人都没有"权利"来复制或者出版该书了。国会图书馆里的藏书，比美国国内其他任何一栋建筑里面的藏书都要多。

看一看家里的照相机、留声机，或者家中其他的机器设备，看你们能不能找出"专利"这个词来。美国国内任何一个发明了新颖、有用之物的人，无论他发明的是一支自来水笔、一架飞机还是一台捕鼠器，都会送上一件所谓的"样品"，到华盛顿市另一座叫作"专利局"的建筑里去，并且要求获得专利。如果发明的东西的确新颖，并且以前从未有人发明过同类之物，"专利局"便会授予发明者独家生产并销售这种东西的权利。这种权利，就叫专利。其中有些样品非常古怪。有个人发明的一件样品，竟然是一台用两条铁腿走路的蒸汽发动机。小的时候，我也发明过一种"迅速复原"的手帕呢。擤完鼻涕之后，我放开手帕，一根橡皮筋便会把手帕拽回我的口袋里去。不过，我并没有获得这种手帕的专利。

游行队伍！士兵！乐队！飞扬的旗帜！华盛顿市里一条叫作"宾夕法尼亚大道"的宽阔街道上，曾经举办过一些最为盛大的游行活动，这条大街，人们通常都简称为"大道"。其实，它也可以称为"游行大道"。它从国会大厦开始，延伸到

"dollars" with the same two letters, written one on top of the other, with the bottom of the "U" cut off—thus, $.

Paper money and postage-stamps are printed in another building.

"You see that man over there turning the handle of that printing-press?" says the guide who shows you around. "He makes a million dollars a day!"

"Whew! He must be the richest man in the World."

"Oh, no. He only gets $5 a day."

The money made out of silver, and gold, and copper is made in another city—not in Washington—at a place called the Mint.

When I was a boy I had an old bookcase which I called my museum. In it I had a starfish, some shells, a bird's nest, a "gold" rock, and so forth. In Washington there is a large museum called the National Museum in which there is a huge collection of all sorts of curious and remarkable things from all over the World.

There are many white houses in the country, but next door to the Treasury is a White House that is different from any other, for in this house the President lives. There is a picture of it on the $20 bill. From the back porch of The White House the latest President of the United States can look across his back yard and see a monument to the First President—-Washington. The Washington Monument is the highest piece of stone work in the World. It's like a giant finger, five hundred and fifty-five feet high. It seemed a mile high, but it is really only about a tenth of a mile high—not even as high as a low mountain.

了大约一英里之外的另一栋建筑，那座大厦的样子，就像是一家大型的银行。这栋建筑，叫作财政部大楼。在面值十美元的纸币上，就印有这座大楼的照片。财政部大楼里，保存着美国的货币。我们将美国缩写成U. S.，并且也用这两个字母来书写"美元"的符号：将它们叠起来，然后切掉U字的底部，就变成了$[1]。

美国的纸币和邮票，却是在另一栋大楼里印制的。

"大家看到那边那个转动印刷机手柄的人了吗？"带领你们参观的导游说。"他每天都会印出一百万美元来呢！"

"嗬！那他一定是世界上最富有的人了。"

"噢，可不是那么回事。他每天的工资只有五美元。"

银币、金币和铜币，则是在华盛顿以外的另一座城市里，在一个叫作铸币厂的地方制造出来的。

小的时候，我曾经有过一只旧书柜，并称它是我的博物馆。书柜里，我存放了一只海星、一些贝壳、一个鸟巢、一块"金"石头，以及诸如此类的东西。而在华盛顿，也有一座大型的博物馆，叫作"国家博物馆"，里面收藏着从世界各地搜集来的、各种各样古怪而非凡的东西。

美国国内，有许多白色的房子，但紧挨着财政部大楼的，却是一座与众不同的

---

[1]　注意，美元符号本是一个大写的S中有两条竖线，但后来演变出了中间只有一竖的符号，表示以美元为单位的货币，比如Can $（加拿大元）、HK $（港币）等。

No man has ever been able to build as high as God. Though there is an elevator, I used to run up the stairs, two steps at a time, to the top of the monument—just for fun—to see how quickly I could do it, and whether I could beat the elevator. Boys are like that. They will run a race with anything. I could beat the elevator down by jumping half a dozen steps at a time, but not up. My heart did the beating going up.

There is a long pool of water at the foot of the Washington Monument in which you can see the monument as in a mirror. At the other end of this pool is a marble building with columns all around the four sides. It was built in honor of Abraham Lincoln, the sixteenth President after Washington. It is probably the most thrilling memorial ever built to a

白宫

你们有朝一日也有可能住进那里呢

华盛顿纪念碑

它似乎有一英里高

"白房子"，因为住在里面的，是美国总统。在面值二十美元的纸币上，就印有这座房子的照片。从白宫的后阳台上，在任的美国总统既可以眺望自家后院的景色，还能看到美国第一任总统华盛顿的纪念碑。华盛顿纪念碑，是世界上最高的一座石制艺术品。它就像是一根巨大的手指，有五百五十五英尺[1]高呢。虽说看上去似乎高达一英里，可实际上它却只有差不多十分之一英里高，甚至还没有一座小山那么高。有史以来，还没有人能够建造出像上帝所造之物那样高的建筑。尽管纪念碑里有电梯，但我以前经常沿着楼梯跑上去，一次跨过两级台阶，爬到纪念碑的顶上去，这样做只是为了好玩，只是为了看一看我能跑多快，能不能打败那部电梯。男孩子就是那样的。他们会为了任何东西来比赛。下来的时候，我一次可以跳下六级台阶，因此可以超过电梯，但上去的时候就不行了。往上跑时，我的心跳会不断加快，弄得上气不接下气。

华盛顿纪念碑的脚下，有一个长长的水池，它就像一面镜子，人们可以在池中

---

[1] 英尺（foot），英制长度单位。1英尺约合0.3048米，5280英尺为1英里。

human being. There is a picture of Lincoln on the $5 bill and on the other side a picture of his Memorial. Lincoln was born in a tiny house made of logs, so small that the whole house could be put in one room of your home. No boy was ever poorer, or had less money or less chance, and yet he became President of the United States. While he was President two parts of the United States fought a terrible war with each other and almost became un-United, but Lincoln kept the States together. That's why this beautiful building was built in his honor. The only thing in the building is a statue of Lincoln sitting in a chair. He looks down on the crowds of people who visit him, as if his spirit were inside that figure of stone.

林肯纪念堂

看到纪念碑的倒影。这个水池的另一端，是一座大理石建筑，其四面都有圆柱环绕。这座建筑，是为了纪念华盛顿之后、曾任美国第十六届总统的亚伯拉罕·林肯而修建的。

它很可能是有史以来为纪念一个人类而修建起来的、最令人激动的一座纪念馆了。在面值五美元的纸币上，一面印有林肯的头像，而另一面就是他这座纪念堂的照片。林肯出生于一座小木屋里，那座小木屋实在是太小了，你们家里的一个房间就可以容纳下来呢。再也没有其他的孩子比他更穷，或者比他更没有钱、机会更渺茫的了，可尽管如此，后来他还是成了美国的总统。他担任总统的时候，美国的南北两个地区之间爆发了一场可怕的战争，使得整个国家差一点儿就四分五裂，可林肯却维护了美国的统一。人们之所以修建这座美丽的建筑来纪念他，原因就在于此。纪念堂里唯一的物品，就是一尊坐在椅子里的林肯雕像。他俯瞰着前来瞻仰自己的那一群群民众，仿佛他的精神永远活在那尊雕像里。

7 Mary's Land, Virginia's State, and Penn's Woods

Did you ever trade a top for some marbles or an apple for an orange? Long before there was any Washington or any United States there used to be trader Indians living on the shores of the river that flows by Washington. These Indians paddled their canoes up and down the river and traded with other Indians, swapping things they had for things they wanted—beads for furs, bows for arrows, corn for potatoes. In the Indian language the name for Traders was Potomac, so we call the river after these trader Indians, the Potomac River. The Potomac separates two States with girls' names: Maryland and Virginia. They are named after two queens. The Potomac Indians paddled their canoes down the river till they came to a much broader piece of water. This piece of water was so big it seemed to them like the ocean, and they called it "the Mother of Waters," which in their own language was "Chesapeake." You can see it on the map. Chesapeake Bay is not the ocean, but it is the biggest bay in the United States.

Did you ever eat snails or terrapin or frogs' legs? Some people like them. The Indians found oysters growing in the Chesapeake Bay. At first no one thought of eating oysters—they didn't look good to eat. But one day an Indian who was very hungry broke an oyster-shell open and ate the oyster inside. It tasted good and it didn't hurt him, so others began to eat oysters, and now almost every one likes oysters, either raw or cooked. Oysters grow

第7章 "玛丽之地" "弗吉妮亚之州" 和 "宾的森林"

你们有没有过用陀螺换弹珠，或者用苹果换橙子的经历呢？在什么华盛顿、什么合众国都还没有出现的很久以前，流经如今华盛顿的那条河流两岸，曾经生活着许多的印第安商人。那些印第安人划着独木舟在河上来去，与其他印第安人进行贸易，就是用自己已有的东西，换取他们想要的东西，比如用珠子换取毛皮，用弓换箭，以玉米换取土豆。在印第安语里，"商人"称为"波托马克"，因此后来我们便用这些印第安商人的名称，将那条河称为"波托马克河"。波托马克河隔开了两个具有姑娘名字的州，即马里兰州和弗吉尼亚州。那两个州，是以两位女王的名字来命名的。波托马克河沿岸的印第安人，划着他们的独木舟沿河而下，最终来到了一片宽阔得多的水域。那片水域非常广袤，在他们看来就像是大海似的，因此，他们便把这片水域称为"百川之母"，在印第安语里，就叫"切萨皮克"。你们可以在地图上看到这个地方。其实，切萨皮克湾并不是海洋，而是美国境内最大的一个海湾。

你们有没有吃过蜗牛、水龟或者青蛙腿呢？有些人可喜欢吃这些东西了。印第安人发现切萨皮克湾里出产牡蛎。起初，没有人想过要去吃牡蛎，因为那种东西看上去并不好吃。可后来有一天，一位饥肠辘辘的印第安人打开了一只牡蛎壳，吃掉了里面的牡蛎肉。牡蛎肉的味道很鲜美，也没有给他带来什么不适，所以其他人便

in other parts of the World too, but many people say that those in the Chesapeake Bay are the largest and best, but they are not supposed to be good unless they are eaten during the eight months that have an R in their names. They are good in March but not in June.

Near "the Mother of Waters" are two cities. One is named Annapolis. The other is named Baltimore. Annapolis means Anna's City, and it too was named after a queen. That makes three places—Anna's City, Mary's Land, and Virginia's State—named after queens. Annapolis is the capital of the State of Maryland, just as Washington is the capital of all the States. At Annapolis the United States has a school for teaching boys to be sailors and fit to fight the sea battles of the United States if the country should ever have any. This school is called the Naval Academy. Some of the best boys chosen from each State in the United States go to Annapolis. They study all about boats and fighting and about geography; they visit other countries and learn to command ships.

Baltimore is the largest city in Maryland. It was named after an English lord. The first railroad in our country started in Baltimore, and as it ran from Baltimore to the State of Ohio, it was called the Baltimore & Ohio, or the B. & O. for short. Baltimore is famous for the Johns Hopkins University and Hospital. Boys come from all over the World to study at the "Hopkins," and people come from all over the World to be treated at the "Hopkins Hospital."

A man named Penn once owned the State just north of Maryland. It was then all woods, so it was called Pennsylvania, which means Penn's Woods. But ages before Penn's Woods

开始跟着吃牡蛎了。如今，无论是生吃还是煮熟了，几乎每个人都很喜欢吃牡蛎了呢。虽说世界上其他一些地方也出产牡蛎，可许多人都说，切萨皮克湾里出产的牡蛎个头最大、质量最为上乘，不过人们也认为，只有在含有英文字母"R"的那八个月份里[1]，这儿的牡蛎吃起来才口味最佳。比如说，在三月份（March）吃口味上乘，但若是在六月份（June）吃，口味就不好了。

距"百川之母"不远的地方，有两座城市。其中一座叫作安那波利斯，另一座叫作巴尔的摩。"安那波利斯"指的就是"安娜之城"，也是根据一位女王的名字命名的。因此，美国总共有三个地方，即"安娜之城"、"玛丽之地"和"弗吉妮亚之州"，都是以女王的名字命名的。安那波利斯是马里兰州的首府，就像华盛顿是合众国的首都一样。在安那波利斯，美国有一所学校，专门将男孩子培训成能打海战的水兵，以备美国爆发海战时所需。这所学校，叫作海军学院。美国各州都会选拔出一些最优秀的男孩子，并把他们送到安那波利斯的海军学院里去深造。他们会全面学习舰船、作战和地理方面的知识，他们会出访其他的国家，并且学会指挥战舰。

巴尔的摩是马里兰州最大的城市。它是以一位英国贵族的名字来命名的。我国的第一条铁路，就是在巴尔的摩兴修起来的。由于它从巴尔的摩通往俄亥俄州，因

---

[1] 即一月（January）、二月（February）、三月（March）、四月（April）、九月（September）、十月（October）、十一月（November）和十二月（December），它们的英文名称中都含有r这个字母。其他几个月份中都不含有r。

other woods were there—huge forests of trees and giant plants growing high and thick and fast. More ages passed and these forests died and became buried and mashed down under the ground and turned into black rock. More ages passed and men dug up this black rock, and by accident they found that unlike other rock this rock would burn. Of course it would burn, because, as we know now, it was really only hardened wood—which we call coal.

There are two kinds of coal. One is called hard and the other is called soft. Soft coal doesn't mean soft like a cushion; it means it crumbles easily. Hard coal is the best; soft coal is dirtier and smokier, but is a great deal cheaper. Why is it that the best things almost always cost the most? In the eastern part of Pennsylvania the coal that comes out of the ground is *hard*; in the western part it is *soft*.

Hundreds of thousands of men, called miners, work underneath the ground, where it is like night all day long, digging out the coal to run steam-engines and to heat our houses. They have been digging away for years and years, so that there are huge hollow places underneath parts of Pennsylvania.

Coal is in layers underneath the ground and between layers of rock like the chocolate in a chocolate layer-cake. But there are also iron mines in Pennsylvania, and iron is not in layers; it is all mixed through the rock under the ground and is called ore. To get the iron out of the ore, men build huge fires under the ore and the iron melts and runs out, like water, into troughs which they make in the ground to catch it. When the iron cools, the blocks of iron are called "pigs"—perhaps because they are about the size of pigs—or

此被称为"巴尔的摩—俄亥俄铁路",或者简称"巴—俄铁路"。巴尔的摩还因为该市有约翰·霍普金斯大学和约翰·霍普金斯医院而著称。世界各地都有孩子来到"霍普金斯大学"就学,而世界各地也都有病人来到"霍普金斯医院"接受治疗。

马里兰州北部的那个州,原本为一个叫作"宾"的人所有。当时,那里全都是森林,因此被称为"宾夕法尼亚",意思就是"宾的森林"。不过,在"宾的森林"出现的很久以前,那里就有其他的森林了,并且面积广袤,各种树木和巨型植物都高大、茂密且生长迅速。过了许多年之后,那些森林都枯死了,并且被埋到了地下,挤压成了黑色的岩层。又过了许多年后,人们挖掘出了这种黑色的岩层,并且在无意中发现,与其他岩层不同,这种岩石竟然能够燃烧。它们当然能够燃烧啦,因为如今我们都知道,它们实际上不过是硬化了的木材罢了,我们称之为"煤炭"。

煤炭分为两种。其中一种叫作硬煤,另一种叫作软煤。"软煤"可并不是指这种煤炭像垫子那样柔软,而是指它们很容易粉碎。硬煤的品质最佳,软煤非但比较脏,而且燃烧后产生的烟雾也较多,但它比硬煤要便宜得多。为什么品质最好的东西,费用几乎总是最昂贵呢?宾夕法尼亚东部地区出产的是硬煤,而西部地区出产的则是软煤。

有成千上万个叫作"矿工"的人,都在暗无天日的地下工作,将煤炭开采出来,供蒸汽发动机运行,以及为我们的房子供暖。他们已经年复一年地开采了很久的时间,因此宾夕法尼亚州的部分地区下面,全都留下了一个个巨大的空洞。

煤炭是一层一层地分布在地下岩层之间的,就像多层巧克力蛋糕上的那一层层

perhaps because a pig goes into a trough.

To get iron out of iron ore you must have heat, and to have heat you must have something to make heat with, like coal. Some places have iron ore but no coal, and some places have coal but no iron. It is as if some boys who wanted to play baseball had a ball but no bat, and some other boys had a bat but no ball. But Pittsburgh, in the western part of Pennsylvania, had both iron and coal near-by. That is like boys who have both a hat and a ball.

From the ore they make iron, and from the iron they make steel, and from the steel they make rails for railroad tracks and beams for tall buildings and bridges to cross rivers.

A name that is in the Bible is the name of a city, Philadelphia. It means the City of Brotherly Love. This name was' chosen to give to the largest city in Pennsylvania, in fact, the third largest city in all the United States, but I don't know whether it suits or not. Philadelphia was the capital of the United States before there was any Washington, D. C., but now it isn't even the capital of its own State. Here in an old building, called Independence Hall, is the bell that rang

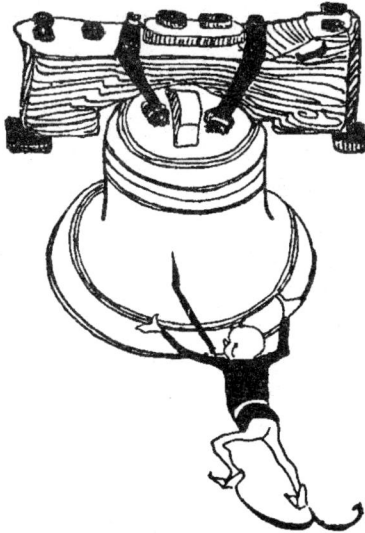

"自由大钟"已经开裂了

巧克力一样。不过，宾夕法尼亚州也储有铁矿，而铁矿却不是成层分布的，铁矿与地下的岩石全都混杂在一起，这种岩石就称为铁矿石。为了从矿石中开采出铁矿，人们在矿石下生起大火，使得铁矿石熔化，然后像水一样流淌出来，流进人们在地上建造的、用于接住铁水的那种槽子里。铁水冷却后形成的铁块，被称为"生铁锭"；之所以如此称呼，或许是因为它们的形状与猪差不多，或许是因为猪喜欢跑到饲料槽子里去的缘故吧[1]。

要想从铁矿石里提炼出铁来，必须对铁矿石加热才行，而要想加热铁矿石，就必须有某种能够产生热量的东西，比如煤炭才行。有些地方储有铁矿石，却没有煤炭；有些地方储有煤炭，却没有铁矿石。这就好比是一个想要打板球的孩子有球却没有球棒，而其他孩子则是有球棒却没有球一样。不过，位于宾夕法尼亚州西部的匹兹堡却既储有铁矿，附近地区也出产煤炭。这就好比是那些既有球棒、又有球的孩子了。

人们从铁矿石中开采出铁，然后将铁提炼成钢，再用钢材制造出铁路所用的铁轨、高楼大厦里的梁桁，以及横跨河流的桥梁来。

---

[1] 英语中，"生铁（锭）"用pigs表示，此词亦可指"猪"，因此作者才进行此种猜测。

out the news when the United States was first made a country. It is now cracked, so will not ring any more, but is more treasured than any bell in the United States that *can* ring.

The biggest bathtub in the World is not far from Philadelphia. It is an ocean bath called Atlantic City, on the coast of New Jersey. People from all over the World go there to take salt baths and sun baths and to be amused. There is a boardwalk miles long and as wide as a street close by the ocean, and along its side is every kind of thing to amuse you and your "stummick." If you want to see a board "walk," go to Atlantic City.

费城这个城市的名称，来自《圣经》。它的意思就是指"兄弟友爱之城"[1]。人们选择了这个名称，来给宾夕法尼亚州最大的、实际上也属于全美第三大的这座城市命名，可我不知道，这样做合不合适。在哥伦比亚特区的华盛顿出现之前，费城曾经是美国的首都，而如今，这里连本州的首府也不是了。费城有一栋叫作"独立大厅"的旧楼，正是里面的一座大钟敲响，宣告了合众国最初建国的消息。虽说这座大钟如今已经开裂，因而没法再敲响了，可它比美国现存的、任何一座能够敲响的大钟，却都要宝贵哩。

世界上最大的浴场，位于距费城不远的地方。那是一个海上浴场，叫作"大西洋城"，就在新泽西州的海滨。世界各地的人纷纷来到这里，享受盐浴、日光浴以及休闲娱乐。离海边很近的地方，有一条长达数英里、并且像街道那样宽阔的木板路，两侧全都是各种各样、让你们觉得有意思并且能够让你们"大快朵颐"的东西。如果你们想要看到一块会"走路"的木板，那就去大西洋城吧。

假如你们想要看到一块会"走路"的木板，
那就去大西洋城

---

[1] 费城（Philadelphia），原属小亚细亚西部吕底亚的一座古城"费拉德尔菲亚"，在《圣经》中曾有提及。

8 The Empire State

Several countries together are called an "Empire." So New York State is often called the Empire State, because it has as many people, who do as much business and make as much money, as several countries put together.

Down at the corner of New York State is New York City, the second largest city in the World, with more shops, more hotels, more people, and more money than any other city on this side of the World, and with more tall buildings than on any side of the World. It was named after a city across the ocean called York, but *New* York is now hundreds of times bigger than old York. It is the city of millionaires and millions who are not. People from all over the world come to New York hoping to be millionaires too. Some used to think the streets were paved with gold, and were disappointed when they found them just asphalt.

The main part of New York City is on an island which the Indians called Manhattan. White men bought it from the Indians and paid them about $24 for the whole island—not in money, for the Indians didn't know what money was, but in beads and ornaments worth $24. A piece of ground only large enough to stand on would now cost many times more than what the whole island once cost. That may seem a big price for a small piece of ground, but a plot of ground is not like a sheet of paper, without thickness. The owner

第8章 帝国之州

好几个国家合并起来之后，就称为一个"帝国"。纽约州通常被人们称为"帝国之州"，因为这个州人口众多，他们所从事的生意、赚到的钱财，都有好几个国家合起来那么多。

纽约州的南部一角，便是纽约市，它是世界上的第二大城市，其中的商店、旅馆、人口、财产，比西半球上其他任何一座城市都要多，而其中的高楼大厦，也超过了全世界其他任何一座城市。它是用大洋彼岸的一座叫作"约克"的城市来命名的，可如今的"新约克"，即纽约市，却要比旧的约克市大上了数百倍呢。这是一座既有许多百万富翁，也有数百万普通民众的城市。世界各地的人都纷纷来到纽约，希望自己也在这里变成一位百万富翁。有些人曾经以为，纽约市的街道上全都铺着黄金，因此待到发现该市的街道不过就是柏油路之后，他们都大失所望呢。

纽约市的主城位于一座小岛上，印第安人称这个小岛为"曼哈顿岛"。后来，白人从印第安人手中买下了这个小岛，当时，白人只花了大约二十四美元，就买下了整个岛屿。当然，白人支付的并不是现金，而是价值二十四美元的珠子和装饰品，因为印第安人那时还不知钱为何物。如今，一处巴掌大小、仅能供人站立的地块，价钱也会比当时整座小岛的价钱贵上许多、许多倍了呢。对于一小块土地来说，这似乎已经是一种高价了，可一块土地，却并不像一张没有厚度的纸张。地块

owns everything above and below the ground—down to the center of the earth and up to the sky. That is why men in New York build buildings up to the sky—"sky-scrapers" we call them—for a fifty-story building takes up no more land than a one-story building.

To me there is nothing in the World made by the hand of man more wonderful than New York's giant buildings. They are marvelous, magnificent, awe-inspiring, stupendous, amazing, overpowering, thrilling, Brobdingnagian. Have you read "Gulliver's Travels"? Brobdingnag was the land of the giants. They stand unmoved by thunder and lightning, by wind, storm, or tempest, and they look down on their creators—mites of men who, with their hands of only five fingers, have built them. New York's motto is "Excelsior," which means "Higher", and that is the motto of its builders. There is a saying, "Great oaks from little acorns grow," and one of the greatest of these buildings—sixty stories high—was built from the nickels and dimes made by Woolworth's Five and Ten Cent Stores. The most marvelous building of all is called the Empire State Building. It is one hundred and two stories high, taller than any other building in New York City, or in America, or in the whole World.

One group of high buildings in New York might be called the capitol of the World. After

纽约的天际线

所有者拥有地上和地下的一切，下至地心、上至苍穹，一切都是地块所有者的。纽约市的人之所以会修建高耸入云的大楼（我们称这种大楼为"摩天大楼"），原因就在于，一栋五十层高的大楼所需的土地面积，并不比一栋一层楼的建筑多。

在我看来，人类在世界上手工建造出来的东西，没有什么比纽约的这些高楼大厦更加奇妙的了。它们神奇非凡、宏伟壮丽、令人惊叹、巨大无比、令人称奇、令人无法抗拒、令人激动，一座座都像巨人国里的巨人似的，耸立在那里。你们有没有看过《格列佛游记》这本书呢？这本书里提到的巨人国，就是一个巨人的国度。这些高楼大厦屹立在那里，不为雷鸣电闪和狂风暴雨所动，高高地俯瞰着下面的人们，正是那些小如虫蚁的人，用自己那双只有五个指头的手，建造了这些高楼大厦。纽约市的座右铭是"不断向上"，意思就是"追求更高"，而这也正是修建那些高楼大厦的人的座右铭。有一句谚语说得好："参天橡树，也是从小小橡果长成的。"而那些最了不起的建筑中，有一座高达六十层，竟然都是用伍尔沃斯公司"五分和一角商店"里所用的那种分币和角币凑起来建成的呢。其中最令人称奇的一栋大楼，叫作帝国大厦。它有一百零二层楼高，曾经比纽约市、全美国乃至整个世界上的其他大楼都要高。

纽约有一组高楼群，堪称整个世界的国会大厦。第二次世界大战结束之后，世界上的绝大多数国家都希望找到某种途径，来避免爆发第三次世界大战。这些国家

World War II most of the countries of the World wanted to find some way of keeping a third World War from happening. These countries each sent men to meet together as our States send men to Congress. At their meetings they discuss matters that are of interest to all the countries of the World. When any country quarrels with another these people try to have them settle their quarrel without fighting. This congress is called the United Nations. The United Nations decided that New York City would be the best place to have its meetings and carry on its business. So there it built its offices. When the buildings were dedicated, or solemnly set apart for United Nations use, the speeches were broadcast in twenty-six different languages.

At a meeting of the United Nations each speaker speaks in his own language, yet he can be understood by all the other people there, for everyone wears earphones and hears a translation of the speech in the language he understands. Of course the people who do the translation must know two languages, for they have to listen in one language and speak into a microphone in another language. What they speak into the microphones is what is heard in the earphones. Millions of other people watch the United Nations meetings on television.

On a little island in New York Harbor is a huge bronze statue called the Goddess of Liberty holding aloft a torch-light. Her hand is over sixteen feet long. What a hand to shake! One finger is eight feet long. What a finger for a ring! Her nose is four and one-half feet long. What a nose for smelling! Her mouth is a yard wide. What a mouth for talking!

便各自派出代表来举行会议，就像我国各州派出代表参加国会那样。在会议上，他们将对关乎世界上所有国家的重大问题展开讨论。如果一个国家与另一个国家发生了冲突，那么这些代表就会想方设法，尽量让两国不要开战便解决分歧。这个"国会"，就叫"联合国"。联合国认为，纽约是一个最适合于举行联合国大会、行使联合国职能的地方，于是便把办公室建在这里。这组楼群专门拨给（或者说正式交付）联合国使用之后，代表们在联合国大会上的发言，便用二十六种不同的语言进行广播了[1]。

在联合国大会上，每位发言者说的都是本国的语言，可与会的其他代表全都听得懂，因为每位代表都会戴上耳机，听到用他们听得懂的语言所翻译出来的发言。自然，那些从事翻译工作的人必须懂得两种语言才行，因为他们必须听一种语言，然后再对着麦克风说另一种语言。他们对着麦克风所说的内容，也就是代表们在耳机中听到的内容。还有其他数百万的人，都是通过电视收看联合国大会呢。

纽约港内的一个小岛上，有一尊巨大的青铜雕塑，叫作"自由女神像"，女神手里高举着一个火炬。她的手掌就有十六英尺长。这样的一只手，叫人怎么去握呀！其中一根手指就长达八英尺。要是戴上戒指的话，那个戒指得有多大呀！雕像的鼻子，有四英尺半长。用这么大的鼻子来闻气味，该有多神奇呀！雕像的嘴有一码[2]宽。这张嘴巴说起话来，该有多响亮呀！你们可以从雕像内部爬到女神的脑袋

---

[1]　联合国大会正式的工作语言只有六种，即汉语、英语、法语、俄语、阿拉伯语与西班牙语。

[2]　码（yard），英制长度单位。1码相当于3英尺，约合0.9144米。

You can climb up on the inside into the Goddess's head and arm, and a dozen people can stand inside her torch. Ships pass by her, and their passengers crowding the deck greet her with a thrill of "My Country, 'Tis of Thee, Sweet Land of Liberty," and wave her farewell as they leave for afar, perhaps never to return.

On one side of Manhattan Island is the Hudson River and on the other side is the East River. A bridge was built across the East River by stretching ropes made of steel from one side of the river to the other and hanging the floor of the bridge from these steel ropes. This is called a suspension bridge. It is called the Brooklyn Bridge because at the other end of it on Long Island is another big city called Brooklyn. Brooklyn is now a part of New York City. Such bridges had been built over small streams before, but this was the first big, long bridge built in this way. It is suspended in the air so high above the water that even the greatest ships easily pass beneath it.

At first people were afraid to cross the Brooklyn Bridge, for, said they, "A bridge hung on ropes, even if made of steel, will fall." It swayed and shook as trucks and cars rumbled over it, and it still does—but still hangs. Several other bridges have been built over the East River and the Hudson River to New York City. Also, tunnels have been dug *under* the Hudson. The tunnels are called "Tubes" because they are like big tubes under the river.

自由女神像

雕像的鼻子有四英尺半长。用这么大的鼻子来闻气味，该有多神奇呀

和胳膊那里去，而雕像所举的火炬里面，也可容纳十二个人呢。船只从雕像旁边经过，乘客们都挤到甲板上来对着她欢呼："我的祖国，也属于你，美妙的自由国度。"如果是离开美国去往远方，或许永远都不再返回时，乘客们就会挥手向雕像告别。

在曼哈顿岛的一侧，流淌着哈德逊河，而岛的另一侧，则是东河。东河上修建了一条跨河大桥，这座大桥，是将钢索从河流的这一侧拉到对岸，再用这些钢索将桥面悬吊起来。这种桥梁，叫作悬索桥。这座大桥叫作"布鲁克林大桥"，因为大桥那一端的长岛上，还有一个叫作布鲁克林的大城市。如今，布鲁克林变成了纽约市的一个区。以前，人们在一些较小的河流上也修建过这种悬索桥，但布鲁克林大桥却是第一座用此种方法修建起来的大型长跨度悬索桥。它悬在空中，距水面很高，因此连最大的船只也能轻松地从桥下穿过去呢。

起初的时候，人们都很害怕，不敢跨过布鲁克林大桥，他们都说："用绳索悬挂的桥梁，哪怕用的是钢索，也会垮掉的。"卡车和小汽车经过大桥上面时，大桥会摇晃、震动，如今依然这样，可大桥却依然悬挂在那里。东河以及通往纽约市区的哈德逊河上，后来又修建了好几座跨河大桥。而且，人们还在哈德逊河的下方修建了隧道。这些隧道被称为"管道"，因为它们就像是河流下面的一条条巨大管道似的。

Two of the most famous streets in the World run the length of Manhattan Island and still farther north. One is named Broadway and the other Fifth Avenue. Broadway was at first only a short street, but it seemed very broad, so they called it that. Broadway, however, is now so long that it might better be called "Longway." One part of it is lighted so brightly at night by thousands of electric lights and flashing electric signs that it is often called "The Great White Way." Fifth Avenue is a famous street of once fashionable homes, and many of the finest and most expensive shops are there, so that Fifth Avenue has come to mean Fashion Avenue. The streets of New York are so crowded that most of the people travel from their homes to their work by trains that run in tunnels underground. These underground tunnels are called Subways.

In spite of the fact that land in New York City is worth more than any other land in the World, there are two big parks where city people may have a little country. Central Park is fifty blocks long and several blocks wide, and Bronx Park has a wonderful Zoo where there are strange and curious animals which hunters have brought alive from the jungles, mountains, deserts, and wildernesses of far-off lands.

A man from across the ocean once landed in New York and spent the day seeing the sights. Just before dinner he said he would like to drive

布鲁克林大桥

起初，人们都很害怕，不敢跨过布鲁克林大桥

世界上最有名的两条街道，都穿过了整个曼哈顿岛，并且继续向北延伸。其中一条叫作"百老汇"，而另一条则叫"第五大道"。百脑汇大街起初只是一条很短的小街，但看上去宽阔得很，因此人们便给它起了个"百老汇"[1]的名字。然而，如今的百老汇大街却已经变得很长，因此可能称它为"长街"更合适了。其中有一段路，晚上灯火通明，数千盏电灯、闪烁的电子广告牌相互竞辉，因此还经常被人们称为"大白路"呢。第五大道是一条曾经以时尚之家而著称的街道，那里有许多最优秀、最昂贵的商店，因此后来第五大道也开始指"时尚大道"了。纽约市内的街道都非常拥挤，因此绝大多数人都是乘坐在地下隧道里运行的列车上下班。这种地下的隧道列车，就叫地铁。

尽管纽约市内的土地比世界上其他任何一个地方的土地都要值钱，但该市还是开辟了两个大型的公园，从而让城里人也可以感受到一点儿乡村风情。中央公园有五十个街区那么长，几个街区那么宽，而布朗克斯公园里还有一个奇妙的动物园，里面养着许多陌生而奇怪的动物，都是猎人们从遥远国度的丛林里、山脉上、沙漠中和荒野处捕捉来的。

---

[1] 百老汇（Broadway）一词，是由表示"宽阔"的broad和表示"道路"的way复合而成的，"百老汇"属于音译。

out and see Niagara Falls, which he had heard were the most wonderful falls in the World. When he was told that it would take all night on a fast train to get to Niagara, he couldn't understand.

"But isn't Niagara in New York?" he asked.

"Yes," was the reply, "but not in New York City. Niagara is all the way across the State of New York."

On the west edge of New York State are two great lakes with Indian names—Lake Erie and Lake Ontario. Lake Erie on the map looks lower than Lake Ontario, but it really is much higher. So the water from Lake Erie falls over a high and broad cliff to reach Lake Ontario. This waterfall is called Niagara, and though there are other falls in the World higher and other falls broader, Niagara is the most beautiful and most famous, and people go from all over the World to see it. The roar of the water as it thunders over the edge can be heard for miles, and when the sun is shining there is always a rainbow in the spray that rises from the bottom of the falls. Thousands of people view the falls each day, and of each thousand —

358	say	**"Isn't it wonderful!"**
247	say	**"Isn't it grand!"**
136	say	**"Isn't it beautiful!"**
93	say	**"Isn't it lovely!"**
45	say	**"Isn't it pretty!"**

　　有个外国人曾经横渡大西洋，来到纽约，观赏了一整天的风景。就在吃晚饭之前，他说自己想开车出去，去看一看尼亚加拉大瀑布，因为他听说那是世界上最神奇的瀑布。当有人告诉他说，坐快速列车也得花上整整一个晚上才能到达尼亚加拉之后，他简直无法理解。

　　"尼亚加拉不是在纽约吗？"他问道。

　　"是的，"有人回答说，"但它不在纽约市。要穿过整个纽约州，才能到达尼亚加拉大瀑布呢。"

　　纽约州的最西端，是两个具有印第安名称的大湖，即伊利湖和安大略湖。在地图上看去，伊利湖的位置比安大略湖要低，但它的实际地势，却要比安大略湖高得多。因此，伊利湖的湖水便从一个高耸而宽阔的悬崖一泻而下，注入了安大略河。在这个悬崖边形成的那道瀑布，就叫尼亚加拉大瀑布，尽管世界上还有比它更高、更宽阔的瀑布，可尼亚加拉大瀑布却是其中最美丽、最著名的，世界各地的人都纷纷前来一睹其风采。湖水跃过悬崖边缘而下时发出的轰鸣之声，数英里以外都听得到，如果艳阳高照，那么瀑布底部喷溅上升的水雾，往往还会形成一道彩虹。每天都有成千上万名游客来观赏这道瀑布，而每一千名游客中，就有

　　三百五十八位会说："真是不可思议呀！"

　　二百四十七位会说："太壮观了！"

　　一百三十六位会说："真美呀！"

　　九十三位会说："太可爱了！"

24 say "Ah!"
And the rest say "Oh!"

A part of Niagara is caught in a huge bucket as it falls, and the falling water turns giant wheels in the bottom of the bucket. The wheels make electricity, which is carried on wires to turn the wheels of mills, to run the trolley-cars, and to light the houses and streets in the city of Buffalo near-by, and other places farther away.

For some reason or other, every now and then some man tries to jump the falls in a barrel, and at least one man has done it and lived. But boats on Lake Erie that wanted to go to Lake Ontario couldn't jump the falls. So men dug a river around Niagara Falls from Lake Erie to Lake Ontario and put water steps in it so that boats could go downhill to Lake Ontario or uphill to Lake Erie. This man-made river is called the Welland Canal.

It may seem strange for a boat to step downhill, but it not only can step downhill, it can step up too. A water step down a hill is called a "lock," and a lock is like a huge bathtub set in the canal. Perhaps you have floated toy boats in your bathtub. If you have, you know that as you fill the tub the boat rises

尼亚加拉大瀑布的一部分

瀑布的轰鸣之声，几英里以外都听得见

四十五位会说：“太漂亮了！”
二十四位会发出“啊！”的惊叹。
其余的人则会发出“呀！”的感叹。

尼亚加拉大瀑布的一部分在下落的过程中，会注入一个巨大的戽斗里，从而驱动戽斗底部那些巨大的轮子。这些轮子能够发电，通过电线的输送，就可以给附近的布法罗市及更远的其他地方提供电力，让磨坊里的轮子转动，以及驱动电车，提供家用照明和街道照明用电了。

出于某种原因，时不时地会有人试图坐在水桶里从这道瀑布上跳下去，起码有一个人干过这样的事情，并且活了下来。不过，伊利湖里的船只要想驶到安大略湖去，却是没法直接从瀑布上跳下去的。于是，人们便绕着尼亚加拉大瀑布挖出了一条从伊利湖通往安大略湖的河流，并且一级一级地注水，从而让船只可以从上游航行到安大略湖里去，或者从下游上溯到伊利湖里去。这条人工开凿出来的河，叫作威兰运河。

一艘船只竟然可以走下山去，这一点看起来似乎很奇怪，不过，船只不但可以下山，还可以上山呢。下山时的梯级提水区，叫作“水闸”，一道水闸，就像是安放在运河里的一个巨型浴盆似的。没准，你们都在浴盆里漂过玩具船吧。要是玩过的话，那你们就会知道，往浴盆里加水时，随着水位升高，玩具船也会上浮，要是

as the water rises, and as you let the water run out of the tub the boat lowers as the water lowers.

Now a canal lock works the same way with large boats as the bathtub with small boats. If a boat wants to go downhill it sails into the lock. The water in the lock is then let out and the boat lowers as the water lowers. When the boat is at the bottom, doors at the end of the lock are opened and the boat sails out on the lower canal. If a boat wants to go uphill it sails into the bottom of the lock through the open doors, the doors are then closed, and the water is turned on. As it fills the lock the boat rises with it, for water will lift anything that will float, no matter whether it be the smallest chip or the biggest ship. Water, just plain water, has more power to lift and lower the largest steamship than even giant machinery would have. It lifts the largest battle-ship as easily and softly as it would the lightest feather floating on the surface—as easily as you might lift a snowflake on your hand.

Boats that wanted to go to New York City—and almost all boats did want to go to New York—once had to go down through the Welland Canal and locks to Lake Ontario, then all the way out the St. Lawrence River, which runs from Lake Ontario to the Atlantic Ocean, then sail down the coast to New York. To avoid this long detour, this long way round, men dug a canal all the way across New York State from Buffalo on Lake Erie to the Hudson River, so that big boats can now cut across from Lake Erie to New York City. This is called the Barge Canal. It's one of the longest canals in the World.

将浴盆里的水放掉，那么，随着水位下降，玩具船也会下沉。

注意，一座运河船闸让大型船只上下航行的原理，与你们在浴盆里让小型玩具船只上下浮动的原理是一样的。假如一艘船想要下坡，它就会驶入水闸。接下来，水闸里的水就会被排掉，而随着水位下降，那艘船只也会下降。当船只到达水闸底部后，水闸一端的两扇门就会打开，船只便可以驶出去，进入较低的那段运河了。如果一艘船想上山，它就会通过那两扇打开的大门驶入水闸底部，然后关上那两扇门，并且开始向水闸里注水。随着河水注满水闸，船只便会上浮，因为河水能够托起任何可以漂浮起来的东西，无论是最小、最小的木片还是最大的船只。水，普普通通的水，在托举或者放下大型汽轮方面，本领甚至比巨型机械还要大呢。它能够轻而易举、平平稳稳地浮起一艘最大的战舰，使之就像是一片漂浮在水面上的最轻的羽毛一样，并且像你们用小手托起一片雪花那样毫不费力。

过去，那些想要前往纽约市的船只（几乎所有船只的确都想要前往纽约呢），都不得不先沿着威兰运河，以及运河里的水闸，一路下行到安大略湖，然后一路驶出圣劳伦斯河（该河从安大略湖一直通往大西洋），再向南航行，沿着海岸驶向纽约。为了避免如此麻烦的长途迂回，人们便开掘了一条贯穿整个纽约州的运河，从伊利湖畔的布法罗开始，一直通到了哈德逊河，这样一来，大型船只如今就可以抄近路，从伊利湖直接驶往纽约市了。这条运河，称为"驳船运河"。它也是世界是最长的运河之一呢。

9 Yankee Land

A pair of shoes, a hat, or an automobile we should not call "New" if they were a year old, but there is a corner of our country which is 300 years old and yet we call it "New." About 300 years ago people from England, across the ocean, came to the northeast corner of the United States and made their homes there. So the six States north of New York, where they settled, we call New England. The Indians tried to call the white people "English," but the best they could say was "Yenghees" or "Yankees," just as a child in trying to say "brother" might say "buddy"—so the people of New England we still call "Yankees." We could put all six States of New England in any one of several States out West; but though the New England States are small in size, they are big in many other things.

The largest and most important city of New England is Boston, named after a town in old England. Many people call Boston "the Hub," by which they mean to say that the rest of the World turns round Boston, for the hub of a wheel you know is the center, around which the rest of the wheel turns. Of course, the World really turns around the North and South Poles and these Poles are the real hubs of the World; so people are only joking when they say the World turns round Boston.

Rocks and cold weather are bad for farming. New England in winter is very cold and

第9章 扬基人之地

一双鞋子、一顶帽子或者一辆汽车，要是用了一年之后，我们就不能再说它们是"新的"了，不过，我国有一个角落，虽说已经有三百多年的历史了，可如今我们却仍然说它是"新的"。大约三百年前，人们从英国漂洋过海，来到了合众国的东北角，并在那里定居下来。于是，我们便把这些人定居的地方，即纽约以北的那六个州，称为"新英格兰地区"。当地的印第安人本想称呼这些白人为"英国人"，可他们却发不准音，充其量只能说出"英基人"或者"扬基人"来，这就好比是一个想要叫"哥哥"的孩子，喊出来的却有可能是"柯柯"一样。因此，如今我们仍然将新英格兰地区的人称为"扬基人"呢。我们可以将新英格兰地区的那六个州，统统装进西部几个州中的任意一个里，不过，尽管新英格兰地区的这几个州面积很小，可它们在其他许多方面却都很了不起。

新英格兰地区最大和最重要的城市，就是波士顿，它是用英国一个小镇的名称来命名的。许多人都把波士顿称为"轮毂"，他们这样叫，意思就是说，整个世界都是在围绕着波士顿运转哩。因为你们都知道，轮毂就是一个轮子的中心，轮子的其余部分都是绕着轮毂在转动。当然，整个世界实际上是绕着北极和南极运转的，南、北极才是世界真正的"轮毂"，因此，人们说世界绕着波士顿运转时，其实只是在开玩笑罢了。

it also is very rocky, so rocky that men make their fences of stones gathered off the fields. The cold and the rocks make it very hard to grow things there, but there are many, many waterfalls in New England, and waterfalls can be used to turn the wheels of factories to make things, so what people chiefly do in New England is to make things for the rest of the United States—thousands of different kinds of things—not big things such as railroad tracks and bridges that they make in Pittsburgh, but small things for a person's use, such as needles and pins, watches and clocks, boots and shoes. If the wheels of the factories are turned by waterfalls they are called mills. Nowadays, most of the waterfalls are used to make electricity, and the electricity is used to run the machinery, but the factories are still called "mills."

When I was a boy my idea of perfect happiness was to go barefoot. In some countries rich and poor alike go barefoot all the time, but in America almost every one wears shoes all the time. One of the chief things they make in these New England mills is shoes. In New England they make enough shoes for every pair of feet in the United States. Shoes wear out, so we can understand why the mills should keep on, year after year, making so many shoes. But in one of the States—the one with the Indian name, Connecticut—they make pins—enough for every man, woman and child in the United States to use 100 every year. What becomes of so many pins, do you suppose? They don't wear out like shoes, and yet they disappear—billions of pins every year.

And clocks and watches—they make millions of them too, though one clock or one

地上多石和天气寒冷，都是不利于种庄稼的。新英格兰地区的冬季非常寒冷，而且那里还到处是石头，以至于人们都可以用从地里捡来的石头砌围墙。寒冷与多石，使得这里很难种出庄稼来。不过，新英格兰地区却有许多、许多的瀑布，而人们则可以利用瀑布去驱动工厂里的机器轮子，来制造产品。因此，新英格兰地区的人从事的主要业务，便是为美国的其他地区制造产品，生产出成千上万种不同的东西来。这些产品，可不是像人们在匹兹堡制造的铁轨、桥梁那样的大型产品，而是个人所用的小型产品，比如缝衣针和别针、钟表和鞋靴等。如果工厂里的轮子是由瀑布驱动的，那么这种工厂就叫"磨坊"。如今，虽说绝大多数瀑布都被用于发电，然后再用电力去驱动工厂里的机械设备，可这些工厂仍然被人们称为"磨坊"呢。

小时候我曾经觉得，最幸福的事情莫过于光着脚丫走路了。在有些国家里，富人和穷人一样，始终都是光着脚丫的，可在美国呢，几乎所有的人始终都穿着鞋子。新英格兰地区这些工厂里生产的一种主要产品，就是鞋子。新英格兰地区生产出了足够全美国所有人穿的鞋子。鞋子会磨损，因此我们也就可以理解，为什么那些工厂能够存在下去，并且年复一年，生产出如此之多的鞋子来。但是，有一个州，即也有个印第安名称的康涅狄格州，生产的别针却足够让全美国的每个男人、女人和孩子每年都用上一百根呢。你们觉得，那么多的别针最后都怎么样了呢？虽说它们可不像鞋子那样会磨破，但最终还是消失不见了，因此，美国每年都要耗费数十亿根别针呢。

watch should last a person a lifetime—little watches for the wrist and little clocks for mantelpieces and big clocks for clock towers.

And spools of thread—enough thread is made in one mill in a single day to wind round the World—that is, over twenty-five thousand miles of thread in one mill in one day!

Where do you spend your vacation? Do you go to the seashore, to the mountains, or "down on a farm"? New England is the vacation land of many people from other parts of the country, because there are so many lakes, waterfalls, and beautiful spots for camps, streams for fishing, and in the Maine woods places for hunting deer and moose. In New Hampshire there are mountains called the White Mountains, and one of these White Mountains, named after our First President, is Mount Washington. It is the highest mountain in this part of the country, and just because it is so high many people like to climb it. Some people are like that. In Vermont, which means "green mountain," there are the Green Mountains, not as high as the White Mountains, but very lovely. All along the New England coast are places where people go to spend the summer, because this part of the country is so cool while the rest of the country is so hot.

钟表、线团、靴子、鞋子、缝衣针和别针

　　还有钟表。这些工厂也生产出了成千上万块钟表，尽管一只钟表其实可以让一个人戴上一辈子，还有小型的腕表、置于壁炉架上的小钟，以及用于钟楼上的大钟。

　　还有一轴轴的线团。一家工厂里一天生产出来的线，就足以绕地球一周，也就是说，一家工厂一天就能生产出长度超过两万五千英里的线来！

　　大家一般都去哪里度假呢？你们是会去海滨、去山区，还是会"下放到农场"里去呢？新英格兰可是美国其他地区许多人的度假胜地，因为那里有大量的湖泊、瀑布，以及适合于野营的美丽景点、适合于垂钓的溪流。而在缅因州的森林里，还有许多适合于狩猎鹿和驼鹿的地方。在新罕布什尔州，有一道叫作"白山"的山脉，其中有一座山峰，还是以美国第一任总统的名字命名的，叫作"华盛顿山"。华盛顿山是美国这一地区最高的一座山峰，而恰恰是因为它高高耸立，所以许多人都喜欢去攀登。有些人就是那样的。在意思是指"绿色山脉"的佛蒙特州，有一条绿色的山脉，虽说它并没有白山山脉那样高耸，景色却极其美丽。整个新英格兰地区的沿海，都遍布着人们的避暑胜地，因为美国其他地区非常炎热的时候，这个地

But the thing that New England is proudest of is its schools and colleges. In their mills they make *Things*, in their schools and colleges they make *Men*. Two of the most noted colleges in the country are in New England—Yale is in Connecticut and Harvard is in Massachusetts. Harvard is the oldest college in the United States.

Sticking out from Massachusetts like a long, bent finger, as if beckoning to people across the water to come to Massachusetts, is a piece of land called Cape Cod. It was named in honor of the codfish, because codfish are so plentiful in those waters, and they are caught and dried in great quantities and shipped everywhere.

The finger of Cape Cod has beckoned to people of other lands than England. People who speak strange languages have come to New England to work in factories and mills, so that now almost one quarter of the people in New England are not from England; they are not Yankees.

·

区却非常凉爽。

不过，新英格兰地区最值得骄傲的一个方面，却还是这一地区的学校和大学。这个地区的工厂里生产物品，而这个地区的学校和大学却是出产人才。美国最著名的两所大学，都位于新英格兰地区，它们就是位于康涅狄格州的耶鲁大学，以及位于马萨诸塞州的哈佛大学。哈佛也是美国历史最悠久的一所大学。

从马萨诸塞州伸出来，就像一根长长的、弯曲着的手指，仿佛是在召唤人们漂洋过海到马萨诸塞州来的那片土地，叫作"科德角"。之所以叫这个名称，是为了纪念鳕鱼[1]，因为那里的海洋中盛产鳕鱼。人们将鳕鱼捕捞起来后大批量晒干，然后再运送到各个地方去。

手指状的科德角，不但召来了英国人，还吸引着其他国家的许多人都来到了此处。一些说着陌生语言的人都来到新英格兰地区，在工厂里面工作，因此，如今新英格兰地区差不多有四分之一的人并非来自英国，自然，他们也不是扬基人了。

---

[1] "科德角"（Cape Cod）中的"科德"（Cod），源自"鳕鱼"（codfish）一词中的cod，"科德角"属于音译。

10 Five Big Puddles

Did you ever wonder what an ant must think of us giants who tread on his ant-hills, or what he must think of a puddle of water?

There are five big puddles of water along the northern edge of the United States—at least they look like puddles on the map—as if a gigantic giant had left his wet umbrella standing and the water had trickled out over the land. We call these puddles "The Great Lakes," for they are the biggest lakes on this side of the World, though a giant with legs a mile long would think them only puddles to wade across. Two of the lakes—the smallest two—I have already told you about. They are Lake Erie and Lake Ontario. Two of the others also have Indian names, Lake Michigan, which means "Great Lake," and Lake Huron. The Greatest Lake of all the Great Lakes is called Superior, which means simply Greater Lake, as we say a boy who is a better football player or who makes better marks is "superior" to some other boy. Lake Michigan is the only one of the Great Lakes that belongs entirely to the United States, as it is entirely inside of the United States. Half of the other four lakes belong to the country north of the United States—the country called Canada—because these other lakes are along the border between the two countries. The United States owns its side of each of these lakes and out to the middle; Canada owns its side and out to the middle.

Lake Superior is not only bigger, it is higher than the other lakes. It empties its water

第10章　五个大水坑

你们以前有没有想过，一只蚂蚁对我们这些踩到蚂蚁窝的庞然大物会有什么感受，它们对一个小水坑又会有什么感受呢？

美国的北部边境，有五个大水坑，起码来说，它们在地图上看上去就像是水坑，仿佛是一个不可思议的巨人将一把湿漉漉的雨伞立在那里，伞上的雨水流淌到大地上，从而形成了它们似的。我们将这些水坑称为"五大湖区"，尽管一个腿长一英里的巨人可能会觉得它们只是小水坑，很容易就能涉水过去，但它们其实却是美洲最大的湖泊呢。其中有两个湖泊，即面积最小的那两个，我在前面已经向你们介绍过了。它们就是伊利湖与安大略湖。另外两个湖泊也都有个印第安名称，即意思就是"大湖"的密歇根湖，以及休伦湖。大湖区面积最大的湖泊是苏必利尔湖，意思就是"更大的湖"，就像我们说一个技术更好的橄榄球员或者一个得分比别人多的球员"优于"其他球员一样。大湖区里，只有密歇根湖完全属于美国，因为只有这个湖完全位于美国境内。其余四个湖泊，都有一半属于美国北方的那个国家，即那个叫作加拿大的国家，因为这四个湖泊正好位于两国的国界线上。美国拥有美国一侧的那一半，加拿大则拥有加拿大那一侧的一半。

苏必利尔湖非但面积最大，地势也比其他四个湖泊都要高。湖水通过一条叫作

into Lake Huron through a little river called St. Mary's, and in this river are falls. These falls in the St. Mary's River are called St. Mary's Jump, because the water jumps, jumps down. These falls are not nearly as high as Niagara Falls, but they are too high for boats to go over the jump, so men had to build canals with locks around the falls to lower boats down and raise them up from one lake to the other. As there are so many boats that want to go down and up, one canal was not enough to take care of all the boats that wanted to go round the falls, so men have built five canals round St. Mary's Jump. St. Mary's Jump in French is Sault Ste. Marie, and as this is so difficult to say, people simply call the falls Soo, the river Soo, and the canals Soo too.

Some of the boats on the Great Lakes are as big and fine as those on the ocean; and they have to be, for the Great Lakes are like small oceans. When you are out, far out, you cannot see land, and at times there are high waves and storms, just as at sea. The chief difference is that the water in the lakes is fresh, not salt.

"Business before pleasure."

A great many people take trips on these big lake boats just as they do on the ocean—for pleasure; but the chief reason for the great number of ships that go from one end of the lakes to the other is not pleasure but business. The business is carrying things, which we call freight. It is much cheaper to send things by ship than by train, for one big ship can carry much more than many trains, and ships do not have to have land and tracks to run on, as trains do. When we send freight by train we also call that "shipping," which seems strange. Every one would ship by ship instead of by train if he could, because it is so much

"圣玛丽"的小河注入休伦湖，一路形成了多道瀑布。圣玛丽河上的这些瀑布，被称为"圣玛丽瀑布"，因为此处的河水，是一级一级地往下跳落的。虽说这些瀑布的落差根本没有尼亚加拉大瀑布那么高，可船只也不可能翻越过去，因此人们也只能开凿带有水闸的运河，绕过这些瀑布，才能让船只下行或者上行，从一个湖泊驶入另一个湖泊。由于下行和上行的船只太多，因此一条运河根本就满足不了所有想要绕过瀑布的船只的需求，故人们修建了五条绕过"圣玛丽瀑布"的运河。在法语里，"圣玛丽瀑布"被称为"苏圣玛丽亚"，但由于这名称太难念了，所以人们只是把这些瀑布叫作"苏"，把圣玛丽河叫"苏"，把那几条运河也叫"苏"。

在五大湖区航行的一些船只，与在大海上航行的那些船一样庞大、一样精美，而它们也必须这样才行，因为五大湖个个都像是小小的海洋呢。大家坐船出湖的时候，到了很远的地方，不但会看不见陆地，有的时候还会有惊涛骇浪和暴风雨，与大海上的情况一模一样。二者主要的不同之处，就在于湖水是淡水，而不是咸水。

"先工作，后享乐。"

有许多的人，乘着这些大型的湖船往来，就像他们在海上航行一样，只是为了享乐。不过，大量船只在湖泊上来去的主要目的，却是为了做生意。这种生意，就是运送东西，即运送我们所称的货物。用船只来运送货物，要比用铁路运送货物便宜得多，这是因为，一艘大船所运送的货物，要比许多节列车运送的货物多得多，而船只也不像火车，无须陆地和铁轨就能来去。我们用火车运送货物的时候，也将

cheaper, but of course you have to be near the water to ship by ship.

Fortunately, eight out of our forty-eight States are on the Great Lakes, although some of the States have only a small "frontage" on a lake. Michigan has the most frontage, by far. It fronts on four of the Great Lakes, all except Lake Ontario.

You remember that the Potomac Indians were great traders, paddling their canoes up and down the river, and swapping things they had for things they wanted. The Indians of the Great Lakes used to do the same thing. Nowadays the white man's huge ships— thousands of times bigger than the Indians' canoes made out of a single log—do the trading. They carry huge loads of freight from one end of the Great Lakes to the other, unloading at different places along the way the things that people want, and loading up with other freight to go back.

Most of the ships start at the far end of Lake Superior at a place called Duluth. Trains loaded with wheat come to Duluth from the wheat-lands west of that city, and other trains loaded with iron ore from mines near-by. Then huge machines on the shores of the lakes, with giant hands of iron, lift whole cars of wheat and ore and dump them into the ships waiting to be filled, as you would lift a toy car of your toy train and empty its load with two fingers. Other ships collect copper ore and also iron from that part of Michigan which is on Lake Superior. They then carry their loads through the Soo Canal and unload at a place called Detroit, between Lake Huron and Lake Erie, or carry their iron ore to Cleveland and Buffalo on Lake Erie. Most of the ships do not go past Niagara Falls.

这种方式称为"货运"，看起来似乎有点儿奇怪。只要做得到，大家都会利用船运，而不会去用铁路运输，因为前者要的成本要低得多，不过，人们当然也得在距水边很近的地方，才能用船只来进行运输。

幸好，美国的四十八个州中，有八个州位于大湖地区，但其中有些州，在湖区实际上只有一小片"临湖地块"。其中，密歇根州的临湖土地面积最大。该州濒临五大湖泊中的四个，只有安大略湖除外。

你们都还记得吧，波托马克河两岸的印第安人都是些很了不起的商人，他们划着独木舟在河上来去，用他们已有的东西，换取他们想要的东西。大湖地区的印第安人，过去也经常这样干。如今，这里则是白人制造的巨型船只在进行贸易了，这些船只，比印第安人用一根圆木制成的独木舟都要大上好几千倍呢。它们把巨大的货物量从大湖地区的一端运送到另一端，一路上在不同的地方将人们想要的东西卸下来，然后再装上其他的货物返回去。

绝大多数船只，都是从苏必利尔湖最西端一个叫作德卢斯的地方出发的。有些火车会将德卢斯市以西产麦区的小麦运送到该市，而其他一些火车又把附近铁矿开采出的铁矿砂运来。然后，湖边一些巨大的机器便用它们那些巨型的铁臂，将整车的小麦和铁矿砂提起来，倒进等待装货的船只中去，就像你们用两个手指拎起玩具火车的一节车厢，将里面的东西倒出去那样。其他一些船只，则会装上密歇根州濒临苏必利尔湖那个地区出产的铜矿，还有铁矿。然后，它们便运送着货物，穿过"苏运河"，再在休伦湖和伊利湖之间一个叫作底特律的地方把货物卸下，或者将

They load up again with things that have been made in New England, or in the east of the United States, or with coal from Pennsylvania, and go back to Duluth.

But when winter comes, all this trading up and down the lakes has to stop, for this part of the country is very cold and ice forms and stops the ships.

A baby is born every second, but in Detroit an automobile is born every minute. Most of the automobiles in the World are made in Detroit. Into one end of a Detroit factory go iron and wood, leather, etc., and out at the other end comes an automobile. Every hour of the day hundreds of automobiles are finished and run out of the factories, to be shipped over the whole World.

I am sitting in a chair that was made from a tree that grew in Michigan, a thousand miles away, before I was born. The upper part of Michigan used to be covered with forests of trees especially suited for making furniture—and more furniture was made there, especially at a place called Grand Rapids, than at any other place in the World. You probably have some Grand Rapids furniture in your own home. Look on the bottom and see if you can find a label "Made in Grand Rapids." So much furniture was made there that men have cut down and used up most of the trees, and only stumps are left. But the people had learned how to make furniture, and so they kept on making furniture, though now much of the lumber has to be brought to Michigan from other parts of the country.

Side by side, like two children trying to peek out of one small window, are two States looking out on Lake Michigan. They are Illinois and Indiana, written "Ill. and Ind." for

铁矿砂运送到伊利湖畔的克里夫兰和布法罗去。绝大多数船只都不会航行到尼亚加拉大瀑布下游去。它们会再次装上新英格兰地区或美国东部地区制造出来的产品，或者装上宾夕法尼亚州出产的煤炭，然后回到德卢斯去。

不过，到了冬天后，湖泊上下游之间进行的这种贸易，就得停下来了，因为这一地区的冬季非常寒冷，湖泊上面会结冰，从而让船只无法航行。

世界上，每时每刻都有婴儿出生，可在底特律，却是每一秒钟都会生产出一辆汽车来。世界上绝大多数汽车，都是在底特律生产的。在底特律的一家工厂里，从这头进去的是钢铁、木材、皮革等东西，从那头出来的就是一辆汽车了。每天的每一个小时里，都有数百辆汽车生产出来，驶出各家工厂，等待着运送到世界各地去呢。

我现在坐的一张椅子，正是用我出生前就生长于一千英里之外的密歇根州的一种树木制成的。密歇根州的北部地区，以前都覆盖着树木茂密的森林，其中的树木尤其适合用来做家具，那里生产出的家具，比世界上其他任何地方都要多，特别是在一个叫作"大急流城"的地方。你们自己家里，很可能就有一两件产自"大急流城"的家具呢。找一找家具的底下，看能不能找到"大急流城制造"的标签吧。由于生产了太多的家具，因此人们砍伐并用光了那里的大部分树木，只留下了一个个树桩。不过，由于那里的人已经学会了制造家具，因此他们便一直在生产家具，只是如今所用的许多木材，都只能从美国的其他地区运送到密歇根州来了。

此地有两个州并排着，就像两个试图从一扇小窗户向外偷看的小孩一样，面对着密歇根湖。这两个州，就是伊利诺伊州和印第安纳州，分别缩写为"伊利州"

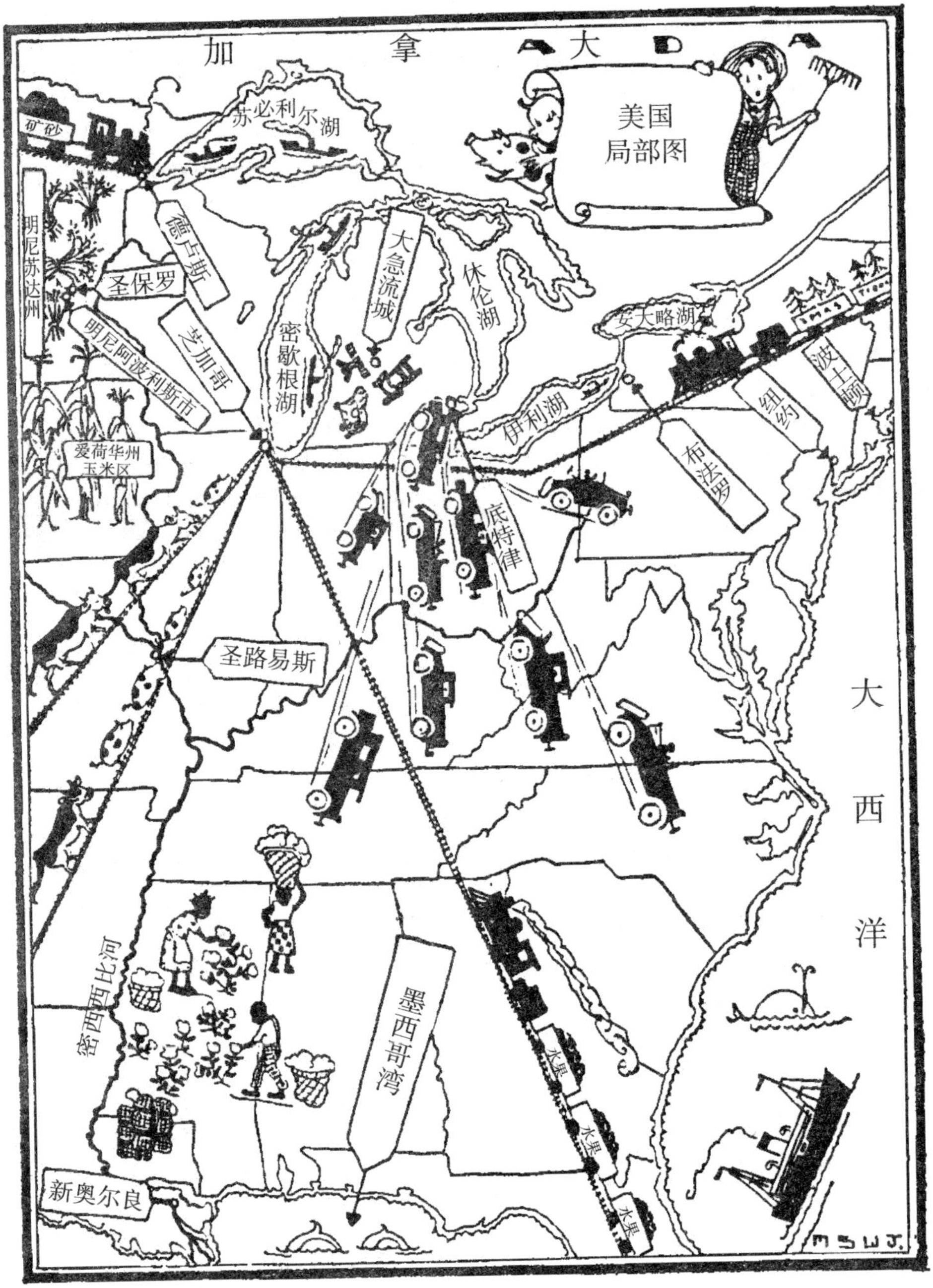

加　拿　大
苏必利尔湖
美国局部图
矿砂
明尼苏达州
德卢斯
圣保罗
明尼阿波利斯市
爱荷华州玉米区
芝加哥
密歇根湖
大急流城
休伦湖
安大略湖
波士顿
伊利湖
纽约
底特律
布法罗
圣路易斯
密西西比河
墨西哥湾
新奥尔良
大西洋

short. The second largest city in the country is in the State of Illinois on the lower end of Lake Michigan. It has an Indian name—Chicago. More trains of cars come into and go out of Chicago than any other city in the World. Most trains going across the United States stop there and start there—freight trains carrying things and passenger trains carrying people.

There are a great many kinds of animals in the World, and yet of all these animals there are only three kinds that people generally eat. These three are the cow, the sheep, the pig. It takes millions of these animals every year to feed all the people in the United States, and millions of these animals are raised in the States near-by and far from Chicago. These animals have to be fed, and the food that is best to make them fat is corn, so whole States grow corn, just to feed cows and sheep and pigs. The State of Iowa grows more corn than any other State, so it is called the Corn State. Some of the corn is shipped to Chicago, but most of it is shipped "on the hoof"—that is, it is fed to the animals and the animals are sent alive to Chicago to be killed. They are kept in big pens called stock-yards until they are killed. From Chicago they are sent in refrigerator cars or ships, everywhere, even to Europe. Chicago is the greatest butcher-shop in the World. The bacon I had for breakfast, the ham sandwich I had for luncheon, and the roast beef I had for dinner came from Chicago.

和"印第州"。美国的第二大城市便在伊利诺伊州内，位于密歇根湖的南端。该市也有一个印第安名称，叫作芝加哥。芝加哥市进出的一列列运送汽车的火车数量，比世界上其他任何一个城市都要多。其中绝大多数跨越整个美国的火车，都是在这里停留，然后再从这里出发的，其中既有运送货物的货运列车，也有运送旅客的列车。

虽说世界上有各种各样的动物，可所有这些动物当中，人们通常吃的都只有三种。这三种动物，便是牛、羊和猪。每一年，全美国的人都要吃掉数百万头牛、羊和猪，而其中的数百万头牛、羊和猪，又都是在美国距芝加哥或近或远的地方养殖出来的。这些动物得吃食，而能将它们喂肥的饲料则是玉米，因此整个美国都种玉米，目的就是为了喂养牛、羊和猪。爱荷华州出产的玉米，比其他各州都要多，因此该州还被誉为"玉米之州"呢。该州出产的玉米，一部分被运往了芝加哥，而其中的绝大部分，却都是运给了那些"待宰之物"，即喂了动物，以及那些活着被运送到芝加哥去屠宰的牲畜。在屠宰之前，那些牲畜都被关在一种叫作"畜场"的大型围栏里。屠宰后，它们又被装到冷冻车或者冷冻船上，从芝加哥出发，运送到各地，甚至是运送到欧洲去。因此，芝加哥是世界上最了不起的屠宰场。我早餐所吃的培根，中饭所吃的汉堡三明治，以及晚餐时所吃的烤牛肉，可全都来自芝加哥呢。

11 The Father of Waters

The biggest *bay* in the United States I told you is called "the Mother of Waters." The biggest river in the United States is called "the Father of Waters." Although the river is called a "father," he is not a Mr. He is a "Miss." In the Indian language he is Miss—issippi, and is spelled in this jingly way:

M
i double s
i double s
i double p
i

which is very easy to learn.

If I asked you to draw a picture of a river, and also of a tree without any leaves on it, you would probably draw the tree this way—a main stem, with big branches, and big branches with little branches, and little branches with tiny branches—like the picture to the left. And you would probably draw the picture of the river as just a wiggly line—now wouldn't you? As a matter of fact, the picture of a tree and the picture of a river should be drawn exactly the same way, for they each have a main stem with big branches, big branches with little branches, and little branches with tiny branches—although you may

第11章 百川之父

我曾经跟你们说过，美国最大的海湾，叫作"百川之母"。而美国最大的一条河流，则叫作"百川之父"。尽管这条河流被称为一个"父亲"，可它并不是一位"先生"（Mr.），而是一位"女士"（Miss）。在印第安语里，此河被称为"密西西比"（Mississippi），而它在英语中的拼写也很有节奏感：

一个M，
一个i，两个s，
一个i，两个s，
一个i，两个p，
再加一个i

很容易记住吧。

假如我要求你们画出一条河流，并且画出一棵上面没有任何叶子的树来，那么你们很可能都会这样来画那棵树：一根树干，加上粗大的树枝，上面再画较小的树枝，上面再画一些更细的树枝，就像下图一样。并且，你们很可能会将河流画成只是一根蜿蜒曲折的线条，是不是这样呢？事实上，树和河流的画法应该是一模一样的，因为二者都有一个主干和粗大的分支，而粗分支上又有小分支，小分支上又有更细小的分支。不过在地图上，大家在一条河流的示意图上可能是看不到所有分

not see all the branches in the picture of a river on the map.

But there is this big difference between a tree and a river:

A tree *grows* from the bottom to the top of its branches.

A river *flows* from the top of its branches to the bottom. The sap runs up a tree, water runs down a river. If a river were just a single line and had no branches at all, it would be just as big at the finish as at the start. It's the river's branches that make it bigger and bigger. The biggest river in the United States, the Mississippi, starts almost at the top of our country, at a little lake called Itasca, in the State of Minnesota, and flows all the way to the bottom of our country, getting bigger and bigger all the time as its branches flow into it, until at last it reaches a corner of the ocean we call the Gulf of Mexico. The Mississippi River really cuts our country into two parts, but the two parts are not the same size. The part west of the Mississippi is about twice as big as the part east of the Mississippi.

The Mississippi River hardly gets a good running start on its long journey south to the Gulf of Mexico before it falls down, and where it falls men have built big mills, the wheels of which are turned by the falling water. These mills, however, are not like those in New England. They do not make things. They grind wheat to make flour to make bread, for more and better wheat grows near where the Mississippi starts and the States near-by than anywhere else in the whole World.

支的。

但是，一棵树和一条河流之间，还是有着下面这种重大的差别：

一棵树，支桠是从树干底下向顶上生长的。

一条河流，水却是从各条支流的顶端流向底下的主干的。树液从下往上，流向树梢；河水则自上而下，汇入主流。如果一条河流就像一根线，没有任何支流的话，那么它的发源之地就会跟它的终止之处一样粗细了。正是有了各条支流，才使得一条河流变得越来越粗、越来越宽阔。美国最大的河流密西西比河差不多发源于美国的最北端，即明尼苏达州境内一个叫作伊塔斯卡的小湖，然后流向美国南方，一路上随着各条支流的汇入而变得越来越宽阔，最后注入我们所称的"墨西哥湾"这个大洋的一角。实际上，密西西比河把美国分割成了两个部分，不过，这两个部分的面积并不相同。密西西比河以西的那个部分，面积达到了密西西比河以东那一部分的两倍左右。

密西西比河刚一开始向南经过漫长的旅程流往墨西哥湾的时候，便陡然下落，而在它下落形成瀑布的那个地方，人们建造了许多大型的磨坊，利用下落的河水来推动磨轮。然而，这些磨坊却跟新英格兰地区的那些磨坊不同。它们并没有制造出任何东西来。它们只是用于将小麦磨成制作面包的面粉，因为在密西西比河源头的附近地区，人们种植了比全世界其他任何地方更多的、品质更好的小麦。

An acre seems to me, who lives in a city, a large piece of ground, a hundred acres seems immense, and a thousand acres seems enormous, but some farms in Minnesota where they raise wheat have as many as *ten thousand* acres of wheat in a single farm! The farmers would never get through planting or gathering the wheat if they did so by hand or even with a horse. So they plow with an engine and often with ten plows in a row, and they use machines for gathering the wheat and for separating the grains of the wheat from the straw, which has to be done before it can be ground into flour.

On opposite sides of the Mississippi near these falls two large cities of almost the same size have grown up. These two cities are connected by a bridge, and they are so nearly the same size they are called Twin Cities. One of them is named Minneapolis, which means "Water City," as Annapolis means "Anna's City"; and the other is named St. Paul. Notice that almost all names around the Great Lakes and the Mississippi are named either after saints or after Indians. That's because priests were among the first to come to this country to make the Indians Christians, and they named places either after the Indians or after the Christian saints.

The water city—Minneapolis—is the greatest flour-making place in the whole World. I have to say "in the whole World" so often, I'm going to use only the first letters from now on—i for "in," t for "the," w for "whole," W for "World"—thus: i.t.w.W. Minneapolis is the greatest flour-making place i.t.w.W. Minnesota and the States near it are the greatest wheat-raising States i.t.w.W.

　　对于居住在城市里的我来说，一英亩[1]可是面积很大的一块土地了，一百英亩土地属于极大，而一千英亩土地则属于无边无际了，可在明尼苏达州一些种植小麦的农场里，单个农场就种植着多达一万英亩的小麦呢！要是人工种植的话，那些农民永远都种不了、也收割不了这么多的小麦，哪怕用马匹来，也做不到。因此，他们都是用一种装有发动机的犁来耕地，并且常常是一次用十张犁排成一行来进行的，而收割小麦、脱粒时用的也是机器，小麦必须先经过脱粒，才能再去磨成面粉。

　　在密西西比河这些瀑布的两岸，出现了两座大小差不多相等的大城市。这两座城市之间，有一条大桥相连，由于两市的大小几乎相同，因此人们还把它们称为"双子城"呢。其中一座，叫作"明尼阿波利斯"，意思是"水城"，就像"安那波利斯"指的是"安娜之城"一样；另一座城市则叫"圣保罗"。注意，大湖地区和密西西比河附近地区，几乎所有的地名，不是用基督教圣徒的名字，便是用印第安名称来命名的。那是因为，一些传教士最先来到美国并将印第安人点化成为基督徒，他们在给地点命名时，要么是用印第安人的名称，要么便是用基督教圣徒的名字。

　　"水城"明尼阿波利斯是整个世界上最大的面粉生产地。由于我必须不停地说"整个世界上"，因此我打算此后只用"全世界"来进行简称。比如，明尼阿波利

---

　　[1]　英亩（acre），英制面积单位。1英亩合4047平方米。

As the Mississippi River flows south toward the Gulf of Mexico it passes other cities, but the biggest one is St. Louis, about half-way down. St. Louis—another saint—is near the two biggest branches of the Mississippi River—the Missouri, which comes in from the west, and the Ohio, which comes in from the east—both rivers named after States and both States named after the Indians. The Missouri is such a big branch that it is hard to tell whether it is a branch of the Mississippi or the Mississippi is a branch of it. Indeed, if you can find where the Missouri River begins you will see that from that point to the end of the Mississippi the river is much longer than the Mississippi itself—it is over 4,000 miles—so the Missouri-Mississippi together is the longest river i.t.w.W.

The Mississippi gets bigger and bigger as it gets more and more branches, and in the spring when the snow melts and the rain rains so hard and flows down into the branches, the river swells and swells until it finally bursts over its banks and floods the country. So, down where this is likely to happen, men have built banks along the river on each side, to hold the water in. These banks are called levees; but sometimes the river grows too big and strong even for these levees to hold it in, and the river breaks through or over the top and floods the country. If there happen to be any farms or houses or towns with people in them, the water washes houses away and drowns people and animals, and destroys thousands upon thousands of farms and other property.

The Mississippi near its end passes the city called New Orleans and at last flows into the Gulf of Mexico. The end of a river where it flows into the sea is called its mouth. I

斯是全世界最大的小麦生产地；明尼苏达州及附近各州，是全世界最大的小麦种植州，等等。

　　密西西比河在向南流入墨西哥湾的过程中，还流经了其他一些城市，其中最大的一座，则是位于该河中下游的圣路易斯。"圣路易斯"又是一位圣徒的名字，该市位于密西西比河两条最大的支流附近：其中一条是密苏里河，它自西向东注入密西西比河，另一条则是俄亥俄河，它自东向西注入密西西比河。这两条支流的名称都与州名相同，也都是用印第安人的名称来命名的。密苏里河非常巨大，因此我们很难说清，究竟是它属于密西西比河的支流呢，还是密西西比河属于它的支流。事实上，假如能够找到密苏里河的发源地，那么你们就会看出，从那个地方起，直到密西西比河的入海口，密苏里河的流程都要比密西西比河本身长得多，竟然超过了四千英里，因此，倘若将密苏里河与密西西比河合起来，它便是全世界最长的河流了。

　　随着汇入的支流越来越多，密西西比河也变得越来越宽阔，到了春季，冰雪消融、春雨如注并流入各条支流之后，密西西比河就会变得越来越宽，河水也会越涨越高，最终决堤，淹没整个乡村。因此，在下游有可能决堤的地方，人们在河流两岸都筑有高高的河堤，以便约束河水。这些河堤，称为防洪堤，不过，有的时候，由于河水上涨得太厉害，连这些防洪堤也约束不了，因此河水便会冲垮堤坝，或者越过堤坝，淹没乡村。如果附近正好有住了人的农场、房屋或者市镇，河水便会将房屋冲走、淹死民众和牲畜，毁掉成千上万座农场和其他的财产呢。

never knew why, because a mouth is where water flows in, not where it flows out. At any rate, the Mississippi has several mouths instead of one mouth, for the water in the river brings along with it so much mud that it settles right in the way of the river's mouth and forms mud islands which the river has to go round, so the river blocks itself.

Where the Mississippi begins in the far north of the United States it is very cold in winter, but as the river flows farther and farther south it gets warmer and warmer and warmer. This warm country is nicknamed "Dixie." When the river is near its end at New Orleans, flowers bloom even at Christmas and it is warm all the year round. Where the river begins you see white people in the fields and on the shores, but when it gets down south in Dixie Land you see more and more colored people working in the fields. The chief thing they are doing is growing cotton, for "Dixie Land," as the song says, is way down south "in the land of cotton," and more cotton is grown here than anywhere else i.t.w.W. Strange to say, there was no cotton in America at first. A cotton plant was brought first to Maryland from the other side of the world and grown only for its pretty flowers.

Cotton grows on a low bush in little white balls, and inside each white ball are troublesome little seeds. The cotton is picked off the bush and then these seeds have to be picked out of the cotton before it can be made into cotton thread, and then into cotton cloth, and then into cotton clothes, sheets, towels—can you think of anything else made out of cotton? Things made of cotton were once very expensive, because it took such a long time to pick the seeds out of the cotton, but a school-teacher—a man—invented a

密西西比河的最末端，流经一个叫作"新奥尔良"的城市，最后注入墨西哥湾。一条河流末端注入大海的地方，叫作河口。我一直都不知道为什么要这么叫，因为"口"应当是指水流汇入河中的地方，而不是河水排出河流的地方。不管怎么说，密西西比河可不止一个河口，而是有好几个河口，原因就是，河水一路携带着许多的泥沙，并在河口中间沉积下来，形成了一些泥沙岛屿，使得河水必须绕流而过，也就是说，河流堵住了自己的去路。

在密西西比河那个位于美国遥远的北方的发源地，冬季气候非常寒冷，但随着这条河流逐渐向南流去，一路上的气候则变得越来越暖和、越来越炎热了。这片暖和的土地，还有个绰号，叫作"狄克西"[1]。这条河在新奥尔良靠近河口的地方，连圣诞节花儿也会盛开，并且一年到头都温暖如春。在这条河的发源地，你们会看到地里和河岸上都是白人在干活，可当它向南流到了"狄克西之国"后，大家就会看到，地里干活的有色人种越来越多。他们主要干的就是种植棉花，因为正如歌谣所唱，"狄克西之国"位于遥远的南方的"棉花地里"，所以这里种植的棉花比全世界其他任何一个地方都要多呢。说来也怪，美国起初是没有棉花的。最初的棉花树，是人们从地球的另一面带到马里兰州来的，并且，当初人们之所以种植棉花，也只是为了观赏这种植物开出的美丽花朵。

---

[1] 狄克西（Dixies），美国南部诸州的别称，尤指1861年美国内战时组成南部联邦的各州，亦可指新奥尔良。

way to pick the seeds out by a machine—an "engine" which the colored people called "a gin," for short, and now cotton goods can be made very cheaply. Indeed, it is now hard to understand how we ever got along without cotton, for this little plant that was once grown only for its flowers is used in more things and in more ways than anything that grows out of the ground. This is why it is often called "King Cotton."

棉花是一种长有白色小球的低矮灌木，而每个白色小球里面，都长有令人烦恼的小棉籽儿。人们将棉花从棉花树上摘下来之后，必须先将这些小棉籽儿挑出来，才能将棉花纺成棉线，再用棉线去织成棉布衣服、袜子和毛巾，你们还能想出其他一些用棉花制成的东西吗？用棉花制成的东西，价格曾经十分昂贵，因为将棉籽儿从棉花中挑出来，要费很久的时间，不过，后来有一位老师（竟然是位男老师），他发明出了一种用机器来挑出棉籽儿的方法。有色人种将他发明的那种"机械装置"简称为"机子"，这样，如今的棉织品才可以很便宜地生产出来了。事实上，我们现在很难理解，当初没有棉花的时候，人们都是怎么过来的，因为人们曾经只是为了观赏其花朵才种植的这种小植物，如今的用处可比地上生长出来的任何东西都要大，用途也更广泛呢。它之所以经常被人们称为"棉花大王"，原因也正在于此。

12 The Fountain of Youth

Birds go south in the winter to get warm. Some people in the cold Northern States do the same. The farthest south they can go in the United States is to the corner State, shaped like a dog's paw, called Florida, which means the land of flowers. On the automobiles that go to Florida you can read the tags of every one of the forty-eight States. People go to Florida in the winter to sit in the sunshine, to bathe in the sea in January, to get rid of shivers, sneezes, and handkerchiefs. It is a winter playground, as New England is a summer playground. I know a man who is supposed to live in Baltimore, but he spends his winters in Florida and his summers in New England, so he only lives in Baltimore a few weeks in between.

The first white people who came to America came to Florida, because they had been told there was a fountain of youth there. The fountain of youth was supposed to be a spring which was said to have magic powers. It was believed if old people bathed in it or drank its water they would become young again. But no one has ever found a fountain of youth in Florida or anywhere else, though many old people after they have spent the winter in Florida say they *feel* young again.

But not everybody in Florida plays all winter long. Many have to work. They have to run the hotels for the people who do come to Florida to play. And a great many others are busy raising "fresh early vegetables" to ship to the cold Northern States, where they would

第12章　不老泉

冬季，小鸟都会飞往南方去过冬。美国寒冷的北部各州中，有些人也是这样的。在美国境内，他们能够去的最南之地，就是东南角上那个形状有如一只狗爪的州，该州叫作"佛罗里达"，意思就是"鲜花之地"。在前往佛罗里达州的那些汽车上，你们可以看到美国四十八个州中每一个州的标记呢。人们在冬季前往佛罗里达，都是为了去沐浴那里的阳光，为了在一月份到海里去游泳，为了摆脱寒战、喷嚏和擤鼻涕的手帕。那里是一个冬季的乐园，就像新英格兰地区是夏季的避暑胜地一样。我认识一个人，他本来住在巴尔的摩，可由于冬天在佛罗里达过，夏天又在新英格兰地区过，因此冬夏两季之间，他只会在巴尔的摩住上寥寥的几个星期呢。

第一批到美洲来殖民的那些白人，首先到达的就是佛罗里达，因为他们听说，那里有一眼"不老泉"。据说，不老泉是一眼具有魔力的泉水。传说中，若是老人在不老泉中洗个澡，或是喝了不老泉里的水，他们就会返老还童。不过，迄今为止还没有哪个人在佛罗里达州或者其他哪个地方发现过一眼不老泉呢，只是许多的老年人在佛罗里达度过了一个冬天之后，都会说他们觉得自己返老还童了。

但是，并非所有的佛罗里达人整个冬天全都无所事事，只管玩儿。他们必须经营好旅馆，招待好那些的确是到佛罗里达来玩儿的人。还有其他的许多人，则忙于

have only canned or frozen vegetables during the winter otherwise. Just as there is a top time, a kite time, a football time, and a baseball time, there used to be certain times or seasons for certain fruits and vegetables; but in most of Florida it is so warm they seldom or never have frost or snow or ice, so they can raise fruits and vegetables the year round. Farmers ship the vegetables they raise out of season to other States, so that people in the North can now have fresh strawberries at Christmas, and asparagus too, and lettuce and radishes every month in the year.

The chief fruits from Florida are oranges and grapefruit, which will grow only where there is no frost. Grape-fruit grows in bunches like big, yellow grapes—that's why it is called "grape"-fruit. Grape-fruit was at first thought not fit to eat—too bitter and not sweet like an orange; but people have learned to like it. More grape-fruit grows in Florida than in any other place i.t.w.W.

Once there was no Florida at all—the United States had no "paw" sticking out into the sea. It grew a paw and this is the way it grew it. The sea was warm and shallow and in the sea there lived millions, billions, trillions of little animals, each like a tiny drop of jelly with a tiny stony speck in the center, or a tiny stony shell on the outside, and millions and billions and trillions

种植运往寒冷的北部各州去的"早熟新鲜蔬菜",否则的话,北部各州的人在冬季就只有罐装或者冷冻的蔬菜可吃了。就像有最适合于玩陀螺的时候、有最适合于放风筝的季节、有最适合于打橄榄球的时候、有最适合于打棒球的时候一样,过去常常也有最适合于吃某种水果或蔬菜的时候或者季节,可在佛罗里达州的绝大多数地区,由于气候非常温暖,很少或者从来都不会有霜、雪或冰冻,因此一年到头都可以种植水果和蔬菜呢。农民将自己种植的反季蔬菜运往其他各州,使得北方的人在圣诞节也可以吃到新鲜的草莓,还有芦笋,并且一年十二个月里都能吃到莴苣和萝卜了。

佛罗里达出产的主要水果,就是橙子和葡萄柚,这两种水果,都只能生长在没有霜冻的地区。葡萄柚长成一串一串的,就像是一串串巨大的黄色葡萄,这也是它之所以被称为"葡萄"柚的原因。人们起初以为葡萄柚不适合于食用,因为它的味道太苦,不像橙子那样甜,可后来人们却慢慢地喜欢上了这种水果。佛罗里达种植的葡萄柚,比全世界其他任何地方都要多。

世界上本来没有佛罗里达这个地方,而美国原本也是没有伸向海中的这只"爪子"的。只是后来美国"长"出了这样一只"爪子",过程则是下面这样的。海洋里很温暖、很浅,并且海洋中生活着无数、无数种小动物,每一种都像一颗小果冻,中心包裹着一个石质的核,或者是外面包裹着一层石质的壳,后来,无数、无

of these little sea animals died. As they died, millions, billions, trillions of these stony specks and shells fell to the bottom of the sea like a snowfall of chalk dust, and this piled up until the water was filled up. This stony, bony, chalky pile is Florida. On this kind of ground of which Florida is made plants grow very well indeed. In fact, this soft, chalky ground is so good for growing things that people dig it up and send it to other States to be put on the ground to make vegetables grow better.

Long, long years ago, before there were any people on the World, our whole country was at the bottom of the sea, and a great deal of our country was made under the sea just as Florida was made, from bones and shells of sea animals. This kind of bone and shell rock—for it is rock—is called limestone, because if you burn it it makes lime. Limestone is really bone-stone; stone made of the bones of sea animals. Then the earth wrinkled and crinkled and rose out of the water and formed our country. We know it was once under the sea because in many places now, high above the sea, even on mountain tops, we find this limestone with shells and bones of fish and other sea animals still showing in it. Marble, the most beautiful of all stone, is a kind of limestone, for it also is made of bone. People build houses and palaces of it and make statues and tombstones of marble or limestone.

Many of the people who go to Florida stop on their trip to see sights, and one of the greatest sights is in Virginia and Kentucky where the rock under the ground is all limestone. The "sights" are huge caves, and in Kentucky they are so large they are called Mammoth Caves. These caves have not been dug out by men but by water. Water, you know, melts sugar; but perhaps you didn't know that water melts rock too—not ordinary

数种这样的海洋小动物都死了。它们死后，无数、无数个这样的石质核和石质壳便落到了海底，就像粉笔灰一样纷纷洒落，堆积起来，直到填满了整个水域。这个堆积起来的、石质而嶙峋且由白垩组成的地方，就成了佛罗里达。在形成佛罗里达的那种土壤上，植物的确生长得非常茂盛。事实上，这种柔软而含有白垩的土壤，非常适合于栽种东西，因此人们还将此处的土壤挖出来，运到其他各州去铺在地上，以便让那里的蔬菜长得更好呢。

很久、很久以前，在世界上还没有出现人类以前，整个美国都还位于海底，因此我国大部分地方都是像佛罗里达那样，是在海底由海洋动物的骨头和贝壳形成的。这种由海洋动物的骨头和贝壳所形成的岩石（没错，就是岩石），叫作石灰岩，因为如果将这种岩石进行煅烧的话，它们就会变成石灰。石灰岩实际上就是骨质岩，也就是由海洋动物的骨头所形成的岩石。接下来，大地开始皱曲、隆起，升出了海面，形成了美国。我们之所以知道这里曾经位于海底，是因为如今在许多高海拔的地方，甚至是山脉之巅，我们都发现了含有贝壳、鱼骨以及仍然看得见其他海洋动物骸骨的石灰岩。所有石头中最美丽的大理石，就是一种石灰岩，因为它也是由海洋动物的骨头形成的。人们用大理石建造房屋和宫殿，还用大理石或者石灰石来制作雕塑和墓碑呢。

前往佛罗里达的许多人，在旅途中都会停下来观光，而其中最了不起的一个景点，就位于弗吉尼亚和肯塔基州，那里所有的地下岩层全都属于石灰岩。这个"景

rock, but it melts limestone, and these caves are in limestone rock. The Mammoth Cave is like a huge cellar underground—a cave so large and high that you could put a whole city with its tall buildings in it. You could easily get lost and wander for miles. Men have been lost and unable to find their way out again and died and their skeletons have been found long years after.

Through the roof of the cave water drips drop by drop, and each drop leaves a bit of limestone, until in the course of time the dripping water makes icicles of rock that hang down from the roof of the cave. Drops of water from each icicle fall on to the floor of the cave, and the limestone gradually piles up and up like a stone post until at last the icicle above meets the post beneath.. The trickling water also forms pools in the bottom of the cave, and in these pools of water live fish that are different from the fish in the water above ground. As it is pitch dark in the caves, these fish have no use for their eyes, so after long, long years they at last grew none. They are blind. Instead of seeing, they feel with the part of their heads where their eyes were.

猛犸洞穴

点"，便是巨型的地下洞穴，而在肯塔基州，由于那些洞穴都极其巨大，因而还被人们称为"猛犸洞穴"呢。那些洞穴可不是人工挖掘出来的，而是被水流侵蚀出来的。大家都知道，水会将糖溶化，但你们可能并不知道，水也会将岩石溶化呢。当然，它并不能溶化普通的岩石，而是只能溶化石灰岩，因此，那些洞穴全都位于石灰岩里。"猛犸洞穴"就像是一座巨大的地窖，是一个又大又高的洞，完全可以把整座城市的高楼大厦全都放进去呢。在洞里，人们一不小心就会迷路，然后不知不觉地走上好几英里远。曾经有人在洞里迷了路，再也找不到出去的路，然后死在里面了，而他们的遗骸，则过了多年才被人们发现呢。

在洞里，水是从洞顶一滴一滴地滴下来的，并且每一滴都会留下一点儿石灰石，随着时间的推移，滴水便形成了一根根的石锥，从洞顶垂下来。每根石锥上面滴下来的水落到洞底后，其中携带的石灰石又会逐渐堆积起来，并且越堆越高，就像一根石柱，最终，上面的石锥便会与下面的石柱连成一体。滴水还在洞底形成了一个个水坑，而在这种水坑里，还生长着一些与地面水体中不同的鱼类。由于洞穴里面漆黑一片，这些鱼类的眼睛没有任何用处，因此千万年过去之后，这些鱼的眼睛最终便完全退化了，变成了没有眼睛的鱼。虽说看不到东西，但它们会用头部原先长有眼睛的那个部位来进行感知。

13 The Covered Wagon

Not so many years ago the Mississippi River was the far edge of the United States. Beyond the Mississippi it was wild, wilder, wilderness. Few people had ever been all the way across our country to the Pacific Ocean. There were wild Indians, wild animals, and high, high mountains in the way. Why did people want to go across the country anyway, and what sort of people were they? They were hunters who wanted to hunt wild animals, they were missionaries who wanted to make the Indians Christians, and they were people who were just inquisitive and who wanted to see what the wilderness was like.

Then one day a man told another, that another man had told him, that another man had told him, that still another man had told him that he had found gold in California, a land way off on the edge of the Pacific Ocean—plenty of gold; all you had to do was to dip it up in pans out of the rivers and pick it out of the sand and water.

Gold! Gold! It was almost as if some one had cried Fire! Fire! Thousands of people dropped their tools, stopped their farming, shut up their shops, loaded their beds and cooking things on wagons, put a cover over the wagon so that they could live under it as under a tent, took along a gun, and rushed for the Far West to hunt for gold. There were no roads, there were no bridges, there were no sign-boards to tell which was the right way— it was just wild, wilder, wilderness. For months and months they traveled. Many of them died of sickness, many were killed by the Indians, many were drowned in crossing rivers,

第13章　大篷车

不久以前，密西西比河还属于美国偏远的边缘地区。密西西比河对岸，全都是荒野一片。当时，几乎还没有人一路横跨整个美国，前往太平洋沿岸。一路上，既有野蛮的印第安人，有各种野兽，还有高耸挺拔的崇山峻岭。那么，人们为什么会想要去横跨整个美国，而横跨美国的又是些什么人呢？他们就是那些想要猎杀野兽的猎人，是那些想要让印第安人皈依基督教的传教士，以及那些完全属于好奇、想要看一看荒野是个什么样子的人。

接下来有一天，一个人对另一个人说，有人告诉他说自己在加利福尼亚发现了黄金。这一消息一传十、十传百地流传开来，而加利福尼亚则是位于太平洋沿岸的一个遥远之地。据说人们发现了很多很多的黄金，只要用盆子从河里捞出沙子，然后从沙子和水中就可以拣到黄金了。

黄金！黄金！几乎就像是有人喊"失火了！失火了！"一样，成千上万的人都放下手头的工具，全都不再种田，关上店门，将床铺和炊具装上马车，给马车盖上篷子，好让自己能够像在帐篷里一样住在其中，再带上一杆枪，急急忙忙地赶往遥远的大西部淘金去了。一路上，既没有马路，没有桥梁，也没有指示要走哪条路的路标，只有一片片荒芜、更加荒芜的原野。他们走了一月又一月。许多人都病死在

many lost their way and died of starvation or of thirst—but many also, at last, reached California, found gold just where they heard it was to be found, and made their fortunes. This was in the year 1849, so these people who went West were called "Forty-niners."

Since that time roads and railroads have been made all the way across the country; great cities have been built where once was only wilderness; and the wild Indians have been tamed. The United States has given the Indians large pieces of land to pay them for having taken other land away from them. These places given to the Indians are called "Reservations", because they are reserved for them, just as a seat in the theater that is reserved for a person is called a "reserved seat."

The first railroad to the Pacific coast took the middle route from Chicago to San Francisco. But you can now take a train from Chicago and cross to the Pacific by the north, middle, or south. It took months when the "Forty-niners" went across in their covered wagons, but now it takes less than one day by airplane.

People used to say, "Go West, Young Man, if you want to make a fortune," and many thousands did go West, not looking for gold, but for farm lands, which were given them free by the United States if they would raise crops. Some of these men who

将他们的床铺和炊具装上马车，
开始向大西部进发

路上，许多人都被印第安人杀害了，许多人在过河之时淹死了，还有许多人则是迷了路，饿死或者渴死了，不过，也有许多人最终还是到达了加利福尼亚，在这个传说中能够找到黄金的地方找到了黄金，并且发了大财。这时正值1849年，因此那些前往大西部的人就被称为"四九年人"。

从那时起，人们便开始修筑一条条横跨整个美国的公路和铁路了，那些曾经只是荒野一片的地方，兴建起了许多的大城市，而野蛮的印第安人，也被制服了。合众国占用了印第安人的土地之后，会偿付给他们大片的土地。交给印第安人的这些土地，就叫"保留地"，因为这些地方是专门留给印第安人的，就像剧院里为某个人预留的位子叫作"保留席"一样。

第一条通往太平洋沿岸的铁路，位于美国中部，从芝加哥通往圣弗朗西斯科。不过，如今你们乘坐列车，从芝加哥经由北部、中部或者南部横跨美国，都可以到达太平洋沿岸了。"四九年人"赶着大篷车西行时，需要耗费好几个月才能到达，可如今坐飞机还用不了一天，就可以到达太平洋沿岸。

人们以前常说："想发财的话，就到西部去吧，年轻人。"的确有成千上万的人前往大西部，可他们并不是去淘金，而是去耕种土地，如果他们能够种出庄稼，

went to Oklahoma and Texas and other places, chiefly west of the Mississippi, found oil oozing out of the ground on their farms. This oil spoiled the land for farming and made the water unfit even for the horses and cows to drink. The land was ruined—no good—so many farmers gave up and moved away.

There are three kinds of oil in the World—vegetable, animal, and mineral. Did you ever play the game called Animal, Vegetable, and Mineral? It's a good game. The "Old Man" shouts, "Vegetable!" and you must name a vegetable, any vegetable—"potato," for instance—before he can count ten. Or he shouts, "Mineral!" or "Animal!" and you must name a mineral or an animal before he counts ten. In this game a mineral is anything that isn't animal or vegetable. But no matter whether he says "Animal," "Vegetable," or "Mineral," you will always be right if you say, "Oil!" for it is one of the few things in the World that can be all three.

The oil from vegetables, like olive oil, and the oil from animals, like cod-liver oil, is good for food, but mineral oil from the rocks under the ground is not good for food. But some one found out that mineral oil could be burned to give light and heat, and then the automobile was invented, and from this mineral oil was made the gasoline to run automobiles. Many other things are now made from this kind of oil—medicine, colors for dyeing, and even perfumes.

People who thought their farms had been spoiled by oil found that the oil was worth a fortune, worth much more than what they could make out of chickens and pigs, or corn

美国就会把土地免费分配给他们。其中有些人来到了俄克拉荷马、得克萨斯和其他地方，主要都是密西西比河以西的地区，在自家的农场上，他们都发现了溢出地面的石油。这种石油，让土地无法再耕种，使得那里的水甚至不适合于饮牛饮马。由于土地荒废，没有用了，因此许多农民便放弃耕作，搬到别的地方去了。

世界上有三种油类：植物油、动物油和矿物油。你们有没有玩过那种叫作"动物、植物和矿物"的游戏呢？那可是一种很不错的游戏啊。玩游戏的时候，"老人"会喊道："植物！"而你则必须在他数到十之前，说出一种植物的名称来，说任何植物都行，比如"土豆"。他若是喊"矿物！"或者"动物！"那你就必须在他数到十之前，说出一种矿物或者动物的名称来。在这种游戏里，"矿物"可以是不属于动物或者植物的任何东西。不过，无论他喊的是"动物"、"植物"还是"矿物"，若是你们回答"油！"的话，就总不会错，因为油正是世界上为数不多的、同时可以归于这三类中的东西之一。

像橄榄油这样的植物油，和像鱼肝油这样的动物油，都是适合于食用的油类，可从地下岩石里开采出来的矿物油，却并不适合于食用。不过，有人却发现，矿物油可以燃烧，可以发出光和热，接下来，人们发明了汽车，便开始用这种矿物油制成汽油，来驱动汽车了。如今，还有许多其他的东西也是用这种矿物油制成的，比如药品、染料，甚至是香水。

一些曾经以为自己的农田被石油毁掉了的人，发现石油也可以让他们赚到钱，赚到比他们养鸡、养猪、种植玉米或小麦更多的钱。有些地方必须打出油井，然后

and wheat. Some wells had to be dug and the oil pumped up, but others sprouted up like fountains—these were called gushers.

This oil that comes out of the rock underneath the ground is called petroleum, which means rock oil. Some of the petroleum companies are nicknamed "Pete" for short, which is a pretty good name because Pete means "rock."

If you take a train by the middle route you cross Iowa, the Corn State, passing through endless fields of corn. You next cross Nebraska and gradually rise higher and higher as the ground slopes gently upward, until you reach the State called Colorado. Colorado means "color red." Colorado is at the foot of the highest mountains in America—they are called the Rocky Mountains. The capital of Colorado is Denver and Denver is just about half-way from Chicago to the Pacific Ocean.

Not so far from Denver you can climb to the top of a Rocky Mountain peak, if you want to and if you have a good heart. The first man who tried to climb this mountain was named Pike, but he gave it up, so ever since it has been called "Pike's Peak." When I was in school we used to try to say this "tongue-twister": "Speak Pike, Speak Pike, Speak Pike" over and over as fast as we could *without saying* "Pike's Peak." We couldn't do it— neither can you! Pike couldn't climb to the top of his mountain, but nowadays thousands of people climb to the top each year just as a "stunt" to see in how many hours they can do it. Pike's Peak is so high that there is snow on the top in the summer as well as in the winter, and it is so high in the air that there is very little air to breathe when you are at the

才能将石油抽取出来，可其他一些地方，石油却会像井水一样涌出地面，这种油井便叫作"自喷井"。

从地下岩石中开采出来的这种油类，叫作石油，也就是岩石里的油之意。有些石油公司还被人们简称为"皮特（Pete）"，这种简称很合适，因为"皮特"的意思就是"岩石"。

假如乘坐中部线路的一列火车，大家就会横跨爱荷华这个"玉米之州"，因而一路上全都是无边无际的玉米地。接下来，你们就会穿过内布拉斯加州，然后随着地势缓慢升高而越爬越高，最终到达那个叫作科罗拉多的州。"科罗拉多"就是"红色"的意思。科罗拉多州位于美国最高的一座山脉，即人称"落基山脉"的山脚下。科罗拉多州的首府是丹佛，而丹佛差不多正好位于从芝加哥到太平洋沿岸的中间。

在距丹佛不远的地方，大家可以爬上落基山脉中某座山峰的山顶，前提当然是你们真想去爬，并且心脏也没有问题。第一个试图爬上那座山峰的人，名叫"派克"；虽说他中途放弃了，可自此以后，人们便将这座山峰称为"派克峰"了。儿时上学的时候，我们曾经常努力说过一首"绕口令"："拼派克，拼派克，拼派克"，尽量快速地说上一遍又遍，还不能说成"派克峰"。[1]我们根本就做不到，

---

[1]　此处属于英文中的绕口令。连续、快速地说Speak Pike（拼派克）后，很容易变成"Pike's Peak"（派克峰）。

top. A great many people cannot stand it at the top; they have to sit down. They gasp for breath as if they had been running, or like a fish out of water; their hearts beat fast and so hard they can hear it drumming in their ears, and they feel faint and weak. There are now an auto road and a railway up to the top, so that you don't have to climb Pike's Peak if you don't want to. The railway track, however, is so steep that an ordinary railway car would slide down like a sled, so the track has small iron steps between the rails, and the car has a wheel that catches into the steps so that it cannot slip backward or run away downhill—it walks up and down the steps.

你们也是做不到的！虽说派克没能登到这座山的山顶，可如今每年都会有数千人爬上去呢，他们这样做，只是一种"噱头"，只是为了看一看，他们究竟要几个小时才能爬到山顶。派克峰海拔很高，因此夏季与冬季一样，山顶都有积雪，又由于它高耸入云，因此登上山顶之后，你们就会觉得那里空气稀薄、呼吸不畅了。许多人在山顶上站都站不了，只能坐下来。他们必须大口大口地吸气，好像自己一直都在跑步似的，或者像一条离了水的鱼似的，他们的心脏跳得很快、很厉害，甚至自己耳朵里都听得见心跳的声音，还会觉得头晕、全身乏力。如今，已有一条公路和一条铁路一直通到山顶，因此，如果不想的话，你们无须亲自攀爬，就能到达派克峰顶了。然而，那条铁路非常陡峭，普通的火车会像雪橇那样往下滑，因此两条铁轨之间还设有一些小小的铁质梯级，以便阻止火车往回滑行或者向山下冲去，也就是说，火车上山下山，都是在"踩"着这些梯级来去呢。

14 Wonderland

"Alice in Wonderland" is a fairy-tale, but there is a real Wonderland out in the West. One of the wonders is a river. It is called the Colorado River, but it is not in the State of Colorado. It is in Arizona.

The river runs deep down in the bottom of the deepest ditch in the World, a ditch a mile deep in places. This ditch is called by the Spaniards a Canyon. You can stand on the edge of the Colorado Canyon and look almost a mile down to what seems a slender little thread of water—the Colorado River—running at the bottom, and yet this little stream has cut this ditch in which it runs—worn it down—all by itself. Here we can see, better than any place i.t.w.W., what the World looks like on the inside if we could dig down into it a mile deep, for here a little river has dug down a mile deep for us. I asked my guide how far it was across to the other side of the Canyon.

"Oh," he replied, "about ten or twelve shouts." That was a new distance to me, for I didn't even know how far one shout was. My arithmetic says twelve inches make a foot and three feet make a yard, but does not say how many feet make a "shout." You can look across to the other side of the Canyon and see the opposite wall almost a mile high—not a plain, blank wall like the wall of a building, but more like the walls of heaven—layers of rock, pile upon pile, colored yellow, red, green, orange, purple, mixed with sunshine and shadow. All of this rock was once under the sea, for it is limestone and sandstone. Each

第14章　仙境

《爱丽丝梦游仙境》只是一个童话故事，可在美国的大西部，却有一个真真实实的"仙境"。其中的奇迹之一，便是一条河。这条河叫作科罗拉多河，可它并不位于科罗拉多州境内，而是位于亚利桑那州境内。

这条河，流淌在世界上最深的一条沟里，在有些地方，这条沟甚至深达一英里呢。西班牙人将这条沟称为"大峡谷"。你们可以站在科罗拉多大峡谷一侧，俯瞰差不多一英里之下：科罗拉多河就像是一道细线，在谷底流淌而过，可正是这条小河，凭一己之力，切入、侵蚀了它所流经的这道峡谷。就算在别处也可以向下挖掘一英里深，但我们在此还是可以比在全世界其他任何地方更好地看到地球内部的模样，因为在这里，一条小河已经替我们向下挖掘了一英里。我曾经问过导游，到大峡谷那一边有多远。

"哦，"他回答道，"大概喊上十声或者十二声那样远吧。"对我来说，这可是一种新的距离，因为我连喊一声有多远都不知道呢。我的数学知识规定，十二英寸是一英尺，三英尺则合一码，可没有说过多少英尺合一"喊"呢。你们可以眺望大峡谷的那一边，看到对面的谷壁高达差不多一英里，那道谷壁，并不是一堵像是建筑物里的那种普通而单调的墙壁，而更像是天堂里的一堵墙壁，它是由岩石一层

layer has been dyed a different color by minerals like iron and copper; if there was iron in the water, it turned the rock the color of iron rust—red; if copper, it turned the rock green.

I once bought a souvenir pencil. In its end was a pinhole, and when you squinted into the hole with one eye, there you saw in all its vastness the Colorado Canyon. It seemed impossible, and yet there it was, stretching off in the distance, mile upon mile, in a picture the size of a pin head!

Some of the branches of the Colorado run in smaller canyons, and high up on the walls of these canyons are houses built in caves in the rock. Once upon a time, long, long ago, people whom we call "cliff-dwellers" built these homes j there to be safe from their enemies.

A giant hop and skip north from the Grand Canyon would bring one to the State of Utah, where there is a great lake, but this Great Lake is different from the five "Great Lakes." The water in the five Great Lakes is fresh, the water in this great lake is salt, so it is called Great Salt Lake, though it is really a little ocean. As in the case of the ocean, rivers run into the Great Salt Lake, but no rivers run out of it.

What makes it salt? The same thing

大 峡 谷

你们可以向下俯瞰差不多一英里远

层堆叠起来的，颜色丰富，有黄色、红色、绿色、橙色、紫色，与阳光和阴影混合驳杂，显得五彩斑斓。这些岩层曾经都位于海底，因为它们都是石灰岩或者砂岩。每种岩层都因为含有像铁或铜这样的矿物质而呈现出不同的色彩：如果水中含铁，那么它就会把岩石变成铁锈的颜色，即红色；如果水中含的是铜，那它就会让岩石呈现出绿色来。

我曾经买过一支用来做纪念品的铅笔。铅笔一端有个小孔，如果眯起一只眼睛，向小孔里望去，就会看到科罗拉多大峡谷那种广袤无垠的景象。这似乎是不可能的，可事实就是如此，在一幅针尖般大小的图画上，科罗拉多大峡谷竟然一英里一英里地向远处延伸着！

科罗拉多河有的支流是在其他一些较小的峡谷里流淌着，而在那些峡谷高高的谷壁上，还有一些房屋，修建在岩石上的洞穴里。那些房屋，都是很久、很久以前我们所谓的"悬崖洞人"修建的，目的是为了让他们不致遭到敌人的侵扰。

从大峡谷往北，经过一个巨大的"三级跳"，我们就会来到犹他州。那里有一个巨大的湖泊，可这个"大湖"，却与那五个"大湖"不一样。五大湖区的湖水都是淡水，可这个大湖里的湖水却是咸水，因此这个大湖便被称作"大盐湖"，不过，它其实就是一个小小的海洋。因为与海洋的情况一样，大盐湖有河流注入，却

that makes the ocean salt.

What makes the ocean salt?

The ground through which rivers flow is salt. If you ever tasted the ground, you would know it, but, of course, I don't suppose you ever have, unless you have fallen and gotten some in your mouth or on your lips. Rivers, as they flow along, wash some of this salt out of the ground, carry it along, and dump it into the ocean. They carry so little salt at a time you would never know by tasting the river water that it was salt at all, but the rivers pour in this ever so little bit of salt all the time, all the time, and so the salt gradually does collect in the ocean and in Great Salt Lake, for there is no way for the salt to go out once it's in the ocean or the lake. The water gets out of the lake as it does out of the ocean—by rising into the air as vapor—evaporating, we call it—but the salt doesn't evaporate, it can't rise into the air, and so it has no way of getting out.

The Great Salt Lake is getting saltier and saltier all the time. It is already much saltier than the ocean. Salt water holds up a person or anything in it much better than fresh water, and the saltier the water the more it holds the person up. So in Great Salt Lake you couldn't drown whether you knew how to swim

崖 居

没有河流排出。

是什么原因，使得这个湖中的水是咸水呢？

这与使得海水成为咸水的原因是一样的。

是什么原因，使得海水是咸的呢？

这是因为，河流流经的土壤是咸的。如果以前尝过泥土的味道，那大家就会明白这一点，但是，除非你们摔倒过，把泥土弄到了嘴里或者粘到了嘴唇上，否则我当然认为你们没有尝过。在一路流淌的过程中，河流会将土壤里的这种盐分溶解，然后一路携带着，最终汇入海洋之中。它们一次只会带走一点点儿盐分，因此你们完全不可能通过尝一尝河水，就感觉出河水的咸味来，不过，由于河流始终都在将这一点点的盐分不断地注入海洋当中，所以海洋和大盐湖里的盐分便开始逐渐地越积越多了：因为一旦注入海洋或者湖中，这种盐分就没有办法再流失出去。湖水逸出的方式，与海水是一样的，那就是变成水蒸气，升到空中（我们称这一过程为蒸发），可盐分却不会蒸发掉，不能升到空中，因而无法流失出去。

大盐湖一直都在变得越来越咸、越来越咸，使得那里的湖水如今比海水都要咸得多了。咸水浮起其中的人或者别的东西的本领，要比淡水大得多，而且，水越咸，它浮起水中之人的力量也越大。因此，在大盐湖里，无论会不会游泳，大家都是不会溺水的。你们既可以在水中站着，也可以坐在水里，还可以像躺在沙发上那

or not. You can stand in the water or sit in the water or lie down on the water as you would on a sofa. You can read the paper or eat your luncheon while sitting in the water, but you have to be very careful not to get any of the water in your eyes or in any small cut you may have on your hands or body, for the salt water is so strong it smarts. Some day the ocean will be as salty as Great Salt Lake, for the ocean too is slowly, very slowly, getting saltier and saltier all the time. Then, even if there were a shipwreck, people would not drown—they would bob about in the sea like corks.

Still farther north, a hop, skip, and a jump from the Colorado Canyon, in the corner of the State of Wyoming, is a place that looks on the map like a little State within the State. It is called Yellowstone Park. There are so many wonderful things in this part of the State— freaks, funny things, and lovely things—that the United States thought people would like to see them, so they made a Park of this corner of the State, with good roads and hotels, for people who wish to see the sights. No hunting is allowed, so wild animals and birds can live and raise families without fear of being killed. There are bears in Yellowstone Park, but as they are not allowed to be hunted or shot, they become very tame and people can even go close enough to photograph them.

The World in that part of the country has not yet cooled off altogether, and it is still very hot not far down under the ground. If a person asked me to have a glass of spring water, I should expect a nice cool drink; but if the spring were in Yellowstone Park the water would probably scald my throat, for there are hundreds of springs in Yellowstone Park heated so hot by underground fires that they boil up and over like a pot on the fire.

样，躺在水面上呢。你们可以坐在水里看报纸或者吃午餐，不过，大家得非常小心才行，不能让湖水进入眼睛里面，不能让湖水浸到自己手上或者身上可能有的任何小伤口里，因为咸水太厉害，会刺得眼睛和伤口生疼生疼。有朝一日，海水也会变得像大盐湖里的湖水那样咸，因为海洋也一直都在慢慢、慢慢地变得越来越咸、越来越咸。到了那时，就算船只在海上失事，乘客也不会溺死了，因为他们会像软木塞一样，浮在海里呀。

再往北去，从科罗拉多大峡谷再来一个三级跳，就到了怀俄明州的一个角上，那里有个地方，在地图上看起来，就像是怀俄明州里面又有一个小州似的。这个地方，叫作黄石公园。怀俄明州的这个地区，有许多、许多的奇妙之处，有奇怪、有趣而可爱的东西，美国觉得人们可能都会想来看一看这些东西，因此便将怀俄明州的这个角落变成了一个公园，并且修建了一条条大路和一座座好旅馆，供那些希望去观赏美景的人用。那里禁止打猎，因此野生动物和鸟儿可以生活在那里，可以繁衍后代，而不用害怕遭到人们猎杀。黄石公园里有熊，但由于禁止猎杀，因此它们都变得非常温驯了，游客甚至还可以走近它们去拍照。

地球在美国这一地区的部分，还没有彻底冷却下来，因此在地面以下不远的地方，温度仍然非常高。要是有人请我喝上一杯井水的话，那么我心里肯定会想，这杯井水一定是凉丝丝的，不过，要是那口井位于黄石公园的话，井水十有八九就会烫伤我的喉咙，因为黄石公园里有成百上千眼井都被地热烧得滚烫，还会像炉子上

There is a big lake in Yellowstone Park called Yellowstone Lake. You can stand on its edge and catch a fish in the lake and, without taking the fish off the hook, drop it into one of the hot springs near shore and cook it. In other places the water is blown up by the steam underneath into fountains. These fountains are called "geysers," and some are quite big and some are quite beautiful. One called "Old Faithful" spouts regularly about once every hour, throwing a beautiful stream of water straight up into the air like a gigantic fire-hose. It does this so faithfully that it seems almost as if a person turned the water on and off, but it has been spouting this way ever since it has been known—never missing an hour, night or day, never forgetting, never running down, more faithful than any human being would or could be.

的水壶那样沸腾起来呢。

　　黄石公园里有一个大湖，叫作黄石湖。你们可以站在岸边，钓起湖中的一条鱼，然后都不用把鱼从鱼钩上取下来，只需直接扔进湖边的温泉中煮熟，就可以吃了。在其他一些地方，井水还会被地下形成的蒸汽冲向空中，形成一座座喷泉。这种喷泉，就叫"间歇泉"，有些间歇泉的规模相当巨大，有些间歇泉则非常漂亮。其中有一座间歇泉，叫作"老忠实"，差不多每个小时都会喷发一次，并且每次都是径直向空中喷出一道美丽的水雾，宛如一条巨大的消防水龙。这座间歇泉始终这样有规律地喷发着，简直就像是有一个人在那里将井水开了关、关了开似的，自从人们发现这眼喷泉之后，它就一直都在这样喷发，从未间断过一个小时、一个昼夜，从不遗忘、从不衰竭，比任何人都要更加忠实呢。

15 The 'Est, 'Est West

A land where they have the b-est, the bigg-est, the fin-est, the high-est, the loveli-est of everything—so they say—the *best* oranges, the bigg-*est* prunes, the fin*est* grapes, the tall*est* trees, the high*est* mountains, the loveli*est* weather—i.t. w.W. No, it's not Paradise. That's the 'est, 'est West.

California was named after an island in an old fairy-tale and in many ways the real California is a fairy-tale land. When gold was found in the rivers there, the story sounded like a fairytale, but it turned out to be a true tale. Many stories they tell nowadays about California still sound like fairy-tales to people in the East. Who would believe that there are trees in California so tall they seem to brush the sky—trees so big around that men have cut tunnels in them for automobiles to go through—trees so old that they were born before Christ was born! It's true, there are. They are called Giant Redwoods. How more wonderful than a fairy-tale it would be if those trees could tell us the true story of what has happened in their long lives!

Let us see how many 'ests we can count in California.

California is the long*est* State in the United States. If you could take up California and put it down on the Atlantic coast it would stretch from Florida to New York. That's one'est.

第15章　最遥远的西部

有一个地方，那里的人们拥有整个世界上最好、最大、最优、最高、最美的一切，比如，他们说，那里有最好的橙子、最大的李子、最优质的葡萄、最高的树木、最高的山脉、最令人愉快的天气。不，这里并不是天堂，而是美国最遥远的西部地区。

加利福尼亚这个州，是用古老童话里一个岛屿的名称来命名的，而从许多方面来看，现实中的加利福尼亚也确实是一个童话般的地方。人们在加利福尼亚的河流当中发现了黄金，这种说法听上去就像是童话故事里才有的事情，可结果却表明，这的确是一个现实版的童话故事。如今，当地人述说的许多经历，在美国东部的人听来，仍然像是一个个童话呢。谁会相信，加利福尼亚的大树会高耸参天；谁会相信，那里有一些树硕大无比，人们甚至在树干里凿出隧道，供汽车通行；谁又会相信，那里有些树极其古老，甚至是基督降生之前长出来的呢！可事实的确如此，那里有这样的树。这些树，叫作"巨型红杉"。要是那些树能够说话，给我们讲述其漫长的一生当中发生的真实故事的话，该比童话故事精彩多少啊！

我们不妨来数一数，看加利福尼亚究竟拥有多少个"最"吧。

加利福尼亚是美国最长的一个州。假如你们能把整个加利福尼亚拿起来，放到

California has the high*est* mountain in the United States. It is called Mount Whitney. That's two 'ests.

California has the low*est* place in America. It's a valley, and the valley is more than two hundred feet lower than the ocean. It is so dry and so hot down in this hollow—this lowest spot—that nothing can live there, either animal or vegetable, except horned toads and lizards, both of which animals love heat—the more heat the better for them. Some people say they can even live in fire—but that's a fairy-tale. This low hot valley is called Death Valley. People usually keep away from it, but some men have strayed into it looking for gold and have lost their way, or some who wanted to get to the other side tried to cross it and before they could get out or reach the other side they have died of heat or thirst. That's why it is called Death Valley. That's longest, highest, lowest—three 'ests.

Besides Death Valley, California has another valley—but this is one of the loveliest valleys. It is called the Yosemite. It is a very deep trough, and streams of water fall over the edge into the trough from many high places. One of these falls turns to mist before it reaches the ground and looks like a huge veil of a bride, so it is called Bridal Veil Falls. Half a dozen of these waterfalls in the Yosemite Valley are higher than Niagara, and two of them tumble headlong a quarter of a mile from the top to the bottom of the valley, the highest falls in America—loveliest valley, highest falls; that makes two more 'ests.

California has, beside these 'ests, the sweet*est* oranges, the sour*est* lemons, the big*gest* grape-fruit, so they say, but they didn't *come* from California; they *went* there. There

大西洋沿岸去比一比的话，它会从佛罗里达一直延伸到纽约呢。这是一个"最"。

加利福尼亚有美国最高的一座山峰。那座山，叫作"惠特尼峰"。这就有了两个"最"。

加利福尼亚有一个地方，是美国海拔最低之处。那是一个峡谷，比海平面还要低两百多英尺。这个峡谷的谷底（即整个峡谷最低的地方）非常干燥、非常炎热，因此除了角蟾和蜥蜴，其他动植物都无法在那里生存，角蟾和蜥蜴都喜欢高温炎热的环境，并且越热越好。有些人吹牛说，他们甚至可以在火中生存，可那不过是神话罢了。这个海拔低、温度又很高的峡谷，叫作"死亡谷"。人们一般都对"死亡谷"敬而远之，但也有一些人曾经进去，到峡谷里去寻找黄金，后来却迷了路；还有一些人则想要越过峡谷，到另一边去，可还没等走出峡谷或者到达峡谷的另一边，他们就热死或者渴死了。这里之所以叫作"死亡谷"，原因就在于此。最长、最高、最低，加起来就有三个"最"了。

除了"死亡谷"，加利福尼亚州还有另一个峡谷，不过，这里却是美国风景最优美的峡谷之一。这个峡谷，叫作"优胜美地"。这是一个非常深邃的峡谷，一条条溪流从许多地势较高的地方顺流而下，在峡谷边缘下落，形成一道道瀑布，注入峡谷之中。这些瀑布里面，有一道甚至还没有到达地面就化成了水雾，看上去像是一匹巨大的婚纱似的，因此被人们称为"婚纱瀑布"。"优胜美地"峡谷里，有六道瀑布的落差都超过了尼亚加拉大瀑布，其中还有两道瀑布水流湍急，从顶端下落到峡谷底部，距离竟达四分之一英里，属于美国落差最大的瀑布。最美的峡谷、落

were no oranges and no lemons growing in America at all before white men came to this country. The first white people to settle in California came from the country of Spain on the other side of the Atlantic Ocean. In Spain oranges and lemons grew, and the people from Spain, called Spaniards, brought over orange and lemon plants and started them growing in California and also in Florida.

The Spaniards built houses like those back in Spain, with white stucco walls and red tile roofs and with the "back yards" in the center of the house. They gave their cities Spanish names—Los Angeles, which means The Angels; and they named many of their cities after saints—San Francisco after St. Francis, Santa Barbara after St. Barbara—for many of the Spaniards were priests, who built mission churches up and down the land.

The City of the Angels is now the largest city on the Pacific coast. Near the City of the Angels is Hollywood, the greats (another 'est) moving-picture place i.t.w.W. There are 365 days in the year, as you know, but in Hollywood they say the sun shines on 400 days a year—fairy-tale land! At any rate, the weather is fine most of the time for taking moving pictures. This is one reason why it is such a good place for making movies, but another is that there are so many different kinds of natural scenery near-by. If they want to make a picture of a ship scene or shipwreck, there is the ocean. If they want to make a picture of the desert with camels and Arabs, there is the seashore. If they want to make a picture in the hot countries, there are palms and flowers. If they want to make pictures of winter scenes, all they have to do is to go to the mountains near-by and there is snow and ice all

差最高的瀑布，加起来就又多了两个"最"。

除了上述这些"最"，人们说加利福尼亚州还出产最甜的橙子、最酸的柠檬和最大的葡萄；不过，这些东西的原产地都不是加利福尼亚州，而是从别的地方引进加利福尼亚州的。在白人到来之前，美国根本就没有橙子和柠檬。最早到加利福尼亚殖民的白人，都来自于大西洋彼岸的西班牙。西班牙国内原本种植有橙子和柠檬，因而西班牙殖民者便把橙子树和柠檬树带到了加利福尼亚和佛罗里达，开始种植这两种果树。

西班牙殖民者所建的房屋，风格跟西班牙国内的建筑差不多：墙壁刷成白色，屋顶铺有红瓦，并且房屋的中央部位还有个所谓的"后院"。他们兴建起城市，并给这些城市起了西班牙名称，比如洛杉矶，意思就是"天使之城"。并且，许多城市都是用圣徒的名字来命名的，比如用圣方济各的名字命名的圣佛朗西斯科[1]，根据圣巴巴拉命名的圣巴巴拉市。由于许多西班牙殖民者都是牧师，因而他们还在这片土地上修建了许多的使命教堂。

洛杉矶这座"天使之城"，如今已经成了太平洋沿岸最大的城市了。离洛杉矶不远，就是好莱坞，这里可是世界上最大的电影生产基地呢（又有一个"最"了）。大家都知道，一年有三百六十五天，可在好莱坞，人们却说一年中有四百天是阳光普照，所以这里真是个童话般的地方啊！反正，那里的天气绝大部分时间都

---

[1]　圣佛朗西斯科（San Francisco），就是我们通常所称的"旧金山"，亦译"三藩市"。

the year round.

The city of San Francisco on the coast north of Los Angeles is nearly as large as Los Angeles. It might have been larger, but not so many years ago a terrible earthquake shook down the city. The quake only lasted a few minutes, but in that few minutes it rocked the city, cracked open the ground, and knocked down buildings as if they were houses of children's blocks, and hundreds and hundreds of people were killed. But the worst thing the earthquake did was to upset stoves and lamps that started one of the worst fires ever known—fires that burned up most of the city. Were the people discouraged? Not at all. They collected their insurance money—and they built the city up again.

San Francisco has one of the finest harbors in the World. Its harbor is a long bay—fifty miles long. Ships enter the harbor from the Pacific Ocean through an opening called the Golden Gate. The city is built on many hills so steep that it is difficult for automobiles to climb them, but houses built on them have lovely views of the ocean, the bay, or the

好莱坞是全世界最大的电影生产基地

是晴朗无云的，很适合于拍摄电影。这就是好莱坞极其适合于拍摄电影的一个原因；而另一个原因则是，好莱坞附近地区还有许多不同类型的自然景观。假如需要拍摄一艘轮船或者一场船只失事的镜头，就可以到太平洋上去拍摄。如果想要拍摄有骆驼和阿拉伯人的沙漠场景，就可以到海滩上去拍摄。要是想拍热带国家的镜头，那里就有棕榈树和鲜花。如果想拍冬景，只需到附近的山上去就行了，因为那些山峰上，终年都覆盖着冰雪呢。

位于洛杉矶以北沿海地区的圣弗朗西斯科这座城市，大小与洛杉矶差不多。它本来应该比洛杉矶大，只是多年以前，这里发生了一场可怕的大地震，将这座城市毁坏了。那次地震只持续了几分钟的时间；可就在那几分钟之内，整座城市都地动天摇，地面开裂，建筑物就像孩子们用积木搭成的房子似的纷纷倒塌，并且导致了成百上千人丧生。不过，此次地震最大的破坏，还是打翻了炉子和灯具，引发了有史以来最大的一场火灾，从而将这座城市的绝大部分都烧成了平地。经此灾难之后，那里的人气馁了没有呢？根本就没有。他们领取到了保险金，于是再次建好了这座城市。

圣弗朗西斯科拥有世界上最好的港口之一。那座港口，是一条长达五十英里

Golden Gate. Across the Golden Gate is a huge suspension bridge much bigger than the Brooklyn Bridge.

Ships enter and leave San Francisco for all the countries on and across the Pacific Ocean. Across the Pacific Ocean are China and Japan, and in days gone by so many Chinese came to the United States and landed in San Francisco that there is a part of the city called Chinatown, where there are Chinese houses and shops and theaters. Many Japanese too came to the United States from Japan, and bought farms where they raised fruits and vegetables.

的海湾。太平洋上的船只，都是穿过一个叫作"金门海峡"的通道，进入这个海湾的。虽说该市建在许多陡峭的山坡上，连汽车都很难爬上去，但把房屋建在山上，却能观赏到大海、海湾或金门海峡的美景呢。金门海峡的上方，横跨着一座巨大的悬索桥，这座桥，比纽约的布鲁克林大桥还要大得多。

进出圣弗朗西斯科的船只，可以到达太平洋沿岸或者对岸的所有国家。太平洋的对岸，是中国和日本。随着时间的推移，许多中国人都来到美国，抵达了圣弗朗西斯科，因此，该市如今还有一个区，叫作"唐人街"，那里遍布着中式房屋、商店和戏院呢。许多日本人也背井离乡，来到了美国，买下了许多的农庄，种植水果和蔬菜。

16 The 'Est, 'Est West (continued)

Here is a riddle for you. What is it that has no legs and yet can jump as high as the Washington Monument? I'll tell you the answer in a minute.

Between Oregon and Washington is a river named Columbia, after Columbus. In the Columbia River are large fish called salmon. Salmon live in the salt ocean, but when Mrs. Salmon wants to lay her eggs she goes way up the Columbia River, far above the falls to fresh water, looking for a quiet place to do so. How can she get by the falls? She jumps the falls. You may wonder how fish without legs can jump at all, and it is peculiar that they can, but they do. They bend their tails into a kind of spring, then flip!—up they go; for a salmon can jump as high as the Washington Monument.

"Are the falls as high as the Washington Monument?"

"No, they are all low."

"But you said a salmon could jump as high as the Washington Monument."

"A salmon *can*, for the Washington Monument can't jump at all!"

Millions of salmon together called "schools" swim up the river and fishermen catch them in nets, but they leave most of them so that they can lay eggs from which little salmon are born, and the little salmon swim down the river and out into the ocean, where they live and grow up until it comes time for them also to lay eggs, and then they in

第16章 最遥远的西部（续）

出个谜语给大家来猜一猜吧。什么东西没有腿，却能跳得像华盛顿纪念碑那样高呢？过一会儿，我再告诉你们答案。

俄勒冈州和华盛顿之间有一条河流，叫作哥伦比亚河，是用哥伦布的名字命名的。哥伦比亚河里有一种大型的鱼类，叫作鲑鱼。鲑鱼原本生活在海洋的咸水当中，但母鲑鱼要产籽的时候，却会沿着哥伦比亚河逆流而上，到瀑布上游很远的地方，去寻找水流平稳、适合产籽的水域。母鲑鱼又怎么能够通过那些瀑布呢？告诉你们吧，它们都是跳上瀑布的。你们可能都很奇怪，没有腿的鱼儿怎么能够跳跃，尽管这是一种很古怪的现象，可这种鱼儿确实能够跳跃呢。它们是先把尾巴弯成弓弦似的，然后猛地一弹，就上去了。鲑鱼能够跳得像华盛顿纪念碑那样高啊。

"那些瀑布的落差都像华盛顿纪念碑那样高吗？"

"不，瀑布的落差都很低。"

"可您说的是鲑鱼能够跳得像华盛顿纪念碑那样高啊。"

"鲑鱼当然能够，因为华盛顿纪念碑根本就跳不起来！"

数百万条鲑鱼聚集在一起，形成所谓的"群"，浩浩荡荡地在河中逆流而上。虽说渔夫会用渔网捕捉，但他们也会放过绝大部分鲑鱼，好让它们产下能够孵出小鲑鱼的鱼子来。而小鲑鱼出生后，又会在河中顺流而下，进入海洋，并在那里

their turn swim up the river, jump up the falls, and are either caught or left to raise more families of little salmon. Salmon meat is pink; we call it salmon color. It is packed in cans. You have probably eaten salmon from the Columbia River yourself.

The oldest fruit in the World is the apple. It is the fruit that grew in the Garden of Eden, but people believe the apple that Eve gave Adam was a very poor one compared to the apples that grow in the State of Washington. People in Washington, D. C.—all the way across the country—buy apples that have been shipped from Washington State—3,000 miles away—for they are so much better than ordinary apples. They are "skookum." That's what the Indians of the Northwest call something very nice—whether it is a girl or an apple.

There are great forests in Washington and Oregon. The forest trees are cut down to make lumber for building houses; and the paper I am writing on was made from trees that grew in Oregon. How do I know that? When I hold the paper up to the light, there is printed in white—we call it a watermark—the word "Oregon."

At the northwest corner of America is a large country that belongs to the United States and yet it is not a State. It is called a Territory. It is Alaska. The highest mountain in North America is there. It is called Mount McKinley. Alaska is so cold, so far off, and so hard to get to, and yet the United States bought it and paid millions of dollars for it, not because it had the highest

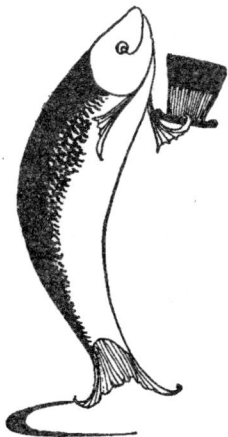

什么东西能够跳得像华盛顿纪念碑那样高呢?

生活、长大,直到它们也准备产籽的时候,便轮到它们在河中逆流而上,跳上那些瀑布,然后要么被渔夫捕住,要么便是留下来产籽、孵出更多的小鲑鱼来。鲑鱼肉呈粉红色,我们把这种颜色称为"肉粉色"。鲑鱼肉都是装在罐头里面的。你们很可能都吃过了哥伦比亚河出产的鲑鱼呢。

世界上最古老的水果,就是苹果。苹果也就是生长在伊甸园里的那种水果,可人们认为,夏娃给亚当吃的那个苹果,与华盛顿州出产的苹果比起来,质量却低劣得很。位于美国东海岸华盛顿特区里的市民买到的苹果,都是从三千英里以外的华盛顿州运来的,因为那里出产的苹果与普通苹果相比,品质要优良得多。它们都是"呱呱叫"。这个词,是西北地区的印第安人用于形容某种非常不错的东西的,他们无论形容的是一位姑娘还是一个苹果,都是用这个词。

华盛顿和俄勒冈两个州,都被广袤的森林覆盖着。林中的树木被人们砍伐下来,当成建筑房屋的木材,而我此时正在写字的纸张,也是用俄勒冈出产的树木制成的。不过,我又是怎么知道的呢?这是因为,如果把纸张举起来,对着光线,我就能看到纸上印有白色的"俄勒冈"字样,这种字样,我们称之为"水印"。

美洲的西北角上,有一大片土地,虽说那里也属于美国,但它并不是一个州。这个地方,被称为"准州"。这个准州,就是阿拉斯加[1]。北美洲最高的山峰就位

---

[1] 如今,阿拉斯加已经成为美国的第四十九个州。

mountain, but chiefly because of the fish in its waters and the fur on its animals, and then one day gold was discovered there.

Gold is a magic word. Again, as in the days of the Forty-niners, thousands of people, when they heard of the gold, left everything and, with nothing but shovels to dig the gold and sieves to strain it out of the water, started off to that far-away place, hoping to make their fortunes before the new year. Many foolishly went off with nothing to live on after they reached Alaska. They didn't seem to know that where the gold was to be found there was no food, nothing to eat, and no stores where one could buy food. Others, more wise, carried cans of food with them, and when the foolish gold-diggers had found gold, the wise ones sold them food for their gold. For a can of beans they often asked hundreds of times what it had cost, and the foolish gold-diggers had to pay it or starve, for they couldn't eat gold and they had to eat or die. So the wise ones came back with the gold which the foolish ones had dug, and the foolish ones were lucky to get back at all.

In the parts of Alaska where fish can be caught for food, Indians live in small villages. In the center of each village they put up a tall pole carved and painted in the forms of birds and animals with big ugly faces. These are called Totem Poles. Each tribe or family has some bird or

"呱呱叫"

于这里，叫作"麦金利山"。虽说阿拉斯加的气候非常寒冷，距美国本土又那么遥远，那么难以到达，可美国还是支付了数百万美元，买下了此地，这并不是因为此地有一座最高的山峰，而主要是因为美国希望获得阿拉斯加周边水域里的出产的鱼类和那里的动物皮毛。而接下来，有一天人们又在那里发现了黄金。

黄金可是一种咒语。就像"四九年人"所处的那个时代一样，一旦听说阿拉斯加发现了黄金，便又有成千上万的人抛下一切，除了挖掘黄金的铲子、用于把黄金从水中淘出来的筛子之外，什么也不带，开始前往这个遥远的地方，希望在新年到来之前发上一笔大财。很多人还非常可笑，连生活用具都没有带，就抵达了阿拉斯加。他们似乎并不知道，发现黄金的那个地方既没有粮食，没有吃的东西，也没有可以买到食物的商店。还有一些人却比较聪明，随身带着罐头食品，因此，当那些可笑的淘金者找到黄金后，这些聪明人就开始用食物换取黄金了。一罐豆子，他们的要价通常都是正常售价的成百上千倍，那些愚蠢的淘金者却不得不用黄金来购买，否则他们就会挨饿，因为他们既不能吃黄金，又必须吃东西才行，不然就会饿死。因此，最终聪明人便带着愚蠢者淘来的黄金满载而归，那些愚蠢的人能够回去，就已经是很幸运的了！

在阿拉斯加那些能够捕鱼为食的地方，土著印第安人都聚居在一些小型的村庄里。他们在每个村庄的中央部位，印第安人都会立起一根高高的木杆，上面雕刻或者绘制着许多丑陋的鸟形或兽形大面具。这种木杆，叫作"图腾柱"。每个部落或者家族，都把某种鸟儿或兽类当成自己的吉祥物，比如鹰或者熊，就像大家可能

animal such as an eagle or a bear for its mascot, as you might call your club "the Lions" or "the Owls," and the Totem Pole is the tribe's sign.

If you should suddenly see at night the whole northern sky hung with curtains of fire and ablaze with flashing flames shooting from the ground far up into the heavens, you might think, as I did the first time I saw it when a boy, that the World was coming to an end. It looked as if the World were on fire and were about to explode. This amazing sight is called the Aurora Borealis or Northern Light, and it may be seen often in Alaska and sometimes, though perhaps only once or twice in a lifetime, much farther south. It is a terrifying sight to those who have never seen or even heard of such a thing before, and yet the Aurora Borealis does no more harm than a beautiful sunset or a rainbow in the sky.

图腾柱

What causes the Aurora Borealis? That's a hard question to answer. Electricity has something to do with it and so have sun spots. Have you ever heard of sun spots? Sometimes a dark spot will appear on the sun and move slowly across it. You can't see sun spots because the sun is much too bright to be stared at. But men who look through telescopes with darkened glass to protect their eyes can see these spots and they can photograph them with special cameras. After a sun spot appears on the sun there is usually a very bright Aurora Borealis.

That's all I can tell you. A little girl once asked, "What is a thought made of?" That's a hard question to answer too.

把你们的俱乐部叫作"雄狮俱乐部"或者"猫头鹰俱乐部"一样，而"图腾柱"，就是每个部落的标志。

假如哪一天晚上，你们突然看到北方的天空中腾起一道火帘，熊熊燃烧着的火舌从地面高高地喷向空中，那你们可能会认为，世界末日到了，我小时候第一次见到那种情形后，曾经也是这样以为的呢。那种情形，就像是地球失了火，马上要爆炸了似的。这种令人诧异的景象，叫作"北极光"，阿拉斯加经常能够看到北极光，有的时候更往南的地方也能看到，只是比较罕见，一生中也就一两次罢了。对于那些以前从未见过、也从未听说过这种东西的人来说，北极光可是一种非常恐怖的现象，不过，就像美丽的日落或者空中的彩虹那样，北极光也不会给世人带来什么危害。

北极光是怎样形成的呢？这个问题可不容易回答。电与它有关，而太阳黑子也是如此。你们有没有听说过，什么是太阳黑子呢？这是指，有的时候，太阳表面会出现一个黑色的斑点，并且缓慢地从太阳表面一侧移动到另一侧的现象。大家用肉眼是看不到太阳黑子的，因为太阳太过明亮，没法直视。不过，人们通过装有能够保护眼睛的深色玻璃的望远镜，却能观看到这些斑点，并且用特殊的相机拍下来。每当太阳上出现黑子后，通常随后就会出现非常明亮的北极光。

我能告诉你们的，就只有这些了。一个小姑娘曾经问我说："思想是由什么组成的呢？"这也是一个不易回答的问题啊。

17 Next-door Neighbors

There is a saying that "Good fences make good neighbors," but that depends on the neighbors. North of the United States is a country bigger than the United States called Canada. It stretches across America from sea to sea, from the Atlantic to the Pacific, and there would have to be a fence 3,000 miles long if there were a fence, but there is none—nothing but an imaginary line. An imaginary line is a line on the map but not on the ground. On this imaginary line the two countries set up a stone on which they said something like this, "Canada and the United States agree never to fight"; that's all—a gentlemen's agreement. It is called the "Peace Stone."

Boys often say "findings is keepings." The French people found Canada, but England thought she had a better right to it, so she fought for it and took it away from the French. That was a long time ago, but there are a great many French still in Canada, and in the city of Quebec more people speak French than English.

I once had a Newfoundland dog. He was woolly and big and ate as much as a man. Newfoundland dogs came from an island on the Atlantic side of Canada which an Englishman found, and so he called it New-found-land. Newfoundland is now a part of Canada.

Just off the coast of Newfoundland is a shallow part of the sea called the Grand Banks.

第17章　隔壁邻居

有句老话，说"好篱笆出好邻居"，不过，这也取决于邻居好不好。美国的北方，有一个国土面积大于美国的国家，叫作加拿大。该国也横跨美洲大陆，西面是太平洋，东面是大西洋，因此，两国之间要是修上一道篱笆的话，那么这道篱笆就必须有三千英里长才行呢。当然，两国之间实际上是没有什么篱笆的，除了一条想象中的界线，什么也没有。这条想象中的界线，只存在于地图上，而不是画在现实中的地面上。两国在这条想象中的界线上立了一块石碑，上面刻着像"加拿大与美国一致同意永不开战"之类的话，那就够了，因为它完全就是一种君子协定。这块石碑，就叫"和平石"。

男孩子们常说"谁找到，就归谁"。加拿大原本是法国人发现的，可英国却觉得，自己更有权力拥有加拿大，因此便发动战争，从法国人手中夺取了加拿大。这当然是很久以前的事儿了，可如今，加拿大仍然还生活着大量的法裔民众，而在魁北克市，说法语的人也比说英语的人还要多。

我曾经养过一条纽芬兰犬。它全身毛茸茸的，体型巨大，食量跟人一样大。纽芬兰犬产自加拿大东边大西洋上的一个岛屿，那个岛屿是一个英国人发现的，因此他把该岛命名为"新发现之地"，音译过来就是"纽芬兰"了。如今，纽芬兰也隶属于加拿大。

But the Banks are under the water. It is a great fishing ground, but men go fishing there, not for pleasure, but for business. Thousands of small boats go off and stay off and do not return until they have caught all the fish they can carry. It is often very foggy on the Grand Banks, and sometimes big ocean steamships coming over from across the Atlantic Ocean cannot see the small fishing boats and run into them and sink them with all on board.

Canada is big in size but small in number of people. There are not as many people in all of Canada as there are in the State of New York. Most of the people in Canada live as close along the edge of the United States as they can, because it gets very cold in winter farther north than that. Close to the United States people do pretty nearly the same things and raise the same things as people south of the border in the United States. For instance, Canada raises more wheat than any other country in the World except the United States.

One of the biggest concerns in Canada is a railroad company called the Canadian Pacific. The railroad runs all the way across Canada from the Atlantic Ocean to Vancouver on the west coast of Canada. But it doesn't stop at the Oceans. It has big steamers that cross the Atlantic Ocean and it has big steamers that cross the Pacific Ocean. The Canadian Pacific owns all the hotels along the railroad, too. Along one part of the railroad there is very wonderful scenery—beautiful mountains and lakes. Lake Louise, in the Rocky Mountains, is so beautiful that many people go there on their vacations or on their wedding journeys.

No woman likes a wild animal such as a fox or wolf close to her, but as soon as the

　　纽芬兰岛海岸外，有一片浅海区，叫作"大浅滩"。不过，这片浅滩却位于水下。那里是一处了不起的渔场，人们到那里去捕鱼，并不是为了消遣，而是为了生意。成千上万条小船来到大浅滩，停在那里，直到捕获的鱼儿再也装不下，才会回去。大浅滩上经常浓雾弥漫，因此，有的时候横渡大西洋的那些巨型远洋轮船看不到小渔船，就会撞上去，使得渔船连同上面的渔民一起沉入大海。

　　加拿大国土面积广袤，可人口却不多。加拿大的全国总人口，还不及美国纽约这一个州的人口呢。绝大多数加拿大人都尽可能地居住在靠近美国边界的附近地区，因为再往北去，冬季就会变得极其寒冷。居住在靠近美国边界地区的加拿大人，从事的工作、种植的作物，跟边界以南的美国人差不多是一样的。比如说，加拿大的小麦产量就位居世界第二，仅次于美国呢。

　　加拿大最大的企业，是一家叫作"加拿大太平洋"的铁路公司。该公司运营的那条铁路横跨整个加拿大，从大西洋沿岸一直通到了西海岸的温哥华。不过，这条铁路并非是两端分别到达大西洋和太平洋沿岸就止步了。该公司既有横渡大西洋的巨型轮船，也有横渡太平洋的巨轮。铁路沿线的旅馆，也都归"加拿大太平洋"铁路公司所有。在铁路沿线的一个地区，一路上都是非常奇妙的风景，既有壮美的山脉，又有秀丽的湖泊。落基山脉中的路易斯湖风景非常瑰丽，因此还有许多人前去度假或者度蜜月呢。

　　没有哪个女子，会喜欢让狐狸或者狼这样的野兽近身，可一旦这些野兽死了，她们却很喜欢用野兽皮毛制成的衣服，愿意花高价钱去购买。加拿大有一个巨大的

animals are dead she loves their skins close to her and will pay high prices to get them. There is a big bay in Canada, almost as big as the Gulf of Mexico; it is called Hudson Bay and named after the man who discovered it. He is the same man who discovered the Hudson River, but Hudson Bay and Hudson River have no other connection. Hudson Bay is filled with ice all winter long, and all around Hudson Bay the winters are so cold that men do not live there unless they have to. The chief reason some men do live there is to hunt animals. The animals in that cold country can't buy overcoats, so they grow overcoats on themselves—fur overcoats, which are the very best kind of overcoats. Hunters trap and kill wolves, foxes, and other animals, skin them of their overcoats, and sell them to ladies who can pay big prices for them. This company of people who trap animals and sell furs is called the Hudson's Bay Company.

As we have States, Canada has provinces, but there are only ten provinces in Canada. The chief one is called Ontario, after Lake Ontario. Ontario, however, borders all the other Great Lakes too, except Michigan. In Ontario is the capital of Canada. It is called Ottawa. England sends a man across the ocean to Canada, called the Governor-General, but the people in Canada send men to Ottawa to make their own laws.

As you go north in Canada the country gets colder and colder, till at last it gets so cold that it is too cold even for trees to grow. The trees that grow farthest north hold their leaves and stay green the year round like the pine and spruce. They are called "evergreens." The wood of evergreens is soft. The trees that cannot grow as far north as evergreens drop their

海湾，几乎有墨西哥湾那么大，那里叫作哈德逊湾，是用发现此处的那个人的名字命名的。那个人还发现了哈德逊河，可"哈德逊湾"和"哈德逊河"除了名称之外，就没有什么别的联系了。哈德逊湾整个冬季都会封冻，而附近地区冬季也非常寒冷，因此除非万不得已，否则是没有人愿意在那里居住的。而人们之所以到那里生活，最主要的原因就是，他们要在那里猎杀野兽。那片寒冷之地里的野兽由于不可能买来大衣穿上，因此干脆身上都长出一件"大衣"，长出一件"毛皮大衣"来，这种毛皮，可是最好的大衣呢。猎人用陷阱捕杀狼和狐狸，以及其他的野兽，将它们的皮毛剥下来，再将皮毛卖给那些出得起高价的贵妇。这些捕杀野兽并出售兽皮的人，便成立了"哈德逊海湾公司"。

就像美国分成了一个个州那样，加拿大也分成了一个个省，不过，整个加拿大只有十个省。其中最重要的一个，就是安大略省，它是根据安大略湖的名称来命名的。然而，安大略省实际上却濒临了五大湖中的四个，只有密歇根湖除外。加拿大的首都也在安大略省，叫作渥太华。英国派遣一个人跨洋过海，到加拿大来担任总督，而加拿大人民则派遣代表来到渥太华，代表他们制定法律。

在加拿大境内向北而去，气候会变得越来越寒冷，冷到连树木也无法生长。最北方生长的树木四季都不落叶，像松树和云杉那样，一年到头都郁郁葱葱。这种树木，叫作"常绿植物"。常绿植物的木质都非常柔软。而那些无法像常青树一样在遥远的北方生长的树木，比如橡树和枫树，冬季里则会落叶。这种树木的木质通常都很坚硬。硬木树主要用于制作家具，而软木树则被碾碎制成纸张。

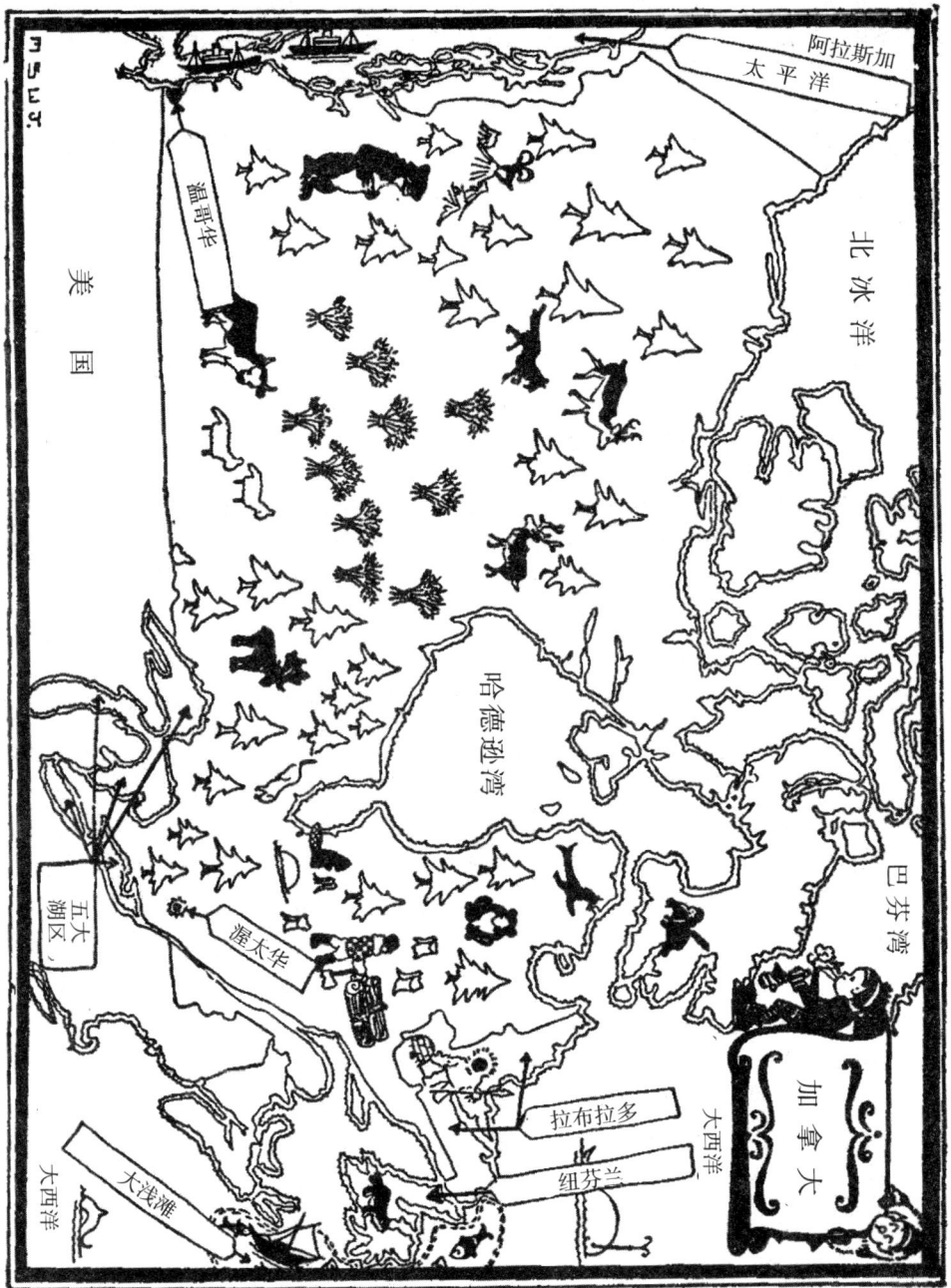

leaves in the winter, like the oak and maple. Their wood is usually hard. The hard-wood trees are used chiefly to make furniture, but the soft-wood trees are ground up to make paper.

The paper on which this book and almost every other book is printed and all the paper used for newspapers is made from wood. A great city newspaper will use up many acres of trees in a single day. It takes as many trees as grow in a space the size of a city block to feed a single paper a single day. So you see how fast trees are being cut down in Canada to keep the presses in the United States going. Day after day miles upon miles of trees are cut down, ground into pulp, made into paper, and shipped to us in large rolls, that we may have the news—only to be burned up the day after. As people are fed wheat, and animals corn, printing presses must be fed trees for their daily meal, year in and year out, without ceasing.

One of the first geography lessons I ever had was about Eskimos, who lived in snow houses and fished through a hole in the ice. One of the homes of the Eskimos is Labrador on the northeastern corner of Canada. The Eskimos are related to the Indians, I'll tell you more about them later.

本书以及几乎其他所有图书所用的纸张，连同一切报纸所用的纸张，都是用木材制成的。一份大型的城市报纸，一天内就要用掉好几英亩的树木呢。需要像一个城市街区那么大面积内生长的树木，才能满足一份报纸一天的用纸量。因此，你们不难看出，加拿大境内树木的砍伐速度需要有多快，才能满足让美国的印刷机开动下去的要求呢。日复一日，树木被大量砍伐，碾成纸浆，制成纸张，然后大卷大卷地运到美国，我们才看得到新闻，可当天过后，这些报纸就毫无用处，只能付之一炬了。就像人们以小麦为食、牲畜以玉米为食那样，印刷机每天必须以树木为食，并且年复一年，无休无止。

我以前在地理课上最先学到的一课，就是关于因纽特人的情况，他们住在冰雪建造的房子里，并且在冰面上凿洞来捕鱼。因纽特人的家园之一，就在加拿大东北角的拉布拉多地区。因纽特人与印第安人有亲缘关系，过一会儿我还将给你们介绍这两个人种的情况。

18 The War-God's Country

Tommy Tinker was eating a slice of bread and butter. He was biting it very carefully round the edges and between bites he looked at it thoughtfully.

"What in the world are you doing!" asked his father.

"I'm biting a map of North America," replied Tommy. He placed it carefully on the tablecloth. "There's Alaska on this corner, Labrador on this corner, Florida on this corner, and Yucatan opposite it." Then he rolled out a little tail of bread and placed it on the other corner. "And there's Lower California."

"I ought to send you from the table for playing with your food," said his father; "but I won't if you can tell me where the Gulf of California is."

"It's not in California," said Tommy. "You didn't catch me that time. It's in Mexico and so is Lower California too—both are in Mexico."

"Right," said his father. "When I was a boy my teacher asked me where the Gulf of California and Lower California were and, though I hadn't studied my lesson, I answered 'California,' for I felt sure that must be right."

"Did your teacher ever show you this one?" asked Tommy. He curved the finger and thumb of his left hand to form the letter "G." "G is for Gulf of Mexico," he said. "My finger is Florida, my thumb is Yucatan and here is Mexico. Do you see it?"

第18章　战神之国

托米·廷克正在吃一块黄油面包。他很小心地把面包的边缘咬掉，并且一边咬，一边若有所思地看着面包。

"你究竟在干什么呀！"他的父亲问道。

"我正在咬出一幅北美洲的地图来，"托米回答道。他把面包小心地放在桌布上。"这个角上是阿拉斯加，这个角上是拉布拉多，这个角上是佛罗里达，正对着它的是尤卡坦半岛。"然后，他又小心地展平一小条面包，并把它放到另一个角上。"这里就是下加利福尼亚半岛了。"

"拿着吃的东西玩，我本该把你赶下餐桌的，"他的父亲说，"不过，要是你能告诉我加利福尼亚湾在哪里的话，我就饶了你。"

"这个海湾可不在加利福尼亚，"托米说。"那一次您就没有骗过我。它在墨西哥境内，而下加利福尼亚半岛也是，这两个地方都在墨西哥境内。"

"对了，"他的父亲说。"我小的时候，老师也问过我，看加利福尼亚湾和下加利福尼亚半岛在哪里，尽管当时没有预习课文，我还是回答说：'在加利福尼亚啊。'因为我以为这个答案肯定是正确的。"

"您的老师有没有给您看过这个呢？"托米问道。他把左手的拇指和其他四个指头弯起来，形成字母"G"的样子。"'G'就代表墨西哥湾，"他说。"其

"They didn't teach me geography that way when I went to school," said his father.

"They don't now," said Tommy. "I made that up myself."

Perhaps you have heard people speak of some place as "God's Country." Well, the country just south of the United States is named "God's Country," but it is the War God's Country. It is called Mexico after the Indians' God of War, Mexitli.

When you cross the line from the United States to Canada you hardly know you are in another country—the people are the same, they talk the same language. But when you cross the line from the United States to Mexico you *do* know you are in another country—the people are different and they talk a different language. Mexico used to belong to Spain across the Atlantic; it now belongs to itself.

I told you there was a Peace Stone on the Canada line and that Canada and the United States agreed long ago never to fight each other. There is no peace stone on the Mexican border line and there have been many fights between the United States and Mexico. Our

墨西哥湾 ←佛罗里达
←尤卡坦半岛
墨西哥地图
您的老师给您看过这个吗？

他手指代表佛罗里达，大拇指是尤卡坦半岛，手背这边就是墨西哥了。您看到了吗？"

"我上学的时候，老师们可不是这样教地理的呢。"他的父亲回答道。

"他们现在也不这样教啊，"托米说。"这可是我自己想出来的。"

没准，大家都听人们说过某个地方是"神的国度"。好吧，美国南边的那个国家，就被人们称为"神的国度"，只不过它是战神的国度。这个国家的名称，是根据印第安人的战争之神"墨西提利"来命名的，叫作墨西哥。

在越过国界线从美国进入加拿大的时候，你们很难知道自己已经进入了另一个国家，因为两国的人是一样的，说的语言也是一样的。可倘若越过边境线从美国进入墨西哥的话，大家却会明明白白地知道，自己已经来到了另一个国家，因为两国的人不同，所说的语言也不同。墨西哥以前是大西洋彼岸的西班牙的殖民地，如今已经独立了。

前面我已经跟你们说过，美、加国界线上有一块"和平石"，并且两国很久以前就一致同意，彼此之间决不开战。可美、墨之间的国界线上却没有什么"和平

States of Texas, New Mexico, and Arizona once belonged to Mexico. Between Texas and Mexico is a river called the Rio Grande, which means River Grand or Grand River. The Rio Grande runs through such a dry country, however, that part of the time there is no river, only a dry place where the river did run, so that people can walk right across from the United States to Mexico in certain places, or at certain times of the year.

When the white people came to America there were Indians living all over our country. The white people pushed the Indians farther and farther off to the corners and out-of-the-way places until now there are so few Indians in the United States that many boys and girls have never seen an Indian except in the circus or on the 5-cent piece. When the white people came to Mexico there were Indians living all over that country too, but in Mexico there still are more Indians now living than there are white people. Many of the white Spanish people have married Indians, so some Mexicans are Spanish, more are Indian, and still more are mixed Spanish and Indian.

The people in the United States speak English and do many things as the people in England do. The people who came to Mexico were white people from Spain. So they speak Spanish and do many things as the people in Spain do.

When the Spanish first came to Mexico they found the Indians there wearing silver necklaces and silver bracelets and silver ornaments, so they knew there must be silver in Mexico. The Spaniards were really looking for gold, but silver was next best, so they set to work to dig for silver and they are still doing so, and even now, more than 400 years

石", 并且两国之间爆发了多场战争。美国的得克萨斯、新墨西哥和亚利桑那等州, 以前都属于墨西哥所有。得克萨斯州与墨西哥之间, 有一条河流, 叫作格兰德河, 意思就是"大河"。然而, 由于格兰德河流经的是墨西哥这样一个干旱少雨的国家, 因此一年中总是有一部分时间根本就没有什么河, 只留下一个干燥的河床, 所以, 人们还可以在某些地方, 或者在一年中的某些时候, 直接跨过河去, 从美国进入墨西哥呢。

白人来到美洲殖民的时候, 如今的美国到处都生活着印第安人。后来, 白人把印第安人越赶越远, 一直赶到一些角落和偏远的地方, 因此如今美国留下来的印第安人极少, 使得许多小朋友除了在马戏团里或者五分钱的硬币上, 都从未见过印第安人呢。当白人来到墨西哥殖民的时候, 该国也到处生活着印第安人, 可在墨西哥, 如今生活着的印第安人, 却仍然比白人多。许多白种西班牙人都与印第安人通婚, 因此如今的墨西哥人里, 有些是西班牙裔, 有些是印第安裔, 而更多的则是西班牙人与印第安人的混血后代。

美国人都是说英语, 而许多的生活、工作习惯也与英国国内的人相似。而到墨西哥殖民的, 却都是来自西班牙的白人。因此, 他们都说西班牙语, 而许多的生活、工作习惯也与西班牙国内的人相似。

西班牙人刚刚来到墨西哥的时候, 发现印第安人都戴着银项链、银手镯和银质装饰品, 因此他们明白, 墨西哥肯定盛产白银。当时, 西班牙人寻找的其实是黄金, 但白银是仅次于黄金的贵重之物, 因此他们便开始挖掘银矿, 如今, 他们仍然

after white people came to Mexico more silver is mined there than anywhere else i.t.w.W. except the United States. Silver mines are in the mountains, the same chain of mountains as the Rocky Mountains in the United States, only in Mexico they are called Sierra Madre.

Up in the Sierra Madre Mountains, in a bowl-shaped valley, is the capital of Mexico. It is called Mexico City, so you don't have to learn a new name. The farther north you go the colder it gets, but not always. The farther south you go the warmer it gets, but not always. But the higher up you go in the mountains the colder it gets—always. Mexico City is so far south you would think it would be very hot, but it is not, because it is so high up in the mountains. They have mild weather in Mexico City all the year round.

Near Mexico City is an old volcano with the peculiar name: Po-poca-tepetl. It sounds something like Po-poca-teakettle. Why didn't they give it an easy name, you may wonder. They did, for in the language of the Indians who named it, Popocatepetl means "smoking mountain." Popocatepetl is so far south we should expect it to be warm, but it is so high that its top is cold and is covered with snow all the year round. Popocatepetl is no longer firing up, but clouds of sulphur smoke pour out of it all the time and sulphur collects in its mouth. Indian workmen climb up the sides of Popocatepetl and climb down inside to get the sulphur, which is used in making matches and medicine and other things.

On the Gulf side of Mexico, along the shore, it is very warm indeed, very damp and unhealthful, so no one would live there if he didn't have to; but great lakes of oil were found down under the ground, along the shore near a city called Tampico, and men have

在这样做，因而即便是到白人在墨西哥殖民了四百多年之后的现在，该国开采出来的白银，也比全世界除美国之外的其他任何一个国家都要多。银矿都位于山区里面，该国的山脉与美国境内的落基山脉属于同一山系，只是到了墨西哥之后，这条山脉就叫作"马德雷山脉"了。

在马德雷山脉高处一个有如碗状的峡谷里，坐落着墨西哥的首都。这个首都，叫作墨西哥城，很简单吧，你们不用再记一个新地名了。一般来说，越往北走，气候就越寒冷，可也并非始终都是这样；一般来说，越往南走，气候就越炎热，可也并非始终都是这样。不过，如果是在山里的话，那么越往上走，气温就会越低，这一点却是始终如此。墨西哥城地处那么远的南方，因此大家可能会以为，那里应该炎热得很吧，可实际上并非如此，因为该市坐落在海拔很高的山上，一年四季，墨西哥城的天气都温暖宜人呢。

墨西哥城附近，有一座古老的火山，这座火山还有个古怪的名称，叫作"波波卡特佩特"。大家很可能会感到奇怪，为什么没有给它起个好记的名称呢？人们原本的确给它起了个容易的名称，因为在印第安语里，"波波卡特佩特"指的就是"冒烟的山峰"。波波卡特佩特火山也是地处遥远的南方，因此我们可能也以为那里炎热得很，可实际上，由于地势很高，因此那座火山的山顶非常寒冷，一年到头都有积雪呢。虽说波波卡特佩特火山如今不再猛烈喷发了，但它还是在不断冒出含硫的烟雾，而火山口也积聚了大量的硫黄。印第安工人会从波波卡特佩特火山一侧爬上山顶，然后爬到火山口里去取硫黄，用于制造火柴、药品或者其他的东西。

美 国

墨 西 哥

墨 西 哥 湾

大 西 洋

坦皮科

剑麻

波波卡特佩特火山

墨西哥城

古 巴

加 勒 比 海

白银

太 平 洋

巴拿马运河

中 美 洲

墨西哥
和
中美洲

南 美 洲

dug wells through the ground to get the oil. It is so close to the sea that tank ships can fill up with the oil and carry it to the United States and other places in the World. It is much cheaper to send oil by ship than by train, for one tank ship will carry as much as a thousand tank cars.

The thumb-like piece of Mexico is called Yucatan. In Yucatan grows a plant with tall sword-shaped leaves. From these leaves a fiber that looks like long gray hair, called sisal, is obtained. It is used to make rope and twine. From the juice of another plant that grows in Yucatan, chewing-gum is made.

墨西哥靠近墨西哥湾一侧的沿海地区的确非常炎热、潮湿，对人体健康不利，因此除非万不得已，也没人会愿意在那里生活，不过，在距一个叫作"坦皮科"的城市不远的沿海地区，人们在地下发现了许多巨大的油田，故在那里向下钻出油井，开采出了石油。由于那里紧邻大海，因此开采出来的石油可以装满油轮，然后运送到美国和世界各地去。用油轮运送石油，成本要比用铁路运输便宜得多，因为一条油轮的装载量，就比得上一千节油罐车呢。

墨西哥那个像是大拇指的地方，叫作尤卡坦半岛。尤卡坦半岛上生长着一种高高的植物，叶子形状如剑。从这种叶子里，人们发现了一种像是灰白长发似的纤维，叫作剑麻。人们用剑麻来制造绳索和麻线。而口香糖，也是用生长在尤卡坦半岛上的一种多汁植物制造出来的呢。

19 So Near and Yet so Far

N-A-M-E-R-I-C-A and S-A-M-E-R-I-C-A are two names printed in large letters across my map of North America and South America. Namerica and Samerica sound like brothers: Nam and Sam Erica. They look as if the Creator had pulled them just as far apart as He could without pulling them quite in two. They are held together by a little piece of land called Central America, and the very thinnest part of Central America—the part as thin as a leaf stem—is called the Isthmus of Panama: spelled "isthmus," but sounded "ismus."

On one side of the Isthmus is the Atlantic and on the other side the Pacific Ocean, so near to each other and yet so far. Ships that wanted to get from one ocean to the other couldn't get across this little strip of land— they had to go the long way round, all the way round the bottom of Samerica, thousands of miles out of the way. There was no way at all round the top of Namerica, for both land and ice were in the way up there. It seemed a terribly long distance for a ship to have to go just because it couldn't cross this little strip of land. It was as if you were motoring and the road came to a river and there was no bridge, and a sign said "Detour 10,000 miles." It was the longest detour i.t.w.W. Naturally, people tried to find a way not to make that detour. Some men suggested wheeling ships across the Isthmus. They said, "Let us lift a ship out of the water on a kind of huge elevator, then put it on a huge truck, push it across the Isthmus to the other ocean,

第19章 既近又远

在我的地图上，有用粗体横向标注出的"北美洲"与"南美洲"字样。听上去，"北美洲"与"南美洲"就像是两兄弟。好像是上帝将它们尽力拉开，最终却没有将它们完全拉断似的。南、北美洲之间，由中美洲这个狭长地带相连，而中美洲最狭窄的地方，就是地图上窄得像树叶叶梗似的那个地方，叫作巴拿马地峡，"地峡"一词拼作isthmus，可听起来就像是ismus呢。

巴拿马地峡的一侧是大西洋，另一侧是太平洋，两大洋之间一方面相距极近，而另一方面却又是如此的遥远。那些想要从一个大洋驶进另一个大洋的船只，根本没法越过这片狭长的陆地，它们只能绕很远的路，一直绕过南美洲的最南端，要多跑数千英里的水路，才能做到这一点呢。而北美洲的北端呢，船只根本就没法绕过去，因为那里既有陆地阻挡，又有冰雪覆盖。仅仅是因为没法穿过这片狭窄的陆地，一艘船便不得不多跑那么远的路，可真是糟糕啊。这种情形，就像是你们开着汽车，来到一条河边，可那里却没有桥，只有一个标志，上面写着"绕道一万英里"似的。这可是世界上绕得最远的一条路呢。于是，人们自然就会努力去找出一种办法，以便不用绕那么远的路。有些人提出，可以给轮船装上轮子，穿过巴拿马地峡。他们说："咱们不妨用一台巨型起重机，将船吊出水面，然后将船只装在

then lower it into the water again by another huge elevator." But it seemed simpler to cut a canal across the Isthmus so that a ship might sail straight through from one ocean to the other. On the map this looked easy enough—just a snip with the scissors or a nick with a knife; but that little stem of land was over thirty miles across and there were mountains in the way too.

They have many earthquakes in Central America, and if one of these earthquakes had only cracked the Isthmus of Panama across and broken Namerica and Samerica apart it would have been very convenient; but earthquakes don't do helpful things like that—they make cracks where you don't want them.

Why did ships want to get from one ocean to the other, anyway? Why shouldn't those on one side stay on that side, and those on the other side stay on the other side? Well—your mother goes downtown shopping for things to wear and things to eat and furniture for the house; so ships go shopping—shipping, shopping—around the World. Ships from the countries around the Atlantic Ocean go shopping to countries around the Pacific Ocean for tea and China dishes and silk stockings. And ships from countries around the Pacific Ocean go shopping to the countries around the Atlantic Ocean for things they want and haven't got. That's one reason why ships wanted to get from one ocean to the other, and they didn't want to go the long way round, ten thousand miles out of the way, if they could possibly help it. So at last a company of men from France on the other side of the ocean, who knew how to dig canals—for they had already dug a long canal—started to dig a canal across the Isthmus.

一辆大卡车上，带着它穿越地峡，到达另一个大洋边，然后再用另一台巨型起重机将船只放下水去。"不过，开掘一条横跨巴拿马地峡的运河，使得船只可以径直驶过，从一个大洋进入另一个大洋，却似乎更加简单。从地图上来看，这个办法非常容易，用剪刀咔嚓一剪或者用刀子一划就行了，可实际上，那条小茎般的地峡宽达三十多英里，并且上面还有山峰呢。

中美洲地震频繁，要是来一场地震，将巴拿马地峡横向震裂，将南、北美洲分裂开来的话，那就非常方便了。可是，地震却不会干这样有益的事情，只会在大家不想要的地方弄出裂缝来。

那么，船只为什么想要从一个大洋驶入另一个大洋中去呢？为什么在大西洋上航行的船只不能留在大西洋里，而在太平洋上航行的船只不能留在太平洋里呢？好吧，你的妈妈会到市中心去购买穿的、吃的，以及家具，因此，船只也得去购物才行，在全世界边运送、边收购。大西洋周边国家的船只，会到太平洋沿岸的国家去采购茶叶、瓷器和丝袜等东西。而太平洋沿岸各国的船只，则会到大西洋沿岸国家去采购各国想要却买不到的商品。这就是船只想要从一个大洋驶入另一个大洋的原因之一，而只要做得到，船只自然就不会想去绕上一万英里远的水路。因此，大西洋彼岸一群明白如何开掘运河的法国人（因为他们已经开挖过一条长长的运河了），最终便开始挖掘一条横跨巴拿马地峡的运河。

如今巴拿马地峡所在之处，以前原本是世界上最不卫生的地方。这一点对生活

Now the Isthmus of Panama used to be the most *un*healthful place i.t.w.W. The Indians and black men who lived there didn't seem to mind it, but with white men it was different. One out of every three white men who went there died of fever. The company of men from France set to work and worked for several years on the canal, but so many of their men died and so much money was spent and so little canal was dug that at last they gave it up, stopped digging.

Later the United States rented from the little country of Panama a piece of land forever, a piece of land ten miles wide like a belt right across the Isthmus. This belt of land is called the Canal Zone. But before the United States started to dig the canal they said, "We must make the Canal Zone a healthful and fit place for white people to work so that they won't die as soon as we send them down there." So they sent a famous doctor down to the Canal Zone to see if he could make the Zone a more healthful place for white men to live in.

This doctor found out that what made the Isthmus so unhealthful was—what do you suppose?—nothing but little mosquitos. These mosquitos were different, however, from those we have that merely leave an itchy spot where they bite. The mosquitos down there were of an entirely different kind. Some of them were town mosquitos and some were country mosquitos. The country mosquitos gave people malaria, which was bad enough, but the worst kind of mosquitos were the town mosquitos. They gave people a terrible disease called yellow fever—a disease that turned people yellow and killed almost every one who caught it. So the doctor said I'll find out how to get rid of the mosquitos and keep

在那里的印第安人和黑人来说，似乎并不要紧，可对于白人来说，却不是那样了。到那里去的白人当中，有三分之一的人都死于发烧。那群法国人开始挖掘运河，并且一干就是好几年，可由于因病而死的人太多、花的钱太多，而运河掘进速度却很缓慢，因此他们最终还是放弃，不再挖掘运河了。

后来，美国向巴拿马这个小国永久租用了一块土地，那块土地有十英里宽，就像是一条正好横跨了整个地峡的腰带似的的。这片有如腰带似的土地，叫作"运河区"。不过，在美国动手开凿这条运河之前，他们说："我们必须把运河区建成一个卫生且适合于白人工作的地方才行，目的是让他们不会一来到这里就死掉。"因此，美国派了一个非常有名的医生到运河区去，看他能不能把运河区变成·个更卫生的、适合于白人生活的地方。

那位医生找到了巴拿马地峡如此不卫生的原因，你们猜一猜，原因是什么呢？只是一种小小的蚊子，除此之外就没什么了。然而，这种蚊子与平常叮了我们之后只会留下一个痒包的蚊子可不一样。那里的蚊子是一种完全不同的种类。其中有一些属于城市蚊子，还有一些属于乡下蚊子。乡下蚊子会让人们得上疟疾，这种疾病本来就够厉害的了，但最可恶的还是城市里的蚊子。它们会让人们得上一种叫作"黄热病"的可怕疾病，这种疾病会让得病的人全身变黄，并且差不多会让所有患者丧生。那位医生说，我会找到办法来消灭这些蚊子，不让它们再害人性命的。于是，他先是寻找这些蚊子，然后又找出了消灭这些蚊子的办法。对于城市蚊子，他

them from killing the people. Accordingly, he went after the mosquitos first, and this is the way he killed them. The town mosquitos he killed with sulphur smoke—sulphur from Popocatepetl—and the country mosquitos he killed with oil—oil from Mexico too. Then he cleaned up the marshes and other places where the mosquitos lived and raised their enormous families, so that they had no place to live, and in these ways he changed the Canal Zone from the most unhealthful place i.t.w.W. to one of the most healthful places i.t.w.W.

Then, and not until then, the United States went ahead and made the Canal. They didn't cut the land straight through, however, as the French had started to do, so that the Atlantic and Pacific could run together—that would have meant too much digging, even with dynamite, for dynamite blows up land, and the land has to be carried away after it is blown up. So the United States dug a ditch across the Isthmus on top of the land and used a river and a lake already there to keep this ditch filled with water. At each end of this ditch or canal they made locks to raise ships from the sea at one end, and to lower them to the sea at the other. So ships now go across from one ocean to the other, but most of the way they sail on fresh water, for neither ocean runs into the other. Namerica and Samerica are not cut apart—they are still joined and always will be, until the Creator does the separating.

是用硫黄烧烟熏死，就是用从波波卡特佩特火山采下来的硫黄；对于乡村里的蚊子，他则是用同样从墨西哥出产的石油杀死的。接下来，他又将蚊子生活并滋生出大量后代的沼泽以及其他地方清除干净，使得蚊子没有地方可以生存，用这些方法，他终于把世界上最不卫生的运河区，变成了世界上最卫生的一个地方。

接下来，也直到那个时候，美国才继续施工，开凿出了巴拿马运河。然而，美国人并不是像法国人起初那样干，不是对直挖掘运河的。要是那样干的话，就算有了炸药，挖掘的工程量也会太大，因为炸药虽然能够炸开地面，但炸开之后，土石也得运到别的地方去才行。因此，美国只在地面上挖掘出了一条横跨地峡的沟渠，并且利用了本已存在的一条河流和一个湖泊，使得那条沟渠里永远都注满了水。在这条沟渠或者运河的两端，人们修建了两个船闸，用于将一端的船只升出海面、而在另一端又把船只放入海中。因此，如今的船舶虽然可以从一个大洋航行到另一个大洋，但一路上绝大部分都是在淡水里航行，因为大西洋和太平洋的海水都没有注入运河里面去。所以，南、北美洲并没有分开，它们仍然连在一起，并且日后也仍将如此，除非上帝动手来将它们分开。

20 Pirate Seas

I was once on a train leaving Baltimore when a man asked me where I was going. I told him I was going to Baltimore. He looked at me as if I must have made a mistake and exclaimed, "You are on the wrong train; this train is *leaving* Baltimore."

"I know that," I replied, "but I'm going to Baltimore the long way round, round the World to Baltimore. I'm going west to get east."

On the other side of the World from us are some islands called "The Indies." People had always gone to the Indies, far, far away, by traveling toward the east. Columbus thought he could go in just the opposite direction—toward the west—and reach the Indies that way. People said it was foolish to go west to get east, but Columbus believed the World was round, and if it were round he knew he could get to these islands by going west just as well as by going east. So he sailed, and he sailed, and he sailed, always toward the setting sun, and at last he did come to some islands. He thought these islands were the Indies, so he named them the "West Indies." As a matter of fact, we know, but he didn't know, that he hadn't gone half far enough to reach the Indies. He didn't know that even if he had gone on farther, Central America would have been in the way, anyway.

Living on these islands were men with red skins, painted faces, and feathers in their hair, and Columbus called them Indians. Other people called these Indians "Caribs,"

第20章　海盗出没的海域

有一次，在一趟从巴尔的摩发出的列车上，有人问我要去哪里。我说要去巴尔的摩。他看着我，仿佛我一定是搞错了，然后大声说道："您坐错火车了吧，这趟火车可是从巴尔的摩发出的呢。"

"我知道啊，"我回答道，"可我打算绕上一大段路，绕过整个地球去巴尔的摩呢。我打算往西边走，到东方去。"

地球上与我们美国相对的那一面上，有一些岛屿，叫作"印度群岛"。以前，人们一直都是往东而去，走上很远、很远的水路，才能到达印度群岛。哥伦布认为，他可以朝着相反的方向航行，并且用这种办法向西到达印度群岛。人们都说，要到东方去，却向西行，这是一种愚蠢的做法，可哥伦布却相信地球是圆的，他很清楚，如果地球是圆的，那么向西航行也可以像向东航行那样，最终到达这些岛屿。于是，他便动身起航了，他不停地航行、航行，始终朝着日落的方向而去，最终的确来到了一些岛屿上。当时他以为这些岛屿就是印度群岛，于是便将它们命名为"西印度群岛"。事实上，我们都知道，他那时才走了一半，根本就没有到达印度群岛。不过，就算他继续航行，走得更远，他也是不会明白这一点的，因为不管怎么说，中美洲都会挡住他的去路。

这些岛屿上生活着的人，都有着红色的皮肤，脸上绘着油彩，头发里还插着

which means "brave," because they were brave, and the blue sea which surrounded these islands they called the Caribbean Sea—the sea of the Caribs.

Columbus was looking for a new *way* and he found it, but after Columbus other men came along looking for gold and silver and they found that. Some they found in Mexico and some they found in South America, and some they took away from the Indians who had already found it. They robbed them, that's all. This gold and silver—treasure—found and stolen, they loaded on ships and started back to Spain.

But many of those ships bearing treasure never reached Spain. Pirates—sea robbers—lay in wait to rob the land robbers. It was better sport to rob robbers than to rob the poor Indians. These pirates were bold and bad and cold and cruel. They wore blood-red sashes round their waists, blood-red handkerchiefs round their necks, and blood-red handkerchiefs round their heads. They hung huge rings in their ears and huge bracelets on their arms, and they were "armed to the teeth"—whatever that means. They hid behind these little islands in the Caribbean Sea, and when they saw a treasure ship coming from afar they hoisted a black flag to their ship's mast, a flag with a skull and two bones crossed on it, and sailed forth and captured the ship, its treasures, and its crew. They made the crew slaves, or if the pirates didn't want any more slaves, they made their captives "walk the plank"—that is, walk blindfolded out on a plank set over the ship's edge. They would reach the end and suddenly step off into the sea and be drowned. Then the pirate would load the treasure he had captured into a huge iron-bound chest, sail back to his

羽毛，哥伦布称他们为印第安人。可其他一些人却将这些印第安人称为"加勒比人"，就是"勇士"的意思，因为这些印第安人都很勇猛，他们还把环绕着这些岛屿的那片蓝色大海称为加勒比海，即"加勒比人之海"的意思。

哥伦布寻找的是一条新航线，并且他的确找到了；而哥伦布之后，其他人前往那里却是为了寻找黄金和白银，并且他们也找到了。他们在墨西哥找到了一些，在南美洲发现了一些，并且还从已经发现了黄金、白银的印第安人手里拿走了一些。他们完全是抢劫印第安人，就是那么回事。找到或者抢到黄金、白银之后，他们便将这种所谓的财宝装上船，开始返回西班牙。

不过，运载着这些财宝的许多船只，后来却一直没有回到西班牙。海盗——即海上的强盗——埋伏在路上，等着劫掠那些在陆地上进行抢劫的人。这些海盗全都胆大包天、道德败坏、冷酷无情，并且残忍无比。他们的腰间系着血红的腰带，脖子上系着血红的手帕，头上绑着血红的头巾。他们的耳朵上都戴着巨大的耳环，胳膊上戴着巨大的手镯，并且"武装到了牙齿"（不管这是什么意思）。他们都躲藏在加勒比海上的这些小岛屿后面，一看到有宝船从远处驶来，便会在桅杆上升起一面黑色的旗子，旗子上还飘着一个有两根骨头交叉的骷髅图案，然后驶上前去，夺取宝船，抢劫船上的珍宝，俘虏船员。他们把船员当成奴隶，要是海盗不需要更多奴隶的话，他们就会让俘虏"走跳板"，也就是说，蒙上俘虏的眼睛，让他们去走一块搭到了船舷之外的木板。俘虏走到木板的尽头后，便会突然踏空，掉入海里淹死。然后，海盗会把夺得的财宝装进一个巨大的铁皮箱里，驾船回到自己的那个小

little island, and bury the treasure chest in a hole in the sand. He would mark the spot on a map with an X so that he might find it when he wanted it, and so that no one else could find it.

These pirates are gone long years ago, and the ships that sail the blue Caribbean have now no fear of pirates any more, and few of these ships carry anything that pirates would want. But the sea is so blue and the weather so warm and the islands so lovely that many people make voyages to the Pirate Seas just for pleasure. I did once myself.

I left New York when it was snowing and in two days I was on an island called Bermuda, where it was warm and sunny. Easter lilies were growing in the fields, and new potatoes and onions. Farmers were raising them to send to shivering New York so that Americans might have warm-weather flowers and warm-weather vegetables long before warm weather itself came.

Another two days' sailing south and I was on another island called Nassau, the capital of a group of islands called the Bahamas. In Nassau sponges are gathered from the bottom of the sea and sent back to U.S. for US to USe. Would you believe that the sponges you use were once alive? They were once like jelly with the sponge inside. Men dive down into the sea and tear the live sponges off the rocks where they grow. Then they wash off the jelly-like part and what is left is the sponge.

Another one of the Bahama Islands is the little island on which Columbus first landed— the most famous little island i.t.w.W. A monument marks the spot where he stepped out

岛上，在沙滩上挖一个洞，将装满财宝的箱子埋起来。海盗会在地图上将藏宝地用一个大写的X标注出来，以便自己需要的时候可以找到，并且让其他人发现不了。

这些海盗在很多年前就早已销声匿迹了，因此如今航行在碧蓝的加勒比海上的船只，不用再担心遇上海盗了，并且，这些船只所运载的物品，也都是海盗不想要的东西。不过，由于大海蔚蓝、气候温暖、岛屿可爱，因此许多人都只是为了消遣而坐船来到这个曾经有海盗出没的海域。我自己就去过一回呢。

我从纽约动身的时候，天上还是大雪纷飞，可两天之后，我就来到了一个叫作"百慕大"的岛屿上，那里气候温暖，阳光普照。那儿的田野上盛开着百合花，生长着新鲜的土豆和洋葱。农夫们正在采摘，将它们运送到寒风瑟瑟的纽约去，使得美国人在天气回暖之前，就能够看到热带的花朵，吃到热带的蔬菜了。

坐船再往南走了两天之后，我就来到了另一个岛屿，那个岛屿叫作"拿索"，是巴哈马这个群岛国家的首都。在拿索，人们从海底捞出海绵，并将它们运回美国，供我们使用。你们相信吗，大家所用的海绵曾经都是活着的呢。它们本来像是一团果冻，里面包裹着的就是海绵。人们潜到海底，将活着的海绵从它们生长的岩石上撕下来。然后，他们再把外面那种果冻状的部分洗掉，剩下的就是海绵了。

巴哈马群岛中，还有一个便是哥伦布最先到达的那个小岛，它也是全世界最著名的一个小岛呢。上面有座纪念碑，标出了哥伦布横跨大洋、在茫茫大海上航行了那么久之后，走下自己的那艘小船，在沙滩上跪下来，感谢上帝指引着他安全到达了新世界的那个地方。当时，他用自己的救世主的名字，把这个小岛命名为"神圣

of his little boat after his long voyage across the ocean, kneeled down in the sand, and thanked God for directing him safely to the New World. He called the island after his Saviour, "Holy Saviour," which in Spanish is San Salvador.

There are three large islands of the West Indies—tit-tat-to, three in a row. There is also another island a little smaller, and many, many very small islands besides in the Caribbean Sea.

The largest island of all the West Indies—the first one of the tit-tat-to, three in a row islands—is Cuba. Columbus found the Indians in Cuba carrying burning torches in their mouths. They breathed in the smoke and blew it out again in a most strange and amazing fashion, as if they were dragons. It seemed an extraordinary thing for people to do—to breathe in smoke of a burning weed, for that was what it was; yet they seemed to enjoy it. No one across the water had ever seen such a sight before—people breathing fire. But now people all over the World copy the red Indians of Cuba. The weed was called tobacco. Tobacco is now grown in many parts of the World, but the finest tobacco i.t.w.W. for cigars still grows in Cuba, and Havana, the capital of Cuba, ships "Havana" cigars everywhere.

People from Spain went to live in Cuba and Cuba belonged to Spain until not so many years ago, but now Cuba belongs to itself.

Almost all vegetables and fruits in the World have sugar in their juice; they are sweet. Some have a great deal, some have very little. But two vegetables have such sweet juice

救世主", 在西班牙语里就叫"圣萨尔瓦多"。

西印度群岛有三个大岛, 并且这三个岛屿还连成了一串。那里还另有一个较小的岛屿, 而且, 除了加勒比海里的岛屿, 还有许多、许多很小的岛屿。

西印度群岛里最大的那个岛屿, 即连成一串的三个岛屿中的第一个, 就是古巴岛。哥伦布发现, 古巴岛上的印第安人嘴里都叼着一个燃烧着的火把。他们把火把产生的烟吸进肚子里, 然后再呼出来, 样子极其古怪和惊人, 仿佛他们全都是龙似的。竟然将燃烧着的草产生出来的烟吸进去(因为那种东西就是草), 人们干这样的事情, 似乎很不寻常吧, 可是, 印第安人却好像很喜欢这种东西呢。在大洋彼岸, 还从未有人见过别人将火吸进肚子里这样一种景象。不过, 如今世界各国的人都纷纷效仿古巴岛上那些红皮肤印第安人的做法了。那种草, 叫作烟草。虽说如今各地都种植烟草, 可世界上质量最佳的烟草, 却仍然产自古巴, 而古巴首都哈瓦那出产的"哈瓦那牌"雪茄, 也远销世界各地。

后来, 西班牙人便来到古巴殖民和生活了, 因此, 直到不久以前, 古巴还是西班牙的殖民地, 但如今古巴已经独立了。

世界上所有的蔬菜汁和水果汁里都含有糖分, 因为它们都是甜的。有些蔬菜和水果含有大量糖分, 有些蔬菜和水果的含糖量则很少。不过, 有两种蔬菜, 由于它们的汁液里含糖量很大, 因此人们大量种植, 以便用它们的汁液来制糖。这两种蔬菜, 就是甜菜和甘蔗。大家都知道甜菜是个什么样子吧。甘蔗则有点儿像是玉米秆。人们将甘蔗里的汁液榨出来, 然后烧开并制成食糖。古巴种植的甘蔗, 比全世

that they are raised for the sugar that can be made out of their juice. These vegetables are the beet and sugarcane. You know what a beet looks like. Sugarcane looks something like stalks of corn. Men press the juice out of the cane and boil it to make sugar. In Cuba they grow more sugar-cane than any other place i.t.w.W.

The Island of Haiti—the tat of the tit-tat-to islands—although it is not large, has two little countries on it. Both these countries are republics like the United States, with presidents and senators and representatives chosen by the people, but their presidents are colored and their senators and representatives are also colored. That may seem strange until I tell you that the people on the island are colored too.

When Columbus died he was buried on this island of Haiti. Many years after, men dug up what they thought were Columbus's bones and sent them back to Spain, where they are kept in a great cathedral. But many people say they were not Columbus's bones at all that they took back, but some one else's, and that Columbus's body still lies in Haiti.

Puerto Rico, the third of the tit-tat-to islands of the West Indies, belongs to the United States. In Puerto Rico they raise tobacco too, but there seems to be some difference in the land, for they can't seem to raise quite as good tobacco as the people in Cuba do.

Jamaica is a small island south of the tit-tat-to islands. It belongs to England. In Jamaica they grow many of the bananas that we eat. They are picked when they are still green, but by the time they have been shipped to the United States and are put in the fruit shops on sale they are yellow and ripe—sometimes. If you eat them before they are ripe, you may

界其他国家都要多。

海地岛是连成一串的那三个岛屿里的第二个，尽管这个岛不大，但上面却有两个国家。那两个国家都是像美国这样的共和国，都有人民选举出来的总统、参议员和众议员，只不过他们的总统都是有色人种，参议员和众议员也都是有色人种罢了。在你们看来，这一点可能有点儿奇怪，可我告诉你们吧，海地岛上的居民也全都是有色人种呢。

哥伦布去世后，就埋葬在这个海地岛上。许多年后，人们将据说是哥伦布的那具遗骸挖了出来，送回西班牙，保存在一座大教堂里。可很多人都说，送回来的根本就不是哥伦布的遗骸，而是别人的遗骸，他们都说，哥伦布的遗体仍然留在海地。

西印度群岛中连成一串的那三个岛屿中的第三个，就是波多黎各，它归美国所有[1]。虽然波多黎各人也种植烟草，但此处的土质似乎有所不同，因为这里似乎种植不出古巴那样优质的烟草来。

牙买加是位于这三个岛屿南边的一个小岛。它隶属于英国管辖。我们所吃的香蕉，大部分都是由牙买加人种植的。这些香蕉还是青色的时候，人们便将它们采摘

---

[1] 波多黎各原本是西班牙的殖民地，但在美西战争（1898年）后，变成了美国的殖民地。虽说此后该国人民进行了多次起义，想要独立，但都被镇压下去了。因此，直到现在，该国都是美国的自由联邦。

need a little Jamaica ginger, which is good for "tummy aches"—that comes from Jamaica too.

Tobacco and sugar, sponges and early vegetables, bananas and lilies!—pirates would have turned up their noses in disgust if they had captured a ship laden with such a cargo!

下来，待它们运到美国、摆到水果店里出售时，有的时候就已经变黄、变熟了。要是吃了没有熟透的香蕉，你们可能就得吃点儿牙买加姜才行，因为它对"肚子疼"有好处，而这种姜，自然也是产自牙买加了。

　　烟草和糖、海绵和时鲜蔬菜、香蕉和百合花！要是俘虏到了一条装载着这些东西的船只，海盗们肯定会讨厌地嗤之以鼻呢！

21 North South America

South America looks like a carrot, a turnip, a top, a funnel, a leaf, a fig, a pear turned upside down, a paddle, a lamb chop, a leg of mutton, an ice-cream cone—but the only thing it really looks like is: South America. The stem is Panama; the hook at the bottom is called Cape Horn.

From the tip top to the tip toe of South America, from Panama to Cape Horn, stretches a long wall of high mountains called the Andes. It is the highest range of mountains in the Western Half Ball, and it is the longest range of mountains i.t.w.W.

Columbus, who discovered America, had only one country named after him. This country is in South America nearest Panama, nearest the stem by which South America seems to hang to Central America. It is called Colombia, spelled with two o's instead of an "o" and a "u."

When white men first came to the northern shore of South America they found a land next to Colombia where the Indians lived in houses built on stakes in the water. This reminded them of a city in Italy across the ocean, called Venice, where the houses are built in the water, so they named this new country Little Venice, which in the Spanish language is Venezuela. Off the shore of Venezuela is a peculiar island called Trinidad. On this island is a lake—but the lake has no water in it. Instead of water there is a kind of tar called

第21章　南美北部

在大家的眼中，南美洲看上去就像是一根胡萝卜、一棵大头菜、一个陀螺、一个漏斗、一片树叶、一个无花果、一个倒着的梨、一片桨、一块羊排、一条羊腿或者一个蛋筒冰淇淋，可它的样子，实际上却只像一种东西，那就是南美洲自己。南美洲的头顶，就是巴拿马，而最底端的那个钩子，则叫"合恩角"。

从最顶端到最底端，从巴拿马到合恩角，绵亘着一条高高耸立的山脉，即安第斯山脉。这是西半球最高的山脉，也是全世界最长的一条山脉。

世界上只有一个国家，是用发现美洲的哥伦布这个人物的名字来命名的。这个国家位于南美洲，距巴拿马最近，距似乎把南美洲吊在中美洲上的那根"茎"也最近。这个国家，叫作"哥伦比亚"，注意，拼写起来，"哥伦比亚"（Colombia）一词里有两个"o"，而不是像"哥伦布"（Columbus）那样只有一个"o"和两个"u"。

白人第一次抵达南美洲北部的沿海地区之后，发现了与哥伦比亚接壤的一个国度，那里的印第安人，都是住在水面上用柱子支撑起来的房屋里。这让他们想起了大洋彼岸意大利一个叫作威尼斯的城市，那里的房屋也都是建在水里的，因此，他们便把新发现的这个小国命名为"小威尼斯"，而在西班牙语里就是"委内瑞拉"。委内瑞拉沿海，有一个叫作"特立尼达"的奇特岛屿。该岛上有一个湖泊，可那个湖泊里却没有水。湖中存着的不是湖水，而是一种叫作"沥青"的焦油。人

asphalt. This asphalt is dug up and loaded on to ships and brought to the United States to make roadways.

The three little countries next door to Venezuela are called the three Guianas. They belong to three different countries in Europe. In fact, they are the only countries in South America that do belong to countries outside of South America. The first Guiana belongs to England, the second belongs to Holland, the third belongs to France.

In British Guiana far back in the wilds is a waterfall nearly five times as high as Niagara, yet so far away from everything that hardly any white men have ever seen it or even heard of it. It's name is Kaieteur. Just for fun ask your father if he knows what Kaieteur is.

The line around the middle of the World, if there were a line—which there isn't—is like the belt around a very fat man. It is called the Equator. The Spanish for Equator is Ecuador. Ecuador is also the name of a little country in South America that straddles the Equator. We should expect it to be very hot there, for the nearer the Equator one goes the hotter it usually gets; but most of Ecuador is high up in the Andes Mountains, so high up that it is quite cool all the year round. The capital of Ecuador is Quito, pronounced Key-toe. From Quito you can see two of the highest volcanoes in the World. They have names that sound strange to us; both begin with "C." Chimborazo is the name of the higher, but it no longer smokes or sends forth fire. The other is Cotopaxi, not quite so high but still very much alive, for fires inside have not gone out.

们把这种沥青挖出来，装到船上，运到美国来铺马路。

紧挨着委内瑞拉的，是三个小国，并且它们都叫"圭亚那"。它们是欧洲三个不同国家的领地。实际上，整个南美洲只有这三个国家，才真正属于非南美国家的领地。第一个圭亚那隶属于英国，第二个圭亚那属于荷兰，第三个则属于法国[1]。

在英属圭亚那内陆的茫茫荒野中，有一座瀑布，其落差几乎达到了尼亚加拉大瀑布的五倍，可由于它与世隔绝，因此白人几乎从未见过这座瀑布，甚至都没有听说过呢。这座瀑布，叫作"凯厄图尔瀑布"。不妨纯属为了开开玩笑，问问你们的父亲，看他们知不知道"凯厄图尔"是什么吧。

假设有那么一条线，绕过整个地球的中部（实际上是没有这样一条线的），那么它就会像一个胖子的腰带似的。这条假设出来的线，叫作"赤道"。在西班牙语里，"赤道"就叫"厄瓜多尔"。厄瓜多尔也是南美洲横跨赤道的一个小国的名称。我们应该会想，那里可能非常炎热吧，因为一个地方距赤道越近，那里的气候也会越炎热，不过，由于厄瓜多尔绝大部分地区都位于高高耸立的安第斯山脉上，海拔极高，因此一年到头都相当凉爽。厄瓜多尔的首都是基多。在基多，大家可以看到世界上海拔最高的两座火山。这两座火山的名字，在我们看来非常古怪，它们都是用字母"C"开头的。其中，较高的那座火山叫作"钦博拉索山"，但如今这座火山已经不再喷发了。另一座叫作"科托帕希火山"，尽管它的海拔没有前者那

---

[1]　如今，荷属奎亚那已经独立，叫作"苏里兰"。

It seems strange that from this far country in the mountains, from Ecuador, something comes which you eat or drink, perhaps every day—chocolate and cocoa. They are both made from beans which grow in a large pod—a pod as big as a melon. These pods grow, not on branches, but right on the trunk of the tree. This tree is called the ca-ca-o tree. Notice how cocoa and cacao are spelled: See-o see-o-a comes from the see-a see-a-o-tree. Cocoa does not come from the cocoanut-tree. The cocoanut-tree is an entirely different tree that bears cocoanuts but not cocoa.

The Indians of Ecuador are very wild and savage. They are called head-hunters. One family or tribe will fight another tribe whenever they want something they haven't got—wives, perhaps—or simply because they want to fight. When they kill a man they cut off his head and save it for a souvenir, as the American Indians used to cut off a man's scalp and save it as a souvenir or trophy. The Indian who has the greatest number of heads is considered the greatest fighter. They often fight, not with bows and arrows, but with huge blow-pipes—as long as a man—using clay balls or little darts which have been dipped in poison. With these blow-pipes they can kill men and animals. These savage Indians catch fish for food, not with a line or net, but by putting poison in the streams where the fish are. The poison kills the fish and they float on the top, but it doesn't spoil them for eating.

The Indians of Ecuador are the most savage Indians now known, hut in the country just south of Ecuador, in the country called Peru, once lived the most civilized Indians ever known. They lived not in tents or wigwams or huts, but in palaces, and they were very

样高，如今却仍然很活跃，因为火山内部的火还没有熄灭。

没准大家每天吃的、喝的一些东西，比如巧克力和可可饮料，都产自这个地处遥远山区的国家，这一点似乎很令人觉得奇怪。这两种东西都是用一种大型的豆荚，一种大如甜瓜的豆荚制成的。这些巨型豆荚，并不是长在枝头上，而是长在树干上。那种树，就叫可可豆树。注意，"可可饮料"（cocoa）与"可可豆"（cacao）的拼法不同，可可粉源自可可豆树。还有，可可并不是长在椰子树上的[1]。椰子树是一种完全不同的树，上面结的是椰子，而不是可可豆。

厄瓜多尔的印第安人非常野蛮，非常残暴。因此，人们还称之为"猎头者"。无论何时，一个部落或者家族只要想掠夺自己没有的东西，比如老婆，或者仅仅是因为想打仗，便会与另一个部落开战。杀死一个人以后，他们还会把死者的头颅砍下来，留作纪念品，就像美国的印第安人以前也会把自己杀死的人的头皮剥下来，留作纪念品或者战利品一样。头颅留得最多的印第安人，就会被誉为最了不起的勇士。他们经常打仗，但他们用的不是弓箭，而是一种与一个人身高差不多长的巨型吹管，发射土球或者用毒药浸泡过小飞镖。用这种吹管，他们既可以杀人，也可以猎杀野兽。这些野蛮的印第安人也捕鱼为食，但他们不是用钓丝或者渔网来捕鱼，而是向有鱼的溪流中投毒。毒药把鱼儿毒死之后，鱼儿便会浮到水面上来，不过，

---

[1] 作者这样说，是因为英语中的cocoa（可可）与cocoanut（椰子）两个词容易让小朋友们产生混淆。

特立尼达
委内瑞拉
圭
亚
那
英属
荷属
法属
哥伦比亚
赤道
可可
厄瓜多尔
橡胶树
印加遗址
秘鲁
巴
西
咖啡豆
奎宁（即金鸡纳霜）
锡
玻利维亚
大
西
洋
里约热内卢
太
平
洋
硝酸钠
智
利
巴
拉
圭
桑托斯
乌拉圭
碘
阿
根
廷
南美洲
麦哲伦海峡
火地岛
M.S.W.J.

intelligent and very rich. They were called Incas and their capital was named Cuzco. The Incas had great treasures of gold and silver, and when the Spaniards first came to South America looking for gold or silver they found it in Cuzco already mined. All they had to do was to take it away from the Incas. This was easy because the Spaniards had guns, and the Incas, who had no such thing, were no match for them in a fight. So the Spaniards won and simply helped themselves to the gold, and made the Incas work in the mines for more. However, the joke was on the Spaniards, for many of their ships sailing back to Spain with their stolen treasure were captured by the pirates.

Many of the Spaniards who stayed in Peru married Indian women, so now most of the people in Peru are a mixture of Spanish and Indian.

There is little left of Cuzco, except ruins of the old Inca palaces. The present capital of Peru is Lima, but Lima beans don't come from there. A medicine that is often given for fever does come from Peru, however. The Indians found that the bark of a certain tree when stewed in water made a kind of tea that was good for fever. When the white man came, he found it was good for fever too. So now the bark of this tree is gathered and sent to other countries to be used in making medicine to cure fevers. The medicine is called quinine.

In the United States loads are usually carried on freight trains or trucks but in the Andes Mountains they are usually carried on the backs of a little animal called a llama. A llama is something like a small camel without a hump.

这种毒药并不厉害，毒死的鱼儿还是可以吃的。

厄瓜多尔的印第安人，是迄今所知最为野蛮的印第安人，不过，就在厄瓜多尔南边那个叫"秘鲁"的国家里，却曾经生活着人类所知文化最为发达的印第安人呢。秘鲁的印第安人并非居住在帐篷、活动窝棚或者茅屋里，而是住在宫殿里，并且，他们都非常聪明、非常富有。这些印第安人叫作印加人，而他们的首都则叫库斯科。印加人拥有黄金、白银等大量财宝，因此当西班牙人首次到南美洲来寻找黄金和白银时，他们发现库斯科的金银全都已经开采出来了。因此，他们只需从印加人手里夺取就行了。这样做很容易，因为西班牙人有枪有炮，而印加人却没有这些武器，在战斗中根本就不是西班牙人的对手。于是，西班牙人大获全胜，非但可以随意掠夺黄金，还迫使印加人到矿井里去干活，为他们开采出更多的黄金来。然而，上帝却跟西班牙人开了一个玩笑，因为运载着掠夺而来的财宝驶回西班牙的那些船只中，有许多都被海盗劫走了。

留在秘鲁的许多西班牙殖民者都娶了印第安女子，因此，如今绝大多数秘鲁人都是西班牙人和印第安人的混血后裔。

除了印加人那些宫殿的废墟，库斯科几乎没有留下什么遗迹了。如今，秘鲁的首都是利马，不过，"利马豆"[1]可不是产自那里。然而，有一种通常用于治疗发烧的药品，却的确产自秘鲁。印第安人发现，有一种树的树皮，煮水之后就成了

---

[1] 利马豆（Lima beans），即青豆。

Have you ever heard of a man named Simon Bolivar? Probably not, but in South America every boy and girl knows him as you know George Washington. In fact, he is often called the George Washington of South America. Just as England once owned the thirteen colonies, Spain once owned a great part of South America. Then this man Bolivar, Simon Bolivar, who lived in Venezuela, thought, as a great many others did, that Spain was not treating his country right. Bolivar had been in the United States and had heard how the United States once belonged to England and how George Washington had led the revolution against England until the United States belonged to itself. So Bolivar went back to South America and started a revolution to make his country and other countries of South America independent of Spain. He had a very hard time of it, indeed. Again and

美 洲 驼

安第斯山区的大量货物都由小小的美洲驼来运送

一种可以治疗发烧的茶。白人到来之后，也发现这种树皮熬出来的水对治疗发烧有作用。于是，如今人们便把这种树皮收集起来，送到其他国家去制作治疗发烧的药品。这种药品，叫作"奎宁"。

在美国，我们通常都是用货运列车或者卡车来运载货物的，可在安第斯山脉，人们通常却是用一种叫作"美洲驼"的小型动物来运送货物的。美洲驼有点儿像是一头小骆驼，只是它们没有驼峰罢了。

大家听没听说过，有一个叫作西蒙·玻利瓦尔的人呢？很可能都没有听说过吧。不过，在南美洲，每个小朋友却都知道这个人，就像你们都知道乔治·华盛顿似的。实际上，他还经常被人誉为南美洲的乔治·华盛顿呢。正如美国最初那十三个殖民地曾经隶属于英国那样，南美洲的大部分地区曾经也隶属于西班牙。后来，这个玻利瓦尔，生活在委内瑞拉的西蒙·玻利瓦尔，也像绝大多数人一样认为，西班牙没有很好地对待他的祖国。玻利瓦尔到过美国，听说了美国曾经隶属于英国，以及乔治·华盛顿如何领导人民起来革命、对抗英国并最终使美国获得独立的情况。于是，返回南美之后，玻利瓦尔便发动了一场革命，想让祖国和其他南美国家

again he had to flee for his life, but again and again he returned to South America and at last succeeded in making five countries of South America independent of Spain. After he died one of these countries that he had freed changed its name from High Peru to Bolivia, after him. Bolivia is one of the few countries in the World that do not touch the sea, from which there is no way to get to the sea by boat.

Much of the tin in the World comes from mines in Bolivia. Tin pans and tin cans are not made of pure tin—it would cost too much if they were. They are made of iron and simply plated with tin. Pans and cans made of iron would rust and so be unfit for food, but tin doesn't rust and that's why the pans and cans are covered with a thin coating of tin. When this thin tin wears off, the iron rusts easily enough, and that's why most tin cans you see on the ash pile are rusty; the tin has worn off..

Between Bolivia and Peru there is a very large lake. Its name sounds funny, like a person stuttering. It is Ti ti ca ca. It is the highest lake of its size i.t.w.W. I once built a rowboat in my cellar. When I had finished it I found it was so big I couldn't get it out of the house. So I had to take it apart, carry it outside, and put it together again. There are steamers on Lake Titicaca, but in order to get them there from where they were built they had to be taken to pieces and carried up the mountains to the lake, piece by piece, and there put together again.

摆脱西班牙的统治，获得独立。他当然经历了一场非常艰难的斗争。他不得不一次又一次地逃命，但他一次又一次回到南美，并且最终成功地让五个南美国家摆脱了西班牙的统治，获得了独立。去世之后，他所解放的那些国家里，有一个国家还根据他的名字，将本国的国名从"高秘鲁"改成了"玻利维亚"呢。玻利维亚是世界上少数不临海的国家之一，也就是说，从该国出发，是没有水路可以到达大海的。

世界上绝大部分的锡，都产自玻利维亚的锡矿。锡锅、锡罐都不是用纯锡制成的，要是用纯锡的话，成本就太高了。它们实际上都是铁制的，只是外面镀了一层锡罢了。铁锅、铁罐都会生锈，但锡却不会生锈，铁锅、铁罐外面之所以都要镀上一层薄薄的锡，原因就在于此。这层薄锡剥落之后，里面的铁很快便会锈蚀，你们在垃圾堆上看到的绝大多数锡罐之所以全都锈迹斑斑，就是因为上面的镀锡磨掉了。

玻利维亚和秘鲁两国之间，有一个巨大的湖泊。这个湖泊的名字听上去很有意思，就像一个人口吃似的。它叫"的的喀喀湖"，是全世界此种大小的湖泊中海拔最高的一个。我曾经在自家的地窖里造出了一条划艇。造完之后我却发现，划艇太大，没法弄到屋外去。于是，我只得将划艇拆卸开来，一件件拿到屋外去，然后再组装起来。的的喀喀湖上有轮船行驶，可为了将船只从厂家运到这个湖上，船只也只能拆卸成许多部件，运到位于高山之上的湖边，然后再在那里一件一件地重新组装起来呢。

22 Rubber and Coffee Land

Mountains make rivers. If a continent were flat—absolutely flat and level like a table—there would be no rivers. Rain falling would run off the continent like water poured on a table. The water running off the Andes Mountains makes the greatest river in the World—not the longest, but the biggest. The name of this river also begins with an "A". It is called the Amazon. On the map the Amazon looks like a vine with many branches. It gets so broad and wide as it goes on that you cannot see across it. The Amazon empties more water into the ocean than any other river i.t.w.W.

You may wonder why, with all the big rivers in the World pouring water into the ocean all the time, the ocean does not fill up and run over as a bathtub would fill up and run over if you left the water running into it all the time. It is because the water in the ocean is always turning into vapor, rising high into the air and making clouds. The clouds rise over the sea, then blow over the land, then turn to rain: the rain falls on the ground, a great part of it is taken up by trees and plants but the rest runs into the rivers, the rivers flow into the ocean and then the same thing goes on over and over again—rivers, ocean; ocean, clouds; clouds, land; land, rivers; rivers, ocean; ocean, clouds, and so on forever and ever. No water is ever lost in the World. It may be in a different place, but there is never any more nor any less water in the World than ever has or ever will be.

第22章　橡胶与咖啡之国

河流发源于高山。如果一个大陆是平平坦坦的，即绝对水平，就像桌面一样的话，那么这个大陆上就不会有河流。雨水落到这个大陆上后，就会跟我们往桌子上倒水那样，四处漫延。安第斯山脉上流下来的水，形成了世界上最大的一条河流，注意，是最大，而不是最长。这条河流的名称，与"安第斯山脉"一样，也是用字母"A"开头的，叫作"亚马孙河"。在地图上，亚马孙河看上去就像是一根有着许多分枝的葡萄藤。这条河又宽又大，一眼望不到对岸。亚马孙河注入海洋中的水量，比全世界其他任何一条河流都要多。

你们可能会感到奇怪，世界上有这么多的大河，一直都在将河水注入海洋当中，海洋为什么不会被注满和干涸，为什么不会像一个浴缸，你们加水后就会注满，而放水后就会干涸那样。这是因为，海水始终都在蒸发、升腾到空中，然后形成云朵。云朵起初飘在海洋上方，然后被风吹向陆地，接下来形成降雨。雨水落到地面上后，大部分都被树木、植物所吸收，其余的则注入河流当中，而河流则一路将河水注入海洋，然后，再一遍又一遍地重复这一过程：河流→海洋，海洋→云朵，云朵→陆地，陆地→河流，河流→海洋，海洋→云朵，周而复始，永远循环下去。地球上的水分，是永远都不会流失的。虽然水分可能处于不同的地方，但地球上如今的水量与过去或者将来的水量相比，既不会多，也不会少。

All the great rivers in South America flow into the Atlantic Ocean—none flows into the Pacific, because the Andes Mountains lie so close to the Pacific edge there is no room for great rivers on that side.

The Amazon runs through a country by the name of Brazil. Brazil is the biggest country in South America. It is bigger than the whole of our United States! People called the country Brazil after a tree growing there. The brazil-tree is used for making a colored dye. But it would have been more fitting if the country had been named "Rubber" or "Coffee," for more rubber-trees and coffee-trees grow in Brazil than do brazil-trees.

The land around the Amazon River is called "Selvas"—which means "woods." It is not only woods but jungles and swamps, and it is very wild, hot, damp, and unhealthful. It is so hot and damp that everything grows big and thick and fast—so big that water lilies grow leaves as big as the top of a dining-room table; so thick that a man can hardly make his way through; and as fast as *Jack the Giant Killer's* beanstalk.

There are many animals but few men in the Selvas, and the men are mostly Indians. There are many monkeys, the kind organ-grinders use. There are parrots, which sailors catch and teach to speak and bring back home. There are butterflies and moths of great size and beautiful colors that a boy would love to have for his collection. There are huge snakes called boa-constrictors, that look like heavy vines hanging from branches to fool other animals which they catch, coil around, and hug to death, then swallow whole and go to sleep for a week or month while the meal is being digested. There are animals that hang

南美洲所有的大河，全都汇入了大西洋，没有一条是注入太平洋的，这是因为，安第斯山脉距太平洋沿岸非常近，那一侧并没有形成大河的空间。

亚马孙河流经了一个叫作巴西的国家。巴西是南美洲面积最大的国家。该国的国土范围，甚至比我们美国还要辽阔呢。人们是根据那里生长的一种树木，而将该国叫作巴西的。"巴西苏木"可用于制造一种染料。不过，该国要是叫"橡胶"或者"咖啡"可能更加合适，因为巴西栽种的橡胶树和咖啡树，要比"巴西苏木"更多。

亚马孙河沿岸的陆地，被称为"热带雨林"，也就是"林地"的意思。那里并非只有森林，还有丛林和沼泽，并且，那里既荒无人烟、炎热潮湿，又很不卫生。那里非常炎热、非常潮湿，因此所有植物都长得又大、又密、又迅速，比如，那里的荷叶大如餐桌桌面，林木密得连人都钻不过去，生长起来快得就像是"巨人杀手杰克"的豆茎呢[1]。

热带雨林中有许多的野生动物，而人类却不多，并且主要都是印第安人。那里有许多的猴子，就是在街头演奏手风琴的人带着的那种猴子。那里有鹦鹉，水手们抓到鹦鹉后，会教它们说话，然后带回家里去。那里有体型巨大、色彩漂亮的蝴

---

[1] 巨人杀手杰克（Jack the Giant Killer），根据英国童话、民间传说《杰克与豆茎》及《巨人杀手杰克》改编而成的美国电影。杰克是英国亚瑟王统治时期的一个小伙子，既勇敢又聪明，由于杀死巨人而扬名。他曾用母牛换来几颗豆子，那些豆子一夜间便发芽长大，豆茎高耸入云，通往一个陌生的世界。

from trees by their toes like a boy on a trapeze, and even sleep upside down; lazy, sleepy animals that never seem to be awake, and move, when they do move, so slothfully they are called "sloths." There are animals like dragons, called "iguanas." There are huge bullfrogs whose croaking sounds like the roar of lions. And there are mosquitos, the country mosquitos that give you malaria. You may wonder why any one goes to the Selvas at all. They go a-hunting for animals for museums and zoos, but the chief thing they go hunting for is the juice or sap of a tree that grows wild in the Selvas.

White people found the Amazon Indians playing with balls that bounced and bounded. They had seen nothing of the sort before. These balls, they found out, were made of the sap of a tree. That gave the white man the idea that this sap might be used to make balls for white children and white men to play with—babies' balls, tennis-balls, golf-balls. Then they found that lumps of it would rub out—so they called it rubber—and that they could make rubber erasers, automobile tires, rubber bands, and rubber boots of it. Soft rubber and hard rubber and pully rubber and springy rubber are all made from the sap of the rubber-tree by treating it in different ways as a cook makes taffy and gum-drops and caramels by cooking sugar in different ways.

Men go through the Selvas and wherever they find a rubber-tree they cut notches in the tree trunk and fasten a cup underneath to catch the tree's sap, which flows out from the notches like blood out of a cut finger. Then they go round again and empty the cups of rubber sap into a bucket and carry it to their camp. When they have collected enough sap

蝶和蛾子，男孩子们都很乐意收藏它们的标本呢。那里有一种叫作"王蛇"的巨型蟒蛇，从树枝上垂下来，就像一根根巨大的葡萄藤似的，能够骗过它们捕食的动物，它们会缠在猎物身上，把猎物勒死，整个儿吞下去，然后再睡上一个星期或者一个月的时间，边睡边消化食物。那里有一种用脚趾抓住树枝倒悬起来的动物，就像男孩子们在秋千上倒悬时那样，它们甚至还能倒悬着睡觉呢。这种懒惰、嗜睡的动物，似乎从来都没有醒来过，也不会挪动，就算它们真的走动起来，也是很懒散的，因此人们都称之为"树懒"。那里还有一种像龙的动物，叫作"鬣蜥"。那里有一种巨型牛蛙，它们呱呱大叫起来的时候，声音简直就像是狮吼。那里也有蚊子，就是那种会让人得上疟疾的城市蚊子。你们可能会感到奇怪，人们为什么要到热带雨林里去。人们去那里，是为了替博物馆或者动物园捕猎动物，不过，他们前往寻猎的，主要还是生长在热带雨林里的一种野生树木的汁液，或者说树液。

　　白人发现，亚马孙地区的印第安人会用一种能够弹跳起来的球玩游戏。他们以前都没有见过那种东西。他们发现，这种球是用一种树木的树液做成的。白人心想，这种树液可以用于制造供白种小朋友或者大人玩耍的球类，比如娃娃球、乒乓球、高尔夫球。后来，他们又发现，一块这样的东西能够擦掉字迹，因此他们便把这种东西叫作"橡胶"，它可以制成橡皮擦子、汽车轮胎、橡皮筋，以及胶鞋。软橡胶、硬橡胶、伸缩橡胶和弹力橡胶，都是利用橡胶树的汁液，根据不同的方法制造出来的。这就好比是一位厨师，用不同的方法，可以把食糖做成太妃糖、橡皮糖、饴糖等不同糖果一样。

they take a stick, pour some of the sap on it, and dry it over a fire. They do the same thing again and again until there is a big lump of rubber on the stick. These lumps of rubber they pile into canoes and carry down the Amazon River to larger boats that carry the rubber to the United States and to other countries.

But there is something that grows in Brazil that begins with a "C"—that almost every family in the United States has at breakfast each morning. Can you guess what it is? It's coffee. Coffee doesn't grow in Brazil wild as the rubber-tree does. In fact, coffee didn't grow in Brazil at all until some men brought coffee bushes from across the ocean and planted them in Brazil. They planted them on high ground near the shore, not in the Selvas. They found that the high ground and the weather were just exactly right for growing coffee, and now much more coffee grows in Brazil than in the place where coffee came from first, and indeed more than in any other place i.t.w.W.

Coffee grows on a small tree, and the coffee berries look something like cherries. Inside of each cherry-like berry are two seeds. These seeds are coffee, but before coffee can be made into a drink the coffee seeds must be toasted brown and then ground to powder.

One New Year's Day a long time ago a man was sailing along the coast of Brazil when he came to what seemed to be the mouth of a river. As it was the first day of January he named the place River of January, which in his language was Rio de Janeiro. It turned out to be no river; hut the city that grew up at that place is still called Rio de Janeiro, and it is the capital of Brazil. In the harbor of Rio, as it is called for short, there is a huge rock

人们在热带雨林中穿行，看到一株橡胶树，就在树干上划出一道口子，并在口子下面绑上一个杯子，把流淌下来的树液收集起来，这种树液，会从划出的口子流淌出来，就像我们手指割破了会流出血来似的。过后，他们会再次来到树下，将那些装满了橡胶树液的杯子倒到一只桶子里，然后带回营地去。收集到了足够多的橡胶树液后，他们又会拿出一根棍子，倒上一些树液，然后在火上烤干。他们一遍又一遍地这样做，直到棍子上结起一大块橡胶。然后，他们再将这些橡胶块堆到独木舟上，运着它们顺亚马孙河而下，然后装上大船，运到美国和其他各国去。

不过，巴西还生长着一种以字母"C"开头的东西，是几乎每一个美国家庭每天早上吃早餐时都要吃到的东西。你们猜得到那是什么吗？就是咖啡啊。在巴西，咖啡可不像橡胶树那样属于野生的。事实上，以前巴西根本就不种植咖啡，只是后来有些人将咖啡树从大洋彼岸带到巴西之后，巴西人才开始种植。他们把咖啡树种在沿海地区的高地上，而不是种植在热带雨林里。他们发现，高海拔地区和那里的天气情况，都正好适合于种植咖啡，因此，如今巴西出产的咖啡量，比咖啡原产地的产量都要大得多，事实上比全世界其他任何一个地区出产的咖啡都要多呢。

咖啡生长在一种矮小的树木之上，而咖啡豆的样子，也有点儿像是樱桃。每一颗樱桃状的浆果里，都有两粒种子。这两粒种子，就是咖啡豆，不过，在制成饮料之前，人们还得先把咖啡豆烘成棕色，然后磨成粉末才行。

在很久很久以前的一个元旦，有个人正沿着巴西海岸航行，来到了一个似乎属于一条河流的河口。由于那天是元旦，因此他就给这个地方起名为"一月河"，而

which is called "The Loaf of Sugar," and as you see Rio from a ship the mountains back of the city look like a "Sleeping Giant," and that is what they are called.

More coffee is shipped from Rio than from any other place i.t.w.W., except another place on the coast of Brazil just south of Rio. This other place is called Santos. The cup of coffee your father drinks in the morning probably comes from either Rio or Santos. If coffee and cocoa could talk, and tin cans and asphalt streets and rubber tires, as such things do in fairy-tales, what tales they could tell of their homes and travels!

用他自己的语言来说，就是"里约热内卢"，这里，就是如今巴西的首都[1]。在简称"里约"的这个港口，有一块巨大的岩石，叫作"甜面包"，而从船上往里约港看去，该市背后的山脉就像是一个"睡着的巨人"，而那座山脉，也正是叫作"睡巨人"呢。

除了里约热内卢，还有一个地方也盛产咖啡，叫作桑托斯。你们的父亲早上喝的那杯咖啡，很可能要么是来自里约热内卢，要么来自桑托斯呢。如果咖啡和可可能够说话，而锡罐、柏油街道和橡胶轮胎也能够像童话故事里的东西一样说话，那么它们将会述说关于其产地和旅途中的多少故事啊！

爸爸早餐时喝的是产自巴西的咖啡

---

[1] 如今，巴西的首都是巴西利亚。

23 Silver Land and Sliver Land

We give babies names when they are born, but sometimes when the babies grow up the names do not fit them. "Charles" means "strong" and "Ruth" means "beautiful," but when Charles grows up he may not be strong, and Ruth may not be beautiful. You never can tell. When white people came to South America to the land south of Brazil they saw Indians there wearing silver bracelets and silver necklaces, and they supposed there must be a great deal of silver in the land, so they named the country "Silver Land," which in their language is "Argentina." But Argentina turned out to have very little silver, yet we still call it Silver Land just the same.

Although Argentina has little silver, the people there have a great deal of money; in fact, they have more money than any other country in South America. They do not get the money out of the ground, but they make it by selling wheat and meat, so it would have been a more fitting name if they had called Argentina "Wheat Land" or "Meat Land" instead of "Silver Land," but not nearly so pretty. In Argentina there are enormous farms where they grow wheat and corn, and enormous fields called pampas where they raise cattle and sheep. The men that look after these cattle and sheep we should call "cowboys," but there they are called "gauchos." Gauchos wear ponchos. A poncho is a kind of square blanket with a hole in the center through which the gaucho sticks his head. He uses it as a

第23章　白银之国与狭长之国

宝宝一出生，我们就会给宝宝起个名字，不过，有的时候，宝宝长大后，当时所起的名字却会不再名副其实了。"查尔斯"这个名字，是"强壮"的意思，"露丝"则是指"美丽"，可查尔斯长大后却可能并不强壮，而露丝长得也并不美丽。这种事情，大家永远都没法说得准。当人们来到南美洲，来到巴西以南的那片土地之后，他们看到那里的印第安人都戴着银手镯、银项链，因此他们认为，当地肯定储有大量的白银，于是便将那个国家命名为"白银之国"，在西班牙语里，就叫作"阿根廷"。但结果表明，阿根廷可没有多少白银，不过，我们却照样称之为"白银之国"呢。

尽管阿根廷没有多少白银，可当地人却很有钱，事实上，阿根廷人比南美洲任何一个国家的人都要富裕。他们的钱，并不是来自地下的矿产，而是通过出售小麦和肉类挣来的，因此，要是把阿根廷叫作"小麦之国"或者"肉类之国"，而不是"白银之国"的话，虽说听起来没那么漂亮，却可能更加合适呢。阿根廷非但有许多种植小麦和玉米的巨型农场，还有面积广袤的土地，叫作"潘帕斯大草原"，可以喂养牛羊。我们本该把这些喂养牛羊的人称为"牛仔"才是，可在那里，他们却被称为"加乌乔人[1]"。加乌乔人身上都穿着南美披风。所谓的南美披风，就是一

---

[1]　加乌乔人（gaucho），指居住于南美大草原上的印第安人和西班牙人的混血种族。

coat by day and as a blanket by night. A gaucho always carries a big knife, which he uses as a sword, as a hatchet, or as a table knife.

Corn feeds the cattle. Cattle makes meat and meat makes money. From the skin of the cattle leather is made, and from the wool of sheep cloth is made, and from both money is made.

Argentina is so much like the United States in a great many ways that it is often called the United States of South America. Both countries are alike in this—that they have hot weather part of the time and cold weather part of the time. But there is this big difference: in Argentina they have winter when the United States is having summer, and summer when the United States is having winter. In Argentina Christmas comes in hot weather and snow and ice in July and August. They have flowers and vegetables and vacations in January and February, and snow and ice and sledding and skating in July.

The capital of Argentina is often called the New York of South America, as it is the largest city of South America, as New York is the largest city of North America. Its name, however, is not New York but "Good Airs," or, in Spanish, "Buenos Aires." It is on the Plata River, which is another name that means silver. So we

加乌乔人

加乌乔人身穿南美披风

块方方正正的毯子，中间有个洞，加乌乔人把脑袋从这个洞里穿过去，披风就穿到身上了。加乌乔人白天把它当成外套，晚上则把它当成毯子。加乌乔人总是随身带着一把大刀，既把它当成剑、斧子，也把它当成餐刀。

牛羊以玉米为食。牛羊杀掉后变成牛羊肉，而牛羊肉则会带来收入。牛皮可以制成皮革，羊毛则可以织成布料，这两种东西也都可以带来收入。

阿根廷在很多方面都跟美国非常相似，因此还经常被人们称为南美洲的美国。两国有一个相似之处，那就是：两国都有一段时间天气炎热，然后都有一段时间天气寒冷。不过，两国却有一个巨大的差异：阿根廷处于冬季的时候，美国正值夏天；而阿根廷正值夏天的时候，美国却处于冬季。在阿根廷，圣诞节的时候天气炎热，而七、八月份却是冰雪交加。一、二月份的时候，该国鲜花盛开、蔬菜遍地，人们纷纷休假；而到了七月份，该国却是冰雪漫天，适合于乘坐雪橇、去滑雪了。

阿根廷的首都，经常被人们誉为是南美洲的纽约，这是因为，它是南美洲最大的城市，而纽约则是北美洲最大的城市。然而，这个首都的名字却不是"纽约"，而是"良好空气"，在西班牙语里，就叫"布宜诺斯艾利斯"。该市坐落在拉普拉塔河上，"拉普拉塔"就是西班牙语里意指"白银"的另一个词。因此，"良好空气"这座城市，就是坐落在"白银之国"的"白银之河"上。

have the city of Good Airs on the Silver River in Silver Land.

In most of the other countries of South America there are many more Indians and Indians mixed with white men than there are white people, but in Argentina most of the people are white. That's another reason why it is like the United States; but Argentina was settled by people from Spain, not from England, so the people speak Spanish and not English.

Up the Silver River from Argentina, tucked in between the larger countries are two little countries called Uru-and Para-guay. Uruguay and Paraguay are similar to Argentina in many ways. They raise sheep and cattle and gauchos with ponchos. In Paraguay they raise a tree from the leaves of which a kind of tea is made. It is called Paraguay tea or mate. It is the chief drink of the gauchos, and many people in South America drink it instead of real tea. It was thought so good that they tried to sell it to other countries. But other countries didn't care for it as much as for regular tea or coffee. Grown people are like children: what they like they like; what they think they won't like they don't like. Most people in the United States like soda-water, but people in other countries usually do not.

The Andes Mountains separate Argentina from a very long and narrow country on the Pacific shore named Chile. Argentina is called the Silver Land. Chile is so long and thin it is sometimes called the Sliver land. Chile doesn't mean chilly; it means Land of Snow, for most of Chile is mountains, and the mountains are so high there is snow on their tops all the time. Chile and Argentina were once going to war in spite of the wall of mountains between them, but they made an agreement, as Canada and the United States did, that

在南美洲其他的绝大多数国家里，印第安人以及印第安人与白人通婚形成的混血人口加起来，都要比白人人口多得多，可阿根廷的人口，却主要是白种人。这就是我们说该国与美国类似的另一个原因，不过，在阿根廷殖民的都是西班牙人，而不是英国人，因此该国的人都说西班牙语，而不是说英语。

从阿根廷沿着"白银之河"而上，有两个小国家，它们夹在两个较大的国家之间，分别叫作乌拉圭和巴拉圭。乌拉圭和巴拉圭两国，在很多方面都与阿根廷相似。三个国家的人们都喂养牛羊，都有穿着南美披风的加乌乔人。巴拉圭人还种植一种树，树上的叶子可以制成一种茶，这种茶，就叫"巴拉圭茶"，或者叫"冬青茶"。加乌乔人喝的，主要就是这种茶，而南美还有很多的人都喝这个，而不喝真正的茶。他们觉得这种茶非常好，因此想方设法地要把这种茶卖到其他国家去。不过，其他国家的人却并不像喜欢普通的茶或者咖啡那样喜欢巴拉圭茶。成年人也像小朋友一样，他们觉得喜欢的，就会很喜欢，而觉得不喜欢的，就不会喜欢。绝大多数美国人都很喜欢喝苏打水，可其他国家的人通常却不喜欢喝这种东西呢。

安第斯山脉把阿根廷与一个位于太平洋沿岸、叫作"智利"的狭长国家隔了开来。阿根廷被称为是"白银之国"。智利由于又长又窄，因此有时会被人们称为"狭长之国"。"智利"（Chile）这个词，可不是"寒冷"（chilly）的意思，它指的是"冰雪之地"，因为智利绝大部分地区都是山区，而那些山脉全都高耸入云，故而山顶会终年积雪。尽管两国间有山脉相隔，可智利和阿根廷之间曾经还打

they would not fight. They set up on top of the Andes Mountains a huge bronze figure of Christ holding a cross—they melted their cannons to make it—and on the base they put words which say something like this: "Sooner shall these mountain crags crumble to dust than Chile and Argentina shall go to war with each other—they have sworn it at the foot of Christ." They have had no fights since. What a pity such an easy way to stop fighting cannot be used everywhere!

Chile is so long and so thin and has so many mountains it hardly seems a country worth fighting for, but in spite of what seems to be, Chile makes a lot of money. This may seem still more surprising when I tell you that the northern part of Chile is a desert where it often does not rain for ten years at a time. That doesn't sound like very good land, but it is one of the richest lands in the World. You would never guess why. Of course, nothing will grow there because it is a desert, and there are no diamonds nor gold. It is on account of something you probably never heard of. This something you never heard of is called Nitrate of Soda. It is a kind of salt that was once in the sea. The reason it is so valuable is because farmers all over the World buy it to put on their fields, as it makes vegetables grow so much better. Strange it doesn't grow anything where it is found; but that is because there is no rain there and nothing will grow without rain. But it is lucky there is no rain, for if there were rain the Nitrate of Soda would melt. This part of Chile is like a long narrow trough. It was once under the sea, then there was an earthquake, and this part of the bottom of the sea rose up and made land; the water in the trough evaporated and left this rough kind of sea salt called Nitrate of Soda. Iodine comes from there too; and who

算开战呢，不过，后来两国间签署了一项协定，就像加拿大和美国那样，同意两国不再交战。两国在安第斯山脉顶上，用熔化大炮后形成的铜液，制作出了一座巨大的青铜雕像，雕像描绘的是手持十字架的基督，而在雕像基座上，还铭刻着这样一句话："智利和阿根廷两国在基督脚下发誓，哪怕高山峭壁化为尘土，两国也永不开战。"自那以后，两国间就的确没有发生过战争了。没法将这样一种简单的、阻止战争的办法推广到世界各地去，是一件多么遗憾的事情啊！

智利形状既狭长，地势又多山，似乎是一个不值得为之去发动战争的国家，不过，尽管看似如此，智利其实却非常富裕呢。倘若我告诉你们说，智利北部还是一片沙漠，那里经常十年都不下一场雨，那么该国非常富裕这一点，可能就更令人惊讶了。听上去，那里并不是一处很肥沃的土地，可实际上，那里却是世界上最富裕的地方之一。大家是永远都猜不出个中原因的。自然，由于是沙漠，因此那里是什么也种植不了的，并且，那里也不出产钻石或者黄金。该国之所以富裕，靠的全是一种你们十有八九听都没有听说过的东西。这种你们从未听说过的东西，叫作"硝酸钠"。它是一种曾经存在于海洋中的盐类。之所以如此贵重，是因为全世界的农民都要买这种东西去给地里施肥，是因为硝酸钠能够让蔬菜长得更加茂盛。奇怪的是，出产硝酸钠的地方却什么也种不了，可种不了的原因，却是因为当地没有雨水，而没有雨水的话，就什么也长不出来。不过，幸亏那里不下雨，因为要是那里下雨的话，硝酸钠便会溶化掉。智利的这个地方，就像是一条狭长的沟槽。那里

doesn't know that stinging brown stuff that your mother puts on cuts?

The Valley of Paradise is in Chile—only it isn't what you would think Paradise would be. It is the chief seaport of Chile, and it is not very lovely and not very healthful. In Spanish it is called Valparaiso.

The capital of Chile is up in the mountains where it is cool and healthy. It is called Santiago, which means St. James.

Columbus tried to go around the World, but didn't. The first man whose ship went around the World was named Magellan. Magellan sailed across from the other side of the ocean, as Columbus had done, but he went on until he bumped into America. Then he went along down South America, trying to find a way to get through to the Pacific Ocean. He sailed up the Amazon, thinking he might get through there, but he couldn't. Then he sailed up La Plata, thinking he might get through there, but he couldn't. Then when he had nearly reached the tip of South America he at last found a way through to the Pacific. This way through was quite crooked, but we call it a strait and we have named it after him—the Strait of Magellan. He saw many fires on the land at his left, whether they were from volcanoes now no longer burning, or made by the Indians, no one knows. At

安第斯山上的基督

在基督脚下，两国发誓永不开战

原本位于海底，后来发生了一场地震，海底的这一部分隆起，升出水面后变成了陆地，而待沟槽中的水蒸发掉之后，便留下了这种叫作硝酸钠的海盐。这里还出产碘，你们的妈妈，都应该给你们的伤口上抹过那种棕色的、弄得你们生疼生疼的东西，所以谁不知道碘呢？

"天堂谷"也位于智利，只是这里可不是你们所想的那种"天堂"。那是智利的第一大海港，既不是很可爱，也不是很卫生。在西班牙语里，那里就叫"瓦尔帕莱索"。

智利的首都位于海拔很高的山区，那里气候凉爽，也很卫生。该市叫作"圣地亚哥"，就是"圣徒詹姆斯"的意思。

哥伦布曾经想要环游世界，却没有成功。第一个驾船进行环球航行的人，名叫麦哲伦。麦哲伦像哥伦布一样，驾船从大西洋的彼岸横渡过来，不过，他却一直坚持航行，直到抵达了美洲。接下来，他一路航行到了南美洲，试图找出一条通往太平洋的航线来。他曾经沿着亚马孙河逆流而上，以为可以从中穿过去，可实际上那里是不可能通过的。后来，他又沿着拉普拉塔河而上，以为可以从中穿过去，可实际上也不能。接下来，待差不多到达了南美洲的最南端之后，他终于发现了一条进入太平洋的水道。这条水道非常曲折，可我们还是称之为海峡，并且根据麦哲伦的

any rate, he named it Fireland, which in Spanish is Tierra del Fuego. The Indians he saw on the right, which is now the southern part of Argentina, had such big feet he called them the big-feet people, which is "Patagonians."

For hundreds of years other ships followed this same way through that Magellan had taken, for though some went entirely around the outmost island at the tip of South America—the tip called Cape Horn—it was so stormy that way and so rough and dangerous that most ships used the strait. On this strait a little town grew up—a sort of filling station—just to supply ships with provisions they needed to keep on with their voyage, for there were no other places anywhere near, and it was a long voyage down South America on the Atlantic side and up again on the Pacific side. This little town was called Sandy Point, which in Spanish was Punta Arenas. It is the farthest south city in the whole World. As most ships now go through the Panama Canal, Punta Arenas does less business as a filling station, but a new business is taking the place of filling. They raise sheep on Tierra del Fuego, and the wool is brought to Punta Arenas to be shipped to other parts of the World.

名字，将其命名为"麦哲伦海峡"。经过此处的时候，他看到左手边的陆地上有许多的火堆，那些火堆，究竟是如今不再燃烧的火山喷发出来的，还是印第安人点燃的，就没人知道了。反正，后来他把那儿叫作"火地岛"，而在西班牙语里，则叫"迪拉德尔菲格"。而在右边的陆地上，即如今阿根廷的南部，他看到印第安人都长着一双大脚，因此称这些印第安人为"大脚族"，在西班牙语里，就叫"巴塔哥尼亚人"。

后来的数百年里，其他船只都是沿着与麦哲伦相同的路线从大西洋驶入太平洋的，因为尽管也有一些船只完全绕过了南美洲最底下的那个岛屿（南美洲的最底端叫作合恩角），但那条航线经常刮起暴风雨，海浪汹涌，危险重重，所以绝大多数船只都是经由这条海峡来去。于是，海峡沿岸逐渐形成了一个小镇（这是一种补给站），给过往船只补充继续航行所需的给养，因为附近没有任何一个可以获得补给的地方，而船只到达这里时，已经沿着南美洲的大西洋海岸向南航行了很远的距离，沿太平洋海岸向北则还有很长的一段航程。这个小镇，叫作"桑迪角"，在西班牙语里叫作"彭塔阿雷纳斯"。它是整个世界上位置最南的一座城市。由于如今绝大多数船只都是取道巴拿马海峡，因此作为一个补给站的彭塔阿雷纳斯港，业务量已经大大减少了，不过，一种新的行业也正在取代原来的补给业务。人们开始在火地岛上养绵羊，然后把羊毛送到彭塔阿雷纳斯，再运送到世界其他地区去。

24 The Bridge Across the Ocean

When you go to Europe you have to take two things with you besides your ticket and your luggage. I wonder if you can guess what they are. You have to take plenty of money, but not of your country, as it wouldn't be any good, but of the kind used in the country to which you are going; and the second thing you have to have is a passport. A passport is a little book with only one picture in it—your own—and very few pages. The reading is not a story—it gives you permission to land in the country to which you are going. It is like a ticket of admission: Admit only the person whose picture is in the book. They won't let you go aboard the ship or airplane unless you have a passport, and they won't let you get off the ship unless you have a passport.

It is about 3,000 miles across the Atlantic Ocean from New York, the largest city in the New World, to London, the largest city in the Old World.

Columbus took over a month to cross the Atlantic Ocean from Europe to America.

We can cross in less than a week by ship.

We can cross in less than a day by airplane!

But there is something that crosses the ocean faster than that and does it every day and is always on time. You would never guess what it is. It's the sun. The sun crosses from London to New York in five hours and does it every day.

第24章　跨海大桥

如果要到欧洲去的话，那么除了船票和行李之外，你们还必须带上两种东西才行。不知道大家猜不猜得出，这两种东西是什么。你们必须带很多的钱，但不是你们本国的钱，而是大家打算前往的那个国家的钱，因为你们本国的钱到了那里以后就没法使用了，大家必须带上的第二种东西，就是护照。所谓的护照，就是一个小小的本子，上面只有一张你们自己的照片，和寥寥的几页纸。护照上面所写的文字，可不是一个故事，而是让你们进入所去国的许可。这就像是一张入场券，只允许护照上印有照片的那个人进入。除非拥有护照，否则人们就不会让你们上船或者上飞机；除非你们拥有护照，否则人们也是不会允许你们下船或者下飞机的。

从"新大陆"最大的城市纽约，横跨大西洋，到达"旧大陆"最大的城市伦敦，有差不多三千英里远。

哥伦布花了一个多月的时间，才横渡大西洋，从欧洲到达美洲。

我们如今坐轮船的话，则用不了一个星期。

可要是坐飞机的话，连一天都用不了！

不过，有一种东西，横渡大西洋的速度更快，并且每天都在横渡，还始终都会准时到达大洋彼岸。你们永远都猜不出来。这种东西，就是太阳。太阳每天都会从伦敦开始，五个小时后便会照射到纽约，并且天天如此。

The people in London, when the sun reaches its highest point in the sky over their heads, set their clocks at 12 o'clock—midday. Five hours later the sun has reached New York and the people there set their watches at 12 o'clock too, because that's what 12 o'clock means: "when the sun is highest in the sky." While the sun has been crossing the ocean all the watches and clocks in London have been ticking along, so it is 5 o'clock in London when it is 12 o'clock here in New York. That is, London clocks are five hours ahead of our clocks.

When you sail for London you have to set your watch ahead each night when you go to bed, so that when you reach London your watch will be five hours ahead of the time you started with. You will then be just right with London time when you reach London. When you sail back you must put your watch back too. If you telephoned to London now at 10

海洋

什么东西五个小时就可以横越大洋，并且天天如此呢

伦敦人把太阳正好运行到他们的头顶、达到最高位置的时候，定为钟表上的十二点，也就是正午。五个小时后，太阳到达纽约上空，于是纽约人也把这个时候定为钟表上的十二点，因为十二点的意思，就是"太阳在空中处于最高位置的时候"。由于太阳在横跨大西洋的过程中，伦敦的所有钟表一直都在嘀嗒嘀嗒地走个不停，因此纽约这里十二点钟的时候，伦敦时间就已经是下午的五点了。也就是说，伦敦钟表上的时间，比美国纽约钟表上的时间要快上五个小时。

因此，当大家前往伦敦的时候，每天晚上睡觉前都得把手表拨快才行，这样，到达伦敦的时候，你们手表上的时间才会比出发时的时间快上五个小时。而当大家返回美国的时候，也必须把手表调慢才行。假如大家在此刻的上午十点钟往伦敦打电话，并且问接电话的人那边是什么时间的话，他们就会回答你们说，那边已经是下午三点钟了。

船上的大钟，虽然样子跟我们家里的闹钟毫无二致，但报时的方式却不一样。

o'clock in the morning and asked them what time it was they would say 3 P.M.

The clocks on board ship look the same as our clocks at home, but they strike differently. Our clocks, as you know, strike once for 1 o'clock, twice for 2 o'clock, and so on, but on board ship a clock strikes two bells for each hour from 1 o'clock to 4 o'clock, when it strikes eight times. It strikes one bell more for the in-between halves of the hour. Then it starts all over again—one stroke at 4:30, two at 5, and so on—never more than eight strokes altogether.

"A watch" on board ship doesn't mean only a watch that you put in your pocket. It means something else too. A ship doesn't stop going at night. A ship must keep on going, night as well as day, so the men, the officers and crew who run the ship, take turns at running the ship, as they can't stay awake all the time, and their turns are called "watches," because they must be wide awake and watching when it is their "watch." Some men are running the engines, some are steering the ship, and some are just watching out to see that they do not run into other ships while the others are sleeping.

How can the captain, when he leaves New York, know the way to go to London, when all the ocean in front of him as far as he can see on every side is just broad flat water or rolling waves or thick fog, with no sign-posts to guide him?

Right in front of the steering-wheel is a box in which is a little pointer that, no matter how much the ship rises and falls, or twists and turns, or rears and plunges, always points one way. The box with its pointer is called a compass. You know what a magnet is—a

大家都知道，家里的钟表响一声表示一点，响两声表示二点，并且依此类推，可轮船上的大钟却不同，从一点到四点的时候，每响两声代表一个小时，即到四点钟的时候，钟会响上八声。而在整点之间的半点钟，钟还会再敲一次。接下来，就会重复这一过程，即四点半钟敲响一次，五点钟响两声，依此类推，也就是说，反正大钟的每个整点最多不会响过八声。

船上的"值班人员"，可不单是指你们口袋里的那种怀表[1]。它还有别的意思。轮船在夜间也会继续航行。不论昼夜，轮船都必须一直往前行驶，驾船的船长和船员们也不能始终不睡觉，因此他们会轮流驾驶船只，这种轮流制度，就叫"值班"，而这些人在"值班"的时候，必须完全清醒，密切注视着前方才行。其中有些人负责轮船的发动机，有些人只是负责瞭望，以免撞上其他轮船，而其他的人却都呼呼大睡去了。

那么，船长在驶离了纽约之后，在面前的大海极目所至四周全都是平坦而白茫茫的水面，或者巨浪滔天，或者浓雾弥漫，又没有路标可以指引的情况下，他又怎么知道哪个方向是往伦敦而去的呢？

在船只舵轮的前面，有一个盒子，里面有一根指针，无论轮船在海上是下沉还是上浮、是歪歪扭扭还是左转右转、是高高立起还是一头往下扎去，这根指针始终

---

[1] 英语中的"手表，怀表"（watch）一词，还有"值班（人员），密切观察（的人员）"等义，作者在此是提醒小朋友不要把watch的这两种意思混淆起来。

little thing like a small horseshoe that pulls needles and nails to it. Well, near the North Pole there is a spot on the World like a magnet and this spot pulls all the compasses on the World toward it. So that spot on the World that pulls all the compasses toward it is called the Magnetic pole, though there is no pole. This Magnetic pole is where the stem would be if the World were an orange or an apple, though there is no stem.

The captain knows from the way the compass points which way he must go to reach England. He doesn't follow the way the compass points—that would bring him to the Magnetic pole.

When it's fine weather at sea the passengers have a fine time too. They play games, they dance, they take photographs, they write letters and post-cards, they read books, they eat five meals a day, they lie in long steamer chairs wrapped up in rugs, and look out over the ocean or talk or sleep. Now and then porpoises, that look like big fishes, swim along the side or just ahead of the ship, and jump out of the water and dive in again, as if they were running a race with the ship. Occasionally a mountain of ice may be seen floating in the sea, many many times bigger than the ship, called an iceberg. It has broken away from the frozen part of the ocean far up north and floated down. And then at times a whale like a little island may rise out of the water, spout a fountain into the air, then sink out of sight again.

Sometimes, but not often, the sea is so smooth it is like glass, no wind and no waves except those which the ship itself makes. That's why the Atlantic Ocean is sometimes

都指向同一个方向。这个带有指针的盒子，就叫"指南针"。大家都知道磁铁吧，那是一种有点儿像是小型的马蹄铁，能够吸住针啊、钉子之类物品的东西。注意，地球的北极有一个地方，就像磁铁一样，吸引着世界上所有的指南针全都指向那个地方。所以，让全世界所有指南针都指向它的那个地方，就叫"磁北极"，可实际上，那里并没有什么"极点"。如果把地球看成是一个橙子或者一个苹果的话，那么这个"磁北极"就是橙子或者苹果的柄了，当然，那里实际上也是没有什么"柄"的。

根据指南针所指的方向，船长便知道轮船必须朝哪个方向行驶，才能到达英国了。当然，船长并不是驾驶着轮船跟着指南针所指的方向前进，因为那样的话，轮船到达的就是"磁北极"了啊。

如果海上风平浪静、天气晴朗的话，船上的乘客就能够尽情地玩乐了。他们可以玩游戏，可以跳舞，可以拍照，可以写信、写贺卡，可以看书，可以每天吃上五顿饭，可以裹着毯子躺在甲板上的折叠式长椅上，远眺海景、与人交谈或者睡觉。时不时会有一种像大鱼似的海豚，在轮船的一侧或者在船头游过，跃出海面，然后再一头扎进海中，仿佛在跟轮船比赛似的。偶尔还可以看见巨大的冰块在海上漂浮着，它们的尺寸都要比轮船大上许多倍，叫作"冰山"。这种冰山，是从遥远北方大海上封冻的地方脱落下来，并一路向南漂浮过来的。而且，偶尔还会有大如小岛般的鲸鱼跃出水面，向空中喷出一道水雾，然后又沉到水下去不见了。

有时，海面也会平滑如镜，除了轮船本身激起的浪花之外，可以说是风平浪

called "The Big Pond." But then again the wind blows, clouds rise, rain pours down, the waves rise up higher and higher until the sea is all moving hills and valleys of water, and the ship pitches up and down and rolls and tosses from side to side. It is necessary to put fences on the dining tables to keep the dishes from sliding off, and of course many people are seasick. The ship slides down one water hill and rises up the next water hill, and, big though it is, seems almost to turn over. But it seldom does turn over or sink unless it runs into an iceberg or another ship and smashes a hole in its side.

But it isn't rough weather that the captain fears most of all. It is a sea fog, especially when he knows there are other ships near, for when there is a fog he cannot see his way at all. It is like groping your way about in the dark at night, only the ship has no arms. The captain slows the ship down till it barely moves. He starts a big, deep horn a-blowing by clock-work, and it blows about once a minute regularly day and night as long as the fog lasts, which may be for several days, while sailors peer over the ship's side listening and looking. They can hear another ship's fog-horn some distance away, but often they cannot see another ship only a few feet away. When at last the fog clears off, land may be in sight—England.

We can tell land is near long before we actually see it. How do you suppose? Large white birds called sea-gulls come out to meet the ship, but not as friends come out to welcome you. They are looking for food that they know is dumped overboard from the ship's kitchen. Just before we do land a man comes out in a small boat to meet the big

静，可这种情况并不常见。人们有时会把大西洋称为"大池塘"，指的就是大西洋风平浪静的时候。不过，海上一会儿就是风起云涌了，大雨滂沱，海浪越卷越高，整个大海全都变成移动着的水山水谷，轮船则会上上下下，大起大伏，左摇右摆起来。轮船餐桌的四周都必须装上栏杆才行，以免盘子碗碟掉落下去。自然，许多人还会晕船。轮船从一个浪尖上滑行下去，然后再爬升到另一个浪尖顶上，尽管轮船很大，可看上去就像要翻了似的。不过，轮船很少倾覆或者沉没，除非是撞上了冰山或其他的船只，把船上撞出一个大洞来才会如此。

但是，船长们最害怕的，可不是海上的恶劣天气。他们最害怕的，是海上的大雾，而当他们知道附近还有其他船只也在航行的时候，则尤其如此了，因为起雾之后，他们根本就看不清前面的水路。这就像是大家在伸手不见五指的晚上摸索着走路似的，只是轮船没有胳膊伸出去摸索罢了。在这种情况下，船长便会让轮船的速度慢下来，直到差不多相当于停下来。接着，船长便会启动一个用发条吹响的、又大又长的喇叭，并且差不多每分钟鸣响一次，不分昼夜，直到大雾消退，这种大雾，可能会持续好几天呢。而船员们则会在船舷的两侧仔细倾听，并且仔细观察。他们听得见不远处航行的另一条船只鸣响的雾角，但经常要到两船相距只有几英尺远的时候，才能看得到对方。待大雾终于消退之后，陆地便会映入眼帘：那就是英格兰。

此时，就算是还没有看到，我们也知道陆地不远了。你们觉得，这是为什么呢？有一种叫作海鸥的白色大鸟，会到海上来迎接船只，当然，这种迎接可不像是

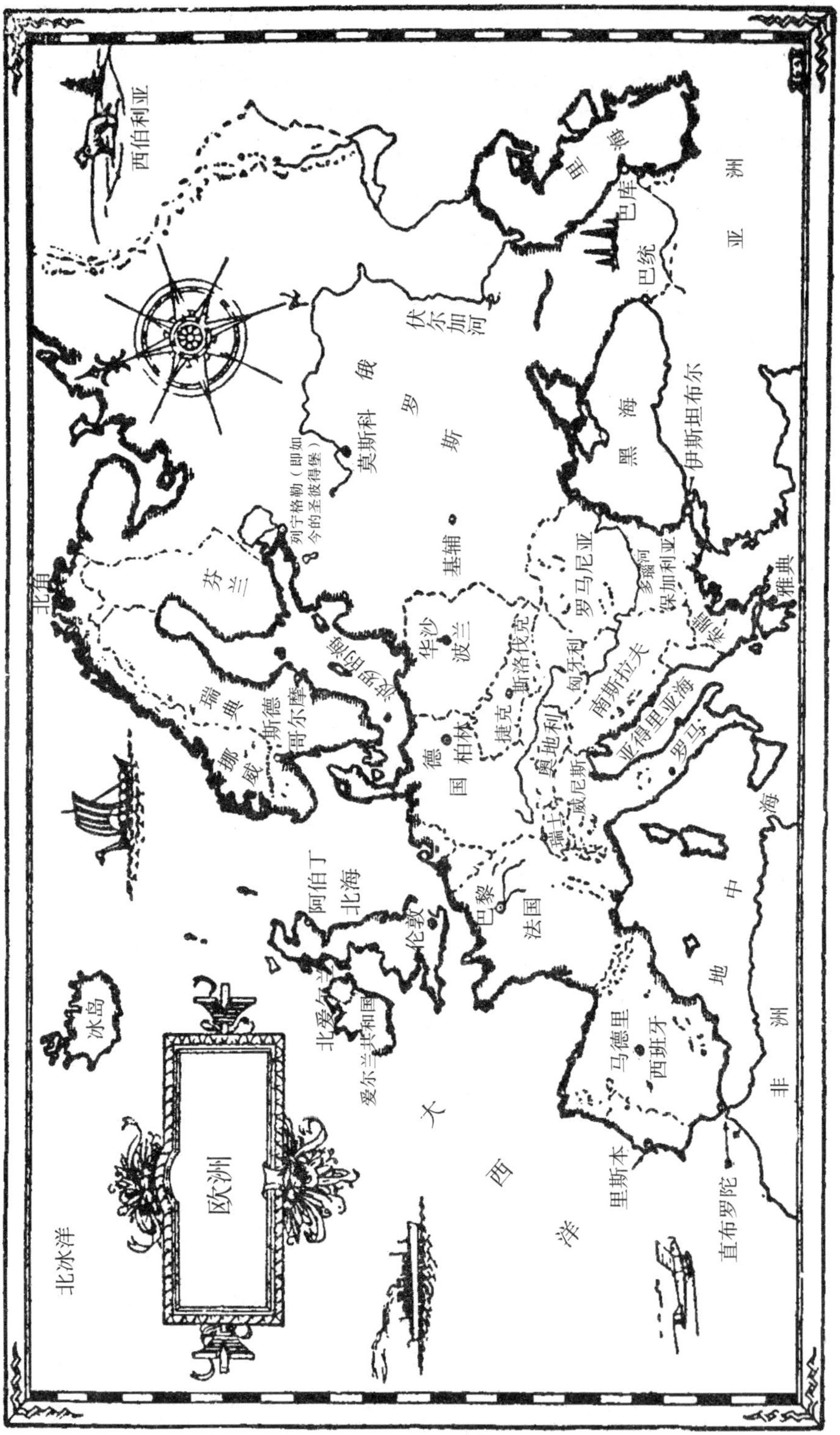

西伯利亚

亚洲

里海

巴库

巴统

伊斯坦布尔

黑海

俄罗斯

伏尔加河

莫斯科

北角

芬兰

瑞典

挪威

哥尔摩

列宁格勒（即如
今的圣彼得堡）

基辅

华沙

波兰

斯洛伐克

罗马尼亚

多瑙河

保加利亚

南斯拉夫

雅典

德国

柏林

捷克

奥地利

匈牙利

威尼斯

亚得里亚海

罗马

阿伯丁

北海

伦敦

巴黎

法国

冰岛

北爱尔兰共和国

爱尔兰共和国

大西洋岸

马德里

西班牙

里斯本

直布罗陀

地中海

非洲

北冰洋

欧洲

ship. The big ship doesn't stop; it lets down over the side a ladder made of rope and the man grabs hold of the rope, kicks the boat away, and climbs aboard. Who do you suppose he is? Why do you suppose they take him aboard? He is the new captain of the ship. He is called the pilot, and it is his job to bring the ship into the harbor. A big ship is so big it can't sail into the dock itself; it has to have small boats called tugboats push and pull it. A broad gang-plank is laid like a bridge across from the dock to the deck and the passengers and their baggage go ashore. The people in England speak English, so you can ask questions and understand their answers, though their language sounds strange to us and our language sounds funny to them. They call it "an American accent." You must show your passport and you must open all your bags and let a man examine everything inside before he will let you go on. So you must have nothing you don't want him to see. This man is called a customs officer. You may have to pay for some things you have. This that you have to pay is called a "duty."

朋友们出来迎接你们啊。它们是出来寻找食物的,因为它们知道,轮船上的厨房会把剩饭剩菜倒进大海里。就在我们登陆之前,会有一个人驾驶着一条小船,出来迎接大型轮船。大轮船不会停下来,它只会在船舷一侧放下一架用绳索搭成的梯子,而那个人则会抓住绳梯,把那艘小船踢开,然后爬上大船。你们觉得,那个人是干什么的呢?你们觉得,轮船上的人为什么要他上船呢?那个人,就是大船的新船长,称为"领航员",他的职责,就是把轮船引入港口内。由于轮船体型巨大,因此它本身是没法直接驶到码头边上去的,所以,人们必须用一种叫作拖船的小船,又推又拉,才能让轮船靠岸。然后,人们会在码头和甲板之间架上一块像桥一样的跳板,乘客们便带着各自的行李,走过跳板上岸了。英国人说的是英语,因此大家有问题都可以问他们,也听得懂他们的回答,不过,他们的话音我们听起来会觉得很奇怪,而听到我们所说的话,他们也会觉得很好笑呢。他们会说我们有"美国口音"。大家必须出示自己的护照,必须打开所有的行李,让一个人彻底检查完,他才会让你们走。因此,你们必须确保自己没有携带违禁物品才行。这个人,叫作海关关员。你们可能还会因为携带了某些东西而要付钱呢。大家可能必须支付的这笔钱,就叫作"关税"。

25 The Land of the Angles

England is an island.

Angles once lived on the island—no, not Angels—but people called Angles.

So it was called Angle-land.

We now spell it England But we call it "Ingland."

There are, however, two other countries on the island—Wales and Scotland—as well as England; so we should call the whole island "Great Britain." Next door to the island of Great Britain is another island. It is Ireland.

A ship, when it reaches England, cannot land its passengers wherever it chooses. There are only certain places. The shore may be too shallow and the ship would run aground and turn over, or the shore may be too rocky or too high with cliffs. Most people who go to England usually land on the west side at a place called Liverpool—Liver pool: what a peculiar name!—or at Southampton, which we can tell from the name is on the south side of England; or at London, which is on the east side. If they land at London the ship must go up a river spelled Thames but called "Temz." English people spell many things one way and pronounce them another. The Thames runs right through London, but big ships cannot go up any farther than London Bridge. Have you ever played the game "London Bridge is Falling Down"? Well, London Bridge has fallen down several times, but each

第25章 盎格鲁人之国

英格兰是一个小岛。

这个岛上，曾经生活着"盎格鲁人"，不，不是"天使"，而是一个叫作"盎格鲁"的民族[1]。

于是，这里便被称为"盎格鲁人之地"，如今我们则称之为"英格兰"。

然而，这个岛上除了英格兰，还有另外两个国家，即威尔士和苏格兰，于是，人们便将整个岛屿称为"大不列颠岛"。紧挨着大不列颠岛，还有另一个岛屿，叫作爱尔兰。

一艘船只抵达英格兰后，无论选择什么地方，都是没法让船上的乘客登岸的。那里可以登岸的地方不多。英格兰的沿海地区，要么太浅，船只会搁浅、倾覆，要么就是岩石众多或者悬崖峭立。绝大多数前往英格兰的人，要么是在该岛西部一个名字古怪、叫作"利物浦"的地方，或者是在南安普敦（从名称我们就能看出，这里位于英格兰的南部）上岸，要么就是在英格兰东部的伦敦登陆的。假如在伦敦靠岸，那么船只还必须逆着一条叫作泰晤士的河流而上才行。许多的东西，英国人拼写起来是一回事，可说出来却又是另外一回事了。泰晤士河从伦敦市穿城而过，但

---

[1] 在英语中，"盎格鲁"（Angle）与"天使"（Angel）两个单词词形相近。

time it has been built up again; and the London Bridge that is there now I don't believe will ever fall.

London was a city when Christ was born, but it was then so small and so far off that Christ never heard of it. London is now the largest city i.t.w.W.

New York is tall, London is broad. New York buildings climb to the sky, fifty, seventy, a hundred stories high. London buildings seldom go higher than a few stories, but the city spreads out in every direction, mile after mile. People travel about London chiefly on buses, double-decker ones with seats on top as well as inside, but they also travel about London on trains that run under the ground.

London is the capital of England. The capit-o-1 of England—the building—is, of course, in London and it is on the banks of the Thames. It is called the Houses of

"伦敦桥要倒了！"

许多大型轮船却只能到达伦敦桥那里，之后就没法再逆流而上了。你们有没有玩过"伦敦桥要倒了"这个游戏呢？注意，伦敦桥倒了好几次，可每次倒塌之后又重新建好了，如今伦敦桥仍然屹立在那里，而我也相信，它永远都不会再倒塌呢。

基督降生的时候，伦敦就已经是一座城市了，可因为当时该市还很小，并且地理位置遥远，因此基督才从未听说过这座城市。如今，伦敦却是全世界最大的城市了。

纽约是一座高楼大厦林立的城市，伦敦则是一个不断向四周扩张的城市。纽约的建筑物都高耸入云，有五十、七十甚至一百层高。伦敦的建筑物通常都不高，只有寥寥数层，可整个城市却向四面八方扩展，一英里一英里地扩张。在伦敦旅行时，人们主要是乘坐公共汽车，就是那种上面和里面都有座位的双层巴士，不过，人们也可以乘坐地铁列车到伦敦的各处去。

伦敦是英国的首都。英国的国会大厦自然也位于伦敦，并且坐落在泰晤士河边。英国的国会大厦叫作"议会大楼"，也就是"议事的地方"。这里非但是英国人议事的地方，也是他们为英国制定法律的地方。英国虽由国王统治，但人民却

Parliament, which means the Houses of Talk. It is the place where people not only talk but make the laws for England. A king rules over England, but the English people send men to Parliament to make their laws. As I had lived in sight of our Capitol in Washington for many years, I thought all capitols had to have domes, just as all cows had horns. It was therefore a shock for me to see that the English Capitol, the Houses of Parliament, had no dome—only square towers with a large clock in one of them, with a huge bell, called "Big Ben," that strikes the hours.

There is, however, another great building in London that does have a dome like our Capitol. But that building is a church and it is called St. Paul's. Indeed, it is said that the dome of our Capitol at Washington was copied from St. Paul's, for St. Paul's was built long before there was a Capitol at Washington, long before there was a Washington, and even long before there was a United States. They once had a great fire in London—they still call it the Great Fire, for it burned up most of the city. That was about three hundred years ago. Then a man with the name of a bird, Wren—Christopher Wren—built up much of the city that had been burned down. He built beautiful churches and other buildings; so people say it was well the old city was burned down, for it gave them the chance to make a beautiful city. St. Paul's was one of the churches that Wren built.

During World War II thousands of buildings were destroyed

大本钟

用于报时的大本钟

派代表加入议会来制定法律。由于多年里一直看着美国的国会大厦，因此我曾经以为，各国的国会大厦一定全都建有穹顶，就像牛全都有角似的。所以，在看到英国的国会大厦，即议会大楼没有穹顶时，我还吃了一惊呢。英国的议会大楼上，只建有几座四四方方的塔楼，其中一座塔楼上还安着一座大钟，叫作"大本钟"，是用来报时的。

然而，伦敦还有一座了不起的建筑，上面的确建有一个像美国国会大厦那样的穹顶。可那栋建筑是一座教堂，叫作"圣保罗大教堂"。实际上，据说美国华盛顿国会大厦上的那个穹顶，就是仿照"圣保罗大教堂"的穹顶修建的，因为圣保罗大教堂建成的时间，要远早于华盛顿建起国会大厦、远早于美国建起华盛顿市，甚至远早于美国建国呢。伦敦曾经发生过一场大火灾，人们如今仍然称之为"伦敦大火"，因为那场火灾把伦敦绝大部分城区都烧成了平地。那场火灾，发生在大约三百年之前。后来，一个叫作克里斯托弗·雷恩的人，重建了城中被大火烧毁的许多地方，"雷恩"这个名字，本是指一种叫作"鹪鹩"的鸟类。他修建了许多美丽的教堂，以及其他的建筑，因此，如今人们还说，伦敦老城被烧毁是件好事，因为火灾给了他们兴建一座美丽城市的机会。圣保罗大教堂，就是雷恩修建的教堂之一。

在第二次世界大战期间，伦敦有成千上万座房屋都被德军投下的炸弹摧毁了。

by bombs dropped on London by the Germans. Many of Christopher Wren's churches were among the buildings burned or smashed by the bombs, but he had built so many that there are still some left. The people of London called these terrible bombings the Blitz. Great numbers of people were killed. The Blitz will be remembered, like the Great Fire, for hundreds of years to come, but no one can ever say, as they said about the Great Fire, that it was a good thing for the city. The only good thing about the Blitz was the bravery shown by the people of London.

A church that Wren didn't build, a very old one, is called Westminster Abbey. Westminster Abbey is not only a church; it is also a tomb for famous people. In it are buried the most famous English people who have ever lived and died—kings and queens, great writers, great poets, great musicians, great soldiers. After World War I a soldier who had died on the battlefield in France, but whose name no one knew, was buried in Westminster Abbey to honor all those who had died without name or fame for a great cause. The place is called the Tomb of the Unknown Soldier.

In Westminster Abbey is a chair in which all the kings of England sit when they are crowned kings. It is called the Coronation

圣保罗大教堂有一个像华盛顿美国国会大厦那样的穹顶

被炸弹焚毁或者炸毁的房屋中，也包括了克里斯托弗·雷恩兴建的许多教堂，不过，由于他修建了许多这样的教堂，因此其中一部分仍然幸存下来了。伦敦人将那一场场可怕的轰炸总称为"大轰炸"。许多人都在大轰炸中丧了命。虽然像"伦敦大火"一样，"伦敦大轰炸"在接下来的数百年间也会被人们牢记心间，但没有人可以像评价"伦敦大火"那样，说"大轰炸"对伦敦来说是件好事。"伦敦大轰炸"唯一的好处，就是让伦敦人民体现出了大无畏的精神。

伦敦有一座历史非常悠久的教堂，叫作威斯敏斯特教堂，但它并不是雷恩修建的。威斯敏斯特教堂并非只是一座教堂，还是许多英国名人的墓地呢。这座教堂里面，安葬着英国有史以来一些最著名的人物，比如国王和王后、伟大的作家、伟大的诗人、伟大的音乐家、伟大的战士等。第一次世界大战过后，一位在法国战场上捐躯的无名士兵也被安葬在威斯敏斯特教堂里，以此来纪念那些为了一种伟大的事业而献身的无名烈士。那个地方，就叫作"无名烈士墓"。

威斯敏斯特教堂里有一把椅子，是英国所有国王加冕[1]登基时都坐过的。这把

---

[1] 加冕（crown），指把皇冠戴到国王的头上，以代表国王登基、掌握大权的一种仪式。西方信奉基督教的君主制国家里，国王加冕时，通常都是由教皇来将皇冠戴到国王的头上。

Chair. Underneath the seat of the Coronation Chair is a large stone. Why the stone underneath the chair seat? Well, hundreds of years ago the country North of England named Scotland was separate from England. When the kings of Scotland were crowned they used a large stone for a seat. So when England and Scotland became one country, the people took the stone of Scotland and put it under the Coronation Chair of England, so that the king could sit on both seats while he was crowned king of both countries.

The oldest building in London, built long before the Great Fire, is one which from its name sounds like only part of a building. It is called the "Tower." In the times long ago the Tower was a prison in which were put many famous people. Even princes and queens were put in this prison, and some of them were put to death. It is now a museum where are kept many interesting curiosities of those days—the steel armor that soldiers and their horses, and even their dogs, wore; the block and ax with which prisoners' heads were cut off; and wonderful jewels which the kings wore in their crowns—huge diamonds and rubies as big as walnuts. The Queen's crown is there on a white satin pillow. It is studded with jewels and a huge diamond called the "Koh-i-noor," which means "mountain of light." This stone was supposed to bring bad luck to any man who owned it, so

加冕宝座

国王同时坐在两个宝座之上

椅子，叫作"加冕宝座"。加冕宝座之下，是一块巨大的石头。为什么加冕宝座下要放这样一块大石头呢？注意，几百年前，英格兰北边那个叫作苏格兰的国家曾经是独立于英格兰的。苏格兰国王加冕时，是用一块巨石当作宝座的。因此，待后来英格兰和苏格兰统一成了一个国家之后，人们便把苏格兰的那块巨石拿过来，放到了英格兰的加冕宝座之下，以示英王可以坐在两个宝座之上，加冕成为两国的君主。

伦敦城内最古老的建筑，是距"伦敦大火"很久以前修建起来的，而从名称来看，它似乎还只是一栋建筑物的一部分呢，这座建筑，叫作"伦敦塔"。在古时候，伦敦塔曾经是一座监狱，里面关押过许多著名的人物。这座监狱，连王子和女王也关押过，其中有些人后来还都被处死了呢。如今，这里已是一座博物馆，保存着当时许多有意思的奇珍异物：有旧时士兵身上所穿以及他们的战马甚至是小狗所披的铁制盔甲，有砍掉囚犯脑袋的木砧和斧头，有国王们所戴皇冠之上镶嵌着的奇妙珠宝，比如巨型钻石和大如胡桃的红宝石。那里也保存着英国女王的王冠，它放在一个绸缎垫座上。那顶王冠上装饰着许多珠宝，还有一颗叫作"科依诺尔"的巨型钻石，"科依诺尔"的意思，就是"光明之山"。这颗钻石，据说会给拥有它的任何男子带来噩运，所以如今拥有它的才是一个女人，即英国女王。伦敦塔里的卫兵，叫作"禁卫军"，如果有人强行打开存放珠宝的盒子，伦敦塔的各个小门与大

a woman now owns it—the Queen. The guards of the Tower are called "Beef-Eaters" and should any one break into the cases in which are the jewels, the doors and gates of the Tower would automatically clang shut and the thief be caught a prisoner.

Did you ever collect stones or stamps, butterflies or coins? Well, grown-ups have collected treasures and curiosities from all over the World and brought them together in a wonderful museum, and the largest i.t.w.W. It is called the British Museum.

It is said that if all the streets in London were strung out in one line they would reach round the World. No one could ever know the names of all the London streets, not even the London policemen, who are called "Bobbies" and who are supposed to know everything. They may have to look for a street in a little book which they carry in an inside pocket. But every one knows the names of some of the streets— they are either so famous or so funny. There is Threadneedle Street and Cheapside. There is Pall Mall and Piccadilly, where are fine houses, hotels, clubs, and palaces. There is Fleet, Strand, Regent, and Bond Streets, which are shopping streets. There is Oxford Circus and Piccadilly Circus, but there is no "circus" there. A circus is simply a big open space where streets cross, and which we should call a Square or a Circle.

他们被称为"禁卫军"

门就会自动关上，而窃贼则只能束手就擒了。

大家有没有收集过漂亮的石子、邮票、蝴蝶标本或者是硬币呢？注意，大人们已经收集到了世界各地的珠宝和奇珍异物，并且将它们集中存放在一个令人称奇、属于全球最大的博物馆里。这座博物馆，就叫"大英博物馆"。

据说，要是将伦敦所有的街道都排成一列的话，其长度可以环绕地球一周。没有人对伦敦的所有大街小巷了如指掌，连伦敦的警察也不是全都清楚，他们被称为"博比"，本来是应该什么都知道的。他们可能也得掏出口袋里随身携带着的一个小本子，到那上面去查找某条街道呢。不过，其中有些街道却是众所周知的，因为它们或是大名鼎鼎，或是非常有意思。比如，蓓尔美尔街和皮卡迪利街就是如此，因为这两条大街上林立着许多豪宅、旅馆、夜总会和宫殿。再如弗利特街、河岸大街、摄政街和邦德大街，它们都是赫赫有名的商业街。还有牛津广场和皮克迪利广场，不过，这两个地方当然没有"马戏团"[1]。广场只是一个有街道交汇的大空地，我们本该称之为街心广场或者环形街道的。

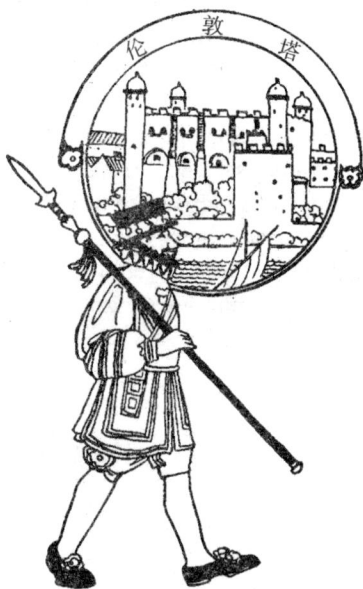

[1] 英语中，circus既可指"圆形广场"，亦可指"马戏团"。

26 The Land of the Angles (continued)

I once asked an Englishman if he lived in London.

"Why does every American think that every Englishman lives in London?" he replied—and he sounded rather vexed. "There are other places in England besides London.

There is *Chester* and Man *Chester*,

There is Nor *wich* and Har *wich*,

There is Ox *ford* and Guild *ford*,

There is Birm *ingham* and Nott *ingham*,

There is Cam *bridge* and Tun *bridge*,

There is North *ampton* and South *ampton*,

There is Ply *mouth* and Yar *mouth* and Wey *mouth* . . ."

And as he gasped for breath I cried, "Please don't tell me all the 'wiches and 'fords and 'mouths in England."

"Well," said he, "there are over thirty million people in England who don't live in London and I am one of them."

But nearly every Englishman, no matter where he does live, goes to London some time in his life. You can get to London in a day from any place in England, for the island is so small and trains are so fast.

第26章　盎格鲁人之国（续）

我曾经问一个英国人，看他是不是住在伦敦。

"为什么每一个美国人都会以为，每一个英国人都是住在伦敦呢？"他回答道，并且显得很生气。"除了伦敦，英国还有很多的地方呢。

有切斯特和曼彻斯特，

有诺威奇和哈威奇，

有牛津和吉尔福德[1]，

有伯明翰和诺丁汉，

有剑桥和唐桥，

有北安普敦和南安普敦，

有普利茅斯、雅茅斯和韦茅斯……"

趁着他换气的时候，我叫了一声："千万别把英国所有带'威奇'、'福德'和'茅斯'的地方全说给我听啊。"

"好吧，"他说，"反正，英国有三千多万人口没有住在伦敦，而我恰好就是

---

[1] 这里每一行所列举的地名，后缀都是相同的。Oxford（牛津）一词中的ford本指"浅滩，渡口"，我国前人将其意译为"津"（也是"渡口"的意思），因此才与后面音译的Guildford（吉尔福德）显得不一样，但实际上它们都含有ford这个词尾。

Railroads were invented by an Englishman, and some of the fastest trains i.t.w.W. run in England. Their trains look different from ours. They seem much smaller and lighter and the cars are divided into rooms instead of being one long room like ours. Each room has half the seats facing forward and half facing backward, so that half of the people have to ride backward. Some of these rooms are labeled "1st class," but most are "3rd class." People pay more to ride in a 1st class room than they do in a 3rd class room. The 1st class has cushioned seats and there is more space for each person. The 3rd class has wooden seats without cushions, and more people are put in a room. The English railroad trains run on the left hand side of the road. Most Americans are right-handed, and we say "Keep to the Right," but most Englishmen are right-handed too, yet they say "Keep to the Left." You would be arrested in England if you drove or rode on the right hand side as we do here.

Our country roads usually have fences alongside, but in England the country roads usually have hedges. Sometimes the hedges are like those that grew up round *Sleeping Beauty's* castle, so thick and so high that you cannot see through them or over them, and the houses behind them are hidden, all except perhaps the roof. Sometimes the roofs are quite different

要是驾车靠马路的右侧行驶，
大家就会被警察逮起来

其中的一员呢。"

不过，无论住在哪个地方，几乎每个英国人在一生当中的某个时候，都会到伦敦去的。从英国国内的任何地方，大家都可以在一天之内抵达伦敦，因为大不列颠岛很小，而如今的火车跑得又那么快。

铁路是一个英国人发明出来的，而英国也拥有全球速度最快的火车。他们的火车，样子与美国的火车可不同。英国的火车，看上去要比美国的火车要小得多、轻得多，并且车厢里也被分隔成了一个个小房间，而不像美国的列车那样，每节车厢就是一个长长的房间。其中有些小间标上了"一等车厢"，但绝大多数小间都属于"三等车厢"。乘坐一等车厢的票价，要高于三等车厢的票价。一等车厢里的座位都是软席，每个人所占的空间也较大。三等车厢里的座位则是没有软垫的木制座位，并且每个小间里坐的乘客数量也比较多。英国的火车，都是靠铁路的左边行驶。绝大多数美国人都习惯于用右手，因此我们会说"靠右行驶"，而绝大多数英国人虽说也习惯于用右手，可他们却会说"靠左行驶"。要是在英国开车时也像在美国那样靠右行驶的话，大家就会被警察逮起来呢。

美国的公路两侧，通常都立有栅栏，可英国乡间公路的两侧，通常却是树木形

from ours—made of piles of straw, which are called "thatch." You would hardly think thatch roofs would keep the rain out, but they do; and you would think they would burn up easily, but they don't. The houses themselves are seldom built of wood, because there is very little wood in England to build them of. Almost all of them are built of stone which comes out of the ground, or brick made out of the ground. In America there is a great deal of wood, but in England there is little wood, for there are very few forests, hardly any big ones, and they are usually kept like a park. The country is so old the trees have nearly all been cut down. The trees that are left are so valuable that people do not often cut them down to use them for building houses. In America a wood house is cheaper than a stone or brick house. In England a stone or brick house is cheaper than one made of wood.

Among the sights which people go to see in England are the churches and cathedrals. Few churches in America are a hundred years old. There are few churches in England that are not a hundred years old, and many of the cathedrals are more nearly a thousand years old. Most of the people in England are Episcopalians, so most of the churches in England are Episcopal. In fact, the Episcopal Church is called the Church of England.

Two of the greatest universities in the world are in England. They play each other football, but not baseball. Instead of baseball they play a game called cricket, and they have rowing matches. One of these universities is on River Thames where oxen used to wade across or "ford" the river, and so is called Ox-ford; the other university is by the River Cam where a bridge crosses, so this is called Cam-bridge.

成的篱笆。有的时候，公路两侧的树篱会像《睡美人》[1]里面绕着城堡生长的树篱那样，长得又密又高，从中间和上面都无法透视，根本就看不到它们后面的房屋，可能充其量也只看得到树篱后面的房顶呢。当地房屋的屋顶完全与美国房屋的屋顶不同，它们都是用一堆堆的稻草盖成，叫作"茅屋"。你们可能很难相信，茅草屋顶能够避风挡雨，可它们的确能够，你们可能还会以为，茅屋很容易着火，其实却不是那样的。那些房子本身很少用木材建造，因为英国木材稀少，没法用树木来盖房子。几乎所有的房屋，都是用地上的石头修建起来的，或者是用泥土制成的砖块建造而成的。美国木材丰富，英国却没有什么木材，因为英国的森林面积很少，几乎没有什么大型森林，因此森林通常都是用作公园。该国历史非常悠久，因此那里的森林几乎都已经砍伐殆尽了。留下来的那些树木便变得极其珍贵，所以人们不常将它们砍伐下来去建房子。在美国，用木材建造一座房子的成本，比用石头或者砖块来建造房子的成本要低。而在英国，用石头或者砖块建造起来的房子，成本却比用木材建造出来的房子要低哩。

人们到英国去观光的景点，其中就包括了那里的教堂和大教堂。很少有哪座美国教堂的历史达到了一百年。可在英国，却是很少有哪座教堂的历史不到一百年，而且，许多大教堂的历史差不多都达到了一千年。由于英国绝大多数人都是圣公会

---

[1]　《睡美人》（Sleeping Beauty），欧洲著名的童话故事，讲述了一位公主因中魔咒而在城堡里沉睡百年、最后被一位王子吻醒的故事。这个童话有诸多版本，其中最著名的是法国作家夏尔·佩罗于1697年出版的《鹅妈妈的故事》中收录的版本，以及《格林童话》中的版本。

Many of the World's greatest writers whose stories you read and whose poetry you have learned lived in England, and the greatest English writer i.t.w.W., William Shakespeare, lived there at a place called Stratford-on-Avon.

But the chief business of England is "making things"—as the chief business of New England in America is "making things." In New England there is neither coal nor iron to make the things with; both have to be brought from somewhere else; but in Old England there is a great deal of both coal and iron. Coal makes the fire to run the machinery and iron makes the things; so in England they make everything that can be made of iron, from huge engines to small penknives. At Sheffield they make a great quantity of table knives and silver-plated ware called "Sheffield." Look at your own table knives and silver-plated ware and see if any of them have the label "Made in Sheffield" stamped on them.

In England they also make a great deal of cloth—cloth made of wool from the backs of sheep that are raised in England, and cloth made from cotton which is not grown in

索尔兹伯里大教堂

这是世界上最漂亮的一座教堂尖顶

教徒，因此英国的绝大多数教堂也都是圣公会教堂。事实上，圣公会还被称为"英国国教"呢。

有两所属于全世界最了不起的大学，都位于英国。这两所大学之间经常进行足球比赛，但不会进行棒球比赛。两校之间会进行一种叫作板球的比赛，并且还会举行划艇比赛。其中一所大学位于泰晤士河边，由于以前经常有牛在那里涉水过河，或者"渡过"河去，因此被称为"牛津"；另一所大学则位于剑河边上架有一座桥梁的地方，因此被称为"剑桥"。

世界上许多最伟大的作家，曾经都住在英国，大家也都看过他们所著的小说、背过他们所写的诗歌。全世界公认的、最伟大的英国作家威廉·莎士比亚，就住在英国一个叫作"埃文河畔斯特拉特福"的地方呢。

不过，英国最主要的产业还是"制造东西"，就跟美国新英格兰地区的主要业务也是"制造东西"一样。新英格兰地区没有制造业所需的煤和铁，两者都得从别的地方运过来；可在老英格兰，却有大量的煤和铁。煤炭可以燃烧，从而驱动机器，铁则可以制成其他物品，所以，英国人生产的，便是从巨型发动机到小铅笔刀的一切铁器。在设菲尔德，人们生产出了大量的餐刀和镀银器具，使得"设菲尔德"成了这些东西的代名词。看一看你们所用的餐刀和镀银器具，看上面有没有贴

England but brought there all the way from the United States.

There are farms in England too, but not enough is raised on the farms to feed the English people one day a week. Most of the food has to be brought to them from other countries across the sea. The English eat a great deal of mutton and roast beef. "The Roast Beef of Old England" has been celebrated in song and story. One story is that a certain King of England thought steak from the loin of the beef was so good that he called it "Sir Loin," as he would a knight or a lord, and that's why we still call it sirloin steak to-day. It's a good story but I'm afraid it isn't a true story.

The King of England is king of many more people than just those who live in Great Britain. Englishmen explored and conquered and settled in far-off places all over the World in times gone by. England owned countries in every continent and at first the laws for all these countries were made in London. Now, however, many of these countries that belonged to England govern themselves and make their own laws. They have become independent countries but they have kept the King of England as their king. This big family of countries all over the World with the same king, the king of England, is called the British Commonwealth of Nations. The country of Canada, that I told you about earlier, is a member of the British Commonwealth of Nations.

着"设菲尔德制造"的标签吧。

英国人也生产出了大量的布匹，其中既有用英国人喂养的羊身上的羊毛所制成的布料，也有用英国并未种植而是从美国一路运送过去的棉花所制成的布料。

英国也有农田，不过，该国全部农田种植的粮食，还不够所有英国人每周吃上一天的呢。绝大部分粮食，都得经由海上，从别的国家运来。英国人消耗掉了大量的羊肉和烤牛肉。人们所写的歌曲和小说中，还歌颂过"老英格兰的烤牛肉"呢。传说，有位英国国王觉得用牛腰肉做成的牛排是一道美味，因此还将这种牛排封为"腰肉勋爵"，就像他封别人为骑士或者勋爵似的，这也是我们如今仍然将那种牛排称为"沙朗牛排"的原因呢[1]。这是个很好的传说，但我觉得这恐怕并不是真事儿。

英国国王手下的臣民，可比仅仅生活在大不列颠岛上的人口要多得多。在过去的历史长河中，英国人曾经前往全球许多遥远之地，进行探险、征服和殖民。英国在各个大洲都有属国，而那些属国里的法律，起初也都是在伦敦制定出来的。然而，那些曾经臣服于英国的属国里，有许多都已经开始自治和制定本国的法律了。它们已经变成了独立自主的国家，但仍然承认英王就是它们的国王。这个由世界各地的国家组成、拥立同一个国王即英国国王的大家庭，就叫作"英联邦"。

---

[1] 沙朗牛排（sirloin steak），即用牛腰里脊肉做成的一种牛排，亦译"西冷牛排"。"沙朗"一词是音译，由"勋爵"（sir）与"腰肉"（loin）合成，如果意译的话，就是"腰肉勋爵牛排"了。

27 The Englishman's Neighbors

Here is the longest name I know. It has fifty-eight letters. It is LLANFAIRPWLLGW YNGYLLGOGERYCHWYRNDROBWLLLLANTYSILIOGOGOGOCH. It looks as if a child had been playing on a typewriter and had pounded out the letters at random. But it is a real name, the name of a town in Wales—a little country on the same island with England. It means "Church of St. Mary, in a hollow of white hazel, near a rapid whirlpool, and near St. Tysilios Church, which is near a red cave." People who live there or direct letters there usually call this place simply "Llanfairpwll," for short—and that's long enough. I'd rather call it "Gogogoch"! Wales is now a part of England, but once upon a time it was not. The people in Wales spoke a different language—a difficult language with many long names hard to pronounce, with many "ll's" and "w's" and "y's" all mixed together.

An English king at last conquered Wales, and in order to make the people he had conquered satisfied and happy he told them he would give them a ruler who was born

第27章　英国人的邻居

这里有一个我所知的最长的地名。它由五十八个英文字母组成，写出来就是：Llanfairpwllgwyngyllgogerychwyrndrobwllllantysiliogogogoch。这就好像是一个孩子在玩打字机，随机打出来的字母似的。不过，这可是一个真实的地名，是威尔士一个小镇的名称呢，威尔士是与英格兰同处于大不列颠岛上的一个小国。这个地名的意思，就是："红岩洞边圣田西路教堂湍急旋涡附近白榛树林山谷中的圣马利亚教堂。"不过，那里的人，或者是往那里写信的人，通常都只将其简称为"兰韦尔普尔"（Llanfairpwll），可就算如此，这个地名也是够长的了。我倒是宁愿叫它"果果果奇"（Gogogoch）呢！如今，威尔士已经成了英国的一部分，可在以前，它却不属于英国。那时，威尔士人说的是一种不同于英语的语言，那种语言很难，既有许多又长又拗口的名称，还夹杂着诸多的"ll"、"w"和"y"。

去往"红岩洞边圣田西路教堂湍急旋涡附近白榛树林山谷中的圣马利亚教堂"镇

我所知的最长地名，是威尔士一个小镇的名称

in Wales and couldn't even speak a word of English. The people in Wales were pleased at that, for they thought the king would give them one of their own countrymen to rule over them. But the king's own son was born in Wales—of course, he was a baby and he couldn't speak a word of English, nor of any other language either. So the king made him the ruler of Wales and the king called him the Prince of Wales. Ever since then the King of England's first-born son, the one who will be king when his father dies, has been called the Prince of Wales. Nowadays few people of Wales can speak their own "mother-tongue," for all the children learn English in the schools. Many people study other languages besides their own, but it isn't necessary to know Welsh in order to travel in Wales, for every one speaks English even if he speaks Welsh too.

The game of golf first started in Scotland, the country north of England, on the same island, and some of the finest golf-courses i.t.w.W. are there. Scotland is the land of the Scots and it once had a separate king. The Scotch men used to wear—and some do today—shawls of bright-colored squares, and skirts instead of breeches, and stockings rolled down, leaving their knees bare even in the coldest weather—and they have a great deal of cold weather in Scotland. The Scotch families are called Clans and each Clan has a special design called a plaid in which its shawls and skirts are woven. A great many Scotch names and words are different from English, and yet similar. They call a baby a bairn, and boys and girls they call lads and lassies, and a pretty girl they call a bonnie lassie.

The Scots have a peculiar musical instrument called a bagpipe. It's a bag made of a

后来，一位英格兰国王最终征服了威尔士，为了让征服的威尔士人感到满意和高兴，这位英格兰国王便对他们说，他会让一位出生于威尔士、甚至不会说一句英语的人来统治威尔士。听到这个，威尔士人都很高兴，因为他们以为，这位国王会让一个威尔士人来统治他们。可是，那位国王的儿子就是在威尔士出生的，当时还是个婴儿，自然是一句英语也说不了，也不会说其他任何一种语言。于是，那位国王便让自己的儿子当上了威尔士的统治者，称之为"威尔士亲王"。自那以后，英国国王的长子，就是在父亲死后要继承王位的那个儿子，一直就叫威尔士亲王了。如今，再也没有几个威尔士人会说他们自己的"母语"，因为孩子们在学校里学的都是英语。许多人都会去学习除母语之外的其他语言，可为了到威尔士去旅行，却并不是非得懂威尔士语才行，这是因为，就算有人说威尔士语，那里的人也全都会说英语啊。

高尔夫球这种运动，起源于与英格兰同处一岛、并且位于英格兰北边的苏格兰，因此，如今全球最好的一些高尔夫球场，也都在苏格兰。所谓"苏格兰"，意思就是"苏格兰人的国度"，以前，苏格兰也有本国的国王哩。过去的苏格兰人常常穿着绘有色彩亮丽的方形图案的披肩，身穿短裙而不是裤子，袜子则是往下卷到小腿上，哪怕是最冷的日子，也会让膝盖裸露在外面（苏格兰天气寒冷的日子可不少），而现在，也仍然有人那样穿着打扮呢。苏格兰人的家族，称为"部族"，每个部族都有一种叫作"格子"的特殊图案，并且会用这种图案编织披肩和短裙。许多苏格兰人的名字都与英国人不同，当然，二者之间还是有某种相似性的。他们把

pig's skin and it has a pipe to blow it up as you would a balloon, and there are several horns attached to the bag. The player puts the bag under his arm, keeps blowing it up to keep air in it, and at the same time squeezes out the air with his arms so that it blows the horns, making a peculiar squeaky music.

Some of the greatest ships in the World such as those that cross the ocean are made in Scotland, at a place called Glasgow on the River Clyde, on the west side. Glasgow is the second largest city on the island, but the capital of Scotland is on the other side, the east coast. It is called Edinburgh. The Presbyterian Church started in Scotland and most of the people in Scotland are Presbyterians, just as those in England are Episcopalians.

We call white potatoes "Irish" because they raise and eat so many potatoes in Ireland, the island to the west of Great Britain. In fact, Ireland is shaped something like an Irish potato. But they had no potatoes at all in Ireland and no one there had ever seen or heard of a potato before Columbus discovered America. Potatoes were born in South America and were brought over and raised in Ireland.

The island of Ireland is divided into two parts. The small northern part is called Northern Ireland and is part of the United Kingdom of Great Britain and Northern Ireland. That means the King of England is king of Northern Ireland as well as of England, Scotland, and Wales.

婴儿叫作幼儿，把男孩和女孩分别叫作小伙和姑娘，并把一个美丽的女孩子称为漂亮姑娘。

苏格兰人有一种很古怪的乐器，叫作"风笛"。这种乐器，是用猪皮做成包状，然后用一根管子将它吹起来，就像你们吹气球似的，而且，包上还装有好几个喇叭。演奏者将包夹在一只胳膊底下，一边往里吹气，把包吹得鼓起来，同时一边用胳膊挤出包中的空气，使之吹响那些喇叭，从而发出一种古怪的、吱吱作响的音乐。

苏格兰人吹出一种吱吱作响的音乐

世界上最大的一些船舶，比如远洋轮船，都是在苏格兰西部一个位于克莱德河上、叫作"格拉斯哥"的地方建造出来的。虽说格拉斯哥是大不列颠岛上的第二大城市，但苏格兰的首府却位于另一侧的东海岸上。那里叫作"爱丁堡"。基督教长老会发源于苏格兰，因此绝大多数苏格兰人都是长老派信徒，就像很多英格兰人都是圣公会教徒一样。

我们之所以将马铃薯称为"爱尔兰土豆"，是因为在大不列颠岛西边的爱尔兰岛上，爱尔兰人大量食用马铃薯。事实上，爱尔兰岛的形状也有点儿像是一颗马铃薯呢。不过，在哥伦布发现美洲之前，爱尔兰原本可没有马铃薯，当地人也根本没有见过或者听说过什么马铃薯。马铃薯原产于南美洲，只是人们把它带回了欧洲，才开始在爱尔兰种植起来的。

The Irish are great story tellers and fairy-tale tellers, and they say that once upon a time long ago a giant in the north of Ireland built a magic bridge from Ireland all the way across to Scotland; and to prove the story true they show you thousands of stone posts from the shore out into the sea—all there is left of the bridge—that look as if they had been driven down into the sea by a pile driver. These stone posts running out into the sea are called the Giant's Causeway, which means the Giant's Bridge.

Have you a handkerchief in your pocket? Is it made of linen or cotton? If it's a "party" handkerchief it is probably made of linen and came from Ireland. Linen is made from the fiber of a plant called flax. Flax is much stronger and more silky than cotton, but it costs more. Flax grows especially well in the country around Belfast, which is the capital and chief city of Northern Ireland. In Belfast, they make more linen, and especially fine linen, than anywhere else i.t.w.W.—handkerchiefs, napkins, and tablecloths.

Most of the people of Northern Ireland are Presbyterians like the Scots or Episcopalians like the English, for their ancestors, many years ago, moved to Northern Ireland from Scotland.

The other part of Ireland, the south part, used to belong to England too. But the Irish people there never liked being ruled by the English and so they started a country of their own, with a city named Dublin for its capital. It is often said that the people in Dublin speak better English than even the people in England do. There is another language used in southern Ireland besides English. It is called Irish and is the language spoken long ago by the ancient Irish people before they spoke English. Some of the Irish coins and postage

这个爱尔兰岛，分成了两个部分。北部较小的那一部分，叫作北爱尔兰，是"大不列颠及北爱尔兰联合王国"的一部分。那就意味着，英国国王除了是英格兰、苏格兰和威尔士三地的国王，也是北爱尔兰的国王。

爱尔兰人都是一些非常擅长于讲故事、讲述童话的人，他们说，从前有个巨人在爱尔兰的北部修建了一座神奇的桥梁，从爱尔兰一直通往苏格兰。为了证明这个故事是真的，他们还会带着大家去看海边一直向海中延伸的数千根大石柱，说它们就是那座大桥遗留下来的，那些石柱，都像是被一台打桩机打到了海中似的。这些延伸到了海中的石柱，叫作"巨人堤"，意思就是"巨人之桥"。

你们口袋里有没有带着手帕呢？手帕是亚麻布还是棉布呢？如果手帕是"杂色"的，那么它很可能是用亚麻布制成，并且产自爱尔兰呢。亚麻布是用一种叫作亚麻的植物所含的纤维织成的。亚麻布比棉布更加牢固，也更加柔滑，但成本也较高。在北爱尔兰首府贝尔法斯特周围的乡村，亚麻生长得尤其茂盛。因此，贝尔法斯特生产的亚麻布，尤其是细亚麻布，比如手帕、餐巾和桌布，比全球其他任何地方都要多。

绝大多数北爱尔兰人，都是像苏格兰人那样的长老派信徒，或者像英格兰人那样的圣公会教徒，这是因为，他们的祖先都是很久很久以前从苏格兰迁到北爱尔兰的。

爱尔兰岛的另一部分，即南边的那个部分，以前也隶属于英国。不过，那里的爱尔兰人却始终不愿意接受英国人的统治，便建立了一个属于他们自己的国家，把一个叫作"都柏林"的城市当作首都。人们常说，都柏林人的英语，讲得甚至比英格兰人都要地道呢。除了英语，爱尔兰岛南部还有一种语言。这种语言叫作爱尔兰

stamps have Irish words on them.

The country that the Irish formed is a republic with a president, and the King of England now is no longer their king, as kings of England used to be.

Farther south than Dublin is another city with the strange name of Cork, and at some distance another place called Kilkenny. The Irish are famous for their quick wit. Once a man named Kenny was drinking a bottle of ginger-ale, when he swallowed a piece of the cork and nearly choked to death. Some one said to him, "That's not the way to Cork." "No," said Kenny, between coughs, "that's the way to Kilkenny."

Near Cork is an old ruined castle called Blarney. There is a certain stone high up in the wall of this old castle, and the story goes that if you kiss this stone you will be able to say very pleasant and nice things to people. People go long distances to kiss this Blarney stone, although they can only do it by lying on their backs almost upside down. So when a person says something to us that is very flattering, we reply, "Oh, you must have kissed the Blarney stone."

Almost all the people of the Republic of Ireland are Roman Catholics, for their families have lived there since before the time of Christ, and missionaries from Rome taught them Christianity over a thousand years ago.

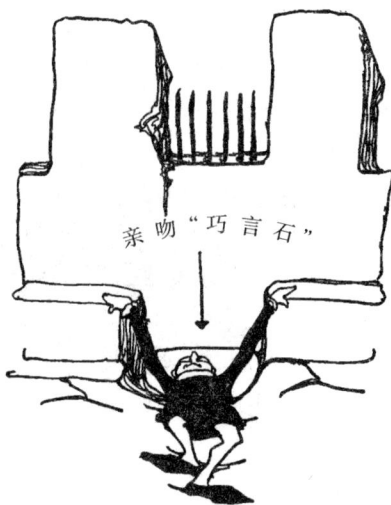

亲吻"巧言石"

人们从世界各地赶来亲吻"巧言石"

语，是很久很久以前古爱尔兰人还没有学会说英语之前所说的语言。如今，爱尔兰的一些硬币和邮票上面，还印有爱尔兰文字呢。

爱尔兰人建立的那个国家是个共和国，设有一位总统，如今，英国国王并不像过去那样是爱尔兰共和国的国王了。

距都柏林很远的北部，还有一个城市，它的名称很奇怪，叫作"科克"，而距这里不远的另一个地方则叫"基尔肯尼"。爱尔兰人一直以机智著称。有一次，一个叫作基尼的人正在喝一杯姜汁汽水，突然咽下了一块软木塞，差点儿噎死了。有人对他说："那样可到不了科克。""不，"肯尼一边咳嗽，一边回答道，"那条路是去基尔肯尼的。"[1]

科克附近，有一座废弃的古城堡，叫作"布拉尼"。这座古堡城墙上的高处，有一块石头，据说只要亲吻一下那块石头，大家就能够对别人说出非常令人愉快、非常讨人喜欢的话来。于是，人们便不远千里而来，去亲吻这块"巧言石"，可他们只有仰面躺下去，把身体几乎倒立起来，才能亲吻到那块石头。因此，如果有人向我们说奉承话，我们就会这样回答："哦，您一定是亲吻过'巧言石'了吧。"

[1] Cork（科克）一词也可指"软木塞"，而Kilkenny（基尔肯尼）一词可看作kill（杀死）和Kenny（肯尼）两个单词的组合，因此这里的对话都属双关，体现出了爱尔兰人的机智和幽默。

Ireland is often called the Emerald Isle because an emerald is a very beautiful green stone and Ireland has so much rain the country is very green. That's why green is the national color. Their flag is green, white, and orange, and a kind of clover, called the shamrock, which grows there, is their national leaf.

You have all heard of St. Patrick, who was supposed to have driven the snakes out of Ireland. Well, the British flag has three crosses worked together like a monogram. One is the cross of St. George of England, the second is the cross of St. Andrew of Scotland, and the third is the cross of St. Patrick.

爱尔兰共和国内，差不多所有人都是罗马天主教徒，因为他们的祖先自基督降生之前就已经生活于此，从罗马而来的传教士早在一千多年前就已经向他们传播过基督教教义了。

爱尔兰通常被人们称为"翡翠之岛"，因为翡翠是一种非常美丽的绿宝石，而爱尔兰雨水充沛，因而整个国家都是绿油油的。该国的国色是绿色，原因也在于此。他们的国旗是绿、白、橙三色，而一种生长在该国、叫作三叶草的苜蓿，则是他们的国花。

大家都听说过圣帕特里克[1]吧，传说是他把恶蛇赶出了爱尔兰。注意，英国国旗上有三个十字架，它们交织在一起，就像是一种图案组合的文字似的。其中一个十字架代表的是英格兰的圣乔治，第二个代表苏格兰的圣安德鲁，第三个则代表着圣帕特里克。

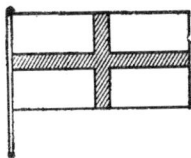

圣乔治十字架

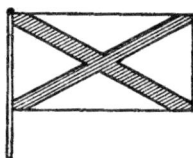

圣帕特里克十字架

圣安德鲁十字架

---

[1] 圣帕特里克（St. Patrick，约385—约461），爱尔兰的守护圣徒。

28 Parlez-vous Français?

I know a boy who has never been to school and who has never had a French lesson in his life, but who can speak French fluently. He's no brighter than you are, either. How do you explain that? It's because he was born in France. He is a French boy. But there was a time when every one who was anybody, no matter in what country he was born, could speak French. The English kings and nobles and educated people all spoke French; they spoke English only to their servants.

France is only two dozen miles from England—twenty-four miles—but there is water between the two countries and no bridge. The water between England and France is called the English Channel. It might just as well have been called the French Channel, for it doesn't belong to either England or France. The finest swimmers in the World, both men and women, have come from all over the World just to try to swim across the English Channel. But only a very few have been able to do it. A boat takes only about an hour to cross and an airplane takes even less time.

When you cross over to France you usually leave a place on the English side called Dover and land at a place on the French side called Calais, because this is the shortest distance. It's short, but often so very rough that every one is seasick—then it seems very long. Some day perhaps a tunnel will be made underneath the English Channel. People usually speak of this as the Calais-Dover route, and there is an old catch question, "What

第28章　您会说法语吗？

我认识一个小男孩，他从来没有上过学，一生中也没有去听过一堂法语课，却能够说流利的法语。当然，这个小男孩也并不比你们更聪明。那么，你们又怎么解释这种现象呢？这是因为，那个小男孩是在法国出生的。他就是一个法国小朋友。不过，曾经有过一个时期，无论出生在哪个国家，大家都会说法语呢。以前，英国的历代国王、贵族以及受过良好教育的人，全都是说法语，他们只是在跟手下的仆从说话时，才会说英语。

法国与英国之间，相距只有二十四英里远。不过，两国间却是一片水域，而水域上方也没有修建桥梁。英、法两国间的这片水域，叫作"英吉利海峡"。其实，那里叫作"法兰西海峡"也是没有问题的，因为这条海峡既不属于英国，也不属于法国。世界上的一些游泳高手，其中既有男的，也有女的，都曾从世界各地赶来，只是为了横渡英吉利海峡。不过，只有极少数游泳高手能够游过去。一艘船舶，只需一个小时左右便可横渡过去，而乘坐飞机的话，则用时更少。

横渡英吉利海峡到法国去时，人们通常都会从英国一个叫作"多佛"的地方出发，然后在法国一个叫作"加来"的地方上岸，因为从多佛到加来的航程最短。虽说航程很短，但一路上海浪汹涌，所有乘客都会晕船，因此会显得很是漫长呢。

is the shortest route from England to France?" One usually answers "Calais-Dover," but that is wrong, for the shortest way to France is "Dover-Calais." Some people cross a longer way, landing at other places on the French side. Havre is one of these places. Havre is at the mouth of a river spelled "Seine," but called "Sane."

When you land in France you see French flags flying; they are red, white, and blue, the same colors as our own flag, but their flags have only three stripes and the stripes are up and down, not from side to side, and the colors are backward—blue, white, red, instead of red, white, blue. The street signs and signs on the buildings are in a different language, the people are talking a different language, and of course the money is different too. It is called "francs."

You have probably heard some one say, "You look like your father or mother," but they don't say that your father or mother looks like you. Well, up the River Seine is the capital and largest city of France, spelled "Paris," but called "Paree" by the French people. Some call it the most beautiful city i.t.w.W. People often say some other very beautiful city looks "like Paris," but they never say Paris looks like any other city.

London is up a river too, but it is only a short way and quite large ships can get up to London. But Paris is a long distance up the Seine, and the river is too shallow and too narrow for large steamships to go up so far, although smaller boats can do so. The Seine runs straight through Paris, or rather I should say it runs crooked through Paris, for it curves as it passes through.

On a small island in the river is a great church—a cathedral, built to the Virgin Mary,

将来，人们可能会在英吉利海峡底下修建一条隧道[1]。人们常常把这条航线说成是"加来—多佛线"，并且还有一个古老的脑筋急转弯："从英国前往法国的最短路线是什么？"人们通常都会不假思索地回答说："加来到多佛啊。"可这个答案是错误的，因为前往法国的最短路线是"多佛到加来"。有些人会绕上一段更长的水路，然后在法国一侧的其他地方上岸。其中有个地方，叫作"勒阿弗尔"。勒阿弗尔位于塞纳河的入海口。

在法国上岸之后，大家就会看到飘扬着的法国国旗了，法国国旗与美国国旗一样，是红、白、蓝三色旗，只不过法国国旗上只有三道条纹，并且条纹是竖向而非横向排列的，以三色为背景：从左到右依次为蓝、白、红，而不是红、白、蓝。然后，大家便会看到，街道上的路标、建筑物的招牌上，用的都是一种不同的文字，人们口中说着的是一种不同的语言，而该国的货币自然也是不一样的。法国的货币，叫作"法郎"。

大家很可能都听到有人这样说过："你长得像你爸爸或者你妈妈。"但别人不会说你们的爸爸、妈妈长得像你们。注意，法国最大的城市兼该国的首都叫作"巴黎"，它位于塞纳河上游。有些人说，巴黎是全球最美丽的一座城市。因此，人们常说其他某座非常美丽的城市看上去"像是巴黎"，可他们绝不会说巴黎看上去像其他城市。

伦敦也位于一条河流上，但那里距河流的入海口很近，一些大型船只都能逆流

---

[1] 英吉利海峡隧道（The Channel Tunnel）已于1994年5月6日开通，是世界第二长的海底隧道和最长的海底铁路隧道，它大大缩短了欧洲大陆往返英国的时间。

whom the French call Notre Dame, which means Our Lady. Notre Dame was built many hundreds of years ago of stone and stained glass, with two towers in front and a thin spire in the center "like a finger pointing to heaven." Long props made of stone hold up the roof. They are called flying buttresses, and if these props were taken away the roof would tumble down. Around on the edge of the roof of Notre Dame are perched strange animals made of stone. They are hideous creatures, different from any real animals you have ever seen or heard of, part bird, part beast, part devil. They are called "gargoyles," and they were made as hideous as possible and put there on the edge of the roof because it was thought they would scare away evil spirits from the church.

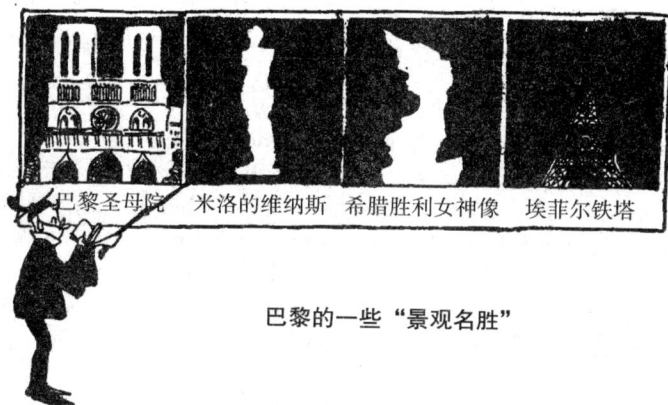

巴黎圣母院　米洛的维纳斯　希腊胜利女神像　埃菲尔铁塔

巴黎的一些"景观名胜"

而上，到达伦敦。可巴黎距塞纳河的入海口却很远，而这条河又太浅、太窄，大型轮船没法逆流而上，不过，一些较小的船只还是能够抵达那里的。塞纳河正好穿过巴黎市区，更准确一点来说，是在巴黎市内蜿蜒而过，因为在流经巴黎时，塞纳河拐了许多的弯。

塞纳河中的一个小岛上，有一座了不起的教堂。那是一座大教堂，是为了纪念圣母玛利亚而修建的，法国人称她为Notre Dame，翻译过来，就是"我们的夫人"。这座圣母院，是人们在几百年前用石块和彩色玻璃建成的，正面建有两座塔楼，中央则有一个又细又高的尖顶，"就像一根直指苍穹的手指"。圣母院的屋顶，由许多石制的长柱子支撑着，这些支柱叫作"飞扶垛"，要是撤掉这些扶垛的话，屋顶便会垮塌下来。圣母院屋顶的四周，立着许多奇怪的石制动物雕像。它们都是一些很丑陋的生物，与大家在现实生活中见过、听说过的所有动物都不一样，部分是鸟、部分是兽，还有部分则是魔鬼。这种东西，叫作"怪兽雨漏"，之所以尽可能将它们雕得面目丑陋，并把它们放在四周屋檐上，是因为人们觉得它们可以将所有的恶鬼吓走，使之不敢到教堂来。

巴黎还有一座有名的教堂，是为了纪念《圣经》中的另一位玛利亚而修建的，人们称她为"抹大拉的玛利亚"[1]。这座纪念"抹大拉的玛利亚"的教堂，人们只

[1]　抹大拉的玛利亚（Mary Magdalene），基督教《圣经》中的人物。传说耶稣曾替她驱出身上的七个恶鬼，后来当耶稣受难时，门徒都逃走了，可她却一直跟在耶稣身边，看着耶稣受苦、断气和下葬。其故事散见于各福音书中。

There is another famous church in Paris built to that other Mary in the Bible known as Mary Magdalene. This church to Mary Magdalene is called simply "The Madeleine," which is the French for Magdalene. It is a much newer church than Notre Dame but it is much overlooking. It is built like the old temples they used to build before Christ was born—before they had any churches. The Madeleine has stone columns all around the outside, but it has no windows, no towers, no flying buttresses, no spire, no dome.

Once upon a time France had kings and queens and princes and princesses, and along the Seine are many beautiful palaces in which they lived. Now, however, France has no more kings and queens or princes. It has a President as we have, for France is a republic as we are. So the old palaces are now used for museums or art galleries or libraries. One of the greatest of these palaces is the Louvre, and in the Louvre are many famous pictures and statues.

A photograph is never worth much—even though it may be a good likeness and the person famous. But a painting, even though not a good likeness and the person unknown, may be worth a fortune. One of the great pictures in the Louvre is the painting of a smiling woman called Mona Lisa. It is one of the most valuable paintings i.t.w.W., but it was once upon a time stolen right off the wall in the Louvre where it was hanging. It was a foolish thing to steal, for the thief could not sell it nor even show it to any one. All the World looked for the picture, but it was a long time before it was found in another country and put back again in the Louvre, where it is once more.

是称之为"玛德莱娜教堂",因为"玛德莱娜"就是法语中的"抹大拉"一词。虽然这个教堂的历史比巴黎圣母院短得多,但它的外表却要比后者古旧得多。这座教堂的建筑样式,就像是基督降生之前,世界上还没有任何教堂之前,人们经常修建的那种神庙。玛德莱娜教堂外部,四周都立有许多的石柱,可整座教堂却既无窗户、塔楼、飞扶垛,也没有尖顶和穹顶。

很久以前,法国也有国王和王后,有王子和公主,如今,塞纳河沿岸还有许多非常美丽的宫殿,就是他们当时生活的地方。然而,法国现在已经没有什么国王、王后和王子了。该国像我们美国一样,也有总统,因为法国也成了美国这样的共和国。所以,原来的那些宫殿都被改成了博物馆、画廊或者图书馆。其中最大的一座宫殿叫作"罗浮宫",如今,罗浮宫里还保存着许多著名的画作和雕像呢。

照片值不了什么钱,就算照片拍得与实物非常相似,就算被拍者是一个名人,也是如此。而一幅画作,哪怕画得与实物不像,哪怕画中描绘的是个默默无闻的人物,也有可能值一大笔钱呢。罗浮宫里保存的最伟大的一幅画作,描绘的是一个微笑着的、叫作"蒙娜·丽莎"的女子。这也是全世界最珍贵的一幅画作,不过,它曾经还被人从罗浮宫的墙上盗走过哩。盗走这幅画是一件非常愚蠢的事情,因为窃贼既卖不出去,甚至也不能给任何人看这幅画。此后,全世界的人都在寻找这幅画,但过了很久,人们才在另一个国家里找到了这幅画,并把它重新放回了罗浮宫里原先挂着的那个地方。

人们都相信世间有许多的神灵,就像善良或者邪恶的妖精,并且按照传说中

People believed there were many gods who were like good and bad fairies, and statues were made of them as they were supposed to look. Two of the greatest statues i.t.w.W. are in the Louvre. One is a marble figure of the goddess Venus. Venus was the goddess of Love, and this statue of her was made more than 2,000 years ago, but was found not many years ago on an island called Melos, so it is called the Venus of Melos. The other figure, like an angel with outspread wings, is called "Victory." Victory too was made before Christ was born. Venus has lost her arms and Victory has lost her head, but, in spite of that, both figures are more beautiful than most real people who have both arms and head.

The Capitol of France has neither a dome like our Capitol nor towers like the English Capitol. There is, however, a building in Paris with a dome something like that of our Capitol and St. Paul's in London, but it is neither a church nor a Capitol. It is the tomb of France's two greatest soldiers. One was named Napoleon, and he lived at the same time as our George Washington. He was at one time emperor before France had presidents. His bones are in a large marble chest under this dome. The other soldier is General Foch—the leader of the armies in World War I.

The tallest tower in the World is in Paris near the banks of the Seine. It is called the Eiffel Tower and it is about a thousand feet high. It is made of iron and stands on four tall iron legs. You can look between its legs and see whole buildings as if the tower were a giant straddling them.

的样子，给这些神灵制作了雕像。世界上最伟大的两座雕像，都存放在罗浮宫里。其中一座就是女神维纳斯的大理石雕像。维纳斯是爱神，这尊雕像制作于两千多年前，只是不久前才被人们在一个叫作米洛的岛屿上发现，因此就叫"米洛的维纳斯"。而另一尊雕像则像是一个张着双翼的天使，叫作"胜利女神像"。这尊胜利女神像，也制作于基督降生之前。虽说那尊维纳斯雕像上没有胳膊，而这尊胜利女神像则缺了脑袋，但这两尊雕像却比现实生活中绝大多数有头有胳膊的人都要更加漂亮呢。

法国的国会大厦，既没有像美国国会大厦那样的穹顶，也没有像英国议会大楼那样的塔楼。然而，巴黎有一座建筑，虽然有一个与美国国会大厦和伦敦圣保罗大教堂那样的穹顶，可它却既不是教堂，也不是国会大厦。那是法国两名最伟大的战士的陵墓。其中一位战士叫作拿破仑，他与美国的乔治·华盛顿生活在同一个时代。法国变成共和国、选举总统之前，拿破仑曾经当过该国的皇帝。他的遗骨用一个大型的大理石棺材盛放着，埋在那个穹顶之下。另一位战士，就是福煦将军，他曾是第一次世界大战期间法军的元帅。

世界上最高的一座塔，位于巴黎塞纳河边不远的地方。这座塔，叫作"埃菲尔铁塔"，差不多有一千英尺高。该塔全用钢铁建成，立在四根高耸的铁腿上。大家可以从铁塔的四条腿之间望过去，看到对面的所有房屋，仿佛这座铁塔是一个踩在它们上面的巨人似的。

29 Parlez-vous Français? (continued)

There are two French words which I know you know, even if you don't speak French. One is "Boulevard" and the other is "Avenue." You have probably always thought they were English words, but they are both French words. Paris has many Boulevards and one of the finest Avenues in the World. This Avenue is lined with trees and rims directly toward the setting sun, and was thought beautiful enough to be a street in Paradise, so it was called the Champs-Elysées, which means "The Fields of Paradise."

In London a square is called a Circus, but in Paris it is called a Place, as if spelled "Plass." The most beautiful Place in Paris is the Place de la Concorde. In the center of this Place is a monument made of one single tall stone standing on end. It is called Cleopatra's Needle. The Place de la Concorde is at one end of the Champs-Elysees and at the other end is a beautiful arch like a huge gateway across the avenue. It is called "L'Arc de Triomphe," which it is easy to guess means The Arch of Triumph. No automobile nor carriage may pass through this Arch of Triumph, however, for underneath it in the pavement is the tomb of the French Unknown Soldier, and from this tomb a flame flickers day and night—a flame to be kept burning forever to the memory of the brave Frenchmen who died in the World Wars.

第29章　您会说法语吗？（续）

我知道，有两个法语单词，就算不会说法语，你们也全都认识。其中一个就是"林荫大道"（Boulevard），另一个则是"大街"（Avenue）。大家很可能一直都以为这两个词是英语里的单词，可实际上它们却是法语单词。巴黎有许多的林荫大道，还有世界上最美丽的大街之一，这条大街，两边都是树木，并且笔直地通向日落的方向，人们觉得它非常美丽，完全可以称得上是天堂中的街道，因此叫它"香榭丽舍大街"，意思就是"天堂之地"。

在伦敦，人们将广场叫作Circus，可在巴黎，广场却被称为Place。巴黎最漂亮的广场，就是协和广场。这个广场中央，有一座用一整根长石制成，然后直立起来的纪念碑。这座纪念碑，叫作"克里奥帕特拉之针"。协和广场位于香榭丽舍大街的一端，而大街的另一头，则是一道美丽的拱门，就像是横跨大街的一扇巨型大门似的。这座拱门，叫作"凯旋门"，它的意思我们不难猜出，就是指"胜利的拱门"。然而，这座凯旋门下，是不允许汽车和马车通行的，因为

凯旋门之下，是法国无名烈士墓

The French people love beautiful things. They love beautiful pictures and beautiful sculpture and beautiful buildings, and they know how to make them; so young men and women from our country and from other countries go to Paris to learn from the French how to make beautiful things—to become painters and sculptors and architects.

But the French love beauty in everyday things as well—in such everyday things as hats and clothes and cooking and manners. French hats and French clothes and French cooking and French manners are famous. Strange to say, the most famous French dressmakers are men. Also, strange to say, the most famous French cooks are men too. We call them "chefs." Our dressmakers go to Paris to study and copy the fashion in clothes and the style in hats, and we get French chefs for our finest hotels and restaurants. Perhaps you have noticed that the bill of fare in many of our restaurants is printed in French. That is because our cooks copy not only the way the French cook but the names of the dishes they cook. The French can make delicious soup out of a piece of bread and a bone. In America soup is just soup, but in France soup is called potage or consommé instead of soup—it sounds better, and anything that sounds better you expect will taste better, too, and it usually does.

法国最著名的厨师都是男士

凯旋门下的人行道下，是法国的无名烈士墓。这座墓中，火炬日夜燃烧，永远不熄，以此来纪念那些在两次世界大战中英勇牺牲的法国人。

法国人民都热爱美丽的事物。他们热爱美丽的画作、美丽的雕塑、美丽的建筑，并且知道如何去绘画、雕刻和建造，因此，美国和其他国家的年轻人都纷纷来到巴黎，向法国人学习如何制造美丽的东西，学习如何当画家、当雕刻家和建筑师。

不过，法国人也热爱日常生活当中的美，比如帽子、衣服、厨艺、礼貌等日常事物中的美。法国帽子、法国服饰、法国厨艺和法国人的礼仪，都是赫赫有名的。说来也怪，法国最著名的一些裁缝都是男士。说来还怪的是，法国最著名的一些厨师也是男士呢。我们称这些厨师为"大厨"。美国的裁缝都会到巴黎去学习，仿效那里的服装时尚和帽子风格，而法国的大厨也会被请到美国一些最好的旅馆和饭店里去工作。或许大家都已经注意到，美国许多饭店里的菜单上，印的都是法文。这是因为，美国的厨师不但效仿了法国厨师的厨艺，还把法国大厨所做的菜品名称也一股脑儿拿了过来。法国厨师可以用一片面包和一根骨头做出美味的汤品来。在美国，汤就是汤，可在法国，汤却被称为"浓汤"或者"清汤"，而并非只是统称为汤。这种名称更好听，凡是名称好听的食物，大家也会期待它的味道更好，而事实也常常如此。

When we eat our meals we almost always do so indoors, where we can see no one else and no one else can see us. But the French often eat out-of-doors, on the sidewalk or overlooking the sidewalk, where they can see every one and every one can see them, and that's where many of their most famous restaurants are placed.

The French drink a great deal of wine with their meals, much as we drink milk or coffee or tea, and there are many great farms in different parts of France where they raise grapes from which they make the wine. These farms are vineyards—called "vinyards."

Cloth is made out of several things—linen, cotton, wool, and silk; linen, cotton, and wool are chiefly for use, but silk is chiefly for beauty. In Ireland cloth is made out of linen, in England cloth is made out of cotton and wool, but in France cloth is made out of silk for beauty's sake. Linen and cotton are made from plants, wool is made from sheep, but silk is made from a little caterpillar. We call this caterpillar a silkworm, but he is not really a worm at all. A worm is born, lives, and dies always a worm, but a caterpillar turns into a beautiful moth or butterfly if let alone. Most caterpillars, however, we try to kill, for they eat the leaves of trees and other green things. But silkworms are so valuable that people feed them leaves and raise them as our farmers raise chickens. The silk caterpillar likes a special kind of leaf—the leaves of the mulberry-tree. So in the valley of a river in France called the Rhône the French people grow mulberry-trees—not for the mulberries but for the leaves, which they gather and feed to the silkworms.

After the silk caterpillar has eaten, he spins a fine thread of silk almost a quarter of a

我们吃饭的时候，通常都是在屋里吃，这样，我们既看不到别人，别人也看不到我们的吃相。不过，法国人却经常在户外吃饭，餐桌要么是摆在路边，要么就是俯瞰着下面的人行道，这样，他们看得见其他的人，而其他的人也能看见他们。法国许多最著名的饭店，也都是设在这样的地方呢。

法国人除了吃肉类，还会喝很多的葡萄酒，就像我们喝牛奶、咖啡或者茶那样，因此，法国各地都有许多大型的农庄，农民在其中种植葡萄，再用葡萄酿酒。这些农庄，就叫"葡萄园"。

有好几种东西，都可以用来制作布匹，比如亚麻、棉花、羊毛和丝绸，其中，人们用的主要是亚麻、棉花和羊毛，而丝绸则主要是为了好看。在爱尔兰，布匹都是用亚麻织成的，英国则用棉花和羊毛制作布料，可法国的布料，却都是为了好看而用丝绸制作出来的。亚麻和棉花都是产自植物，羊毛产自绵羊，可丝绸却是产自一种小小的毛虫。我们把这种小毛虫叫作"蚕"，不过，蚕其实根本就不是一种蠕虫。蠕虫从出生、长大一直到死去，始终都是一条蠕虫，可蚕这种毛虫，要是不管它们的话，它们最终就会变成美丽的飞蛾或者蝴蝶。然而，绝大多数毛虫都会被我们人类想方设法杀死，因为它们会吃掉树叶和其他绿色植物的叶子。蚕却很珍贵，人们会用树叶来喂养它们，就像农民喂养鸡鸭一样。蚕喜欢吃一种特殊的树叶，即桑树的叶子。因此，在法国一条叫作"罗纳河"的河流流域，法国人种植了大量的桑树，他们不是为了要吃桑树上结出的桑葚，而是为了要采摘桑叶。他们把桑叶收集起来，然后喂给蚕吃。

mile long out of his own body, as a snider spins a spider web out of his own body. The silk caterpillar winds himself up in this thread as he spins it round and round and round until he is completely covered up and looks in his cover of silk thread something like a peanut. Then he goes to sleep inside, and if he waked up he would come out a moth; but they don't let him wake up. They boil him while he is asleep, till he is soft, and then they unwind the thread which he has wound round himself and use it to make silk cloth, silk stockings, silk ribbons, and all the silk things that women love. On the River Rhône is the greatest place in Europe for making silk. It is called Lyons.

The River Rhône flows south into a gulf called the Gulf of Lyons, which is a part of the Mediterranean Sea. The chief city on the Gulf of Lyons is Marseilles. It is the next largest city to Paris, but it was a city long before there was any Paris, for it was a port for ships that sailed the sea long, long ago, and it still is one of the great ports for ships. It is near, but not quite at, the mouth of the Rhône.

Another thing that women love is perfume—sweet perfume! The French are famous for making perfume from flowers and from sweet grasses and even from weeds. French perfume is very expensive, because it often takes a whole field of flowers to make but a very few bottles of perfume. A dollar for a thimbleful! It always seemed wonderful to me that both flowers and their perfume come out of the ground—that the beautiful colors and sweet perfume are both made from mud!

French farmers raise other things, of course, besides grapes and silkworms and flowers

蚕吃饱桑叶之后，就会从身体里吐出一种很细的丝线来，这种丝线差不多可以长达四分之一英里，就像蜘蛛从体内吐出来结成蛛网的那种蛛丝。蚕一圈一圈又一圈地吐出蚕丝，把自己缠绕起来，直到全身都被蚕丝裹住，最终形成一个看上去有点儿像是花生的蚕茧。接下来，蚕便会在茧里开始睡觉，待它醒来之后就会变成一只飞蛾，不过，人们可不会让蚕睡醒。他们会趁着蚕在茧里睡觉的时候，就把蚕茧放到沸水里煮，让蚕茧变软，然后将蚕绕在自己身上的丝线解开抽走，用于制作丝绸布料、丝绸袜子、丝绸缎带，以及女性热衷于的所有丝绸制品。罗纳河两岸，有着欧洲最大的丝绸生产地。那里就是里昂。

罗纳河向南注入了一个叫作"里昂湾"的海湾，这个海湾是地中海的一部分。里昂湾沿岸最大的城市是马赛。马赛也是法国仅次于巴黎的第二大城市，但该市的历史却比巴黎要悠久得多，因为很久很久以前，马赛就是一个海港，供在大海上航行的船只停泊，而如今那里也依然是一个大型海港呢。马赛距罗纳河入海口不远，但并没有正好位于该河的入海口处。

女性喜欢的另一种东西，便是香水，气味芬芳的香水。法国人以用鲜花、香草甚至是野草制作香水而著称。法国香水非常昂贵，因为通常要用一整片地里的鲜花，才能制作出寥寥几小瓶香水来。一美元只能买到一丁点儿香水呢！我一直都觉得非常奇妙，因为鲜花和鲜花所制成的香水都产自地上：五彩缤纷的鲜花和气味芬芳的香水，竟然都是产自泥土之中！

当然，除了种葡萄、养蚕、栽种用于制作香水的鲜花，法国农民也种植其他

for perfume. They raise many of the same things that our own farmers raise. Most of the people in France are farmers, but they don't live in farm-houses on their farms; they live in houses in a village and walk out and back to their farms, which often are a long way off.

When I was five years old I was given a penny bank, "to save for my old age." When, at the age of twelve, I had a hundred dollars, I felt like a millionaire. The French are very saving. Even a man who earns very little saves some of that little, so that even poor people have money saved up for their old age when they can no longer work.

A girl saves her money so that when she marries she will have enough to buy furniture and perhaps a house or even more. This is called her "dot." Sometimes her father and mother give it to her, and sometimes the girl earns it herself; sometimes her "dot" is only a few hundred dollars, sometimes it is thousands of dollars, but seldom can a girl marry who hasn't some "dot." "And they lived happily ever afterward."

的东西。他们所种的作物，许多都与美国农民所种的一样。绝大多数法国人都是农民，但他们并不是住在农田边上的农舍里，他们都是住在村里，都是出村去地里劳作后再回到村中的家里，因为农田通常离村庄都有很长的一段距离。

五岁的时候，大人给了我一个零钱罐，要我"存钱养老"。因此，到了十二岁的时候，我就攒了一百美元，觉得自己像是个百万富翁了。法国人都非常节俭。即便是一个挣钱不多的人，也会从微薄的收入中拿出一部分存下来，所以，即便是穷人也有存款，供自己老了之后、不能再工作的时候花。

小姑娘也会存钱，以便日后结婚的时候，有钱去买家具，没准还会去买一栋房子或者更多的东西。这种存款，叫作"嫁妆"。有的时候，父母会给女儿送嫁妆，有的时候，嫁妆则是姑娘自己挣来的；有的时候，这种"嫁妆"只有几百美元，有的时候却会有数千美元。不过，一位姑娘结婚的时候没有"嫁妆"，这种情况却很少见。"从那以后，他们就幸福地生活在一起了"。

女士们都到巴黎去购买漂亮的帽子和衣物

30 The Land Below the Sea

Bells and Battle-fields don't seem to go together, but north of France is a land of Bells and Battle-fields, called Belgium.

The bells are in the towers of churches, of town halls, and of other buildings. The bells in Belgium strike the hour, but they do more than that—they play a tune every hour or oftener. And on Sundays and holidays a bell-ringer, seated at a keyboard as at an organ, plays all sorts of hymns and tunes on the bells, so that every one in the town can enjoy the music without leaving his own home. The music is broadcast without a radio. Some of the bell sets have as many as fifty bells of different sizes and sounds—little bells that make high notes, and big bells, as big as a man, that make deep, low notes. The bells themselves don't move; the bell clapper moves instead. The clappers are fastened by wire to keys like those of a piano or organ, and as the player touches the keys the clappers strike the side of the bell. When a bell concert is being given, all noises in the streets near-by are forbidden—no honking of horns nor loud shouting allowed—so that nothing will spoil the music for those who are listening.

Bells and Battle-fields! Belgium has been the battle-field of Europe—not battles fought by the Belgians themselves, but by other countries of Europe. In the two World Wars Belgium was a chief battle-ground of the French and German soldiers, and thousands

第30章　低于海平面的国家

大钟和战场，二者似乎扯不上什么关系，但在法国的北方，却有一个"大钟和战场之国"，叫作比利时。

比利时的大钟，都是安放在教堂塔楼上、市政大厅里和其他的建筑物里。比利时的大钟虽说也会报时，但其作用却不仅如此，因为它们每个小时都会演奏一曲音乐，有时演奏频率还会更高。在星期日或者节假日里，一名敲钟人会坐在电子琴前，就像坐在风琴前面一样，用大钟演奏出各种各样的旋律和曲调来，从而让市镇里的所有人足不出户，就能欣赏到美妙的音乐。这种音乐，不用广播便能传得很远。有些编钟竟然由多达五十座大小不一、声音各异的钟组成，比如发出高音的小钟，以及有一个人高、发出低音的大钟。这些大钟本身不会移动，但钟锤能够移动。钟锤用铁丝与那种像钢琴或者风琴的琴键相连，因此演奏者敲击琴键时，钟锤便会敲击大钟的一面。在举行钟声音乐会的时候，附近所有的街道都不准发出任何噪音，既不准汽车鸣喇叭，也不准人们高声大叫，以便不让噪音破坏听众欣赏音乐的心情。

大钟和战场！比利时一直都是欧洲的战场，不是比利时人本身参战的战场，而是其他欧洲国家参战的战场。在两次世界大战中，比利时都是法、德两国士兵交战的一个主要战场，在战争中，成千上万栋建筑被毁，给比利时造成了巨大的损失。一百多年前，法国一个叫作拿破仑的伟大将领，在比利时一个叫作滑铁卢的地方，

of buildings were wrecked and an immense amount of damage done. A little over a hundred years ago a great French General named Napoleon, who I told you was buried in Paris, fought one of the greatest battles in history at a place in Belgium called Waterloo. Napoleon was beaten at Waterloo, and beaten so badly that we now use the word "Waterloo" to describe almost any big defeat, whether it is a defeat of an army in battle or of a team in a game. We say "A tennis champion has his Waterloo" or "A football team has its Waterloo."

B. B. B. The capital of Belgium also begins with a "B." It is Brussels. Perhaps you have heard of Brussels lace, Brussels carpets, or Brussels sprouts. They all come from Brussels.

Another city of Belgium beginning with a "B" is Bruges. Bruges has many streets of water with bridges crossing them, and boats instead of carts, although there are paved streets also. See how many things in Belgium begin with a "B":

Belgium

Bells

Battle-fields

Brussels

Bruges

Bridges

Boats

Belgium is hilly on the side near France, but on the opposite side it is very low. On this

打了一场历史上最伟大的战役，我在前面已经跟你们说过，拿破仑死后安葬在巴黎。在滑铁卢之战中，拿破仑被打败，并且是一败涂地，因此如今我们还在用"滑铁卢"这个词来形容任何一种惨败，不管是一支军队在战斗中惨败，还是一支球队在比赛中惨败，都可以用这个词来形容。我们可以说，"一位网球冠军遭遇到了他的滑铁卢之战"，或者说"一支橄榄球队遭遇到了其滑铁卢"。

比利时的首都，也是用字母"B"开头的，叫作"布鲁塞尔"。没准，你们都听说过"布鲁塞尔花边"、"布鲁塞尔地毯"或者"布鲁塞尔芽菜"了。这些东西，都是产自布鲁塞尔。

比利时还有一个城市，也是用字母"B"开头的，那就是布鲁日。布鲁日市内有许多水道，上面都架有桥梁，尽管该市也有许多用卵石铺就的街道，但人们通常都是乘坐小船而不是大车出行。现在再来看一看，比利时有几个方面是用字母"B"开头的吧：

比利时（Belgium）

大钟（Bells）

战场（Battle-fields）

布鲁塞尔（Brussels）

布鲁日（Bruges）

桥梁（Bridges）

小船（Boats）

low side it joins the land of the Dutch people, which is called Holland. Holland means "hollow land," and it is so named because in many places it is even lower than the sea. Banks or walls called dikes had to be built to hold the water back, and windmills with big sprawling wings had to be built inside the dikes to pump the water out and keep it out. Water won't run off the ground in Holland, for there is no low place for it to run to; it would have to run uphill. So it has to be pumped off.

The dikes that hold back the sea have to be very big and very strong to stand the pounding of the waves against them, for the slightest break or hole in the dike would soon burst open and the water would flood the country, and cover houses and drown the people, so they have men to watch the dikes all the time to mend any broken places as soon as they are made.

But long, long ago—about seven hundred years ago—there was a terrible storm, and the North Sea did break through and it drowned thousands upon thousands of people and the villages and houses in which they lived. Ships now sail and fish now swim where these drowned villages lie, and this inland water is called the South Sea,

人们修建了许多叶片巨大的风车，来将
陆地上的水排出去

比利时靠近欧洲大陆的那一侧多山，而相对的那一侧地势却非常低矮。在地势低矮的这一边，该国与荷兰毗邻。"荷兰"（Holland）一词，指的就是"空心之地"（hollow land），而之所以得名如此，是因为荷兰许多地方的地势甚至比海平面还要低。所以，荷兰不得不修建一道道防波堤来挡住海水，并且不得不在防波堤里侧建造许多翼展巨大的风车，来将防波堤内侧的水排出去，不让海水漫进来。荷兰的雨水不会在地面往下流，因为没有更低的地方可以排出这些雨水，必须让雨水向上流才行。所以，就只能用泵将雨水抽出去。

挡住海水的那些防波堤必须修建得非常巨大、牢固，能够抵挡海浪对它们的拍击才行，因为防波堤上哪怕是一条极其细小的裂缝或者一个极其细小的孔洞，也有可能在很短的时间内猛地爆开，这样，全国便会海水肆虐，房屋和民众纷纷被淹了。所以，荷兰会派人时时刻刻地巡视防波堤，一旦发现哪里出现了破损，便马上进行修补和加固。

不过，很久、很久以前，即差不多七百年以前，出现了一场可怕的暴风雨，因此北海海水的确冲破了这些防波堤，倒灌进来，淹死了成千上万的荷兰人，淹没了他们所住的村庄和房屋。这些被淹村庄的所在之处，如今已是一片汪洋，既有船只来去，也有鱼儿出没了，由此形成的这片内陆水域，被称为"南海"，而在荷兰语里，就叫"须德海"。不过，如今荷兰人民正在计划修建防波堤，再次将北海的海

which in Dutch is the Zuyder Zee. But the Dutch people are planning to build dikes and shut off the North Sea once again and pump the water out. This will make dry land where the Zuyder Zee now is; so some day, not many years from now, there will be no Zuyder Zee, no South Sea, and where fish now swim and ships now sail will be houses and farms.

Where we have roads and streets, in Holland they have canals. In the summer, boats sail on the canals and in the winter the people skate on them. Children skate to school and men skate to work. What fun!

In Holland they don't have many horses; they use dogs to haul and bicycles to carry. Dogs eat less than horses, they don't have to have stables, and bicycles don't have to have garages. Dogs can be trained like horses to haul small carts, large enough to carry milk cans. Sometimes, however, when a cat comes along, there is trouble.

Though there are few horses in Holland, there are many cows. They have black and white cows called Holsteins. Holstein cows give a great deal of milk, more milk than any other kind of cow. The milk is used for making cheese, for which Holland is famous. The cheese is made in big pieces and then varnished so that it will keep a long time. They have markets in which nothing but

有的时候，要是闯过来一只猫，那就糟了

水挡住，并将内陆的海水用泵抽出去。这会让如今须德海所在的地方变成旱地，因此，在不久的将来，荷兰将不会再有什么"须德海"，不会再有什么"南海"，而如今鱼儿嬉戏、船舶航行的地方，也会重新变成房屋和农田了。

我国有许多的马路和街道，而荷兰却有许多的运河。夏季，这些运河里船来船往；而到了冬季，人们就会到运河上去滑冰。小朋友们可以滑冰去上学，大人们则可以滑冰去上班。多有意思啊！

荷兰人养的马匹不多，因为他们习惯于用狗来拉东西，用自行车来运东西。狗吃的粮食没有马儿多，也不用为它们修建马厩，而自行车则不需要车库。人们可以把小狗训练得像马儿一样，去拉小型的大车，而大型犬还拉得动牛奶罐呢。然而，有的时候，要是闯过来一只猫，那就麻烦了。

尽管荷兰的马匹不多，但该国喂养了大量的奶牛。那种奶牛，身上的毛色都是黑白相间的，叫作"荷斯坦奶牛"。荷斯坦奶牛产奶量大，比其他任何一种奶牛的产奶率都要高。人们用牛奶来做奶酪，因此荷兰的奶酪鼎鼎有名。荷兰人把奶酪制成大块，然后把表面打磨光滑，使之能够保存很长的时间。那里有些市场，竟然除了奶酪，其他什么都不卖呢，这种市场，就叫"奶酪市场"。

荷兰人都喜欢把家里收拾得干干净净。他们的厨房，通常也兼做客厅和餐厅。他们屋里屋外不停地擦洗，连人行道也不放过，有的城市里，连街道也会擦洗呢。

cheese is sold—cheese markets.

The Dutch keep their houses very clean. The kitchen is usually the living-room and dining-room too. They scrub and scrub and scrub, outside as well as inside, even the sidewalks, and in some towns even the street. The cow sheds are often part of the house and are kept just as clean as the houses, with white curtains at the windows, and hooks to hold up the tails of the cows while they are being milked. People wear wooden shoes, because Holland is such a damp country, and they take them off and leave them at the door, as we do overshoes, before entering the house. In some places in Holland the men wear trousers as big as pillow-cases and the girls wear very big skirts and white bonnets. In the large cities, however, the people dress about the same as we do.

Dam means a dike, and as there are so many dikes in Holland there are many towns' and cities' names ending in "dam." Amsterdam and Rotterdam are the two largest cities.

Amsterdam is a city of diamonds. The diamonds are not found in Holland but are brought there from Africa. When they are taken out of the diamond mines in Africa they don't look like diamonds but look like pebbles, and you would never guess they could be made into anything beautiful. But at Amsterdam they are made into the beautiful sparkling jewels that we know. A diamond is the hardest thing in the World. You cannot cut it with a steel tool nor grind it on a grindstone; you cannot scratch it with sandpaper nor make a mark on it with a file. The only thing that will cut a diamond or scratch a diamond is another diamond. So in Amsterdam they chip one diamond with another diamond and polish it into a many sided jewel with diamond dust.

牛圈通常都与家中的房子挨在一起，也会保持得像家里那样干净，窗户上挂着白色窗帘，而在挤奶的时候，甚至还有专门用于把牛尾马钩起来的钩子。那里的人都穿木屐，因为荷兰是一个非常潮湿的国度，进屋之前，人们都会在门口脱下木屐，就像我们进屋前会把套鞋脱下，放在门外一样。在荷兰的有些地方，男子都穿枕套般宽松的裤子，而姑娘们则会穿很宽大的裙子，戴着白色的帽子。然而，在大城市里，荷兰人的穿着打扮却跟我们是一样的。

"大坝"（Dam）的意思，就是"堤坝"，由于荷兰的堤坝太多，因此许多的城镇名称后面，都带有"大坝"这个后缀。阿姆斯特丹和鹿特丹，就是该国最大的两座城市。

阿姆斯特丹号称"钻石之城"。不过，那里的钻石并非产自荷兰，而是从非洲运过来的。在非洲的矿场上开采出来之时，它们的样子根本就不是钻石，而是像鹅卵石，此时，你们可能永远都想象不到，它们能够制成什么美丽的东西。可到了阿姆斯特丹后，它们就会被加工成美丽无比、熠熠生辉的宝石，变成我们所知的钻石。钻石是世界上最坚硬的东西。我们无法用铁制工具去切割，也没法用磨石去磨碎钻石，我们无法用砂纸去打磨它，也无法用锉刀在钻石上面划出一道印子来。唯一能够切割或者打磨一颗钻石的工具，便是另一颗钻石。因此，在阿姆斯特丹，人们就是用一颗钻石来切割另一颗钻石，并用钻石粉来把钻石打磨成一颗多边形宝石的。

31 Castles in Spain

When I was a boy I used to plan the kind of home I would have when I grew up and had plenty of money. It was to have a gymnasium in the attic, a zoo for pets in the cellar, a museum of curiosities in the parlor, and a soda-water fountain in the dining-room. My mother used to say that was my Castle in Spain, and when I asked her what a Castle in Spain was, she said, "Any wonderful home—in your mind."

But Spain is a real place, a real country, and there are real castles there even now.

The map of Europe is like a puzzle-picture. If you turn it around or look at it sideways you will see a little old woman with a big head, a humpback, and a long leg kicking a football into the sea. The head is called Spain, and the cap that Spain is wearing on the front of her head is called Portugal. Where the head joins France there is a collar of mountains called the Pyrenees.

At one time Spain not only looked like the head of Europe, she really was the head of Europe, for she owned a great part of Europe. Then there came a time just after Columbus discovered America when Spain was the head not only of Europe but of all the World. She then owned a great part of North America and all of South America, except Brazil. So she was the greatest country i.t.w.W. Now, however, Spain doesn't even own all of Spain. On the map Spain seems to be rubbing her nose against the nose of Africa, as some savages

第31章　西班牙的城堡

我小的时候曾经盘算过，等我长大了、有了很多钱之后，要买一栋什么样的房子。那栋房子的阁楼上必须有一个健身房，地下室里必须有一个能够养宠物的小动物园，客厅里必须有一个存放奇珍异物的小博物馆，而餐厅里则要有一个源源不断地喷出苏打水的喷泉。妈妈听了之后，经常说那是我的"西班牙城堡"（即白日做梦），而当我问"西班牙城堡"是什么意思时，她回答说："凡是想象出来的神奇家园，都叫这个。"

不过，西班牙却是实实在在的地方，一个真实存在的国家，而且，即便是到了如今，那里也还有真正的城堡呢。

欧洲的地图，就像是一幅拼图。如果把它转动一下，或者从侧面看去，就会看到一个脑袋很大、个子很矮小的老太太，她驼着背，一条腿还在将一个足球踢向海中。这个老太太的"脑袋"，叫作西班牙，而她脑袋前边戴着的那顶"帽子"，叫作葡萄牙。要是把她的"脑袋"与法国连起来看的话，她的"衣领"就是比利牛斯山脉了。

曾经有过一个时期，西班牙的样子非但像是欧洲的脑袋，而实际上也是欧洲各国的领袖，因为当时西班牙占领了欧洲的大部分地区。接下来，就在哥伦布发现美洲之后，又有一个时期，西班牙非但是欧洲的领袖，还成了整个世界的霸主。当

rub noses when they meet. This nose of Spain is called Gibraltar, but Gibraltar does not belong to Spain; it belongs to England.

Gibraltar looks like a nose on the map, but if you were in a boat out on the Mediterranean Sea, Gibraltar would look like a long, high rock. Between it and Africa there is a narrow strip of water called the Strait of Gibraltar. It is only about thirteen miles

西班牙地图看上去就像是一位老太太

时，该国占领了北美洲的大部分地区，以及除巴西之外的整个南美洲。因此，该国就成了全球最大的国家。然而，如今西班牙却连本国的土地也丧失了一部分呢。在地图上，西班牙似乎正在将自己的"鼻子"与非洲的那个"鼻子"相碰，就像一些野兽相遇时要相互碰碰鼻子那样。西班牙的这个"鼻子"，叫作"直布罗陀"，可

across. It is about half as wide as the Strait of Dover, but powerful currents are pulling and pushing in and out from the Atlantic Ocean, and only recently has any one been able to swim across it. Inside of the Rock of Gibraltar, England has cut hallways and rooms and windows with long-distance guns in them, and placed her soldiers there to watch out over the water, and in time of war to fire on any one England does not want to pass through the water-gate.

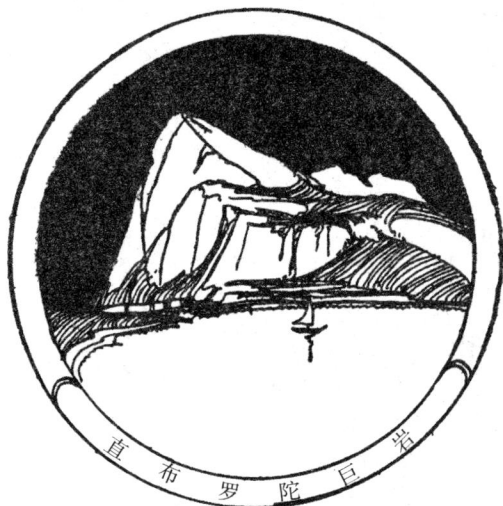

这块岩石里，隐蔽着一个巨大的要塞，
里面部署有兵力和大炮

Long years ago most all of the World that people knew was chiefly around the edge of the Mediterranean Sea. Sailors at that time thought it dangerous to go outside this gate, the Strait of Gibraltar, into the great ocean, and—so the story goes—they set up Pillars on each side of the Strait like gate-posts. They called them the Pillars of Hercules, and they put up a sign to warn sailors that it was dangerous to go beyond these Pillars. The sign said "Non Plus Ultra," which meant "Nothing More

如今，直布罗陀已经不再属于西班牙，而是英国的领土了。

虽说直布罗陀在地图上像是一个"鼻子"，可要是你们乘坐船只在此处驶出地中海的话，直布罗陀看上去就会像是一块又长又高的岩石。直布罗陀与非洲之间，是一片狭窄的水域，叫作"直布罗陀海峡"。这条海峡只有大约十三英里宽，差不多只有多佛海峡的一半宽，不过，由于来自大西洋的强大洋流不停地进出海峡，因此到了最近才有人从中游过去呢。在直布罗陀这块大岩石里面，英国开凿出了许多的走廊、房间和窗户，里面部署有射程很远的大炮，并且驻扎有兵力，来监视这片水域，这样，到了战时，他们便可以向英国不希望进出这个海峡的任何船只开火了。

很久以前，人们所了解的世界，绝大部分都集中在地中海沿岸。传说中，由于那时的水手认为，驶出直布罗陀海峡这扇地中海的"大门"，进入那片更辽阔的海洋是很危险的，因此他们便在海峡两边立起了两根巨大的柱子，就像门柱似的。他们将这两根柱子称为"海格力斯之柱"[1]，还在那里竖起了一块标牌，警告水手们

---

[1] "海格力斯之柱"（Pillars of Hercules），海格力斯是古希腊神话中宙斯与阿尔克墨涅所生之子。他力大无比，因完成了天后赫拉所要求的十二项任务而获得永生。这些任务中，有一项便是到西方牵回巨人革律翁的牛群，这是海格力斯往西出行最远的一次，其终点即是所谓的"海格力斯之柱"。直布罗陀海峡两侧对峙的两座峭壁，被古人认为正是海格力斯此次西行的终点，故后人就用此名指代直布罗陀。

Beyond." It was supposed that not far outside the Pillars of Hercules the ocean came to an edge where you would tumble off down, down, down to bottomless nothing. Columbus did not believe any such foolishness; he was not afraid. He sailed from Spain, starting from a place outside the Pillars of Hercules called Palos. He sailed on and on and on until, as you know, he came to America.

Just before Columbus sailed from Spain there were people living there called Moors, who had come across from Africa and made their home in Spain. The Moors were different from other people in Europe. They believed in a man named Mohammed and a god whom they called Allah. The Moors built beautiful palaces, but they were different from Christian palaces. The Moorish princes lived in one of these palaces on a hill in the city of Granada, which is not far from Gibraltar. The palace in Granada was called the Alhambra.

The Christians in Spain didn't like the Moors, so they fought them, and at last the Christians drove the Moors out of Spain, drove them across the Strait of Gibraltar back into Africa whence they had come. The Spanish Queen received Columbus in the Alhambra and bade him good-by before he started out for the New World, but no one now lives there. It is still there on the hill at Granada and Spain keeps it as it once was, so that people may visit it. The walls, instead of being plastered or painted, are covered with colored tiles. The doorways, instead of being square, are shaped like a horseshoe, and its court-yards have splashing fountains and walled-in pools where the Moorish princesses

说驶出这两根柱子之后就会很危险。那块标牌上写着这样一句话："不可越过"，意思就是"此地之外就是虚无"。人们认为，船只驶出"海格力斯之柱"不远，就会来到海洋的边缘，然后一头向下跌去，一直跌到深不见底的虚无之中去。哥伦布可不相信这些愚蠢的迷信，他什么也不怕。于是，他从西班牙动身，从"海格力斯之柱"外边一个叫作帕洛斯的地方启航了。他驾驶着船只不停地航行、航行，而大家也都知道，后来他终于到达了美洲。

就在哥伦布从西班牙出发开始航海之前，该国还生活着一个叫作"摩尔人"的民族，他们都是从非洲横渡过来，然后在西班牙定居下来的。摩尔人与欧洲其他的民族都不一样。他们信仰的是一个叫作"穆罕默德"的人，以及一个他们称之为"安拉"的神灵。摩尔人兴建了许多美丽的宫殿，而这些宫殿也与基督教风格的宫殿大不相同。摩尔人的王子们，都住在格拉纳达市一座小山上的宫殿里，那里离直布罗陀不是很远。格拉纳达的这座宫殿，叫作"阿尔罕布拉宫"。

西班牙的基督徒都不喜欢摩尔人，因此向摩尔人发动了战争，最终，基督徒将摩尔人逐出了西班牙，将他们赶过了直布罗陀海峡，赶回了非洲老家。西班牙王后曾经在阿尔罕布拉宫接见过哥伦布，并在他动身前往"新大陆"之前跟他道别，可如今，没有人再住在那座宫殿里了。它仍然屹立在格拉纳达那座小山之上，西班牙人也一直保持着它的原貌，以便人们能够前去参观。宫殿里的墙壁上既没有粉刷灰泥，也没有绘制壁画，而是盖着彩色的瓷瓦。宫殿门廊的样子并不是方形的，而是有点儿像马蹄铁，并且庭院里还有水花四溅的喷泉，以及围起来的水池，摩尔人的

used to bathe instead of in bathtubs.

A city in Spain called Seville has a great Cathedral, the second largest church in the World. It was built, of course, after the Moors had been driven out of Spain, as it is a Christian church, built where there once was a Moorish church. In this Cathedral are buried what are supposed to be the ashes of Columbus, though we think, as I told you before, that they are not his ashes at all, but the ashes of his son, and that his real ashes are in Haiti.

Moorish women used to wear veils over their faces. It was thought immodest for them to go out on the street with their faces uncovered. The Spanish women often wear veils too, but they wear them over their heads instead of hats, and some of the veils made of lace are very beautiful and very costly. They also wear very big and high combs in their hair and bright-colored silk shawls over their shoulders, and in summer carry beautiful fans, for it gets very warm in Seville—so warm that during the middle of the day no one goes out-of-doors who doesn't have to. In our country young children take naps during the day, hut in Spain grown-ups take naps too, after their midday meal, only they call a nap by the very pretty name "siesta."

她的头发上插着一把高高的梳子，头上和肩膀上则披着一块长长的头巾

公主们以前都是在这个水池里洗澡，而不是在浴缸里沐浴呢。

西班牙有座叫作"塞维利亚"的城市，那里有一座大教堂，规模位居全球第二。自然，这座大教堂是在摩尔人被赶出西班牙之后修建的，因为它是一座基督教堂，并且修建在一座摩尔人教堂的原址之上。据说，哥伦布的骨灰就安葬在这座大教堂里，不过我却认为，正如前面跟大家说过的那样，安葬在这里的可能根本就不是哥伦布的骸骨，而是他儿子的骨灰，至于哥伦布的真正遗骸，却仍然留在海地。

摩尔女子的脸上，常常都罩着面纱。摩尔人认为，女子不戴面纱便到大街上去抛头露面，是一种很不庄重的行为。西班牙妇女经常也戴着头巾，但她们的头巾不是戴在帽子上方，而是戴在头上，其中一些头巾还有金银边饰，非常漂亮，也非常昂贵。她们的头发上会插着一把很大很高的梳子，肩膀上则披着颜色亮丽的丝质披巾，夏天还会带上漂亮的扇子，因为塞维利亚的夏天非常炎热，中午时分如果不是非得如此，人们就不会到户外去。在我们美国，小朋友们白天都会午睡，可在西班牙，大人吃过中饭后也会去午睡，只是他们的午睡有个非常漂亮的名字，叫作"午后小憩"。

32 Castles in Spain (continued)

When I was a boy I once climbed over a fence into a field, and before I knew it a bull was dashing toward me. I barely had time to scramble back over the fence again—a narrow escape; I didn't see any fun in it at all. But in Spain on Sundays and holidays great crowds of people go to an outdoor theater called the bull-ring to see men fight bulls.

The people sit on seats outside a fence that shuts in a sandy field, and from that safe place they watch the bull-fights. A gate is opened into the field and a big, wild bull rushes in. A man called a bull-fighter goes to meet him with a red cloak in his hand and waves it in the face of the bull. This makes the bull mad, so with lowered horns he charges the red cloak. The bull-fighter jumps to one side just as the bull reaches him, and the angry bull, unable to turn quickly, passes him by. The bull-fighter teases the bull in this way again and again. After worrying him in various ways, as a cat plays with a mouse, the bull-fighter kills the bull with a thrust of a long sword. It seems to us very cruel, but in Spain they say we kill bulls for meat and do not give any one the fun (?) of seeing them killed.

A bull-fighter has to be very brave and very skilful, and his foot must not slip on the sandy ground, or he cannot dodge the bull and he will be killed. Almost every city and town in Spain has a bull-ring, as almost every city in the United States has a baseball field or a stadium, for bullfighting is a national sport, as baseball or football is our national

第32章　西班牙的城堡（续）

小的时候，我曾经翻过一道篱笆，跑到一块地里去，可是，还不待我明白是怎么回事，一头公牛便朝我冲了过来。我费了好大的劲，勉勉强强才从篱笆上爬了出来，真是死里逃生呀，这件事情，我可看不出哪里有什么意思。但在西班牙，很多很多的人却会在星期天或者节假日里，到一个叫作"斗牛场"的露天剧场去看斗牛呢。

看斗牛的时候，观众都是坐在一块封闭式沙地周围的栏杆外边，坐在这样一个安全的地方，他们就可以安安心心地观看斗牛比赛了。人们把一扇通到场地里面的大门打开后，一头体型巨大、疯狂乱窜的公牛就会跑进场中。一个叫作斗牛士的人迎上前去，手里拿着一块红斗篷，在公牛面前挥动。这样做，会激怒公牛，所以，公牛便低下来，用牛角向那块红斗篷顶过去。就在公牛即将顶到他身上时，斗牛士往旁边一跳，那头发怒的公牛由于无法迅速转弯，便一下子从斗牛士身边冲过去了。斗牛士用这种方式，一遍又一遍地捉弄公牛。就像猫捉弄老鼠一样，用各种各样的方法折磨了公牛一遍之后，斗牛士最终还会用长剑猛地一刺，把公牛杀死。这种情景，在我们看来是很残忍的，可在西班牙，人们却会说，我们杀牛吃牛肉，却没给任何人带来观赏杀牛场景的乐趣呢。你们说，这种事情有乐趣可言吗？

斗牛士必须非常勇敢，必须技术高超，而他的脚也不能在沙地上打滑，否则便无法躲开公牛，会被公牛顶死。西班牙几乎每个城镇里都有一个斗牛场，就像美国

sport. Even boys play bullfighting, one making believe he is the bull and the other the bull-fighter.

Every country seems to have certain games they like to play best. In Spain the girls do not jump rope, but they dance instead, and keep time by clicking little clappers on their fingers, often singing as they do so. The clappers look like big chestnuts and so are called castanets, which means chestnuts. They dance in twos and fours on the sidewalk, in the parks and squares, wherever our children would jump rope or play hop-scotch. Even in the great Cathedral of Seville the choir boys dance with castanets in front of the altar at certain church festivals. It is the only place in the World where any one dances in church.

Spanish houses have no front yard nor back yard nor side yard, but an inside yard with the rooms all around it. This inside yard is called a patio and it is often a living-room and dining-room for all who live in the house.

As you ride through Spain on a train you can see from the car window a very peculiar looking tree—different from any tree that grows in our country. This is the cork-tree. The little and big corks we use for bottle stoppers don't grow on trees as cherries or peaches do. They are made from the bark of a kind of oak. The bark is cut off from the tree in

斗牛士用一块红色斗篷捉弄公牛

几乎每座城镇里都有一个棒球场或者体育场一样，这是因为，斗牛是西班牙的一种全国性体育活动，就像棒球或者橄榄球是美国的全国性体育运动一样。连西班牙的小男孩，也会由一个小朋友假装公牛、由另一个小朋友假装斗牛士，来玩斗牛游戏呢。

似乎每个国家都有本国国民最喜欢玩的一些游戏运动。西班牙的小姑娘不会跳绳，而是跳舞，并且会敲击手上所拿的小响板来打拍子，常常还边打拍子边唱歌。那种响板，样子就像是大颗的栗子，叫作"卡斯塔内"，也就是"栗子"的意思。她们会两个一组或者四个一组，在人行道上、公园里和广场上跳舞，而美国的小朋友呢，则会在这些地方跳绳或者玩跳房子的游戏。即便是在塞维利亚大教堂里，唱诗班的孩子们在某些宗教节日里，也会在祭坛前打着响板跳舞呢。放眼全世界，只有这里的人们才会在教堂里跳舞。

西班牙的房屋都没有什么前院、后院或者侧院，而是有一个四周都是房间的内院。这种内院叫作"天井"，通常既是一家人的客厅，也是餐厅。

如果坐火车穿越西班牙的话，大家从车窗往外看去，就会看到一种样子非常古怪的树，它们与美国的树完全不一样。这种树，叫作"软木树"。不过，我们用于做瓶塞的那种大大小小的软木塞，并不是像樱桃或者桃子那样，是树上结出来的。它们都是用软木树的树皮制成的。人们把软木树的树皮大块大块地割下来，然后再

large pieces and cut up into big and little corks. The tree then grows another coat of bark, but it takes nine years to grow a thick enough bark to be cut again. So every cork you use is nearly as old as you are, or older.

Cork-trees live to a great age, much longer than people do. But another tree you see in Spain grows to be still older. It is the olive-tree, which bears a fruit that looks something like green cherries. It is said that olive-trees have been known to live and bear fruit for a thousand years! Olives have been used as food since Bible times and long before that, and yet many people have to learn to like them. Olives are also pressed to make olive oil, which we use in salad dressing, for no other kind of oil is quite as good for food. In Spain they often use it instead of butter, and it is also made into a very pure soap called Castile soap, which you may have used.

Winners of games long ago used to be crowned with a wreath made of olive leaves, and in time of war, messengers bringing peace used to carry an olive branch. In certain parts of Spain you can ride all day long on a train and see olive-trees, olive-trees, olive-trees, from morning to night, till you wonder what the people can do with so many. They use a great many olives themselves, for olives are often bread and

把它们切成大大小小的软木塞。然后，软木树又会长出一层新的树皮来，但是，要过九年，这种树上才会长出一层厚厚的、足以再次切割下来做软木塞的树皮。因此，大家所用的每个瓶塞，年纪都跟你们差不多，没准还会比你们大呢。

她们不跳绳，而是打着响板跳舞

软木树的生长寿命很长，比人类的寿命还要长得多。不过，你们在西班牙还会看到一种树，它们的寿命就更长了。这种树，就是橄榄树，它结出的果实，样子有点儿像是青樱桃。据说，橄榄树能够生长和结果一千年之久呢！自《圣经》时代以及之前很久以来，人们一直都把橄榄当成食物，不过，也有许多人是不得不开始喜欢这种东西的。人们还会用橄榄榨出橄榄油来，我们用橄榄油当沙拉调味汁，因为橄榄油是最好的一种食用油。西班牙人常常吃橄榄油而不吃黄油，并且，人们还用橄榄油制成了一种非常纯净的肥皂，叫作"橄榄皂"，大家可能都用过呢。

很久以前，人们常常是给比赛中的优胜者戴上一顶用橄榄叶编成的桂冠，而到了战时，那些带来和平消息的信使手里，常常也会持一根橄榄枝。在西班牙的某些地区，游客坐着火车可以看上一整天的橄榄树，从早到晚，触目之处除了橄榄树还是橄榄树，以至于大家都会奇怪，那里的人种这么多橄榄树干什么。西班牙人本身就要消费掉大量的橄榄，因为橄榄往往就是他们的黄油面包、肉和蔬菜，不过，他们也会向没有橄榄树的世界各国出口数百万罐橄榄和橄榄油。

西班牙首都的人都说，那里是一座可以与巴黎媲美的城市。西班牙的首都位于

butter, meat and vegetables to Spaniards, but they send millions of bottles of olives and olive oil all over the World to other countries that have none.

One of those cities that says it is like Paris is the capital of Spain. It is near the center of the country. It is called Madrid. Old Madrid had narrow streets and small houses. New Madrid has broad boulevards and big buildings, and if you did not hear the people speaking Spanish you might think you were in Paris or even in New York. In old Spain men used to say all the time "Manyana," which means "tomorrow," for they put off everything they could until to-morrow. New Spain says "Do it now." When you are in Madrid and say you live in America, they think you mean South America, and that of course you speak Spanish, for to a Spaniard "America" means South America. A Spaniard who has made his fortune in South America comes "home to Madrid" to live on what he has made, for a house in Madrid is his "Castle in Spain."

Sometimes two brothers have families and live in the same house, but usually they get along better if they live in separate houses. Portugal and Spain are like two brothers. They speak a language that is alike and the people are alike in other ways, but they have never been able to get along together, though they tried it once for a little while. In both countries they like dancing and music. In both countries they raise cork and olives. In both countries they like bull-fights—though in Portugal they do not kill the bull, and they wrap the points of his horns so that he can't kill.

该国中部，叫作"马德里"。老马德里市中，街道狭窄，房屋狭小。新马德里市则有许多宽阔的林荫大道和一栋栋高楼大厦，要是听不到当地人说西班牙语的话，大家可能还会以为自己身处的是巴黎，或者甚至是纽约呢。以前的西班牙人总是在说"曼雅那"（Manyana），就是"明天"的意思，因为他们会把所有能够推到明天的事情都推到第二天再去做。不过，如今的西班牙人却会说"现在就做"了。在马里德旅行的时候，如果大家说自己住在美洲，那么他们会以为你们是南美人，并且以为你们肯定会说西班牙语呢，这是因为，在西班牙人看来，"美洲"指的就是南美洲。西班牙人在南美洲发了财后，便会"回到马德里的家中"，用自己挣到的钱来生活。在马德里买上一座房子，就是西班牙人的"梦想"。

有的时候，西班牙人会是两兄弟带着各自的家人生活在同一栋房子里，不过，要是分开生活的话，兄弟之间的关系通常都会更好一些。葡萄牙和西班牙就像是两兄弟。两国说一种相似的语言，两国民众在其他一些方面也很相似，但是，尽管曾经短暂地努力过，两国却从来没能和睦相处。两国民众都喜欢跳舞，都喜欢音乐。两国都有软木树和橄榄树。两国民众都喜欢斗牛，只是葡萄牙人最后不会将公牛杀死，还会用布将公牛的尖角包裹起来，使得它没法伤人。

33 The Land in the Sky

The lowest country in Europe is Holland.

The highest country in Europe is the land of the Swiss people, called Switzerland.

There is hardly a hill in the whole of Holland. The country is as flat as a ball-field.

There is hardly a hill in the whole of Switzerland. The hills are all mountains—the highest mountains in western Europe—mountains so high that there is snow on their tops all the year round, in summer as well as winter. They are called the Alps.

But you can't have a hole in a doughnut without the doughnut, and so you can't have a mountain without a valley. The mountain tops in Switzerland are white, but the valleys are green, and cows with tinkling bells graze over the fields. The melting snow from the mountain tops makes beautiful waterfalls and babbling, tinkling brooks in the valleys.

Have you ever seen the snow on the roof of a house suddenly slide off and fall to the ground? That is called an avalanche. But suppose the roof of the house were a mile long like the side of a mountain, and suddenly the snow covering it slipped and fell into the valley beneath. That is an avalanche such as they have in Switzerland; and sometimes avalanches bury people and houses and even whole villages beneath.

Some long and wide valleys are filled with snow that has turned to ice. The ice filling these long valleys, like a river frozen to the bottom, is called a glacier, and the biggest of

第33章　空中国度

欧洲地势最低的国家，是荷兰。

欧洲地势最高的国家，则是瑞士人生活的那个国度，叫作"瑞士"。

荷兰全境几乎没有一座小山。该国就像一个棒球场那样平坦。

瑞士全境也几乎没有一座小山。该国境内的山，全都是大山，属于西欧地区海拔最高的一条山脉，而且，这条山脉高耸入云，因此不论冬夏，山顶都常年积雪。这条山脉，叫作"阿尔卑斯山脉"。

不过，正如要是连炸面圈都没有的话，大家就不可能在炸面圈上弄出一个洞来那样，要是没有山谷，那就没有大山了。瑞士的山顶全都白雪皑皑，可山谷中却是绿草如茵，牛羊在地里吃草，牛铃清脆悦耳。山顶融化的雪水，在山谷中形成了一道道美丽的瀑布，和一条条水声潺潺、叮咚作响的溪流。

大家有没有见过，屋顶上的积雪在突然之间滑下来，掉到地上的情景呢？那种现象，叫作"雪崩"。不过，大家不妨假设屋顶有一英里长，就像一片山坡，然后想象想象上面覆盖的积雪突然滑下来，掉入下面山谷之中时的情形。瑞士的雪崩，情况正是如此，有的时候，这种雪崩还会将下面山谷里的人、房屋甚至整个村庄都掩埋起来呢。

在一些又长又宽的山谷中，全都是已经结成了冰的积雪。冰雪填满了这些长长

these glaciers have names just as rivers have.

Most rivers start from springs, but in Switzerland they usually start from the melting ice under a glacier. One of these big glaciers in Switzerland is called the Rhône Glacier. From under the end of the Rhône Glacier, as from an ice cave, flows a cold stream of melting ice. This stream grows larger and larger as it flows on down the valley and is joined by other streams of melted snow and ice. It is then called the Rhône River. It runs on until it reaches a big, broad valley, which it fills and forms a lake—the largest lake in Switzerland—called Lake Geneva.

The Rhône flows out again on the other side of Lake Geneva, down through France past Lyons and the mulberry-trees and silkworm farms and silk manufactories I told you about, and at last empties into the Mediterranean Sea.

Another river with the same name as the Rhône, all except one letter, is the Rhine. It, too, starts from underneath a glacier, but flows north between France and Germany, through Holland, and empties into the North Sea.

There are many people in the World who think it great sport to climb mountains— the higher the mountain and the more difficult and the more dangerous it is, the more they like to climb it. Now the highest mountain in the Alps is Mont Blanc, which means White Mountain. Part of it is in Switzerland, but the top is in France. Every summer many people climb Mont Blanc and other mountains in the Alps. These mountain-climbers use long poles with spikes on the ends to catch on the ice, and they wear heavy shoes with

的山谷，就像是一条从上到下全都封冻了的河流，叫作"冰川"，而那些最大的冰川也像河流一样，各有各的名称。

绝大多数河流，都是发源于山泉之间，可瑞士的河流，通常却是发源于冰川下面融化的雪水。瑞士境内有一座大冰川，叫作"罗纳冰川"。从罗纳冰川末端的下方，流出了一条由融化的冰水形成的寒冷溪流，它就像是从冰洞中流出来似的。在流向下方山谷的过程中，由于不断有其他冰雪融化后形成的溪流汇入，因此这条小溪变得越来越大了。这条溪流，就叫"罗纳河"。罗纳河继续往前流去，然后注入一个又大又宽的山谷，在那里形成了一个湖泊，那是瑞士境内最大的湖泊，叫作"日内瓦湖"。

然后，罗纳河从日内瓦湖的另一侧继续往下流去，向南穿过法国，经过我在前面已经向大家提到过的里昂、桑树和养蚕的农场、丝绸生产厂，最后注入了地中海。

还有一条河流，它的名称听起来与罗纳河差不多，叫作"莱茵河"。这条河也发源于一座冰川之下，但它是在法、德两国之间向北流去，经由荷兰，最后注入北海。

世界上有许多人都觉得，爬山是一种很不错的运动，山越高、路越险、爬起来越费劲，他们就越喜欢去爬。如今，阿尔卑斯山脉的最高峰是"勃朗峰"，也就是"白峰"的意思。这座山峰，虽说有一部分位于瑞士境内，但其顶峰却在法国境内。每年夏季，都有许多的人来攀登勃朗峰，攀登阿尔卑斯山脉的其他山峰。这些

hobnails; and they take along guides who know the way to go and the way to climb, and they are tied together so that if one slips over a ledge the others may pull him back. But every summer people lose their lives in such mountain-climbing. They slip and fall and are dashed to their death or they are covered by an avalanche and buried alive under the falling pile of snow.

Probably the hardest of all Swiss mountains to climb is a mountain that looks like a huge horn. It is called the "Matterhorn." Only the most skilled and the most daring ever attempt to climb it, though the only thing you can do after you have risked your life to reach the top is to admire the view. The reason most people climb it, however, is simply so they can say "I've done it."

So many people go to Switzerland to see the giant snow-covered mountains, even if they do not climb them, that the Swiss people have built hotels wherever there is a fine view of a mountain, or a waterfall, or some other wonderful or beautiful sight. There are thousands of such hotels all through Switzerland, so that the chief business of the Swiss people seems to be hotel-keeping, and they keep them very well indeed. In fact, it is said they are the finest hotel-keepers in the World. They are

人们冒着生命危险登上顶峰

登山者，全都带着一根底端有尖刺、能够扎进冰里的长杆，穿着一双沉重的、装有鞋钉的登山鞋。他们还会请一些知道路线、懂得登山技术的人来当向导，然后用绳索把所有的人都绑成一串，这样，万一有人滑下岩石的话，其余的人就可以把他拽回来。不过，每年夏季都有人在这样的登山活动中丧生。他们要么是滑倒、跌落并摔死，要么便是雪崩之时被压在积雪下，被掉下来的一堆堆积雪活埋了。

瑞士所有山峰中最难攀登的，很有可能是一座外形有如巨角的山峰。这座山峰，叫作"马特峰"。只有那些本领最高、胆子最大的人，才敢试着去攀登这座山峰，可冒着生命危险终于爬到山顶后，他们唯一能做的事情，不过就是欣赏眼前"一览众山小"的景色罢了。然而，绝大多数人前去攀登的原因，却只是为了让自己能够说："我做到了。"

就算人们不去攀爬，也有无数游客到瑞士来欣赏这些白雪皑皑的山峰，所以，瑞士人在凡是能够看到山峰、瀑布或者有其他妙景美景可赏的地方，全都修建了旅馆。瑞士全境，有成千上万座这样的旅馆，因此，瑞士人的主要业务似乎就是开旅馆，而他们在这方面也的确干得很不错。事实上，人们都说瑞典人是全世界最优秀的旅馆经营者呢。当然，在其他一些方面，瑞士人也同样赫赫有名。比如说瑞士的牛

famous for other things too: Swiss milk chocolate, which you have probably eaten; Swiss cheese with big holes in it, which you may have eaten; Swiss wood-carving, and cuckoo-clocks and cowbells and music boxes.

Most countries have an army and a navy as we have police and a watch-dog to keep out burglars. But Switzerland is one of the few countries in the World that has no seashore. So she can't have a navy, and she doesn't have to have much of an army either, because the mountains are like great walls to keep out the enemy. Switzerland kept out of both World Wars, although every country around her was fighting.

Switzerland is completely surrounded by other countries. On one side is France, on the other Germany, and on another Italy. So the Swiss have no language of their own. On the side nearest Italy they speak Italian, on the side nearest Germany they speak German and on the side nearest France they speak French. In fact, many Swiss people speak all three languages.

To get into Switzerland or out of Switzerland, or from one part of Switzerland to another, you don't have to climb the mountains. You can go over the low places between the high mountains, but many of these low places are a mile or more high, so they are not so very low at that. These low places are called passes. One of these passes is named the Simplon; and Napoleon, the French general I told you about, once crossed the Simplon Pass with his army into Italy. But you can now go under and through the mountains, for in many places long tunnels have been built.

奶巧克力，大家很可能都吃过；瑞士奶酪，上面有一个个大洞，大家可能也吃过；还有瑞士手表、瑞士木刻、瑞士的布谷鸟钟、牛铃以及八音盒，全都有名得很哩。

绝大多数国家都有自己的陆军和海军，它们的作用，就像我们用警察和看门狗来阻止窃贼偷东西那样。不过，瑞士却是世界上为数不多的、没有海岸线的国家之一。因此，该国不可能有海军，而且，该国也没有必要拥有大量的陆军兵力，因为那里的山脉就像是一道道巨大的墙壁，可以将敌人拒之门外。在两次世界大战中，瑞士都没有参战，可其周围的邻国，却一个个全都参战了。

瑞士全境，都被别的国家所包围着。一面是法国，一面是德国，而另一面则是意大利。因此，瑞士没有本国的语言。靠近意大利那一面的瑞士人说意大利语，离德国那一面最近的瑞士人说德语，而距法国那一侧最近的瑞士人则说法语。实际上，许多瑞士人这三种语言都会说。

当然，要想进出瑞士，或者从瑞士的一个地区到另一个地区去，大家也不一定非要翻山越岭。你们可以从两座高山间的低凹之处通过，不过，很多低凹之处都有一英里或者更高，所以它们其实并不算是低凹。这些低凹之处，叫作"山口"。其中，有处山口叫作"辛普朗山口"，前面我跟你们说过的那位法国元帅拿破仑，就曾率领手下的军队，从辛普朗山口挺进到了意大利呢。不过，如今人们可以从山脉底下通过了，因为许多地方都修建了长长的地下隧道。

其中最长的一条隧道，就是"圣戈特哈德"隧道。开凿这条隧道的工人，先是从那座山的两侧掘进，然后两洞正好在山腹中央合龙。有些人称赞说，从一座山相

One of the longest tunnels is St. Gothard. The men who built it started to dig from both sides of the mountain, and the two holes they dug exactly met in the middle. Some people said it was wonderful that two tunnels, each miles long, dug from opposite sides of a mountain, should meet. The men replied, "Not at all. It would have been wonderful if the tunnels hadn't met. We are not moles digging blindly. We had figured it out beforehand and we knew where we were digging."

But the longest tunnel in the World is under the Simplon Pass. At one end of this tunnel is Switzerland and at the other end is Italy. It is over twelve miles long. I have been under the pass riding in a train through this tunnel and I have been over the top of the pass carried by my own two legs. It takes sixteen minutes to go through the tunnel. It took me part of two days to climb over.

Near the top of the Simplon Pass is a house called a hospice where I once spent the night. It is a house where certain priests, called monks, live, and the reason the hospice was built there and the reason the monks live there is to provide a shelter for travelers and a place where they may rest safely in case they should be caught in a storm.

Few people now cross the pass, for it is so easy and so quick and so safe to go through the tunnel; but before the tunnel was made underneath there was no other way for people to go from Italy to Switzerland but over the top of the pass, and many people were traveling that way all the time. Snow-storms and blizzards were likely to happen almost any time, summer or winter, and often travelers would be lost and frozen to death. These

对的两侧各挖一个长达数英里的洞，而两个洞竟然能够在山腹中央刚好接上，这种技术太神奇了。可那些工人却回答说："根本就不神奇。要是隧道两侧合不起来，这才奇怪呢。我们事先都经过了计算，因此知道朝着哪个方向掘进。"

不过，世界上最长的隧道，则是辛普朗山口下面的那条隧道。这条隧道，一端是瑞士，另一端则到了意大利。整条隧道有十二英里多长。我曾经乘坐火车到达这个山口之下，穿过了那条隧道，我也曾经凭借自己的两条腿，从那座山口的顶上翻过去。坐火车穿过那条隧道，用了十六分钟。我徒步翻越那个山口，却用了差不多两天。

距辛普朗山口顶上不远的地方，有一座叫作"救济院"的房子，我曾经在那里过了一夜。那座房子，以前是一些叫作"修道士"的牧师居住的地方，而把救济院建在那里，修道士们会住在那里，目的就是为了给旅行者提供一个住处，让旅行者可以在那里安全地休息，以免他们困在暴风雪中。

如今，很少有人再去翻越那个山口了，因为坐车走山下的隧道，既轻松快捷，又非常安全。不过，底下那条隧道建成之前，人们除了翻过此处山口，就没有别的办法从意大利前往瑞士了，因此，许多人一直都是沿着这条道路来去的。几乎不管什么时候，无论是夏季还是冬季，山上都有可能刮起暴风雪，因此旅行者们常常会迷路、冻死。而住在这座救济院里的那些善良修道士，就是辛普朗山口上的救生员。他们沿着山路修建了许多的小茅屋，还养了许多体型巨大、体格强壮、非常聪明的"圣伯纳"犬，训练它们在山上刮起暴风雪的时候从救济院出发，去搜救那些可能已经被大雪压倒、迷路或者掉进了厚厚积雪中的旅行者。圣伯纳犬的脖子上会

good monks living in the hospice were the life-savers of the mountain pass. They had built little huts along the mountain pathway and they had large, strong, intelligent dogs called St. Bernards who were trained to go forth from the hospice when there was a storm, and search for travelers who might have been overcome, lost their way, or fallen in the snow. A dog would carry, strapped to his neck, a barrel filled with bread and wine. His sense of smell was so strong he could find a man even though buried in the snow, shake him back to his senses, and drag him to the nearest hut, to wait for food and drink until the storm should stop. The Simplon Hospice is one of the few places in the World where any one, whether he be rich man or poor man, saint or sinner, will be housed for the night, fed, and taken care of for nothing, without question and without charge.

Do you know the story of William Tell? Well, Switzerland has many lakes, but the most beautiful one is called the Lake of Light—Lake Lucerne—and on the shore of Lake Lucerne is a little church marking the spot where William Tell is supposed to have shot the apple off of his young son's head.

圣伯纳犬不会伤害你们。它是你们的好朋友

挂着一个小桶，里面装满了面包和葡萄酒。圣伯纳犬的嗅觉非常灵敏，甚至能找到一个埋在雪下的人，将被埋者摇醒，并把被埋者拖到最近的一座小茅屋里，等待暴风雪平息之后，修道士们再送来食物和饮水。辛普朗山救济院，是世界上为数不多的、任何人都可以过夜的地方之一。无论是富翁还是贫民，无论是圣徒还是罪人，都可以不用付出任何费用便在那里过夜，得到修道士们的悉心照料，修道士们不会问你们任何问题，也不会收取任何费用。

你们听没听说过威廉·退尔[1]的故事呢？注意，瑞士有很多的湖泊，而其中最美丽的一个，则被称为"光明之湖"，也就是"卢塞恩湖"。卢塞恩湖畔有一座小教堂，那里还标出了据说是威廉·退尔射中小儿子头上苹果的地方哩。

---

[1] 威廉·退尔（William Tell），瑞士民间传说中的英雄和农民起义领袖。传说十三世纪时统治瑞士的总督非常残暴，竟然把自己的帽子用杆子顶着，放在闹市，勒令过往民众向其鞠躬。农民射手退尔经过时拒不行礼，总督便叫人将一个苹果放在退尔小儿子的头上，要退尔向苹果射箭。退尔射中后，拿出另一支箭，说如果第一箭没有射中，就会用第二支箭射杀总督。总督逮捕了退尔，但在押解途中，退尔射死了总督并逃脱。后来，退尔带领瑞士人民起来斗争，获得了自由。

34 The Boot Top

You've heard of the "old woman who lived in a shoe, who had so many children she didn't know what to do." Well, there is a boot in which live not only many children but millions of children and millions of men and women too. It is called Italy. It is the largest boot in the World and yet it is not large enough to hold all its children, so a great many of them have come over to America. The very first one of them to come over was Christopher Columbus, over four hundred years ago. He sailed from Spain, but he was born in Italy and lived in a city at the top of the boot, called Genoa. A part of his house is still standing in Genoa, and there is a statue of him just outside the railroad station. Ships still sail from Genoa to America, but they know where they are going now and Columbus didn't.

On the other side of the boot top is another city. It is not *near* the water, nor *by* the water, nor *on* the water, but *in* the water. It is built on many little islands, and the streets are water with bridges across them. This city is called Venice. The water streets are called canals, and the main street, which would be a broad avenue if it were paved, is called the Grand Canal. Instead of automobiles or carriages, the people have to use boats. These boats are painted black and in the center there is a little cabin like a closed automobile. In the very front there is a queer thing with teeth which looks something like a big comb standing on end. These boats are called gondolas, and a man called a gondolier stands

第34章　"靴子"顶上

大家都听说过"老太太，住鞋子，儿太多，没法子"[1]这首童谣吧。注意，世界上有一只"靴子"，里面非但是住了许多的孩子，住了数百万个孩子，还住着数百万的成年人呢。这只"靴子"，叫作"意大利"。虽说它是世界上最大的一只"靴子"，可它还不够大，装不下意大利所有的孩子，因此，许多意大利孩子便来到了美洲。其中第一个来到美洲的，就是四百多年前的克里斯托弗·哥伦布。虽然是从西班牙动身航海的，但他出生于意大利，并且住在这只"靴子"顶端一个叫作"热那亚"的城市里。如今，热那亚仍然保存着哥伦布故居的一部分，而热那亚火车站外，也屹立着一尊哥伦布的雕像。如今，仍然有船只从热那亚驶往美洲，而船上的人也都知道自己要航向哪里，但是，哥伦布那时却并不清楚这一点。

这只"靴子"顶端的另一侧，还有一座城市。那座城市并不临水，不在水边，不在水面之上，而是位于水中。该市建在许多小岛之上，城中的街道都是水路，上面架有桥梁。这座城市，就叫"威尼斯"。城中的水上街道，都叫运河，而其中的主街则叫"大运河"，要是铺上石子的话，那里本来应该是一条宽阔的大街呢。威

---

[1]　这是世界最早的英国儿歌集《鹅妈妈童谣》里的一首童谣，原标题是《An old woman in a shoe（住在鞋子里的老太太）》。

back of the little cabin and rows the gondola with one long oar. There are no "stop" and "go" signs at the canal crossings, so the gondoliers, as they come to a crossing, call out a funny "ooh," and if there is a gondolier coming from the cross canal he calls back so that they will not run into each other. There are no honking horns, no rumbling wheels—Venice is almost silent except for singing and music.

Long ago where Venice now is there were many little islands but no city. Some people, called Veneti, were troubled by a wild tribe from the north. So they moved to these islands to get away from these annoying tribes. The Veneti cut posts made of cedar wood, which does not easily rot, and drove them down into the water, and on top of these posts they built their houses. The Veneti lived chiefly on fish, which they caught in large numbers, because all they had to do was to drop a line or net out of the front door. In fact, they caught so many fish they could not eat them all. So they gathered salt by drying sea-water and salted the fish so that they would keep.

As the Veneti lived on the water they had to be good sailors, and they were. So they sailed to all corners of the Mediterranean Sea, selling their salt fish and selling salt too, and bringing back in payment silk gowns and rugs and jewels. Then people from all over Europe came to Venice to buy these things which the Veneti had brought back in exchange for this fish and salt, and Venice became the greatest shopping-place, the greatest market, in Europe. So the Venetians, as the Veneti came to be called, kept on getting richer and richer. They built beautiful palaces along the canals, and as they believed a certain saint

尼斯人在市里来去，只能乘坐小船，而不能乘坐汽车和马车。那些小船都被漆成了黑色，中央有一个小舱，就像一辆封闭的汽车。船头装着一种有齿的奇怪之物，样子就像是一把竖着的梳子。这些小船，就叫"贡多拉"，一个叫作"船夫"的人站在小舱后面，用一根长桨划着贡多拉前进。在运河的交叉之处，并没有"停止""前进"之类的交通标志，因此船夫将贡多拉划到一个交叉口的时候，就会很滑稽地喊上一声"噢"，如果另一条运河里也有一名船夫正划船而来，他就会同样地回应一声，从而使得两船不至于撞上。他们不用呜呜直叫的喇叭，那里也没有隆隆作响的车轮声，除了歌声和音乐，威尼斯几乎静寂无声呢。

很久以前，如今威尼斯所在的那个地方，还是很多的小岛屿，没有城市。一些叫作"威尼蒂族"的人当时正遭受北方一个野蛮部落的袭扰。于是，他们便搬到这些岛屿上，远离了那些令人恼火的部落。威尼蒂人将一些难以腐朽的雪松树削成木桩，打到水下，然后在木桩上面修建房屋。威尼蒂人主要是捕鱼为食，他们只需在前门垂下一根钓丝或者撒下一张网，就可以捕上许多许多的鱼儿来。事实上，他们捕到的鱼儿，根本就吃不完。于是，他们又通过晒干海水来制盐，然后将吃不了的鱼肉腌制、保存起来。

由于威尼蒂人住在水上，因此他们必定都是优秀的水手，而事实也正是如此。于是，他们便驾驶着船只，前往地中海沿岸各地，出售他们的腌鱼，也出售食盐，换取丝绸服装、地毯和珠宝并带回来。接下来，欧洲各国的人便纷纷来到威尼斯，购买威尼蒂人用腌鱼和食盐换回来的这些东西，因此威尼斯便变成了欧洲最大的购

had brought good luck to them and their city, they built a beautiful church to him. This saint was St. Mark. They found his bones and buried them in this church underneath the altar. St. Mark's Church is different-looking from any of the churches I have told you about so far. It has five domes, one on each side and one big dome in the center, but these domes are not like those of St. Paul's or the Capitol—they are shaped like an onion.

Pictures are usually painted with paint, and you have probably never seen colored pictures made without paint. But the inside of St. Mark's, and the outside too, is covered with hundreds of pictures, not made with paint but out of bits of colored stone and gold and colored glass. Such pictures are called mosaics. They will not fade nor peel off, nor wash off, as painted pictures might do.

As you might have a dog for a pet, St. Mark was supposed to have had a lion for a companion, so on top of a column, out in front of his church, the Venetians put a bronze statue of a lion with wings. Over the door of the church there are four horses. They are not live horses, yet they have traveled far. They were made about the time of Christ, out of bronze, and they have been carried away by one ruler and another

威尼斯的圣马可教堂

物地和最大的市场。后来，人们开始将威尼蒂人叫作威尼斯人，而威尼斯人也变得越来越富有了。他们在运河沿岸修建了许多美丽的宫殿，由于相信一位圣徒给他们和这座城市带来了好运，因此他们还修建了一座美丽的教堂来进行纪念。这位圣徒，名叫"圣马可"。威尼斯人找到了圣马可的遗骸，并

他们修建了这座教堂来纪念圣马可，认为是圣马可给他们带来了好运

将遗骸安葬在这座教堂的祭坛下面。圣马可教堂的样子，与迄今为止我跟你们说过的所有教堂都不相同。这座教堂建有五座穹顶，每边一个，而且中央还有一个大穹顶，不过，这些穹顶可不同于圣保罗大教堂或者国会大厦的那种穹顶，它们都呈洋葱形。

画作通常都是用颜料绘制的，因此，你们很可能从来没有见过不用颜料绘成的彩色画作。不过，圣马可教堂的内墙和外墙上，却绘有几百幅这样的画作呢，它们都不是用颜料绘制的，而是用五颜六色的小石子、黄金和彩色玻璃镶嵌而成。这种画作，叫作"马赛克"。它们既不会褪色，不会剥落，也不像用颜料绘制的画作那样会被雨水冲掉。

据说，圣马可曾经有一头雄狮做伴，就像你们养小狗当宠物似的，因此在圣马可教堂正门外边的一根柱子顶上，威尼斯人还安放了一尊青铜雕像，就是一头长有翅膀的雄狮。而教堂门口的上方，还有四匹马儿。虽说它们不是真马，而是雕像，

威尼斯的贡多拉

圣马可教堂里的
飞狮雕像

叹息桥·

from one place to another, and finally back again to Venice.

The largest piece of land in Venice is a paved square in front of St. Mark's. In this square there are flocks of pigeons, and they are so tame they will alight on your hand or shoulder to be fed. People have pictures taken of themselves with pigeons on their head and shoulders and at their feet. Once upon a time Venice was saved from an enemy by a message brought by a carrier-pigeon, and ever since then Venetians treat pigeons as sacred, and they would arrest and punish any one who harmed a pigeon. Did you know that a pigeon discovered America? Yes, that's a fact, for in Italian "Columbus" means "pigeon." So his real name is Christopher Pigeon.

Venice is now only a city, but it used to be like a little country all by itself. It made its own money and it had its own ruler, who was called a Doge (dozhe), which means Duke. A Doge ruled like a president and lived in a palace like a king, and punished people who had done wrong, like a judge. Just across the water street from the Doge's palace was the prison, and connecting his palace with the prison was a covered bridge. When a man was sent to prison by the Doge he crossed over this bridge, sighing and

可它们走的路却非常遥远。它们是与基督在世差不多同一个时期，用青铜制作出来的，后来被一些统治者接二连三地带到了一个又一个地方，最终才重新回到了威尼斯。

威尼斯市内最大的一处陆地，就是圣马可教堂前面那个铺有卵石的广场。广场上有着一群群的鸽子，它们都非常温驯，会飞到游客的手掌或者肩膀上，让游客喂食呢。人们纷纷拍照，将自己头上、肩上、脚下全都是鸽子的那一刻留存下来。很久以前，威尼斯曾经因为一只信鸽带来的消息而在敌人手下逃过一劫，因此，自那以后，威尼斯人便将鸽子视为圣鸟，凡是伤害鸽子的人，都会被逮起来，受到惩处。

你们知不知道，是一只"鸽子"发现了美洲呢？是的，这是事实，因为意大利语里的"哥伦布"，就是"鸽子"的意思。所以，哥伦布的真名，其实应该叫"克里斯托弗·鸽子"。

如今的威尼斯，只是一座城市，但是，以前它却像一个完全独立自主的小国家呢。当时，威尼斯有自己的货币，有自己的统治者，叫作"总督"，意思就是"公爵"。总督治理威尼斯的方式，就像如今的总统；他住在一座宫殿里，就像一位国王；而他惩处起那些犯了错误的民众来，又像是一位法官。总督府所在的那条水上街道的对面，就是监狱，而总督府与这座监狱之间，则有一条廊桥相连。每当总督将一个人送进监狱去的时候，那个人就会走过这条廊桥，并且边走边叹息、边抱

groaning, so it came to be called the "Bridge of Sighs."

Theaters are sometimes named "The Rialto," but *The* Rialto is not a theater. It is a bridge in Venice over the Grand Canal. It has shops along its sides. Venice was the shopping-place of Europe, and the Rialto was the department store of Venice, where every kind of thing was sold. There is a play written by William Shakespeare, the English author, called "The Merchant of Venice." The story is about a man who had a shop on the Rialto.

The Venetians made their living in the first place out of two commonplace things right at hand—fish and salt. That was the start of their fortune. There was also a great deal of another commonplace thing right at hand too—this was sand. Sand seems to have very little value, but the Venetians found out that they could make glass out of sand by melting it in a furnace with something else. They found out too that they could blow this melted glass as one blows soap-bubbles, and by blowing the glass in this way into different shapes they made wonderfully beautiful bottles, vases, beads, and drinking-glasses. The glass-blowers became as famous as any artist who could make beautiful paintings or beautiful music, and the glass-blowers made fortunes besides, for people everywhere sought their work and paid high prices for it. They were the most important people in Venice. A specially fine glass-blower was as important as the Doge himself—one glass-blower was made a Doge—and some of their daughters even married princes.

Venice is now no longer a country by itself. It is now only one city in Italy, but people go from all over the World to see St. Mark's and the Doge's palace, to bathe at its

怨；因此，后来人们便将这座廊桥叫作"叹息桥"。

有的时候，我们会把剧院林立的地方称为"里亚尔托"[1]，不过，"里亚尔托"实际上并不是指一座剧院。它是威尼斯大运河上的一座桥。这座桥的两边都有商店。威尼斯是欧洲的购物广场，而里亚尔托桥就是威尼斯的百货商店，因为那里什么东西都卖。英国作家威廉·莎士比亚曾经写过一部戏剧，叫作《威尼斯商人》，写的就是一个在里亚尔托桥上开有一家商店的人的故事。

起初，威尼斯人是靠身边两种普通的东西，即鱼和食盐为生的。他们的财富，正是始于这种谋生方式。不过，当时他们身边的另一种普通之物也不少，那就是沙子。如今在我们看来，沙子似乎没什么用处，可威尼斯人却发现，把沙子和其他东西放进炉子里加热，熔化后可以制成玻璃。他们还发现，可以把这种熔化后的玻璃吹起来，就像你们吹肥皂泡那样。用这种方法，可以把玻璃吹制成各种不同的形状，从而让他们制造出了许多神奇而美丽的水壶、花瓶、珠子和玻璃水杯。于是，玻璃匠人便变得和那些能够绘制精美画作、谱写美妙音乐的人一样声名鹊起了，而且，玻璃匠人都发了财，因为各地的人都在寻找由他们制作出来的玻璃制品，并且花大价钱买下来。他们都成了威尼斯最重要的人物。一位技艺精湛的玻璃匠，会跟总督大人本身一样重要，曾经还有一位玻璃匠被任命担任威尼斯总督，而一些玻璃

---

[1] 里亚尔托（The Rialto），在美国英语中特指纽约百老汇附近的剧院区。亦译"丽都街"。此处译者是为了让读者明白它与威尼斯的"里亚尔托桥"是同一个词，才将其音译成"里亚尔托"。

wonderful beach nearby called the Lido, to ride in gondolas on its canals, and listen to musicians who on warm moonlight nights sing and play on stringed instruments. Venice is one of the places in the World where every girl thinks she would like to spend her honeymoon when she is married.

An American girl once sent a postal card home: "Here I am in Venice. It is wonderfully beautiful—the golden palaces, the gorgeous sunsets, the enchanting music. I am sitting in a gondola on the Grand Canal and drinking it all in!" We speak of a person "thirsting" for knowledge or beauty, but one would have to be very thirsty to drink in the Grand Canal.

The "Boot" lies in the Mediterranean Sea, but the part of the sea that borders Venice is called The Adriatic. Venice is so beautiful it is known as the "Queen of the Adriatic." Fame and fortune made from fish and salt and ships and sand!

匠的女儿，甚至还嫁给了王子呢。

如今，威尼斯已经不再是一个独立的国家了。虽说它如今只是意大利的一座城市，但世界各地的人还是络绎不绝地前往威尼斯，去参观圣马可教堂和总督府，到附近一个叫作"利多"的奇妙海滩上去游泳，去乘坐在运河里穿梭的贡多拉，去聆听音乐家们在炎热的月夜唱歌和弹奏弦乐。而且，威尼斯也是全世界所有姑娘都希望结婚时能到那里去度蜜月的地方之一呢。

一位美国姑娘曾经给国内寄了一张明信片，上面写道："我到威尼斯了。这里极其美丽，有金碧辉煌的宫殿，有灿烂瑰丽的日落，有令人陶醉的音乐。我正坐在大运河上的一艘贡多拉里，尽情地享受着这一切！"我们会说一个人"渴望"获得知识或者观赏美景，可一个人必须极其渴望，才会"尽情地"去欣赏整条大运河呢。

虽说意大利这只"靴子"位于地中海里，但环绕在威尼斯四周的那片海域，却叫"亚得里亚海"。由于威尼斯那么美丽，因此世人还称之为"亚得里亚海的皇后"呢。这就是鱼儿、食盐、船舶和沙子给那里带来的名望和财富啊！

给鸽子喂食

35 The Gates of Paradise and the Dome of Heaven

Down the length of Italy like the back of a sea monster is a ridge of mountains called the Apennines. To get from one side of Italy to the other side you have to go over, under, or through these Apennine Mountains, and trains do all three; over, under, through, winding in and out of one tunnel after another. There are forty-five tunnels in going just from Venice to a city across the Apennines called Florence.

Florence is a girl's name meaning "flowering," but Florence is also the name of this city. As the train comes into Florence it curves around the city and you see above the housetops, near the center of the city, a large dome that looks like the hub of a wheel about which the train is turning. Next to the dome is a big, square tower. Both the tower and the dome were built before Columbus was born. The dome looks like the dome of St. Paul's in London, but, as a matter of fact, this dome is not like St. Paul's. The dome of St. Paul's is like it, and so is the dome of the Capitol in Washington like it, and so are all the other domes of that kind in the World like it, for this dome in Florence was the first one of that kind ever built and all others are copies.

Little domes and flat domes had been built before, but when the people of Florence were building a cathedral they wanted a different kind of dome on it, a dome that would be bigger and better than any other dome i.t.w.W. They wanted a dome so big that no one

第35章 天堂之门与天堂之顶

意大利从北到南有一条山脉，看上去就像是一只海怪的背影，叫作"亚平宁山脉"。要从意大利的一侧到达另一侧，人们必须翻过亚平宁山脉，或者从亚平宁山脉之下，或者从亚平宁山脉之中穿过去，而如今，这三种方式的火车都有：火车或是在山上，或是在山下，或是山中，蜿蜒着出了这个隧道，又进那个隧道。从威尼斯到达亚平宁山脉另一侧的佛罗伦萨市，一路上就要经过四十五条隧道呢。

"佛罗伦萨"本是一个女性名字，意指"花儿般盛开"，不过，它同时也是一座城市的名称。火车驶入佛罗伦萨的时候，会拐上一个大弯，绕城而行，因此，旅客可以看到，在鳞次栉比的屋顶上，在靠近市中心的地方，有一个巨大的穹顶，就像是一个轮毂，仿佛火车正在绕着这个轮毂拐弯似的。紧挨着那个穹顶，有一座巨大的、四四方方的塔楼。这个穹顶和这座塔楼，都是哥伦布出世之前修建起来的。这个穹顶，看上去很像伦敦圣保罗大教堂的穹顶，可实际上，并非是它像圣保罗大教堂的穹顶，而是圣保罗大教堂的穹顶像它，而且，美国华盛顿国会大厦的穹顶，以及世界上其他同类的穹顶全都像它，因为佛罗伦萨的这座穹顶，是历史上修建的第一座此种穹顶，其他所有的穹顶都是仿照它的样式修建起来的。

当然，在此以前，人们也修建过一些小型的穹顶和平穹顶，不过，当佛罗伦萨人打算建造一座大教堂的时候，他们却想给大教堂修建一座不同的穹顶，希望这座

knew how to build it. Now a dome is built out of pieces of stone, and the stones have to cover a space beneath without falling, just like a bridge or an arch. No cement is strong enough to stick stones together so that they will not fall when placed across an open space, but if the stones can be held up by some wooden framework until every stone is in place, the wooden framework underneath can then be taken away and the stones will not fall, for all the stones push downward at the same time, and as all push downward together they get wedged in so tight that none can fall through. It is like a jam of people all trying at once to get through a door: they get so wedged in that none can go through.

But the dome on the Cathedral of Florence was to be so big no one knew how to hold it up while it was being built. It would have taken a whole forest of trees to build a big enough framework underneath. Some one said, "Let's pile up a mountain of dirt and put pennies all through the dirt, then build the dome on top of this mountain. After the dome has been built people will cart away the dirt in order to get the money out of the dirt and that will leave the dome standing alone." But this very foolish scheme was never tried.

At last two artists who were rivals said they knew a way to build the dome, but neither one would tell how he would do it. One artist was named Brunelleschi. As Brunelleschi is such a long name, I'm going to call him Mr. B. for short. The other artist was named Ghiberti, and I shall call him Mr. G. Mr. B. got the job and Mr. G. was made his helper. Mr. G. didn't like to be only a helper, so he went about saying that Mr. B. did not really know how to build the dome at all, and would never finish it.

穹顶比世界上其他任何一座穹顶都更大、更好。他们希望修建一座巨大的穹顶,可当时却没人知道如何来修建。注意,穹顶是用一块块的石头建成的,这些石块必须盖住下面的一定范围,就像一座桥梁或者拱门似的,不能垮塌下来。没有哪种混凝土,强度足以将石块紧紧地黏结在一起,使得它们盖住某个空间的时候不会垮塌下来,不过,要是可以用木架子支撑起来,待每块石头都安放就位后,再拆掉木架的话,那么石块就不会掉下去了。因为这样一来,所有石块都会同时向下压,挤在一起,从而紧紧地相互嵌在一起,哪块石头也掉不下去了。这种情形,就像是一堆人同时尽力要从一扇门里挤出去似的:由于人挤人,彼此紧紧地嵌在一起,所以哪个人也挤不过去。

但是,由于佛罗伦萨大教堂的这座穹顶实在太大,因此没人知道,在修建的时候该怎样才能将它支撑起来。要砍掉一整片森林,才能在下面扎起一个足够巨大的木架子。有人献计说:"不妨堆起一大堆土,在土里到处都埋上钱,再在这个土堆顶上修建穹顶。待穹顶建好后,人们为了找到土里的钱,就会来挖这土堆,并将土运走,这样,等下面的土全部运走之后,穹顶就立起来了。"不过,这个非常愚蠢的计划一直都没有人去尝试。

最后,两位互为对手的艺术家都说,他们有办法修建穹顶,可谁也没把自己的办法说出来。其中一位艺术家叫作布鲁内莱斯基。由于他的名字太长,因此我打算只简称他为"布先生"。另一位艺术家叫作吉贝尔蒂,我称他为"吉先生"。布先生接下了这一任务,而吉先生也受命去当布先生的助手。但吉先生不乐意只当助

Mr. B. and his men went on with the work for some time, until the sides of the dome reached the place where the stones had to be built over the center to cover the vast space beneath. This was the hard part, for the sides of the dome had to meet in the middle with nothing underneath to hold them up. Mr. G. kept on with his talking against Mr. B., and even made fun of him, until Mr. B., tired of being nagged in this way, made believe he was sick and stopped work. Time went on and Mr. B. staid home—still sick—and the dome stood unfinished. Mr. G. said, "Oh, Mr. B. isn't really sick; he is only making believe he is sick—as a school-boy sometimes does—because he doesn't know how to go on." So the people of Florence went to Mr. B.'s house and begged him to go on with the dome.

"I'm sick," said Mr. B. "Mr. G. knows so much about building a dome, let him go on with it."

So the people went back to Mr. G. and told him to go ahead. Then Ghiberti tried, but he was able to go only a little way and couldn't go any farther.

So then the people went back to Brunelleschi again.

"If you'll make that Ghiberti keep still and not say another word," said Mr. B., "I

布先生是唯一知道如何修建这座"天堂之顶"的人

手，因此他开始到处散布，说布先生其实根本就不知道如何修建这座穹顶，因此穹顶永远都不可能建成。

布先生带领手下的人工作了一段时间，完成了前期工作，只待把石块在中心部分搭建起来，盖住下面那个巨大的空间了。这是最困难的部分，因为他必须在下面没有任何支撑的情况下，让穹顶各面在中央位置合拢起来。吉先生仍然在说布先生的坏话，甚至还嘲笑他，布先生厌烦了听这种坏话，便假装生了病，停工不干了。时间一天天过去，布先生一直待在家里"养病"，穹顶也一直都没有完工。吉先生又说："噢，布先生并不是真的病了，他是在装病，就像小学生有时会干的那样，因为他不知道怎么干下去了。"于是，佛罗伦萨的人便来到布先生家里，恳请他继续修建穹顶。

"我生病了，"布先生说。"吉先生不是很了解怎么修建穹顶吗，让他来建好了。"

于是，人们便回去找吉先生，让吉先生接手干下去。接下来，虽然吉先生全力以赴，可他只能再往上修建一点点，却无法继续修建下去。

于是，佛罗伦萨人便再次回过头去请布鲁内莱斯基。

"如果你们能让吉贝尔蒂老老实实地待着，不再说一句话，"布先生说，"那我就接着干下去。"他的确做到了，完成了世界上第一座、也是最美丽的一座此种穹顶，直到今天，也没有人确切地知道，他当时究竟是怎么修建的呢。

will go on as I started," and he did, finishing the first and one of the most beautiful domes of its kind i.t.w.W., and no one to this day knows exactly how he did it.

Although Ghiberti was such a poor "sport," he was, however, a great sculptor. Right across the street from the cathedral with the dome which Brunelleschi built is a low, six-sided building called a baptistery, because they baptized children there. The doors of this baptistery are made of bronze, and on these doors Ghiberti made bronze figures and scenes of some of the Bible stories. One of these pictures in bronze shows Abraham about to sacrifice his son on the altar as he was told to do by God.

"They are fit to be the gates to Paradise!" said another great Florentine artist when he saw these doors. The artist who said this was named Michelangelo, and he lived in Italy at the same time as Columbus. Columbus was never at home; he was away from Italy almost all his life, discovering new countries. But Michelangelo never left Italy; he stayed at home. He spent his whole life there making beautiful drawings, paintings, sculptures, and buildings, for an artist in those days did every kind of artistic work, from making necklaces to churches, as well as painting and sculpture.

One day Michelangelo found a block of marble which some one had thrown away because it had a crack in it. Michelangelo said that he saw in this block of marble the figure of young David, so he set to work with his chisel and cut the figure of the young shepherd boy out of the marble. In Florence there are two huge copies of this statue several times bigger than a man, and in thousands of other places in the World there are

　　尽管吉贝尔蒂是一个如此没有 "风度" 的人，可他也是一位伟大的雕塑家。就在布鲁内莱斯基修建的那座带有穹顶的佛罗伦萨大教堂的街对面，有一栋低矮的六面建筑，它叫作 "洗礼堂"，因为佛罗伦萨人都是在那里为孩子举行洗礼[1]的。这座洗礼堂的门都由青铜铸成，吉贝尔蒂在这些大门上制作了《圣经》故事中的许多青铜人物雕像和场景。其中有一幅青铜画，描绘的是亚伯拉罕[2]正在按照神的指示，准备把儿子献祭到祭坛上。

　　"它们完全可以做天堂里的大门呢！" 另一位伟大的佛罗伦萨艺术家看到这几扇大门后，如此说道。说这话的那位艺术家，名叫米开朗琪罗，他住在意大利，与哥伦布属于同时代的人。哥伦布一直都没有待在国内，他几乎一生都不在意大利，而是在不停地发现新的国家。可米开朗琪罗却从未离开过意大利，一直都待在家乡。他一生都在创作精美的素描、油画、雕塑作品和建筑物，因为几乎每一种艺术作品，从制作项链到修建教堂，以及绘画、雕塑，当时的艺术家全都精通。

　　有一天，米开朗琪罗发现了一块大理石，那是别人扔掉的，因为那块大理石上

---

　　[1]　洗礼（baptize），基督教的一种入教仪式。仪式中，主礼者口诵经文，把水滴在受洗者额上，或将受洗者身体浸在水里，表示赦免入教者的 "原罪" 和 "本罪"，并赋予 "恩宠" 和 "印号"，使其成为教徒。亦称 "浸礼"、"圣洗圣事" 等。

　　[2]　亚伯拉罕（Abraham），传说中犹太教、基督教和伊斯兰教的先知，是上帝从地上众生中挑选出来并给予祝福的人，同时也是希伯来族和阿拉伯族的共同祖先。他奉神命将爱子以撒献祭给耶和华的故事，见于《旧约圣经》。

small copies in plaster, and you may have one of these copies in your own home.

Many of these beautiful works of art are kept in buildings that used to be palaces. The palaces in Florence look more like prisons than palaces. They were built that way, not to keep people in, but to keep people out. In olden times rich families lived in these palaces, and they were not good neighbors, for one family frequently quarreled or fought with another, so the palaces had to be strong as forts.

There are no water streets in Florence like those in Venice, but through Florence flows a river called the Arno, and across it are several bridges. On one of these bridges, called the Ponte Vecchio, which means the Old Bridge, are shops as on the Rialto in Venice. Most of the shops sell ornaments and souvenirs made out of silver, mosaic, leather, and

佛罗伦萨的维奇奥桥（老桥）

"老桥"的商店里出售纪念品

比萨斜塔

有朝一日它总会倒塌

有一条裂缝。米开朗琪罗说，他从这块大理石上看出了年轻时的大卫[1]，之后，他便拿起自己的凿子，开始雕塑，用这块大理石雕刻出了那位年轻的牧童。在佛罗伦萨，现在还有两座仿照这尊雕像制成的巨型雕塑作品，它们的尺寸都比真人大了好多倍，而世界其他许多地方也都有这尊雕像的小型石膏复制品，没准你们家里也有一尊呢。

　　如今，这些美丽的艺术作品当中，有许多都存放在以前的那些宫殿里。佛罗伦萨的宫殿，样子更像是监狱，而不像是宫殿。它们之所以建成那样，是因为这些宫殿不是让人进去住的，而是为了让人进不去。在古代，一些富有的人家都住在这些宫殿里，他们可不是和睦的邻居，因为一个家族经常会跟另一个家族争吵、打仗，因此这些宫殿必须建得像堡垒那样牢固才行。

　　佛罗伦萨与威尼斯不一样，市里并没有水上街道，不过，有一条河从佛罗伦萨穿城而过，叫作"亚诺河"，河上还建了好几座桥。其中有一座桥叫作"韦奇奥

---

[1] 大卫（David，约公元前1050年—约公元前970年），传说中以色列的第二位国王。他本是犹大支派耶西的第八个儿子，生于伯利恒，是一个牧羊人。后来他战胜了腓力斯丁人哥利亚，因而受到扫罗王的赏识。扫罗战死后，他当上了犹太王，并在公元前1000年左右建立了统一的以色列王国，定都耶路撒冷。大卫死后，由所罗门继承王位。他的故事，见于《旧约圣经·撒母耳记》等。

tortoise-shell, for this is the kind of art work that present-day Florentines make to sell to the thousands of travelers that visit the city.

Towers are built to stand erect—straight up and down—as boys and girls are. But not far from Florence is a city named Pisa, which has a very peculiar tower that leans to one side. It is called the Leaning Tower of Pisa. The tower was built to stand straight, but the foundation has sunk on one side, so that the tower slants over as it were going to fall. It has stood that way for hundreds of years, but is gradually leaning more and more, and if it cannot be stopped, some day it will fall.

You remember I told you that marble was made from the bones of sea animals; but all marble is not alike—some is so coarse you can even see the bones in the stone. But near Pisa are stone mines called quarries, from which are cut blocks of stone of a very fine and smooth kind of marble called from the name of the place, Carrara. Ever since the time of Christ men have been cutting out blocks of marble from these quarries, and people send all the way to Carrara from this country and other countries when they want especially fine marble for a building or n mantel or a piece of sculpture.

桥", 就是"老桥"的意思, 桥上设有许多商店, 情形就跟威尼斯的里亚尔托桥一样。其中绝大多数商店都出售银制饰品和纪念品、马赛克画、皮革制品, 还有玳瑁制品, 因为如今佛罗伦萨人的谋生之道, 就是制作此种艺术品, 卖给成千上万来到该市观光的游客哩。

一般的塔都是建得笔直的, 即上下笔直, 就像小朋友们的站姿那样挺拔。但是, 距佛罗伦萨不远的地方, 有一个叫作"比萨"的城市, 那里却有一座非常古怪的塔, 朝一面侧着。那座塔, 就叫"比萨斜塔"。这座塔原本是建得上下笔直的, 可由于底下的地基向一侧下沉了, 因此塔身便开始慢慢倾斜, 好像随时都会倒下来似的。这座塔已经斜着立在那里几百年了, 如今还在逐渐地越斜越厉害, 要是不停下来的话, 它总有一天会倒塌的。

大家都还记得吧, 我曾经跟你们说过, 大理石是海洋生物的遗骸形成的, 不过, 大理石却并非是完全一样的。有些大理石非常粗糙, 甚至看得见石头里面有海洋生物的遗骸。但距比萨不远的地方, 却有一些叫作"采石场"的石矿, 从这些采石场里, 人们开采出了一种非常纯净、非常光滑的大理石, 并且根据该地的地名, 将这种大理石叫作"卡拉拉大理石"。自基督降生的那个时代以来, 人们便一直在这些采石场里开采大理石了, 当世界各国的人需要特别优质的大理石来建造房屋、制作壁炉或者创作雕塑的时候, 他们就会不远万里, 派人到卡拉拉来购买这种大理石呢。

36 The Dead and Alive City

Two thousand years ago you could start out on any road anywhere, and if you kept on going far enough you would at last come to a great city in Italy called Rome, for at that time "all roads led to Rome." Rome was then the largest, the richest, the most beautiful, the most important city in the World. It was the capital of the World.

Rome was built on seven hills, and seven was supposed to be a lucky number. Through Rome runs a river called Tiber, whose waters the Romans thought were ruled over by a god called Father Tiber, to whom they prayed to save them from drowning and shipwreck.

The old Rome of that time is now dead, mostly in ruins, but there is a saying that Rome will live forever—that it is "Eternal"—and though old Rome is in ruins, there is a new Rome. The new Rome, however, is no longer the capital of the World. It is now only the capital of Italy.

Rome is still the capital, however, of all Roman Catholics in the World, and the head of all the Roman Catholic churches in the World lives there. He is called the Pope, which means "Papa."

St. Peter is supposed to have been crucified and his bones buried in Rome. It is said that on this spot a religious service has been held every single day since the time of St. Peter to

第36章   新旧罗马

两千年前，人们可以从任何一个地方的任何一条道路出发，一直走下去，最终来到意大利一座叫作"罗马"的大城市，因为那时可谓"条条大路通罗马"。当时，罗马是世界上最大、最富裕、最美丽和最重要的城市。可以说，当时的罗马就是世界的首都呢。

罗马城建在七座小山之上，因而人们认为，"七"是个很吉利的数字。一条河从罗马穿城而过，叫作"台伯河"，古罗马人认为，台伯河是由一个叫作"台伯始祖"的神灵掌管着，因此古罗马人都会向这个神灵祈祷，让神灵保佑他们不会溺死，不会沉船。

当时的那个古罗马城，如今已经不复存在，绝大部分都成为废墟了。不过，有一句老话说，罗马会获得永生，也就是"永恒"存在下去，因此，尽管古罗马已经变成一片废墟，那里却又出现了一个新的罗马。然而，新罗马却不再是世界的首都了。如今，它只是意大利的首都。

不过，罗马仍然是全世界所有罗马天主教徒的首都，而全世界罗马天主教会的最高首领，也仍然住在那儿。这位首领，叫作"教皇"，就是"父亲"的意思。

传说，圣徒彼得[1]被钉死在十字架上后，他的遗骸就葬在罗马。据说，安葬他

---

[1] 圣徒彼得（St. Peter，？—约64），基督教早期领袖人物之一，位列耶稣的十二门徒，也是十二使徒中安德烈的哥哥。

the present—that is, for about 1,900 years. At first these services had to be held in secret at night, for most of the Romans did not believe in Christ, and any one who did was likely, if caught, to be thrown into prison or even put to death. But over this same spot, many hundreds of years later, was built the largest church in the World. It is called St. Peter's.

On the top of St. Peter's is an immense dome copied after Brunelleschi's dome in Florence, but much larger. It was built by that great artist Michelangelo, who, I told you, was an architect as well as sculptor and painter. St. Peter's is so large that on the roof is a village of small houses, a village in which live the caretakers of the church.

The front door of St. Peter's is never closed night or day, but just to the right of that door is another door of bronze that is never opened except every twenty-five years. It is called the Holy Door and it is walled up with stone. At the end of every twenty-five years this wall has to be taken down in order to open the door.

St. Peter's is so large that thirty services can be carried on at one time without one interfering with another. Inside the church everything is huge, to match the building. The statues of angels are the size of giants and the doves are the size of eagles. There is a bronze statue of St. Peter himself seated on a throne. This is one of the few statues there of natural size. Good Catholics from all over the World, when they come to St. Peter's, kiss the statue's bronze foot. So many millions have kissed it that they have kissed away all his toes.

At Easter and at other celebrations the inside walls of St. Peter's are hung with crimson silk, thousands of candles burn, choir boys chant and altar boys swing smoke of burning

遗骸的那个地方，自圣彼得那个时代一直至今，每天都会举行一场宗教仪式，也就是说，这种仪式已经举行一千九百多年了呢。起初，这种仪式只能在夜间秘密举行，因为当时绝大多数古罗马人都不信奉基督，而任何信奉基督的人要是被人抓住了，可能就会关进监狱，甚至被处死。不过，就在同一个地方，几百年之后，却建成了世界上最大的一座教堂。这座教堂，就叫"圣彼得大教堂"。

圣彼得大教堂上面，有一座巨大的穹顶，它是仿照布鲁内莱斯基在佛罗伦萨完成的那个穹顶建造的，只是比后者要大得多。这座穹顶，就是我在前面告诉过你们的那个伟大艺术家米开朗琪罗建造的，他既是一位建筑师，又是一位雕塑家和画家。圣彼得大教堂占地面积广袤，顶上的小房子竟然形成了一个村庄，而那些守护这座大教堂的人，便全都住在这个村庄里。

圣彼得大教堂的前门，不论昼夜，都是始终敞开着的，不过，就在这扇大门的右边，还有一扇青铜大门，每隔二十五年才会打开一次。这扇青铜大门，叫作"圣门"，它的四周还修有一道石墙，将它封堵起来。到了每个二十五年末，人们必须拆掉这堵石墙，才能打开"圣门"呢。

圣彼得大教堂非常巨大，一次就可以举行三十场礼拜仪式，并且彼此之间不会相互干扰。教堂内部，一切东西都硕大无比，这样才能与整座教堂的大小相匹配。其中的天使雕像宛如一个个巨人，而鸽子雕像也仿佛是一只只雄鹰。教堂里面，有一尊描绘圣彼得坐在宝座上的雕像。那是整座教堂里为数不多、真人大小的雕像作品之一。世界各地善良的天主教徒来到圣彼得大教堂后，都会去亲吻这尊青铜雕像

incense to the high roof, while hundreds of priests in gorgeous robes and cardinals in red caps and red gowns and the Pope himself, the head of all the Catholics in the World, in glistening white, move in stately procession down the main aisle to the high altar, over the spot where, 1,900 years before, St. Peter himself was crucified and a Christian would have been afraid to show himself for fear of being killed.

The Pope lives next door to St. Peter's in an immense house called the Vatican. Your house may have a dozen rooms, or perhaps even a score, but it is said that the Vatican contains more than a thousand rooms. There are so many rooms that probably no one has ever counted them all. Many of the large rooms are filled with famous pictures and sculpture. They are art museums which people may visit. One room is the Pope's private chapel. It is called the Sistine Chapel. Michelangelo painted pictures on the ceiling and walls of this chapel. In order to see the pictures on the ceiling comfortably you have to lie flat on your back or look at them in a mirror held in your hand.

Before the time of St. Peter, when people believed in many gods, another church was built in Rome "To All the Gods." This building is still standing. It is called the Pantheon, which means "All Gods." The Pantheon too has a dome, but it is not like St. Peter's. The dome of St. Peter's is like a giant cup turned upside down. The dome

圣彼得大教堂的穹顶

圣彼得大教堂是世界上最大的教堂

的脚。由于被数百万信徒亲吻过，因此如今这尊雕像上的脚趾都被人们吻没了。

到了复活节和举行其他宗教仪式的时候，圣彼得大教堂的墙壁上都会悬挂红色丝带，点上数千支蜡烛，唱诗班的小朋友齐声吟唱，祭坛侍童则挥舞着焚香，让烟雾飘向高高的屋顶，几百位牧师全都身穿华丽的长袍，主教们头戴红色的帽子，身穿红色的法袍，而身为全球天主教徒首领的教皇本人，则身穿洁白的衣服，随着庄严肃穆的队伍，在主过道上向祭坛走去。祭坛高高在上，那里正是一千九百多年前圣彼得在十字架上受难，而有位基督教徒却因为担心自己被杀而不敢现身的地方。

教皇住在圣彼得大教堂隔壁一栋叫作"梵蒂冈"的巨大房子里。你们家里可能有十二间房，或者甚至有二十个房间，可梵蒂冈里，据说有一千多个房间哩。那里的房间太多，很可能没有人去数过。许多大房间里，全都摆满了著名的画作和雕塑作品。它们都是一些艺术博物馆，人们也可以前去参观。其中有个房间，是教皇自己的小礼拜堂。这个礼拜堂，叫作"西斯廷教堂"。米开朗琪罗给这座教堂的天花板上、墙壁上绘制了许多的画作。要想舒舒服服地欣赏天花板上的那些画作，游客们必须仰面躺在地上，或者手里拿一面镜子，从镜子里观察才行。

圣彼得降生之前的那个时期，人们信仰多个神灵，因此罗马还修建了另一座教

of the Pantheon is like a giant saucer turned upside down. There are no windows at all in the Pantheon, but there is a large hole in the top of the saucer called an "eye" which looks toward heaven, and through this eye the sun shines and the rain falls. It is so high above the floor, however, that the rain scarcely wets the floor beneath, but evaporates before reaching it.

Most of the buildings in Rome that were built about the time of Christ are in ruins, but the Pantheon is still almost the same as it was when first built. Around and about the very old buildings the dust and dirt and rubbish of the city had collected for two thousand years and had gradually piled higher and higher until the ruins were twenty feet or more lower than the present city, so that it has been necessary to dig them out.

In those days long ago there was a great market-place in Rome called the Forum. Around the Forum were beautiful palaces, court-houses, temples, and arches. The arches were built so that generals, when they returned from the wars they had fought and won, might ride in triumph through them. One of these arches is called the Arch of Titus. Titus was a Roman Emperor who destroyed the capital city of the Jews called Jerusalem and this arch was built to celebrate the event. Another arch is the Arch of Constantine. Constantine was the first Emperor of Rome to believe in Christ. That was not until three hundred years after Christ had died.

提图斯凯旋门

这是为了向摧毁了耶路撒冷的提图斯
致敬而修建的

堂，来"供奉所有的神灵"。那栋建筑物，叫作"万神殿"，意思就是"众神之殿"。万神殿也建有一座穹顶，可它的样子却与圣彼得大教堂的穹顶不同。圣彼得大教堂的穹顶，就像是一个倒扣着的巨杯。而万神殿里的穹顶，则像是一个倒扣着的巨型浅碟。万神殿里没有一扇窗户，只是穹顶中央有一个直视苍穹、叫作"眼睛"的大洞，而阳光和雨水则会透过这只"眼睛"洒落下来。然而，由于这个大洞离地面太高，所以雨水很少打湿下方的地板，因为还不等雨水落到地上，就蒸发掉了。

虽说罗马城中绝大多数始建于基督降生之前的建筑，如今都已成了一片废墟，但万神殿的样子，却仍然跟它刚刚建成时差不多。在这座历史悠久的建筑周围，城市里的尘土、垃圾已经积聚了两千年，越堆越高，使得古城的废墟比如今的新城低了二十多英尺，因此人们必须向下挖掘，才能看到以前的废墟了。

很久以前，古罗马有一个很大的市场，叫作"广场"。古罗马广场周围，全都是些美丽的宫殿、法院大楼、神庙和拱门。之所以修建拱门，是为了让将领们在战场上打完胜仗归来的时候，可以骑着马儿趾高气扬地从拱门底下走过。其中有一座拱门，叫作"提图斯凯旋门"。提图斯是古罗马的一位皇帝，曾经摧毁了犹太人那个叫作"耶路撒冷"的首都，而这座拱门，就是修建起来庆祝那场胜利的。还有

The old Romans had a peculiar idea of fun. They liked to watch fights between men and wild animals such as lions and tigers, and they liked to see the men and animals kill each other. Sometimes the men were prisoners who had been captured in battle, sometimes they were just Christians whom the Roman Emperors wanted to put to death. So a great stadium was built where the Romans could sit in safety and watch these fights as we watch football or baseball games. This stadium is called the Colosseum and, though it is partly in ruins, most of it is still standing and you can still see the dens where the wild animals were kept before they were let loose into the arena.

As the Christians were afraid to worship above ground where the Romans would see them, they hid in secret cellar-like places where they could worship as they pleased. Just outside of Rome, underneath the ground, are miles upon miles of these cellar-like rooms where they worshiped and where they were buried when they died. They are called Catacombs. Millions of the Christians were buried in the Catacombs.

古罗马斗兽场

一头曾经在斗兽场里杀死过基督教徒的狮子幽灵

一座拱门，就是"君士坦丁凯旋门"。君士坦丁是第一位皈依了基督教的古罗马皇帝。他皈依基督教的时候，已经是基督去世的三百年后了。

古罗马人对于娱乐，有一种非常古怪的观念。他们喜欢观看人和狮子、老虎这样的野兽搏斗，并且喜欢看到人和野兽相互杀死对方。有的时候，参与搏斗的人是战场上掠来的俘虏，有的时候则是罗马皇帝想要判处死刑的基督徒。于是，他们修建了一座巨大的露天体育场，古罗马人可以坐在那儿安全地观看搏斗，就像我们观看橄榄球比赛或者棒球比赛一样。这座露天体育场，叫作"斗兽场"。尽管如今这里的一部分已经变成了废墟，但大部分却仍然屹立着，因此大家仍然看得见其中的小房间，野兽被人放出来上场之前，就关在这些小房间里。

由于基督徒都不敢在地上做礼拜，不敢被古罗马人看到，因此他们都藏身于一个秘密的、地窖似的地方，在那里，他们可以尽情做礼拜。就在古罗马城外的地下，有数英里长的这种地窖式房间，基督徒曾经在里面做礼拜，并且死后也被埋葬在里面。这种房间，叫作"地下墓穴"。有好几百万基督教徒，全都安葬在这些地下墓穴里呢。

罗马"地下墓穴"内景

37 A Pile of Ashes a Mile High

A pile of ashes is not usually very beautiful,, and if it is in your back yard it is usually very ugly. But in Italy there is a pile of ashes which every one thinks beautiful, though it is nearly a mile high and though it is in the back yard of a city called Naples. It is on the beautiful Bay of Naples, and people have built their homes and hotels around the bay so as to get a view of this pile of ashes, which is called Mount Vesuvius, though it's not really a mountain at all.

In olden days when grown-up people believed in fairy-tales they said that a lame blacksmith lived down under the ground, that he kept a huge furnace burning there to heat the iron with which he worked. His name they said was Vulcan, and the smoke and flame that came out of the ground and the ashes that piled up above the ground were from his fires. So we call these mountains of ashes, through the top of which fire and smoke pour forth, volcanoes, after Vulcan.

There are volcanoes in many places in the World, but Vesuvius is the best known of all. We now know that volcanoes are huge fiery furnaces beneath the ground, hut we also know that no man nor fairy nor god is down there keeping them burning. Some volcanoes in other parts of the World have burned out, but the fires of Vesuvius have not. Vesuvius is always smoking and burning. We can see smoke or steam coming out of its top in the

第37章 一英里高的灰堆

通常来说，一堆灰烬的样子都不会漂亮，如果这堆灰烬还是堆在你们家后院的话，那么它看起来通常就会很丑陋了。但在意大利却有一堆灰烬，尽管它有一英里高，并且尽管它位于一个叫作"那不勒斯"的城市后院，可大家都觉得它非常漂亮呢。这堆灰烬，位于美丽的那不勒斯湾上，而人们也沿着整个海湾定居下来，并且修建起了旅馆，以便能够看到这堆灰烬，这堆灰烬叫作"维苏威山"，可它其实根本就不是一座山呢。

从前，就是连大人也相信童话故事的时候，他们说有个跛腿的铁匠住在地下，一直烧着一个大大的火炉，用于烧红他要打的铁。据说，这个铁匠叫作"伏尔甘"，而从地下冒出来的烟和火苗，以及地上堆积起来的灰烬，就是伏尔甘的火炉形成的。因此，我们便把这些有灰烬的、顶上喷出烟雾和火苗的山，根据伏尔甘的名字，叫作"火山"[1]。

世界上许多地方都有火山，但维苏威火山却是其中最著名的一座。如今我们已经知道，火山都是地下一个个炽热的巨大熔炉，但我们同时也知道，那里没有任何

---

[1] 火山（volcano）一词由"伏尔甘"（Vuclan）一词变形而来，但我们是用意译的方法，而非音译。

day and we can see the firelight come out of its top at night, but usually it does no more damage than a huge smoking chimney would. But every now and then the fires start burning fiercely and rock and ashes are shot up into the air, and pieces of rock are blown to such fine powder that they float in the air like dust. This dust may float for months in the air and for thousands of miles to other countries far off from the volcano from which it comes. Strange to say, it is this dust from volcanoes that often makes the sunsets such brilliant colors.

The fire in volcanoes is hotter than any fire we can make. We can make a fire so hot that it will melt copper and iron, but we can't make a fire so hot that it will melt rock. A volcano fire melts rock as easily as if it were butter. The rock that the volcano melts flows over the top like a pot boiling over and runs down the sides in streams that gradually harden into rock as they cool off. This rock is called lava, and as there is plenty of lava around Naples the people there use blocks of lava to pave their streets.

Some years ago I was in Naples after Vesuvius had been firing up. The streets of Naples were filled with what looked like gray snow. The gray snow was

维苏威火山和那不勒斯湾

在那不勒斯附近，有一个差不多高达一英里的灰堆

人、精灵或者神灵来让这些熔炉始终不熄。世界其他地方的一些火山都已经熄灭了，可维苏威火山却没有。维苏威火山一直都在浓烟滚滚，一直都在熊熊地燃烧着。白天我们看见见山顶上冒出的烟雾，晚上看得见山顶冒出的火光，而这座火山通常也只是像一根巨大的烟囱罢了，不会给人们造成更大的危害。但山顶的火会时不时地猛烈燃烧，将岩石和灰烬喷向空中，并将许多石块都炸成极细的齑粉，使它们像灰尘一样飘浮在空中。这种灰尘，可以在空中飘浮数月之久，飘浮数千英里之远，飘到距火山很远的其他国家。说来也怪，正是这种火山灰，经常让落日显示出如此瑰丽奇幻的色彩呢。

火山上的火，温度比我们所生的任何炉火都要高。人工生起的火，温度可以高到熔化铜、铁，但我们生不出一堆温度高到可以熔化岩石的火来。火山熔化起岩石来，就像是熔化黄油那样轻而易举呢。被火山熔化的岩石飘浮在顶上，就像一个烧开了的水壶，然后顺着山坡，像小溪一样往下流，并在冷却的过程中逐渐石化成岩石。这种岩石，就叫"火山岩"，由于那不勒斯周围有许多火山岩，因此那里的人还用大块大块的火山岩来铺街道呢。

几年之前，就在维苏威火山喷发后不久，我曾经到过那不勒斯。那不勒斯的大街小巷里，全都像是盖上了一层灰色的积雪。这种灰色的积雪，就是火山喷发后落下来的火山灰，只是这种灰不会像雪花那样融化，只能扫拢来，用车子运走，倒

dust that had fallen from the volcano, but it would not melt like snow and had to be carted away and dumped into the Bay of Naples. I wanted to see what the inside of a volcano looked like. There had been a railway almost to the top, but it had been wrecked. So I climbed from the bottom to the top, though it took half a day to do so, for at each step my feet sank deep into the ashes. I looked over the edge, down into the fiery mouth of the volcano. Every now and then pieces of rock would shoot high into the air and, looking up, I would dodge those that fell near-by. Entirely too many were falling around me, so I started back down the side of the volcano. I didn't walk down, I jumped, for each step I took was like jumping off a house, and at each step I fell, only I didn't hurt myself when I fell, for I sank into the ashes up to my knees, up to my waist, up to my neck. It was great fun, like jumping into a pile of hay, only it was oh, so dirty! It took me half a day to go up—it took me about ten minutes to come down—but hours to wash off the ashes when I was down, and my clothes were utterly ruined.

Some birds build their nests on the tops of chimneys, but it seems strange that people should build their homes at the foot of a volcano that may blow up and destroy them at any time. Yet long, long ago people built a city at the foot of Vesuvius, nearer even than Naples. It was called Pompeii. All of a sudden one

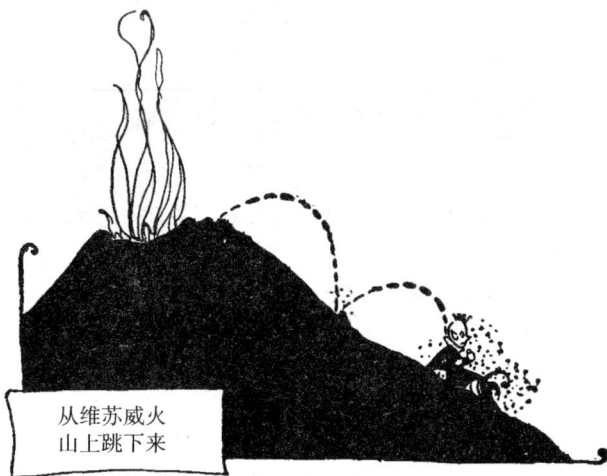

从维苏威火
山上跳下来

山顶太热，于是我从山坡上跳了下来

进那不勒斯湾里。我想看一看火山内部是个什么样子。山上本来修有一条铁路，差不多到达了山顶，可此时这条铁路已经被火山喷发破坏了。于是，我便徒步从山脚向山顶爬去，我花了半天工夫才爬上去，因为每走一步，我的双脚都会陷入深深的火山灰里。到达山顶后，我站在火山边上，探过身子，向那个烈焰滚滚的火山口里看去。时不时还会有一块块岩石高高地喷向空中，我只能仰起头来看着，躲避落在不远处的石块。由于身边落下的石块实在太多，于是我开始返回，沿着火山山坡往下走。下山时根本没法走，只能跳跃，因为我每走一步，都像是在从房顶上跳下来一样，并且每走一步都会摔上一跤，不过，摔倒的时候我却没有受伤，因为我是摔在深达膝盖、腰部甚至脖子的火山灰里。那种感觉太有趣了，就像是跳进一堆干草那样，只是，噢，实在太脏了！我用了半天时间才爬到山顶，只花了约十分钟便下了山，可洗掉下山时沾在身上的火山灰，却花了我好几个小时，而我身上的衣服也完全不能再穿了。

有些鸟儿会在各家各户的烟囱顶上筑巢，不过，要是人们把自家的房子建在一座火山山脚下，而这座火山任何时候都有可能将房子炸坏、摧毁的话，这一点似

day Vesuvius began to burn and boil and then blew up. Before any one in Pompeii knew what was going to happen, before any one had time to move from the spot where he was working or playing, Vesuvius had poured down on this little city its deadly fire and smoke and gas, and every one was killed where he stood and buried deep in dust and ashes. There the city and its people lay buried for almost two thousand years. Not so very long ago the city was dug out, its houses and temples and theaters were uncovered, and travelers can now visit the ruins, walk through the streets, and go into the houses and shops where once upon a time people went about their daily tasks and pleasures without a thought that the end of the World was coming to them in the twinkling of an eye.

No one knows when Vesuvius may do the same thing again, but the people in Naples never seem to think of such a thing; they don't worry; they go about the streets singing happily; in fact, it's one of the few cities in the World where people sing on the streets.

We may hear people whistling on the street in this country, but seldom, if ever, do we hear them sing on the streets. Singing may not be a sign of happiness at all, but people in Naples sing and sing, especially at night. Taxi drivers sing, ragged street urchins sing, beggars sing, and they sing songs you hear at concerts or in the opera. One of the greatest singers that ever lived, who now is dead, but whom you can still hear singing on the phonograph, was once a street urchin in Naples. Then he came to America. His name was Caruso.

The Italian language is the language of singing, the language of music. Some one has said you can't help singing if you speak Italian. Even the sheet music we use in this

乎就很奇怪了。但是，很久、很久以前，人们竟然还在维苏威火山脚下建立了一座城市，并且它的位置比那不勒斯更靠近这座火山呢。那座城市，叫作"庞贝"。有一天，维苏威火山突然喷发起来，火光熊熊、熔岩翻滚，然后爆炸了。不待庞贝城里的人明白即将发生什么，不待城里的人从工作或者玩耍的场所转移，维苏威火山喷发出的炽热熔岩、浓烟和有毒气体，便倾泻到了这座小城里，所有的人全都当场死亡，埋到了深深的火山灰下。那座古城和其中的居民，便在此处埋藏了差不多两千年。不久前，人们将这座古城发掘出来，其中的房屋、神庙和戏院等场所重见天日，而游客如今也可参观这处废墟，走过古城的街道，进入原来的那些房屋和商店了，以前，古城里的人曾经在这些房屋和商店里工作、做家务或者玩耍，根本没有想过世界末日会在转瞬之间降临到他们身上呢。

如今，没人知道维苏威火山什么时候会再这样喷发一次，而那不勒斯人也似乎从未想过这个问题。他们一点儿也不担心，他们愉快地唱着歌儿，在大街小巷上来去，实际上，那里也是世界上为数不多的、居民会在大街上唱歌的城市之一。

在美国，虽然我们可以听到人们在大街上吹口哨，但要说听到人们在大街上唱歌，这种事情就算有，也是很少见的。唱歌可能根本就不算是感到快乐的一种标志，可那不勒斯人却在不停地歌唱，而且尤其喜欢在晚上唱歌。那里的出租汽车司机会唱歌，大街上衣衫褴褛的流浪者会唱歌，乞丐也会唱歌，而他们所唱的歌曲，就是大家在音乐会或者剧院里面听到的那些歌曲。人类历史上最伟大的一位歌手，曾经就是那不勒斯街头的一位流浪者呢，虽说他如今已经辞世，但你们仍然可以在

country is usually written in Italian and the directions for playing are given in Italian. In Italian almost every word ends in a vowel, that is, in a, e, i, o, or u. Piano and 'cello, soprano and alto are Italian words. Even Naples ends in a vowel, for in Italian it is called Napoli.

The name "Goat" is neither pretty nor musical and it wouldn't sound well in a song, but across the Bay of Naples is an island the name of which in English is goat; but in Italian it is "Capri," and songs are sung about "Bella Capri"—the beautiful Capri—the beautiful Goat Island.

In the rocky shore of Capri there is a sea cave which you can only enter in a rowboat through a low opening. The opening is so low you have to duck your head, and if the waves are high you can't go through at all. The cave is called the Blue Grotto, for inside this rocky cave the water is such a beautiful clear blue that it seems almost as if your boat were floating on sky instead of on water. What makes it so blue? If you dip some of the water up in a bottle to take home as a souvenir—as I have known people to do—the water is just as colorless as the water in your own bathtub.

留声机里听到他的歌声。这位歌手后来移居到了美国；他叫卡鲁索[1]。

意大利语是一种有如唱歌般好听的语言，是一种音乐般的语言。有人说过，人们在讲意大利语的时候，会情不自禁地唱起来歌来呢。连美国所用的散页乐谱，通常也是用意大利语写的，并且演奏技法用的也是意大利语。在意大利语里，差不多每个单词都是用元音结尾，即用a，e，i，o或者u结尾的。比如"钢琴"（piano）、"大提琴"（'cello）、"女高音"（soprano）和"女低音"（alto）等词，全都是意大利语里的词汇。连"那不勒斯"这个地名，也是用元音结尾的，因为在意大利语里，这座城市叫"拿波里"（Napoli）呢。

"山羊"这个词既不漂亮，不悦耳，放在歌曲里也不好听。但在那不勒斯湾对面，却有一个小岛，它的名字翻译成英语，就是"山羊"的意思，而在意大利语里，这个小岛叫作"卡普里"。那里还有很多关于"贝拉卡普里"的歌曲，翻译成英语，就是"美丽的卡普里"，也即"美丽的山羊之岛"的意思。

卡普里岛沿海多石，那里有一个海边洞穴，人们必须划着小船，从一处低矮的开口里才能进去。那个口子很矮，船上的人不得不把头低下来才能通过，如果浪高风大的话，那里根本就无法通过了。这个洞穴，叫作"蓝洞"，因为在这个怪石嶙峋的洞穴内部，海水呈现出一种瑰丽而澄明的蓝色，小船仿佛是在碧空之中而不是在水面之上漂浮着。是什么东西，让那里的海水如此碧蓝呢？大家要是用装上一瓶水，带回家做纪念品的话（我知道有人那样干过），那么瓶中的海水就会像你们自家浴缸里的水一样，完全是无色的了。

---

[1]　卡鲁索（Kalusuo Enrico Caruso，1873—1921），著名的意大利男高音歌唱家。1895年在家乡那不勒斯初次以男中音登台演唱《浮士德》，1898年扮演了《费杜拉》一剧中的罗列斯，开始演唱男高音。后旅行热那亚、圣彼得堡等地演唱，深受欢迎。1904年赴英国修道院花园歌剧院演出，一举成名。毕生刻苦磨炼，演出歌剧五十余部，后定居美国，在纽约的十年内演唱过六百余场，随时能够演出的曲目达五百多首。

38 Wars and Fairy-Tales

Though Italian is the language of music, the people of Germany are quite as musical as the Italians. But their music is very different from the music of the Italians. Some of their music is warlike, big and loud, and yet some of it is gentle and sweet, and the most famous cradle songs and Christmas carols have been written by Germans. "Silent Night, Holy Night" is one. Musical plays are called operas. Some of the greatest operas in the World have been composed by Germans.

Cradle songs and Christmas carols don't seem to go well with fighting. But the Germans, besides being very musical, have also been very warlike. You have all heard of the two terrible World Wars, World War I and World War II. Most of the countries of the World took part in these two wars. In each war Germany fought almost all the other countries in the World and, even with almost all the rest of the World against her, she nearly won both times.

After World War II the countries that had beaten Germany divided Germany up to keep her from starting any more wars. Russia took Eastern Germany. The United States, Great Britain, and France ruled Western Germany. So there came to be two Germanies, West Germany and East Germany.

Which do you like better, fairy-tales or true stories? Some of the World's best fairy-tales have been made in Germany. Stories, poems, songs, and operas have been written

第38章 战争与童话

意大利语是一种音乐般的语言，而德国人也像意大利人一样热爱音乐。不过，德国音乐与意大利音乐有很大的不同。虽然德国有些音乐充满了好战情绪，音调大而洪亮，但也有一些音乐温柔而动听，世界上最著名的一些摇篮曲和圣诞颂歌，都是德国音乐家创作出来的。《安静的夜晚，神圣的夜晚》就是其中的一首。音乐剧又叫歌剧。世界上最伟大的一些歌剧，也是德国音乐家创作出来的。

摇篮曲和圣诞颂歌，似乎与战争并不相配。可德国人除了热爱音乐，还非常好战。大家都已经听说过那两次可怕的世界大战，即第一次世界大战和第二次世界大战了吧。全球绝大多数国家都参与了这两次大战。其中每一场大战，德国差不多都是与世界其他各国作战，并且，尽管差不多世界其余各国都在与之作战，德国却差点儿两次都打赢了呢。

第二次世界大战过后，打败了德国的那些国家将德国分成了两个部分，目的是让该国无法再发动战争。俄罗斯占领了东德。美国、英国和法国则控制了西德。于是，世界上便出现了两个德国，即西德和东德。

在童话和真实发生的故事之间，你们更喜欢哪一种呢？世界上一些最优秀的童话故事，也是德国人创作出来的。德国人创作出了许多的小说、诗歌、歌曲和歌

about fairy people and real people who once lived on the hills and in the caves by the side of a river in Germany called the Rhine. The Rhine starts from a glacier in the Swiss Alps and runs north along the west side of Germany and through Holland.

On both sides of the Rhine are steep hills and rocks and on top of these hills are castles built many years ago. The men who built these castles were called robber barons, and they built their castles on these hills so that they could rob and would be safe from their enemies. The poor people, who lived down in the valleys, had to give part of the things they raised to the barons; if they did not do so, the barons would swoop down on them with their men and take what they wanted and destroy the people's homes. The people knew it was useless to attack the barons because of their strong castles. Most of these castles are now in ruins, because it is too hard to get to them and to keep them in repair, and no longer can any one treat the poor people the way the barons did.

Cologne is a kind of strong perfume. It is named for a city on the Rhine called Cologne. Cologne means colony, for it was once a colony of Rome. The house in which I live took seven months to build, but there is a Cathedral in Cologne that took seven hundred years to build!—the longest time of any building in the World.

世界上一些最优秀的童话故事都来自德国

剧，描述了那些生活在德国莱茵河畔的小山上或者洞穴中的仙人以及现实人物的故事。莱茵河发源于瑞士境内阿尔卑斯山脉上的一座冰川，沿着德国西部向北而去，还流经了荷兰。

莱茵河两岸，全都是陡峭的山峰和岩石，许多年以前，人们还在这些山峰之巅修建有城堡。修建这些城堡的人，叫作"强盗贵族"，这是因为，他们将自己的城堡建在这些山峰上，目的是为了能够掠夺财物，同时也是为了能够安全地躲过敌人的攻击。而居住在山谷之中的贫苦百姓，必须把所种粮食收成的一部分交给这些贵族，要是不这样做的话，那些贵族就会带领手下的人来袭击百姓，然后把他们想要的东西洗劫一空，将老百姓的房子毁掉。老百姓知道，去攻打这些贵族是没有用的，因为贵族们的城堡都坚固得很。其中绝大多数城堡如今都已变成了废墟，因为人们很难爬到那些城堡里去对其进行维修，而且如今也没有人能够再像以前那些贵族一样对待贫苦百姓了。

"古龙"是一种气味浓烈的香水牌子。这种香水，是根据莱茵河畔一个叫作"科隆"的城市命名的[1]。"科隆"（Cologne）本指"殖民地"（colony），因为

---

[1]　"古龙"和"科隆"是同一个词，都是Cologne，只是为了区分它们，人们才将其译成不同的名称。

Cologne is a city famous for its Cathedral but the most famous German city is Berlin. Before World War II Berlin was one of the finest and clearest cities in the world. It had broad tree-lined avenues, great handsome stone buildings, parks and statues. It was also the capital of Germany. But by the time World War II was over, much of Berlin was a wreck. Many of its finest buildings were in ruins, destroyed by bombs dropped from airplanes during the war. Berlin is in Eastern Germany, the part of Germany ruled by the Russians after the War, but the United States, Great Britain, and France as well as Russia govern Berlin. The Russians had fought on our side during World War II, but after the War was over they became very unfriendly to the United States and Great Britain. They even said that the countries ruling Western Germany could not use the railroad or auto roads to Berlin. The people of Berlin had to be fed, so the United States and Great Britain flew tons and tons of food and coal into the city by airplanes day after day for a year and a half. Finally the Russians realized they could not keep out the Americans and British and opened the railroad again. This carrying of supplies to Berlin was called the Berlin Airlift because the supplies were lifted through the air from Western Germany

莱茵河畔的城堡

这些城堡里曾经住着强盗

那里曾经是古罗马的殖民地。我家的房子花了七个月才建好，可在科隆有一座大教堂，却整整花了七百年才建成呢！它可是世界上所有建筑物中耗时最长的一座呢。

虽说科隆是一个以拥有一座大教堂而著称的城市，但德国最闻名遐迩的城市，却是柏林。第二次世界大战以前，柏林本是世界上最美丽、最干净的城市之一。那里有宽阔的街道，两侧绿树成荫，有非常漂亮的石制建筑，并且公园密布，雕像成群。那里也是德国的首都。不过，到了第二次世界大战结束的时候，柏林的大部分地方却都变得千疮百孔了。其中许多精美的建筑都成了废墟，被战争期间空投下来的炸弹毁掉了。柏林本来位于东德，就是第二次世界大战后由俄罗斯统治的那一部分，不过，后来它却是由美国、英国、法国和俄罗斯四国共管。俄罗斯在第二次世界大战期间，本来是站在我们美国这一方与德国作战的，可战争结束后，该国对美国和英国却很不友好起来。俄国人甚至不允许统治西德的那些国家使用通往柏林的铁路和公路。可柏林人民必须吃饭呀，因此美、英两国用飞机昼夜不停地向柏林空投了成百上千吨的食物和煤炭，并且这种情况整整持续了一年半。最终，俄国人认识到，他们没法挡住美国人和英国人，于是再次开放了通往柏林的铁路和公路。此次向柏林空投给养的行动，叫作"柏林空运"，因为给养都是通过空运，从西德投往柏林的。

科隆大教堂花了七百年才建成

to Berlin.

Sticking up off the map of Germany like a thumb is a little country called Denmark. On one side of it is the North Sea; on the other side is another sea called the Baltic. Germany fronts on the North Sea and on the Baltic Sea too, but this little thumb of land does not belong to Germany. The Germans had to go all around this country in order to get from the cities on the North Sea to the cities on the Baltic Sea, so they cut off the thumb by digging a canal across the bottom of it. It is called the Kiel Canal.

在地图上，德国北面那个像竖起的手指的地方，是一个叫作"丹麦"的小国。该国一侧是北海，一侧却是另一个海域，叫作"波罗的海"。德国的边境西达北海，同时还濒临波罗的海，但这个大拇指般的小国，却并不属于德国。由于德国人必须绕过这个小国，才能从北海沿岸各市经由水路到达波罗的海沿岸城市，于是他们便在该国的最南边开凿了一条运河。这条运河，就叫"基尔运河"。

39 The Great Danes

When anything annoyed my uncle he used to cry out, "*Skagerrack and Kattegat!*" It sounded terrible, for I didn't know then that Skagerrack and Kattegat were merely the names of the narrow waterway around Denmark from the North Sea into the Baltic Sea and that Kattegat simply meant "the cat's throat" and Skagerrack meant "Skager throat."

There are two chief pieces to Denmark. One piece is the thumb-like land called Jutland, because a people called the Jutes used to live there. The other piece is a little island right alongside of Jutland called Zealand. You don't have to be a good guesser to know that Zealand means "Sea Land." On this island is Copenhagen, the capital of Denmark. Copenhagen means "Merchants' Harbor," because merchants with their ships used to stop there on the way from the North Sea to the Baltic. But there are not as many ships now as there used to be, for instead of going through the Skagerrack and Kattegat, many ships take the short cut through the Kiel Canal. Copenhagen is the only big city that Denmark has—there are no other large cities.

You probably have heard of a "Great Dane," a kind of big dog that comes from Denmark. But the people in Denmark are called Danes, and there is one great Dane whom you probably know and whose stories you have probably read. He wrote "The Little Match Girl" and "The Ugly Duckling." The man who wrote those fairy-tales lived in

第39章　了不起的丹麦人

每当有什么事情惹恼我叔叔的时候，他都会大声喊道："斯卡格拉克和卡特加特！"这句话听上去吓人得很，因为那时我还不知道，斯卡格拉克和卡特加特只是一条环绕着丹麦、从北海通往波罗的海的狭窄水道，并且"卡特加特"一词原本只是指"猫的喉咙"，而"斯卡格拉克"则是指"斯卡格的喉咙"。

丹麦全境主要分成了两个部分。其中一个部分就是那个像拇指般的陆地，叫作"日德兰半岛"，因为那里曾经生活着一个叫作"日德兰"的民族。另一个部分则是日德兰半岛沿岸的一个小岛，叫作"西兰岛"。估计大家都不需要动什么脑筋，就猜得出"西兰"的意思是指"海上陆地"吧。丹麦的首都哥本哈根，就坐落在这个小岛上。"哥本哈根"就是"商人之港"的意思，因为从前的商人在率船从北海前往波罗的海地区时，半路上通常都会在这个海港停靠。不过，如今这里已经没有过去那么多的船只了，因为许多船只不用再经由斯卡格拉克海峡和卡特加特海峡，而是可以抄近路，经由基尔运河进出波罗的海了。哥本哈根是丹麦唯一一座大型城市，除此之外，该国就没有别的大城市了。

你们很可能都听说过"大丹犬"吧，它指的可不是人，而是一种产自丹麦的大型犬类。生活在丹麦的人，被称为"丹麦人"，其中还有一位很了不起的丹麦人，大家很可能都听说过，并且阅读过他所写的故事呢。他创作过《卖火柴的小女孩》

Copenhagen. His name is Hans Christian Andersen. The Danes like the name "Christian." Ten of their kings have been named Christian.

But over a thousand years ago the Danes were not Christians, and many were pirates who sailed the seas and robbed other lands. They are now, of course, no longer pirates; but they are still great sailors. In some towns almost every person is either a sailor, a ship-builder, or connected with shipping in some way.

The Danes who stay at home are chiefly engaged in the butter and egg business. They raise cows to make butter and chickens to lay eggs and they send butter and eggs to other countries that haven't enough. Danish eggs have the date when they are laid stamped on them, so that every one may know how fresh or how old they are. Danish butter is so good and brings such high prices that the Danes send most of it away, and they themselves usually eat an imitation butter made out of fat or grease.

Denmark is one of the healthiest countries in the World. People live longer there than in almost any other country; so the moral of this is, if you want to live long, go to Denmark.

Denmark, though such a little country, used to own two islands that were perhaps ten times as big as itself. These two islands are far away from Denmark in the cold north; one is a little island called Iceland and the other is a big island called Greenland. Greenland still belongs to Denmark, but Iceland no longer does. Most people cannot see why Denmark should want either island, for Iceland is full of volcanoes and many hot springs—which seems strange, for ice and fire do not seem to go together—and Greenland

和《丑小鸭》。这位创作童话故事的丹麦人，就住在哥本哈根，名叫汉斯·克里斯汀·安徒生。丹麦人都很喜欢"克里斯汀"这个名字。该国曾经有十位国王，都叫"克里斯汀"呢。

但是，一千年以前，丹麦人却还没有皈依基督教，其中有很多人都是海盗，常常到别的国家去劫掠财物。当然，如今丹麦人不再当海盗了，不过，他们仍然都是些了不起的水手。在许多城镇里，居民或是水手、造船工人，或是从事着某种与航运相关的工作。

而那些待在国内的丹麦人，从事的主要是与生产黄油和鸡蛋相关的工作。他们喂养奶牛来制造黄油，养殖小鸡来下蛋，然后，他们再把黄油和鸡蛋出口到这两种产品不足的其他国家。丹麦所产的鸡蛋上面，都印有每只鸡蛋产下的日期，从而让每个消费者都很清楚，一只鸡蛋是新鲜蛋还是陈蛋。丹麦所产的黄油品质非常好，售价昂贵，因此丹麦人把绝大部分黄油都用于出口，而自己则吃一种由脂肪或者油脂制成的人造黄油。

丹麦是世界上最宜居的国家之一。丹麦人的寿命比其他绝大多数国家的人都要长，因此，有条格言曾说，如果你们也想长寿的话，那就该去丹麦生活。

尽管丹麦是一个很小的国家，但该国曾经拥有过两个岛屿，这两座岛屿的面积之和，可能达到了丹麦本土面积的十倍呢。这两个岛屿，都位于距丹麦非常遥远、气候寒冷的北方，其中一个小岛叫作"冰岛"，而另一个大岛则叫"格陵兰岛"。如今，格陵兰岛仍然隶属于丹麦，可冰岛却不是这样了。绝大多数人都不明

is chiefly ice. I think it would be more exact if Greenland were called Iceland and Iceland were called Volcano Land. I used to know a boy who was very fat, but all his friends called him "Skinny." That is like calling this ice-covered land Greenland, so I think it was called Greenland for a joke. Only along one edge of Greenland do we find any land at all showing. The ice in Greenland is about a quarter of a mile thick, covering the land, and where the ice comes down to the water's edge big chunks often as big as a church break off and float away in the sea. They are then called icebergs, which means ice mountains.

There are Eskimos living in Greenland. You may well wonder what the Eskimos in Greenland live on, for they can't raise any of the vegetables we have to eat. They live chiefly on fish out of the sea and animals and birds. There are millions of birds called "auks" which fly so low and so thick over the land that the Eskimos catch them with a net as you would catch butterflies. They can catch enough to last them for many months, and as all out-of-doors is a refrigerator the birds that are caught can be kept on ice without having the ice man call every day. Eskimos use the auk's soft feathers to line their clothes to keep themselves warm and comfortable, for the thermometer sometimes goes to seventy degrees below zero. Another bird, the eider-duck, has still softer feathers. They are called "down." Eider-down is one of the softest and lightest things imaginable and makes the best filling for bed quilts, as it is both light and warm. Eskimos eat the eider-duck's eggs, too, and they gather thousands of them at a time.

Instead of beef, the Eskimo eats the flesh of an animal called the musk-ox. The musk-

白，丹麦为什么要拥有这两个岛屿，因为冰岛火山密布，上面还有许多的温泉（这一点似乎很奇怪，因为冰与火似乎没什么联系），而格陵兰岛上则主要是冰雪。我倒觉得，要是把格陵兰岛叫作冰岛，而把冰岛叫作火山岛的话，可能会更加贴切呢。我曾经认识一个小男孩，他长得胖乎乎的，可朋友们却全都叫他"瘦子"。这种情况，正如把一个冰雪覆盖的地方叫作"格陵兰"一样[1]，因此，我觉得人们之所以把这里称为"格陵兰"，纯粹是为了好玩。格陵兰岛上，只有一侧边缘才有从冰雪下露出来的陆地。格陵兰岛上的冰雪，差不多有四分之一英里厚，盖住了整个大地，而在冰雪层延伸到海边后，大块大块的冰雪还会掉落海中，随着海水漂浮而去。这些脱落的冰块，常常有一座教堂那么大哩。因此，人们便称这些如山一般大的冰块为"冰山"。

格陵兰岛上，生活着因纽特人。大家可能会感到奇怪，格陵兰岛上的因纽特人靠什么生活，因为他们种植不了我们必须食用的任何一种菜蔬。他们主要是从海中捕鱼、在陆上猎杀野兽和飞禽为食。那里有数不清的、一种叫作"海雀"的鸟儿，它们飞得很低，离地面很近，并且密密麻麻、铺天盖地，因此因纽特人用一张网就可以捕捉到，就像你们用网子逮蝴蝶那样。他们一次就可以捕捉到足够吃上好几个月的鸟儿，而他们的屋外就是一个天然的大冰箱，把捕到的鸟儿放在冰上就行，根本无须每天都叫送冰的人来。因纽特人还会用海雀柔软的羽毛来给衣服做衬里，让

---

[1]　"格陵兰"（greenland）这个地名如果意译的话，就叫"绿地"，因此作者才说格陵兰岛的名称与实际情况不符，说他认为人们之所以给那个岛屿起这个名称，是为了好玩。

ox has hook-like horns and a shaggy long-haired coat to keep himself warm in the terrible cold. His coat makes him look big, but when he is killed and the coat removed, there is only a poor little lean animal left inside.

There is another animal which the Eskimo hunts. It lives both in the water and on the land and has tusks like an elephant. It is called a walrus. It is also caught for meat, but chiefly for its ivory tusks, which are two big teeth that hang far down out of its mouth.

What the Eskimo likes best to eat, however, is not lean meat but fat. A big, greasy strip of fat to him is as delicious as a banana to us. Fat food keeps people warm, and nature in its wonderful way makes fat taste good to the Eskimo because it makes him warm. People in warm countries don't like fat food because it would make them warm when they want to be cool.

One of the most valuable furs that ladies wear is made from the coat of the seal, another animal that lives both in the water and on the ice. The Eskimo uses the sealskin to make his tents in which he lives in the summertime. The winds are so terribly strong in parts of Greenland that a tent has to be anchored down by heavy stones to keep it from blowing away. In the wintertime, however, the Eskimo makes his hut of blocks of stone—if he can find any; but if he can't, he cuts blocks of snow and makes a bowl-shaped house of that instead. Of course, his house is hardly large enough to stand up in and has only one room and no windows, so that he has to light it inside with a fire built right on the ground, or by a lamp made out of a hollowed stone with a wick soaked in the grease or fat of the animals

自己穿得暖暖和和、舒舒服服，因为那里的气温有时会低至零下70华氏[1]度呢。那里还一种鸟儿，就是"绒鸭"，它们的羽毛则更加柔软，叫作"鸭绒"。鸭绒是人们能够想到的最柔软、最轻的东西之一，它们既轻便、又暖和，所以是做被子时最好的填充物。因纽特人也吃绒鸭下的蛋，他们一次就可以捡到成千上万个鸭蛋呢。

因纽特人不吃牛肉，而是吃一种叫作"麝牛"的动物肉。麝牛长有两个钩子一样的角，全身都长满了蓬松的、在极端寒冷的天气里具有保暖作用的长毛。这身长毛让它们显得体型巨大，但宰杀并将长毛剔除干净之后，里面剩下的，却是一具瘦得可怜的牛尸了。

因纽特人还猎杀一种野兽。那是一种水、陆两栖的动物，长着大象那样的长牙，叫作"海象"。因纽特人猎杀海象，虽说也是为了得到海象肉，但主要还是为了获得象牙，所谓的象牙，其实就是海象嘴边向下伸展得很长的两颗大牙齿。

然而，因纽特人最爱吃的并不是瘦肉，而是肥肉。对于因纽特人来说，一块油乎乎的大肥肉极其美味，就像我们觉得香蕉很好吃那样。高脂肪的食物可以让人们保持暖和，而大自然也用一种神奇的方法，使得肥肉成了因纽特人的美食，因为这会让他们保持身体暖和。热带国家的人之所以不喜欢吃油腻的食物，就是因为这种食物会让他们在想要凉快的时候，全身却暖和得很。

---

[1] 华氏（Fahrenheit），西方国家常用的一种温度计量单位，以32℃为冰点，212℃为沸点，略作°F。它与我们常用的摄氏温度（Celsius，略作℃）之间的换算关系为：1°F=1℃×9/5+32。所以，此处的零下70华氏度，就相当于零下56.67摄氏度。

he has killed.

The only tame animals the Eskimo has are the Eskimo dogs, which look very much like wolves and may be cousins of the wolves. The Eskimo uses dogs hooked up to his sled, instead of a horse and carriage or automobile. Four or eight or more dogs are harnassed together and make a team. Almost all of our dogs love water; they will run and jump into a pool or into a river if given half a chance. But the Eskimo dog is afraid of water, and though he can swim he will not go into it unless he is whipped into it, and not even then if he can run away. The Eskimo, however, is not afraid of the water even when blocks of ice are floating in it. He has a canoe called a kayak which is completely covered, all except a place in the center where he sits and paddles. It is water tight, so that even when upset no water can get in. The Eskimos are experts at paddling, and they have water sports in which an Eskimo upsets his kayak on purpose and rolls over and over in the water just to show off.

女士们身上最珍贵的一种毛皮大衣，就是用海豹毛制成的，海豹是另一种两栖动物，生活在水中和冰上。因纽特人会用海豹皮来搭帐篷，夏季的时候，他们就住在这种帐篷里。格陵兰岛上有些地方的风力非常巨大，帐篷必须用大块的石头固定在地上，才不会被大风吹走。然而，到了冬季，要是找得到石头的话，因纽特人便会用石头搭建小屋，要是找不到石头，他们就会切割出大块大块的冰雪，用冰块堆出一座形状像碗的房屋来。当然，他们搭建的这种房子都很小，一个人站在里面连腰都直不起来，并且，这种房子通常都只有一个房间，没有窗户，因此里面必须依靠一个地灶发出的火光，或者是点上一盏油灯来照明才行。他们的油灯，是用一块中空的石头做成的，上面有一根灯芯，浸在宰杀动物后获取的油脂或者脂肪里。

因纽特人驯养的唯一一种动物，就是爱斯基摩犬，这种狗的样子很像是狼，可能与狼是同族吧。因纽特人把狗拴在雪橇上，让它们拉着雪橇前进，而不是用马拉大车或者开着汽车。他们把四条、八条或者更多的狗拴在一起，形成一个团队。我们所养的小狗，几乎全都喜欢戏水，只要有机会，它们就会跑进或者跳进池塘、河流里耍上一番。可是，爱斯基摩犬却很怕水，尽管会游泳，但它们不会主动跳进水里，除非主人用鞭子逼着，并且要是躲得开的话，哪怕有鞭子逼着，它们也不会下水。然而，因纽特人却不怕水，就算水里漂浮着巨大的冰块，他们也不害怕。他们有一种叫作"皮筏子"的独木舟，除了上面有一个让人坐着划桨的地方之外，整个船身都用兽皮裹得严严实实的。这种船不透水，因此哪怕是翻了，水也不会进去。因纽特人都是些划桨高手。他们还有一种水上运动：一个因纽特人会故意将皮筏子翻过来，并且连人带船在水中不停地翻滚，以此来炫耀自己的本领呢。

坐在皮筏子里的因纽特人

40 Fish, Fiords, Falls, and Forests

Have you a good imagination? I mean, when there are clouds in the sky, can you see giants or galloping horses or rabbits with long ears or other things? Then look at the map on page 260 and tell me what it looks like:

Turn it on the side. Do you see what I see? A WHALE, with his mouth open, ready to swallow little Denmark. Skagerrack and Kattegat are the whale's throat.

My geography calls this whale the "Scandinavian Peninsula"—that's a big name, but then a whale is a big animal. The geography calls the back of the whale Norway, and it calls the other side Sweden. Norway plus Sweden equals Scandinavian Peninsula.

Perhaps the reason I thought of a whale was because there are so many real whales in the sea near Norway. Now a whale is the largest fish there is, you know, only it isn't a fish. Fish lay eggs as chickens and birds do, only much smaller and many more, but a whale mother doesn't lay eggs. She has babies as a cat has kittens. Besides, a whale has to have air to breathe and must come up to the top of the water as you would have to do if you were swimming under the water. A fish wouldn't do that, for he couldn't do that, so you see a whale is not a fish.

The whale eats little fish called herring, lots of them at one gulp, bones and all. There are millions, billions, trillions of herring in the sea, and millions, billions, trillions more

第40章 鱼儿、峡湾、瀑布和森林

大家的想象力丰不丰富呀？我的意思是说，倘若天空中飘着朵朵白云，你们从中看得出巨人、奔马、耳朵长长的兔子或者其他东西吗？接下来，就请看一看下面这幅地图，然后跟我说说，它看起来像是什么吧：

将地图沿着一侧翻转过来。你们看到了我看到的东西吗？我看到了一条鲸鱼，它正张着嘴巴，准备将小小的丹麦一口吞下肚去呢。斯卡格拉克海峡和卡特加特海峡，就是这条鲸鱼的喉咙。

在地理学上，这条鲸鱼叫作"斯堪的纳维亚半岛"，这可是个很长的地名，不过，鲸鱼本身也是一种大型动物呀。鲸鱼的背部，在地理上一半叫作"挪威"，而另一半则叫"瑞典"。挪威和瑞典，合起来就构成了斯堪的纳维亚半岛。

或许，我之所以看出了一条鲸鱼的样子，原因就在于挪威附近海域里有许多的鲸鱼吧。注意，大家都知道，鲸鱼是世界上最大的动物，但它并不是一种鱼类。鱼类会像母鸡、小鸟那样产卵，只是鱼卵比鸡蛋和鸟蛋要小得多、数量也要多得多罢了，可鲸鱼妈妈却不会产卵。母鲸会像母猫生小猫那样，生出小鲸鱼来。此外，鲸鱼必须游到水面上来呼吸空气，就像你们在潜水时必须浮上去换气一样。鱼类则不会这样，而且鱼类也没法这样，因此，你们就不难看出，鲸鱼并不属于鱼类。

鲸鱼以一种叫作"鲱鱼"的小鱼为食，它一口就能吞下无数条鲱鱼，并且是一

than that. They live together in enormous crowds called "schools," but one school of herring has more pupils than all the schools in the World; so, although the whales eat some herring, there are plenty of herring left for us to eat. The Norwegian people catch herring in nets, then they salt, smoke, or dry them to make sure they will keep almost forever without spoiling. Then they send these dried herring all over the World to be sold. I had a

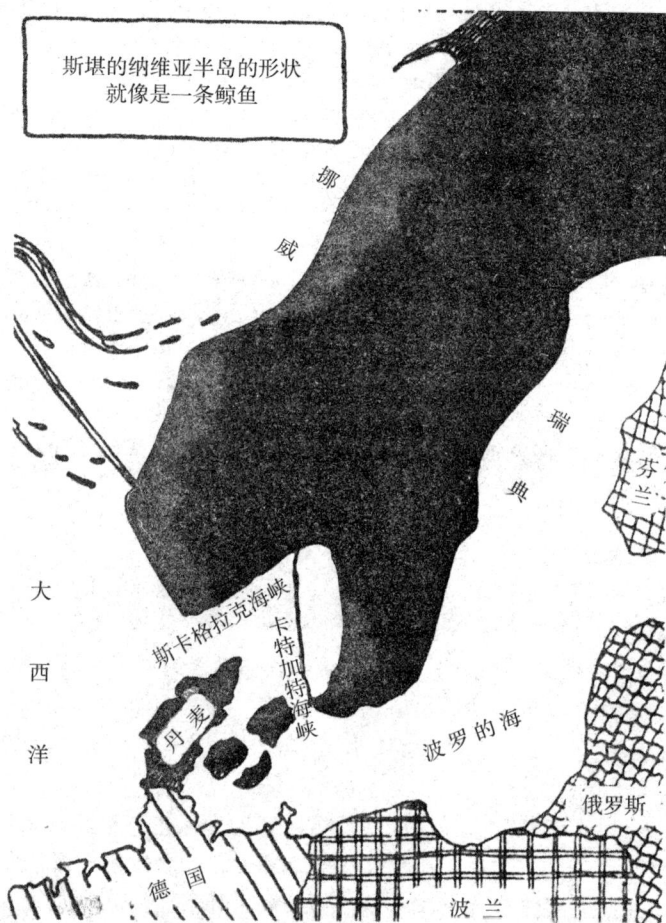

斯堪的纳维亚半岛的形状就像是一条鲸鱼

挪威

瑞典

芬兰

大西洋

斯卡格拉克海峡

卡特加特海峡

丹麦

波罗的海

俄罗斯

德国

波兰

古脑儿吞下肚去。海洋中的鲱鱼，多到以万亿计，数不胜数。它们都聚集在一起生活，形成一个个巨大的"鱼群"，不过，一群鲱鱼的数量，比全世界所有学校里的学生加起来还要多呢[1]。因此，即便是鲸鱼吞食掉一些，也还会剩下大量的鲱鱼，够我们来吃的了。挪威人都是用渔网捕捞鲱鱼，然后再腌渍、熏制或晒干，确保鲱鱼可以永久保存而不会变坏。接下来，他们又把这种加工好的干鲱鱼运送到世界各地去卖。今天早上我就吃了一条鲱鱼，许多年前，这条鲱鱼没准就在挪威海域里游

---

[1] 英语中"鱼群"一词与"学校"一词相同，都是school，故作者这样说。

herring for breakfast this morning which may have been swimming round Norway years and years ago—it has been kept all that time.

I also ate a thousand eggs for breakfast this morning. That sounds impossible, but it's really so—only they were not *hen's* eggs, but herring eggs, for the mother herring carries her eggs inside of her—thousands of them. The herring's eggs we call "roe."

The seashore of Norway is not smooth and level like a bathing beach. There are mountains all along the edge right in the water and the sea fills the valleys between these mountains. These valleys filled with water are called "fiords."

Norway is so far north we would expect the water in these fiords to be very cold in the winter; and we know what happens when water gets very cold—it freezes and turns to ice. But, strange to say, the water in these fiords does not freeze. The reason it doesn't freeze is because the sun shines down on the water in the Gulf of Mexico, several thousand miles off. You may wonder what the Gulf of Mexico several thousand miles off has to do with Norway. Well, the boiler way off in my cellar heats the water in the pipes and that heats the radiator in the farthest room in my house. In the same way the sun heats the water in the Gulf as if it were a big boiler and from this Gulf a warm stream of water, called the Gulf Stream, flows as if it were a river in the ocean, all the way across the ocean from the Gulf of Mexico to the shore of Norway and warms the fiords. In the warm water of the fiords the herring schools have a fine recess until a whale or a fisherman comes along.

The north*est* city in the World is in Norway and the name of this city ends in *est*, too. It

来游去，然后被人捕捞上来，保存了这么些年呢。

今天早餐时，我还吃掉了一千个"蛋"。听上去，这种事情似乎是不可能的，但情况确实如此，只是它们并不是母鸡产下的鸡蛋，而是鲱鱼蛋，因为母鲱鱼的蛋都在肚子里存着，达数千个之多。鲱鱼的蛋，我们称之为"鱼子"。

挪威的沿岸地区，可不像海水浴场那样平坦。挪威的沿海，全都是一条条从海中拔地而起的山脉，山脉之间的山谷里则全是海水。这种注满了海水的山谷，叫作"峡湾"。

由于挪威地处遥远的北方，因此我们可以想见，这些峡湾里的海水到了冬季必定会非常寒冷，而我们也知道，海水变得非常寒冷之后会发生什么，那就是封冻起来，变成冰。可是，说来也怪，这些峡湾里的海水却不会结冰。之所以不会结冰，是因为阳光照射着数千英里以外的墨西哥湾里的海水。你们可能会觉得很奇怪，数千英里以外的墨西哥湾与挪威有什么关系。这么说吧，我家那台安装在地窖里面的锅炉会将管道里面的水加热，从而使得我家与地窖相距最远的一个房间里的暖气片也变热了。同理，太阳将墨西哥湾里的海水加热，使之变成了一个大型的锅炉，因此一股温暖的、叫作"湾流"的海水便从这个海湾出发，像海洋里有一条河流那样，一路穿过大西洋，从墨西哥湾流到了挪威沿海，使那些峡湾里的海水变热了。除非有鲸鱼或者渔夫到来，否则峡湾里那种温暖的海水，就是鲱鱼理想的栖身之所呢。

世界上位置最北的城市就在挪威，叫作"哈默菲斯特"。墨西哥湾流似乎流到

is Hammer*fest*. The Gulf Stream seems to end at Hammerfest and it dumps on the shore sticks of wood, some of which have floated like toy boats in a river all the way from the Gulf of Mexico. The people gather this "driftwood" and use it to make fires. Ordinary wood burns with a yellow flame, but wood that has drifted for a long time in the sea-water gets filled with salt from the water and when dried and burned gives off flames colored blue and green and purple, so that driftwood makes especially beautiful fires in open fireplaces.

You have probably tasted cod-liver oil—and hated it—but you were told it was very good for you, and it is. The cod is a much bigger fish than the herring, but of course not nearly as big as the whale. One of the playgrounds of the cod is near Norway, round some islands called "The Lofodens." Fishermen catch shiploads of cod, press the oil out of their livers, and bottle it for your good health. The bones of the cod they have no use for, so they take them out—and this is quite a job, for there are a great many—and then they dry the flesh of the cod to make food. Here is a sentence that sounds funny unless you put in a period where it belongs, and then it makes perfect sense: "A codfish was swimming round the Lofoden Islands a month after all its bones had been taken out." Where would you put the period to make sense?

哈默菲斯特后便止步了，它把许多木头带到这个地方的海滨，其中有些木头还像河里的玩具船一样，是从墨西哥湾一路漂到这里来的呢。当地人将这种"浮木"收集起来，用于生火。普通木头烧起来，火焰是黄色的，可在海中漂浮了很久的浮木，由于浸透了海水中的盐分，晒干后烧起来的时候，火焰就会变得五彩缤纷，有蓝色、绿色和紫色。因此，如果在开放式的壁炉里烧这种浮木，你们就能看到极其美丽的火焰。

大家可能都吃过鱼肝油，并且很不喜欢它的味道吧，不过，大人会告诉你们说，鱼肝油对你们的身体有好处，事实也的确如此。鳕鱼是一种比鲱鱼体型大得多的鱼类，但它们当然没有鲸鱼那么大。鳕鱼喜欢嬉戏的一个海域，就在挪威附近，是一群小岛周围的海域，那群小岛，合称为"罗弗敦群岛"。渔民们捕捞了一船又一船的鳕鱼，将它们肝里的油榨出来，装在瓶子里，喝了这种东西，就能让你们保持身体健康。鳕鱼的骨头没有什么用处，因此人们还得将鱼骨剔出来，这可是件不容易的事情，因为鳕鱼体内的骨头很多，然后，人们再把鳕鱼风干，作为食物。下面这句话，听起来会很可笑；但是，如果你们在其中合适的地方加上一个句号，那么整句话就会言之有理了："一条鳕鱼围着罗弗敦群岛游来游去一个月后它全身的骨头都被剔掉了"。你们会在哪里加上一个句号，使整句话说得通呢？

41 Fish, Fiords, Falls, and Forests (continued)

The "fishiest" city in the World is in Norway on a fiord. The city and the fiord are both called Bergen. The fishermen from the Lofoden Islands and the fiords bring their catches to Bergen—boatloads of big fish and little fish, thick fish and thin fish, white fish and black fish—to sell and to ship everywhere.

Bergen is also another "est" besides the "fishiest." It is the wett*est* city in Europe. People carry umbrellas or raincoats all the time, for you scarcely ever see the sun, and when it is not raining it is getting ready to. It takes a lot of rain, if caught in a bucket, to make as much as an inch deep of water. Perhaps you have seen it rain so hard that the streets were flooded and at the crossings the rain has been over your shoe tops, but probably it has rained less than an inch in any one spot, such as in a bucket. Of course, when rain runs off the roof and pours down on to the street the water has run together from a large space, but very few cities have a rainfall of more than a few feet in a whole year. Bergen however has a rainfall of six feet in a year. This is enough rain to drown every man, woman, and child in the city if it all came down at once, but fortunately it does not.

As nearly every family in America has an automobile, nearly every family in Norway has a boat. The Norwegians always have been famous sailors.

Long, long ago the Norwegian sailors were called Vikings, which, however, does not

第41章 鱼儿、峡湾、瀑布和森林（续）

世界上最"有鱼腥味儿"的城市，就坐落在挪威的一个峡湾边。这座城市和这个峡湾，都叫"卑尔根"。来自罗弗敦群岛和峡湾地区的渔民，纷纷带着他们捕捞到的鱼儿来到卑尔根市，一船船的鱼儿大小不一、粗细各异、黑白混杂，卖出之后，就会被运送到世界各地去。

除了最"有鱼腥味儿"，卑尔根市还有一个"最"。它是欧洲雨水最多的一个城市。人们每时每刻都随身携带着雨伞或者雨衣，因为那里几乎看不到太阳，就算此时没有下雨，那么随时都会下雨。如果用桶子接着的话，那么需要下很大、很久的雨，才能在桶中盛起一英寸深的雨水来。你们可能都看到过下大雨吧，街道一下子被淹没了，十字路口的水都漫过了人们的鞋面，不过，这种大雨很可能在任何一个地方，比如一只水桶里，落下来的雨量还不到一英寸深呢。当然，雨水从屋顶流下，淌到大街上之后，实际上是把大范围内的雨水全都集中到了一起，不过，世界上却少有几座城市，全年的降水量会超过几英尺。然而，卑尔根市每年的降水量却达到了六英尺。这种降雨量，若是集中一次性落下来，足以淹死该市里的每一个男人、女人和孩子呢，但幸运的是，情况并不是这样的。

就像美国几乎每个家庭都有一辆汽车那样，挪威几乎每个家庭都拥有一艘小船。挪威人可一直都是闻名遐迩的水手啊。

mean Vi-"kings," but "Vik"-ings, and that means "fiordmen." One of the greatest of these Vikings was a man named Leif, son of Eric, called Leif Ericson. Leif Ericson lived about a thousand years ago. He and his men sailed across the ocean and landed in America five hundred years before Columbus discovered America, but he didn't think much of the country, and when he went back to Norway he said little about it.

In later times there have been famous sailors and discoverers too in Norway. Men up there live so near the top of the earth that they have tried to go all the way to the top, to the point where if you stood still you would turn exactly around on the spot where you stood once every twenty-four hours. That point is the North Pole. Such men have risked their lives—and many have lost them—in trying to reach the poles. Two famous Scandinavian explorers, Nansen and Amundsen, tried—they didn't lose their lives, but they didn't reach the North Pole either. An American named Peary was the first man to reach the North Pole. Amundsen, however, tried to reach the South Pole and he succeeded. He was the first man to reach the South Pole. Since then airplanes, and a Norse airship too, have crossed the North Pole, but they didn't stop there.

佩里是第一个抵达北极的人

很久很久以前，挪威的水手都叫"维京人"，也就是"峡湾人"的意思。这些维京人当中，最了不起的一位名叫列夫，他是埃里克的儿子，因此全名为"列夫·埃里克森"[1]。列夫·埃里克森生活在距今大约一千年前。他和手下的人驾着船只漂洋过海，在哥伦布发现美洲的五百年之前就抵达美洲，不过，他并没有重视这个地方，因此回到挪威后，几乎没有说起过美洲。

后来，挪威也涌现出了许多著名的水手和发现者。由于这里的人生活在距地球顶端那么近的地方，因此他们曾经想方设法地要到达那个顶端，到了那个地方，若是站着不动的话，那么每隔二十四个小时，你们就会在原地转上一圈。那个地方，就是北极。这些人冒着生命危险（许多人都丢掉了性命），想要到达北极。有两个著名的斯堪的纳维亚探险家，即南森和阿蒙森，也这样尝试过，不过，他们虽然没有送命，可最终也没有抵达北极。一个叫作佩里的美国人，是世界上第一个成功抵达北极的人。然而，阿蒙森后来又试着前往南极，而这一次他却成功了。因此，他就是世界上第一个成功抵达南极的人。自那以后，有许多飞机，以及一艘挪威的飞

---

[1] 埃里克森（Ericson）一词是由"埃里克"（Eric）和"儿子"（son）合成的。

Later Amundsen started for the North Pole in an airplane and was never heard from again.

You have overshoes to wear when you go out in the snow, but every one in Norway and Sweden has a pair of long wooden runners called "skis," which he straps to his shoes when he goes out. With these on his feet he coasts over the top of the snow, making a sled of himself—sliding down slopes and pushing himself along on level ground with a pole, as if it were a cane.

Have you ever seen a white blackbird? No one has. Have you ever seen white coal? They have a lot of it in Norway and Sweden. On the tops of the mountains there are vast fields of snow and ice like frosting on a huge cake, but as this snow and ice sinks down to the valleys it melts and the water falls in streams like rain running off a roof down a waterspout. This water falling is used in Norway and Sweden to turn wheels and the wheels turning are used to run sawmills and machinery, just the same as if the wheels were turned by steam-engines run with coal fires. Norway and Sweden have no black coal, but the waterfalls do much the same thing; they run machines, and so people speak of their waterfalls as "white coal."

But white coal won't do one thing that black coal will do—it won't heat. In the northern part of Sweden there are iron mines. This iron is particularly good for making tools that have to have sharp edges, like knives and razors. But there is no black coal to melt the iron out of the ore, so they ship most of the ore to England, where there is plenty of coal, and there the English make fine cutlery from it.

Perhaps you have seen pictures of pine-trees in the snow or covered with snow.

艇，都曾飞过北极上空，不过，它们都没有在北极停留过。后来，阿蒙森又乘坐一架飞机向北极进发，此后就音讯全无了。

要是到雪地里去的话，你们都会穿上套鞋，可挪威人和瑞典人却都有一双长长的木制滑板，叫作"滑雪板"，出去的时候就把它们绑到自己的鞋子上。他们脚下踩着滑雪板，可以在雪上滑行，让自己变成一副雪橇，滑下山坡了，而在平路上，他们则用一根杆子推着自己往前走，就像那是一根手杖似的。

你们有没有见过白色的乌鸦？你们又见没见过白色的煤炭呢？在挪威和瑞典两国，这种煤炭有很多。那里的山顶上有大片大片的冰雪，就像一个巨型蛋糕上的糖霜似的，不过，这些冰雪沉到下面的山谷之中后，就会融化，而雪水则会形成一条条溪流往下而去，就像雨水顺着屋顶上的排水管往下排出似的。这种落差很大、由雪水形成的瀑布，在挪威和瑞典两国用于驱动一些轮子，来发动锯木机和其他的机械设备，这样做的原理，跟用燃煤带动蒸汽发动机来驱动轮子的原理是一样的。挪威和瑞典都不出产黑色的煤炭，但两国的瀑布却发挥出了燃煤一样的作用，它们能够发动机器，因此人们便把这些瀑布叫作"白煤"。

不过，有一个方面，黑色煤炭做得到，"白煤"却做不到，那就是"白煤"无法加热。在瑞典北部，有许多的铁矿山。那里出产的铁，尤其适合于制造具有锋利边缘的工具，比如刀子和剃须刀。可那里却没有煤炭，无法将铁矿砂熔化来提炼铁，于是，挪威人便将绝大部分矿砂都运往英国，因为英国拥有丰富的煤炭资源，

Anyway, pine-trees and snow seem to go together, and a great part of Norway and Sweden is covered with forests chiefly of pine-trees. Pine-trees—tall, straight ones—make fine masts for ships, flag and telegraph poles, and lumber for building. They also make fine match-sticks, and millions of match-sticks can be made out of a single tree. If you will look on a box of matches that you may find at your home, you will probably see the words "Made in Sweden" printed on it. The smaller trees the Swedes grind up into pulp, which is used to make paper, for almost all paper nowadays—whether it is newspaper, wrapping-paper, or the paper you write on—is made of wood-pulp rolled thin. So the people in Sweden cut down trees, saw them up into logs, slide them into the streams, and float them down to the sea, and there they ship them all over the World. But they take good care to plant little trees for every large tree cut down, so that there will always be more trees.

他让自己变成了一副雪橇

而英国人又用这种铁矿，制造出了精美的餐具。

　　或许，大家都看见过在雪中屹立或者积雪压枝的松树的照片吧。不管在什么情况下，松树和白雪似乎都是相得益彰的，挪威和瑞典两国的大部分地区都覆盖着森林，而其中的林木主要就是松树。高耸而挺拔的松树非常适合于做船只上的桅杆、旗杆和电线杆，以及建筑所用的木材。它们也很适合于做火柴棍，一棵松树，就可以生产出数以百万计的火柴棍来。看一看家里的火柴盒，你们可能就会发现，上面印着"瑞典生产"的字样呢。瑞典人还把那些较小的树碾成纸浆来造纸，因为如今所有的纸张，无论是报纸、包装纸还是写字所用的纸，全都是用木制纸浆薄薄地卷摊而成的。瑞典人把树木砍伐下来，锯成圆木，将它们滑入河中顺流而下，漂进大海，然后再装船运往世界各地。但他们同时也细心地呵护着森林，每砍伐掉一棵大树，就会种上许多小树，这样，那里就会有更多的树木，永远可以采伐了。

42 Where the Sun Shines all Night

In "Through the Looking-Glass" the story of "The Walrus and the Carpenter" starts this way:

The sun was shining on the sea,
Shining with all his might: . . .
And this was odd, because it was
The middle of the night.

Sun shining at midnight! You probably think this can't be true and is only a joke, but it is true up at the top of Norway and Sweden. At the top of Norway is a great rock sticking out into the Arctic Ocean. It is called the North Cape, and although there is no town there, people make long journeys from other lands to the North Cape to see the sun shining on the sea in the middle of the night.

You have always been told that the sun rises in the east and sets in the west, and probably you have never seen it do anything else; but the boys and girls in the north of Norway and Sweden know differently, for up there the sun doesn't rise in the east and set in the west. It goes completely round the house low down in the sky near the ground and keeps on going round and round this way every day for six months and in that time never sets—is never out of sight—there is always daylight for six months. But the sun gradually

第42章　太阳整夜不落的地方

在《爱丽丝镜中奇遇记》当中，《海象与木匠》[1]的故事是这样开头的：

太阳照耀着海洋，

发出了全部光芒……

说来真是奇怪，

因为当时正是午夜时光。

太阳竟然在午夜照耀着！你们很可能会觉得，这种情况不可能是真的，只是一个笑话罢了，不过，在挪威和瑞典两国的最北方，这种现象却是事实呢。挪威的最北部有一片巨大的礁石，延伸到了北冰洋里。这个地方，叫作"北角"，尽管那里并没有城镇，但人们却不远万里，纷纷从世界各地来到北角，一睹午夜时分太阳照耀着海洋的奇观。

从小时候起，大人就一直教给你们，说太阳总是从东方升起、从西方落山，并且你们看到的情况也一直如此，可挪威、瑞典两国北部的小朋友们了解到的情况，却与你们的不一样，因为在那样遥远的北方，太阳并不是从东方升起、从西方落山

---

[1]　《海象与木匠》（the Walrus and the Carpenter），是《爱丽丝镜中奇遇记》（《爱丽丝梦游仙境》的姊妹篇）中第四章里的一首长诗，它以梦幻般的笔法，讲述了海象、木匠和牡蛎之间的故事。

gets closer and closer to the ground as it goes round the sky and then at last sinks out of sight below the edge of the World, and there it stays out of sight for another six months and for six months it is night.

How can such a thing be? Isn't it the same sun we see here?

Yes, of course it's the same sun; there's only one sun. But we are living on the side of the World and we can't see the sun when it goes round to the other *side* of the World. If, however, we climb up the side of the World to the top where the North Cape is, we can see the sun go all the way round. It is as if you lived on the side of a hill and some one went round the hill and came back on the other side. You could see him go off one way and come back the other way, but you couldn't see him when he was on the other side. If, however, you went to the top of the hill you could see him all the way round.

The land at the top of the World is often jailed "The Land of the Midnight Sun," because the sun shines at midnight. It might just as well be called "The Land of the 10-o'clock-at-night Sun," for the sun shines at every hour of the night as well as every hour of the day. And it also might be called "The Land of the Midday Night," for when the sun is going round out of sight below the edge of the World it is dark every hour of the day as well as of the night.

This "Land of the Midnight Sun" is the land of the Reindeer—Santa Claus Land. In this land of snow and ice very little grows except moss, and the Reindeer is the only animal that can live on moss. The people that live there are called Lapps. They look something

的。太阳会低低地在天空中绕着小朋友们家的房子转，离地面很近，并且始终如此，不停地转上六个月，在这段时间里，太阳永远都不会落山，人们什么时候都看得到太阳，因此那里总是有六个月的白天。不过，随着太阳在空中运行，它会离地面越来越近，最终从地平线上落下去，再也看不到了，这样，人们又会有六个月的时间完全看不到太阳，从而出现六个月的黑夜。

这种情况是怎么可能发生的呢？那里的太阳，与我们在这里看到的，究竟是不是同一个太阳呢？

是的，当然是同一个太阳，因为世界上本来就只有一个太阳。只是因为我们住在地球的一侧，因而看不到太阳转到地球另一侧之后的情形罢了。然而，如果我们沿着地球的这一面一直向北，爬到地球顶端"北角"所在的那个地方，那么我们就看得见太阳运行的整个过程了。这就好比你们住在大山的一侧，有人绕着那座山，走到另一侧再绕回来。然而，如果你们爬到山顶的话，就看得见那个人绕行这座山的情况了。

地球最北端的陆地，经常被人们称为"夜半太阳之地"，因为那里到了午夜时分，也仍是阳光灿烂。由于无论黑夜白天，每个小时都是阳光普照，故将那里称为"晚上十点太阳之地"也不妨。我们也可以称之为"正午黑夜之地"，因为待太阳转到地平线以下、再也看不到了之后，无论白天黑夜，那里就都是伸手不见五指了。

这个"夜半太阳之地"，也是驯鹿的国度，是圣诞老人的国度。在这片冰雪覆

like Eskimos, and both look like the Chinese, so we think they probably were Chinese long, long ago. The Lapps and the Reindeer live together in the same hut—the Reindeer is like a horse, a cow, a sheep, and a dog all in one. The Lapp harnesses the Reindeer to his sled, he gets milk from her, he kills her and eats the meat, and then he uses her skin to make himself and his family fur coats and tents.

But the people who live in the rest of Norway and Sweden are the same kind of people as you and I, only some of them are much smarter and better educated. I know a Swede who speaks twelve languages, I know of a Swede who invented a way of separating cream from milk without skimming it, and I know of two Swedish boys who invented a machine for making ice with heat.

一位拉普人和他养的驯鹿

这里是圣诞老人的国度

盖的大陆上，除了苔藓，几乎寸草不生，而驯鹿则是唯一一种能够靠苔藓生存下来的动物。生活在那里的人，叫作"拉普人"。他们的样子，有点儿像是因纽特人，而且，拉普人和因纽特人都很像中国人，因此我们认为，很久很久以前他们可能都是中国人呢。拉普人和他们所养的驯鹿，都住在同一座小屋里，对于他们来说，驯鹿就像是一种集马匹、奶牛、绵羊、小狗于一身的动物。拉普人会用驯鹿拉雪橇，会挤驯鹿奶喝，会把驯鹿宰了吃鹿肉，还会用驯鹿的皮给自己和家人做毛皮大衣、做帐篷呢。

不过，生活在挪威、瑞典两国其他地区的人却与你我一样，只是他们当中有些人更精明，接受的教育更好罢了。我认识一个瑞典人，他竟然能说十二国外语。我也听说，一个瑞典人发明了一种不用脱脂就将从牛奶中分离出奶油的办法。我还听说，有两个瑞典小男孩发明了一种用加热法制冰的机器。

瑞典和挪威原本是一个国家，由一位国王统治着，但如今它们是两个独立的国家，每个国家都有自己的国王和首都了。

在你们爷爷一辈所用的地理书上，挪威的首都叫作"克里斯汀亚那"，可后来人们把这个名称改了。在地图上那条鲸鱼的喉咙下方，大家就可以找到挪威的首都。那里如今叫作"奥斯陆"。瑞典的首都则与"瑞典"（Sweden）这个国名一

Sweden and Norway used to be one country with one king, but now they are separate countries and each has a separate king and a separate capital.

In the geography your grandfather used, the capital of Norway was named Christiania, but the name was changed. You will find it on the map way down the throat of the whale. It is now called Oslo. The capital of Sweden begins with an "S," as Sweden does. It is Stockholm. Both Oslo and Stockholm are on the water, but they are not touched by the Gulf Stream, so the water in their harbors is frozen over nearly all winter and ships cannot go and come at that time. Stockholm is often called the Venice of the North, because like Venice it has many streets of water.

Mary and John are our commonest names. The Scandinavians like some names for their children better than others. Ole is one name they like especially well. Hans is another, and Eric and Peter are others. We sometimes make a family name by adding "son" to John to make Johnson. The Scandinavians add "son" or "sen" to their names to make family names, as Eric*son*, Ole*son*, Han*sen*, Peter*sen*, Nan*sen*, Amund*sen*. If you were in Wisconsin or Minnesota and looked in the telephone book you would find thousands of such names. That is because many, many Swedes and Norwegians have come to our country and settled in that part of our country which is most like their country.

Many common Norse words look like English words misspelled:

lamp is lampe
house is hus

样，是用"S"开头的，叫作"斯德哥尔摩"（Stockholm）。奥斯陆与斯德哥尔摩两市都位于海边，但墨西哥湾流并没有到达这两个地方，因此两市的海港几乎整个冬季都会封冻，船只无法通行。斯德哥尔摩常被人们称为"北国威尼斯"，因为那里与威尼斯一样，也有许多的水上街道。

"玛丽"和"约翰"，是我们这种英语国家里最常见的名字。斯堪的纳维亚人在给自己的孩子起名时，也有他们比较喜欢用的一些名字。他们尤其喜欢"奥勒"这个名字。还有便是"汉斯"、"埃里克"和"彼得"。我们有时会在一个名字之后加上"儿子"（son）一词，从而形成一个姓，比如，在"约翰"（John）后边加上"儿子"（son），便成了"约翰逊"。斯堪的纳维亚人也喜欢在名字后边加上"son"或"sen"来形成一个姓，比如"埃里克森"（Ericson）、"奥尔森"（Oleson）、"汉森"（Hansen）、"彼得森"（Petersen）、"南森"（Nansen）和"阿蒙森"（Amundsen），等等。如果你们是住在美国的威斯康星州或者明尼苏达州的话，那么查一查电话黄页，就会发现成千上万的这种名字呢。那是因为，有许多、许多的瑞典人和挪威人都移民到了美国，并且定居在美国最像他们祖国的那个地区。

在挪威语里，有许多词汇的样子都好像是英语单词，只是拼写错了，比如：

英语里的"灯"（lamp），被拼成了lampe；

英语里的"房屋"（house），被拼成了hus；

英语里的"奶牛"（cow），被拼成了ko。

cow is ko

They haven't copied us, we have copied them, for long ago Norse sailors settled in England, and after thousands of years we still use some Norse words changed very little.

Long years ago the men of Scandinavia were fierce fighters, who drank a strong liquor called "mead" and used the skulls of their enemies for cups. They believed in fairy-tale gods and goddesses. Thor, they believed, was a god who made the thunder and lightning. Tiu was the god of war. So they named some of the days of the week after their gods; Tiu's day, Thor's day, Woden's day, Fria's day. Strange to say, four of the sever days of our week are still named after these Scandinavian gods, for those wild people who believed in those gods are the great-great-grand-fathers of many of us. Tuesday is Tiu's day, Thursday is Thor's day, Friday is Fria's day and Wednesday is Woden's day—that's why we still have a "d" in Wednesday which we might forget in spelling, as we do not sound it now. Most people have forgotten that, our week-days are named after heathen gods, but some think that we should not use such heathen names, so they use numbers instead of names for the days of the week, as in Bible times.

Dynamite, you know, is something used to blow up things. It was invented by a man who lived in Sweden some years ago. When he died he left a lot of money and said that the interest from this money was to be given every year to the men or women who, no matter in what country they lived, had done the most for the World during that year. So each year judges go over all the things that have been done and choose those men or women

　　并不是挪威人模仿了我们的英语，而是我们模仿了他们的挪威语，这是因为，很久以前有许多挪威水手定居到了英国，因而几千年过去了，我们仍在使用一些做出了细微改变的挪威语词汇。

　　古时候，斯堪的纳维亚的男子个个都是凶猛善战的勇士，他们喜欢喝一种叫作"蜂蜜酒"的烈性酒，并且用敌人的头盖骨做酒杯。他们信奉神话故事里的神灵。他们相信，托尔是雷电之神，蒂乌是战神。于是，他们便用这些神灵的名字，给每个星期中的几天命了名，比如"蒂乌之日"、"托尔之日"、"沃登[1]之日"、"弗里亚之日"。说来也怪，我们一个星期当中，倒有四天仍然是用斯堪的纳维亚人的这些神灵来命名的，他们之所以那样干，是因为他们相信，那些神灵是我们当中许多人的祖先。如今，星期二就是"蒂乌之日"，星期四是"托尔之日"，星期五是"弗里亚之日"，而星期三则是"沃登之日"了，英语中所用的"星期三"（Wednesday）这个单词里仍然有个字母d的原因，也在于此，而我们在拼写时常常会漏掉这个字母，因为它如今不再发音了。绝大多数人都已经忘记，我们的工作日是用异教神灵的名称来命名的，但也有一些人认为，我们不该再用这种异教名称，因此他们便用数字来称呼每个星期的那七天，就像《圣经》时代一样，而不再用名称来称呼一周的七天了。

---

　　[1] 沃登（Woden），日耳曼神话中的主神，在北欧神话中拼作Odin。下文中的"弗里亚"（Fria）则是主司婚姻和生育的女神，在北欧神话中拼作Frigg。

who have done the most for the good of the World and give them the money. This man was named Nobel and the money is known as the Nobel Prize. Two of our Presidents— Theodore Roosevelt and Woodrow Wilson—won the Nobel Prize for Peace and so did an American Negro, Ralph Bunche. You yourself could win the Nobel Prize if you ever did something big enough and fine enough. Do you think you ever will?

　　大家都知道，炸药是用来把东西炸开的。炸药是许多年前由一个瑞典人发明出来的。这个瑞典人死后，留下了一大笔钱，并且还留下遗言说，这笔钱的利息用于奖励那些在每一年中为世界做出了最大贡献的人，而不管这个人是男是女、是哪个国家的人。于是，一些评审员便会仔细审视每年世人获得的所有成就，并且选定那些为整个世界做出了最大贡献的人，给他们颁发奖金。那位瑞典人名叫诺贝尔，因此世人便将这个奖项称为"诺贝尔奖"。我们美国有两位前总统，即西奥多·罗斯福和伍德罗·威尔逊，以及一位美籍黑人拉尔夫·本奇，都曾获得过诺贝尔和平奖。要是你们也干出什么重要而优秀的成绩来的话，那么你们也可以获得诺贝尔奖了。你们觉得，自己将来会不会那样呢？

43 The Bear

When I was a boy the story I liked best was one about wolves in Russia. Some Russians in a sleigh were driving across the snow, when they were attacked by a pack of hungry wolves. The men whipped up their horses, but the wolves drew nearer and nearer. When the wolves were just about to spring upon the sleigh the men threw out food, which the wolves stopped a moment to devour, allowing the sleigh to get ahead. But the wolves caught up and again food was thrown out and again and again, till there was no food left. See if you can guess the end of the story, or make up an ending of your own.

Naturally, I used to think of Russia as a land of wolves, though for some reason people call Russia "The Bear."

Russia is a huge country—it is the largest country in Europe—it is as large as all the other countries of Europe put together, and in the far north there are wolves, snow, and sleighs. But there is also a middle Russia which is not so cold and a southern Russia which is quite warm.

In the north of Russia it is so cold that even in summer when the snow has gone and the ground has thawed out on top, the ground underneath remains frozen stiff, and, though grass and even flowers grow above, the ground below remains hard and icy. These frozen lands are called "tundras," and there are thousands of miles of such tundras across the

第43章　熊的国度

小的时候，我最喜欢的一个故事，与俄罗斯的狼有关。故事说，几名俄罗斯人正驾着雪橇越过茫茫雪原，突然遭到了一群恶狼的袭击。那些人不停地用鞭子催赶马儿快跑，但狼群还是越逼越近。就在狼群即将跳上雪橇的时候，他们把食物扔下雪橇，狼群便停了一会儿，去撕咬食物，因而雪橇便跑到狼群前面去了。可不久之后，狼群再次追了上来，雪橇上的人便再次扔下了食物。这样，一次又一次，最后雪橇上再也没有食物可扔了。看你们能不能猜到这个故事的结局吧，或者，你们也可以自己编一个结局出来。

自然，过去我曾经以为，俄罗斯是一个遍地是狼的国家，可是，不知出于什么原因，人们却把俄罗斯称为"熊的国度"。

俄罗斯国土广袤，是欧洲最大的国家，面积差不多有欧洲其他国家面积的总和那样大，而该国遥远的北部，则是一个狼群、冰雪和雪橇的世界。不过，俄罗斯中部地区的气候没有那么寒冷，而俄罗斯南部的气候还非常炎热呢。

俄罗斯北部地区的气候严寒，就算是到了夏季，冰雪消融、地表解冻之后，地表以下也仍然冻得非常严实，尽管地面上长出了花草，地下却仍然冻得硬邦邦的。这种冰冻的土地，叫作"冻土带"，而在俄罗斯北部地区，竟然绵亘着数千英里的冻土带哩。

north of Russia.

At the top of Russia is a sea called "White" and at the bottom of Russia a sea called "Black." The White Sea, I suppose, is called "White" because it is frozen over most of the year and covered with snow—and yet, during a few months of the summer when the ice in it has melted, great ships sail into the White Sea, bringing in loads of all sorts of goods to the one great port on this sea—a city called Archangel—a name that makes one think of heaven.

You may wonder why people live in such far-off places, why they don't move to other places that are more comfortable. But people live where they can make a living, and cities usually start with a few houses and more and more houses are built until there is a city. But there is a great city farther south than Archangel which was built all at once—to order. It was built by a man named Peter, who was one of the rulers of Russia. They were called "czars." Peter wanted to live by the water so that he could sail ships, just as you might like to go to the seashore to sail boats, so he built a city by the sea, with streets, shops, houses, and palaces, and then, as he was a czar who could make people do what he wanted, he made people come and live in this city. Peter had been named for St. Peter, so he called his city St. Petersburg, which meant St. Peter's City. That was two hundred years ago.

When Russia was fighting in World War I the people of St. Petersburg said that they wanted a real Russian name for their city, for "burg" was the German name for city, and they were fighting the Germans, so they called it Petrograd, which was the Russian name

俄罗斯的北边有一个海洋，叫作"白海"，而俄罗斯的南方也有一个海洋，则叫"黑海"。我猜想，白海之所以叫"白海"，是因为那里一年中的大部分时间都是封冻的，上面覆盖着冰雪的缘故，不过，夏季还是有那么几个月，海上的冰雪会消融，大型船舶便会运载着各种各样的货物驶入白海，来到海边的一个大型港口。这个港口城市叫作"大天使城"[1]，听到这名称，会令人情不自禁地想到天堂呢。

大家可能会觉得奇怪，人们为什么会住到这么遥远的地方来，他们又为什么不搬到其他一些更加舒适的地方去。其实，人们是可以在哪里谋生，便会住在哪里。通常来说，一个地方最初都是寥寥几座房子，然后房子越建越多，最后就形成了城市。不过，在"大天使城"以南很远的地方，有一座大城市，却是根据命令一下子建成的。那座城市，是一个叫作"彼得"的人兴建的，他是俄罗斯的君主之一。过去，俄罗斯的君主都叫"沙皇"。彼得希望住在水滨，以便自己能够划船，就像你们都喜欢到海边去划船似的，因此他便在海边兴建了一座街道、商店、房屋、宫殿林立的城市，然后，由于他是当时的沙皇，能够命令臣民按照自己的旨意去行事，所以他又命令臣民们来到这座城市里生活。彼得自己的名字是根据圣彼得起的，因此他便把这座城市命名为"圣彼得堡"，意思就是"圣彼得之城"。这一事件，发生在两百多年之前。

在俄罗斯参与第一次世界大战的期间，圣彼得堡的人都说，希望他们所生活

---

[1] 大天使城（Archangel），现多音译为"阿尔汉格尔"，即俄罗斯的阿尔汉格尔斯克。

for Peter's City. But the people got tired of the war and all of a sudden they said they would not fight any more; they had a revolution, killed the czar and set up a government of their own. They wanted the city of Petrograd called for the leader of the revolution, a man named Lenin, so they changed the name of the city again to Leningrad, which meant Lenin's City.

St. Petersburg
Petrograd   } was built to be the capital of
Leningrad

Russia, but if was so cold there they moved the capital to a city still farther south near the center of Russia that had been the capital before. This city is called Moscow.

The revolutionists took the palaces and homes of the wealthy and turned them into hospitals and public buildings. They took the land of the rich and lent it out to farmers and workers. These revolutionists were known as Communists. The provinces and districts of Russia combined as the Union of Soviet Socialist Republics, which is governed from the capital at Moscow.

In Moscow there is a big walled-in place with houses and palaces and churches called the Kremlin. It is from the Kremlin that Russia is ruled, so the Kremlin is really the capitol, though it is not just one building like our Capitol in Washington. The churches in the Kremlin are not used as churches now for after the Revolution the Communists turned them into museums and government buildings just as they did the palaces of the wealthy.

的这座城市有一个真正的俄罗斯名称，因为"堡"本是一个德语名词，指的就是"城市"。何况，当时俄国正与德国交战，因此人们便将圣彼得堡改成了"彼得格勒"，在俄语里就是"彼得之城"的意思。不过，后来人们都厌倦了战争，因此突然之间便说自己不想再战了，他们发动了一场革命，杀掉了沙皇，成立了一个自己的政府。他们希望将彼得格勒市改名，改成此次革命的领袖、一个叫作"列宁"的人的名字，因此便再次将该市改名为"列宁格勒"，也就是"列宁之城"的意思。以前的圣彼得堡、彼得格勒，后来的列宁格勒，原本是作为俄国的首都而兴建的，可由于那里的天气实在是太过寒冷，因此俄罗斯人便将首都迁到了南边靠近俄国中部地区的一座城市，那里以前一直都是俄罗斯的首都。那座城市，就叫"莫斯科"。

革命党人占领了宫殿和富人的家，然后将这些地方改成了医院和公共建筑。他们没收了富人的土地，然后再将这些土地出租给农民和工人。这些革命党人被称为共产党。俄罗斯以前的各个省和地区都联合起来，组成了"苏维埃社会主义共和国联盟"，接受首都莫斯科的管辖。

在莫斯科，有一个四周为围墙环绕、里面有房屋、宫殿和教堂的地方，叫作"克里姆林宫"。统治俄罗斯的，就是克里姆林宫，因此，克里姆林宫实际上是该国的国会大厦，尽管它并不像美国华盛顿的国会大厦那样只有一栋建筑。如今，克里姆林宫内的教堂不再用作教堂了，因为革命之后，共产党人把教堂全都改成了博物馆和政府办公大楼，就像他们把那些有钱人的宫殿全都改成了公共建筑一样。

Near the walls of the Kremlin is a great open paved space called Red Square. On one side of Red Square is a flat-topped building which is the tomb of Lenin. The Russians have the largest army i.t.w.W. and they often have parades of soldiers which pass through Red Square past the chief Russian rulers who stand on top of Lenin's tomb to see the soldiers march by.

The square is called Red Square because red is the color of revolution and the people who govern Russia adopted it as their color. Russia's flag is red. The Communists don't believe in any religion.

The Russian people love music and they love their land of Russia. Some of the best music in the whole World has been written by Russians. Whenever a group of Russians are working together they are apt to sing. Russian soldiers sing on the march, workers in the fields sing together as they work, sailors sing on their ships. Even those poor people who are kept like slaves in prison camps sing, though their songs are not gay but sad.

在克里姆林宫的院墙附近，有一个巨大、空旷、地上铺有卵石的广场，叫作"红场"。红场一侧有一座平顶建筑，那里就是列宁墓。俄国拥有世界上规模最大的陆军，并且经常举行阅兵活动，也就是说，让士兵们列队走过整个红场，经过那些站在列宁墓顶上观看阅兵的主要领导人身边。

这个广场之所以叫作红场，是因为红色是俄国革命的颜色，所以，统治俄罗斯的那些人便把红色定为整个国家的颜色。俄国的国旗是红色的。共产党人不信仰任何宗教。

俄罗斯民族热爱音乐，也热爱俄罗斯这片土地。全世界最优秀的一些音乐作品，就是由俄罗斯人创作出来的。不管什么时候，只要是一群俄罗斯人一起干活，他们都会唱起歌来。俄国士兵在行军时会唱歌，农民们在地里干活时会唱歌，水手们在船上也会唱歌。

44 The Bread-Basket

In the north of Russia the ground is white with snow.

In the south of Russia the ground is black—almost as black as coal—because the soil is so rich, probably the richest in the World. So this part of Russia is called the Black Earth Land. In parts of our country the rich soil usually goes down only a few inches before there is rock or clay, on which nothing will grow, but in Russia the rich soil is so deep that you could dig down in some places three or four times your height before striking rock or clay in which nothing grows. In America many farms wear out, because there is such a thin layer of the rich soil that it is soon used up. This is the case on many farms in New England that were in use two hundred years ago but are now used up, and so little will grow on them that the farmers move away and leave their farms, for they are no longer any good. In Russia, however, the rich soil never seems to wear out. Their farms are thousands of years old and still there is enough of this soil to grow food.

In the Black Earth Land they raise great quantities of wheat and, as bread is made from wheat, this part of Russia is often called the Bread-Basket. There is one thing the farmers raise that may seem strange—that is, sunflowers—acres and acres of them. But they do not raise them for their flowers; they raise them for their seeds. They eat sunflower seeds as we eat peanuts; but the chief thing they do with them is to press the oil out of the seeds,

第44章 粮仓

在俄罗斯的北部地区，地上都覆盖着皑皑的白雪。

而在俄罗斯的南部地区，地上却是黑的，几乎跟煤炭一样黑，因为那里的土壤非常肥沃，很可能还是世界上最肥沃的土壤呢。因此，俄罗斯的这一部分，便叫"黑土带"。在我国的许多地区，肥沃土壤层通常都只有数英寸厚，再往下便是什么都种不了的岩石或者黏土层了，可在俄罗斯，沃土层却非常厚，有些地方甚至深达一个人身高的三四倍，再往下才是什么都种不了的岩石或者黏土层呢。美国的许多农田都已经"老化"了，因为那里的沃土层太薄，肥力很快就用光了。新英格兰地区的许多农庄正是这种情况。两百年前，那些农庄上都种着作物，可如今它们的肥力都已经耗尽，上面几乎种不了什么庄稼，因此那里的农民便纷纷搬走，把农庄留下，因为农庄再也没有什么用处了。然而，俄罗斯那种肥沃的土壤，却好像永远都不会耗尽肥力。虽说那里的农场都有几千年的历史了，可如今却依然有足够的沃土来种植粮食作物呢。

俄罗斯人在"黑土带"种植了大量的小麦，因为人们所吃的面包都是用小麦制成的，因此人们常常把俄罗斯的这一地区称为"面包篮子"。当地农民还种植一种可能看似奇怪的作物，并且大片大片地种植，这种作物就是向日葵。不过，人们种植向日葵，可不是为了收获向日葵的花朵，而是为了得到葵花籽。他们都喜欢吃葵花

for this oil is good for salad, for making soap and other things.

The largest lake in the World is in the corner of Russia next to the Black Sea. Rivers run into it but none run out of it, and so the lake is salt. It is called the Caspian Sea, for it is like a little ocean.

As the *March Hare* in "Alice in Wonderland" said, "You can draw water out of a water-well, so I should think you could draw treacle out of a treacle-well," and in the same way you get oil from an oil-well. At the city of Baku on the side of the Caspian Sea there are so many oil-wells and so much oil that it seems to get into everything. You see it, smell it, feel it, and taste it. As there are no rivers flowing out of the Caspian Sea, no ships can get to the ocean from Baku, so a way had to be found to carry the oil to a place where ships could come and get it. The nearest place where a ship could come was over seven hundred miles away, a place called Batum on the Black Sea, so they laid a huge pipe seven hundred miles long to carry the oil from Baku to Batum, where it is put into boats called oil tankers and carried away.

The highest mountains and the longest river in Europe are both in Russia. The mountains are the Caucasus, on the southern edge of Russia, between the Black and the Caspian Seas. They are higher than the Alps.

Most rivers we say "run," but the longest river in Europe is also the slowest. It is the Volga. It moves so slowly it is hard to tell whether it is going or coming. It "walks" into the Caspian Sea. In the Volga River big fish are caught called sturgeon. The sturgeon's

籽，就像我们都喜欢吃花生一样，不过，俄罗斯人种植葵花籽最主要的目的，还是用葵花籽榨油，因为葵花籽油很适合用来拌沙拉，适合做成肥皂或者其他的东西。

世界上最大的湖泊，就坐落在俄罗斯紧邻黑海的那个角上。河流注入这个湖泊，可湖泊里却没有河流泄出，所以这个湖泊就是一个咸水湖。这个湖泊叫作"里海"，因为它就像是一个小小的海洋。

《爱丽丝漫游仙境》中的"三月兔"曾说："既然可以从水井里汲出水来，那么我有理由相信，你也可以从糖浆井里汲出糖浆来。"同理，从一口油井里自然也可以打出石油来。里海之滨的巴库市有许多许多的油井，人们开采出了大量的石油，仿佛那里到处都有石油似的。人们非但看得到石油、闻得到石油、触得到石油，还尝得到石油呢。由于那里并没有从里海流出的河流，从巴库没有船只可以通往大海，因此人们必须找出一条道路，才能将石油运送到一个船只可以到达和运送石油的地方。由于船只能够到达的最近之地也在七百英里以外，在黑海之滨一个叫作"巴统"的地方，因此俄罗斯人便铺设了一条长达七百英里的巨型管道，来将石油从巴库输送到巴统，然后，他们在巴统把石油装上一种叫作"油轮"的船只，用油轮把石油运走。

欧洲最高的山脉和最长的河流，都位于俄罗斯境内。这条山脉叫作"高加索山脉"，位于俄罗斯南部边境，夹在黑海和里海之间。这条山脉的海拔，比阿尔卑斯山脉还要高呢。

对于绝大多数河流，我们在描述的时候都会说"流动"，可欧洲最长的那条

eggs are called caviar, and caviar is considered a great delicacy, though one usually has to learn to like it. Caviar is probably the most expensive food there is—a very little costs so much: a pound of caviar costs almost a hundred times as much as a pound of beefsteak—perhaps that is one reason why people like it.

The most precious metal in the World is not silver, not gold, but a metal called platinum. Platinum looks something like silver, but there is so little of it that it costs more than gold. On the eastern edge of Russia, which is also the eastern edge of Europe, there is a range of mountains called the Ural Mountains; they are not very high, in fact they are not much more than hills. In these mountains platinum is found.

There is a peculiar kind of rock found in Russia. The rock is like bundles of silky threads, which can be made into a kind of cloth. It is called asbestos. As asbestos cloth is made from rock it will not burn. A king long ago had a table-cloth made of asbestos. People didn't know about asbestos at that time, so the king used to amaze his dinner guests by throwing the tablecloth into the fire after dinner was over, then after awhile taking it out unburned. We use asbestos to cover hot pipes, for firemen's suits, and for roofs of houses, as it will not burn, no matter how hot it is heated. Asbestos is also found in parts of the United States and Canada.

河流，却是流动得最慢的一条河。由于河水流速非常缓慢，因此很难分清河水究竟是往上流呢还是往下流。这条河，最终慢条斯理地注入了里海。这条河，就叫"伏尔加河"；人们在河中捕捞到了一种大鱼，叫作"鲟鱼"。鲟鱼的卵，叫作"鱼子"，尽管一个人需要逐渐习惯才会喜欢，可如今人们都公认，鱼子是一种非常美味的食品呢。鱼子酱很可能是世界上最昂贵的食物了，因为一点点儿鱼子酱，就要卖上一大笔钱：一磅[1]鱼子酱，售价差不多达到了一磅牛排的一百倍，人们之所以喜欢吃，原因之一可能也就在于此吧。

世界上最贵重的金属，不是白银，不是黄金，而是一种叫作"铂"的金属。铂金的样子有点儿像是白银，但由于地球上的储量很少，因此铂金的价格要比黄金更贵。在俄罗斯的东部边缘，也就是欧洲的东部边缘，有一条叫作"乌拉尔山"的山脉，那条山脉的海拔不是很高，实际上跟一座座小山差不多。不过，人们在这条山脉中却发现了铂金。

人们还在俄罗斯发现了一种罕见的岩石。那种岩石的样子，就像是一捆捆的丝线，还能制成一种布料呢。这种岩石，叫作"石棉"。由于石棉布是用岩石制成的，因此不会着火。从前，一位国王有一块用石棉布制成的桌布。由于当时的人并不了解石棉，所以那位国王在大宴宾客的时候，常常会待宴会结束后，把那块桌布扔进火里，过会儿再拿出来，让大家看到它不会着火，从而令宾客大吃一惊呢。如今，我们一般用石棉来包裹热力管道、制作消防服以及盖在屋顶上，因为无论怎么加热，石棉都不会烧起来。美国和加拿大的部分地区也发现了石棉。

---

[1] 磅（pound），英制重量单位。1磅约合0.454千克。

45 The Iron Curtain Countries

There are thousands of cities and towns in the World that neither you nor I have ever heard of, yet millions of people call these cities and towns *home*. These same people probably have never heard of the town or city where you yourself live.

Between Russia and the rest of Europe are nine little countries, some of them not very important, but all of them most important to the people who live in them; and yet many people may live their whole lives and perhaps never hear of some of these places—unless they collect postage stamps. Six of these countries end in "ia" and two end in "land."

Finland is the largest of these in-between countries. It lies between Russia and the Scandinavian Peninsula. Finland means Marsh Land, for it is a land of marshes and lakes. It is like Norway and Sweden in some ways—it has fiords and it makes paper and matches. It is a republic with a president.

The other "land" country is Poland, which means Flat Land. It is almost as large as Finland. Poland has much farm land and there are iron and coal mines. Many famous musicians have been Poles.

Are you a good speller? How would you spell a cough or a sneeze? South of Poland is a long thin country with a name which sounds funny to us—something between a cough and a sneeze—Czechoslovakia. I have a set of china dishes that has stamped on the bottom

第45章　其他东欧国家

世界上有成千上万座城市，虽然你我都没有听说过，但还是有千百万人称这些城市是他们的家乡。很有可能，那些人也没有听说过你们所生活的城镇呢。

俄罗斯与欧洲其他地区之间，有九个小国家。虽说其中有些国家并不是很重要，但对于生活在这些国家当中的人民来说，它们却都是极其重要的，不过，许多人也可能在一生当中都从未听说过这些地方，除非他们有集邮的爱好。其中有六个国家，它们的名称都是用"ia"结尾，还有两个国家的名称则是用"land"结尾的。

芬兰是这些"中间国家"中面积最大的。该国位于俄罗斯与斯堪的纳维亚半岛之间。"芬兰"（Finland）的意思就是"沼泽之地"，因为该国沼泽密布、湖泊众多。在某些方面，该国与挪威和瑞典很相似，因为芬兰也有峡湾，也生产纸张和火柴。芬兰是一个共和国，设有一个民选总统。

另一个以"land"结尾的国家，就是"波兰"（Poland），意思就是"平坦之地"。该国面积与芬兰差不多。波兰境内有许多农田，并且有铁矿和煤矿。许多著名的音乐家都是波兰人。

你们是不是很少写错别字呢？"咳嗽"、"喷嚏"这些词你们都会写吗？波兰的南面有一个又长又窄的国家，该国的名称听起来也很可笑，与"咳嗽"和"喷

Made in Czechoslovakia, for there they used to make a great deal of china, and glassware too. Perhaps they still do but I can't tell you for sure because, after my dishes were made, Czechoslovakia became an Iron Curtain country.

There used to be a country called Austria-Hungary. Now there are two countries—Austria and Hungary. Through Austria and Hungary runs a famous river—almost as famous as the Rhine. It is called the Danube; and, like the Rhine, the Danube has castles overlooking it, castles in which once lived robber barons. Fairytales and poems and music have been written about the Danube too. One of the most famous waltzes ever written is called "The Blue Danube." The *Blue* Danube runs into the *Black* Sea. The capital of Austria is Vienna. Vienna used to be famous for its restaurants and cooking. Perhaps you have eaten Vienna rolls or been to a Vienna restaurant, even if you have never been to Austria, for we have Vienna rolls and restaurants in the United States too.

The name Hungary makes you think of food, or rather lack of food, but the name doesn't mean *hungry*. It means Land of the Huns. In fact, Hungary should not be hungry, for a great deal of wheat for making bread is raised there. Have you ever eaten a kind of hash called Hungarian goulash? It is very highly seasoned with pepper and spices, and some restaurants in our country serve it. In some of these restaurants orchestras play Hungarian music. It is a kind of music such as the Gypsies dance to—slow and sweet, then fast and furious, with a hop, skip, and jump time.

Have you ever had your palm read or your fortune told? Gypsies are people who

嘘"差不多，叫作"捷克斯洛伐克"。我有一套瓷器盘子，盘底都印有"捷克斯洛伐克制造"的字样，因为该国以前曾经大量出产瓷器以及玻璃制品。如今，该国没准仍然生产这些东西呢，可我不太肯定。

以前，欧洲还有一个叫作"奥匈帝国"的国家。如今，那里分成了两个国家，一是奥地利，一是匈牙利。有一条河流从奥地利和匈牙利两国穿过，非但声名赫赫，还差不多与莱茵河齐名呢。那条河流，叫作"多瑙河"，与莱茵河一样，多瑙河沿岸的山峰之上，也矗立着一座座城堡，里面曾经住着"强盗贵族"。人们也创作了许多的神话故事、诗歌和音乐作品，来歌颂多瑙河。历史上最著名的一首圆舞曲，就叫《蓝色多瑙河》。蓝色的多瑙河，注入了黑海之中。奥地利的首都是维也纳。过去，维也纳以其饭店和烹饪业而著称。即便是你们从来没有去过维也纳，没准你们也都吃过维也纳小面包，或者到维也纳餐馆去吃过饭呢，因为美国国内如今也可以买到维也纳小面包，也有维也纳餐馆了。

"匈牙利"这个国名，会让大家想到吃的东西，或者更准确一点来说，是想到没有吃的东西[1]，但是，这个国名可不是指"饥饿"，而是指"匈奴人的国度"。事实上，匈牙利不可能发生饥荒，因为该国种植有大面积可以制作面包的小麦。你们有没有吃过一种叫作"匈牙利红烩牛肉"的杂碎汤呢？这种汤拌上辣椒和调味料之后，味道十足，我国的一些餐馆里就有这道菜。在一些餐馆里，还会有乐队演奏

---

[1]　"匈牙利"（Hungary）与"饥饿"（hungry）一词只有一个字母之差，故作者才这样说。

wander over the country doing that for a living. Most of the Gypsies come from a country next to Hungary and bordering on the Black Sea called Romania—nowadays frequently spelled Rumania. It is supposed that long ago people from Rome settled in that country and called it Romania from Rome. The language of Romania is still something like the Roman or Italian.

Bulgaria is an Iron Curtain country next to the Black Sea. It has forests and mountains as well as farm land. In the forests live bears, wildcats, and wild boars. The ibex, a kind of wild goat, lives there too. And in the mountains there is a goat-like antelope called the chamois. We get our name for chamois or "shammy" cloths, used for washing automobiles, from this animal. Once chamois cloths were really soft leather from the skin of the chamois, but now we make the cloths from other materials.

An important business of the Bulgarians is perfumery. They raise fields of roses from which they make a very fine and expensive perfume called "attar of roses." It takes a whole roomful of rose petals to make only a tiny bottle of attar of roses, so you can see why attar of roses is expensive.

Albania is a little country where most of the people raise farm crops or cattle and sheep. In parts of Albania the men wear skirts that reach to their knees and stick out all around like a dancer's. The skirts that the men wear in Scotland are made of dark-colored cloths but the skirts worn by Albanian men are white.

Jugoslavia is a country just across the Adriatic Sea from Italy. It has many forests.

匈牙利的乐曲呢。匈牙利音乐，有点儿像是吉普赛人跳舞时的那种音乐，先是节奏舒缓、音调甜美，然后节奏变快、调子激烈起来，并且就像是来了一个三级跳那样，越来越快、越来越激烈。

你们有没有看过手相或者算过命？吉普赛人是一个在世界各地流浪，并且以看手相、算命为生的民族。绝大多数吉普赛人都来自匈牙利一个濒临黑海、叫作"罗马尼亚"的邻国。据说，很久以前，一些古罗马人来到这个国家定居下来，并且根据"罗马"这个名称，把那里命名为罗马尼亚。如今的罗马尼亚语，仍然有点儿像是罗马语或者意大利语呢。

保加利亚也是一个濒临黑海的"铁幕"国家。该国既有森林、山区，也有农田。森林里有熊、野猫和野猪。那里还有一种叫作"巨角塔尔羊"的野生山羊。在保加利亚的山区里，则有一种样子像是山羊的羚羊，叫作"岩羚"。我们用于清洗汽车的羚羊皮布或者"雪米"布，名字就是源于这种动物。以前，羚羊皮布是一种柔软的、真正用岩羚皮制成的皮革，可到了如今，我们则是用其他材料来制作这种布了。

保加利亚人从事的一项重要产业，就是香水制造。他们种植大片大片的玫瑰，然后用玫瑰花制成一种质量上乘、价格昂贵的香水，叫作"玫瑰精油"。需要一整间房子的玫瑰花瓣，才能生产出一小瓶玫瑰精油来，因此，大家就可以看出，玫瑰精油的价格为什么会如此昂贵了。

阿尔巴尼亚是一个小国，该国绝大多数人都是以种植农作物、放牧牛羊为生。

It also has copper mines. In fact more copper is mined in Jugoslavia than in any other European country.

When I hear the name of a place or a person, some one thing usually pops into my head, though that thing may not be at all important.

If I hear "George Washington," the first thing that pops into my head is "cherry-tree."

If I hear "New York," the first thing I think of is "sky-scrapers."

So when I hear "Finland," I think of marshes.

When I hear "Poland," I think of music.

When I hear "Austria," I think of Vienna rolls.

When I hear "Hungary," I think of the Blue Danube.

When I hear "Romania," I think of Gypsies.

When I hear "Bulgaria," I think of chamois and perfumes.

When I hear "Albania," I think of men with skirts.

When I hear "Czechoslovakia," I think of china and glass.

When I hear "Jugoslavia," I think of copper.

她会给你们算命

在阿尔巴尼亚的一些地区，男子会穿着垂膝短裙，并将短裙整个儿撑起，就像是跳舞的人所穿的那种裙子。苏格兰男子穿的短裙，都是用暗色布料制成的，可阿尔巴尼亚男子穿的短裙，却都是白色的呢。

南斯拉夫是一个隔着亚德里亚海与意大利相望的国家。该国森林密布，还储有铜矿。事实上，南斯拉夫开采出来的铜矿，比欧洲其他国家都要多。

每当我听到一个地名或者人名之后，脑海里通常马上就会浮现出某种东西来，尽管那种东西可能根本就不重要。

比如，要是听到"乔治·华盛顿"这个人名的话，首先浮现在我脑海里的东西，就是"樱桃树"。

要是听到"纽约"这个地名的话，我首先想到的东西，就是"摩天大楼"。

所以，要是听到"芬兰"这个国名，我就会想到沼泽。

要是听到"波兰"，我就会想到音乐。

要是听到"奥地利"，我就会想起维也纳小面包。

要是听到"匈牙利"，我就会想到蓝色的多瑙河。

要是听到"罗马尼亚"，我想到的就是吉普赛人。

要是听到"保加利亚"，我就会想起岩羚和香水。

要是听到"阿尔巴尼亚"，我就会想起那些穿裙子的男子。

要是听到"捷克斯洛伐克"，我就会想到瓷器和玻璃。

46 The Land of the Gods

The first book I ever read was Æsop's Fables. Æsop was a slave who lived in a little country called Greece. Æsop the slave wrote such famous fables that his master set him free. The book I read was in English, but the Fables were first written in Greek.

Greece is so small that if I pointed to it on the map down at the corner of Europe it would be entirely covered by the tip of my finger. But small as it is, it was at one time the greatest country, its people were the greatest people, and its language the greatest language in the World. When the rest of the people in Europe were ignorant savages the people in Greece were writing the greatest books, building the most beautiful buildings, making the most beautiful statues, and teaching the most famous schools that have ever been. There is one Book that was first written in Greek but is now printed in over eight hundred languages, and more people have read it than any other book in the World. It's the Bible—the New Testament part.

But the people of Greece didn't at first believe in the Bible or Christ. They didn't believe in only one god but in many gods, who they said lived above the clouds on the top of a mountain called Olympus. The mountain is still there, but if you should climb to the top you wouldn't find any gods. When the sun shone the Greeks said that the god Apollo was driving his golden chariot across the sky. When the rain fell they said another god, Jupiter, was watering the earth, and when the lightning flashed they said he was angry and

第46章   诸神之地

我小时候看的第一本书，就是《伊索寓言》。伊索原本是一个奴隶，生活在一个叫作"希腊"的小国家里。由于伊索这个奴隶创作出了许多赫赫有名的寓言故事，因此主人后来释放了他，让他获得了自由。我看的那本是英文版，但《伊索寓言》最初却是用希腊语写出来的。

希腊非常小，要是我用手指在地图上点到位于欧洲东南角的这个国家上，指尖就会将希腊完全遮住。可尽管面积小，曾经有过一段时间，希腊却是世界上最了不起的国家，希腊人民是世界上最了不起的民族，而希腊语也是世界上最了不起的语言呢。当欧洲其他地区的人还是无知而野蛮的民族时，希腊人却在创作出最伟大的书籍、修建最漂亮的房屋、制作最精美的雕像，以及在世界上最著名的学校里讲学了。有一本书，最初是用希腊文写成的，如今却已印成了八百多种语言，并且读者人数超过了世界上其他任何一本书呢。这本书，就是《圣经》，就是其中的《新约全书》部分。

不过，希腊人起初并不信仰《圣经》或基督。他们信仰的不是一神教，而是多神教，他们称，有许多神灵都住在奥林匹斯山顶上的云端里。奥林匹斯山如今仍然屹立在那里，不过，若是爬到山顶上去的话，你们是看不到任何神灵的。太阳升起的时候，古希腊人会说，那是太阳神阿波罗正驾着他那辆金色的战车越过天空。下

throwing thunderbolts. They believed that there was a god of love and that there was a god of war and that there was a god of almost everything in the World.

Greece is in two chief parts, like a tiny North and South America, which were once joined by a thin stem of land called the Isthmus of Corinth, only four miles across. In the northern part was, is, and probably always will be a great city called Athens. The people in Athens thought that one goddess in particular looked after their city. She was the goddess of wisdom called Athene Parthenos, so they named their city Athens, after her first name; and on the top of a high hill they built the most beautiful temple in the World to her and called it the Parthenon, after her last name. Inside of this temple they placed a huge statue of her, made of gold and ivory. The statue has now disappeared, nobody knows where, and the building itself was blown up in a war and is now in ruins. The beautiful sculptures on this temple were taken down and carried away to London and are now in the British Museum. So if you want to see what beautiful statues the Greeks once made, don't go to Athens—go to London. On the side of the hill on which is the Parthenon and all through the city of Athens are other temples to their many gods. These temples had no domes nor spires like Christian churches, but columns around the outside.

The marble for these buildings and statues they got from a hill near Athens called Mount Pentelicus. Some one has said the reason the Greeks long ago made such beautiful statues and buildings was because they had such beautiful marble to work with; but there is still beautiful marble on Mount Pentelicus, and yet no one seems able to make such

雨的时候，古希腊人会说，那是另一位神灵，即朱比特，正在向大地洒下甘霖；而若是电闪雷鸣，他们又会说，这是朱比特发起怒来，正在将霹雳砸向大地。他们认为，天堂里有一位爱神，一位战争之神，还有一位掌管世间一切的神灵。

希腊由两个主要的部分所组成，它们就像是微型的南、北美洲一样，曾经由一片狭窄的、叫作"科林斯地峡"的陆地相连，那里只有四英里宽。在北部地区，过去、现在都有一个伟大的城市，叫作"雅典"，并且，将来这个雅典很可能还会永远存在下去。雅典人认为，有一位女神尤其眷顾这座城市。她就是智慧女神，叫作"雅典娜·巴台农"。因此，人们便根据这位女神的名字，给那座城市起名为雅典，他们还在一座小山顶上为这位女神修建了一座世界上最精美的神庙，并且用女神的姓为其命名，称之为"巴台农神庙"。在这座神庙里，人们还安放了一尊巨大的、用黄金和象牙雕制而成的雅典娜雕像。如今，这尊雕像已经不知所踪，没人知道它到哪儿去了，而神庙本身呢，也在一场战争中被炸毁，只剩下一片废墟了。后来，人们把神庙上那些精美的雕塑作品全都取下来，运到了伦敦，存放在大英博物馆里。因此，如果想看一看古希腊人制作出来的那些精美雕塑，你们就不要去雅典，得去伦敦才行。巴台农神庙所在的那座小山上、雅典城的大街小巷里，还有雅典人为其他神灵而修建的许多神庙。这些神庙，都没有基督教堂那样的穹顶或尖顶，但神庙外部都立有许多石柱。

修建这些神庙和制作雕像所用的大理石，都是从雅典附近一座叫作"彭忒利科斯山"的小山上开采出来的。有些人说，古希腊人之所以制作出了如此精美的雕

beautiful things of it any more.

People long ago used to go to a place called an oracle to have their fortunes told. At Delphi not far from Athens was one of the most famous oracles. There was a crack in the ground from which gas was always escaping. Over this crack in the ground sat a goddess called a Sibyl and over the goddess a little temple was built. The escaping gas put the goddess to sleep, just as the gas a doctor or dentist uses puts people to sleep so they won't feel any pain; then the goddess began to talk in her sleep and would mumble answers to the questions asked her. People came from all over the World to hear what the oracle had to tell them. The Delphic Oracle, like the statue of Athene, has now gone—no one knows when, nor how, nor where.

Did you know that you could speak Greek? Well, when you say "music," "museum," or "amusements" you are speaking Greek, for all three words are named from nine beautiful

雅典的巴台农神庙

世界上最漂亮的神庙如今已成废墟

像，之所以修建了许多如此漂亮的建筑，是因为他们有如此优质的大理石可用，不过，虽说如今彭忒利科斯山上仍然可以开采出优质的大理石，却似乎无人能够再制作出如此精美的东西了。

以前的人，常常去一个叫作"神谕处"的地方算命。距雅典不远的德尔斐，就有一个最著名的神谕处。那儿的地面上有一条裂隙，里面不停地冒出气体来。在这条裂隙上，坐着一个叫作"女巫"且广受尊敬的女子，上方则建有一座小小的神庙。裂隙中冒出的气体会让女巫昏昏欲睡，就像病人去看大夫或者牙医时，大夫或牙医会用一种气体让病人睡觉，使病人感觉不到疼痛似的，接下来，女巫便会说起梦话来，要是有人提问的话，她还会含含糊糊地进行回答呢。世界各地的人都纷纷前来，聆听神谕对他们的启示。德尔斐神谕处就像雅典娜的那尊雕塑一样，如今也已不复存在了，谁都不知道是它是什么时候、如何消失的，也不知道如今这个神谕处到了哪里。

大家知不知道，你们其实都会说希腊语呢？注意，你们在说"音乐"、"博物馆"或者"文娱活动"的时候，就是在说希腊语，因为它们都是根据"缪斯"这个名称而来的，缪斯是一位漂亮的女神，曾经住在德尔斐一眼山泉的附近。这眼山泉叫

goddesses called "Muses," who used to live near a spring at Delphi. This spring was named Castalia, and it was supposed that those who drank from the spring would be able to write music and poetry. The Castalian spring is still there, and sheep and goats as well as men drink its cool waters, but now it does no more than quench the thirst of men and beasts.

Long before the time of Christ, athletic meets used to be held in Greece once every four years. These were called Olympic Games, and champions in running and jumping and other sports from all over Greece used to compete for a prize, which was a simple crown made of laurel leaves. There is a huge stadium in Athens where such games and races were held, but it had fallen to ruins. Not so many years ago a Greek who had made a fortune and wanted to do something splendid for his home city repaired and recovered the old stadium with marble, and again the Olympic Games were held there.

Near Athens there is another hill called Mount Hymettus, where was found a very delicious kind of honey. It is said to taste like flowers and it was supposed to be the food the gods lived upon—they called it "ambrosia." You can still get the same honey in the restaurants in Athens, but there are no more gods to feed on it.

Greece of today is famous for—what do you suppose? For poetry? No. For music? No. For sculpture? No. For beautiful buildings? No. My geography says it is famous for "currants." Currants are little dried grapes that are used in cakes and puddings. Currants are named from Corinth, the stem that joins north and south Greece, or rather, I should say, the stem that used to join them, for the Greeks have cut a canal four miles long straight through the

作"卡斯塔利亚泉",据说凡是喝过其中泉水的人,都能创作出美妙的音乐和诗歌来。如今,卡斯塔利亚泉仍在,而且除了当地的人,连绵羊、山羊也都是饮用其中沁凉的泉水呢,不过,除了能够让人们和牲畜解渴,那里的泉水就没有任何作用了。

距基督降生很久以前,希腊就开始每隔四年举行一场运动会了。这种运动会,叫作"奥林匹克运动会"。举办运动会的时候,希腊各地在跑步、跳高以及其他运动项目上的优胜者,都会前来争夺奖品,可当时的奖品,不过是用月桂树叶编织而成的一顶花冠罢了。雅典建有一座巨大的体育场,比赛就是在这个体育场里举行的,不过,后来这座体育场倒塌了,成了一片废墟。不久之前,一位希腊人发了大财之后,希望为家乡做点儿有意义的事情,便用大理石修复和重建了这座古老的体育场,于是,奥运会便再次开始在这个体育场里举行了。

雅典附近,另外还有一座山,叫作"伊米托斯山",那里出产一种味道非常鲜美的蜂蜜。据说,这种蜂蜜的味道就像是鲜花,因此,人们认为这种蜂蜜是天上神仙的食物,从而称之为"仙馐"。在雅典的饭店里,人们仍然可以品尝到这种蜂蜜,不过,现在自然不会有更多的神仙来享用"仙馐"了。

如今的希腊最享盛名的是——你们猜一猜,是什么呢?诗歌?不对。音乐?不对。雕塑艺术?不对。漂亮的建筑?不对。我的地理书上说,该国以"加仑子"而著称。加仑子其实就是那种很小的、用在蛋糕和布丁上面的葡萄干。加仑子这个名称源于科林斯,也就是那个把希腊南、北两个部分连接起来的狭长地带,或者更准

isthmus so that boats can now sail across Corinth without going all the way around Greece.

There is a lunch-room downtown kept by a young Greek who has come to America to make his fortune. He calls it the Delphi Restaurant. Last week I went in for luncheon, and just for fun I asked him if he had any ambrosia. "No," said he, "we have corned beef and cabbage today."

确一点来说，是以前把这两个部分连接起来的狭长地带，因为后来希腊人开凿了一条横跨这条地峡、长达数英里的运河，所以如今船舶不用再绕过整个希腊，便可以直接驶过科林斯地峡了。

市中心有一家小吃店，那是一个到美国来挣钱的希腊年轻人开的。他把这家小吃店起名为"德尔斐餐馆"。上个星期我去那里吃午饭的时候，曾经开玩笑地问他，店里有没有"仙馐"。"没有，"他回答说，"今天我们只有腌牛肉炒卷心菜。"

47 The Land of the New Moon

Every place is east of some other place. America is east of China. Europe is east of America. But the only place called "THE East," with a capital THE, is the land east of Europe. This land east of Europe is the continent of Asia. It's the biggest continent of all.

Long years ago in fairy-tale days a god in Asia was in love with a beautiful girl whose name was Europa. Now a god was not supposed to love a human being, so the god turned himself into a snow-white bull and, persuading Europa to get on his back, he ran away with her. At last the bull came to a strait of water and swam across it with Europa still on his back. On the opposite side of the strait where the bull landed with Europa on his back was a great new continent, and to-day we call this continent Europe—after Europa.

People who do not believe in fairy-tales say, however, that Europe is a name that simply means The Land Where the Sun Goes Down, and they say that Asia, the land from which Europa and the bull came, means The Land Where the Sun Gets Up.

The strait across which the bull carried Europa we still call Bull-Carry Strait, for in the Greek language "bull-carry" is Bosporus, and Bosporus is the name on the map.

People built a city where Europa landed, and about a thousand years afterward a Roman Emperor named Constantine, who was the first Christian emperor, moved his capital from Rome to this city and it was called after him, Constantinople.

第47章　新月之地

任何一个地方，都会位于某个地方的东面。美洲在中国的东面。欧洲在美洲的东面。不过，唯一一个被称为"东方"，并且属于专有名称的地方，就是欧洲东面的那片大陆。欧洲东面的这片大陆，叫作"亚洲"。亚洲是世界上最大的一个洲。

在神话传说中，很久很久以前，亚洲有一位神仙，爱上了一个叫作欧罗巴的美丽姑娘。注意，神仙是不应当爱上一位凡人的，因此那位神仙便把自己变成了一头雪白的公牛，并且说服欧罗巴骑到了它的背上，带着她私奔了。最后，这头公牛跑到了一个全都是水的海峡边，然后让欧罗巴骑在它的背上游过了这条海峡。到了海峡对面，这头公牛便驮着欧罗巴，登上了一个伟大的新大陆，因此，如今我们就根据欧罗巴的名字，称这个大陆为"欧洲"了。

然而，那些不相信神话故事的人却称，"欧洲"这个名称只是指"太阳落下的地方"，他们还说，欧罗巴和那头公牛出发的地方，即亚洲，指的就是"太阳升起的地方"。

而公牛驮着欧罗巴游过去的那条海峡，我们却仍然称之为"牛带海峡"，因为在希腊语里，"牛带"一词是"博斯普鲁斯"，因此地图上这里如今就叫"博斯普鲁斯海峡"了。

人们在欧罗巴上岸的地方修建了一座城市。大约一千年后，出了一位叫作"君

After another thousand years Constantinople was captured from the Christians by some people from Asia called Turks, who had a ruler called the Sultan. Most of the people in Europe are Christians, but the Turks are not Christians. They do not believe in Christ. They believe in a god whom they called Allah and a man named Mohammed who they say was Allah's messenger on earth. So we call the people who believe in Mohammed Mohammedans or Moslems.

One dark night many years ago an army was approaching Constantinople, but it was so dark the people in the city did not see it and did not know they were about to be attacked. Suddenly the moon shone out from behind a cloud. By the light of the moon the watchmen saw the enemy, sounded the alarm, and the city was saved. Ever since then the Turks have used the new moon on their churches as we do a cross and a new moon and a star on their flag, as these had brought good luck. A new moon is called a "crescent." The Turks have a society, the same society as our Red Cross; but as a cross is a Christian sign, they don't use it, so they call their society the Red Crescent.

One of the largest churches in the World was built in Constantinople before the Turks came. It was called the church of Holy Wisdom, which in Greek is Santa Sophia. Perhaps

士坦丁"的古罗马皇帝，他也是第一位皈依了基督教的皇帝。他将首都从罗马搬到了这座城市，并且用自己的名字，将该市命名为"君士坦丁堡"。

欧罗巴和公牛

那位神仙变成公牛，带着欧罗巴私奔了

又过了一千年后，君士坦丁堡被亚洲的一些土耳其人攻占了，那些土耳其人的君主，叫作"苏丹"。当时欧洲的绝大多数人都是基督徒，可土耳其人却不是基督教徒。他们不信仰基督。他们信仰的，是一个叫作"安拉"的神，以及一个叫作"穆罕默德"的人，他们说，穆罕默德就是安拉在尘世间的信使。因此，我们便把那些信仰穆罕默德的人称为"伊斯兰教徒"，即"穆斯林"。

很久以前一个漆黑的夜晚，一支军队挺进到了君士坦丁堡，可由于天黑，城中的居民并没有看到这支军队，也不知道他们即将遭到袭击。突然之间，月亮从乌云背后露出来，把月光洒满了大地。借着月光，巡夜者发现了敌人，于是拉响了警报，从而挽救了该市。自此以后，土耳其人便在他们的教堂里绘上一个新升的月亮图案，就像我们的教堂里都有十字架似的，他们的国旗上也有一轮新升的月亮和一颗星星，因为这两种东西给他们带来了好运。一轮新升的月亮，称为"新月"。土耳其人还成立了一个社团，性质与我们的"红十字会"相同，不过，由于十字架是基督教的标志，他们不可能用这种标志，因此便将他们成立的那个社团叫作"红新月协会"。

you may know a girl named Sophie. Well, she may be wise or she may not, but her name means wise. When the Turks captured the Christian city of Constantinople they changed Santa Sophia and all the other churches in the city to Mohammedan churches, which are called mosques, and they tore down the crosses on top of the churches and put up in the place of each a crescent. There are now over eight hundred mosques in the city. Finally not very many years ago they changed Constantinople's name to Istanbul.

You might think it would be better if I hadn't told you the old name of Istanbul. Then you would have one less long name to remember. But Constantinople was the name of the city for a much longer time than Istanbul has been. Even now Constantinople is a better-known name than Istanbul. I won't, however, tell you what the city was called before it became Constantinople. Two names are enough to learn about any city. So if you want to know Istanbul's earliest name you'll have to ask some one or find it in some other book.

The Turks also built, close to each mosque, one or more candle-shaped towers, called minarets. About midway of a minaret is a balcony, and five times a day a priest appears on this balcony and calls the people of the city to prayer. This is done instead of ringing church bells as they do in Christian churches, for Mohammedans do not use bells, even in their own homes. When they want to call a servant they clap their hands. The first call to prayer is about five o'clock in the morning—sort of an alarm clock—when the priest says, "Come to prayer. Prayer is better than Sleep."

Not many people get up at that time to pray, however. When he calls out, a very good

世界上最大的一座教堂，位于土耳其人占领之前的君士坦丁堡。那座教堂叫作"圣智堂"，在希腊语里叫作"圣索菲亚大教堂"。大家没准都认识某位名叫"索菲"的小姑娘呢。好吧，她可能聪明，也可能不聪明，可不管怎样，她的名字都是指"智慧"。土耳其人占领了君士坦丁堡这座信奉基督教的城市之后，便把"圣索菲亚大教堂"以及市里的其他教堂全都改成了伊斯兰教的清真寺，拆掉基督教堂顶上的十字架，然后再安上一个新月标志。这座城市里，如今有八百多座清真寺呢。最终，就在不久之前，他们又把君士坦丁堡改名为"伊斯坦布尔"了。

大家可能会觉得，要是我没有把伊斯坦布尔的原名告诉你们的话，可能会更好。这样一来，你们要记的，就是一个较短的地名了。不过，这座城市叫作君士坦丁堡的时间，可比它叫作伊斯坦布尔的时间要长得多哩。即便是到了如今，"君士坦丁堡"这个名称，也仍然比"伊斯坦布尔"要有名得多。然而，我不会把这座城市叫作君士坦丁堡以前的名称再告诉你们。要了解这座城市，只需知道这两个名称就够了。因此，如果大家想知道伊斯坦布尔最早的名称，那你们就得去问别人，或者到其他图书中去查阅了。

紧挨着每座清真寺，土耳其人还修建了一个形状像是蜡烛的塔楼，叫作"宣礼塔"。每座宣礼塔的中部都有一个阳台，一位阿訇每天都会来到这个阳台上五次，召唤市里的人去做祷告。这就像是基督教堂里用钟声来召唤人们做祷告一样，可穆斯林不用大钟，哪怕家里也不用。需要叫仆人的时候，他们就会拍拍手掌。第一次祷告是在早上五点钟左右，此时，阿訇就像是一座闹钟那样，会大声呼唤："来做

Mohammedan goes into the nearest mosque to pray, or he gets down on his knees and bows his head till it touches the ground. Whenever he goes into a mosque he must first wash his face, hands, and feet, so almost every mosque has a pool or fountain, sometimes on the steps, sometimes in the courtyard, where the people can wash before they enter. For this reason also there are a great many fountains throughout Istanbul. They are not for drinking—they are not for beauty; they are for washing. The mosques are for men only. Women used to be allowed in little hidden cells in the mosque, where they could not be seen, for women and children were supposed neither to be seen nor heard. The Mohammedans' Sunday is our Friday. The Mohammedan goes to the mosque every day if he can, but always on Friday.

An inlet from the Bosporus cuts into Istanbul in the shape of a horn. It is called the Golden Horn, and across the entrance a great chain used to be stretched to keep out ships which the Sultan did not wish to enter. Across the Golden Horn is a bridge called Galata. I have told you of some of the most famous bridges in the World: Brooklyn Bridge, London Bridge, the Rialto and the Ponte Vecchio. Galata bridge is one of the *oldest* and most famous

他们把教堂改成了清真寺

祷告吧。祷告比睡觉更有益。"

　　然而，没有很多人会在那个时候就起来做祷告。阿訇召唤时，凡属非常虔诚的穆斯林，都会来到离家最近的清真寺去做祷告，或者跪下双膝，低下头来，直到额头碰地。进入一座清真寺之前，穆斯林必须洗脸、洗手、洗脚，因此几乎每一座清真寺里都有一个水池或者一座喷泉，水池或者喷泉有的时候建在台阶上，有的时候建在院子里，人们进入清真寺之前都可以在其中进行沐浴。因此，伊斯坦布尔城里就有许多、许多的喷泉。它们不是用来提供饮水，也不是用来衬托美景，而是用来洗浴的。只有男子才能进入清真寺。女性通常可以到清真寺里一些隐蔽的小间里去做祷告，这样的话，别人就看不到她们，而原因就是人们认为，清真寺里不应当看到女人和小孩，也不能听到她们的声音。穆斯林的星期日，就是我们的星期五。要是做得到的话，穆斯林每天都应当到清真寺里去做祷告才是，不过，人们通常都只在星期五才去。

　　博斯普鲁斯海峡有一个小湾，它伸进了伊斯坦布尔市，样子就像是一只喇叭。这个小海湾，叫作"金角湾"，而在入口的海面上，还横着一条巨大的铁链，用于阻止苏丹不想接纳的那些船只。金角湾上还有一座大桥，叫作"加拉太桥"。我在

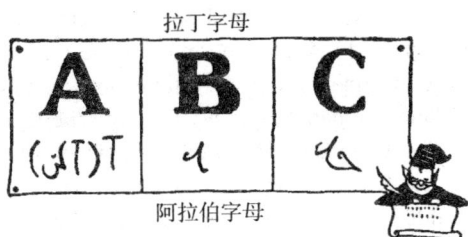

拉丁字母

阿拉伯字母

土耳其文字已经发生了变化

bridges of the World. All day and all night people of every nationality, every color, every dress, and every language pass in an unending stream. Every one on one side seems to want to get to the other side, which makes me think of the old riddle, "Why does a chicken cross the road?"

Turkish writing looks something like shorthand and is very hard to read and to write. But because it is so difficult and so different from the letters of Europe, Turkey began to use an alphabet like ours, and every one under forty years of age is now required to learn the new writing.

In fact, Turkey has been made over into a new Turkey. The old ruler of Turkey, the Sultan, ruled alone and whatever he said had to be done whether it was right or wrong. Turkey now has a ruler who rules not alone but with others chosen by the people to rule with him. The women used to think it immodest to go out on the street with their faces

土耳其男女的着装

过去与现在

土耳其人的着装风格也发生了变化

前面已经向大家介绍过世界上一些最著名的桥梁了，比如布鲁克林大桥、伦敦桥、里亚尔托桥和老桥。加拉太桥也属于世界上历史最悠久、最著名的桥梁之一。不同民族、不同肤色、不同服装、说不同语言的人，都在日夜不停、川流不息地经过这座大桥。大桥两边的每一个人，似乎都想到大桥对面去，这种情景，让我想起了一个古老的谜语："为什么小鸡要过马路呢？"

　　土耳其人的文字，有点儿像是速记符号，既难以阅读，又难以书写。不过，正是因为这种文字如此难写难认，与欧洲的文字如此大相径庭，土耳其人后来才开始使用一种与我们相似的字母呢，如今年纪不到四十的人，全都需要学习这种新的文字了。

　　实际上，土耳其也已变成了一个新的土耳其。以前，土耳其由君主苏丹大权独揽，无论是对是错，他的命令都必须执行。而如今，土耳其的君主不再是一人独裁，而是与人民推选出来的其他代表共同统治该国了。以前，土耳其的女性认为，在大街上抛头露面是很不庄重的一件事情，因此她们出去时都会戴上面纱。而如

uncovered, so they wore veils. Now, however, they wear hats and dresses. The Turks used to have many wives, and every house had a separate apartment, called the harem, where all the wives lived together.

You may wonder why the bird we eat at Thanksgiving and Christmas is called a turkey. Turkey was first brought to our country from Mexico, hut people thought it had come from Turkey, so they called it a Turkey bird.

今，她们也戴着帽子、穿着裙子了。以前，土耳其男子常常还娶有多位妻子，而且每家都有一栋独立的、叫作闺房的公寓，供所有妻妾一起居住呢。

大家可能会感到奇怪，为什么我们在感恩节和圣诞节吃的那种禽类叫作"火鸡"[1]。火鸡起初本来是从墨西哥传入美国的，可当时的人却以为火鸡来自土耳其，因此便把它叫作火鸡了。

---

[1] 火鸡（turkey）与土耳其（Turkey）是同一个词，只是"火鸡"为意译，"土耳其"为音译。

48 The Ship of the Desert

There are a few camels in Istanbul, but camels don't belong in Europe. They have to be carried across the Bosporus from Asia, for a camel is said to be the only animal that cannot swim and cannot learn to swim. Most animals, like dogs, swim naturally; they don't have to learn. The camel may not be able to swim, but he can cross deserts, which no other animal can do as well.

The camel is an animal of the desert, and when we see camels we know there must be deserts somewhere near. The camel loves heat and dryness, the sun and sand. Men and most animals, when it is hot, like the cool shade when they rest, but a camel when he rests lies down in the hot sun. He is often called "the ship of the desert," for he is the only "boat" that can carry passengers across the sea of sands. His feet are made like cushions so that they do not sink into the sand. A camel has several pouches inside of his body in which to store up water, as in tanks, for in crossing desert lands he may have to go days at a time without a drink, so he fills up these tanks inside of him.

The camel in Asia has one hump and is called a Dromedary. There are other camels that have two humps. The hump is not a broken back, as it looks—it is made of fat, and when the camel can get no outside food, the fat in his hump helps to feed him as the food in his stomach feeds him.

第48章　沙漠之舟

虽说伊斯坦布尔也有少量的骆驼，但骆驼并不是产自欧洲的一种动物。人们必须将它们从亚洲经过博斯普鲁斯海峡运过来，因为据说骆驼是唯一一种既不会游泳、也学不会游泳的动物。绝大多数牲畜，比如狗，天生就会游泳，它们完全不需要学习游泳。虽然骆驼不会游泳，但它们能够横跨沙漠，在这方面，其他动物的本领可都不如它们呢。

骆驼是一种属于沙漠里的动物，因此，我们一看到骆驼就知道，附近哪儿一定会有沙漠。骆驼喜欢炎热和干旱，喜欢阳光和沙地。要是天气太热的话，人类和绝大多数动物休息的时候都会喜欢阴凉的地方，可骆驼休息的时候，却是直接卧在炎炎烈日之下。人们常常称它们为"沙漠之舟"，因为骆驼是唯一一种可以驮着旅客穿越"沙海"的"船舶"。骆驼的脚天生就像是四个垫子，不会陷入沙里。骆驼体内有好几个肚囊，可以像水罐一样储水，因为在穿越沙漠的时候，骆驼可能一次得走上好多天，期间滴水不进，所以要把身体里的这些水罐储满水才行。

亚洲的骆驼中，只长有一个驼峰的，叫作"单峰驼"。还有一些骆驼，身上则长有两个驼峰。驼峰的样子就是那样，并不是骆驼的背骨折了、肿了起来。驼峰里面全是脂肪，要是没有吃的东西，驼峰里那些脂肪所起的作用，就跟骆驼肚子里那些食物所起的作用相同了。

The camel "follows the leader," almost as in the game, for wherever the leader goes he goes—so when a number of camels are used to carry loads long distances they are tied head to tail in a line, like a train of cars hitched together, often with a donkey at the head of the train like a locomotive to lead them. The donkey has sense, but a camel has little sense; that's why the donkey is made the leader. Such a train of camels is called a caravan. The camel looks very superior—as if no one were as good as he—but he is really a stupid animal with a very small brain. He has, however, an even temper—always mean, ugly, and nasty. He grunts as he walks slowly along on his stilt-like legs. He is trained to kneel and a load is then put on his back, and he will carry great loads with his driver on top of that. If too big a load is put on his back, when kneeling, the camel will not get up at all; but once he gets up he never gives up, no matter how heavy the load. You can then pile anything on him until it crushes him to the ground. When he has all the load he can carry, one straw

骆驼和最后一根稻草

这是压断骆驼脊背的最后一根稻草

骆驼习惯于"追随领导"，差不多就像游戏里一样，因为领头的骆驼走到哪里，其他骆驼就会跟到哪里。所以，在用多头骆驼远距离运送货物的时候，人们会让它们头尾相接地串成一列，就像是首尾相连的一列火车车厢似的，并且最前头通常用一头驴子带路，相当于火车机车的作用。驴子有方向感，可骆驼的方向感却很差，之所以用驴子带路，原因就在于此。这样一列骆驼，叫作"驼队"。骆驼的样子看起来很神气，仿佛世界上没有什么可以与之媲美似的，可实际上却是一种很蠢的动物，脑袋很不好使。然而，骆驼的脾气却非常稳定，总是倔强、暴躁而烦人。当它们迈开四条高跷般的腿慢慢腾腾地走路时候，会发出呼噜呼噜的声音。人们训练它们跪下去，然后把货物放到骆驼背上，它们能驮很多的东西，连赶骆驼的人也会坐在高高的驼背上呢。要是驮的东西太重，那么骆驼跪下去之后，根本就不会再站起来，可一旦站起来，那么无论背上的货物有多重，骆驼都决不会被压得再跪下去。然后，你们就可以把什么东西都堆到它们的背上，直到货物把骆驼压趴下了。

more may be enough to break his back. So when you give some one too much work to do, people say, "It's the last straw that breaks the camel's back."

The camel carries loads for his master, but the camel does more than that. The mother camel gives him milk, and sometimes young camels are used for food. The camel's hair is woven to make blankets and clothes and tents. In our country the best paint brushes are made of camel's hair.

驮上它们承受得起的重量之后，就算加上一根稻草，也有可能把骆驼的脊背压垮。因此，要是让一个干太多的活儿，人们就会说："这是压断骆驼脊背的最后一根稻草啊。"

骆驼可以替主人驮运货物，可它们的作用还不止如此。母骆驼可以产奶，有的时候小骆驼也可以宰杀了来吃。驼毛可以用于编织毯子、衣物和帐篷。在美国，一些质量最好的画笔，就是用驼毛制成的呢。

49 A "Once-was" Country

We call a small boy a "minor" until he grows up. The corner of Asia on the other side of the Bosporus is only a small part of Asia, so we call it Asia Minor. Asia Minor does not touch Europe, although it comes so close to it in two places that a giant could stride across. One of these crossings is the Bosporus; it is only about half a mile wide. The other crossing, called the Dardanelles, is only about a mile wide at the narrowest point. People have swum across the Dardanelles, and floating bridges have been made here by tying boats together, but there are now no bridges from Asia to Europe, and men and animals have to be carried across in boats if they want to get from Asia to Europe or from Europe to Asia.

Asia Minor is a "Once-was" country. It once was the richest part of the whole World; it is now one of the poorest.

Crœsus, who once was the richest man in the World, lived in Asia Minor.

Helen, who once was the most beautiful woman in the World, was stolen away from her home in Greece and brought to a place called Troy in Asia Minor. Here the Trojan War was fought on her account.

Homer, one of the greatest story poets who ever lived, was said to have been born in Asia Minor.

第49章 "曾经存在"的国度

在一个小朋友长大成人之前，我们会称之为"未成年人"。由于博斯普鲁斯海峡另一侧的亚洲一角只是亚洲的一小部分，因此我们称之为"小亚细亚"。小亚细亚与欧洲并不相连，但那里有两个地方，与欧洲之间的距离非常近，巨人一抬腿就能跨过去。其中一个这样的地方就是博斯普鲁斯海峡，那里只有大约半英里宽。另一处则叫"达达尼尔海峡"。虽说人们将船只连到一起，在那里修建了几座浮桥，可并没有修建将亚洲和欧洲连通起来的跨海大桥，因此，人们想要往返于欧、亚两洲的话，就只能用船只将人和牲畜运送过海。

小亚细亚是一个"曾经存在"的国家。这里曾经是世界上最富裕的地区，可如今，这里却变成了世界上最贫穷的地区之一。

克罗伊斯曾经是世界上最富有的人，当时他就住在小亚细亚。

海伦曾经是世界上最漂亮的女子，后来被人从希腊的家中抢走，带到了小亚细亚一个叫作"特洛伊"的地方。为了争夺海伦，这里便爆发了特洛伊战争。

属于人类历史上最伟大的叙事诗人之一的荷马，据说就是在小亚细亚出生的。

使徒圣保罗也出生于小亚细亚的一个小镇里，那个小镇叫作"塔尔苏斯"，圣保罗曾经在那里给士兵们制作过帐篷。

大家很可能都听说过"世界七大奇迹"吧。据说它们是古代人民用人力创造出

St. Paul—the Apostle—was born in a little town in Asia Minor, a town called Tarsus, where he made tents for soldiers.

You have probably heard of the Seven Wonders of the World. They were supposed to be the seven most wonderful things made by the hand of man in Ancient Times. Three of the Seven Wonders were in Asia Minor:

The Temple built to the Goddess Diana was one of these wonders. This Temple was at Ephesus in Asia Minor, and silversmiths made little copies of this wonderful temple to sell as souvenirs to visitors. St. Paul preached against Diana, for whom the Temple was built, because she was a heathen goddess. The silversmiths at Ephesus who made a living out of their souvenirs of the Temple were afraid St. Paul would hurt their business, so they tried to mob him. Nothing is now left of this wonderful Temple of Diana except the floor, and the silver souvenirs have all disappeared; but the letters which St. Paul wrote to men at Ephesus are still read by millions of people, for they are in the Bible.

The greatest tomb in the World was in Asia Minor. It was built by a woman named Mrs. Mausolus, for her husband, Mr. Mausolus. This was another Wonder of which little is left. And yet nowadays we call a very handsome tomb a "Mausoleum" after this tomb of Mausolus.

There is a little island off Asia Minor, called Rhodes. A huge brass statue of the Sun God was built there. It was called The Colossus of Rhodes, for Colossus means huge. It was as tall as a ten-story house. This was a third Wonder, but an earthquake upset the

来的七种最神奇的东西。在这"七大奇迹"当中，有三大奇迹都位于小亚细亚呢：

其中之一，便是为狄安娜[1]女神修建的神庙。那座神庙位于小亚细亚的以弗所，当时，许多银匠都纷纷根据这座奇妙神庙的样子，制作出小型的复制品，当成纪念品来卖给游客。圣保罗曾经四处布道，反对崇拜狄安娜，因为狄安娜是一位异教女神。那些靠制作神庙纪念品为生的银匠担心圣保罗会毁掉他们的生意，便试图围攻他。除了地板，这座神奇的狄安娜神庙如今已经荡然无存，而那些银制纪念品也全都不见踪影了，可圣保罗在以弗所给民众写下的文字，如今却仍然被千百万人所诵读呢，因为那些文字已经加入了《圣经》当中。

世界上最大的一座坟墓，也位于小亚细亚。那座坟墓，是一位名叫"摩索拉斯夫人"的女士为她的丈夫摩索拉斯先生修建的。这又是一处几乎没有留下什么的奇迹。尽管如此，如今我们却仍然会将一座修建得非常美观的坟墓，根据这座"摩索拉斯墓"而称之为"豪华陵墓"呢。

小亚细亚沿海有一座小岛，叫作"罗兹岛"。那里的人曾经为太阳神修建了一座巨大的黄铜雕像。这座雕像，叫作"罗兹岛巨人像"，"巨人"一词，就是"巨大"的意思。这座雕像，有一栋十层楼的房屋那样高呢。它是小亚细亚的第三大奇迹，不过，后来一场地震把这尊雕像震倒了，而雕像摔成的碎片，则被人们卖给了

---

[1] 狄安娜（Diana），古罗马神话中的月亮和狩猎女神，也就是古希腊神话中的阿耳忒弥斯（Artemis）。

statue and its pieces were sold to a junk dealer.

Almost all of the old glory of Asia Minor has gone. We can see the ruins of the wonderful old buildings, but most of the houses now, except those in a few big cities, are made of mud with one door and no windows, and grass often grows in the mud on the roofs.

Asia Minor now belongs to Turkey—in fact, it is about all there is left of Turkey except Istanbul, although before World War I, Turkey owned much more land.

You have probably seen Angora cats—beautiful cats with long hair and bushy tails. They come from Angora, the capital of new Turkey. In the country round Angora is raised a peculiar kind of goat which has long silky hair. The hair from this Angora goat is used to make lovely rugs and shawls which can be bought here in America. Mohair suits which men wear in hot summer weather because they are so thin and cool are made of Angora goats' hair—if genuine.

In Asia Minor is a very crooked river that flows lazily along to the sea, turning this way and that way as if it had no particular place to go. Its name is the "Meander." So when a boy goes lazily along to school, turning this way and that, or when he goes along on an errand and does not go straight there but wanders along as the Meander goes to the

一位废品商。

　　小亚细亚昔日的辉煌，几乎全都一去不返了。虽然我们看得到过去那些奇妙古建筑的废墟，但如今那里的绝大多数房屋，除了少数大城市里的房子，却全都是用泥土筑成的了：只有一扇门，没有窗户，并且屋顶的泥土之中常常还会长出草来。

一场地震，把雕像震到了海里

　　小亚细亚如今属于土耳其，事实上，除了伊斯坦布尔，土耳其也只剩下这里了。但是，在第一次世界大战前，土耳其拥有的领土可要比这多得多呢。

　　大家很可能都看到过"安哥拉猫"吧，这种猫的样子很漂亮，有着长长的皮毛和毛茸茸的尾巴。它们产自新土耳其的首都安哥拉。在安哥拉周围的乡村里，人们还喂养一种非常罕见的山羊，这种山羊，全身的毛又长又丝滑。从这种安哥拉山羊身上剪下的羊毛，用于制作精美的地毯和围巾，如今在美国也买得到。人们之所以在炎热的天气里也能穿"马海毛西服"，是因为制作那种西服的布料又薄又凉爽，而那种马海毛布料，要是货真价实的话，就是用安哥拉山羊的羊毛制成的呢。

　　小亚细亚有一条蜿蜒曲折的河流，它一路懒洋洋地沿着海岸流淌，七拐八弯，

sea, we say he "meanders." Girls sometimes "meander" too.

Figs grow in the valley of the Meander River and dates grow in many parts of Asia. Figs and dates are brought on camel back across to a beautiful city called Smyrna on the Mediterranean Sea, and from there are shipped to us in America. You can probably get at your corner grocery store a package of Smyrna figs or "Dromedary Dates" that have been picked far away in Asia, carried by caravan to Smyrna, and shipped here. Another thing sent us from Smyrna is sponges. Sponges grow in the sea near Asia Minor. Naked men dive for the sponges and pull them off the rocks, where they grow on the bottom of the sea. They gather as many as they can at a time, as long as they can hold their breath.

仿佛没有什么特定的终点似的。这条河流，就叫"米安德河"[1]。因此，如果一个小男孩懒洋洋地走去上学，一路七拐八弯，或者当这个小男孩帮大人跑腿时，不是直来直去，而是像米安德河沿着海岸线蜿蜒前流那样，我们就会说他是在"闲逛"。当然，小姑娘有时也是会"闲逛"的啦。

　　米安德河流域栽种着无花果树，而亚洲许多地方则种植有枣椰树。人们将无花果和枣椰用骆驼驮着，经由地中海海滨一个叫作"士麦那"[2]的美丽城市，再在那里装船，运到我们美国来。在你们家街角的杂货店里，大家很可能买得到一包士麦那产的无花果，或者是从遥远的亚洲采摘下来、经过驼队运到士麦那、然后再装船运到美国来的"单峰驼牌椰枣"呢。从士麦那运到我们这里来的，还有一种东西，那就是海绵。小亚细亚附近的海底，也生长着海绵。那里的人会脱掉衣服，潜到海底去，将海绵从海底的岩石上扯下来。每次，只要憋得住那么久的气，他们都会尽可能地多采集一些海绵呢。

---

[1] 米安德河（Meander），此处属于音译。在英语里，meander一词指"蜿蜒流动，闲逛"。

[2] 士麦那（Smyrna），土耳其西部一港口城市，现名伊兹密尔。

50 A Land Flowing with Milk and Honey

In Sunday school I used to hear of Bethlehem and Jerusalem and other places in the Bible, but I had no idea then that there were any such places with people living in them today. But there are. We call the land where these places are Bible Land, because so much is told about them in the Bible. Bible Land is at the east end of the Mediterranean Sea. The northern part of Bible Land is called Syria, the southern part is called the Holy Land, or Palestine.

There are a great many cities in Syria and Palestine that were alive when Christ was born and are still living, and there are a great many places that are now dead—nothing left of them but ruins. But there is a city mentioned in the Bible that was a thousand years old when Christ was born and yet is still very much alive. It is the oldest city i.t.w.W. Its name is Damascus.

The main street in Damascus was called "Straight," because it was not quite as crooked as its other streets. On both sides of Straight Street are shops, for Damascus was once the greatest shopping city in the East; the shops are called bazaars. Some of the bazaars are not big enough to hold a piano. One department store in New York would hold all the bazaars in Damascus many times over. In these bazaars the people of Damascus used to sell only things they made themselves. They sold gold and silver jewelry, rugs, shawls,

第50章　盛产牛奶和蜂蜜的国度

在主日学校，我经常听到伯利恒、耶路撒冷以及《圣经》中的其他一些地方，不过，当时我可不知道，如今仍然会有人生活在那些地方。不过，事实就是如此。我们将这些地方都称为"《圣经》之地"，而《圣经》中关于这些地方的内容也非常多。"《圣经》之地"位于地中海的东端。它的北部叫作"叙利亚"，南部则叫"圣地"，或者叫"巴勒斯坦"。

在叙利亚和巴勒斯坦，有许多城市在基督降生的时候就已经出现了，而如今也依然存在，当然，也有许多地方如今都不复存在，什么都没有留下，只剩一堆废墟了。不过，《圣经》中曾经提到过一座城市，它在基督降生时就已经有一千年的历史，而如今那里也依然兴旺得很。它堪称是世界上历史最悠久的一座城市。这座城市，叫作"大马士革"。

大马士革的主街叫作"直街"，原因就在于，它不像其他街道那样蜿蜒曲折。"直街"两侧商店林立，因为大马士革曾经是东方世界最大的一座商业城市，人们把这些商店叫作"杂货铺"。其中有些杂货铺很小，还容不下一架钢琴。纽约的一个百货商店，就可以容下大马士革所有杂货铺的好几倍呢。在这些杂货铺里，大马士革人以前只出售他们自己制造的一些东西。他们出售金制和银制首饰、地毯、围巾、刀剑和丝绸，并且什么东西都是用手工打制，因为那里没有机器。现在，虽

swords, and silks, and they made everything by hand, for there was no machinery. Now there is machinery to make all these things, but it is not in Damascus. Many of these things are now made by machinery in England and sent to Damascus to be sold. Often a traveler buys something in a Damascus bazaar only to find on it later the tell-tale words "Made in Birmingham."

A white picture painted on white paper or a red picture on red paper would not show, but in Damascus they used to make a beautiful kind of cloth with designs of the same color as the cloth woven into it by hand. This kind of cloth is called damask, after Damascus. White damask has white designs on it and red damask has red designs, and they do show. You

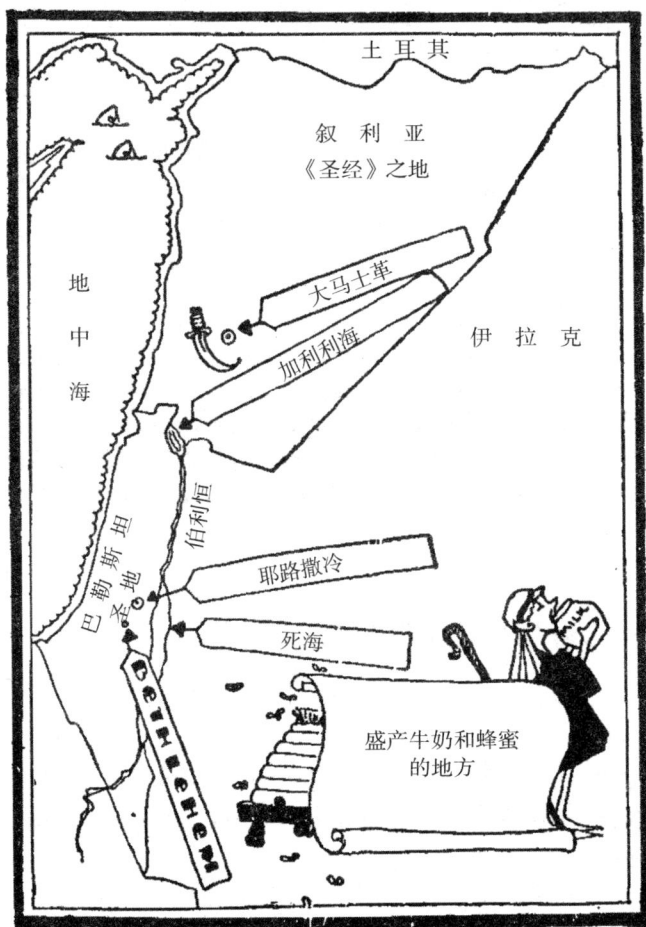

说世界各地都已经有了制作这些东西的机械，可大马士革却还是没有。如今，许多东西都是先在英国用机器制造出来，然后再运到大马士革来出售。游客在大马士革的杂货铺里买到某种东西后，经常会发现上面竟然标着"伯明翰制造"的字样呢。

用白色颜料在白纸上画画，或者用红色颜料在红纸上画画，是看不出来的，不过，在大马士革，人们以前常常制作一种漂亮的布匹，上面带有手工织就的图案，而这些图案所用的线，却与布匹属于同种颜色呢。人们根据大马士革这个地名，把此种布料称为"大马士革织缎"。白色的大马士革织缎上织有白色的图案，红色的大马士革织缎上则织有红色的图案，并且这些图案都看得出来。你们的家里，很可能会有用大马士革亚麻花缎做成的桌布、餐巾或者丝绸椅罩，不过，如今我们购买到的这些东西，全都是机器制造出来的，并且也不是产自大马士革了。

大马士革人以前还经常制造一种镏有金质图案的铁制饰品。这种镏金工艺，

probably have in your own home linen damask table-cloths and napkins or silk coverings on chairs, but the damask that we buy now is made by machinery and does not come from Damascus.

The people in Damascus also used to make a kind of jewelry of iron, with gold designs laid in the iron. This was called Damascene work. Damascene work was much used in decorating swords, and they used to make wonderful swords and knives with edges so sharp they could cut through a bar of iron, so they say. These were called Damascus blades. Soldiers no longer use swords except for show or ornament. Wars are now fought at long distance and soldiers seldom get close enough to use swords.

South of Syria is Palestine, which is also called the Holy Land. On my map there is no room to print the names of even a very few of the places you know. They would run out into the Mediterranean on one side and into the desert on the other, and would be so crowded together that they would cover the little country completely.

You see how small the Holy Land really is. There is a town at the top of the Holy Land with a name like a boy's—Dan. Down at the bottom of the Holy Land is another town called Beersheba; so people often say "from Dan to Beersheba," meaning from top to bottom or from one end of something to the other. Between these two towns the distance is only one hundred and fifty miles and the distance across Palestine is only about fifty miles, so that it would be possible now in one day to go in an automobile up and down and across Palestine.

There are two lakes in Palestine; one is in the north and one is in the south, but both

就叫"大马士革金银镶花工艺"。大马士革金银镶花工艺广泛应用于装饰刀剑,大马士革人以前制作出的刀剑令人叹为观止,刀刃、剑刃都非常锋利,人称削铁如泥呢。那种刀剑,就叫"大马士革刀剑"。如今,除了表演或者用于装饰,士兵们已经不再使用刀剑。如今,战争都是远距离进行,士兵们也很少相互逼近,很少能够达到要使用刀剑的程度了。

叙利亚的南边就是巴勒斯坦,那里也被人们称为"圣地"。在我所用的地图上,就连你们知道的少数几个地名,那里也没有地方可以标注上去。硬要标上的话,这些地名一侧会伸到地中海里去,另一侧则会伸到沙漠里,并且,由于太过拥挤,这些地名还会将巴勒斯坦这个小国完全盖住呢。

因此,你们就能看出,这个"圣地"实际上有多小了。"圣地"的最北端有一个小镇,叫作"达恩",这可有点儿像是一个小男孩的名字呢。"圣地"的最南端是另一个小城,叫作"贝尔谢巴"。因此,人们常说"从达恩到贝尔谢巴",意思就是从头到脚,或者从某种东西的一端到另一端。这两个城镇之间,距离只有一百五十英里,而巴勒斯坦东西边境之间则只相距五十英里左右,因此,如今在一天之内开着汽车从北到南、从东到西跑遍整个巴勒斯坦,是完全没有问题的。

巴勒斯坦境内有两个湖泊,一北一南,并且两个都叫"海"。北部的那个湖,叫作"加利利海"。南部的那个湖则声名赫赫,叫作"死海",因为什么东西在湖里都无法生存,也不能生长在该湖的周围。

are called Seas. The one in the north is called the Sea of Galilee. The one in the south is known as the Dead Sea, for nothing can live in it nor grow around it.

The Sea of Galilee is where Christ walked on the water and where the miraculous number of fish were caught. Many of Christ's close friends were fishermen, and He asked them to help Him teach others, saying He would make them "fishers of men." So a club of Galilee fishermen was started and they used a drawing of a fish as the sign of their society, for, strangely enough, the first two letters of the Greek word for fish were Christ's initials. As in Bible times, they still have sudden storms on the Sea of Galilee and a great many fish are still caught there.

Running from the Sea of Galilee into the Dead Sea is a zigzag river called the Jordan. It was in the Jordan River that John the Baptist baptized Christ, and people so from all over the World to see the spot where this took place, and some to be baptized there themselves. There is always a clergyman on band, ready and waiting, to baptize those who come. Many people fill a bottle with some of the muddy water and take it home to use as "holy water," or in order to baptize their children with water from the same river in which Christ was baptized. The Jordan is very muddy, because it flows very swiftly and washes the mud from the banks and bottom. It empties its yellow water into the Dead Sea, but the Dead Sea, strange to say, is as blue as the Mediterranean.

The Dead Sea is in the bottom of a

基督徒用一条鱼的图案作为社团的标志

加利利海，就是基督曾经在水上行走、渔民曾捕捞到无数鱼儿的那个地方。基督的许多好友都是渔民，基督要求他们协助他向其他人传道，并且说，他会让他们都变成"人类的渔人"。于是，加利利海地区的渔民便成立了一个社团，并且用一条鱼儿的图片做这个社团的标志，说来也怪，希腊语里"鱼"这个词的前面两个字母，也是"基督"这个词的首字母。与《圣经》时代一样，如今加利利海上仍然会突然间风雨大作，而渔民们的捕捞量也仍然非常巨大。

有一条河流，蜿蜒曲折地从加利利海注入死海之中，叫作"约旦河"。正是在约旦河里，"施洗者约翰"替基督实施了洗礼，因此，如今世界各地的人都纷纷前往那里，去瞻仰基督受洗的地方，有些人还会在那儿给自己施洗呢。那里始终都有一位神父，准备着、等待着，为那些前来瞻仰的人施行洗礼。许多人会用瓶子装一点儿混浊的河水，当成"圣水"带回家里去，或者用这种与基督受洗的同一条河流中的水，来给他们的孩子施洗。约旦河的河水非常混浊，因为河水流速很快，冲刷着岸边的泥土，并卷起了河底的泥沙。混浊的河水最终注入了死海，可说来也怪，死海却像地中海那样蔚蓝呢。

死海位于一条非常深邃的峡谷底部，地势极低，因此没有河流可以从中流出，道理就跟水无法往山上流一样。你们可能以为，死海会被汇入的河水注满、溢出，

very deep valley, so low that no water can run out of it, as water cannot run uphill. You might think the Dead Sea would fill up and overflow, but it does not, for the air is so hot and dry that the water in the Dead Sea evaporates as fast as it runs into it. But the river is always bringing in salt, and as salt does not evaporate, the Dead Sea, like Great Salt Lake, is getting saltier all the time. It is saltier than Great Salt Lake, it is ten times saltier than the ocean, and of course no one could drown in it. People don't bathe in the Dead Sea, however, because the water is so salty that if it splashes into one's eyes or touches any scratches or broken skin it stings like iodine put on a cut. There is so much salt around the Dead Sea that nothing will grow there, and even saltwater fish cannot live in the water. We think that the two most wicked cities in the World, Sodom and Gomorrah, were by the Dead Sea. The Bible says they were so wicked that the Lord destroyed them. There is nothing now left of them but desert, with a crust of salt over all. You remember, the Lord told Lot to take his family and flee from Sodom before he destroyed it, and ordered him and his family not to look back. Lot's wife disobeyed and she was turned to a pillar of salt. And a guide will point out a mound of salt that he says is Lot's wife!

罗得的妻子
一根盐柱

罗得的妻子没有听从上帝的吩咐，回
头看了一眼，立刻被变成了一根盐柱

可事实并非如此，这是因为，当地天气炎热、干旱，死海中湖水的蒸发速度要比河水注入的速度更快。约旦河一直都在源源不断地将盐分带入湖中，而盐分又没法蒸发掉，因此死海就像美国的大盐湖一样，一直都在变得越来越咸。死海比大盐湖更咸，要比海水还咸九倍，因此当然不可能有人溺死在里面了。然而，人们是不会到死海里去游泳的，因为湖水太咸，要是溅到眼睛里、浸到伤口或者皮肤破损处的话，就会像往伤口上涂碘酒那样生疼呢。由于死海周围的含盐量太大，因此那里什么也生长不了，连咸水鱼也无法在湖中生存。我们认为，世界上最邪恶的两座城市，即"所多玛"和"蛾摩拉"城，全都位于死海之滨。《圣经》中称，那两座城市极其邪恶，因此上帝把它们全都摧毁了。如今，除了盖着一层盐的漫漫黄沙，那两座城市什么也没留下了。大家都记得吧，上帝在摧毁所多玛城之前，曾经让罗得带着家人逃离那里，并且吩咐罗得和家人都不要回头去看。可罗得的妻子没有听从上帝的吩咐，后来就变成了一根盐柱子。如今，导游还会指着一大堆盐，对游客说那就是罗得的妻子呢！

51 The "Exact Spots"

There are three most famous places in Palestine. The first is the place where Christ was born, the second is the place where Christ lived, and the third is the place where Christ died.

Christ was born in Bethlehem, which is a dirty little village, not at all like the heavenly place with angels hovering over it that you see in pictures and on Christmas cards. Christ's father and mother were traveling and happened to stop in Bethlehem over night when Christ was born. A church was built over the place where Christ was supposed to have been born, and a silver star is in the floor to mark "the exact spot." The fact is that no one knows "the exact spot," but we do know that the church over the supposed spot is the *oldest* church in the World.

Though Christ was born in Bethlehem, He spent most of His early life in another town in Palestine called Nazareth, for Nazareth was His home town and there His father, Joseph, lived and worked. Joseph was a carpenter, and in Nazareth guides point out Joseph's carpenter shop, the work-bench where Christ worked with the saw and hammer and other tools He used. They also point out the kitchen where Christ's mother, Mary, cooked the meals for the family. But just as we cannot believe what the guides tell us about the "exact spot" in Bethlehem, so we cannot believe what they tell us about most of the "exact spots" in Nazareth. There is, however, one exact spot which we can believe. That is a well where

第51章　　"确切地点"

巴勒斯坦境内，有三个极其有名的地方。其中，第一个就是基督降生之地，第二个就是基督生活之地，而第三个则是基督升天之地。

基督出生于伯利恒，那里是一个肮脏不堪的小村庄，根本就不像你们在电影或者圣诞贺卡上看到的那样，根本就不是一个空中盘旋着天使、宛如天堂般的地方。当时，基督的父亲和母亲正在旅游，无意中在伯利恒停下来过夜，而基督就是在那天晚上降生的。后来，人们在据说是基督降生的那个地方修建了一座教堂，教堂的地面上还有一个银色的星形，标出了基督降生的"确切地点"。实际上，没有人知道这个"确切地点"究竟在哪里，不过，我们却的确很清楚，在这个据说之地修建起来的这座教堂，是世界上历史最为悠久的教堂。

尽管基督出生于伯利恒，但他小时候的大部分时间，却是在巴勒斯坦另一座叫作"拿撒勒"的城镇里度过的，因为拿撒勒是基督的故乡，他的父亲约瑟就在那里生活、工作。约瑟是个木匠，如今到了拿撒勒，导游都会给游客指出约瑟的那个木匠铺子，以及基督用锯子、锤子和其他工具干活时的那个工作台。他们还会指出基督母亲玛利亚为家人做饭的那个厨房呢。不过，正如没法相信伯利恒的导游们告诉我们的那个"确切地点"一样，我们也没法相信，导游们对我们所说的、拿撒勒的

they say Mary went to get water, and this may actually be the same well, for there never has been any other place in Nazareth where one could get water. There was no such thing as running water in each house.

The last most important place in Palestine is the city where Christ died—Jerusalem. Christians call it their Holy City. But, strangely enough, the Mohammedans call it their Holy City too, and it was once the capital of the Jews. Mohammed lived about six hundred years later than Christ, and Mohammedans believe some of the same things about Mohammed that Christians believe about Christ. Mohammed was supposed to have died in Jerusalem and to have ascended into Heaven from there. The Moslems captured Jerusalem and kept hold of it for more than a thousand years. During that long time the Christians have tried time and again to get Jerusalem away from the Moslems. Time and time again the Christians from all over Europe formed armies and marched on Jerusalem, trying to take it away from the Moslems, but they were usually beaten; and though they have held the city for a time, the Moslems have always recaptured it, until at last in World War I the English captured Jerusalem.

Jerusalem has probably been destroyed and built up again more times than any

玛利亚在巴勒斯坦打过水的那口井

拿撒勒的女人如今仍然从这口井里打水

绝大多数"确切地点"都是真的。然而，还是有一个确切的地点，我们是可以相信的。那就是他们称玛利亚曾经去打过水的一口井，这口井可能的确是原来的那口井，因为拿撒勒一直都没有别的地方可以打水。当时，各人家里还没有自来水这种东西呢。

巴勒斯坦最后一个极其重要的地方，就是基督升天的那座城市，也就是耶路撒冷。基督徒都把耶路撒冷称为他们的"圣城"。不过，奇怪得很，穆斯林也说这里是他们的"圣城"，并且这里曾经还是犹太人的首都。穆罕默德生活的时期，比基督大约晚了六百年，而穆斯林信仰的穆罕默德的教义，与基督徒信仰的基督的教义也是一样的。穆罕默德据说也是在耶路撒冷去世的，并且在此升入了天堂。后来穆斯林攻占了耶路撒冷，并且占领了一千多年。在那段漫长的岁月里，基督徒一再试图从穆斯林手中重新夺回耶路撒冷。欧洲各国的基督徒一次又一次地组成军队，向耶路撒冷进发，试图从穆斯林手中夺取该城，可经常被穆斯林打败，尽管期间他们也短暂地占领过耶路撒冷，可穆斯林却一次又一次地重新夺回了该城，直到第一次世界大战期间英国攻取了耶路撒冷，这种情况才彻底改变。

与其他城市相比，耶路撒冷很可能是世界上摧毁和重建次数最多的城市。基督降生的一千年前，大卫王修建起了耶路撒冷。接下来，所罗门王在那里修建了许多

other city in the World. King David built Jerusalem about a thousand years before Christ was born. Then Solomon built his magnificent temple there, but not very long afterward Jerusalem was captured and destroyed. Every once in a while Jerusalem has been captured and destroyed and then built up again, so that they say there are really eight Jerusalems, one on top of the remains of the other. That is one reason why it is impossible to know "the exact spots" where so many things mentioned in the Bible took place.

Men say they have found in Jerusalem the tomb of Adam, the first man. They have also found the tomb of Christ—His sepulcher—and right near Christ's tomb they have found in the rock a hole which they say is where the cross was put when Christ was crucified. Over these places they have built a church, called the Church of the Holy Sepulcher. There is one thing, however, that they could not put under this Church of the Holy Sepulcher—that is, the place from which Christ ascended into Heaven, for that spot us on a hill just outside of Jerusalem, called the Mount of Olives.

The Moslems say Mohammed ascended into Heaven too, and not very far from the Church of the Holy Sepulcher is the place. Over this place the Moslems have built a building called the Mosque of Omar, though it really is not a

奥玛清真寺

穹顶之下是一块巨大的岩石，以前人们常常在石上杀牛献祭

金碧辉煌的宫殿，可不久之后，耶路撒冷就被人占领并摧毁了。后来，耶路撒冷不断地被人占领和摧毁，然后又进行重建，因此，如今人们常说，实际上有八个耶路撒冷，并且每一个都是在前一个的废墟之上建立起来的。我们之所以不可能知道《圣经》中提到的诸多之事发生的"确切地点"到底在哪里，原因之一就在于此。

有人说，他们在耶路撒冷发现了人类始祖亚当的墓穴。他们还发现了基督的墓穴，也就是基督的"圣墓"，并且，就在基督圣墓的不远处，他们还在岩石上面发现一个洞，说基督在十字架上受难时，那个十字架就立在这个洞里。他们在此处修建了一座教堂，叫作"圣墓大教堂"。但是，有一件东西，他们却没法埋在这座圣墓大教堂底下，那就是基督升入天堂的地方，原因就是，那个地方位于耶路撒冷城外一座叫作"橄榄山"的小山上。

穆斯林都说，穆罕默德死后也升入了天堂，而他升入天堂的地点，离圣墓大教堂并不远。在这个地方，穆斯林还修建了一座清真寺，叫作"奥玛清真寺"，不过，那里其实根本就不是一个清真寺，也不是奥玛所建。然而，这座清真寺要比圣墓大教堂漂亮得多，事实上，有些人甚至还说，它是世界上最美丽的建筑之一呢。

mosque at all and was not built by Omar. It is much more beautiful than the Church of the Holy Sepulcher, however, and, indeed, some even say it is one of the most beautiful buildings in the World. It is built over the spot where the wonderful temple of Solomon stood. It is made of beautiful marble and tile and has a bowl-shaped dome.

Underneath the Mosque of Omar is a huge rock on which oxen used to be sacrificed. On this same rock Abraham, so they say, was about to kill his son as he was ordered to do by the Lord, who wanted to test him, when an angel sent by the Lord stopped his hand. From this same rock Mohammed ascended to Heaven—so they say. The stone tried to follow him, but the archangel Gabriel held it back; and finger prints of archangels are shown you to prove the story true.

Part of the Temple of Solomon is still standing. It is a piece of the foundation wall.

犹太教的哭墙

这座清真寺，就建在所罗门王那座奇妙的宫殿原址之上。它是用精美的大理石和瓷砖建成，并且有一个碗状的穹顶。

穹顶之下是一块巨大的岩石，以前人们常常在石上杀牛献祭。人们还说，就是在这块巨石上，亚伯拉罕正准备按照上帝的吩咐杀死自己的儿子（上帝这样做，是为了考验亚伯拉罕），突然上帝派来一位天使，拦住了他。据说，穆罕默德也是在这块岩石上升天的。那块巨石本想跟着他一起升天，可"大天使"加百利[1]却挡住了它，如今，导游还会给游客看"大天使"留在石上的手指印，以此来证明这个传说是真的呢。

所罗门王修建的那座神庙，如今有一部分仍然屹立在那里。那是一堵挡土墙。

---

[1] 加百利（Gabriel），《圣经》故事中替上帝把好消息告诉世人的天使，属于七大天使中的报喜天使，参见《但以理书》《路加福音》等。

Ever since the temple was destroyed Jews have gone there to weep and to pray that their country, which the ancient Romans took from them, would be restored to them. It is called the Wailing Wall. Jews lived in many countries but there was no Jewish country that they could call their own. After World War II, however, the United Nations voted to divide Palestine into two parts. One part, they said, should be for Jews and would be the country that Jews for two thousand years had prayed to have. The other part, the United Nations said, should be for the many Arab Mohammedans who lived in Palestine. So at last the Jews had a country of their own. They named it Israel. Israel is the part of Palestine on the east next to the Mediterranean Sea. The western part of Palestine became part of the Arab country of Jordan. Jerusalem, which is the holy city for both Mohammedans and Jews, was divided also. The western and newer part of Jerusalem belongs to Israel and the eastern and older part belongs to the Mohammedans.

Israel is a republic. Though some of the oldest cities in the World are in Israel, the Jews made one of the newest cities in the World the capital of the new country, the city of Tel Aviv. Tel Aviv has modern buildings and wide straight streets and it is very clean and neat, much different from the old cities with their narrow, dirty streets. Many Jews from other countries have gone to live in Israel. They are welcome there, for Israel is the home land of the Jews.

自从那座神庙被毁之后，犹太人便一直前往墙下哭泣哀悼，祈祷他们那个曾经被古罗马人占领的国家能够重新回到自己的手中。这堵墙，就叫"哭墙"。犹太人散居世界各国，一直都没有一个属于他们自己的犹太国。然而，第二次世界大战过后，联合国提出将巴勒斯坦分成两个部分。联合国称，其中一个部分应当给予犹太人，应当成为犹太人已经祈祷了两千多年的那个国家。联合国又说，另一部分应当成为一个容纳那些居住在巴勒斯坦的阿拉伯穆斯林的国度。于是，犹太人终于有了一个属于他们自己的国家。他们把这个国家命名为"以色列"。巴勒斯坦的西部，则成了约旦这个阿拉伯国家的一部分。而同属于穆斯林和犹太教圣城的耶路撒冷，也进行了分割。耶路撒冷城较新的西部归以色列，而较老的东部则归穆斯林。

以色列是一个共和国。尽管世界上历史最悠久的一些城市都位于以色列，但犹太人却把世界上最现代化的一座城市，即特拉维夫城，当成以色列这个新兴国家的首都。特拉维夫市内有现代化的建筑、宽阔笔直的街道，并且非常干净、整洁，与原来那些古城里街道狭窄、肮脏不堪的情景形成了天渊之别。许多犹太人纷纷离开其他各国，到以色列来生活。他们都受到了热烈的欢迎，因为以色列就是犹太人的家园啊。

52 The Garden of Eden

Of course, you have heard of the Garden of Eden, haven't you? When I was a boy I thought that when I was old enough to travel I should like to go and see it for myself. I should like to see whether or not the angels with fiery swords were still there. So I asked my Sunday school teacher where the Garden of Eden was. "It's in the Bible," said she. That didn't help me much. But grown-up people have been looking for the Garden of Eden for a great many years and some say they have found it, or rather that they have found the place where it once was, for it does not look like a garden now, much less like a Paradise.

If you were in Damascus and asked a man on the street, "How do you get to the Garden of Eden?" he might think you were crazy, or maybe he might say, "I'm a stranger here myself." But if he did know the way, he would point to the east and say, "You cross the desert and keep going straight ahead toward the rising sun. In about a month, if you are going by camel, or in a couple of days, if you are going by automobile, you will come to a muddy river. This river is called the Euphrates. Cross the Euphrates and go on a short distance and you will come to a second muddy river. This second muddy river is called the Tigris. These two rivers flow into each other, and near the place where the two rivers join, there you'll find the Garden of Eden. You can't miss it."

There is no garden there now and you may wonder how there ever could have been a

第52章 伊甸园

大家当然都听说过伊甸园了，对不对？我小的时候曾经想过，等我长大了，可以旅行之后，就应当去亲自看一看这个地方。我想要看一看，那里是不是还有携带着火焰之剑的天使。于是，我便问主日学校的老师，伊甸园到底在哪里。"在《圣经》里啊。"她回答道。这个答案对我可没多少用。不过，大人们多年来一直都在寻找伊甸园，有些人还称他们发现了这个地方，或者更准确一点来说，是发现了伊甸园曾经所在的地方，因为如今那里看上去可不像是一个花园，更别说像是天堂了。

假如大家身处大马士革，问街上的一位行人："要怎样才能到达伊甸园呢？"那位行人可能会觉得你们都疯了，或者他没准会这样回答："我对这里也不熟。"不过，要是那人真的知道怎么走的话，他就会指着东方，说："您穿过沙漠，一直朝着太阳升起的方向走。要是骑骆驼的话，差不多一个月后，要是坐汽车的话，则只要几天之后，您就会来到一条泥泞的河边。那条河，叫作'幼发拉底河'。跨过幼发拉底河，走上不远的路，您就会来到第二条混浊不堪的河流边上。这第二条泥泞的河流，叫作'底格里斯河'。这两条河流相互交汇，而在距两河交汇之处不远的地方，您就会看到伊甸园了。您不会找不到的。"

如今，那里可没有什么花园了，并且大家甚至可能会觉得奇怪，那里以前怎

garden there, for most of it is now mud, and, when there has been no rain for a long time, just baked mud ground, which looks as little like a Garden of Eden as you could possibly imagine. Nevertheless, people think this is where the Garden of Eden once was. They even point out an old apple-tree that once bore some apples and say, "That's the original tree." They think the Great Flood took place between these rivers. They think that Noah lived down there somewhere, that he built his ark down there, and that the Flood came and flooded all this valley between the two rivers, and when the Flood was over, the Ark was left high and dry on the top of Mount Ararat, a mountain way up above where the rivers rise. This valley between the two rivers was called Mesopotamia, because "Meso" means "between" and "potamia" means "rivers." But it is now called Iraq, and that is the name you will see on the map.

On the Tigris River, high up, there used to be a big city called Nineveh, and on the Euphrates, farther down toward where the two rivers meet, there used to be another big city called Babylon. I say "used to be," for although these two cities were the largest cities in the World before Christ was born, they have almost completely disappeared.

Have you ever built on the beach or in a sand pile a town of houses and streets

有些人说，他们找到了伊甸园

么可能有一个花园，因为那里全都是泥，要是长时间没有下雨的话，就会是一片干泥地，样子与大家想象中的伊甸园根本就不像。尽管如此，人们还是认为，那里就是以前伊甸园所在的地方呢。他们甚至会指着一棵以前结过果实的老苹果树，说："它就是最初的那棵树。"他们相信，"大洪水"就发生在那两条河流之间。他们还认为，挪亚住在此处以南的某个地方，并在那里建造出了方舟，"大洪水"爆发时，淹掉了两河之间的这片河谷，而当洪水退却之后，那艘方舟便搁浅到了地势很高、很干燥的亚拉拉特山顶上了，因为当时洪水一直涨到了山顶呢。两河之间的这片流域，叫作美索不达米亚（Mesopotamia），其中的"美索"（Meso）指的是"之间"，而"不达米亚"（potamia）指的就是"河流"。不过，这里如今叫作"伊拉克"，而你们在地图上看到的也是这个名称了。

在底格里斯河的上游，曾经有过一座大城市，叫作"尼尼微"，而在幼发拉底河的下游，靠近两河交汇之处，曾经也有过一座大城市，叫作"巴比伦"。我之所以说"曾经有过"，是因为尽管二者是基督降生以前世界上最大的两座城市，但如今它们几乎都已经消失得无影无踪了。

and then some big bully has come along, tramped on it, stamped on it, and kicked it to pieces? Well, Nineveh and Babylon look as if some giant had come along and stamped all over them and kicked them all to pieces, for about all there is to be seen of them now are piles of dirt. Men have been digging in the piles for many years and they have found buried under the dirt some of the things the people of these cities once had in their homes and shops and schools and palaces, for these cities had some of the finest houses and palaces ever built. The walls and gardens of Babylon were once one of the Seven Wonders of the World, but practically nothing is now left of them.

Though Nineveh and Babylon are gone—their names are not even on the map—there are today two big cities on the Tigris that are very much alive, with people living in them. One of these cities is just across the river from where Nineveh used to be. It is called Mosul. You know what muslin is, don't you? Well, muslin was first made in Mosul, so this kind of cloth was called "Mosulin," which became muslin.

Not many years ago people discovered oil in the country round Mosul, enough oil to run all the automobiles in the World. The difficulty was to get the oil to the automobiles. Pipe lines were built from the oil wells to the Mediterranean Sea miles away. The oil is pumped through the pipes and then is loaded on ships. The ships are really floating tanks and so are called tankers. The tankers carry the oil to America and to Europe.

Mosul is a Moslem town. On the great mosque there is a minaret that leans, something like the Leaning Tower of Pisa. People say that Mohammed was once passing this minaret

　　大家有没有过在海滩或者沙堆上堆好一个有房屋、街道的小镇，然后某个大块头坏蛋走过来，在上面踩啊踏啊，踢得你们所堆的小镇七零八落的经历呢？好吧，尼尼微和巴比伦的情况，正像是某个巨人走过来，在两城上面乱踩一通，将它们全都踩得粉碎似的，所以两地如今都只剩下一堆堆黄土了。多年来，人们一直在这些土堆下面进行挖掘，发现了黄土下面埋藏着两地古代居民曾经用过的一些家具，还有商店、学校和宫殿，因为这两座城市里，的确曾经有过人类历史上修建得最为精美的一些房屋和宫殿。巴比伦的墙壁和花园，曾经还属于"世界七大奇迹"之一呢，可如今，那里却几乎什么也没有留下。

　　尽管尼尼微和巴比伦都已经消失在历史的长河中，连两地的名称也不再出现在地图上了，但如今的底格里斯河上，又出现了两座兴旺蓬勃、人们安居乐业的大城市。其中一座，就在尼尼微原址的河对岸，叫作"摩苏尔"。大家都知道"平纹细布"是什么东西，对吧？注意，平纹细布最初就是在摩苏尔生产出来的，因此人们叫这种布料为"摩苏尔细布"，后来就演变成平纹细布了。

　　不久前，人们在摩苏尔周围的乡村发现了石油，并且那里的储量足供全世界的汽车所用。但要将这些石油开采出来，用于汽车上，却是个难题。人们修建了输油管道，从油井一直通到数英里之外的地中海海滨。他们用泵将石油泵入管道，然后装上船只。这些船只实际上就是漂浮在水上的油罐，因此叫作"油轮"。然后，油轮再将石油运送到美国和欧洲去。

　　摩苏尔是一座信奉伊斯兰教的城市。该市的大清真寺里，有一座斜着的宣礼

and it bowed to him and was never able to get entirely straight again—it's still leaning.

Have you ever read the stories of *Ali Baba* and *Sindbad the Sailor*? Down the Tigris River below Mosul is another big city called Bagdad. The people you see there on the streets look like the people you see in the pictures in the "Arabian Nights." Bagdad in summer is one of the hottest places you can imagine. It is sometimes 125°, and you know that 100° is about as hot as we can stand. The streets used to be like narrow alleys, dirty and smelly. But after World War I, England ruled over Iraq and Bagdad and the English made great changes. They built a wide street right through the city and called it New Street. They put in electric lights and ice factories which Bagdad had never had before. Then they had the people vote for a king, and Iraq has been a kingdom ever since. It is still under the protection of England, however, and a few Englishmen stay there to help train the army of Iraq.

巴格达市内的一条街道

难题：找出阿里巴巴和四十大盗来

塔，有点儿与比萨斜塔相似。人们都说，穆罕默德有一次经过了这座宣礼塔，宣礼塔向他鞠躬，此后便没能再直立起来了，如今，这座宣礼塔仍然倾斜着呢。

大家有没有看过《阿里巴巴与四十大盗》和《辛巴达历险记》呢？在底格里斯河的下游，过了摩苏尔，还有一座大城市，叫作"巴格达"。要是去了那里的话，你们在大街上看到的人物，就会很像大家在《一千零一夜》的插图里看到的那些人物了。夏季的巴格达，是我们能够想象到的最炎热的地方之一。那里有的时候气温会高达华氏125°，而大家也都知道，气温达到华氏100°，就会热得我们受不了呢。那里的街道，以前就像是一条条狭窄的小巷子，又脏又臭。不过，第一次世界大战结束后，英国曾经统治过伊拉克和巴格达，因此英国人让这座城市有了很大的改观。他们修建了一条贯穿整座城市的宽阔大街，称之为"新街"。他们开通了电灯，开设了冰厂，都是巴格达以前从未有过的。接下来，他们又让民众投票选举出了一位国王，自那以后，伊拉克就成了一个王国。然而，如今伊拉克仍然处于英国的保护之下，并且还有一部分英国人留在那里，协助训练伊拉克的军队[1]。

---

[1] 1920年，伊拉克沦为英国的"委任统治区"；1921年8月宣布独立，成立伊拉克王国，在英国保护下建立费萨尔王朝；1932年获得完全独立；1958年费萨尔王朝被推翻，成立了伊拉克共和国。

53 The Land of Bedtime Stories

Have you ever been thirsty—really thirsty? Very few people in our country ever have. Have you ever gone for more than one whole day without a drink of water? Some people have gone without food for days and even weeks, but no one ever has gone without water for as long as a week. Suppose that you lived in a country where there is not a single river nor lake in the whole land, where it seldom, if ever, rains, where there is practically no water to drink and even less for washing—a country that is almost surrounded by water, but water you can't drink because it is salt—a country that is a desert except for a little fringe around the edge and damp spots here and there. That country is Arabia, the home of the Arab people. How can any one live there? The answer is that people can only live along the edges or in those few spots where there is water. These spots are called oases. Dates are bread and butter, meat and dessert to an Arab. Dates grow on palm-trees, so the Arabs plant palm-trees in deep holes in order that their roots may be far down where the ground is a little damp. The well-to-do Arab has a camel, because that is the only animal that can stand hardships such as lack of food and water for any length of time; also, he has a few goats or sheep and a horse. The Arab horses are small but they are swift runners. Some say they are the finest in the World, and many of our race-horses have come from Arab stock.

第53章　睡前故事之国

大家有没有过极其口渴的时候，就是实在渴得受不了的那种时候呢？在我们美国，有过此种经历的人很少。大家有没有过在大于一整天的时间里不喝一口水的经历呢？有些人曾经数天不吃东西，甚至是好几周不吃东西，然后什么事情也没有，不过，无人能够在一周的时间里不喝水却依然活着。假设你们生活在这样的一个国家里：该国境内没有一条河流，也没有一个湖泊，很少下雨，而就算下了雨的话，雨量实际上也很小，几乎没有饮用水，而用于洗漱的水就更少了，虽说这个国家周围全都是水，却都是无法饮用的海水，除了四周一小圈，以及零散分布的湿润之地，该国境内全都是沙漠。这个国家，就是"阿拉比亚"，即"阿拉伯人的家园"。一个人，怎么可能在那样的地方生存下去呢？答案就是，人们只能在沙漠边缘或者那些为数不多的、有水的地方生活。这些地方，叫作"绿洲"。对于阿拉伯人来说，椰枣就是面包和黄油、肉类和甜点。椰枣长在棕榈树上，阿拉伯人在地上挖出一个个深坑来种植棕榈树，以便让树根深入到地下稍微湿润一点儿的地方。家境殷实的阿拉伯人，都有一头骆驼，因为它是唯一一种能够忍受诸如食物和饮水缺乏、令人无法支撑很长时间等艰苦条件的牲畜，而且，这种人家通常还有几头山羊、绵羊或者一匹马。阿拉伯马的体型很小，但跑得很快。有些人还说，阿拉伯马是世界上最好的马，因此美国许多的赛马，都是来自阿拉伯地区呢。

The Arabs are very much like all boys and girls in one particular—they love to listen to good stories, especially at night. They can't get enough of them. Once upon a time there was a king in the old days long ago when kings could put to death whomsoever they wished. This king had a wife whom he was going to put to death the next morning, but she told him a bedtime story which so interested him he wanted to hear another. So, on condition that he would spare her life one more day, she promised to tell him another story the next night. And again, day after day, he postponed putting her to death in order that he might hear another story at night. This she kept on doing for one thousand nights and one night more for good measure until the king could no longer live without her stories, so his queen was saved. Some of the most famous of these stories have been translated into English. They are called the "Arabian Nights."

Arabia was the birthplace of Mohammed, the man who started the Mohammedan religion. Mohammed was born in a place called Mecca about six hundred years after Christ was born. He was a camel-driver for a rich widow, who fell in love with him and married him. Mohammed thought he was called by God to be His messenger. His wife and friends believed in him, but his neighbors did not, so they ran him out of Mecca. He fled to the next town, Medina, where he preached to the

阿拉伯人的马匹、绵羊和山羊

阿拉伯人有一个方面与所有的小朋友都非常相似，那就是他们都喜欢听好的故事，尤其是在晚上来听。他们是怎么听也听不够。从前有一位国王，生活在很久以前的古代，那时国王还可以随心所欲地处死一个人。这个国王有一位妻子，他本打算第二天早上就处死她。不过，当天晚上她给国王讲了一个睡前故事，因为故事非常有意思，所以国王还想再听一个。于是，王后对国王说，只要让她多活一天，她就答应第二天晚上再给国王讲一个故事。这样，日复一日，国王为了在晚上能够听到妻子再讲个故事，便一次又一次地推迟了处死王后。王后连续讲了一千个晚上的故事，并且还多讲了一个晚上，直到国王不听她讲故事就活不下去的程度，于是，王后便得救了。其中最著名的一些故事，都已经翻译成了英语。它们合起来，就叫《一千零一夜》。

阿拉比亚是穆罕默德的出生地，穆罕默德就是那个开创了伊斯兰教的人。距基督降生差不多六百年后，穆罕默德在一个叫作"麦加"的地方出生了。他长大以后，成了替一位有钱寡妇赶骆驼的人，寡妇爱上了他，后来还嫁给了他。穆罕默德相信，自己受到了上帝的召唤，要去当上帝的信使。妻子和朋友们都很信任他，可邻居却不是这样，便把他赶出了麦加。他逃到了邻近的一座城市"麦地那"，然后在那里向民众布道。不久之后，就有成千上万的人信奉他的教理，服从他的教义了，如今，信奉穆罕默德的人数，达到了信奉基督的人数的三分之一左右。穆罕默德认为，麦加是世界的中心。虽说耶路撒冷也是穆斯林的圣城之一，但麦加才是其中

people, and before long there were millions who followed him and obeyed his teachings, and now to-day there are about one third as many people who believe in Mohammed as believe in Christ. Mohammedans think Mecca is the center of the World. Jerusalem is one of their holy cities, but Mecca is their holiest of holies. Medina, which means simply "The City," is second only to Mecca in holiness. The Mohammedans think that one prayer said at Medina is worth a thousand prayers said anywhere else, so Mohammedans send long distances to have prayers said for them in Medina.

The Mohammedans have commandments as the Christians do. We have ten; they have four or more. One of their commandments is to pray five times a day; another is to give a present to every beggar who asks—it doesn't matter how little—it may be less than a penny; a third is to fast for a month each year—that's something like Lent; and a fourth is to make a trip to Mecca some time during their lives. Such a trip is called a pilgrimage, and every Mohammedan, no matter where or how far off he lives, hopes to make a pilgrimage to Mecca some time before he dies. A great Mohammedan king named Aaron the Just once made the trip from Bagdad to Mecca—hundreds of miles—all the way on foot, but as he was a king, the whole way was covered with carpet for him to walk on!

Have you ever seen a "shooting-star" in the sky? Most shooting-stars usually burn up before they reach the ground, but some do not. At Mecca there is a mosque and inside this mosque is a black stone called The Kaaba. The Mohammedans say this stone was sent down from heaven, and that may be true, for it is probably a shooting-star that fell to the

---

最为神圣的地方。"麦地那"这个名称，本义只是指"城市"，可实际上，它却是仅次于麦加的穆斯林圣地。穆斯林都认为，在麦地那祷告一次，相当于在其他地方祷告一千次，因此，如今的穆斯林都会不远万里，请人在麦地那为他们做祷告呢。

穆斯林也有像基督教那样的戒律。我们基督徒有"十诫"，他们则有"四诫"或者更多。他们的第一条戒律，就是每天要祷告五次；还有一条戒律，就是要送给每个开口乞讨的乞丐一件礼物，但礼物大小并不要紧，可以是连一分钱也不值的东西；第三条戒律就是每年都要斋戒一个月，这有点儿像是基督教的"大斋节"[1]；第四条戒律则是一生中应当去麦加一次，此种旅程，叫作"朝拜"，每一位穆斯林，不管住在哪里，不管所住之地距麦加有多遥远，都希望自己死前某个时候能够去麦加朝拜一次呢，有位叫作"正直者哈伦"[2]的、了不起的穆斯林国王，曾经从巴格达前往麦加朝圣，一路有数百英里，全是步行，可由于他是国王，因此一路上全都铺了地毯，供他在上面行走呢！

---

[1] 大斋节（Lent），基督教的斋戒节期。《新约圣经》载，耶稣开始传教前，曾在旷野守斋祈祷四十昼夜。该节期始于"圣灰节"，终于"复活节"的前一天，总共四十六天。教徒在此期间应守四十天斋戒，一般于星期五守大斋和小斋，周日不守，所谓斋戒，就是少量摄食，以鱼代肉。节期内教堂祭台上不供花，教徒也不举行婚配，停止娱乐。新教多数宗派不守此节日。亦称"封斋节"。

[2] 正直者哈伦（Aaron the Just），即哈伦·拉希德（Haroun al Rashid，约764—809），阿拉伯阿拔斯王朝第五任哈里发（即国王）。在他统治的二十三年间，国势强盛，经济繁荣，文化发达，首都巴格达成为阿拉伯帝国的政治、经济、文化中心和文人学士荟萃的著名城市。

ground before it burned up. The Mohammedans think, if they kiss this stone, all their sins are forgiven and they will go to Heaven and have a high place there when they die. They say this stone was once white, but it has been turned black by all the sins that have gone into it from the countless kisses of Mohammedans. A railroad one thousand miles long has been built from Damascus to Medina, and there is now a bus line from Medina to Mecca, but this railroad and bus are only for pilgrims, for none but Mohammedans are allowed in either city—Mecca or Medina.

I have told you of a White Sea and a Black Sea. Here is a Red Sea. It is a long, narrow sea bordering Arabia. I don't know why it's called Red, unless it is because it's red hot, for I have been there, and the water is as blue as the Mediterranean. There is a little strip of land that used to separate the Red Sea from the Mediterranean, but men have dug a canal through this strip of land so that ships may pass from the one sea to the other. This strip of land is the Isthmus of Suez and the canal across it is called the Suez Canal.

通往麦加

哈伦·拉希德

一路上数百英里都铺了地毯，供国王在上面行走

大家有没有见过天空中一闪而逝的"流星"呢？绝大多数流星在坠到地上之前，就已经焚毁了，但还有一些则没有。麦加有座清真寺，里面有一块黑黝黝的石头，叫作"克尔白"。穆斯林都说，这块石头是天堂送来的，的确可能如此，因为这很可能是一块还没有燃烧殆尽就掉到了地上的流星陨石。穆斯林们认为，要是亲吻这块石头的话，他们的所有罪孽就会得到赦免，死后就会升入天堂，并且在天堂里享有尊贵的地位。他们都说，这块石头以前是白色的，但如今因为亲吻它的穆斯林数不胜数，这些人的罪孽转移到石头上，就把石头染黑了。人们修建了一条从大马士革通往麦加、长达一千英里的铁路，而如今从麦地那到麦加也有了一条公交线路，不过，这条铁路和公交线路只用于运送朝圣者，因为麦加和麦地那这两座城市都只允许穆斯林进入呢。

我在前面已经跟你们说过一个白海、一个黑海了。这里则有一个红海。它是一个又长又窄、濒临阿拉比亚的海洋。除非是因为那里天气炎热（我曾经去过那里），否则我就不知道，人们为什么把这里叫作"红海"，而红海中的海水，其实也像地中海那样湛蓝。那里有一片小小的陆地，曾经将红海与地中海隔了开来，可后来人们在这处陆地上开凿了一条运河，从而让船舶可以在红海和地中海之间来去了。这块条状的陆地，叫作"苏伊士地峡"，而其中开凿的那条运河，就叫"苏伊士运河"。

The Suez Canal is one of the most important canals ever dug. It is important because, before it was dug, this little isthmus that tied together the two big continents of Africa and Asia, barred the way to ships and they had to go all the way round Africa to get to the east side of the World. It is a water gateway to the east part of the World and England owns it.

The driest city in the World is at the lower end of the Red Sea. It is called Aden. Aden is often called the Gibraltar of the East, for the English own Aden too, and they hold on to it even though it is so dry, because then they can say who shall or shall not pass through the Red Sea. Three gateways for ships between the Atlantic and the Indian Oceans—Gibraltar, Suez, Aden—and England owns all three!

There are no springs nor lakes nor rivers at Aden, and often it does not rain there for years, so the people cannot get drinking-water in any of the usual ways. But the English have found a way. They boil the sea water to get the salt out of it and store it in huge tanks so that they have plenty of fresh water all the time.

You may never have heard of Arabia till now, yet you write Arabic every day of your life, for all the figures we use are Arabic—1, 2, 3, 4, 5. There are only ten figures, as you know, but with those ten figures you can make any number from one to a billion, or more.

Arabia seems far away—a dry and desolate land that could have no connection with us—and yet if there had been no Arabia we should have no figures and no "Arabian Nights."

　　苏伊士运河是人类开凿出来的、最重要的运河之一。之所以重要，是因为在开凿之前，这个连接亚、非两大洲的小地峡阻挡了船只的去路，船只必须绕过整个非洲，才能到达地球的东面。因此，苏伊士运河便是从地球西面通往东面的大门，如今，它归英国所有。

　　世界上最干旱的城市，就坐落在红海的南端。这座城市，叫作"亚丁"。人们经常称亚丁是"东方的直布罗陀"，而亚丁也归英国所有，并且尽管那里如此干旱，英国人还是坚守着那里，因为那样的话，他们就有权决定哪些船只可以通过红海了。因此，船只从大西洋通往印度洋，就要经历三道门户，即直布罗陀、苏伊士运河与亚丁，而这三道大门，都在英国手里呢！

　　亚丁既没有泉水、湖泊，也没有河流，并且那里经常是数年不下雨，因此亚丁人是没有办法按照常规的方式获取饮用水的。不过，英国人找到了一种办法。他们将海水煮沸，滤掉其中的盐分，然后用巨型水罐将淡水储存起来，从而时时都有淡水可用了。

　　直到此前，大家可能都没有听说过"阿拉比亚"这个地方，不过，你们的一生当中，每天都会用到阿拉伯文呢，因为我们所用的数字，如1，2，3，4，5，就是阿拉伯数字。大家都知道，总共只有十个阿拉伯数字，但是，你们可以用这十个阿拉伯数字，写出从一到十亿乃至任意一个更大的数字来。

　　对我们来说，阿拉比亚似乎非常遥远，似乎是一个与我们不可能有什么联系的干旱、荒凉之地，不过，要是没有阿拉比亚的话，我们就不会有阿拉伯数字，也不会有《一千零一夜》了。

54 The Lion and the Sun

Have you ever seen a Persian cat? They are big, beautiful animals with soft thick hair. They come from Persia.

Persia is one of those "once-was" or "used-to-be" countries too. It used to be the greatest country i.t.w.W., yet many people now do not even know exactly where Persia is and can't even find it when they look for it on a map—for the Persian name for Persia is Iran and most maps now say Iran instead of Persia. As I look around me in my home where I'm writing this, I find, to my surprise, I can count nearly a dozen things that have come from Persia or are connected with Persia, though before I began to count I should have said not a single thing Persian did I own.

The rug at my feet was made in Persia, entirely by hand. It was woven of woolen threads in beautiful colored designs and must have taken some Persian many months, perhaps a year or more, to make. Some Persian rugs are said to have taken one person the whole of his lifetime to make.

My wife has a silken shawl also woven by hand in Persia. The silkworms were raised there, the cocoons unwound, the silk spun into thread, dyed in many colors, and then woven into this shawl.

She has a ring set with greenish blue stones, called Turquoises. A turquoise is the birth-

第54章　狮子与太阳

大家有没有见过波斯猫呢？这是一种体型很大、样子很漂亮的动物，身上有着柔软而厚实的皮毛。它们产自波斯。

波斯也是一个"曾经存在"或者"过去存在"的国家。波斯曾经是世界上最大的国家，然而，如今仍有许多人却连波斯的准确地点在哪儿都不知道，甚至在地图上也找不到这个国家呢。这是因为，在波斯语里，"波斯"一词就是"伊朗"，如今绝大多数地图上，标注的都是"伊朗"，而不是"波斯"了。在家中编写本书时，我环顾了一下四周，惊讶地发现，我家竟然数出十来件产自波斯或者与波斯有关的东西来，尽管在开始数之前，我本来该说自己连一件产自波斯或者与波斯相关的东西都没有。

我脚下踩着的地毯产自波斯，并且完全是手工编织而成的。它是用棉线编织的，上面有一些精美的图案，一定是某位波斯人花了好几个月，没准还是花了一年或者更久的时间编织出来的。据说，有些波斯地毯还是一个人花费毕生的心血制作出来的呢。

我的妻子有一条丝质围巾，也是波斯人手工织就的。那里的人养殖桑蚕，剥开茧子，将蚕丝纺织成线，染出五颜六色，然后再织出了这条围巾。

她还有一个镶嵌着绿蓝色宝石的戒指，此种宝石，叫作"绿松石"。绿松石

stone of December, and they too come from Persia. In some countries of the East people wear turquoises to keep away what is called the "evil eye." They believe that some persons can do them harm by looking at them, and the turquoise prevents this "evil eye" harming them.

On my wife's dressing-table is a small thin bottle of perfume called attar of roses. In some parts of Persia they grow the most beautiful and fragrant roses and from their petals this perfume is made.

I have a scarf-pin in which is a pearl that came from an oyster that was brought up from the bottom of the Persian Gulf by a naked diver.

My bath slippers—big, sloppy slip-ons, with heels turned down—are Persian.

The electric light I am writing under is a Mazda lamp, and Mazda was the old Persian god of light.

In my bookcase is a book called "The Rubáiyát." It is a book of poetry written by a Persian named Omar Khayyám.

For breakfast I might have had a melon, and melons were first grown in Persia. Our melons are grown from seeds brought many years ago to this country from Persia.

What I did have for breakfast were peaches, and these too were first grown in Persia. Peach-stones were brought to this country and from these our first peach-trees were grown.

If I had a Persian cat this would complete the picture, but I have a dog instead.

是十二月份的诞生石[1]，也产自波斯。在一些东方国家里，人们佩戴绿松石是为了挡住所谓的"邪恶之眼"。他们认为，有些人能够用双眼紧盯的方式对他们造成伤害，而绿松石则能够不让这种"邪恶之眼"伤害到他们。

我妻子的梳妆台上，有一个小而扁的瓶子，里面装着一种叫作"玫瑰油"的香水。在波斯有些地方，人们种植出了最漂亮、最芳香的玫瑰，而这种香水，就是从玫瑰花瓣里提炼出来的。

我有一个领带夹，上面有一颗珍珠，这颗珍珠，是一位赤身裸体的潜水者从波斯湾海底捞起的一只牡蛎体内取出来的。

我的浴室拖鞋也产自波斯，那是一双尺寸很大、很宽松的便鞋，鞋跟很矮。

我在写字时所用的电灯，灯泡是"玛兹达"牌，而玛兹达正是古代波斯的光明之神呢。

我的书柜里有一本书，叫作《鲁拜集》。那是一本诗集，是一个叫作欧玛尔·海亚姆的波斯诗人写的。

我在早餐的时候可能会吃上一个柠檬，而柠檬最初就生长在波斯。我们的柠檬，是用许多年前人们从波斯带到美国来的柠檬种子栽培出来的。

早餐时我还吃了桃子，而桃子最初也产自波斯。后来，人们将桃核带到了美

---

[1] 诞生石（birth-stone），指象征诞辰吉祥的宝石，从1月至12月分别为：石榴石、紫晶、血纹绿宝石、金刚石、绿宝石、珍珠、红宝石、缠丝玛瑙、蓝宝石、蛋白石、黄玉和绿松石。

Persia is called the Land of the Lion and the Sun, and the Persian flag has a lion and a sun on it. I do not know why there a lion, but the sun is on it because the people of that country used to worship the sun. The sun was their god. They also worshiped the stars, moon, and fire, so we call them fire-worshipers, but they call themselves Parsees. The fire-worshipers' chief god was called Mazda and that is where we get the name for our electric-light bulbs. According to their religion, everything that was light was good and everything that was dark was bad. A few Persians are still fire-worshipers, but most are now Mohammedans.

The good part of Persia, like the little girl who had a little curl, is very, very good, but the bad part is horrid. In the part that is good, beautiful roses, fine melons and peaches grow, but much of Persia is desert. Most rivers get bigger and bigger as they flow along, but the Persian rivers get smaller and smaller and at last dwindle away to nothing. There are a great many mountains in Persia, and when the melted snows come down from these mountains they form streams, but many of these streams do not empty anywhere; they just dry up; they have no mouths.

Did you ever play charades? Here is a word we used to act out when I played charades, though we pronounced the word incorrectly. In the first act two girls would play drinking tea. In the second act

国，从而用它们培育出了美国的第一棵桃树。

如果我有一只波斯猫的话，那么一切就完美了，不过，我养的却是一条小狗。

波斯被称为"狮子和太阳之国"，因而波斯的国旗上也印有一头狮子和一个太阳的标志。我不知道为什么会有一只狮子，但波斯国旗上之所以有个太阳，是因为该国的人以前崇拜太阳。太阳就是他们的上帝。他们也崇拜星星、月亮和火，因此我们称之为"拜火教"教徒，可他们却自称为"帕西人"。拜火教的主神叫作"玛兹达"，而美国的"玛兹达"牌电灯泡，就是得名于此。按照他们的那种宗教，凡属光明的东西都是好的，凡属黑暗的东西都是坏的。如今，少量波斯人仍然信仰拜火教，但绝大多数波斯人都是穆斯林了。

波斯好的方面极其好，就像一个有着小小卷发的小姑娘一样，而不好的方面则极其恐怖。好的方面有种植美丽的玫瑰啦，有优质的柠檬和桃子啦，可波斯很多地方都是沙漠。绝大多数河流在滔滔前行的过程中都会变得越来越宽阔，可波斯的河流却是一路越变越小，最终还会因为水量减少而消失不见呢。波斯有很多的崇山峻岭，当这些山上的积雪融化下流之后，就会形成一条条小溪，可那些小溪中，有许多都没有注入任何地方，只到半路就干涸了，因此都没有什么河口可言。

大家都玩过"看手势猜字谜"这种游戏没有呢？有一个词，在我以前玩猜字谜游戏的时候，大家经常用到，可我们经常都会把这个词说错。第一步，两个小姑娘会做出喝茶的样子。第二步，一个小男孩会从房间的这一头跑到那一头。两步加起

a boy would run across the room. The two acts made the capital of Persia. Can you guess it? It is "Tehran." Another charade can be acted out in only one act. A boy runs across the room and then points to himself. Can you guess this one? It is "Iran," the Persian name of the country.

The ruler of Persia is called, not a king, but a Shah. Once upon a time the Shah could do anything he wished with his people. He could take all their money away from them and put them to death, if he wished to do so; but all that has long been changed. In Tehran is the most famous jeweled throne in the World. It is called the Peacock Throne. It is made of solid gold and the back is in the form of a peacock's tail studded with rubies, emeralds, and sapphires—red, green, and blue precious stones.

All jewels, such as diamonds, rubies, and emeralds, come out of the ground—all except one. But one jewel does not come out of the ground. It comes out of the water, out of an oyster. This jewel is the pearl. The oyster makes a pearl around a grain of sand that has gotten into his shell and annoys him. So at the center of each pearl is a tiny grain of sand. It takes an oyster four or five years to make a pearl the size of a pea. In the Persian Gulf the finest pearls are found. The oysters are not good to eat, but are gathered for the pearls that are to be found in them. Men dive for the oysters, staying under the water long enough to go down to the bottom, gather a basket of oysters and come up to the top—as long as they can hold their breath. You can probably hold your breath only half a minute, but a pearl-diver can hold his for a minute or longer, and it is said that some have been able to

来，谜底就是波斯的首都。你们猜出来了没有呢？谜底就是"德黑兰"[1]。还有一个字谜游戏，只需一步就可以表演出来。一个小男孩从屋子的这头跑到那头，然后指着自己。这个字谜，你们猜得出来吗？答案就是"伊朗"，也就是该国在波斯语里的名称。

波斯的君主不称"国王"，而称"沙"。从前，伊朗王可以随心所欲地对待手下的臣民。他可以将臣民手中的钱财全部掠走，并且只要愿意，就可以处死臣民，不过，那种情况早已变了。世界上最著名的一张镶有宝石的王座，就在德黑兰，叫作"孔雀宝座"。这张宝座是用纯金制成，背面是孔雀尾巴的形状，上面镶嵌着红宝石、绿宝石和蓝宝石，也就是红色、绿色和蓝色的宝石。

所有珠宝，比如钻石、红宝石和绿宝石，全都是从地下开采出来的，只有一种例外。有一种珠宝并不是来自地下。它来自水中，是从牡蛎当中采集出来的。这种珠宝，就是珍珠。牡蛎会在进入自己体内、让它觉得很不舒服的一粒沙子周围形成一颗珍珠。因此，每颗珍珠的中心，都有一粒很小的沙子。一只牡蛎，需要花上四年或五年的时间，才能形成一颗豌豆大小的珍珠呢。波斯湾里出产最优质的珍珠。那种牡蛎的味道不太好吃，但人们把它们集中起来，采集它们体内的珍珠。人们也会潜水去寻找牡蛎，只要憋得住气，他们就会尽可能长久地待在水里，下潜到海

---

[1] 作者是指，"德黑兰"（Tehran）由英语中的"茶"（Tea）、"小男孩"（he）和"跑"（ran）三个单词组合而成。下文中的"伊朗"（Iran）则是由"我"（I）和"跑"（ran）这两个单词组合而成。

do so for an hour—but that is a fairy-tale. A little boy wrote this composition telling how it is done: "They clamp clothes-pins on their noses and stuff wax in their earses to keep out the waterses. Then they fasten heavy stones to their feetses and jump overboard from small boatses." Many pearl-divers lose their lives each year. They burst a blood vessel or are drowned or stung to death by a poisonous fish called the ray. But millions of dollars' worth of pearls are gathered each year to ornament the necks and fingers of queens and ladies all over the World.

底，捡起一篓子的牡蛎，然后再浮到水面上来。你们十有八九只能憋半分钟的气，可一位潜水采珠员却能憋上一分钟，甚至憋得更久，据说，有的潜水采珠员还能憋上一个小时呢，但这只是传说罢了。一个小男孩写了下面这样一篇作文，来说明人们是如何潜水采珠的："他们把领带夹子夹在鼻上，把蜂蜡塞在耳朵里，防止耳朵进水。接下来，他们又给脚绑上大石头，从小船里跳下水去。"[1]每年都有很多的潜水采珠人丢掉了性命。他们要么是血管爆裂、溺水而死，要么就是被一种叫作"鳐"的毒鱼刺死了。不过，每年还是有价值数百万美元的珍珠被采集上来，用于去装点全世界那些女王、贵妇的脖子和手指呢。

潜水采珠员

潜水采珠员憋气的时间比你们久上两倍

---

[1] 由于这是小男孩所写的作文，原文中就存在一些属于小朋友常见的问题，因此翻译时也适当做了加工。

55 Opposite-Feet

There is a shop downtown with a department in the basement, underneath the sidewalk. The sidewalk is made of thick glass, and as you look up you can see the feet of the crowds of people as they pass overhead. If the World were made of glass and you could look down through it in the same way, you could see the bottoms of the feet of the crowds passing by on the other side of the World. It is the "Opposite-feet" Land. That sounds awkward, so grown-ups call it "The Antipodes," which means exactly the same thing—"opposite-feet." The Opposite-feet Land on the other side of the World is a pie-shaped country called India. It is the half-way country—halfway round the World. You go away from home till you reach India, then, though you keep on going, you are coming back. I went west around the World and a friend of mine went east. We both started at the same time and met in India. When I landed at a place called Calcutta, there he was on the dock waiting to greet me. From Calcutta we used to get a kind of cloth which we called, from the name of the place, calico.

When I say "Indians" you probably think of tommyhawks, colored feathers, and war-paint. But you are thinking of American Indians—the kind that were in our country before the white man came. There are only a few of these Indians left. They belong to the red race.

第55章　脚掌相对之地

市里有一家商店，那里人行道的下面还有一层。这条人行道是用厚厚的玻璃建成的，站在底下抬头往上看去，可以看到熙熙攘攘的人群在你们头上经过时的一只只脚掌。如果地球是透明的，那么你们同样可以往下看去，看到地球另一面人群经过时的脚底。对面就是那个与我们"脚掌相对"的地方。这种说法听起来有点儿不太合适，因此大人们都叫它"对跖地"，它与"脚掌相对"的地点完全就是一码事儿。地球那一面与我们脚掌相对的地方，是一个样子像是馅饼的国家，叫作"印度"。这是一个处在"半路上"的国家，也就是说，它位于我们环绕世界一周的半路上。环游世界时，你们从家里出发，一直走到印度，然后，尽管在继续往前走，可实际上你们却是往回返了。假设我向西环游世界，而我的一个朋友则向东走。我们两人都在同一时间出发，然后就会在印度碰面。当我到达一个叫作"加尔各答"的地方时，我的朋友已经在码头上等着迎接我了。以前我们经常买到一种产自加尔各答的布料，并且根据该地的名称，将这种布料叫作"加尔各答印花棉布"呢。

当我说"印度人"的时候，大家很可能都会想到印第安战斧、彩色羽毛，以及战斗之前涂在身上和脸上的那种油彩。不过，你们想到的是美洲的印第安人[1]，也

---

[1]　英语中，"印度人"和"印第安人"是同一个词，都是Indian。

There is another kind of Indian that belongs to the white race, the same as we do, and there are more than twice as many of them as there are people in our whole country. They get the name "Indians" from the name of the country where they live—India. India is the country that Columbus was trying to reach by going the other way around the World. When he bumped into America he thought he had reached India, so he called the people he found here Indians. He did not find out until later that America was not India at all, but a new and unknown land, and that the people were really not Indians at all, but Red Men.

India is shut off from the rest of Asia on the north by the highest wall of mountains in the World; they are called the Himalayas, Him-al-ay-as. The highest mountain on the face of the globe is in this range; it is called Mount Everest, after an English engineer named Everest, who measured its height. No one has ever been to the top, yet we know exactly how high it is. An engineer can find out such things. He can tell exactly how high a tree, a church-steeple, or a mountain is without leaving the ground. This mountain is twenty-nine thousand and two feet high—more than five miles high. The top and sides of Mount Everest are covered with snow and ice which never melts away and will always be there until the crack of doom.

Men have tried and tried again to climb to

产自加尔各答的印花棉布

就是白人来到美洲之前，曾经生活在我们美国的那种土著人。如今，这种印第安人幸存下来的不多了。他们都属于红种人。

但印度人与我们一样，属于白种人，并且他们的人数达到了美国总人口的两倍多。他们之所以叫作"印度人"，是因为他们生活的那个国家叫作印度。印度就是哥伦布从地球的另一面绕过去，想要到达的那个国家。来到美洲之后，他以为自己到的是印度，于是就把自己在这里找到的那些人称为"印第安人"。直到后来，他才发觉美洲根本就不是印度，而是一个新的、未知的大陆，并且发现，那里的土著根本就不是印度人，而是红种的美洲原住民。

印度的北部，有一道世界最高的峻岭之墙，将该国与亚洲的其他地区隔离开来了，这道山脉，叫作"喜马拉雅山"。地球表面最高的山峰，就坐落在喜马拉雅山脉当中，这座山峰，叫作"珠穆朗玛峰"，是用一个曾经测量过此峰高度的英国工程师的名字"埃佛勒斯特"命名的[1]。虽说迄今为止还没有人到达过珠峰峰顶，但我们却知道此峰的准确高度。一位工程师就能做到这一点。工程师站在地上，可以

---

[1] "珠穆朗玛峰"的通用名称是Mount Everest，音译过来就是"埃佛勒斯特峰"。"珠穆朗玛峰"属于我国所起的名称。

the top and many have lost their lives in attempting the climb, but no one has ever been able to get there. The top reaches so high up into the sky that there is very little air up there, and men have to take along canned air to breathe. If they attempt to climb without canned air, they are able to take but a single step and then must stop to breathe many times, like a dog panting for breath, and every few steps they must rest awhile before going on. Two Englishmen, after weeks of struggling up the sides of the giant mountain, got nearer than any other human being ever had before—within a few hundred feet of the top. A companion whom they left at their last stop watched them as they plunged upward in their last desperate struggle, and then—whish!—an icy blast of snow and sleet swept them from sight—forever. The native people think a goddess lives at the top and that she will let no one climb to her, and that it brings bad luck and even death to try to reach such a holy place.

At the other end of the Himalaya Mountains is a high valley which is so beautiful that poets call it a vale instead of a valley. It is the Vale of Kashmir. "Who has not heard of the Vale of Kashmir," says one poet, "with its roses, the brightest the earth ever gave?" Beautiful lakes with snow-topped mountains, and roses, roses

珠穆朗玛峰是世界上最高的山峰

准确地说出一棵树、一座教堂尖顶或者一座山峰的高度来。这座山峰有两万九千零两英尺高，超过了五英里呢。珠峰峰顶和山坡上全都覆盖着冰雪，这些冰雪永不融化，会恒久存在，直到世界末日来临。

人类已经一而再、再而三地尝试过要爬到珠峰峰顶，并且有许多人都在尝试攀登的过程中丢掉了性命，可尽管如此，还是没有人能够到达那里。由于峰顶高耸入云，因此那里空气非常稀薄，登山者必须携带罐装空气才能呼吸。要是不带罐装空气就去攀登的话，他们走上一步就得停下来呼吸多次，就像一条小狗呼呼地喘气那样，并且每走上几步，就得停下来休息一会儿，才能继续往上爬呢。有两位英国人，曾经在这座高山的山坡上苦苦挣扎着攀爬了好几个星期，到达的地方比其他任何人都更加靠近山顶，距山顶只有几百英尺了。在最后一个休息地留下的那个同伴，一直看着他们拼尽最后一丝力气向上爬去，然后嗖的一声，一阵冰冷的雪和冰雹一下子将他们卷得看不见了，并且是永远也看不见了。珠峰底下的当地人认为，峰顶住着一位女神，这位女神不允许任何人爬到她那里去，因此，想要攀登到这样一个神圣之地去，就会给人带来噩运，甚至是死亡。

喜马拉雅山脉的另一端，有一个高高的峡谷，那里的景色非常秀丽，因此诗人都称之为"溪谷"，而不是平平常常地称之为"峡谷"呢。那里就是克什米尔谷。

everywhere. It seems as if this should have been the Garden of Eden instead of that sun-baked mud bank between the Tigris and Euphrates.

If you will look at your map of Asia carefully you will see something strange about two of the countries that touch India. The country next to India on the west and the country next to India on the east have the same name, Pakistan. How can two separate countries have the same name? The answer is that Pakistan is one country in two parts. Until after World War II these two parts called Pakistan were both a part of India and all India belonged to England. The people of India, like people almost everywhere, wanted to rule themselves. So finally the English said they would give up India and turn the country completely over to the Indians. This pleased the people of India but there was one trouble with the plan. Most of the people of India believed in a religion called the Hindu religion but a great many others were Mohammedans. These two religions didn't mix very well. The Hindus wanted India to remain one big country when it became independent. The Mohammedans didn't want one big country for they knew then the Hindus would do most of the ruling as there were more Hindus in India than Mohammedans. The Mohammedans wanted the country split into separate Mohammedan and Hindu countries. Then the Mohammedans could have a country of their own and not have to be part of a Hindu country. They almost went to war about it but finally both sides agreed to make two countries out of India, a Mohammedan country to be called Pakistan and a Hindu country to keep the name of India.

"哪有世人,不知克什米尔谷,"一位诗人曾经如此吟唱道,"不知其中玫瑰,尘世之间最为亮丽?"美丽的湖泊,山顶的皑皑白雪,并且还有玫瑰,遍地的玫瑰。似乎伊甸园应该是在这里,而不是底格里斯河与幼发拉底河之间那片被太阳烤得干干的泥地才对呢。

如果大家仔细看一看亚洲地图,你们就会发现,与印度接壤的两个邻国有个地方很是奇怪。印度西面的邻国与东面的那个邻国国名相同,都叫巴基斯坦[1]。两个独立的国家,怎么可能用同一个国名呢?答案就是,巴基斯坦这个国家分成了两个部分。直到第二次世界大战结束后,这两个叫巴基斯坦的地区都还是印度的一部分,而整个印度则隶属于英国。印度人与世界各地的人一样,也希望实现自治。因此,英国最后终于答应不再统治印度,并打算将该国全部交由印度人去统治。这让印度人觉得非常高兴,不过,这个计划中还存在一个麻烦。绝大多数印度人都信仰一种叫作"印度教"的宗教,但还有许多其他的人是穆斯林。这两种宗教信仰没有很好地融合起来。印度教徒都希望,该国独立后能够继续是一个大国。可该国的穆斯林却不想要一个大国,他们非常清楚,那样一来,印度教徒便会掌握绝大部分的统治权,因为该国信奉印度教的人要比信奉伊斯兰教的人多。所以,穆斯林希望将该国分成为两个独立的国家,一个信奉伊斯兰教,另一个信奉印度教。那样的话,穆斯林就会拥有一个属于自己的国家,而不必成为一个信奉印度教的国家的一部分

---

[1] 如今印度东边的邻国是孟加拉国。

Now the Mohammedans lived mostly on the western and on the eastern sides of India and the Hindus lived mostly in the middle. So Pakistan became a new country with two separate parts, an eastern part and a western part with the new country of India in between. For Pakistan it must be something like living in a house with the kitchen on one side of the street and the living room on the other side. But it seems to work.

Both India and Pakistan are members of the British Commonwealth of Nations.

了。为此，双方还差点儿诉诸战争呢，不过，双方最终还是一致同意将印度分成两个国家，信奉伊斯兰教的那个叫作巴基斯坦，而信奉印度教的那个国家则仍然叫作印度。

如今，穆斯林主要生活在印度的东、西两侧，而印度教徒则主要生活在印度的中部地区。于是，巴基斯坦便成了一个分成了两个部分的新国家，有一个东部地区和一个西部地区，中间则隔着印度这个新国家。对于巴基斯坦人来说，这种感觉一定像是生活在一栋客厅在街这头、厨房却在街那头的房子里吧。不过，这样安排还真的管用呢。

印度和巴基斯坦两国，都是英联邦的成员国。

56 Opposite-Feet (continued)

India is divided into states like the United States and many of these states have separate rulers called rajahs. Many of the rajahs, however, are more interested in showing off and in having a good time than they are in ruling. They love jewels, such ac diamonds and pearls, and they collect them as you might collect marbles, though one of their diamonds may be worth a million times what one of your precious marbles is worth. They own some of the largest and finest jewels that have ever been found. We think of diamond and pearl necklaces as something that only women wear, but when the rajahs appear before their subjects or ride in processions, as they love to do, they dress themselves up with their wonderful gems, some of them as big as walnuts, and wear collars of pearls, rubies, sapphires, and emeralds. In such processions a rajah rides on an elephant, which is dressed up too. The rajah sits on top of the elephant under a canopy that is so high in the air he has to use a stepladder to climb up.

Elephants are considered sacred in India, and even though there are many wild ones, it is against the law to shoot one. So men hunt them, catch them, and tame them without shooting them. Hundreds of men form a long line around the place where there are elephants and beat drums and blow horns to frighten them. The elephants move away from the noise and, unknowingly, toward a pen that is left open to catch them. In this way they

第55章　脚掌相对之地（续）

就像美国一样，印度国内分成了许多的"邦"，并且其中许多的邦都有各自独立的统治者，叫作"王公"。然而，许多的王公对炫耀和享乐比对统治臣民更感兴趣。他们喜欢诸如钻石、珍珠那样的宝贝，因此会像你们收集弹珠那样去搜罗珠宝，只不过，他们的一颗钻石，可能会比你们最贵的一颗弹珠还要值钱一百万倍呢。他们拥有人类历史上发现的一些最大、最精美的珠宝。我们觉得，钻石和珍珠项链都是女士佩戴的东西，可印度这些王公在手下臣民前现身或者带领手下游行（他们很喜欢这样干）的时候，也会用那些精美的宝石将自己打扮起来呢，其中有些宝石大如胡桃，并且他们还会佩戴饰有珍珠、红宝石、蓝宝石和绿宝石的项圈。在这种游行活动中，王公会坐在大象背上，而那头大象也会打扮得花枝招展。王公坐在大象背上驮着的一顶华盖之下，由于华盖太高，所以王公还得用梯子才能爬上去。

印度人认为大象是一种神圣的动物，因此，尽管当地有许多的野象，可射杀野象却是违法的。于是，人们便在捕猎、抓住野象之后将其驯服，而不去射杀它们。捕猎野象时，都是几百个人排成一列，将有野象的地方围起来，然后敲锣打鼓、大吹喇叭，将野象惊起。象群会被噪音驱赶着，不知不觉地朝着一道开着口子、用于关住野象的围栏走去。于是，野象会被这种震天的噪音赶入围栏，然后人们再把围栏关上。捕住野象之后，人们还须将它们驯服才行。这可不是一件容易的事情，因

are driven by the terrible racket into the pen, which is then closed. After they are caught they must be tamed. This is not an easy job, for some elephants are very dangerous and can easily stamp a man to death. Once tamed, however, an elephant can be used like a camel in Arabia, a horse in Europe, or an automobile, a tractor, or a piece of machinery in our country. An elephant will wind his trunk around a log and load it on a train or ship, much as a machine called a derrick would do.

One of the things a rajah likes best to do is to hunt tigers. The tiger—a huge, orange-colored cat with black stripes—is a fearful creature. He lives in the jungles of India, and when he is hungry he raids villages and kills domestic animals and people. A rajah going forth to a tiger hunt takes good care that he is in no danger. He and a party of friends, with hundreds of servants, go out into the jungle and climb to a safe place in a tree where a platform has been built. The servants then go through the jungle beating pans and drums and anything that will make a noise, keeping up a terrific din to scare the tiger along toward the rajah and his party of friends. When he comes within range they fire upon him from above. They then take his skin home to cover the floors or walls of the rajah's palace.

王公坐在一头同样打扮得花枝招展的大象背上

为有些野象非常危险，能够毫不费力地踩死一个人。然而，一旦驯服，大象便可以像阿拉比亚的骆驼、欧洲的马匹，或者汽车、卡车、我们美国的机器那样，供人们来驱使了。大象可以用鼻子卷起一根圆木，并将圆木装到火车或者船只上去，很像是一台起重机呢。

王公最喜欢做的事情之一，就是猎虎。老虎是一种皮毛呈橘色而有黑色条纹的大型猫科动物，也是一种非常可怕的野兽。老虎生活在印度的丛林里，一旦找不到吃的，它们就会袭击村庄，咬死家畜和村民。当然，王公出去猎虎时，会小心翼翼地确保自己不会遇到危险。王公会带上一帮朋友，连同好几百名仆人，来到丛林当中，爬到一棵树上的安全之处，他的手下，早就在树上搭建好了一个平台。然后，仆人们便会敲着盘子、大鼓以及任何可以发声的东西，不停地发出巨大的噪音，把老虎吓得一路朝着王公及其朋友所在的地方而去。待老虎进入射程范围之后，王公及其朋友们便会从树上向老虎开枪。然后，他们会把老虎皮拿回家去，铺在王公宫殿里的地上，或者是挂在墙上。

虽然印度国内存在着一百多种不同的宗教，但正如我在上一章告诉你们的那样，绝大多数人都是印度教徒。印度教徒相信，他们死后，灵魂会附在动物或者另一个人的身上，重新回到这个世界。他们之所以善待那些有用的、健壮的动物，这也是一个原因。印度教徒相信，要是行善的话，他们死后，就会在刹那之间突然获

There are over a hundred different religions in India but, as I told you in the last chapter, most of the people are Hindus. A Hindu believes his spirit comes back into this World in the shape of an animal or of another person. That is one reason why useful or good animals are treated well. A Hindu thinks that if he is good he will, when he dies, suddenly, in a twinkling, be born again—rich or in the shape of a good animal; if he has been bad, he will, when he returns, be poor or in the shape of a bad animal. When I look into the kindly eyes of my dog who wags his tail, puts out his paw, and whines "*m-m-m*," I can almost believe as the Hindu does that some human being, perhaps a rajah, is in his dog body.

On the west side of India is a big city called Bombay, but Bombay does not look much different from any other large city in Europe. The buildings look much like the buildings in London or New York.

But if you travel north from Bombay for about two days you will come to a town with two buildings like none other in the World. This town is called Agra. One building is a tomb, the other is a mosque. The tomb was built by a Mohammedan prince for one of his four wives who was his favorite. It is called the Taj Mahal, and some think it the most beautiful building in the World. I had come half-way round the World to see this sight and had traveled days in

我曾经绕过半个地球，去参观泰姬陵

得重生，并且重生后会变成富人，或者变成一头健壮的动物，而若是作恶的话，他们重生之后就会变成穷人，或者变成一头不中用的动物。当我养的那头小狗对着我摇动尾巴、伸出爪子、发出呜呜的叫声时，要是与之对视的话，我差不多就会像印度教徒那样，相信某个人（没准还是一位王公）的灵魂，就附在这头小狗的身上呢。

印度西部有一个大城市，叫作"孟买"，不过，孟买的样子，跟欧洲其他的许多大城市并没有什么太大的不同。该市里的建筑，都很像伦敦或纽约的高楼大厦。

但是，如果从孟买动身，向北走上大约两天的时间，你们就会来到另一座城市，那里有两栋建筑，与世界上的其他建筑都不相同。那座城市，叫作"阿格拉"。其中有一栋建筑是一座陵墓，而另一栋则是一座清真寺。这座陵墓，是一位信奉伊斯兰教的亲王替自己四位妻子中他最宠爱的那一位修建的。它叫"泰姬陵"，有些人还认为，它是世界上最美丽的一座建筑呢。我曾经绕过半个地球，去参观这一名胜，并且在滚滚热浪中走了好多天，那个时候，人们可都是像担心被闪电击中那样，害怕自己中暑呢。当时，我是在一轮满月之下去瞻仰泰姬陵的，由于只顾观赏，我还一脚踩进了一个池子当中。那里水深过膝，而待我好不容易爬出水池，走下一个平台时，又扭伤了脚。不过，这一切都是值得的。只是在我看来，世界上最精美的建筑并不是泰姬陵，而是同样位于阿格拉的那座"珍珠清真寺"。虽然不知道天堂中的建筑是个什么样子，但我相信，就算是天堂里的建筑，也美不过

such terrific heat that a sunstroke was as much to be feared as a stroke of lightning. I saw the Taj by the full moon and was so busy looking that I stepped into a pool of water up to my knees, and I had hardly clambered out when I stepped off a platform and sprained my ankle. But it was worth it. And yet to me the most beautiful building in the World is not the Taj. It is the Pearl Mosque, which is also at Agra. I don't know what the buildings in Heaven look like, but I don't believe they could be more beautiful than the Pearl Mosque.

On the east side of the country is the sacred river of India; it is called the Ganges. It has several mouths and at one of these mouths is Calcutta. Calcutta is in India but most of the mouths of the Ganges are in Pakistan.

Farther up the sacred river is the sacred city of the Hindus. It is called Benares. No one but a Mohammedan may go to the sacred city of Mecca, but any one may go to Benares. Benares is built on the banks of the river, and covering the banks are long stone steps leading down into the river. Hindus come from all over India to bathe in the Ganges at Benares, not to wash away dirt but to wash away sins. They go in about waist-deep and, filling a bowl with the sacred water, pour it over their heads. Especially do they come to the Ganges when they think they are about to die. Good Hindus are not afraid to die. In fact, if they are miserably poor and unhappy they are glad to die, for if their sins are washed away they expect, by dying, they will immediately be changed into the body of a happier creature.

The Hindus do not bury those who die; they burn their bodies on bonfires. Those who die in Benares are burned on the steps that lead down to the river, and so many are burned

"珍珠清真寺"呢。

印度的东部，流淌着该国那条叫作"恒河"的圣河。恒河有好几个河口，加尔各答就位于其中的一个边上。尽管加尔各答位于印度，但恒河的绝大多数河口却都位于巴基斯坦。

在这条圣河遥远的上游，有一座属于印度教的圣城。这座城市，叫作"贝拿勒斯"。圣城麦加只允许穆斯林进入，但圣城贝拿勒斯却是任何人都可以去。贝拿勒斯位于恒河沿岸，那里的河岸上，全都铺着长长的石制台阶，向下一直通到河里。印度教徒从全国各地来到这儿，到贝拿勒斯的恒河里来沐浴，但他们沐浴，并不是为了洗去身上的尘垢，而是为了洗涤身上的罪孽。他们会下到齐腰深的河水当中，用一个碗盛满圣水，浇到自己的头上。尤其是当一些人觉得自己活不久长了的时候，他们更会来到这里。善良的印度教徒是不害怕死亡的。实际上，如果一贫如洗、过得很不幸福的话，他们还很乐意死去，因为一旦洗去自己的罪孽，他们便希望自己死去之后马上转世，让灵魂附到一种更加幸福的动物身上。

印度教徒不会将死者埋葬，而是会点起篝火，将死者的遗体火化。那些死在贝拿勒斯的人，遗体都会在通往恒河的那些台阶上进行火化，由于那里火化的人太多，因此出售木柴去给人火化，还变成了当地人的一种常规生意呢。一个人越有钱，死后火化时的那堆篝火就可以点得越大，不过，那些死者常常都很穷酸，没有留下什么钱来，连火化遗体所需的寥寥几根木柴也买不起呢。

印度人口众多，所以粮食经常不足，尽管穷人每天除了几把米，就不需要别的

there that men make a regular business of selling wood for these funeral fires. The richer a man is, the bigger fire he can have when he dies; but often a man is so poor he has not left even enough money to pay for the few sticks of wood necessary to burn his body.

There are so many people in India that often there is not enough food to go around, and though the poor people live on little but a few handfuls of rice a day, thousands upon thousands starve to death for lack of even this little food. The rajahs and well-to-do people look fat and well-fed, but the poor people are usually as thin as skeletons, and as they often wear hardly any clothes, you can see every bone in their lean bodies.

From rajahs with their millions' worth of jewels to the poor wretch who dies without two sticks of wood to burn his body, that is the "opposite-feet" land.

South of India is an island called Ceylon, where men wear skirts and combs in their hair. Much of our tea comes from there. Near Ceylon are the greatest pearl fisheries i.t.w.W.—greater even than those of the Persian Gulf. Many of the rajahs' famous pearls have been found there, and even I have a black pearl that came from there. It is supposed to bring good luck whether you wear it or whether you don't. I don't.

The Indians are famous magicians, and at Colombo in Ceylon I saw some of their tricks. An Indian placed his wife in a basket, covered it with a shawl, stabbed through it in every direction, and then uncovered her alive and smiling. I saw him put a seed in a flower-pot and while you watched it it grew to a plant. How do they do such things? You can only guess just as everyone else does.

什么东西来生活，可还是有成千上万的人连这点儿米也没有，因而活活饿死了。王公贵族和家境富裕的人，样子都是肥头大耳、吃得很好，可穷人通常却都是骨瘦如柴，并且，由于他们平时基本上不穿什么衣服，因此大家都数得清他们那种羸弱之体上的每一根骨头。

从拥有价值数百万美元珠宝的王公贵族，到死后连火化遗体的两根木柴也没有的穷苦百姓，这就是"对跖之地"的现实情况。

印度南面有一个岛屿，叫作锡兰[1]；那里的男子都身穿短裙，头发上还插着梳子。我们所喝的茶，很多都产自那里。锡兰附近，有一个全世界最大的采珠场，它的规模甚至比波斯湾里的那些采珠场还要大。印度王公贵族们的许多著名珍珠，都是产自那里，连我也有一颗产自那里的黑珍珠呢。据说，无论戴不戴在身上，黑珍珠都会给人带来好运。我就没有把这颗黑珍珠戴在身上。

印度人都是些赫赫有名的魔术师，在锡兰的科伦坡，我曾经看过他们的魔术表演。当时，一名印度人把自己的妻子放进一个篮子里，用一块披巾盖住篮子，并且用刀子从各个方向刺进篮子里，然后再揭开披巾，让大家看他的妻子非但活蹦乱跳，而且面带微笑呢。我还看到，他把一颗种子放进一个花瓶里，然后让大家看着这颗种子慢慢地长成一株植物。他们是怎么做到这种事情的呢？你们只能像其他人一样去猜想了。

---

[1] 锡兰（Ceylon），斯里兰卡的旧称。

57 The White Elephant

There was once an Indian prince named Gautama. Gautama was rich and had everything in the World he wanted, so he grew up gay and light-hearted. He had never seen any poor people, nor known any misery in his life, so he thought everyone in the World was just as well off and just as happy as he. Then one day when he was grown up he went on a trip and, to his amazement, saw for the first time in his life people who were sick, poor, and unhappy. The sights he saw filled him with such pity that he gave up all he had and spent the rest of his life helping the needy. As Gautama went about from place to place he preached that certain things were right and certain things wrong. People began to call him Buddha, which meant "the one who knows," and to worship him, and thus started a religion called Buddhism. This was about five hundred years before Christ.

After Buddha died, Buddhists sent missionaries to other countries to teach the people Buddhism too, just as Christians now send missionaries to other lands to teach Christianity. After a long while most of the people in India got tired of Buddhism and took up other newer religions. Many became Mohammedans, but in the countries east of India they still held to Buddhism, although now this worship has become chiefly a worship of idols.

The two countries next door to India are Burma and Thailand. A Mohammedan church

第57章 白象

印度曾经有一位叫作"乔达摩"的王子。乔达摩很有钱，得到了他在世间希望拥有的一切，所以非常快乐、无忧无虑地长大成人了。他从来没有见过穷人，也不知道穷人的生活有多悲惨，因此，他以为世界上的每一个人都像他那样生活优裕、无忧无虑。接下来，他长大成人之后，有一天出去旅行，却平生第一次惊讶地看到了那些生病、贫困而不幸的人。目睹了此种情景之后，他的心里充满了怜悯之情，于是，他放弃了自己所有的财产，然后终生开始帮助穷人。乔达摩在漫游各地的过程中，一直宣传某些事情是正确的、某些事情是不对的。于是，人们开始称他为"佛陀"，就是"知一切者"的意思，并且开始崇拜他，从而开创了一种叫作"佛教"的宗教。此时，正值基督降生的五百年左右之前。

佛陀死后，佛教徒派了许多教士前往其他国家，去向当地的人宣传佛教，就像如今的基督教徒会派使徒前往其他国家去传播基督教那样。过了很久之后，绝大多数印度人都厌倦了佛教，便开始信奉其他一些较新的宗教去了。许多人都变成了穆斯林，不过，在印度东边的那些国家里，尽管佛教如今已经变成了一种主要崇拜神像的宗教，可还是有许多人信奉这种宗教。

印度隔壁的两个国家，就是缅甸和泰国。伊斯兰教的教堂叫作清真寺，佛教的教堂叫作寺院。在缅甸首都仰光市（缅甸已于2005年迁都内比都），就有这样一座

is called a mosque, a Buddhist church is called a pagoda. In the capital of Burma—a city called Rangoon—is one of the largest and most wonderful of these pagodas. This pagoda is called the Shwe Dagon Pagoda. It looks like a giant ice cream cone turned upside down and is nearly as high as the Washington Monument. It is built of brick, but the outside is covered with sheets of solid gold—a glorious, dazzling sight in the sunlight. Around the bottom of the pagoda are little cell-like rooms in each of which is an idol, and underneath the center of the pagoda is a box in which, it is said, there are eight hairs from the head of Buddha. On the tip top of the pagoda is—what do you suppose? A church would have a cross, a mosque a crescent, but the pagoda has an umbrella!—with little tinkling bells hanging to it.

Rice is the chief and almost the only food of most of the people in Asia. They eat boiled rice just so, without sugar or cream, and they eat it for breakfast, luncheon, and dinner. Rangoon is the chief rice market of the World.

The people in Burma and Thailand are more like the Chinese than like the people in India. Burma is a republic but Thailand is a kingdom. Until after World War II, Thailand was named Siam. Then the people changed the name of this

通往仰光大金寺的道路

它像是一个巨大的、倒立着的冰淇淋蛋筒

规模非常巨大、极为奇妙的寺院。那座寺院，叫作"大金寺"。它的样子，就像是一个巨大的、倒立着的冰淇淋蛋筒，高度则跟华盛顿纪念碑差不多。它本来是一座砖结构的寺院，可寺院的外墙上，却覆盖着纯金打造的金片，因此在阳光底下呈现出一片瑰丽无比、令人目眩神迷的景象。寺院地基的四周，建有许多小单间似的房间，每个房间里面都有一座佛像，而整座寺院正中间的地下，还有一个小盒子，里面据说放着佛陀的八根头发。在寺院的尖顶上，有一个——你们猜一猜，是什么呢？一座基督教堂上面会有一个十字架，一座清真寺上面会有一个新月标志，可一座寺院上面却有一把伞！并且，这把伞上还挂着许多叮当作响的小铃铛呢。

大米几乎是亚洲所有人的主食，也差不多是他们唯一的食物。亚洲人只是把米饭煮熟了就吃，既不加糖，也不加奶油，并且早、中、晚三餐都是吃米饭。仰光就是世界上最主要的一个大米市场。

缅甸和泰国人都与中国人比较像，而不那么像印度人。缅甸是一个共和国，而泰国则是一个王国。直到第二次世界大战过后，泰国都叫"暹罗"。后来，人们便把这个暹罗国改成了泰国。要是一个人突然之间改了个名字，比如从"琼斯先生"改成了"贝克尔先生"，那么在一段时间内，人们仍然会觉得他是琼斯先生，

country of Siam to Thailand. If a man suddenly changed his name from Mr. Jones to Mr. Baker some people would still think of him as Mr. Jones and call him Mr. Jones instead of Mr. Baker. Many people still call Thailand, Siam.

Once, the King of Siam could do anything he wanted with his people. That is what is called an absolute monarchy. When I was a boy, if any one acted very "bossy" or ordered others around, we used to say, "Who do you think you are? The King of Siam?"

But now the King of Thailand has to rule according to the laws of the country and cannot do just as he pleases the way his ancestors used to do.

The Buddhists believe that when they die their souls go into the bodies of animals. The kings' souls they think go into the bodies of white elephants, so in Thailand the White Elephant is sacred. The white elephants are, however, more gray than white. Once any white elephant found in a herd had to be presented to the King to bring good luck to him and to the kingdom. Because these royal white elephants did no work, we have come to call something we may have that is of no use, and yet we must keep and take care of, "a white elephant." A friend of mine has an old worn-out automobile that will not run, that he can neither sell nor give away, and as it takes up space in his garage he calls it his "white elephant."

In Burma the ordinary gray elephant is used as we use an automobile, truck, or tractor and costs about the same as an

飞翔的天使

暹罗
跳舞的姑娘

并且仍然叫他"琼斯先生",而不会称他为"贝克尔先生"。同样,如今仍然有许多人把"泰国"叫作"暹罗"呢。

以前,暹罗的国王可以随心所欲地对待本国的臣民。这种制度,就叫"绝对君主制"。小的时候,要是有人表现得非常"专横",或者将他人指挥得团团转的话,我们经常就会这样说:"你以为自己是谁呀?难道你是暹罗国王不成?"

不过,如今泰国的国王必须按照该国法律来进行统治,不能再像以前的历代国王那样为所欲为了。

佛教徒认为,他们死后,灵魂也会进入动物的体内。他们认为,国王的灵魂会进入白象的体内,因此在泰国,白象可是一种圣兽呢。然而,白象其实更多的是呈灰色,而不是呈白色。以前,凡是人们在象群里发现的白象,都必须进贡给国王,以便给国王和整个王国带来好运。由于这种属于皇室的白象不用干活,因此后来我们便把那些虽然没用、但必须保留并照管的东西,也叫作"白象"了。我的一位朋友有一辆再也开不了、破旧不堪的老爷车,既卖不掉,也送不了人,在车库里还占地,因此,他也称这辆汽车是他的"白象"呢。

在缅甸,那些普通灰象的用途,就像我们的汽车、卡车或者拖拉机一样,并且一头大象的价格也跟一辆汽车差不多。大象可以驮人,可以运送东西,可以举起木

automobile does. An elephant carries people, he carries loads, he lifts logs, he plows. A driver sits on the elephant's head and taps him on one side or the other to let him know just what he is to do and he does it. He works regular hours and knows when it's time to start work and when it's time to quit. It is as if he belonged to a labor union, and he will not work at all unless he has had one or more baths each day!

We always say wood will float, but there is a kind of wood in Burma that is so heavy it will not float. It is called "Teak." They use teak instead of other woods in making furniture, for white ants eat up and destroy anything made out of softer woods. One of the jobs that elephants are used for is hauling, lifting, and loading the heavy logs of teak. I thought I should like to have an elephant myself, so I bought a nice one and brought it all the way home. There it is on my table now. It's made of bronze.

Stretching down from Thailand like an elephant's trunk is a long peninsula known as the Malay Peninsula. Just about half a mile offshore from the top of this "trunk" is a bit of an island called Singapore. It was at one time nothing but a jungle in which poisonous snakes and terrible tigers lurked. The owner tried to give it away to get rid of it and couldn't. Later, however, he sold it to an Englishman named Raffles for almost nothing, and England built a city there. Why do you suppose England wanted such a place at all? Because this spot was another gateway for ships going east or west. There is, as you will see, a narrow passageway between the islands, and this was the only good way for ships to go. Just as in the case of Gibraltar, Suez, and Aden, England wanted to control it. In World

头，可以耕田。赶象人坐在大象的脑袋上，拍拍这边，再拍拍那边，好让大象知道自己要干什么，再按照赶象人的命令去做。大象每天都有固定的工作时间，知道自己该从何时开始干活，何时又该停止干活。不过，大象就像是加入了一个工会组织似的，每天不洗上一个或者多个澡的话，根本就不会去干活！

我们总是说，木头在水上会浮起来，但缅甸有一种木材却非常沉重，在水里根本就浮不起来。这种木材，叫作"柚木"。那里的人都用柚木做家具，而不用其他的木料，因为用其他质地较软的木料打制的家具，都会被白蚁啃坏。人们叫大象干的一种活儿，就是拉拽、举起和装卸这种沉重的柚木。我曾觉得，要是自己也有一头大象就好了，所以便买了一头中意的带回了家。此时，它就站在我的餐桌上呢。其实，那只是一尊用青铜制成的大象雕塑。

从泰国往南，是一个像大象鼻子那样延伸着的、长长的半岛，人称"马来半岛"。从这个"大象鼻子"的顶端往海里去上差不多半英里，有一个小小的岛屿，叫作"新加坡"。那里曾经荒无人烟，全是丛林，里面出没的都是毒蛇和老虎。当时这个小岛的主人想把小岛送给别人，以便摆脱麻烦，可没能办到。然而，后来他却把小岛卖给了一个叫作"拉弗尔斯"的英国人，价格差不多相当于免费，于是，英国便在那里兴建起了一座城市。你们觉得，英国究竟为什么想要这样一个地方呢？原因就在于，这里是船舶向东或者向西航行的又一道门户。大家可以看到，那里的岛屿之间有一条狭窄的水道，也是那里适合船舶来去的唯一一条水道。与直布罗陀、苏伊士及亚丁等地的情形一样，英国也想要控制这条水道。在第二次世界大

War II the Japanese captured Singapore, not with ships from the sea, but with soldiers from the land side of the city. When the Japanese were finally beaten in the war, England again took control of Singapore. Singapore is now one of the most important stopping-places for ships, and in the lobby of the great hotel called "Raffles" you may now see people from all nations of the earth.

Singapore is almost on the Equator—it is almost half-way between the North and South Poles. Sailors call the Equator "The Line." When you cross "The Line" for the first time you are supposed to be baptized by Father Neptune, the god of the sea. So I was baptized when I crossed it and this was the way it was done. As I stepped out on deck a sailor suddenly appeared on each side of me. One caught me by my arms and the other by my legs and, lifting me in the air, they threw me, with all my clothes on, into a big pool of water that had been made out of canvas on the deck of the ship. Then when I clambered out of the pool, sputtering for my breath, they shoved me into the end of a long canvas pipe, through which I had to crawl. When I came out at the other end they gave me a whack on the back with a paddle. Then I was taken before Father Neptune, a man seated on a throne and dressed up in a bath-robe with a pasteboard crown set on the side of his head, a pitchfork in his hand. He handed me a diploma, as if I were graduating from college, saying that I had been duly baptized and initiated and was now "a regular fellow" in the society of those who had crossed "The Line."

Near the Malay Peninsula are the East Indies and the Spice Islands, which Columbus

战期间，日军曾经占领过新加坡，但他们不是乘坐船只从海上攻占，而是派士兵从该市的陆地一侧占领这里的。当日军最终在此战中被打败之后，英国便重新控制了新加坡。如今，新加坡已经成为远洋船舶最重要的停靠港之一，而在该市那家"拉弗尔斯"大酒店的大厅里，你们也可以看到世界各国的人呢。

新加坡差不多坐落在赤道之上，也就是差不多位于从地球北极到南极的半路上。水手们都将赤道称为"界线"。据说，首次跨过这条"界线"时，人们还应当接受海神"尼普顿"的洗礼。因此，我越过赤道的时候，也接受了洗礼，当时的情形的确是这样的。我走出船舱，来到甲板上之后，左右两边突然分别冒出了一位水手。其中一位抓住我的两只胳膊，另一位抬着我的两条腿，把我高高地举了起来，然后，他们使劲一扔，便连人带衣服，把我扔进了甲板上一个用帆布围成的大水池里。接下来，等我从水池里爬出来，气急败坏地喘息着的时候，他们又把我推进了一条用帆布围成的管道里，管道很长，我只能从中爬过去。待我从管道那一端爬出来之后，他们又用船桨在我的背上重重一击。接着，他们便把我带到了海神"尼普顿"的面前。那是一个人装扮出来的：他坐在宝座上，身上披着浴袍，头上斜斜地戴着一顶用硬纸板做成的王冠，手里拿着一把铁叉。他把一份证书递给我，好像我是一名大学毕业似的，说我已经充分地接受了洗礼，入了门，如今已经成为那些越过"界线"之人所组成的那个团体中的"合格一员"了。

距马来半岛不远，就是哥伦布曾经想要到达的"东印度群岛"和"香料群岛"了。苏门答腊的形状有点儿像是一根粗大的雪茄，而制造雪茄外皮的那种烟草，正

tried to reach. Sumatra, which is shaped something like a fat cigar, is where the tobacco is grown for making the covers for cigars. Java, another one of the East Indies, was once famous for its coffee. I had looked forward to getting a good cup here, but I tried in a number of places and finally got a cup, but the coffee had come from Brazil!

In Java I saw bats as big as eagles and butterflies as big as your two hands.

是产自这里。爪哇岛是东印度群岛中的又一个岛屿，曾以那里出产的咖啡而著称。我曾经渴望着在这里能够喝上一杯优质的咖啡，便找了许多地方，并且最终得到了一杯，可定睛一看，那杯咖啡竟然产自巴西！

在爪哇岛上，我还看到过大如鹰隼的蝙蝠，以及有你们两只手掌那么大的蝴蝶呢。

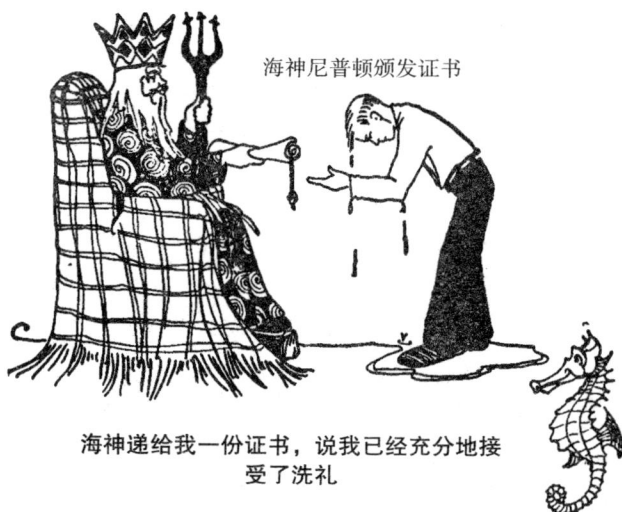

海神尼普顿颁发证书

海神递给我一份证书，说我已经充分地接
受了洗礼

58 Where the Thermometer Freezes Up

Most thermometers have numbers down to forty degrees (40°) below zero. There the numbers stop, for when the mercury gets down to that point it freezes up. But there are few places in the World where it ever gets as cold as that. The coldest place in the World is not at the North Pole; the coldest place in the World, where the thermometer does go below 40° and freezes up, is in the country called Siberia.

Siberia is a huge country north of China. In the north of Siberia the sun never rises all winter long. It is night, as it is in Norway and Sweden. But there is no Gulf Stream to warm the land, so it gets much colder than 40° below zero, and they have to use a different kind of thermometer to measure how cold it is. In one place it goes to 90° below zero, which is the coldest place i.t.w.W. People can't grow fur on their skins to keep themselves warm as animals can, so when they go outside they must cover themselves from top to toe with animal skins or they would freeze to death in a few moments.

But all of Siberia is not like this. There is a top, a middle, and a bottom part. Few people live in the northern part, however. It is so cold that no trees grow there and the ground is frozen solid many feet down. In the summer it gets very warm, and the thermometer sometimes goes just as high above zero as it goes below in the winter; that is, to 90°. The ground then thaws out on top and moss and a few other things grow for a short while,

第58章 极寒之地

绝大多数温度计上的刻度，都只到了华氏零下40°。再往下，就没有刻度了，因为温度要是比这再低的话，水银就会冻起来。不过，世界上有几个地方，气温甚至达到了华氏零下40°，确实极其寒冷呢。世界上最冷的地方，并不是北极，世界上最冷、测出来的气温的确低于华氏零下40°并且会让温度计冻结起来的地方，叫作"西伯利亚"。

西伯利亚是中国北边一个面积广袤的地区。在西伯利亚北部，太阳在整个冬季里都不会升起。与挪威和瑞典一样，这里的整个冬季都是夜晚。不过，这里却没有墨西哥湾流来让土地变暖和，因此气温会变得比华氏零下40°还要冷得多，所以，人们还得用一种不同的温度计，才能测出那里究竟有多冷。有个地方的气温甚至低至华氏零下90°，是全世界最寒冷的地方呢。由于人们的皮肤上没法长出毛皮来，没法像动物一样保暖，因此在外出的时候，他们必须用兽皮从头到脚裹得严严实实才行，否则的话，过不了多久他们就会冻死。

但是，并非整个西伯利亚地区都是如此。这一地区，分成北部、中部和南部三个部分。然而，没有多少人生活在西伯利亚的北部。那里太过寒冷，树木都无法生长，地上则有着数英尺深、结结实实的冻土层。到了夏季，那里会变得暖和起来，有时温度计测出的零上气温会像冬季测出的零下温度一样，也就是说，那里夏季的

though the ground underneath still stays frozen. Siberia is larger than the United States. It belongs to Russia, but there are people from other countries living there too.

The middle part of Siberia is not nearly so cold, and there great forests have grown, and in the forests live wild animals such as foxes, wolves, sable, and ermine, which have beautiful thick coats of fur to keep themselves warm. Trappers hunt these animals just for their furs, to be made into coats to keep people warm. One small animal, called the ermine, has a snow-white coat and a tail with a black tip. The ermine hates dirt or anything that will soil his white fur, so he keeps himself spotless. It is for this reason that the official robes of judges and kings are made of the fur of the ermine, as a sign that they too must be pure and clean in heart and mind. The skins of many such animals are sewn together to make a single cape or coat, which then looks white with little black tails spotted regularly over it.

一位身穿白鼬王袍的国王

这种叫作"白鼬"的小动物与绝大多数小男孩都不同，
因为它们不喜欢脏东西

The longest railway in the World is built through the bottom part of Siberia. It is so long it takes two weeks to

气温有时会达到华氏零上90°。这样，土地表层便会解冻，而苔藓以及寥寥几种其他植物便会生长出来，短暂地成活一阵子，不过，地表之下的土壤却仍然封冻着。西伯利亚的面积比整个美国还要大。它是俄罗斯的领土，但那里也生活着来自其他国家的人。

西伯利亚的中部地区并没有那么寒冷，因此那里生长着广袤的森林，而森林里则生活着像狐狸、狼、黑貂、白鼬这样的野兽，它们都有漂亮、厚实的皮毛来保暖。猎人们用陷阱捕捉这些野兽，只是为了得到它们的皮毛，以便用它们的皮毛制成大衣，来给人们保暖。一种叫作"白鼬"的小动物，全身的皮毛都雪白晶莹，只在尾巴上有一个小黑点。白鼬很不喜欢肮脏的地方，不喜欢那些会弄脏其白色皮毛的东西，所以会让全身不长一点儿斑纹。正是由于这个原因，法官和国王的官服都是用白鼬皮毛制成的，以此来表示他们的心灵和思想也必须像白鼬毛一样纯洁而干净。要用许多白鼬皮缝在一起，才能制成一件披肩或者大衣呢，这种披肩或大衣，看上去就像是雪白的底子上规则地点缀着许多黑色的小尾巴。

世界上最长的一条铁路，就修建在西伯利亚的南部地区。那条铁路极其漫长，要花上两个星期的时间，才能从其一端到达另一端。这条铁路，在太平洋沿岸的一

go from one end of it to the other. One end of it on the Pacific Ocean is called Vladivostok and the other end in Russia is Moscow. It is called the Trans-Siberian Railway, which means the Across Siberia Railway.

Most of the people in Siberia live along this railway, and yet one may travel for hundreds of miles without seeing a town or even a house. Often the towns are far from the railroad, so that there is a long drive from the station to the town. The engines that draw the trains are fired by wood instead of coal, and along the railroad there are piles of wood at which the train stops to get fuel, as a car would stop to get gasoline. The chief Siberian cities end in "sk." They are Omsk, Tomsk, and Irkutsk.

A stranger once asked a man on the street how far it was to the railway station. The man replied, "If you keep on going the way you are headed it is twenty-five thousand miles, but if you turn round it's two blocks."

How far do you suppose it is to Siberia from our country?—how many miles away would you say?—eight thousand?—ten thousand miles? As a matter of fact, it is only about fifty miles—yes, that's right, fifty miles—for the short way is across to Alaska. Between Siberia and Alaska is a narrow strip of water called Bering Strait, and when this is frozen over, one could walk across from Asia to America. On the map there is also a long string of islands that look like stepping-stones, but one would have to be a giant to walk across that way. Some say that the Indians and Eskimos in Alaska and the United States may have come across Bering Strait from Asia long, long ago, and that they look

端叫作"符拉迪沃斯托克"[1]，而另一端则位于俄罗斯境内的莫斯科。这条铁路，叫作"西伯利亚大铁路"，也就是横跨西伯利亚的大铁路。

虽说西伯利亚的绝大多数人都居住在这条铁路沿线，但一个人可能沿着铁路走上几百英里远，却看不到一个小镇，甚至也看不到一座房屋呢。那里的市镇通常都距铁路很远，因此开车从车站到镇里都要用很长的时间。那里用于牵引列车车厢的机车，都是用木柴生火，而不是烧煤，因此铁路沿线放着一堆堆的木头，以备火车停下来加燃料，就像汽车停下来加油一样。西伯利亚那些主要的城市名称当中，都带有一个"克"字，比如鄂木斯克、托木斯克和伊尔库茨克。

有个外地人曾经在大街上问一个人，到火车站有多远。那个人回答道："要是您径直朝着现在您走的这条路走下去的话，就有两万五千英里，可您要是拐上一个弯的话，那就只要走两个街区。"

大家觉得，美国距西伯利亚有多远呢？你们说说，有多少英里？八千英里？一万英里？事实上，美国与西伯利亚相距只有五十英里，是的，没错，就是五十英里，因为从阿拉斯加跨过海去就到了。西伯利亚和阿拉斯加之间，是一片狭窄的水域，叫作"白令海峡"，这个海峡封冻起来后，人们就可以徒步穿过此处，从亚洲走到美洲了。在地图上，那里还有一长串的岛屿，就像一级级台阶似的，不过，只有巨人，一步才能跨那么远。有的人说，阿拉斯加和美洲的印第安人、因纽特

---

[1] 符拉迪沃斯托克（Vladivostok），俄罗斯联邦东南部港市，中国传统称之为"海参崴"。

something like the Chinese because they once came from that country.

Before World War I, when Russia had a czar, people who hated the czar or were supposed to hate the czar, or who had said anything against the czar, or even thought anything against the czar, were made prisoners, torn away from their families and friends, and sent to far-off Siberia to work in the mines. Many of them perished before reaching there. Most of them never returned.

After World War I there was a revolution. The people rose up and threw out the Czar's government. The new government was taken over by a group of Russians called Communists. These Communists killed the czar and his family and most of the well-to-do people of Russia. The Communists made many changes. They started schools. They killed all farmers who owned large farms and gave their land to many poor people to farm. They started factories and opened stores and built railroads and airlines. They made large dams across the rivers so they could use waterpower to send electric current to the factories.

人，可能都是在很久、很久以前从亚洲越过白令海峡而来的，他们之所以都有点儿像中国人，是因为他们的祖先就是从那个国家迁徙过来的。

第一次世界大战爆发之前，俄罗斯还是由沙皇统治的时候，那些憎恨或被人认为是憎恨沙皇的人，那些说了什么反对沙皇的话语的人，甚至是心里对沙皇不满的人，全都被投入了监狱，与家人和朋友分离，然后送到遥远的西伯利亚的矿井里去干活。许多人还没有到达那里就死了。其中绝大多数人再也没有回去。

第一次世界大战过后，俄国爆发了一场革命。人民揭竿而起，推翻了沙皇政府。新政府的大权，被一帮叫作"共产党人"的俄国人夺取了。这些共产党人处死了沙皇及其家人，还处死了俄国绝大多数家境富裕的人。共产党人进行了许多改革。他们开设了学校。他们处死了那些拥有大量土地的地主，然后将地主的土地分给了许多贫苦百姓去耕作。他们兴建了工厂，开设了商店，并且修建了铁路，成立了航空公司。他们在河流上修建了许多大坝，利用水力来发电，然后把电力送到工厂里去。

59 A Giant Sea-Serpent

When the World was young and people believed in sea-serpents they used to say there was a huge sea-serpent a thousand miles long in the sea near China. Wherever the humps on the sea-serpent's back stuck out of the water they looked like islands, and whenever the sea-serpent twisted or turned in his age-long sleep the islands would shake. Yet, long ago people from China went to these islands on the sea-serpent's back and made their homes there, in spite of the fact that he was squirming in his sleep. We now know that these islands are simply old volcanoes in the water, most of which have burned out, and when they shake, as they still do almost every day, we know that the shakes are just earthquakes. We call these islands on the sea-serpent "Japan" and the people "Japanese." The Japanese, however, don't call their island Japan; they call their country of islands "Nippon," which means the Land of the Rising Sun. Of course, the sun rises in other lands too, but when the Japanese went to Japan it was, for them, the land where the sun rose. So their white flag has on it the picture of a red sun with rays.

The Chinese and the Japanese both belong to the yellow race. But the Japanese are as different from the Chinese in most ways. The Japanese are quick to learn and quick to copy. The Japanese used to copy the Chinese writing, the Chinese Buddha, the Chinese way of eating with chop-sticks, for they knew no other people and no other country but

第59章　巨大的海蛇

远古之时，人们相信世间存在着海蛇，并且经常说，中国近海有一条长达一千英里的巨大海蛇。无论什么时候，只要这条海蛇弓起背来、浮出水面，样子都像是一座座小岛，无论什么时候，只要这条海蛇扭动身子，或者在睡梦当中翻个身，那些小岛便会地动山摇。不过，很久以前，中国人便来到了海蛇背上的这些小岛，并且，尽管这条海蛇仍然一边睡觉、一边不停地扭动，他们还是在那里安下了家。如今我们都知道，那些岛屿完全是由海底的古老火山喷发后形成的，其中绝大多数火山都已熄灭，如果这些岛屿晃动起来（如今，那里几乎每天仍会这样），我们也都知道，那不过是地震罢了。我们将这些位于海蛇背上的岛屿叫作"日本"，而生活在那里的人则叫"日本人"。然而，日本人自己可没有把他们生活的那些岛屿称作"日本"，而是将这个岛国称作"Nippon"，意思就是"太阳升起的地方"。当然，太阳也会在其他大陆上升起，不过，最初的日本人来到日本之时，这个地方在他们看来，就是太阳升起的地方。因此，他们那面白色的国旗上，还印有一轮向四周发出光芒的太阳呢。

中国人与日本人都属于黄种人。不过，日本人在绝大多数方面都与中国人不同。日本人长于学习、敏于模仿。日本人曾经模仿了中国人的文字、中国的佛教、中国人用筷子吃饭的习惯，因为在当时，除了中国人和中国，他们并不了解其他的

China and, like the Chinese, they kept all others out of their country. It was as if they had put up a sign, "No Admittance."

Now, for some reason or other, most people whenever they see a sign "Keep Out" want to "Go in"—like Mary, Mary quite contrary, they want to do what they are told they musn't. They are curious or inquisitive and they want to know and see why there is "No Admittance." So, over a hundred years ago, an American naval officer named Commodore Perry went to Japan and tried to get in. He took with him a shipload of presents from our country for the Japanese Emperor, presents such as the Emperor had never seen or known of before. The Emperor was so pleased with the presents that he wanted to buy more and to know more about countries that could make such things. So Commodore Perry said to the Emperor, "Let the American people come in to your country and we will sell you these things and buy other things from you." The Emperor agreed, and so the country was opened for trade and the eyes of the Japanese were opened too, for until then they had had no idea of what was going on in other countries except China. They were amazed to hear about railroad trains, the telegraph, and the marvelous machines that we had. Then Japan sent thousands of her brightest young men to our country and to the countries of Europe to learn about such things, and they returned and taught their own people, who were extraordinarily quick to learn. It was not long before they had copies of everything that we had. They made their country an up-to-date country. But if some one sets out to copy some one else he is apt to copy the bad things as well as the good. And that's what the Japanese

民族和其他的国家，并且，他们将所有外国人都拒之于国门之外。这种情况，就好比是他们在国门立起了一块牌子，上面写着"禁止进入"似的。

注意，不知道是什么原因，绝大多数人只要看到"不准进入"的牌子，便都想"进去"看上一看，他们就像是"玛丽，玛丽，十分叛逆"那样，都想去干点儿别人不让他们去干的事情。他们要么是好奇心重，要么是求知欲强，反正都想看一看，这里为什么会有一块"禁止进入"的牌子。于是，一百多年前，一位叫作佩里准将的美国海军军官前往日本，想要进入该国。他率领的船只上，携带着美国送给日本天皇的一船礼物，而且，这些礼物全都是日本天皇以前从未见过、也没有听说过的新奇之物。天皇看到那些礼物后很高兴，希望购买更多的这种东西，并且更多地了解这些东西的生产国的情况。于是，佩里准将便对天皇说："如果您让美国人民来到贵国的话，我们就会将这些东西卖给您，然后购买贵国生产出来的其他商品。"天皇同意了，于是该国便开放了贸易，而日本人的眼界也因此而大大打开了，因为直到那时，除了中国，他们对其他国家的情况仍然一无所知呢。听到我们拥有铁路列车、电报和其他那些神奇的机器后，他们都大感惊讶。接下来，日本便从国内遴选出数千名最聪明的年轻人，把他们送到了美国以及欧洲各国，去学习这些东西，而回国之后，他们又将这些知识传授给了学习能力极强的本国人民。不久之后，他们便仿制出了我们拥有的所有东西。他们让日本成为一个现代化的国家。不过，如果一个人从一开始就模仿他人的话，这个人也很容易良莠不分，好的坏的一起模仿。日本人的所作所为，正是这样。他们并非只是仿制了西方国家的电车、

did. They not only copied trolley-cars, electric lights, and automobiles. They copied battleships and airplanes and tanks and guns. They built a great big up-to-date army. Then they started a great big up-to-date war by dropping bombs on American ships in Hawaii. After the Japanese were beaten in the war they were not allowed to have a big army nor to build war machines like battleships, tanks, and guns.

One of the first things the Japanese copied was a baby carriage to carry grown-up people. In Japan they have very few horses, because horses eat too much. So an American sailor, living in Japan, made for his wife a large baby carriage that could be pulled by a man, for in Japan a man was cheaper than a horse. The Japanese called it a Jinrikisha, which means a "man pull car," or a Pullman car. It seems strange that the parlor cars on our trains are also called Pullman cars. This "rickshaw," as it is called for short, seemed such a good idea that the Japanese made thousands of them, and they are now used instead of taxis or private cars. The men who pull them are called coolies, and a coolie will dog-trot almost all day long, pulling a rickshaw behind him, without getting tired. As you see a rickshaw going away from you down the street, the coolie is hidden all but his legs, so that it looks as if the rickshaw itself were trotting along with a pair of legs of its own.

In the cities many of the men wear clothes like ours, but most of the people, both men and women, still wear kimonos like those our mothers and sisters often wear in their own homes.

There are two important holidays for Japanese boys and girls. The one for girls comes

电灯和汽车，而且还仿制了战舰、飞机、坦克和大炮。他们成立了一支规模庞大的现代化军队。接下来，他们又发动了一场大规模的现代化战争，向位于夏威夷的美国军舰投下了炸弹。日本人在这场战争中被打败之后，国际社会就不再允许他们拥有一支大型的军队，也不允许他们再兴建像战舰、坦克和大炮这样的战争武器了。

日本人最初仿造的东西中，有一种就是用于运载成年人的婴儿车。因为马匹要吃太多的粮食，所以日本国内马匹很少。于是，一位住在日本的美国水手便给自己的妻子制造了一辆大型的婴儿车，这种车子可以由一个人拉着跑，因为日本的人力成本比马匹要低。日本人将这种车子称为"人力车"，也就是"人拉的汽车"，或者叫作"拉人车"。美国火车上的特等车厢也叫"拉人车"，这一点似乎很奇怪呢。曾经有过一段时间被人们称为"黄包车"的这种车子似乎很不错，因此日本人制造出了成千上万辆，如今，这种车子已经用于取代出租车或者私人汽车了。拉这种车子的人，叫作"苦力"，一名苦力，几乎整天都拉着一辆黄包车，一路小跑着，却不觉得累。一辆黄包车从你们身边驶过，沿着街道往下跑去的时候，除了两条腿，你们是看不到苦力本人的，因此，这种情景仿佛是黄包车自己长了两条腿，一路小跑着往前去了呢。

在日本的城市里，许多人的穿着打扮都跟我们差不多，不过，其中绝大多数人，不论男女，仍然穿着"和服"，就像我们的妈妈、姐妹在家里经常穿的那种便服。

日本小朋友在一年当中，有两个重要的节日。女孩子的节日是第三个月的第三

on the third day of the third month, that is March third. It is called Doll Day and the girls get out all their dolls, arrange them nicely, and play with them. The one for the boys is on the fifth day of the fifth month, that is May fifth. It is called Flag Day or Kite Day. Big paper kites in the form of a fish called the carp are hung out on poles in front of the houses where there are boys. The carp is a fish that swims upstream against the current, which is a hard thing to do, instead of downstream, which is easy. So the carp is a model for boys—to do the hardest thing, not the easiest.

The Japanese love flowers perhaps more than any people i.t.w.W. and they have holidays when the flowers are in bloom. One holiday comes when the cherry-trees, plum-trees, and peach-trees bloom in the spring, and another when the chrysanthemums bloom in the fall. Every house in Japan has a garden, no matter how small it may be—a tiny imitation of the country-side, with tiny lakes and tiny mountains, and tiny rivers with tiny bridges over them—all so perfectly made that a photograph of such a garden looks like a picture of real mountains and lakes and rivers—like a doll garden. The Japanese grow dwarf trees—oaks and maples—which look in a picture as if they were a hundred feet tall and a hundred years old, but which are actually only a foot or so tall, but may be a hundred years old.

The Japanese school-boys seem to "hunger and thirst" after knowledge. I was looking into a shop window where beautiful Japanese umbrellas were displayed, when a school-boy came up to me and asked me in English if he couldn't act as my guide for a day

天，即三月三号。这一天叫作"娃娃节"[1]，小姑娘都会把所有的洋娃娃拿出来，摆得整整齐齐，跟洋娃娃玩。男孩子的节日则是一年中第五个月的第五天，即五月五号。这一天叫作"国旗节"或者"风筝节"。凡有男孩子的家庭，都会在门口的柱子上挂上一种巨大的鲤鱼形纸糊风筝。鲤鱼是一种喜欢逆流而上的鱼类，逆流而上是件难事，而顺流则很容易。因此，鲤鱼便成了男孩子们的榜样，表示大人希望他们去做最困难的事情，而不是去做最容易的事情。

或许，日本人比全世界的其他任何一个民族都更加热爱鲜花，因此，在鲜花盛开的时候，他们也有节日。其中，一个节日是在春季樱桃、李树和桃树全都竞相开花的时候，另一个节日则是在秋季菊花盛开的时候。日本的每栋房子里都有一座花园，无论房子多小，花园都会布置得就像一个迷你乡村似的，有小湖、小假山、小河，上面还有小桥，一切都配合得完美无缺。要是给这种花园拍上一张照片的话，看上去就跟拍摄的是真山、真湖和真河没什么两样，简直就像是个洋娃娃所用的花园呢。日本人喜欢种植盆景树，比如橡树和枫树，在照片上看起来，它们似乎都有一百英尺高、有一百岁那么沧桑，可实际上，它们却只有一英尺左右高，但树龄倒是可能真的有一百岁了。

日本的学生，似乎都"如饥似渴"地想要学到知识。有一次，我正在商店橱窗里观赏一些漂亮的日本伞，这时一个学生向我走来，用英语问我说，能不能免费给

---

[1] 娃娃节（Doll Day），如今一般称为"女儿节"。

without charge.

"Why," said I, "do you want to show me around?"

"Just to practise speaking English," he replied.

I visited a Japanese school, and a dozen boys gave me their calling cards and asked me to write them when I reached home, promising to reply in English if I did so.

我当一天的导游。

"您想带我到处转转，" 我说， "是为了什么呢？"

"只是为了练习说英语。"他回答道。

我曾经参观过一个日本学校，十几个小朋友都把他们的名片给我，要我回国后给他们写信，并且承诺说，要是我给他们写信的话，他们就会用英语给我回信。

60 Picture Post-Cards

When I came home from Japan I sent picture post-cards to all the Japanese school-boys who had given me their names. I had chosen cards that I thought would give them some idea of the size and importance of our country. One card had a picture of the Capitol at Washington, another Niagara Falls, another skyscrapers in New York. In reply each boy wrote me a letter on thin rice paper and drew or painted or inclosed a picture of some scene or common sight in Japan.

Three of the pictures were of the same thing—a beautiful mountain with a snow-white top. It is the sacred mountain of Japan, called Fujiyama or just Fuji. It is really not a mountain at all but a burnt-out volcano, the top of which is covered with snow. You can see it from afar, and the Japanese love it so they put pictures of it on every conceivable thing they want to ornament—on fans, boxes, trays, umbrellas, lanterns, screens. No movie queen or famous beauty has ever had as many pictures made of her as have been made of Fuji.

There were two pictures of a huge bronze statue of Buddha seated out-of-doors in a grove of trees. It is so large that half a dozen people can sit on its thumbs. The eyes are of solid gold and more than a yard long, and in its forehead is a large ball of solid silver. They call it the Diabutsu. We might call it an idol, but the Japanese make statues of Buddha as we put up monuments to famous men and saints, and their statues of Buddha are to remind them that he was wise and good. His life was an example which even Christians might imitate.

第60章　明信片

从日本回国后，凡是把名字告诉了我的日本学生，我都寄了一张明信片。那些明信片，我都经过了精挑细选，觉得它们可以让日本学生多少了解到美国的面积大小和重要性。有张明信片上是华盛顿国会大厦的照片，有张明信片上是尼亚加拉大瀑布，还有一张则是纽约的摩天大楼。每个孩子都用宣纸给我写了回信，并且还附上了一张画或者照片，上面都是日本的某种风景或者常见的名胜之地。

其中有三张照片，上面拍的都是同一个地方，即一座山顶雪白的美丽山峰。那是日本的圣山，叫作"富士山"。其实，那里根本不是一座普通的山峰，而是一座已经熄灭了的火山，而山顶则覆盖着白雪。从很远的地方就看得到富士山，日本人也非常喜欢这座山，凡是想得到的东西，他们都会用富士山的照片来装饰，比如扇子啦，盒子啦，盘子啦，伞啦，灯啦，屏风啦。任何一个电影皇后或者有名的美人，拍的照片都没有富士山那样多呢。

还有两张照片，上面是一尊巨大的青铜佛陀雕像，坐落在户外的绿树丛中。那尊佛像极其巨大，拇指上就坐得下六个人呢。佛像的眼睛是用纯金打造而成，长达一码多，前额上则是一个巨大的纯银球。日本人称这座佛像为"大佛"。我们可以称之为神像。不过，日本人制作佛陀雕像，就像我们为名人和圣人修建纪念碑一

Here are some of the other pictures which the Japanese boys sent me:

A street scene in Tokyo:

Tokyo is the capital and largest city of Japan and one of the largest cities i.t.w.W. The old capital has exactly the same letters as Tokyo but arranged this way: Kyoto. If you say Tokyo twice you say Kyoto too—TO/KYOTO/KYO. Both Tokyo and Kyoto and all other Japanese cities look quite different from our large cities. There are no sky-scrapers, few buildings are more than two stories high, and most of them are built of bamboo. The reason for this is because the sea-serpent is still shaking himself almost every day, and they have so many earthquakes in these islands that tall houses would be shaken down. When an earthquake does come—and slight ones come almost every day and terrific ones every once in a while—the houses can easily be built up again. The chief damage done by the earthquakes, however, is the result of fires started when lights and stoves are upset. Then thousands of houses may be destroyed.

There are a few big buildings that are built to withstand earthquakes. They are built on underground platforms of concrete instead of on the solid rock of the earth. This keeps them from being torn from their foundations when an earthquake shakes the ground; just as a big loose rock lying on the ground might be shaken but would not be broken apart.

富士山，日本神圣的火山

样，而他们之所以制作佛陀雕像，也是为了提醒自己，佛陀既有智慧，又很善良。

佛陀的一生，是世人的一种榜样，连基督徒也可以去效仿呢。

日本学生回寄给我的明信片上，还有下面这样一些照片：

东京的街景：

东京既是日本的首都和该国最大的城市，也是全球最大的城市之一。日本原来的首都叫作京都，在英语里与"东京"所用的字母完全一样，只是排列顺序不同罢了。要是大家连续说上两次"东京"的话，就会发出"京都"的音来："东/京东（都）/京"。东京、京都以及日本其他的所有城市，样子都与美国的大城市很不一样。日本城市里没有摩天大楼，很少有楼房高过两层，并且绝大多数房子都是用竹子建成的。之所以如此，是因为那条"海蛇"如今几乎每天都仍在颤动，这些岛屿上地震频发，要是房子建得太高的话，就会被震塌。如果确实发生了地震，那么，这种竹子建造的房子也可以轻而易举地进行重建，那里几乎每天都有小震，而每隔一段时间，还会出现一次可怕的大地震呢。然而，地震造成的主要破坏，还是把油灯、炉子震翻之后引发的火灾。那样的话，一次就会焚毁成千上万座房屋。

日本也有少量的大型建筑，是按照抗震标准修建起来的。它们都建在地下的混凝土平台上，而不是建在地下的岩石之上。这样一来，地震发生、地面震动的时候，楼房就不会与地基断裂，它们就像是地上一块松动的大石头那样，地震发生时

A picture of a Japanese house:

Japanese houses make fine bonfires, for they are not only made entirely of wood, but the windows are made of paper and the floors are covered with straw mats. The mats are not made to fit the floor, but the floors are made to fit the mats, which are all of the same size. The rooms are built to fit six mats, ten mats, and so on. In order to keep the mats clean, the Japanese take off their shoes whenever they enter their houses, and walk about the house in their stocking feet. Their stockings are like mittens with a place for the toe, and they would no more think of stepping on the mats with their shoes on than you would of getting into bed with your shoes on.

There are no chairs in a Japanese house, for the Japanese sit on the floor. For us it is very uncomfortable to sit on the floor for any length of time, but the Japanese prefer it, and I have seen them squatting on the floor in railway stations, although there were benches to sit on right alongside. I don't know why, but I've often seen American girls sit on chairs with their feet up under them as if they were sitting on the floor. But I've never seen boys do it. Perhaps girls are part Japanese. The tables in a Japanese house have legs only a few inches high; they are really only trays like the bed trays we use when one is sick, and meals are served by placing such a tray in front of each person as he squats on his heels on the floor. There are no beds either;

这尊雕像是为了提醒他们，佛陀睿智而善良

虽然会左摇右晃，却不会从中裂开。

日本民居的照片：

日本的民居都很适合于用来点篝火，因为它们非但完全由木头建成，而且窗户都是用纸张糊出来的，地板上也盖着草席。日本人不是将草席裁剪得适合于地板，而是将地板制造得适合于铺草席，因为草席的尺寸都是统一的。各个房间建成后，都恰好铺上六块席子、十块席子，诸如此类。为了让席子保持干净，日本人进屋之前都会脱掉鞋子，然后穿着袜子在屋里走动。他们的袜子有点儿像是那种连指手套，包住了脚尖。他们绝对不会穿着鞋子到席子上去踩，就像你们不会穿着鞋子上床睡觉一样。

日本人家里没有椅子，他们都是坐在地板上。对于我们来说，坐在地上无论过多久都会很不舒服，可日本人却很喜欢那样坐着，我曾经见到过，尽管身边有长椅可坐，但一些日本人在火车站却宁愿蹲坐在地上。我不知道那是为什么，不过，我也经常看到，一些美国姑娘坐在椅子上的时候，会把双脚放到身子下面，就像是坐在地上一样。但是，我从来都没有见到男孩子这样坐过。或许，姑娘们都有点儿日本血统吧。日本人家里的桌子，桌腿都只有几英寸高，它们实际上只是一种炕桌，就像是有人生病时，我们所用的那种床几一样。日本人吃饭时，都是把双腿跪在身下，蹲坐在地板上，而饭菜则放在每个人身前的这种桌子上。日本人家里也没有

they sleep on the mats and cover themselves with a padded kimono for a comforter and use a hard wooden block for a pillow.

The Japanese are like elephants. In what way? I'll give you three guesses. They bathe frequently. But what seems to us peculiar, all the family, one after another, bathe in the same tub without changing the water. The tub is shaped like a sawed-off barrel in which there is room to sit but not to lie down. The water is piping hot "to open the pores." After the bather has parboiled himself, he then climbs out and scrubs himself.

A picture of two Japanese carrying a big bucket on a pole which rests on their shoulders:

In the tub—I couldn't see them but I knew—there are live fish. The Japanese eat little meat, because they have few animals such as cows, sheep, or pigs from which meat is made, and because good Buddhists do not believe in eating meat anyway. But fish they do not call meat, and they catch and eat more fish than any other people in the World, even more than the people in Norway. As Japan is all islands, no one lives far from the sea, and fresh fish may be had all the time. Peddlers carry them alive in tubs of water so that the fish will be absolutely fresh.

A picture of fields covered with water in which is growing rice:

Rice is the chief and almost the only vegetable in Japan, and tea is the chief drink. Tea the Japanese drink without either sugar or cream. There are tea-houses and tea-gardens where waitresses called Geisha girls serve tea to customers and then entertain them by dancing and playing on long-necked musical instruments something like a banjo.

Another letter was ornamented with high wooden gateways called Torii, which you see

床，他们都是睡在席子上，用填充了东西的和服当被子，用硬木块做枕头。

日本人像是大象。在哪个方面像呢？我会告诉你们三种猜想。他们经常洗澡。不过，让我们觉得奇怪的是，日本人的全家都是一个接一个地在同一个浴盆里洗澡，而不用换水。他们的浴盆，样子就像是一个锯掉了半截的木桶，洗澡者可以坐在里面，但躺不下去。洗澡水热气腾腾，这是为了"打开毛孔"。把自己煮了个半熟之后，洗澡者就会爬出木桶，用力擦洗身上。

两个日本人用一根杆子抬着一只大水桶的照片：

那个水桶里肯定盛着活鱼，虽说看不到，但我知道。日本人很少吃肉，这是因为该国像母牛、绵羊或者猪这种可以产肉的牲畜很少，而且还因为善良的佛教徒都觉得自己不能吃肉。但是，他们却不把鱼类叫作肉食，所以，他们捕捞和吃掉的鱼类，比世界上其他任何一个民族都要多，甚至比挪威人都要多呢。由于日本全是岛屿，人们都住在离海边不远的地方，因此任何时候都有新鲜的鱼类可吃。小贩们都是用水桶运送活鱼，从而确保鱼儿绝对新鲜。

一幅水田里生长着水稻的照片：

水稻是日本最主要的、差不多也是唯一的作物，而茶则是日本的主要饮料。日本人喝茶的时候，既不加糖，也不加奶油。日本有许多茶楼和茶园，其间有一种叫作"艺伎"的女服务员，她们既会给客人斟茶，也会跳舞，还会弹奏一种琴架很长、有点儿像是五弦琴的乐器，来给客人助兴。

everywhere in Japan, standing sometimes alone, sometimes in line. Torii means a bird rest. They are sacred gateways under which one passes to a temple or shrine.

Still another letter was illustrated with pictures of large stone lanterns such as you often see around Japanese temples and in their gardens. These lanterns give very little light, but they are much more ornamental than our lanterns, and the Japanese think more of beauty than they do of use. They even have a festival of lanterns—the paper kind that we use at garden parties.

Another letter contained a picture of three monkeys carved in wood in the greatest of all Japanese temples at Nikko. One monkey had his paws over his ears, the next over his mouth, and the third over his eyes, meaning: "Hear no evil, speak no evil, see no evil."

A picture of two very fat men squatting on the ground and facing each other in the center of a huge building around which are sitting thousands of people watching:

牌坊或者日式大门

The two fat men are wrestlers. Wrestling is a national sport in Japan, as bull-fighting is a national sport in Spain and football is a national sport in the United States. There are two kinds of wrestling. One kind is done by giants weighing several hundred pounds, who wrestle before crowds such as gather to watch baseball or football games in this country. The wrestlers squat, facing each other like huge bullfrogs, and spend most of their time in this position, each watching for a

还有一封信里，则画着一种叫作"牌坊"的、高耸的木质大门，这种牌坊，你们在日本到处都看得到，有时只有一座，有时则是好几座排列在一起。"牌坊"一词，本指"鸟居"。它们都是"圣门"，从这些牌坊下面通过的人，都是前往神庙或者神殿的。

还有一封信中配有插图，上面画着一些巨大的石制灯塔，大家参观日本的神社或者公园时，经常会看到这种灯塔。这种灯塔发出的光线并不强，它们的装饰性要比我们所用的灯大得多，因为日本人比较重视美观，而不那么重视实用。他们甚至还会举办"灯节"，而他们在灯节上所用的灯，就是我们开花园派对时所用的那种纸质灯笼。

还有一封信里，则附有一幅三只猴子的木雕照片，这三件木雕，全都位于日光市，保存在日本那座最伟大的寺庙里。其中，一只猴子把爪子放在耳朵上，另一只猴子的爪子放在嘴巴上，第三只猴子的爪子则放在眼睛上，它们表达出来的意思就是："勿听恶语，勿说恶言，勿看恶事。"

两个胖子在一座大型建筑的中心相对蹲坐在地上，周围坐着几千观众的照片：

这两个胖子都是摔跤手。摔跤是日本的一种民族性运动，就像斗牛是西班牙一种全民运动、橄榄球是美国的全民性运动一样。日本有两种摔跤。第一种，是由体重达到了数百磅的大块头来当众摔跤，围观的人则与美国去看棒球比赛或者橄榄球比赛的观众没什么两样。摔跤手蹲下身子，相对而立，就像两只巨大的牛蛙，并且

chance to get a grip on the other. The game seems to an American simply one of watching and waiting, for once one gets "a hold" on the other the battle is usually over. Another kind of wrestling is called Jiu-jitsu. It is a trick wrestling, and a little chap, if he knows how, can throw a much larger and stronger person by catching his arm, hand, or leg and twisting it with a quick movement into certain positions that make it impossible for him to resist. I have seen in Japan whole schools lined up two and two, practising the various "throws" with lightning-like movements.

Wrestling is an old Japanese sport. The Japanese, however, copied new sports from other countries along with all the other things they copied. They copied baseball, and crowds at baseball games in Japan are as big as baseball crowds in the United States.

The last letter inclosed a photograph of the Emperor. Many countries have now changed from emperors to presidents but Japan, which has been quick to change in most things, I don't believe ever will change to a president. The same family has been ruling in Japan for two thousand years. Even after being beaten in World War II, the Japanese were allowed by the other countries to keep their Emperor. Before this war the Japanese believed the Emperor was sacred as if he were a god. They still treat him with great respect but are no longer supposed to worship him.

日本的石制灯塔

在大多数时间里都会保持着这种姿势，两人都紧盯着对方，都想瞅准机会抓住对方。这种比赛，在美国人看来，完全就是一种"看着、等着"的比赛，因为一旦一方"抓住"了另一方，比赛通常也就结束了。第二种摔跤则叫"柔道"。这是一种技巧性摔跤，若是掌握了技巧，一个小伙子就可以抓住对方的胳膊、手或者腿，将其猛地扭到某种位置，使对方不可能再行反抗，从而打败一个体型更大、体格比更强壮的人。我曾经在日本的学校里看到过，全校的人都排好队，两个一组，用迅雷不及掩耳的动作，练习着各种不同的"摔"的技巧呢。

摔跤是日本一项历史悠久的运动。然而，日本人在模仿其他东西的同时，也模仿了其他国家许多新的体育运动。他们仿效了棒球运动，因此如今日本的棒球比赛观众，并不少于美国观看棒球比赛的人呢。

最后一封信里，有一张日本天皇的照片。虽说如今许多国家都从设有皇帝的王国变成了设有总统的共和国，但我认为，尽管日本在绝大多数方面都变革得非常迅速，可该国永远都不会变成一个设有总统的共和国。日本已经由同一个皇室统治了两千年的时间。即便是在第二次世界大战中战败之后，战胜国也仍然允许日本保留该国的天皇呢。此战之前，日本人都认为天皇非常神圣，就像上帝一样。如今，他们仍然非常尊重天皇，只是据说不再崇拜他了。

61 Man-Made Mountains

All the continents begin with an "A" except one.

Asia is the largest continent.

Africa is the next largest.

But Africa was an "In-the-Way" continent. It was in the way of those who wanted to get to Asia. Everyone wanted to get around Africa. No one wanted to get to it. Sailors had been shipwrecked on its shores, but few lived to tell the tale of jungles of wild animals and wild black men. Africa was called the Dark Continent because no one knew much about it or wanted to know about it. Like children afraid of the dark, people were afraid of the Dark Continent. On one edge—along the Mediterranean Sea—white men lived, but south of that edge was a great desert that men feared to cross, and south of that wild black men and wild animals. But in one corner of Africa, the corner near Asia and along the Red Sea, white people had been living and mighty kings had been ruling for thousands of years. This corner country is called Egypt.

Have you ever seen a man one hundred years old? I have seen a man five thousand years old—a real man, a little dried up man who was once a mighty ruler of Egypt. He did not want to "turn to dust" when he died, for how then could he rise again from the dead at the Day of Judgment? So he left orders that he should be pickled and wrapped in bandages and a mountain of stone placed over his body to make sure it would not be touched or

第61章　人造山峦

所有的大洲，英语名称都是以"A"字开头的，只有一个洲例外。

亚洲是世界上最大的洲。

非洲是位居第二的大洲。

不过，非洲也是一个"挡路"的大洲。它挡住了那些想要前往亚洲的人的路。大家都想绕过非洲，可没有人想要前往非洲。虽然水手们曾经在非洲海岸沉过船，可很少有人幸存下来，向别人讲述那个全是野兽和黑人的非洲丛林里的情况。非洲被人们称为"黑暗大陆"，因为当时没有人很了解那里，也没有人想要去了解。就像孩子们都害怕黑暗一样，人们也害怕这个"黑暗大陆"。尽管非洲北部沿地中海的那个边缘生活着白人，但那道边缘以南，却是一片广袤的沙漠，人们都不敢穿越，而从这个沙漠再往南去，就只有野蛮的黑人和野兽了。不过，在非洲一角，也就是挨着亚洲和红海沿岸的东北角上，却一直生活着白人，并且有强大的国王统治了数千年。这个位于非洲一角的国家，叫作"埃及"。

大家有没有见过百岁老人呢？我可见过一个有五千岁的人呢，那是一个真正的人，曾经还是埃及一位有权有势的君主，只是如今已经变成一具瘦小的干尸了。他不希望自己死后"化为尘土"，因为要是那样的话，到了最后的审判日，他又怎能从死者中获得重生呢？于是，他便留下遗命，让人们给他的尸体进行防腐处理，然

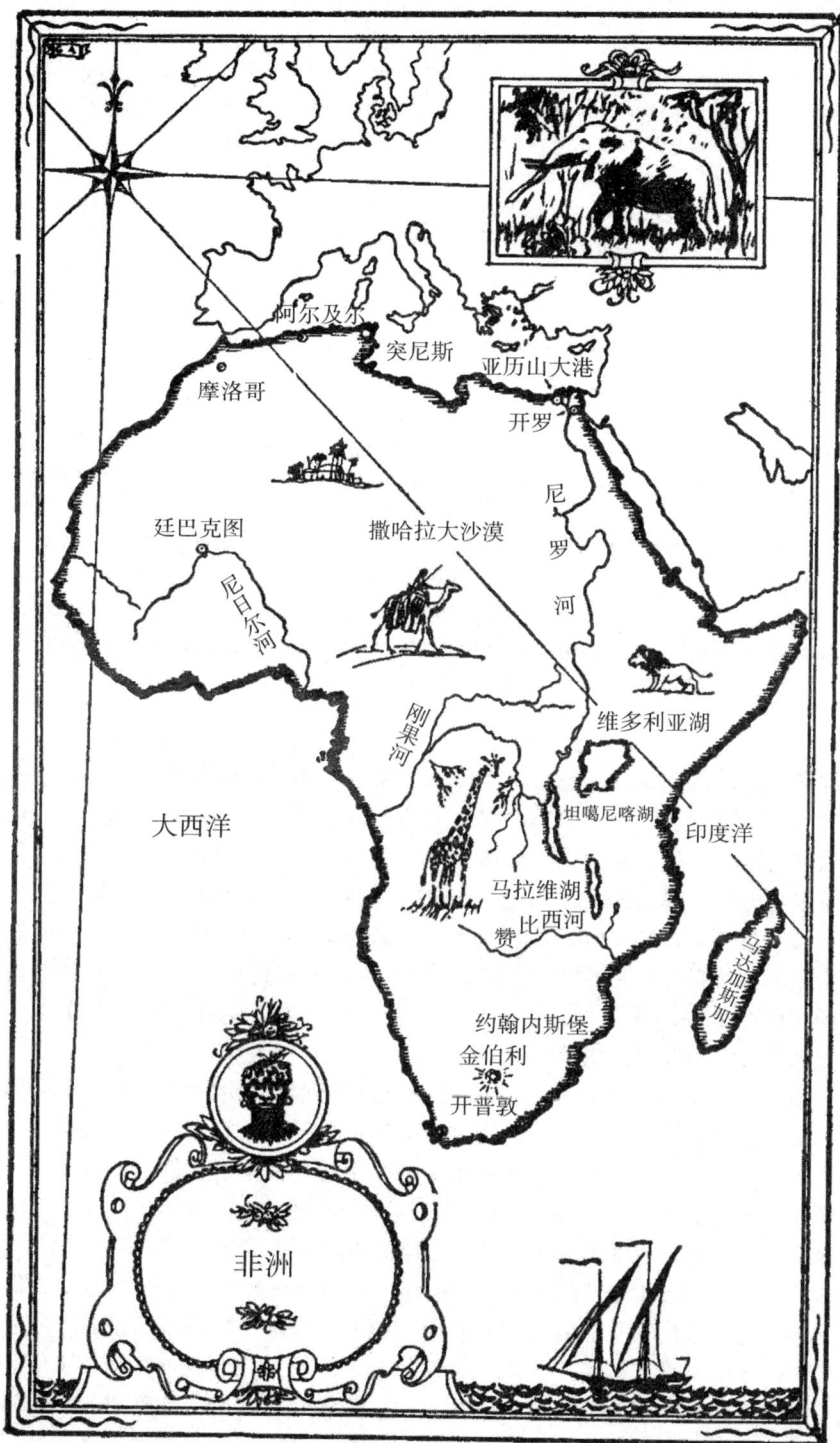

阿尔及尔

突尼斯

亚历山大港

摩洛哥

开罗

尼
罗
河

廷巴克图

撒哈拉大沙漠

尼
日
尔
河

刚
果
河

维多利亚湖

大西洋

坦噶尼喀湖

印度洋

马拉维湖

赞
比
西
河

马
达
加
斯
加

约翰内斯堡

金伯利

开普敦

非洲

moved away. In fact, he built the mountain of stone before he died, to make sure of that part of it. But you can never tell what will happen to you after you are dead, so in spite of the mountain of stone, here he is, a ruler of Egypt whom millions obeyed, now in a case in a museum where anyone can stare at him, and the janitor dusts his face and moves him out of the way to sweep the floor. A pickled man is called a mummy, and the mummies of many such rulers of Egypt are now in museums.

One of the Seven Wonders of the World was these mountains of stone called pyramids, which the kings built when they were alive, to be tombs for themselves when dead. Each king tried to build a bigger and better pyramid than the king before him. The largest pyramid was built by a king called Cheops, who died nearly three thousand years before Christ was born. It is said that it took one hundred thousand people ten years to build his tomb.

The outsides of the pyramids used to be smooth slanting walls, but people have taken out stone from the sides to build other buildings, so that now the outsides of the pyramids are as rough as piled-up heaps of stones and you can climb from stone to stone on up to the top. Cheops's tomb and most of the other tombs or pyramids are of solid rock, with just a small room in the center, which was left for the body of the king and the things he had used when he was alive. The old Egyptians thought they must keep their furniture and other things around them, so that on the Judgment Day, when they should be awakened from their long sleep, they would be all ready to go on housekeeping. After Cheops's body was put into the tomb the passageway leading to it was filled up tight with stone, and all

后用绑带包裹起来，放到一座石山下面，从而确保他的遗体不会被人找到并移走。事实上，这座石山还是他生前就修建好了的，目的就是为了确保他死后，上述过程能够顺利进行。不过，我们是永远都不知道自己死后会发生什么的，因此，尽管有那样一座石山保护着，如今他的遗体却被人转到了这里：那个曾经有数百万人臣服于脚下的埃及君主，如今被人们存放到了一座博物馆的箱子里，任何一位游客都可以瞪着他看，而清洁工还会掸去他脸上的灰尘，并将他搬到一边，来擦洗地板。这种经过防腐处理的人类尸体，叫作"木乃伊"，如今，许多埃及君主的"木乃伊"，都被人们存放到博物馆里了。

"世界七大奇迹"里，有一大奇迹便是这种叫作"金字塔"的石山，埃及国王们都是生前就修建好了金字塔，把金字塔当成自己死后的坟墓。每位国王都想要修建一座比前任国王规模更大、质量更好的金字塔。其中最大的一座金字塔，是一个叫作基奥普斯的国王修建的，这位国王，死于基督降生前差不多三千年左右。据说，他的这座坟墓，用了十万人，花了十年的时间才建成呢。

金字塔的外部，以前都是非常光滑的、倾斜着的石墙，不过，由于人们一直从金字塔的各面取出石头去修建其他建筑，因此如今金字塔的外墙都参差不平，像随便堆砌起来的石堆那样了，人们还可以攀着一块块石头，一直爬到金字塔的顶上去呢。基奥普斯的陵墓和其他绝大多数陵墓，或者说金字塔，都是用实心的岩石建成，只是整座金字塔中央有一个小小的房间，那里是留下来安放国王遗体和国王生

traces of the opening were hidden so that no one could find it and steal his body away. But, nevertheless, someone did find it out, stole his mummy and all the things that had been left there for his use in the next World, and if his soul ever returns it will find no body.

The ancient Egyptians worshiped fairy-tale gods and even animals. Bulls and beetles were sacred and they made mummies of them. Now, however, nine out of every ten people in Egypt are Mohammedans and, instead of building pyramids, they build beautiful mosques.

Close by these big pyramids is the Sphinx, a huge stone figure with the body of a lion and the head of one of the Egyptian kings. In Greece a sphinx was supposed to be an animal with a woman's head that sat by the road and asked passers-by this riddle: "What is it that goes on four feet in the morning, two at midday, and three at night?" If the traveler couldn't tell the answer the sphinx devoured him. At last some one answered, "Man, because he crawls on all fours in the morning of his life, then walks on two feet, and finally on two feet and a cane." The Greek sphinx was a "she." But the Egyptian sphinx is a "he." He has a man's head and he asked no riddles. He was a god of the sun.

前所用之物的。古埃及人认为，他们死后，必须把家具和其他器物都放在尸体旁边，以便到了最后审判日，他们从漫长的沉睡中醒来后，随时都能继续生活。基奥普斯的遗体放进墓穴之后，通往这个墓穴的通道就被人们用石头紧紧地封死，而入口的所有痕迹也都被掩藏起来，从而没人能够找到入口并将他的遗体盗走了。不过，尽管如此，后来还是有人找到了入口，盗走了他的"木乃伊"，以及留在那里供基奥普斯来世再用的所有物品，因此，就算基奥普斯的灵魂确实会重生的话，他也找不到自己的躯体了。

曾经的埃及君主，如今却被存放在博物馆内，清洁工还会将他搬开，来清洁地板

古埃及人崇拜神话传说中的神灵，甚至崇拜动物。公牛和甲虫都是圣兽，古埃及人也会把它们制成"木乃伊"呢。然而，如今十分之九的埃及人都成了穆斯林，因此他们不再修建金字塔，而是修建了许多美丽的清真寺。

紧挨着这些大金字塔的，还有"斯芬克斯"，那是一尊巨大的石雕，身体是狮子，而脑袋则是埃及一位国王的头像。在古希腊，人们认为斯芬克斯是一种长有女子脑袋的动物，它会坐在路边，要路过的人猜下面这个谜语："什么东西早上用四条腿走路，中午用两条腿走路，而晚上则用三条腿走路？"要是答不出来的话，过路的人就会被斯芬克斯吃掉。最后，有个人回答说："是人啊，因为人类小的时候

The Sphinx and pyramids are on the bank of the one and only great river of Egypt, called the Nile. Have you ever heard of crocodile tears? The crocodile is a big alligator-like animal that lives in the Nile, and people used to say that he would catch little Egyptian boys and while he was eating them he would weep as if his heart would break. That's why when you cry, though you don't really mean it, we say you are shedding "crocodile tears"! The Nile splits into several branches before it empties into the Mediterranean Sea, and the land between the branches is called a delta, because it is shaped like the Greek letter "D," which was called delta and shaped like a triangle. You see, people of long ago also called places after common things which they thought had the same shape.

Hardly any rain falls in northern Egypt, but in southern Egypt there are heavy rains in the summer. Then the Nile overflows its banks and floods the country and leaves great quantities of mud. This mud is very rich soil in which the Egyptians grow wheat and a very fine kind of cotton. In the olden times the Nile used to overflow the banks only once a year, and the rest of the year the land would be dry and the people would have to climb down the banks to get water. Not so long ago a huge dam was built far up the

金字塔被称为是"世界七大奇迹"之一

埃及的斯芬克斯和金字塔

是在地上用双手双脚爬着走，长大成人后用两条腿走路，而老年则要拄着拐杖，算是用三条腿走路了。"古希腊的斯芬克斯是位"女性"。但是，古埃及的斯芬克斯却是"男性"。它长着一个男子的脑袋，并且不会要人猜谜语。实际上，他是一位太阳神。

斯芬克斯和金字塔，全都位于一条河流的岸边，那条河叫作"尼罗河"，是埃及唯一的一条大河。大家有没有听说过"鳄鱼的眼泪"这种说法呢？鳄鱼就是一种像是短吻鳄的大型动物，生活在尼罗河里。人们以前常说，鳄鱼会抓住埃及的小朋友，而在吃掉小朋友之前，鳄鱼还会流下眼泪，好像它很伤心似的。你们在假哭的时候，我们之所以会说你们是在流下"鳄鱼的眼泪"，原因就在这里。尼罗河在注入地中海之前，分成了数条支流，而这些支流之间的那片土地，叫作"三角洲"，因为那片土地的样子就像是希腊字母"D"，而这个字母在希腊语中叫"德尔塔"，形状则像是一个三角形。大家看到了吧，很久以前的人也会因为觉得某些东西与地点的形状相同，而用常见的东西来做地名呢。

埃及的北部几乎不怎么下雨，可埃及的南部在夏季却经常下暴雨。这样，尼罗河便会涨水，河水会越过河岸，淹没整个乡村，留下大量的泥土。这种泥土非常肥

Nile at a place called Assuan. This dam holds the water back and forms a deep lake. So now the Nile does not flood lower Egypt all at once; the water is let out by doors in the bottom of the dam as needed. One of the most beautiful of the old temples in Egypt was right in the way when the Assuan Dam was built, but it could not be moved from there, so now the water almost covers it up.

There was once a boy named Aleck. You may know a boy named Aleck too, but this Aleck lived two thousand years ago. He was a great Greek king whose full name was Alexander. He built a city where the Nile flows into the sea and called the city after himself, Alexandria. Alexander has been dead more than two thousand years, but his city still lives and is the chief seaport of Egypt.

Near the beginning of the delta, up the river from Alexandria, is a city called Cairo. It is the largest city in Egypt and also the largest city in the whole of Africa. Even if you were flying over Cairo in an airplane you would know that most of the people there were not Christians but Mohammedans. Can you guess how? In a Christian city you would see church steeples, but in Cairo you see saucer-shaped domes and candle-shaped minarets, for some of the most beautiful mosques in the World are there.

沃，古埃及人在上面种麦子，还种植一种非常优质的棉花。古时候，尼罗河一般每年只会泛滥一次，而其余时间河边的土地都是干燥的，人们必须从河岸上爬下去，才能汲到河水。可不久前，人们在尼罗河上游一个叫作"阿斯旺"的地方修建了一座大坝。这座大坝蓄住了河水，形成了一个深邃的湖泊。因此，如今尼罗河不会再在突然之间淹没下埃及地区了，必要的时候，大坝底下的水闸就会开启，泄掉洪水。修建阿斯旺大坝的时候，埃及一座最精美的古代神庙曾经挡住了人们的去路，可由于神庙无法搬迁，因此如今河水几乎将那座神庙全部淹没了。

很久以前，有一个叫作"亚历克"的小男孩。你们可能认识某个也叫"亚历克"的小男孩吧，可我说的这个"亚历克"，却生活在两千年前呢。他是古希腊一位伟大的国王，全名叫作"亚历山大"。他在尼罗河的入海口修建了一座城市，并且用自己的名字，将这座城市命名为"亚历山大"。虽然亚历山大大帝已经死了两千多年，可如今这座城市却依然生机勃勃，是埃及最大的海港。

在尼罗河三角洲开始形成的南端，即从亚历山大向尼罗河上游走，有一座叫作"开罗"的城市。它既是埃及最大的城市，也是整个非洲最大的城市。即便是乘坐飞机飞过开罗上空，你们也可以看出，绝大多数埃及人都不是基督教徒，而是穆斯林。大家猜得出这是为什么吗？在一座信仰基督教的城市里，大家会看到教堂的尖顶，可在开罗，大家看到的却是浅碟形的穹顶，以及蜡烛状的宣礼塔，因为世界上最漂亮的一些清真寺，可都位于开罗呢。

62 Robber Lands and Desert Sands

It is only a few miles across the Strait from Gibraltar to Morocco, which is the land of the Moors. It's only a few miles in distance but thousands of miles in difference. One morning, after breakfast, I boarded a small boat at Gibraltar, where every one was Christian, wearing "regular clothes" and speaking English, and by luncheon time I was in Morocco across the Strait, where every one was Mohammedan, wearing sheets, and speaking Arabic. It was as if I had walked into a side-show at the circus.

A friend had told me to get a guide named Mohammed, saying he would probably be on the dock. The dock was swarming with white-robed Moors as my boat came alongside, so as I stepped out on shore I shouted:

"Mohammed! Is there any guide here named Mohammed?"

Instantly it seemed to me every one on the dock was crowding around me, waving his hands, and crying out, "I am Mohammed." My friend hadn't told me that Mohammedans often named their children after their prophet and that the name "Mohammed" was about as common in Morocco as the name "John" in New York.

The Moors all looked like pirates and bandits to me, so I took no one for a guide and made my way along the narrow streets alone, jostled and rubbed against by dirty, sore-eyed people and even by lepers, from whom I struggled to get as far away as I could. It

第62章　强盗之国与大漠黄沙

跨过直布罗陀海峡，中间只有几英里的水路，便来到了摩洛哥这个摩尔人的国度。虽说两地近在咫尺，它们之间却有天壤之别呢。一天早晨，我吃过早餐后，就在直布罗陀登上了一艘小艇，前往摩洛哥。直布罗陀的人都是基督徒，他们都穿着"普通的衣服"，说着清一色的英语。到了午饭时分，我就越过直布罗陀海峡，到了摩洛哥，那里的人全都是穆斯林，身上披着床单，嘴里说着阿拉伯语。此时的我，就像进入了马戏团的一个穿插节目里。

朋友让我去找一个叫作"穆罕默德"的导游，说他很可能已经在码头上等着我了。当我乘坐的那艘小船靠岸时，只见码头上人头攒动，全都是身穿白袍的摩尔人；于是，我上岸后，就朝着人群里喊了一声：

"穆罕默德！这里有没有一个叫作穆罕默德的导游？"

刹那间，似乎码头上的每一个人都朝我围了过来，他们挥舞着自己的双手，全都大声喊道："我就是穆罕默德。"我的朋友可没有告诉过我，说穆斯林都喜欢用穆罕默德这位伊斯兰先知的名字给孩子起名，因而在摩洛哥，"穆罕默德"这个名字极其普通，就像纽约的"约翰"这个名字那样多如牛毛呢。

在我看来，摩尔人的样子都跟海盗和土匪差不多，所以我没有要导游，而是独自一人，沿着那条狭窄的街道往前走去，一路上被那些身上肮脏不堪、眼泡红肿、

seemed impossible that these Moors were related to the same Moors who had ruled in Spain before the time of Columbus, and who had built the beautiful Alhambra at Granada.

I had intended to go down to Fez, a city of Morocco, but as there was no railroad I had to have donkeys and a guide and servants. So I went to the American Consul to help me get them. A consul is a man living in each country to take care of the business and the people of his own country.

"You can't go to Fez," said he. "The United States will not let you. There is an Arab bandit lying in wait to capture any American who starts off for Fez."

"But I'd take no money with me for him to steal," said I.

"He doesn't want your *money*," said he, "he wants *you*. Then he'll send the United States a letter saying he's got you and will murder you unless they pay a good price to get you back. You're not worth it, but the United States must look out for its people, so you can't go." That's why I didn't go to Fez, and the only Fez I know is the little red monkey cap, shaped like a flowerpot turned upside down, which the Turks used to wear.

Have you ever heard the song "Home, Sweet Home"? It was written by an American Consul who was homesick for home. He was the American Consul at Tunis—another one of the once pirate countries along the Mediterranean. I don't wonder that he wrote "Home, Sweet Home."

Every continent has deserts, some big, some small, but the biggest desert i.t.w.W. is in Africa, just south of these pirate lands. It is called the Sahara. It is bigger than the whole

甚至是患有麻风病的人推来挤去，对于后者，我是唯恐避之不及，尽量离得远远的。这些摩尔人，似乎不可能跟哥伦布那个时代以前统治过西班牙的摩尔人，跟那些曾经在格拉纳达修建了美丽的阿尔罕布拉宫的摩尔人有什么关系。

我原本打算前往摩洛哥的非斯市[1]，可因为那里没有铁路，所以我只得租上几头毛驴，雇用一名向导和几名随从人员。于是，我便去美国领事馆寻求帮助。所谓的领事，就是派驻每个国家里去负责处理与其祖国相关的事务，并且照料其同胞的人。

"您不能去非斯，"领事说，"美国政府是不会让您去的。那里有一个阿拉伯土匪，正在等着绑架前往那里的美国人呢。"

"可我身无分文呀，他在我身上是抢不到什么东西的，"我说。

"他可不是想要您的钱，"他说，"他想要的是您这个人。接下来，他就会给美国政府写信，说他已经绑架了您，除非政府付一大笔钱给他，否则就要把您杀掉。虽然您值不了那么多的钱，可美国政府必须找到本国的公民呀，所以您不能去。"由于这个，我就没有去成非斯，所以，我对非斯了解甚少，只知道那里有一种红色的圆顶无边小帽，样子像是个倒扣的花盆，也就是土耳其人以前常戴的那种帽子。

大家有没有听过《家，甜蜜的家》这首歌曲呢？这首歌曲，是一位思念家乡的美国领事谱写的。当时，他正担任美国驻突尼斯领事一职，而突尼斯则是地中海沿岸另一个曾经海盗横行的国家。这位领事会谱写出《家，甜蜜的家》这首歌曲，我

---

[1] 非斯（Fez），摩洛哥北部古城，穆斯林的宗教文化中心，非斯省省会。

of the United States. It stretches across Africa from one side to the other, where it touches Egypt. The Sahara is not like the seashore; it is sometimes rocky, sometimes just dry dirt, but it is a place where nothing grows, "deserted" by every living thing. In spots, however, there is water, and in these water spots there are date palms and a few people. These spots are the oases, and some of the oases are many miles broad and long. Men travel from one oasis to another on camels, but there are no roads for them to follow, no guideposts to show the way, and they must follow the compass or the stars as if they were at sea, for like the sea the desert is moving and changing all the time. Strong winds blowing pile up the sand to make a hill here and a valley there, and then the wind changes and what was valley becomes a hill and what was hill becomes a valley. Sandstorms in the desert may be terrible things if the wind blows hard and long, as it often does. Those caught out in a sand-storm may be entirely covered and buried alive as in a terrific hail-storm—only the sand does not melt. Years after their dry bones may be uncovered by the shifting wind and others passing by may see what may happen to them, too, at any time.

阿拉伯土匪

可一点儿也不觉得奇怪呢。

"那里有一个阿拉伯土匪，"他说，"正在等着绑架美国人呢。"

每个大陆上都有沙漠，只是大小不一罢了，可世界上最大的沙漠却位于非洲，就在海盗横行的这些地区以南，叫作"撒哈拉大沙漠"。撒哈拉沙漠的面积，比整个美国都要大哩。它横跨整个非洲，从西非沿海一直延伸到了东边的埃及。撒哈拉沙漠可不像海滩那样平坦，它有的地方全都是岩石，崎岖不平，有的地方又全都是干巴巴的泥地，但整体来说，那里就是一个寸草不生、所有生物都"弃之而去"的地方。然而，其中有些地方还是有水的，而在有水的地方，则生长着枣椰树，并且有人居住。这些地方，就是所谓的"绿洲"，有些绿洲，方圆还有数平方英里呢。人们骑着骆驼，从一处绿洲转移到另一处绿洲，可沙漠里并无道路可循，没有路标指引，人们必须借助指南针或者天上的星星才行，就像是在大海中航行那样，因为沙漠始终都在移动，始终都在不停地变化。沙漠里的大风，吹得沙子在这儿堆成一座小山、在那儿形成一个谷地，然后风向一转，又会将谷地吹成小山，而让小山变成谷地。如果风力强劲且持续时间很长的话（这可是一种司空见惯的现象呢），那么沙漠中的沙暴就会是一种非常可怕的事情了。那些不幸遭遇沙暴的人，有可能被沙子完全吞没和活埋起来，如同身处一场可怕的冰雹风暴当中一样，只不过，沙子可不会融化。多年之后，变化不定的大风可能会让他们干枯的骸骨重见天日，而那些路过的人就会明白，自己随时也有可能遭受同样的噩运呢。

63 Afraid of the Dark

It takes about two months to cross the Sahara Desert by camel from top to bottom, and there is no other way to go than by camel or airplane—no railroads, no auto roads, no roads of any kind. On the southern edge of the desert is a place called Timbuktu. When people want to describe a very long distance they often say, "from Kalamazoo to Timbuktu." Kalamazoo is in Michigan in the United States and Timbuktu is in Africa. Timbuktu is the starting point for caravans going north across the Sahara to the countries along the Mediterranean and it is the ending point for caravans coming from those countries.

The Sahara has no rain, but south of the Sahara is a part of Africa called the Sudan, which has plenty of rain. The Sudan means "the land of the Black People."

When I was a boy we used to say that God made white people in the day and black people at night. Some say black people are simply white people tanned by the sun, which is so hot where they live that the tan never wears off.

The Sudan has one great river called the Niger. Like the Nile, that other great river in Africa beginning with an "N," the Niger fertilizes the land through which it runs. The Niger empties into the great Gulf of Guinea, a name which even intelligent people sometimes mix with Guiana in South America. Along the edge of the Gulf of Guinea are

第63章　黑暗大陆

骑着骆驼从北到南横穿整个"撒哈拉大沙漠"，需要两个月左右的时间；而且，除了骑着骆驼或者乘坐飞机，人们是没有别的办法去穿越的，因为那里既无铁路、公路，也无别的什么道路。撒哈拉大沙漠的南部边缘，有一个叫作"廷巴克图"的地方。人们想要形容一段非常遥远的距离时，经常会说"从卡拉马祖到廷巴克图那样远"。大家都知道，卡拉马祖位于美国的芝加哥，而廷巴克图则远在非洲。廷巴克图既是那些向北穿越撒哈拉大沙漠到地中海沿岸国家去的沙漠商队的出发地，同时也是从那些国家而来的沙漠商队的终点站。

撒哈拉大沙漠里没有雨水，但在撒哈拉大沙漠以南，有一个叫作"苏丹"的非洲国家，雨水却相当充沛。"苏丹"这个词的意思，就是指"黑人的国度"。

我小的时候，人们常常说，白人是上帝在白天创造出来的，而黑人则是上帝在夜晚创造出来的。有些人则说，黑人无非就是皮肤被阳光晒黑了的白人，因为黑人生活的地方烈日炎炎，所以他们晒黑了的皮肤颜色永远都不会褪去罢了。

苏丹境内有一条大河，叫作"尼日尔河"。尼日尔河与非洲另一条同样以英文字母"N"开头的大河，即尼罗河一样，让它流经之地的土壤也变得非常肥沃。尼日尔河最终注入了水域辽阔的"几内亚湾"，就算是聪明人，有时也会把"几内亚"（Guinea）与位于南美洲的"圭亚那"（Guiana）这两个英文地名混淆起来

little countries, all of which except one belong to countries in Europe.

This one country, at the corner of the Gulf of Guinea, is called Liberia. It is like a tiny United States; in fact, it was copied after the United States, but the president and all the people are colored, and the way it came to be so is this:

When our country was first started, the white men wanted some one to do farming and other work for them. So pirates captured black people from the shores of Africa, brought them to the United States, and sold them as slaves, just as the pirates on the Mediterranean captured white people from ships on the sea and made slaves of them. All the colored people in the United States to-day are descended from these black slaves who were brought from Africa. Many people in our country thought these poor slaves, whose fathers and grandfathers had been stolen away from their homes in Africa, should be sent back to their own land. So when Monroe was President of the United States some of our colored people who had been set free and wanted to go "home" were put on a ship and sent back. Home was Home—even if it was a jungle. There they started this little country called Liberia, which means "Land of Liberty." They named their capital Monrovia after President Monroe and named some of their villages after great cities here. Two of their villages they called New York and Philadelphia, although there are but a few hundred people in them. Instead of trying to forget the land where they had been enslaved they imitated it.

As you go farther south in Africa you reach the Equator. This is half-way land between

呢。几内亚湾沿岸都是一些小国家，并且除了其中的一个，其余国家全都是欧洲国家的殖民地。

这个"除外"的国家，位于几内亚湾的一个角上，叫作"利比里亚"。该国就像是一个微型的美利坚合众国，事实上，它就是美国的一个翻版，只是该国的总统和民众全都是黑人罢了。而利比里亚变成如今这个样子，过程则是这样的：

在我们美国建国伊始的时候，白人都希望，既有人来干农活，又有其他的人来为他们工作。于是，海盗们就把非洲沿岸的黑人抓起来，将他们运送到美国，并把他们卖作奴隶，就像地中海上的海盗曾经把乘坐船只在海上航行的一些白人抓起来，然后再把这些白人卖作奴隶一样。如今美国的所有黑人，都是这些从非洲掳掠过来的黑人奴隶的后代呢。美国有许多人都认为，这些奴隶很可怜，他们的父辈、祖辈都是从非洲老家被人掳来的，因此应当将他们放回故土去才是。因此，到了门罗担任美国总统的时候，我国便派出船只，将一些获得了自由并且希望"回家"的黑人送回了非洲。家乡终究还是家乡啊，哪怕那里只有丛林一片。在那里，黑人建立了"利比里亚"这个小小的国家，而"利比里亚"就是"自由国度"的意思。他们根据门罗总统的名字，将首都命名为"蒙罗维亚"，还用美国一些大城市的名称，给他们的一些村庄命名。他们把两个村庄分别叫作"纽约"和"费城"，可那两个村庄里其实只有区区的几百个人。他们没有尽力去忘掉那个曾经奴役过他们的国度，而是模仿了美国的一切。

继续深入非洲南部的话，大家就会来到"赤道"。那里是地球南、北两极之间

the North and South Poles, and the second greatest river in Africa, called the Congo, runs through it. In this part of Africa it is hot and rainy every month in the year. Things grow and keep on growing. Grass grows as high as a room. Vines and trees and everything else grow so thick, so close together, and in such a tangle that one can hardly get through them. It is something like that other Equator land—in South America—the Selvas.

A hundred years ago people knew little or nothing about this part of Africa. It was an unhealthful and a dangerous country for the white man. Many of the black people were cannibals who would kill and eat any white man they caught. The marshes and jungles gave white men fever, and there was a little fly called the tsetse which gave men a disease called sleeping sickness, from which they never awoke. Besides all these terrible things there were fierce wild animals that killed those who escaped other things.

And then there was born in Scotland a boy named David Livingstone. He was just like you or me until he was ten years old. But when he was ten years old he left school and went to work in a cotton mill. There he worked all day from six in the morning until eight at night. If you count this up you will find that it was fourteen hours a day he worked—and he was only ten years old. Every day in the week he worked this way, but when he went home at night he wasn't through working. After his supper he would study until he fell asleep over his books. Livingstone's one idea in life was to be of some good in the world and to help people who were sick and miserable. So he studied to be a doctor. He learned to be a minister as well as a doctor. He was sent to Africa.

的中间地带，而非洲的第二大河流，即刚果河，就穿越了赤道。非洲的这个地区天气炎热，一年十二个月里，月月都多雨。那里什么都长，并且一年四季长个不停。绿草会长得像房间那样高大。藤蔓、树木和其他植物都长得浓密而葱郁，密密麻麻且相互缠织、乱成一团，因此一个人是很难从中间穿插过去的。这里有点儿像是赤道上的另一个地方，那就是位于南美洲的热带雨林。

一百多年以前，人们对非洲的这一地区还所知甚少，或者说根本就不了解这一地区。对于白人来说，这里是一个既不卫生、又危险重重的国家。许多黑人都是"食人族"，会杀死并吃掉他们抓住的每一个白人。那里的沼泽和丛林，会让白人得上黄热病，而且，那里还有一种叫作"采采蝇"的小苍蝇，会让人们患上一种叫作"昏睡症"的疾病，一旦感染，病人就永远不会醒过来了。除了这些可怕的方面，那里还有种种凶猛的野兽，会咬死那些逃过了其他劫难的人。

后来，有个叫作"大卫·利文斯通"的小男孩在苏格兰出生了。十岁以前，他跟你、我都没什么两样。不过，满了十岁之后，他就辍了学，到一家纺织厂里去上班了。在工厂里，他必须工作一整天，从早上六点一直干到晚上八点。大家只要加一加就会看出，他一天要工作十四个小时，而当时他还只有十岁呢。一周当中，他每天都是这样工作的，可晚上下了班、回到家里后，他却还要继续干活呢。吃完晚饭后，他会去学习，一直学到自己趴在书本上熟睡过去。利文斯通的人生目标之一，就是要造福整个世界，去帮助那些生病和可怜的人。于是，他选择了学医。在学医的同时，他也通过学习，变成了一名牧师。后来，他被派到了非洲。

Every one said he would die, he would be stung by the deadly tsetse fly, or he would drink' water that would give him a fever, or he would be devoured by some wild animal. "If I'm going to die," said he, "it doesn't matter which way. I'll have to die some day, but I want to do some good before that day." So he went to Africa.

Thirty years passed and though he went back home several times he always returned to Africa and at last he disappeared. He was given up for lost, and his countrymen thought him dead. But some people in our country got the idea that he might still be alive, so they sent a newspaper reporter named Stanley to look for him. They thought a reporter could find him if anybody could. Stanley landed on the west coast of Africa and asked the black men by signs if any one had seen a white man. Most of the black men said "no"—thirty years was too long a time to remember—in fact, most that were alive then were dead. But some black men said they had heard their fathers say that a white man had once passed through that way, and they pointed toward the east. So Stanley kept on going east and still east. After a long, long while he came to a long, long lake that has a long, long name— Tanganyika. When he reached this lake an old white man came to meet him. Stanley said, "Dr. Livingstone, I presume?" just as if he were greeting a stranger whom he had been sent to meet at the railroad station. Of course, it was Livingstone, and Stanley tried to get him to go back with him.

But Livingstone said, "No, my work is here, teaching the black people about God and curing their bodily diseases. I'll not go back until I'm dead. When I am dead, then I want

大家都说他这回死定了，因为他会被致命的采采蝇叮死，或者喝到会导致他患上热病的饮水，或者被什么野兽吃掉。"如果我一定会死的话，"他却说，"那怎么个死法就不再重要了。我总有一天要死的，但我希望，在死前我能够做一些好事。"于是，他便去了非洲。

一转眼，三十年过去了，尽管期间也回过几次家，但他每次都重新返回了非洲，而最终却音讯全无了。后来，人们以为他失踪了，便放弃了寻找，而同胞们也觉得，他应该是已经死了。不过，美国有一些人却认为他有可能还活着，便派了一个叫斯坦利的记者去寻找他。他们觉得，要说还有人能够找到他的话，那就只有记者了。斯坦利在非洲西海岸登陆后，用手势询问当地的黑人，问他们有没有人看到过一个白人。绝大多数黑人都回答说"没有"，因为三十年的光阴太过漫长，不可能什么都记得，事实上，当时活着的绝大多数人，到了此时都已经不在人世了。不过，有一些黑人却说，他们听父辈们讲过，曾经有一位白人经过了那里，并且他们都指着东方。于是，斯坦利便一直往东而去。走了很久、很久之后，他来到了一个很长、很长的湖泊边上，而那个湖也有一个很长、很长的名称，叫作"坦噶尼喀湖"。来到这个湖畔后，有一位年老的白人前来迎接他。斯坦利说道："我猜，您就是利文斯通医生吧？"好像他是在火车站，跟那个派来接他的陌生人打招呼一样。当然，那人正是利文斯通，于是，斯坦利便努力想让利文斯通跟他一起回国。

可利文斯通却说："不行，我的工作就在这里，就是教导黑人信仰上帝，并且治疗他们的身体疾病。只有死了，我才会回去。将来真的死了之后，我希望能够回

to go home to be buried in England." So Stanley had to return without him.

Two years after that, with no one around him but black men, Livingstone died. He was on his knees at prayer when his black servant boy found him dead. All the black men loved him, and knowing that he wanted to be buried in England, they prepared his body by the sort of embalming they knew and bore it on their shoulders for eight hundred miles—it took two months—until they reached the coast. There they signaled a passing ship and asked that his body be taken to England. In England he was buried in Westminster Abbey, where the famous and great men of the World are buried.

Livingstone was so beloved by the black men that anything he told them to do they would do. His was a magic name. He made black people Christians. He also kept them from eating each other.

他们以为利文斯通已经死了

国，安葬在英格兰。"于是，斯坦利只得一个人回去了。

两年之后，利文斯通就去世了，去世之时，他的身边只有黑人。他是在跪着做祷告的时候，被手下那个小黑仆发现去世了的。所有黑人都爱戴他，因此，在得知他的遗愿是葬回英国之后，他们就用自己所知的防腐措施，对他的遗体进行了处理，接着又用肩膀扛着他的遗体，走了八百英里远的路，花了两个月的时间，来到了海边。然后，他们向一艘路过的船只发出信号，请求船上的人将利文斯通的遗体带到英国。回到英国后，人们便把利文斯通安葬在威斯敏斯特教堂，在这座教堂里埋葬的，全都是一些声名赫赫的伟大人物呢。

利文斯通深受黑人的爱戴，所以黑人对他完全是言听计从。他的名字，在黑人心中充满了魔力。他让黑人变成了基督教徒。他还让黑人不再彼此相食了。

当时有一位阿拉伯酋长，他的名字很可笑，叫作"蒂普·提布"，以前他经常

There was an Arab chief with the funny name Tippoo Tib who used to catch black men as if they were wild animals, chain them, and ship them to other countries to be made slaves. Livingstone with his black men fought Tippoo Tib year after year, until at last he put an end to Tippoo Tib's slave business. This is one of the big things Livingstone did.

Another thing Livingstone did was to make maps of the parts of Africa that no one knew about. He found the greatest waterfall in the World. These falls are twice as high and twice as broad as our Niagara Falls. The falls can be heard twenty miles away. He heard them sounding and resounding long before he reached them and asked the natives what the sound was. They said they are the falls of "sounding mist." He named them Victoria after the Queen of England, who was then living. The Victoria Falls are in the River Zambezi. Far north of Victoria Falls is a lake which is also called Victoria. Victoria Lake is where the Nile begins. The Egyptians had known the Nile River, of course, some three or four thousand years before Christ, but none knew where the Nile began. It might have started in Heaven for all they knew.

抓住黑人，仿佛黑人就是野兽一样，然后用铁链锁住，再用船只将黑人运到其他国家去卖作奴隶。利文斯通带领黑人，与蒂普·提布进行了年复一年的斗争，最终彻底终结了蒂普·提布的奴隶贸易。这就是利文斯通干过的大事之一。

利文斯通所干的另一件大事，就是把非洲一些不为世人所知的地方绘成了地图。他发现了世界上最大的瀑布。非洲这道瀑布的落差和宽度，都达到了美国尼亚加拉大瀑布的两倍呢。瀑布发出的轰鸣之声，在二十英里以外都听得到。当时，他听到了瀑布的巨鸣和回响，可走了很久都没有走到，便问当地的人那是什么声音。当地的人都回答说，那是"能发声音的水雾"落下时的声音。后来，他便根据英国当时还在世的维多利亚女王的名字，将这道瀑布命名为"维多利亚瀑布"。维多利亚瀑布位于赞比西河上。这道瀑布以北很远的地方，还有一个湖泊，也叫"维多利亚"。维多利亚湖正是尼罗河的发源地。当然，埃及人早在公元前三、四千年左右就知道了尼罗河，只是没有人知道尼罗河发源于哪里罢了。他们当时所知的，就是尼罗河可能发源于天上呢。

64 Zoo Land

Have you ever been to the zoo or the circus? How would you like to live in a zoo where the animals were not in cages? The land in Africa on each side of the Equator is like that. A great many of the animals are dangerous, yet some are not.

A lion is a huge cat, hut he is the wildest kind of a wildcat. He is the most terrifying of all wild animals—his roar is enough to "freeze the marrow in your bones," even if he happens to be behind bars in the zoo. No wonder he is feared by all animals and fears none. Other animals have always to be on the watch against enemies, but the lion can lie down and go to sleep without watching or worrying or caring about enemies.

My father used to say if you wanted to catch a bird alive the thing to do is to put a little salt on his tail. But you can't catch lions that way and you can't catch birds that way either. If a hunter wishes to catch a lion *alive* for the zoo or circus, he must catch him in a trap called a snare, which is a pit dug in the ground and covered over with branches and twigs. The lion falls into it and then must be caught with a very strong net. If, however, a hunter wishes to kill the lion, he hides near a water-hole and waits until the lion comes for a drink, or else the hunter kills some harmless animal as you might dig worms for bait to catch fish and places him in the lion's path. One of the animals used for bait is a zebra—a poor, harmless animal that looks like a little pony with stripes. Nature has given the

第64章　动物天堂

你们有没有去过动物园或者马戏团呢？你们乐不乐意住在一个没有把动物关在笼子里的动物园里呢？非洲大陆上位于赤道两侧的那个地区的情况，就像是这样的一个动物园。许多动物都非常危险，但也有一些动物不具危险性。

狮子是一种大型的猫科动物，也是最为凶猛的一种野生猫科动物。狮子是所有野兽当中最令人恐怖的一种，即便是关在动物园的围栏里，它的咆哮也足以"令人毛骨悚然"。难怪，所有的动物都惧怕它，而它却可以目空一切呢。其他动物必须始终对天敌保持警惕，但狮子却可以躺下来睡大觉，完全不用保持警惕，也用不着担心或者在意它们的敌人。

我的父亲以前常说，要是想活捉一只小鸟的话，就必须在小鸟的尾巴上撒点儿盐[1]。但是，用这种方式可抓不住狮子，而且，用这种方式其实也是抓不住小鸟的。要是想给动物园或者马戏团活捉一头狮子的话，猎人就必须设下一个叫作"圈套"的陷阱，也就是在地上挖一个深坑，再在上面铺些树枝进行伪装，才能抓住狮子。狮子掉进坑里后，还必须用一张非常结实的网子将它套住才行。然而，要是想

---

[1] 在英语中，put（a little）salt on sb.'s/sth.'s tail是个习惯用语，指的就是"捉住某人或者某物"，因为只有捉住了，才能往尾巴上撒盐。

北大西洋

地中海

南大西洋

非洲

印度洋

zebra stripes that look like the shadows of tall grass so that he cannot easily be seen. Other animals looking for food will come along too and must be scared away from the bait or killed. The first animal to come along is usually the hyena. The hyena is an animal with a peculiar screech that sounds like a laugh. But he laughs when he is mad, not when he is glad. He is too much of a coward to kill live animals, so he

杀死狮子的话，猎人只需埋伏在水坑附近，等着狮子过来饮水就行了，要不然，猎人也可以杀掉某种没有危害的动物来做诱饵，就像你们挖蚯蚓做鱼饵那样，并把诱饵放在狮子的必经之路上。猎人常常用于做诱饵的一种动物，就是斑马，那是一种可怜的、对人类没有危害的动物，样子就像是身上长有许多条纹的小马驹。大自然让斑马身上长满了条纹，那些条纹看上去就像是高大草木的影子，从而让斑马不易被天敌发现。其他正在觅食的野兽也会来到这里，此时猎人必须将它们吓走，不让它们靠近诱饵，或者必须射杀它们才行。这种野兽当中，最先出现的往往都是鬣狗。鬣狗是一种叫声古怪而尖锐的动物，它们叫起来时，听上去就像是在大笑。不过，鬣狗可不是因为开心，而是因为兴奋，才这样"笑"的。鬣狗的胆子极小，不敢猎杀活的动物，所以只能"守株待兔"，寻找动物的死尸来吃。鬣狗就是丛林中最胆小的动物。

在丛林里，所有动物要么勇敢善斗，要么善于逃跑，否则就必死无疑，那里可没有警察来保护它们呢。

说来也怪，丛林中最勇敢的动物并不是狮子，因为狮子无须勇敢，丛林里最勇敢的动物，就是猴子。

waits until he can find one dead. He is the most cowardly animal in the jungle.

In the jungle every animal must either fight, run away, or be killed; there are no policemen to look out for him.

The bravest animal in the jungle, strange to say, is not the lion—he doesn't have to be; the monkey is the bravest.

When a lion's roar shakes the jungle all the animals start on the runaway from him, but the last to run away are the monkeys. When a hunter who is hiding and waiting for a lion to come along sees the hyena pass by, he knows the lion is far behind, for the hyena is the first to run away; but when at last, after all the other animals have passed by fleeing, the monkeys come along, the hunter knows the lion is close behind. A hunter will not shoot a monkey if he can help it—he looks so much like a child. He will cry like a child when hurt, and if shot try to pull the bullet out with his hands, and that's more than even hunters can stand.

Some animals will not eat meat—only growing things. The giraffe, the animal with a long neck and still longer legs, doesn't eat meat. He eats only what he can reach with his long neck—usually leaves and twigs of trees. When he wants to drink or to eat anything on the ground he must spread his legs apart like a letter "A" so that he can reach the water.

Almost every animal makes some kind of sound. It may be his language. He barks, moos, clucks, bleats, mews, whinnies, croaks, roars, grunts, cries, snarls, chirps, screeches, crows, hisses, whines, laughs, squeals, cackles, squawks, snorts, bellows, or sings. But the giraffe is said to be the only jungle animal that makes no sound.

当狮子的咆哮让整个丛林都为之颤抖时，所有的动物都会吓得屁滚尿流，躲得远远的，而最后才逃跑的，就是猴子了。埋伏在那里、等待着狮子出现的猎人，如果看到鬣狗经过，就知道狮子还在鬣狗身后很远的地方，因为鬣狗见了狮子，就会头一个逃之夭夭，但当其他的动物全都逃走了，猴子出现之后，猎人就会明白，狮子就在后面不远的地方了。只要能够避免，猎人都是不会射杀猴子的，因为猴子的模样很像小孩。它们受伤后，会像孩子一样哭泣，要是遭到枪击的话，它们还会用两只手试着将子弹取出来，这种情景猎人可忍受不了。

有些动物不是食肉动物，而是食草动物。比如长颈鹿就不是食肉动物，它们都长着一个长长的脖子，四条鹿腿则更长。它们只吃自己那个长长的脖子够得着的东西，通常都是吃树叶和嫩枝。它们想要喝水或者去吃地面上的东西时，还必须将四条腿分开成字母"A"那样，才能喝到水、吃到草呢。

几乎每一种动物，都会发出某种声音。这种声音，可能就是它们的语言。动物的叫声五花八门，比如狗会汪汪、牛会哞哞、母鸡咯咯、山羊咩咩、小猫喵喵、马儿嘶鸣、青蛙呱呱、狮子咆哮、小猪哼哼、小鸟啼叫、野兽嚎叫、虫儿唧唧、鸟儿尖鸣、公鸡喔喔、蛇儿嘶嘶，还有的动物则会呜咽悲鸣、哈哈大笑、尖声长叫、叽叽喳喳、嘎嘎乱叫、呼哧呼哧、大声吼叫，或者婉转鸣唱。不过，据说长颈鹿却是丛林里唯一不会发声的动物。

在丛林的河流里，有一种体形肥胖而巨大的动物，叫作"河马"。河马的意思，就是指河里的马儿，不过，它们的模样实际上更像是一头大肥猪。它们和猪一

In the rivers of the jungle lives a huge fat animal called a hippopotamus. Hippopotamus means a river horse, but he is really more like a huge fat pig. Like a pig, he loves to wallow in mud and water. When he lies asleep with perhaps only his back showing above the water he looks like a large rock or a submarine partly under the water. A magician once sold a secret for turning lead into gold. I will tell you the secret and won't charge you anything for it. This is it. "Put the lead in a pot on the fire and stir it for half an hour while you do *not* once think of the word Hippopotamus." If you can do that the lead will turn to gold. Do you think you could do that? Then you don't know how hard it is to try *not* to think of Hippopotamus. Here's another good rule if you want to learn any hard name in geography: try *not* to think of it for half an hour.

Another big clumsy animal is the Rhinoceros. He would take a prize in any Ugly Show. He has very short legs and one or two horns on his nose, and his skin is so thick that a hunter can't shoot him except in the stomach, and he can't shoot him there because his legs are so short his stomach is almost on the ground. When a person is so dumb that nothing we say seems to have any effect on him or trouble him, we say he has a hide like a rhinoceros. I have a peculiar stick and I often ask people to guess what it is made of. They usually say "horn" or "hard rubber," for it will bend. It is really made out of rhinoceros hide. The rhino has very poor eyesight. His little eyes can hardly see at all. He needs glasses. Instead of glasses he has a friend that does his seeing for him. This friend is a little bird called a rhino bird that rides on his back, does his seeing for him, and warns him of

样，都喜欢在泥水里面打滚。河马熟睡的时候，可能只有背部露在水面上，就像水中的一块巨石，或者是一艘半在水下、半在水上的潜艇。有位魔术师，曾经出售过将铅块转化为黄金的秘诀。我把这个秘诀告诉你们吧，并且分文也不收你们的。这个秘诀就是："把铅块放进火上的一个罐子里加热，搅拌半个小时，同时心里一次也不要去想'河马'这个词。"要是做得到这一点，你们就能把铅块变成黄金了。你们觉得，自己做得到吗？你们可不知道，努力不去想"河马"这一点，简直比登天还难呢。在地理课上，如果你们想要记住一个难记的地名，还有一条好的经验，那就是半个小时内，尽量不去想这个地名。

还有一种笨拙的大型动物，那就是犀牛。如果动物界举行"选丑大赛"的话，犀牛每次都会得奖呢。犀牛的四肢非常短小，鼻子上长着一只或者两只角，而且皮粗肉厚，因此除了肚皮，其他地方连猎枪子弹都打不进去，可猎人的子弹是打不到犀牛肚皮的，因为犀牛的四条腿太短，使得它们的肚子差不多都贴到了地面上。要是某个人非常愚笨，似乎我们的什么话都对他不起作用，不会让他觉得烦恼的话，我们就会说他脸皮厚得像犀牛一样。我有一根罕见的手杖，我经常让别人去猜，看它是用什么东西做成的。由于那根手杖可以弯曲，因此人们通常都会说，它是用"牛角"或者"硬橡胶"制成的。实际上，那根手杖是用犀牛皮做的。犀牛的视力很差。它们的那双小眼睛，几乎看不见任何东西。它们都需要戴副眼镜才行呢。不过，它们没有戴眼镜，而是请了一个朋友来当它们的眼睛。这个朋友，就是一种叫作"犀鸟"的小鸟，犀鸟骑在犀牛背上，当犀牛的眼睛，一有危险便会提醒犀牛。

any danger.

The L. F. Ant is another animal with had eyesight. The elephants in Africa are bigger than those in India.

In India they hunt elephants to catch them alive.

In Africa they hunt elephants to kill them.

In India they catch elephants to tame them and put them to work.

In Africa they catch elephants for their tusks, which are teeth sometimes ten feet long. Just suppose you had two front teeth as long as that. These tusks are ivory and they make fine piano keys.

The ivory business is not, however, as good as it used to be—or as bad as it used to be for the elephants—for men have learned to make a kind of ivory out of cotton and other materials. This takes the place of ivory and comes in many forms called plastics. Plastics are much cheaper than ivory and in many cases much better. Ivory turns yellow and cracks as it gets old, but plastics do not.

But the most curious animals in Africa are the human animals—the Black People. They have very funny ideas about beauty, so we think. We have funny ideas, so they think. A white person is all faded out, pale, unhealthy, sickly looking. A black man is a rich, black, coal color. Our ladies wear rings in their ears. Their ladies wear rings in their noses, where they show better. Some hunters had a box of safety-pins. The Blacks begged for the pins, and when they were given to them they pinned them through their noses. An ear-ring isn't

大象是另一种视力很差的动物。非洲的大象，体型比印度的大象更大。

印度人捕象，是为了活捉大象。

非洲人捕象，却是为了杀死大象。

印度人捕住大象，目的是驯服大象，让大象替人们干活。

非洲人捕住大象，却是为了得到象牙，象牙就是大象的牙齿，有时会长到十英尺长。假设一下，你们要是也有两颗这么长的门牙，会是个什么样子吧。象牙呈乳白色，可以制作出优质的钢琴琴键。

然而，如今象牙生意没有过去那么好做了（当然，对于大象来说，情况可能还是跟过去一样糟糕），因为人们已经学会了用棉花和其他材料来制作出一种类似于象牙的东西。这种东西替代了真正的象牙，并且形式多样，叫作"塑料"。塑料的成本比象牙便宜得多，在许多方面也要比象牙好得多。象牙时间久了之后会变黄、开裂，可塑料却不会这样。

不过，非洲最古怪的动物，莫过于那里的人，即黑人了。我们觉得，黑人在"美"这个方面有着许多奇怪的观点。而黑人则认为，我们在这个方面也有着许多古怪的观点。在黑人看来，白人必将逐渐灭绝，因为他们全都脸色苍白、很不健康，一副病入膏肓的样子。而黑人的皮肤呢，却是一种圆润、黝黑、煤炭般的颜色。白人女性都戴耳环。黑人女性戴的却是"鼻环"，因为那样更显眼。有些白人狩猎者，曾经带了一盒安全别针去非洲。那里的黑人恳请狩猎者把别针给他们，可他们得到后，却把别针穿到了自己的鼻子上。对他们来说，耳环不够大。他们在

big enough for them. They make holes in their ears and holes in their lips and gradually work the holes large enough to put their whole hand through the hole. Then they put blocks of wood or something like that in the holes. Our ladies boo their hair. Their ladies arrange their hair in huge topknots and gum it up with blood.

Some white men were building a telegraph line in Africa, but as fast as they built it the Blacks stole the wire to make bracelets, and they would completely cover their arms and legs with the wire. That showed how stylish they were and how smart and how wealthy.

You've probably heard of the little boy who was so sad that he went out into the garden and ate worms. Well, in some parts of Africa the people eat ants and grasshoppers, both raw and toasted, and they He thinks himself very stylish are not sad but glad. But there is one thing that both white and black people like—that is watermelon. Our watermelons first came from Africa.

The music the black people love best is that made by beating on a kind of drum called a tom-tom. They beat it with their hands and fists and will keep it up for hours without stopping; the *thump, thump, thump and boom, boom, boom* seems to charm them. The sound can often be heard for miles, and they can send a sort of wireless message in this way across country to their neighbors. A little girl writing a composition on this subject said, "You can hear them beating on their *tum-tums* for miles!"

非洲黑人

他觉得自己非常时髦

自己的耳朵和嘴唇上打出孔来，然后将孔逐渐撑大，以至于整只手都伸得进去。接下来，他们又会把木块或其他相类似的东西，放进这种孔中。白人女性喜欢剪短发。黑人女性却会把头发扎成巨大的发髻，顶在头上，并且用血将头发胶结起来。

一些白人正在非洲架设电报线路，可他们刚一架好，黑人就会把电线偷走，去做手镯，甚至将胳膊和腿上全都缠满了电报线。在他们看来，这样就会让他们显得非常时髦、非常聪明、非常富有了。

大家或许都听说过这样的一个故事吧：有个小男孩极其伤心，因此走到屋外的花园里去吃蚯蚓。好吧，非洲有些地方的人也吃蚂蚁和蚱蜢，生的熟的都吃，而且，他们并不伤心难过，而是快乐得很。不过，有样东西却是白人、黑人都喜欢吃的，那就是西瓜。我们的西瓜，最初就是产自非洲呢。

黑人最喜欢的音乐，就是敲击一种叫作"嗵嗵"的手鼓。他们会用手掌和拳头敲击手鼓，并且连续敲上好几个小时，"嗵、嗵、嗵"和"嘭、嘭、嘭"的鼓声，似乎让他们如痴如醉。这种鼓声，常常可以传到数英里之外，因此，黑人可以用这种方法，让一种无线信息越过旷野，发送给邻近的部落。一位小姑娘，曾经在她用这个主题写出的作文里说："你们可以听着他们敲击手鼓，走上好几英里的路呢！"

65 The End of the Rainbow

Gold!

It used to be said there was a pot of gold at the end of the rainbow, though no one has ever found it. Yet men have left their business and their families and homes and gone to the ends of the earth in search of gold and to find a short cut to riches, for gold is used for money all over the World, though small coins are not made of it because they would have to be too small and would easily be lost.

The largest gold mines in the World are in South Africa, and more than half of the gold in the World comes from gold mines near a city there called Johannesburg.

Gold is called the king of metals, for though platinum is more valuable, gold can be used for money and for ornament and for other things, and most people think it more beautiful. Pure gold is stamped 24 karat, but pure gold is so soft it wears away too easily and some other metal is usually mixed with it to make it harder. The finest rings and jewelry are usually 18 karat, which means that eighteen parts are of pure gold and six parts are of another metal. Look on a ring or watch and see if you can find the figures 18K or 14K stamped there.

Sometimes gold is found in little lumps which are called nuggets, but usually it is mixed through the rock and doesn't show at all. The rock has to be ground to powder and

第65章　彩虹尽头有金子

金子！

以前的人常说，彩虹的尽头有一罐金子，但迄今为止，却还没有人找到过这罐金子呢。然而，还是有许多人放弃了他们的生意、告别了自己的家人和家乡，到天涯海角去寻找黄金，想要找出一条发财的捷径来，因为全世界的人都把黄金当钱，不过，小型的硬币却不是用黄金制成的，因为硬币太小，很容易丢失。

世界上最大的金矿，全都位于南非，而全球超过一半以上的黄金，也都产自一个叫作"约翰内斯堡"的城市附近的金矿。

黄金被人们称为金属之王，因为尽管铂金更值钱，黄金的用途却更广泛，它既可以当钱用，可以做装饰品，还可以做成其他的许多东西，而且绝大多数人都认为，黄金比铂金更漂亮。纯金通常标为24K[1]，不过，纯金质地太软，极容易损耗，因此，人们为了让它变硬，通常都会往其中加入某种别的金属。最优质的金戒指和金首饰，通常都是18K，这也就是说，其中有18/24为纯金，6/24为另一种金属。观察观察一只戒指或者一只手表，看上面是不是标有18K或者14K的字样吧。

---

[1] K（karat），黄金的纯度单位，24K即为纯金。亦译作"开"。它也可用作宝石（尤其是钻石）的重量单位，相当于carat（克拉，1克拉合0.2克）。

then the gold separated from the powder.

Almost every family has at least one thing that has come from South Africa—a very small thing but a very valuable one. Can you guess what it is? The diamond in your mother's ring. Nearly all the diamonds in the World come from a place called Kimberley in South Africa. They are found in a kind of blue clay in what used to be volcanoes.

Most of the diamonds used to be sent to Amsterdam in Holland to be cut and polished. The reason they are sent there rather than to some other country is because the diamond mines were first discovered by Dutch people living in South Africa. Now, however, many of the diamonds are cut in Kimberley and are all finished there before being shipped to other countries.

Diamonds are made out of the same stuff as coal, and if they were put in the fire would turn to coal. Sometimes people speak of coal as "Black Diamonds." When a diamond is

彩虹的尽头

传说彩虹的尽头有一罐金子

　　有的时候，我们会在一种叫作"块金"的天然小矿块中找到黄金，不过，黄金一般都是混杂在岩石里，根本就看不出来。人们必须把那种岩石磨成粉末，然后才能将黄金从粉末中分离出来。

　　你们几乎每家每户里，起码都有一样东西是来自南非的，虽说很小，这样东西却很值钱呢。你们猜得出是什么东西吗？那就是你们的妈妈所戴戒指上的钻石。几乎全世界所有的钻石，都产自南非一个叫作"金伯利"的地方。钻石是在一种蓝色黏土层里开采出来的；而这种蓝色黏土，存在于过去曾经是火山的地方。

　　以前，绝大部分钻石都是送到荷兰的阿姆斯特丹去进行切割和抛光的。人们之所以把钻石送到这里而没有送到其他国家去加工，原因就在于，是生活在南非的荷兰人率先发现了钻石矿。然而，如今许多钻石都是先在金伯利进行切割和打磨，然后才运往其他国家了。

　　钻石的成分与煤炭是一样的，如果放进火中煅烧，钻石就会变成煤炭。因此，有的时候，人们还会将煤炭称为"黑钻"呢。把钻石放在光下来看，钻石可能会呈纯净的无色，也有可能会呈现出蓝色或者黄色来。其中，纯净无色的那种钻石最为贵重。

held to the light it may look pure white or it may be bluish or yellowish. The pure white diamonds are the most valuable.

The biggest diamond ever found was about the size of my fist. It was called the Cullinan diamond. It was too large and too valuable to be used as a single jewel, so it was broken into two pieces and each piece was cut and polished. The next largest diamond ever found was called the Great Mogul. But the Great Mogul was stolen. Of course, the thief could not sell such a large diamond, for, as there was only one such diamond in the World, every one would know he was the thief. It was something like stealing the picture of Mona Lisa. But the Great Mogul has never been seen since, so the thief must have broken it up into smaller diamonds and sold the pieces.

The owners of the diamond mines take extraordinary care to prevent the black people who dig the diamonds from stealing at least some of those they find. The mines are closed in with a high fence which is closely guarded, and the laborers are not allowed to go home at night but must live inside of the fence for three or four months. When they do leave, the guards, for they are guarded as if in prison, strip them and search their hair and ears and mouths to see that they have not hidden any diamonds away, for even a single diamond would be worth a fortune to one of the black people. They have found so many diamonds at Kimberley that, if they sold them all, diamonds would be too common and too cheap. In order to keep up the price, therefore, the owners of the diamond mines lock up *millions* of dollars' worth and only sell them when people are willing to pay a good price.

迄今为止，人们发现的最大钻石，差不多有我的拳头那么大。这颗钻石，叫作"卡利南钻"[1]。由于这颗钻石的个头太大、太过贵重，不宜做成单件首饰，所以人们将它分成了两块，然后又对每一块进行了切割和打磨。人类迄今发现的第二颗大钻石，叫作"大莫卧儿钻"。不过，"大莫卧儿钻"后来却被人偷走了。自然，窃贼是不可能把那么大的一颗钻石卖掉的，因为全世界都只有一颗这样的钻石，要是拿出去销赃的话，大家都会知道他就是那个"钻石大盗"了。这是一起惊天大案，与油画《蒙娜·丽莎》失窃案有点儿相似。不过，人们此后再也没有见到过"大莫卧儿钻"了，因此，那个窃贼一定是将它切成了许多较小的钻石，然后一颗一颗地卖掉了。

钻石矿场的矿主们都格外小心，防着那些开采钻石的黑人，起码也会防着他们把已经采出来的一些钻石偷走。矿场都有高高的栅栏围住，并且有人严密守卫着，工人们晚上都不准回家，必须留在栅栏里面过上三四个月之久。工人们就像蹲监狱一样被人看守着，待他们离开矿场的时候，守卫还会把他们的衣服剥个精光，检查他们的头发、耳朵以及嘴里，确保他们没有藏着一颗钻石带出去，因为即便只有一颗钻石，对于一个黑人来说，也是一笔很大的财富呢。由于人们在金伯利发现了大量的钻石，因此如果全部卖掉的话，钻石就会变得非常普通，价格也会便宜得很

[1] 卡利南钻（Cullinan diamond），1905年于南非发现的一颗原钻，重达三千一百多克拉，后被人们切割成了九颗主钻。

An Englishman named Cecil Rhodes went out to South Africa for his health. He happened to be there when diamonds were discovered and fortunes were being made, and he found his health and found wealth too. A part of South Africa was named after him: Rhodesia. When Rhodes died he left a great deal of money, part of which was to be used to send some of the best young men chosen from our country and other countries to the great university of Oxford in England. These boys are called Rhodes Scholars.

Cecil Rhodes wanted to build a railroad from the top of Africa to the bottom of Africa, from Cairo in Egypt to Cape Town at the southern point. Most of the railroad has been built since he died. It is called the "Cape to Cairo" Railroad, but more is still to be built. Rhodes was one of the few Englishmen who didn't ask to be sent home when he died. He chose a place in Africa on the top of a mountain to be buried. It was such a high point he called it "The World View."

The capital of South Africa, Pretoria, is like an English city. The chief city is Cape Town, and it too is just like an English city. Only about a hundred years ago these cities were jungle in which only savage black men lived.

If you collect stamps you may have heard of a famous stamp called "A Mauritius" that a collector paid $20,000 for, enough money to buy a good house and lot, yet the only thing he can do with it is put it in a stamp album. Why should he pay so much money for it? Just to show others something he has that no one else has. Mauritius is a little island off the east coast of Africa. There are other islands near Africa. Madagascar is the biggest.

了。为了保持钻石的售价，钻石矿主们便将价值数百万美元的钻石囤积起来，只在顾客愿意出大价钱的时候才出售。

有位名叫塞西尔·罗兹的英国人，曾经为了自己的身体健康而前往南非。人们在南非发现钻石、大发横财的时候，他正好也在那里，于是，他既把自己的身体养好了，同时也发了大财。南非有一个地方，就是用他的名字命名的，叫作"罗得西亚"。罗兹去世之后，留下了一大笔遗产，其中有一部分，就是用来资助一些从美国和其他各国选拔出来的年轻精英到英国的牛津这座了不起的大学去进行深造的。这些年轻人，就称为"罗兹奖学金得主"。

塞西尔·罗兹一直想要修建一条贯穿非洲南北，从埃及的开罗通往非洲最南端的开普敦的铁路。自他去世以来，这条铁路的绝大部分已经建成。这条铁路，就叫"开普敦—开罗"铁路，但还有许多铁路仍在计划建设中。罗兹是为数不多的、没有要求死后将遗体运回祖国安葬的英国人之一。他选择了非洲一个地方的一座山顶，作为自己的埋骨之地。由于那里地势非常高耸，所以他便称之为"观世界"。

南非的首都比勒陀利亚，很像是英国的一座城市。南非的主要城市开普敦，也很像是英国的一座城市。谁能想到，仅仅一百多年之前，这两座城市还都是一片丛林，只有野蛮的黑人生活在那里呢。

如果大家集邮的话，你们可能就会听说过一张叫作"毛里求斯"的邮票，有位藏家竟然花了两万美元将它买下来，这笔钱，足够买下一栋很好的房子和一块很好的地皮了，可那位藏家买下这张邮票，却只能将它夹在集邮册里。他为什么要花

Mauritius is one of the smaller ones. Zanzibar is another small one. Pictures of their stamps you will have in your album, if not the stamps themselves. From Zanzibar come the cloves your mother uses to spice baked apples, pickles, and hams. Cloves look like little burnt match heads, and I don't believe you would ever guess what they really are. They are tiny flower blossoms that grow on the clove-tree!

那么多的钱来买下它呢？理由很简单，不过就是为了炫耀他拥有别人没有的东西罢了。毛里求斯是非洲东海岸的一个小岛国。非洲沿海，还有其他一些岛屿。马达加斯加是其中最大的一座。毛里求斯是其中较小的一座。桑给巴尔则是另一个小岛。你们的集邮册里，就算没有这些国家的真正邮票，可能也会有那些邮票的照片。你们的妈妈用来给烤苹果、泡菜和火腿调味的丁香，就产自桑给巴尔呢。丁香的样子，像是一个个燃烧过了的小火柴头，我觉得，你们永远都猜不到它们是什么东西。其实，它们就是长在丁香树上的小花朵！

66 Fortune Island

Have you ever been homesick? If you haven't, then you have never been far away from home for any length of time, or you never had a home. Just suppose you lived on the other side of the World from your father and mother, from your sisters, brothers, and friends, and were only able to get home once in five or ten years, or maybe never. The English people probably love their homes more and get more homesick than any other people in the World, and yet they go farthest away from home and live there.

There is a big island, so big that it is usually called a continent and so far off from England that it used to take five or six months, a half year, to get to it from England, and even now it takes a month or more by ship. On it lived only wild black men, yet the English people went there, built great cities and now rule over the island. This island is Australia, which means "South Land," for it is far, far south—south of the Equator, where it is summer when it is winter here and night when it is day here. The island was so far away the English thought it would be a good place to send prisoners, to get rid of them, because once there they could not get away and they could not harm anybody but themselves. Many prisoners were sent there and few of them ever came back. Some even died of homesickness, for even a criminal is human and gets homesick.

It was not very long, however, before the English found that this island was too good

第66章　发财之岛

你们有没有得过"思乡病"呢？如果没有的话，那就只能说明大家从来都没有长时间离开过家里，或者是从来都没有离开过家。假设你们在地球的另一面生活，远离了父母、兄弟姐妹和朋友，只能五年或十年回家一次，或者甚至永远都回不了家吧。英国人很可能比世界上其他任何一个民族都要更加热爱自己的家乡，也更加经常地得上思乡病，不过，与世界上其他任何一个民族相比，他们去的地方也距自己的家乡最为遥远，并在那里生活下来了。

世界上有一个巨大的岛屿，因为面积太大，人们通常还称之为"大陆"。而且，该岛距英国非常遥远，以前从英国出发来到这里，常常要用五、六个月，即差不多半年的时间，而即便是到了现在，坐船也要花上一个多月呢。这个岛上，原本只生活着野蛮的黑人，但后来英国人去了那里，他们兴建起了一座座大城市，如今则统治了整个岛屿。这个岛屿，叫作"澳大利亚"，就是"南方大陆"的意思，因为那里地处遥远的赤道以南，当我们这里是冬天的时候，那里却是夏天，而当我们这里是白天的时候，那里却正好是晚上。由于该岛距英国本土实在太远，所以英国人觉得，那是一个关押、摆脱囚犯的好地方，一旦被押送到了那里，囚犯们就不可能再离开，并且除了自己，他们也不可能再祸害到其他人了。英国押送了许多的囚犯到那里，后来几乎没有人回到了国内。其中有些囚犯，甚至是死于"思乡病"，

just for prisoners. The central part of Australia was a desert, but there were gold mines in the desert, and neither a desert nor danger will keep men away when gold, magic gold, is to be found. So a great many young Englishmen went out to Australia in search of gold and to make their fortunes, expecting to return home as soon as they had done so. But they found that it cost more to get the gold than it was worth—it didn't pay. They didn't give up, however. They were bound to make their fortunes in one way or another, so they tried another. In the southeastern part of this island was grass land. Grass was good for raising sheep and cattle, but there were no sheep and no cattle. So the Englishmen sent to England for sheep and cattle. But when the sheep and cattle came it was found that they would not eat the grass—it was not the right kind. And still the Englishmen were not discouraged. "If at first you don't succeed, try, try again." So they sent back again to England and got good grass seed and planted that. And then at last they did succeed, for the grass grew exceedingly well and before long the sheep and cattle turned out to be a "gold mine," better even than the gold mines they had expected to find. From the sheep that they raised they got the finest wool in the World—very long and silky. It was shipped to England and other places to make woolen clothing, and Australia is now the greatest wool-raising country i.t.w.W. And the cattle grew and prospered, and now frozen beef and mutton are sent back to England, which hasn't nearly enough beef of its own.

But not long after the sheep and cattle had gotten a good start a peculiar thing happened. An Englishman carried a pair of pet rabbits out to Australia. The pair of rabbits

因为囚犯也是人，也会想家啊。

　　然而，不久之后，英国人便发现这个岛屿太好了，只用来关押囚犯可不妥当。虽说澳大利亚的中部是一个沙漠，但这个沙漠里却有金矿，一旦发现了黄金，发现了充满魔力的黄金，那么沙漠也好，危险也罢，根本就阻挡不住人们的脚步了。于是，一大批年轻的英国人便纷纷前往澳大利亚，去寻找黄金和致富之路，并且期待着发财之后衣锦还乡。可是，到了后他们却发现，开采黄金的成本超过了所采黄金的价值，很不合算。然而，他们并没有死心。不管用哪种门路，他们都一定要发财，于是，他们又尝试了另一种法子。澳大利亚的东南部，是一片大草原。草原适合于放牧牛羊，可当时那里却既没有牛，也没有羊。于是，英国人便派人回国，把牛和羊引进了澳大利亚。不过，牛羊运来之后人们却发现，它们根本不肯吃那里的草，因为那里的草不适合牛羊吃。尽管如此，那些英国人仍然没有死心。俗话说得好："第一次没有成功不要紧，不要气馁，继续努力。"于是，他们再次派人回到英国，取来了优质的草籽，在澳大利亚种植起来。最后，他们的确成功了，因为新的牧草长势极其良好，而不久之后，牛羊就变成了一种"金矿"，甚至比他们原来希望找到的真正金矿更好呢。他们放牧的绵羊身上，羊毛又长又丝滑，属于世界上质量最好的羊毛。人们将这种羊毛运往英国以及其他地方，去制作毛料衣物，如今，澳大利亚则成了全世界最大的羊毛生产国。而且，那里的养牛业也得到了蓬勃发展，因此现在有大量的冷冻牛羊肉运回牛肉自给不足的英国了。

　　不过，就在澳大利亚的牛羊放牧业刚刚开了个好头之后不久，就发生了一桩

got loose and started to raise families. Now rabbits as well as sheep like grass. But rabbits raise families very, very fast, much faster than sheep or cattle, so before very long there were more rabbits in the country than there were sheep, and there were so many *millions* of rabbits eating up the grass and running wild over everything that there was not enough grass for the sheep. More rabbits and more rabbits and more rabbits—the people could not get rid of them. Men poisoned millions of them and trapped millions more, but for every million killed, millions more were born. It was like some of the plagues that visited Egypt in Bible times. The people built a wire fence all the way across the country to try to pen the rabbits in. But some of them escaped through the fence, so another fence was built.

怪事。一个英国人带着一对宠物兔子，来到了澳大利亚。那两只兔子逃走了，然后开始在外面繁殖起后代来。注意，兔子和绵羊都喜欢吃草。不过，兔子的繁殖速度惊人，比牛、羊的繁殖速度要快得多，所以不久之后，该国兔子的数量就超过了绵羊。由于有数以百万计的兔子，它们非但吃光了青草，还疯狂地破坏一切，因此绵羊的草料就不足了。兔子越来越多，越来越多，越来越多，人们却束手无策，没法消灭它们。虽说人们毒死了数百万只兔子，又用陷阱捕捉了数百万只兔子，可每杀死一批兔子，就有更多的兔子繁殖出来。这就像是《圣经》时代曾经肆虐埃及的那些瘟疫一样。人们沿着全国的乡村建起了一道铁丝网，想要把兔子圈在里面。可有些兔子却逃了出来，所以人们不得不又修建了一道铁篱笆。如今，那里的人们还在大批量地杀死兔子呢。他们将一部分兔肉制成罐头运往英国，还把兔皮也运回英国，去制作婴儿睡袋。但是，人们根本没法彻底消灭这种小东西，并且十有八九，他们永远也做不到呢。

Men are still killing them off by the millions. They pack some of the rabbit meat in cans and send it to England, and they send the skins back also—"a rabbit skin to wrap up Baby Bunting in." But they cannot get rid of the little creatures altogether and probably never will.

The native animals in Australia are very peculiar. One curious animal is the kangaroo, an animal as big as a man. He stands on his two hind legs like a dog begging for food. He uses his tail as if it were a third leg, sitting upon his two legs and tail as if on a three-legged stool. His two front legs are very small and almost useless. He doesn't run along on all fours; he jumps over the ground on his hind legs, making long hops. The mother kangaroo carries her babies in a pocket made of the skin of her stomach; it is a nest and a cradle.

Sailors used to return from long voyages and say they had seen living in the sea beautiful girls—from the waist up—with bodies like fish from the waist down. They called them mermaids. You have heard of them in fairy-tales, of course. Well, there are real mermaids on the west coast of Australia. They do live in the sea, and they do hold their babies in their arms. From a distance a sailor might imagine them beautiful; but close up they do not look like the beautiful girls with fish tails you read about, for they are really ugly animals called sea-cows. How disappointing!

The natives of Australia are black people called "Bushmen." They can't count even up to ten nor write their names nor read a single word. About the only thing they know is how to get food. They wear very little clothing. Instead of clothing they paint their bodies, and they raise bumps on their skin by scratching it with the edge of a shell and rubbing clay into the

澳大利亚本土的动物，全都非常独特。其中有一种古怪的动物，那就是袋鼠，这种动物的体型，有人体那样高大。袋鼠用两条后腿站立，就像一条正在乞食的小狗。它们的尾巴也有用处，就像是它们的第三条腿似的，袋鼠坐在两条腿和尾巴上，就好比是坐在一条三脚板凳上。袋鼠的两条前肢很小，几乎没有什么作用。袋鼠跑动的时候，不是四肢一起用，而是利用两条后腿，在地面上跳跃前进，并且一跳就是好远。母袋鼠会把幼崽放在由其腹部皮肤形成的一个"口袋"里面带着，这个"口袋"，既是幼崽的温床，也是它们的摇篮。

以前，水手们经常要进行远洋航行，回家后，他们都说自己看到过海里住着一些漂亮的姑娘：她们的腰部以上都是漂亮姑娘，可腰部以下的身体却像是一条鱼。水手把这些生物叫作"美人鱼"。大家自然也都在童话里听说过关于"美人鱼"的故事了。注意，澳大利亚的西海岸就有真正的"美人鱼"。它们确实生活在大海里面，也确实会把幼崽抱在两臂之间。从很远的地方看去，水手们可能会把它们想象得非常美丽，不过，要是靠近了再看的话，它们的样子与大家在童话故事中看到的那种长着鱼尾的漂亮姑娘可不像，因为它们实际上还是一种相当丑陋的动物，名字则叫"海牛"。多让人失望啊！

澳大利亚的土著，是一个叫作"布希曼人"的黑种民族。布希曼人都很愚昧，从一数不到十，不会写自己的名字，也念不出一个单词来。他们唯一知道的事情，就是如何找到食物。他们几乎不穿衣物。他们会在身上涂抹颜料，以此来代替衣服，还会用贝壳的锋利边缘划伤皮肤，再将黏土揉进伤处，从而让皮肤上出现疤

scratches. The more bumps they have on their bodies, the more beautiful they think they are.

The Bushmen have a peculiar plaything called a boomerang. It is made of a piece of wood shaped like a new moon. They throw it into the air away from themselves, and it turns round and round like a wheel and, if properly thrown, will come back to the thrower. I have several boomerangs which I have learned to throw. A friend of mine once said, "I hear you know how to throw a kangaroo." "To throw a kangaroo!" said I. "No, not even a Bushman can do that."

The capital of Australia used to be a city called Melbourne. But a new city called Canberra has been built for the capital. It is a made-to-order city. The city was laid out, streets made, a capitol built, and houses put up, and then people moved in. The chief city is Sydney.

The healthiest country in the World is southeast of Australia. It is called New Zealand. You will remember that Zealand is a part of Denmark and you may remember that it is the healthiest country in Europe. New Zealand is made of two big islands that look something like Italy or a boot turned upside down. They do not seem to be far away from Australia on the map, but it takes four or five days to get to them by ship from Australia. In the northern part of New Zealand are natives called Maoris, but they are quite different from the Bushmen in Australia. They used to be cannibals, but they have brains, and they learned so much from the white men that now some of them are as well educated as their teachers, and are even members of the New Zealand Parliament.

瘤。他们还认为，身上的疙瘩越多，自己就越漂亮呢。

布希曼人有一种很罕见的玩具，叫作"回旋镖"。回旋镖是用一块形如新月的木头做成的。布希曼人把回旋镖向空中掷去，回旋镖便会像轮子一样在空中旋转，要是投掷技巧掌握好了的话，回旋镖还会飞回掷镖者的手中。我买过好几个回旋镖，并且学会了掷镖的技巧。一位朋友曾经对我说："我听说您学会掷袋鼠了。""掷袋鼠！"我惊讶地回答道，"不，连布希曼人也不会掷袋鼠呢。"

澳大利亚的首都，以前是一个叫作"墨尔本"的城市。不过，后来人们兴建了一座叫作"堪培拉"的新城，便把这里当成了澳大利亚的新首都。堪培拉是一座经过"定制"的城市。人们先是制定了规划，然后按部就班地铺设街道、兴建国会大厦、修建民居，最后再让居民搬入。澳大利亚的最大城市，则是悉尼。

世界上最卫生的国家，坐落在澳大利亚的东南面。这个国家，叫作"新西兰"。大家应该都还记得，"西兰"是丹麦的一个地区，而且，你们可能也还记得，丹麦是欧洲最卫生的国家吧。新西兰由两大岛屿组成，其形状看上去有点儿像意大利，或者说像一只倒过来的靴子。在地图上，这两个岛屿离澳大利亚似乎都不远，但从澳大利亚坐船去新西兰，实际上却需要四五天的时间呢。新西兰的土著民族都生活在该国北部，叫作"毛利人"，不过，他们与澳大利亚的"布希曼人"却很不一样。他们原先都是"食人族"，但很有头脑，从白人那里学到了很多的东西，因此，如今有些毛利人像白人那样受到了良好的教育，甚至还成了新西兰议会里的议员呢。

67 Cannibal Islands

I suppose you know what cannibals are—savages who kill and eat each other. They used to live on little islands in the Pacific Ocean, which is the biggest, broadest, deepest ocean of all. The Atlantic Ocean has very few islands in it—you could cross the Atlantic without seeing a single island, but in the Southern Pacific Ocean there are thousands of islands, and if you were shipwrecked there you would probably be in sight of one. Many of these islands are so tiny that they are only specks on the map, and some of them are not on the map at all.

If you could drain all the water out of the Pacific Ocean as you drain water out of a bathtub, you would not see a level bottom but thousands of mountains all over the bottom. These mountains were once volcanoes, but they are now drowned by the ocean. Where their tops are high enough to reach above the water you see islands. In the warm water around these islands live the tiny little sea animals called polyps, which I told you made Florida. Their tiny little bones pile up until they reach the top of the water and form rings round these mountain tops. These we call coral islands.

On some of these coral islands live brown-skinned people who once were cannibals; on other islands no one lives. On all these islands grows a tree from which the native gets his food, drink, clothing, house, and furniture. This tree is the cocoanut-palm. I have told you before of that other palm on which dates grow. The *cocoanut*-palm has a tall trunk with all

第67章 食人族之岛

我想，大家都知道什么叫作"食人族"吧，它就是指那些相互残杀并吃掉对方的野蛮人。他们以前都住在太平洋的一些小岛上，在世界四大洋中，太平洋是面积最大、水域最辽阔、海水最深的一个。大西洋上，岛屿很少，因此在横渡大西洋的时候，你们可能一个岛屿也看不到，可南太平洋上却有成千上万座岛屿，万一你们在那里遭遇沉船事故的话，视线范围内很可能就有一个岛屿呢。这些岛屿当中，很多都非常小，在地图上只是一个小小的黑点，还有的小岛，在地图上根本就没有标出来。

如果大家能够像放干浴缸里的水一样，把太平洋里的海水全都放干的话，那么你们看到的海底，不会是平平坦坦的，而是遍布着成千上万座山脉。这些山脉以前全是火山，但如今都被大洋淹没了。如果那些山峰的高度足以让山顶冒出海面，就会形成大家看到的岛屿。在这些岛屿周边温暖的海水里，生长着一种叫作"珊瑚虫"的微型海生生物，就是我在前面告诉过你们的、形成佛罗里达的那种东西。它们的微型骸骨不断地堆积起来，一直伸出海面，从而在这些山脉顶端形成了一种环形的岛礁。这种环形岛礁，我们称之为"珊瑚岛"。

这些珊瑚岛当中，有些岛屿上住着棕色人种，他们从前也属于"食人族"，其他一些岛屿上则荒无人烟。所有岛屿上都长有一种树，土著人的食物、饮料、衣服、房子和家具，全都来自于这种树呢。这种树，就是椰子树。在前文中，我还给

南海的部分岛礁

太平洋

食人族

珊瑚礁

苏禄海

the leaves at the top, and in the center of the cluster of leaves grows a bunch of cocoanuts.

Cocoanuts are about the size of a baby's head. There is a shuck around the outside, and when this is taken off, the nut is inside. Strange to say, the cocoanut has what looks like two eyes, a mouth and a sort of coarse brownish hair. Inside the shell of the cocoanut is white meat, and inside of that is a kind of milk. The natives eat the meat of the nut as we would bread, and drink the milk, so the cocoanut is like bread and milk. From the hair on the nut they make rope and string and cloth and everything that we would make with cotton or silk or wool. From the cocoanut shells they make the cups, saucers, and all other dishes they use. From the leaves of the tree they make short skirts, which are all the clothing they wear. From the leaves they also make the roofs to their houses. Their houses often have no sides—they have roofs of leaves held up by poles made of the cocoanut-tree, and a floor which is raised a few feet off the ground.

When the native tribes had fights with other native tribes they would eat those whom they killed. Missionaries went out to teach them to be Christians, and at first the cannibals ate the missionaries, but many of the natives became Christians and almost all have stopped eating people. The missionaries thought the women were not dressed properly, so they made them wear long dresses called "Mother Hubbards," because they looked like the dress that Mother Hubbard in the nursery book wore. When the native women go to town they wear these dresses, but when they are in the country or want to climb a tree for food, they wrap the dresses around their necks. When the white people went to these islands they took their

大家介绍过另外一种会结枣椰的树，你们都还记得吧。椰子树的树干很高，树叶全都长在顶部，而一串串椰子，就长在密集的椰子树叶当中。

椰子的大小，跟婴儿的脑袋差不多。椰子长有一层厚厚的外皮，而将外皮剥掉后，里面就是椰仁了。说来也怪，剥掉外皮后，椰子上面像是长了两个眼睛、一个嘴巴，以及一撮粗糙的褐色头发似的。椰壳里面长有白色的椰肉，而椰肉里面则是类似于牛奶的椰汁。当地土著会像我们吃面包那样食用椰肉，并且像喝牛奶一样喝掉椰汁，所以椰子对于他们而言，就像我们的面包和牛奶。他们会用椰子上面的"头发"搓成绳子、编成毛线、织成布匹，做成我们用棉花、丝绸或者羊毛可以制成的所有东西。他们会用椰壳做杯子、碟子，以及他们所用的其他餐具。他们会用椰树叶子做短裙，他们身上穿的，也只有这种椰叶短裙。他们还会用椰树叶子来做屋顶。他们房子，通常都没有墙壁，他们都是把椰树叶子做成的屋顶直接搭在用椰树做成的屋柱上，而地板距地面则有数英尺高。

以前，当地的土著部落之间发生战争时，他们会把自己杀死的敌人吃掉。一些传教士前去布道，想让那些土著皈依基督教，一开始的时候，土著人把那些传教士全都吃了。但到了后来，许多土著人都变成了基督徒，并且差不多所有土著都不再吃人了。一些传教士认为，土著妇女的衣着很不雅观，便让她们穿上一种叫作"哈伯德大妈"的长裙，因为这种长裙很像是童书里那位"哈伯德大妈"所穿的裙子。土著妇女进城的时候都会穿上这种裙子，不过，如果是在乡下，或者想要爬上树去找食物，她们就会把裙子缠在脖子上。白人来到这些岛上之后，也带来了某些疾

diseases with them, and the natives, who had never had such diseases before, caught them and many died. They did not seem able to get well even from measles.

The natives live an easy life. They have no money, but they want none, for they have nothing to buy. They do no work, and if they want anything to eat, all they have to do is to climb a tree and get a cocoanut. This is easy, for the trees usually slant, and I have seen boys start at the ground and run up a tree as you might run up a sliding-board.

An Englishman named Captain Cook was the first person to explore these islands and write about them, so one group of islands is named after him.

White men became interested in these islands because they found that the cocoanut meat could be sold in their countries for good prices, so they put the natives to work gathering cocoanuts. It was not necessary to pay them with money, because money meant nothing to them. They wouldn't work for a thousand dollars a day, but they would work for a ten-cent string of beads. They were very fond of jewelry, so the white men paid them with glass beads or with victrolas to amuse them. Shredded cocoanut is called copra and is used in various ways. The cocoanut oil is used for making soap and a sort of butter.

Ships and steamers seldom pass many of these islands, and only at a few of the largest do they ever stop. Many stories have been told of men who were shipwrecked on coral reefs where no one lived, and where they lived alone and waited for years before they saw a sail and were picked up.

Many of these islands are so small that they have no names. Some of the groups, however, are named. There are the Solomon Islands, named so because the discoverers

病，由于土著人以前从未得过这些疾病，所以许多人都受到了感染，还有许多人则病死了。他们得上了麻疹这样的疾病后，似乎也无法痊愈呢。

土著人的生活非常简单。虽说没有钱，可他们并不需要钱，因为他们根本就不用买什么东西。他们没有工作，要是饿了，只需爬上一棵树，摘下一颗椰子就行了。那里的椰子树通常都是斜长着的，所以爬树摘椰子也是小菜一碟，我还看到过，一些小朋友从地上起步，跑到树上去，就像你们跑上一段滑梯那样轻松呢。

一个叫"库克船长"的英国人，是第一个探索这些岛屿并记录下了岛屿情况的人，因此，那里有一个群岛，就是用他的名字命名的。

后来，白人们对这些岛屿开始感兴趣了，因为他们发现，椰肉在他们国内能卖高价，于是，他们便让当地的土著帮他们采集椰子。他们无须付钱给土著人，因为钱对于土著人来说毫无意义。哪怕每天给上一千美元，他们也不会去干活，可要是给他们一串仅值十美分的珠子的话，他们就会乐颠颠地工作去了。土著人非常喜欢珠宝，所以白人只要给他们玻璃珠子，或者用留声机逗逗他们就行了。切碎后风干的椰肉，叫作"干椰肉"，其用途相当广泛。椰子油则可用于制造肥皂和一种黄油。

这些岛屿之间，很少有轮船和汽船经过，并且船舶也只会在少数几座最大的岛屿停靠。有很多的故事和传说，都称人们在那些荒无人烟的珊瑚礁遭遇沉船事故后，就独自在岛上生活，等了好多年才看到一艘船只，然后获救离去。

这些岛屿当中，有很多都太小，连名称也没有。然而，人们也给一些群岛命了

expected to find the wealth of Solomon there; there are the Cook Islands, named after Captain Cook; there are the Fiji Islands, and there are the Samoan Islands, some of which belong to the United States.

One of the largest groups, called the Philippines, once belonged to the United States, but now is a free nation. Near the middle of the Pacific are the Hawaiian Islands, which still belong to the United States. In Hawaii are raised most of the pineapples we eat. Honolulu is the capital of Hawaii, and from Honolulu come some of the greatest swimmers. They spend much of their time in the water, and young boys and girls are able not only to swim like fish but to ride the waves standing on a board. The ukulele, which you probably have heard and seen, is a musical instrument with a Hawaiian name. When a visitor comes to Honolulu the Hawaiians throw garlands of flowers called lei over his head, and when the visitor leaves he throws the lei into the water so that he will return some day. There is one word the Hawaiians use very often; it is "Aloha." It means "Hello, Welcome, Good-by, God bless you."

Aloha!

名。比如"所罗门群岛"，之所以得名如此，是因为发现这个群岛的人原本期待着在那里找到所罗门王的财宝。再如"库克群岛"，它是用库克船长的名字命名的。还有"斐济群岛"和"萨摩亚群岛"，后者中有一些岛屿还隶属于美国呢。

其中最大的一个群岛，叫作"菲律宾群岛"，那里原先是美国的殖民地，但如今已经是一个独立的国家了。太平洋中部附近是"夏威夷群岛"，那里如今仍然隶属于美国。我们所吃的绝大部分菠萝，都是产自夏威夷。夏威夷的首府是火奴鲁鲁，那里涌现出了一些最了不起的游泳健将。那里的人大部分时间都泡在水里，连小朋友也擅长游泳，他们不但像鱼儿一样泳技高超，还能站在一块板子上冲浪呢。大家很可能都听说过、也看见过"尤克里里琴"[1]吧，那是一种乐器，名称其实是夏威夷语。游客来到火奴鲁鲁时，夏威夷人会把一个叫作"花冠"的花环戴到游客的头上，而当游客离去时，游客则会将"花冠"扔到水里，以示自己有朝一日还会回来。夏威夷人经常说的一个词，就是"阿罗哈"。这个词的意思很广泛，可以指"您好，欢迎，再见，上帝保佑您"等等。

阿罗哈！

[1] 尤克里里琴（ukulele），即夏威夷的四弦琴，是类似于吉他的一种小型乐器。亦拼作ukelele。

68 Journey's End

And so back home once more after a trip Around the World in 440 pages! Home, Sweet Home! "'Mid pleasures and palaces though we may roam, be it ever so humble, there is no place like home." Every one feels the same way, whether he is an Eskimo or a Tibetan. Home is where we were born and brought up—whether it is on a block of ice or under a cocoanut-tree.

I once knew an old sea captain. He had been sailing the seas for fifty years. He had been round the World a score of times. He had been in every port from Punta Arenas to Archangel. He could speak a dozen languages. He had been in every land and on every sea; he had been everywhere and had seen everything. For a dozen years he had looked forward to the day when he could at last "settle down" and go home. At last that day came. I never saw any one happier as he headed toward home—the place where he was born—a little village in southern Maryland, near the sea.

A year later I met him again in New York. I never saw any one happier. He was all dressed up, with a flower in his buttonhole as if he were going to be married. "Where are you going?" said I. "I'm sailing, sailing at 12 o'clock," said he, "for a trip round the World!" and I thought he was going to dance a sailor's hornpipe right there on the

第68章　结束旅程

用了好几百页篇幅，进行了一次想象中的环球旅行之后，我们便再次回到了家里！家，甜蜜的家啊！"哪怕在快乐中徜徉，哪怕在宫殿中漫步，就算永远简陋，也没有什么地方，有家里那样舒服"。不管是因纽特人还是西藏人，在这一点上，任何人的感受都是相同的。家，无论是在冰块之上，还是在椰子树下，都是生我们、养我们的地方。

我曾经认识一位老船长。他在大海上航行了五十年。他已经环球航行了二十次。他到过从彭塔阿雷纳斯[1]到阿尔汉格尔的每一处港口。他会说十二种语言。他到过每一座大陆、每一个海洋，他的足迹遍布全球，也饱览了世间万象。十二年里，他一直都在期盼着最终能够"安定下来"、回到家乡的那个日子。这一天终于到来了。我还从来没有见过，有哪个人会比动身回家的他更加幸福的呢，他的出生之地位于马里兰州的南部海滨，是一个小村庄。

一年后，我在纽约又碰到了他。我没有见过比他更幸福的人了。他身穿礼服，打扮得漂漂亮亮，扣眼里还插着一朵鲜花，仿佛那天要结婚当新郎官似的。"您

---

[1]　彭塔阿雷纳斯（Punta Arenas），世界位置最南的城市之一，是智利南极区和麦哲伦省的首府。

street.

"Au revoir," said I. "I thought you were going to settle down at home." "Home," said he, "is a place to come back to," and he waved a jubilant farewell.

要到哪里去呀？"我问道。"我要坐船出海，十二点钟就要出海，"他回答道，"去环球旅行！"当时，我还以为他打算在那条街上跳一支水手们常跳的"角笛舞"[1]呢。

"再会，"我说。"我还以为您打算在家里安安稳稳地待着呢。""家嘛，"他回答道，"就是用于回来的呀。"然后，他就兴高采烈地向我挥手道别了。

---

[1] 角笛舞（hornpipe），以前英国水手中流行的一种舞蹈，人们通常都是伴随着号角（horn）和单簧管（pipe）的音乐起舞。